Waterhole Economies

The only economies that never collapsed

The Economic Principles that Preserved Life and the Planet for Billions of Years and Hunter-Gatherer Societies and Economies for 97% of Humanity's 300,000-Year Existence

Waterhole Economies

The only economies that never collapsed

SAMUEL LAYNE

MAIJAI PRESS

224 W 35th St. Ste 500 #328, New York, NY 10001
www.maijaipress.com
info@maijaipress.com

First published in hardcover, softcover and ebook in 2025

For information about special discounts for bulk purchases,
please contact info@Maijaipress.com.

Publisher's Cataloging-in-Publication Data:
Names: Layne Samuel, author.
Title: Waterhole Economies/ Samuel Layne -
Series: Survival Series -
Includes bibliographical references and index.
Identifiers: LCCN 2023909049 | ISBN 978-1-7337555-5-9 (Hardcover) |
ISBN 978-1-7337555-4-2 (Paperback) | ISBN 978-1-7337555-6-6 (ebook) |
ISBN 978-1-7337555-7-3 (Audio book)

Subjects: LCSH Ecology--Economic aspects. | Economic history--Social aspects. | Economic anthropology. | Environmental economics. | Economic development--History. | Economic geography. | Subsistence economy. | Hunting and gathering societies. | Prehistoric peoples. | Sustainable development. | BUSINESS & ECONOMICS / Economics / General | BISAC BUSINESS & ECONOMICS / Development / Economic Development | BUSINESS & ECONOMICS / Environmental Economics
Classification: LCC HC21. L39 2023 | DDC 330.9--dc23

Illustrations by Sherry Wang, Maijaipress
Book cover design and interior design by Sherry Wang, Maijaipress
Cover Photographs by iStockphoto LP

This book has been composed in Granjon LT Std. and ITC Avante Garde Gothic Pro
∞ Printed on acid-free paper.

10 9 8 7 6 5 4 3 2 1
First Edition
Waterhole Economies (Survival 02) ms x 01 03 2026 01 06 na na 02 c
Printed in the United States of America

ACKNOWLEDGEMENTS

WRITING A BOOK THAT REFLECTS UPON the successes, failures and struggles of humanity as well as the many transitions across our 300,000-year history must inevitably draw upon the writings of numerous historians, scientists, and academics whose contributions I hereby acknowledge. Unspoken in their writings was the implied quest to determine humanity's ultimate outcome—will *homo* sapiens survive, or like all other *homo* species, go extinct. In this book, however, this is the topic. What's different though is where one would look for and find the answers—within the human economy.

But telling this story wouldn't have been possible without Sherry Wang who designed and illustrated the book; Jackie Logue who proofread; and Cindy Coan who indexed the manuscript. Thank you all.

TABLE OF CONTENTS

PART FOUR

TECHNOLOGY AND
HUMAN ECONOMIES

315

CHAPTER 7

Technology and Human Economies

327

PART FIVE

ENERGY AND HUMAN ECONOMIES:
FROM RENEWABLES TO RENEWABLES

361

CHAPTER 8

Energy and Human Economies:
From Renewables to Renewables

369

PART SIX

CLIMATE CHANGE, MIGRATION, AND
HUMAN ECONOMIES

409

CHAPTER 9

Climate Change, Migration, and Human Economies

417

PART SEVEN

HUMAN ECONOMIES AND
HUMAN SURVIVAL

471

CHAPTER 10

Survival-Driven Economies
Were Waterhole Economies

477

Animals converging around a waterhole at Amboseli national park Kenya.
(Source: iStock; Credit: Mongkolchon Akesin)

Introduction

WHAT ARE WATERHOLE ECONOMIES?

Economies that preserved life and the planet for billions of years and hunter-gatherer societies and economies for 97 percent of humanity's 300,000-year existence.

WHY WAS IT ONLY DURING THE LAST 12,000 OF THE more than 300,000 years of human existence that cultures, societies, their economies, and often entire civilizations, collapsed? Was this a consequence of the economic and lifeway changes ushered in by the Neolithic Revolution—that transition from mobile hunting and gathering to sedentary agricultural communities and animal husbandry—that began around that time? If so, what changed? What was it about the hunter-gatherer lifestyle and emergent, primitive societies that enabled survival of their economies and societies for hundreds of millennia while those that have arisen since seem barely able to last a millennium? Again, what changed?

If pre-agricultural hunter-gatherers managed to build such successful economies and societies that lasted for so long, they must have known something about growing societies and building economies—that is, making a living within Earth's habitats and ecosystems—that subsequent humans may have forgotten.

To understand why, we must first understand the societal structures, cultures, and lifeways that gave rise to and cradled the economies and societies they built. What were their economies like? More fundamentally, what does the word "economy" even mean?

Economies, like the biosphere, emerge out of the activities of life. Economies are characterized and shaped by the lifeways, cultures, and societies that species form as they eke out a living *within* Earth's ecosystems and habitats, which form the foundation on which life on Earth evolved and the superstructure within which it operates. Just as there would be no biosphere if there were no life, there would be no economies if there were no living species, including humans, wresting a living within Earth's ecosystems and habitats.

Birds couldn't migrate if there were no air. Fish would neither swim nor breathe if there were no oxygen and no water. Carnivores would not exist if there were no herbivores, and herbivores could not exist if there were no plants, nor plants if there were no soil with nitrogen-fixing bacteria. Nor would humans thrive if there were no oxygen produced first by cyanobacteria, then by plants and phytoplankton through photosynthesis. Similarly, there could be no life if there were no ecosystems and habitats in which to evolve and no economy if there were no life scratching out a living—as economies that shrunk across the globe due to the Covid-19 pandemic lockdowns have demonstrated.

Economies emerge out of the lifeways of species as they try to make a living within Earth's habitats and ecosystems. Then, cultures form and become societal structures that, over time, grow into civilizations. One does not expect to find thriving human economies in the middle of the Sahara any more than one expects to find life, as we know it, on the surface of Mars, and for mostly the same reason—minimal to no life-supporting ecosystems and habitats. Yet many economists still manage to think of economies as something separate and apart from Earth's habitats and ecosystems, whose products and services all too often go uncounted in the numbers comprising the world's economic output.

Human economies can be thought of as an emergent third component in a trio of interdependent components that comprise a *survival-driven Triad of Life*—life, ecosystems, economies. For economies to exist, there must first be life, and for life to exist, there must first be supportive habitats and ecosystems in which to evolve and survive. All three components must coexist for economies to exist—a *triad* of life most modern humans (economists in particular) have failed to recognize or acknowledge. Only since the effects of climate change became apparent did scientists and economists begin to recognize this triad. Remove or impair any component of this triad, and life and economies on Earth would no longer exist. Hence, like survival-driven economies, human economies must also be survival-driven, by design, if they, too, are to survive. Unfortunately, post-Neolithic human economies have been anything but survival-driven.

Rather than being the paragons of capitalism guided by that so-called invisible hand that market economists imagine, human economies must first be seen as integral parts of Earth's habitats and ecosystems, within which they must be survival-driven by design, not market-driven, if we and our economies are to survive. Without Earth's ecosystems and biodiversity remaining intact, there will be no survival, and without survival, there will be no life, and without life to eke out a living, there can be no economies. It's really that simple.

Economies, then, are the set of processes and societal customs that species, including humans, employ interdependently to make a living within Earth's habitats and ecosystems. A successful economy is one that enables the survival of such species, could only survive as long as they do, and therefore, must have their continued *survival* as its highest, if not only, economic goal and outcome. Unfortunately, the human economies that have emerged since the Neolithic Revolution have focused not on survival but on surplus, profits, wealth accumulation, and unending GDP growth—an economic transition that would lay the foundation for all subsequent economic and civilization collapse.

This book will challenge you to rethink much of your understanding about economies and their purpose in human societies. It will help you to discover, explore, and learn about the *survival-driven* role human economies evolved to play in enabling human survival.

Of the types of economies our species has developed over time, which ones have most enabled them and other Earth-life species to survive? According to Encyclopedia Britannica, "history has shown just three ways in which humankind has arranged for its material provisioning: those based on the principle of tradition, those centrally planned and organized according to command, and the rather small number, historically speaking, in which the central organizing form is the market." Which of these three approaches has been the most successful in enabling humans to build and sustain successful economies and societies over geologic time?

Humans have tried all three economic systems, but only one of these, *the traditional economic mode of hunting and gathering,* has enabled humans to survive and thrive without destroying Earth's habitats, ecosystems, and biodiversity—to say nothing of running the risk of destroying humanity itself. This outcome often comes as a huge surprise given the many modern economic theories that might suggest the contrary—indeed, this answer is not what most would have expected. Yet until 12,000 years ago, and for 290,000 of the 300,000 years of our species' existence on planet Earth, traditional hunting and gathering is exactly how human societies and economies managed to survive collapse-free.

Hunter-gatherer economies and societies emerged and developed and eked out a living *inside* Earth's habitats and ecosystems—not *outside* of them, the approach chosen by humans since the Neolithic Revolution and the adoption of agriculture. According to National Geographic, hunter-gatherer culture was (and is, where it still exists, as in Inuit or Kalahari or Bedouin life), "a type of subsistence lifestyle that relies on hunting and fishing animals and foraging for wild vegetation and other nutrients like honey, for food." They adapted by migration or movement to changes in season or climate, sustaining themselves by hunting and gathering. The earliest, and by far the most historically numerous economic systems have been those of hunter-gatherer societies, for which tradition serves as the central means of bestowing order. *So far as is known, all tradition-bound peoples solve their economic problems today much as they did 10,000 years ago.*

There were no special modes of coordination to distinguish the activities of hunting or gathering or the modes of distribution from the rest of social life. *Their economy was essentially a network of provisioning activities that was completely absorbed within and fully integrated into the traditional mode of existence as a whole* and would have included, for example, the once- or twice-daily trek to a nearby waterhole—A provisioning activity that would have ranked top among the experiences a pre-agriculture hunter-gatherer would have come to know.

Treks to the waterhole were an economic activity that was neither optional nor dispensable as their very lives depended on access to a reliable source of water. It would have been the center of all economic activity as their entire lives—hunting, gathering, sharing, eating, playing, and recreation—revolved around planned, unfettered, and safe access to a waterhole. Just getting there and back safely would have been central and would have choreographed the execution of all other economic activities that comprised their day. They essentially lived their lives in an economy shaped by their need to get to a waterhole—*they lived in a waterhole economy.*

Hence, as hunter-gatherers' economies evolved around the daily need to get to a waterhole, their economy became imprinted by the prerequisites of the waterhole. Around these waterholes humans learned that to survive they had to share. Thus, their economies evolved to focus on sharing and surviving. For their economies to work, they had to gain access to the waterhole. But to gain access to the waterhole they had to be willing to share access with other species, and they had to remain alive to do so. Hence these pre-agriculture hunter-gatherer economies developed a singular economic goal and outcome: They became sharing, survival-driven waterhole economies that prioritized sharing, life, and survival above all else.

Until approximately 12,000 years ago, all humans practiced hunting and gathering, and hence all human economies would have been hunter-gatherer waterhole economies. And, if the success of an economic system is measured by its longevity and capacity to enable participating species to both make a living and thrive, as well as survive, then, compared to subsequent economic systems—agricultural economies, that emerged after the Neolithic Revolution, and eventually market economies that are still with us today—it is clear that humans were better off as hunter-gatherers and their economies were more successful as waterhole economies.

Hunter-gatherers saw themselves as integral members of and one with all species that occupied and contributed to the longevity of the habitats and ecosystems they shared, and for whom waterholes were equally indispensable. No single species owned or held continuous control and access to these waterholes. Thus, by necessity, humans had to learn to share with prey and predator alike. Daily access to waterholes wherever they camped would no doubt have forced them to find ways to coexist with other species. In short, they would have seen themselves, their lifeways, and the resulting *waterhole economies* that emerged as an integral part of the habitats and ecosystems in which they evolved, rather than being separate and apart from them.

So, as we asked above, what changed? What was it about the pre-agriculture, hunter-gatherer lifeways that enabled the survival of their waterhole economies and societies for nearly three hundred millennia? And why were the succeeding post-hunter-gatherer nation-states and societies based on agricultural economies—such as the Harappan, Inca, Khmer, Maya, Moshe, Ming, Yang, and Pueblo societies, to name a few—barely able to last a few millennia before collapse? The answer is clear: Historians have linked the collapse of agricultural economies to ecosystem collapse brought on by climate change, the ravaging of the environment, or some combination of these disasters.

Those economies failed and their civilizations collapsed not due to a lack of technology and innovation, destructive politics, or even warfare (though there was much of that to go around). For the most part, they failed when their habitats and ecosystems failed. In a word, those economies and the civilizations they once enabled failed because, unlike pre-agriculture hunter-gatherer waterhole economies, they may never have mastered the wisdom of the waterhole—to prioritize sharing, life, and survival above all else. Instead, they chose to make a living by building their economies *outside of Earth-life ecosystems*. In this way, they operated without regard to the damage they were doing to what scientists today identify as *ecosystem processes and services,* and without regard for the needs of other Earth-life species, the biodiversity upon which those ecosystem processes and services depend.

In this book I attempt to explore further these seemingly forgotten themes. We'll learn about the evolutionary role waterhole economies may have evolved to play, as described in these Parts:

Part One: The Evolutionary Triad of Life. We learn that human economies emerged around waterholes and became waterhole economies that were indispensable to life and survival. These economies became the emergent third component in an Evolutionary Triad of Life—life (of humans and other Earth-life species), habitats and ecosystems, and their economies. We marvel at the indispensable integrating role these waterhole economies evolved to enable. They forced that indispensable collaboration among Earth-life species, ecosystems, and humans that would result in their mutual life and survival.

Part Two: Rediscovering the human economy—driven by norms of sharing, life, and survival. We explore early human waterhole economies, their architecture, and foundations. We discover how these economies became that emergent third property that evolved out of the foraging activities of biodiversity and humans *within* ecosystems. And we see how they would perform that indispensable evolutionary role in enabling and integrating Earth-life species, ecosystems, and human life that would together form the Evolutionary Triad of Life.

Part Three: Transitions. We explore the major transitions human economies would go through during humanity's 300,000-year existence across the geologic epochs of the Pleistocene to the Holocene and through the beginning of the twentieth-first century into the Anthropocene. We learn how these economies would transition from the indispensable evolutionary catalyst of life and survival identified in Part Two to becoming the very opposite: an innovation that is destructive to humanity and other Earth-life species and ecosystems, and that poses a threat potentially worse than a thermonuclear war.

We discover that humans, unfortunately, have made socioeconomic lifeway changes beginning with the Neolithic Revolution that have placed human economies at odds with Earth-life ecosystems and biodiversity, breaking the Evolutionary Triad of Life and threatening our very survival.

We learn, too, that human economies have survived prior bouts of global climate change and have gone through earlier global energy transitions, engendering socioeconomic lifeway transitions from foraging to farming and from mobile to sedentary economies. We also see how these transitioned from *human economies* to *legal-person economies,* in the process becoming the most dangerous threat to human life and survival.

Part Four: Technology and human economies. We examine the role played by technology and innovation throughout human socioeconomic history and note that these seem to have been insignificant in enabling early human survival. On the contrary, while appearing at first to offer great benefits, invariably such leaps have laid the foundations of most of the harms our species has encountered, among which plastics and GHGs stand out, the former for the pervasive pollutants they have become throughout the Earth, and the latter as the cause of global warming that now threatens our very existence.

But the jury is still out about whether any of the many emerging innovations will help humanity escape the existential threats of climate change that legal-person economies, which are rapidly replacing human economies, have engendered.

Part Five: Energy and human economies—how humanity would go from renewables back to renewables. We note the frenzy in modern human economies as societies try to return to the renewable energy sources of the ecosystem that enabled life for 290,000 of humanity's 300,000-year existence—a round-trip transition from renewables back to renewables. Why was there a need to abandon or augment this initial renewable energy source to begin with?

Part Six: Climate change, migration, and human economies. We examine how climate change choreographed human evolution, forcing migrations, foraging, and the formation of mobile human waterhole economies, the first human economies to evolve. Climate stability would go on to enable hunter-gatherer societies and economies for 97 percent of our species' survival.

Part Seven: Survival-Driven Economies: Early human economies were waterhole economies, and they were survival-driven. We examine those early pre-agriculture hunter-gatherer waterhole economies and ask why and how they survived without collapse for most of human existence, exploring what it would take for modern human economies to return to the socioeconomic lifeways that enabled their waterhole economies to survive for most of our species' existence.

In the process we will envision a different kind of human economy, one based on the sharing, *survival-driven* architecture and foundations of the waterhole economy. It would be driven by evolutionary and not market economy values, to build Earth-life economies that ensure the survival of all Earth-life species, the ecosystems that support them, and human life and survival. They would mimic the economies that enabled our pre-agriculture hunter-gatherer forebears to build waterhole economies that did not collapse nor give rise to existential threats such as climate change, and that lasted more than 97 percent of the time humans have existed on Earth.

Given all other Homo species evolved and went extinct, in Book One of this Survival Series we asked, "can Homo sapiens survive, or is extinction inevitable"? Now we explore how early human economies enabled pre-agriculture hunter-gatherer humans to survive 297,000 years collapse-free, for most of our species existence. Then Neolithic Revolution humans emerged and began building their societies and economies differently, and they have collapsed ever since. But who would have thought human survival would depend upon where and how they would build their societies and economies. Here we learn why—but briefly, as James Carville once said, it's "the economy stupid".

PART ONE

The Evolutionary Triad of Life

ECOSYSTEMS, SPECIES, & THEIR ECONOMIES

THE MOST GENUINE MERIT OF SCIENCE, it is said, is its readiness to admit its mistakes. Theories in science are always being scrutinized and reconsidered. Modern research often rejects old ideas, hoaxes, and myths. Even Einstein, who rewrote the laws of nature and completely changed the way we understand the behavior of things as basic as light, gravity, and time, did not always get it right. In 1917 he proposed a static model of the universe, the "Einstein" universe, which was debunked in 1929 when Edwin Hubble discovered that almost all galaxies appeared to be moving away from us (the "Cosmological Redshift"), thereby demonstrating that the universe is constantly expanding.

Unfortunately, though, when it comes to economics, the so-called "dismal science," there has hardly been such willingness to abandon the falsehoods propagated over centuries that came to underpin and often misdirect the socioeconomic lifeways of our species since the dawn of the Neolithic Revolution. This was when early humans abandoned the evolutionary *survival-driven* lifeways embedded in their small, mobile, foraging, and sharing bands for *surplus, profits, and wealth accumulation-driven sedentary* towns and cities that would arise out of farming and animal husbandry, and that evolved and persist to this day.

But while it turned out Einstein could have afforded to have been wrong about his *static universe*, and while numerous cosmological theories about black holes might well be incorrect without leading to the collapse of human civilization, the same cannot be said for false economic theories and the policies they engendered. These have led to the collapse of numerous human societies and their economies over some four hundred generations.

Views of human economies that exclude nature, as Adam Smith and his successors have propounded, have failed to recognize that life itself, as well as all human economies, depend not on the "invisible hand" of a market-driven economy, but on the very visible goods and services provided by Earth-life's ecosystems. The result of this fundamental misunderstanding is catastrophic: Just 3 percent of our planet's ecosystems have escaped the destruction wrought by human economies inspired and built around these misguided socioeconomic lifeways.

In this section you will discover that the first economies were not human economies. Economies did not begin with humanity but burst into existence with the evolution of Earth-life species. These first economies existed only *inside* Earth-life ecosystems, and not *outside* of them as human economies have since the Neolithic Revolution. Earth's original economies were focused on fulfilling a single evolutionary goal and outcome that modern human economies have long since abandoned—the life and survival of the species that gave rise to them. These Earth-life species' economies were part of an *Evolutionary Triad-of-Life* consisting of life, ecosystems, and economies.

Without intact Earth-life ecosystems, there could be no survival; without survival, there would be no life; and without life foraging for a living *within* ecosystems, there would be no economies. This *Survival-Driven Triad of Life* that emerged depended as much on the interconnectedness of its elements as on their mutual dependency. The Triad describes a survival-driven relationship between Earth-life species, its ecosystems, and humanity. This fundamental relational structure is what humans began to abandon four hundred generations ago with the Neolithic Revolution, and what modern humans continue to ignore at our peril.

The Evolutionary Triad Of Life

CHAPTER 1

Earth-life Economies

Economies That Evoled to Enable Life and Survival

CHAPTER 2

Ecosystems

The Foundations of Earth-life Economies

1.

Earth-life Economies

THE ECONOMIES THAT EVOLVED TO ENABLE LIFE AND SURVIVAL

For an economy to exist, life must first exist, and for life to exist, Earth's habitats and ecosystem must also exist.

IF ECONOMIES ARE LIKE THE BIOSPHERE—EMERGENT phenomena of life that arise from the activities of Earth's species as they scratch out a living within habitats and ecosystems—then economies must have emerged long before *Homo sapiens* did. We didn't call them economies, and they wouldn't have been human economies, either. But they were economies nonetheless, *Earth-life species* economies that arose out of the activities of life that inhabited those ecosystems and habitats, most of which humans have since displaced with economies of their own. And it is this view of how an economy emerges—through the indispensable and foundational roles Earth's habitats and ecosystems play in upholding life and the economies created by life—that we will explore. This is not exactly the perspective Economics 101 might offer. It should not be surprising, then, that establishing Earth's habitats and ecosystems were among the earlier tasks in establishing Earth-life species and their economies—even before life itself evolved.

But counting Earth's habitats and ecosystems and the services they provide to life, while indispensable from an Earth-life economy perspective, have never been recognized as necessary and indispensable components by economists, let alone considered foundational to a human economy. Yes, there is plenty of talk about "nature," but such seldom includes humans among what we think of as "nature," any more than we include humans among the species we think of as biodiversity. In everyday speech, "nature" is what we find in the park and "biodiversity" is the wildlife going extinct in the Amazon. Some economists and governments have only just begun to recognize and count habitats and ecosystems and the services they provide as part of an economy, let alone see them as indispensable to all life, including humans—a topic we would have reason to revisit as we dig deeper.

So, long before economists began dreaming up what over the last three hundred years have matured into liberal twenty-first century free-market capitalist economies, the evolutionary process was busy laying the foundations for Earth-life economies. It was terraforming a planet with sustainable-capable habitats that would last for billions of years to ensure the evolution and sustainability of complex animal life and emergent intelligent species like *Homo sapiens*.

And, like a savvy long-term investor, billions of years ahead of everyone and everything else, the evolutionary process began preparing by plowing resources into the galaxy. First, it selected the right type of star, our sun, a class M star that can last the billions of years it would take for life to go from slime to ape-man to spaceman, and perhaps hopefully, even to become an interplanetary species. Next, it ensured it was a mineral-rich, rocky planet with a moon to stabilize its orbit and with outer-orbit planets like Jupiter to shield it from incoming; placed it in a stable orbit in the habitable zone of its star; supplied it with running water on its surface and an oxygen-rich atmosphere with an ozone shield to block DNA-destroying UV and gamma rays; then provided a temperature range suitable for complex animal and human life.

When a planet and its supporting solar system fail to maintain most, if not all, of these requirements, life fails to evolve, or if life evolves, it fails to develop into complex animal life. Too much heat or cold; not enough food and other nutrients; too little or too much water, oxygen, or carbon dioxide; excess radiation; incorrect acidity in the environment; environmental toxins and other organisms—or some combination of these—has repeatedly driven many of Earth's species, including our hominin ancestors, to extinction. And factors like these will take out humans, too, if we continue to rearrange Earth's ecosystems to our liking.

It would seem, then, that the overriding principle guiding Earth's design as a habitat for life, and thereby life's emergent economies, was one thing and one thing only: species evolution, life, and survival, including our own. Earth's design clearly favored species survival and appears to have elevated habitat and ecosystem sustainability, where species must evolve and obtain all they need to survive, above all else. And, as if that were not enough, the evolutionary process even seemed willing to "go all in," betting the prior four billion years of evolution that a lone, emergent intelligent species like *Homo sapiens*, endowed with freedom to choose its own destiny, would ultimately choose survival over self-extinction—a bet not even intrepid Goldstar day traders would likely make.

But why would this evolutionary process go to all the trouble, and even expense, of establishing Earth-life economies in its habitats and ecosystems when most economists don't seem to give a hoot about these things?

Isn't it because it's impossible for economies to emerge and exist without life, and life to emerge and exist without the *a priori* existence of habitats and ecosystems in which they evolve and survive? This process, then, was not just "embedding" economies in life, or in their "societies" as Polanyi prefers. No, it had gone where no economist had gone before, embedding life and the economies they generate firmly in the habitats and ecosystems in which they evolve and survive. Earth's ecosystems and habitats and the services they generate are an integral and indispensable part of all Earth-life economies—whether or not economists can assign a monetary value to them and are certainly not the optional afterthought many economists imagined them to be.

Looking back, though, one can't help but notice that Earth-life species' economies come with a few built-in features seemingly more suited to surviving and eking out a living on planet Earth. These are features that human economies once possessed but no longer have, features no longer associated with human economies.

To begin, Earth-life species economies tended not to remain fixed in the same geographic location as human economies often are today but moved as the community of Earth-life species migrated. Many species migrated in search of food or, like Monarch butterflies, to nest in warmer climates then double back in the spring, or to return to traditional breeding locations as salmon do. As they moved, their societies moved, and so did the tasks of eking out a living that comprised their economy—thus their economies, too, were mobile.

Early human economies were also mobile. For 99 percent of our history, until about 10,000 years ago, there were few, if any, permanent homes, villages, towns, or cities as we know them. Hunter-gatherers migrated as nature dictated, following stocks of food and water, or moving to avoid predators, escape natural disasters, or respond to climate change, as when humans left Africa 70,000 years ago, spreading eventually across the Earth.

It was only 10,000 years ago that humans started farming and building complex cities and nation-states that grew to become the ecosystem- and biodiversity-destroying economies and civilizations we know today. Hunter-gatherer economies, then, were mainly mobile economies.

If hunter-gatherer economies were mainly mobile economies, how different were they compared to modern economies? Very different. They were comparatively small and lightweight but very ecosystem- and biodiversity-friendly, existing entirely within ecosystems and deeply integrated with and dependent upon the Earth-life species dwelling within these ecosystems. They would have had none of the sights, sounds, and odors associated with a modern economy. No CO_2-belching industries and factory towns, no sparkling suburbs, no roads, gas stations, parking lots, police stations, schools, downtowns, or railroad-interconnected cities and towns. No paved streets, electric lights, dental offices, department stores, government buildings, athletic stadiums, bowling alleys, bars, bed-and-breakfast inns, or fast-food restaurants. Nor were there any of the raucous social issues one might encounter in cities and towns across a modern economy.

Each family was at once home, school, hospital, and supermarket, and together with their mobile neighbors, comprised a small, mobile settlement, 20-50 persons or so, that left neither plastic, electronic waste, nor raging forest fires behind. Nor, apart from hunting for food, did they do any harm to Earth-life ecosystems as they picked up their sparse belongings and moved on, leaving hardly a trace. Imagine, if you can, the state of Earth-life ecosystems and biodiversity when our hunter-gatherer forebears started their migration out of Africa, and compare that to their current sad state as revealed in The Millennium Ecosystem Assessment of 2005, and even worse, in the 2021 update entitled The Global Assessment Report on Biodiversity and Ecosystem Services 2021.

Have modern economists thought through how a mobile human economy might work and why such an economy might be better suited to, if not the intended evolutionary model for, supporting life on planet Earth—a planet on which almost all Earth-life species and their economies are mobile? Have they wondered why mobility has been the planet's dominant economic model?

Mobile economies today obviously mean something entirely different. Mention mobile economies and people think digital: smartphones, computers, the Internet, and societal and business operations enabled by electronic communication, that, during the worst of the Covid-19 pandemic, enabled many to stay home yet go to work. This is not quite what a hunter-gatherer would have meant by mobile. Mobile hunter-gatherers were able to migrate with their economies, taking all they needed to survive in the midst of climate change, something that fleeing modern humans wishing or needing to migrate are unable to do.

Those hunter-gatherer economies were at once mobile and self-sustaining. This mobility enabled them to remain small, nimble, and free from numerous domesticated animal zoonotic diseases like Covid-19, many of which would plague their sedentary farming successors. The world has seen at least ten such pandemics, but only after human economies changed from being mobile to becoming sedentary agricultural economies. Mobile economies had neither markets nor money. They were self-regulating and had neither a ruler and laws nor a need for law enforcement. People were caring, and everyone likely knew everyone else; they shared freely the results of the hunt, or of a day out foraging, rather than hoarding the bounty. They thereby avoided the social ills caused by lack of money or food, homelessness, and the boom-and-bust cycles of agricultural and industrial economies that followed.

They also avoided the population growth and explosions seen in subsequent sedentary agricultural to post-industrial economies, a problem that has become a key driver, if not the preeminent driver, of Earth-life ecosystems and biodiversity devastation in the nineteenth through twenty-first centuries. That growth has gone from three million in 10,000 BCE, just before humans became farmers, to eight billion during

November 2022, while simultaneously reducing the carrying capacity of Earth-life ecosystems. In the last 50 years, human population has doubled, the global economy has grown nearly fourfold, and global trade has grown tenfold, together driving up the need for energy and materials, and taking humanity closer to, if not beyond, Earth's current carrying capacity.

There seems also to have been an entirely different economic goal and outcome that may have resulted from the simple fact that those early human economies were mobile. Unlike modern capitalist economies, which focus primarily on endless GDP growth, gain, and wealth, their goal was simple, to remain alive by following the food—the same as all other Earth-life species, then and now. And, as we will later see, remaining alive is an economic objective that economists apparently never considered as the main, if not the only, goal and outcome for a human economy. Otherwise, how can one explain the celebration of a roaring stock market and rising GDP, even as thousands died daily from the ravages of a global pandemic and as even more descend into unemployment and poverty? Clearly human life and survival are neither the goal nor the outcome of any twenty-first century economy.

With nothing even remotely resembling the complexity and financial needs of modern economies, early humans in their mobile egalitarian societies and economies needed neither mayors nor other elected officials and knew neither city nor suburb, homelessness nor food insecurity. They needed neither healthcare, unemployment, nor social security insurance. They would not have experienced inequality, police brutality, gun violence, or any of the numerous mind-numbing social ills found in the modern human society and economy. They could neither ship nor post anything but carried all their belongings. They would have known neither cars nor buses, nor would they have missed the noxious fumes of auto exhaust or the CO_2 that has rapidly polluted and warmed the atmosphere. Fortunately for us, back then, they walked everywhere they went.

Mobile human economies, then, appeared to have done what modern capitalist economies, or any other modern economic system, have so far failed to do—enabled our hunter-gatherer forebears, during those 290,000 years of humanity's 300,000-year existence, to survive within the carrying capacity of the planet. Mobile economies, it turned out, were at once the throttle and the brake that simultaneously controlled human ecosystem products, services, and biodiversity consumption needs, while modulating and restraining its population and civilization expansion, enabling hunter-gatherers to stay within the dynamic population limits of the trophic level they occupied while on their way to becoming Earth's only super-predator.

Before leaving the topic of early mobile human economies it is important to observe that they existed only inside, and not outside of ecosystems as subsequent human economies would locate themselves; and consequently, they were well integrated with the economies of all other Earth-life species with whom they shared those ecosystems. In this way, they were very unlike modern sedentary human economies, almost as if by design.

Here are a few similarities to consider. Almost all Earth-life species and their economies migrated to survive, as did humans for 290,000 years. All species that continued to eke out a living within Earth-life ecosystems (humans did, too, until they became farmers) have had to exist and survive at a population density that can survive within the appropriate trophic level, the level at which a particular species feeds (as predator or producer) to maintain balance within the ecosystem. Post-hunter-gatherer humans came to ignore this balance, perhaps unknowingly, but modern humans, as can be seen from their population explosion, disregarded this balance knowingly. By contrast, Earth-life species and mobile hunter-gatherer humans have not been known to destroy Earth-life ecosystems and biodiversity.

Early humans lived mostly in harmony among the species with which they shared Earth-life ecosystems, and except for meeting food requirements, respected the life of all species. They developed technologies that facilitated their ability to hunt and fish for food, but not technologies designed just to advance growth and profit. They neither invented nor were known to use any man-made hormone disrupting chemicals, nor did anything to Earth-life ecosystems that would have put themselves, other species, or those ecosystems at risk of extinction as modern humans have done and are doing today.

We are all aware of the comparison of Earth with a spaceship, the oft-cited "Spaceship Earth." Our planet is one-of-a-kind in the solar system, and maybe even the galaxy, if not the universe. It might just now be dawning on some that Earth may also have been engineered to function in particular ways and within certain parameters, some of which lie beyond our control. We may also be realizing that to survive and thrive on Spaceship Earth, all Earth-life species evolved to fit and operate within those parameters with "evolutionary precision," and that they are intended to collaborate harmoniously with one another and within the Earth-life ecosystems that function as its life-support systems.

Unfortunately, though, humans seem not to have read the Earth-system user manual, and we are well on our way to dismantling those very life support systems, Earth-life ecosystems, and biodiversity, in a single-focused effort to build our economies. And it might come as a surprise to many, perhaps even to the authors of those hefty multi-year ecosystem and biodiversity assessments, that Earth-life ecosystems and biodiversity exist not just for human well-being or to build human economies but are the life-support systems of the planet that ensure the survival of all Earth-life species—of whom humans are a particularly insignificant fraction that has been around for only an infinitesimally tiny portion of their existence over geological time.

Now that we have seen how the task of laying the foundation for Earth-life economies and the kinds of economies that might work best—mobile economies—let's try to envision a modern human economy the way many economists might—minus the habitats and ecosystem services that many economists seem to think play no role in human economies. Where does one begin?

Karl Polanyi, in his book *The Great Transformation*, tried to envision what early-nineteenth-century economists such as Thomas Malthus and David Ricardo thought of a human economy. (We can be sure some modern economists would be in agreement, too.) Polanyi first wanted us to know what they meant by an economy. He wrote: "the entire tradition of modern economic thought, continuing up to the present moment, rests on the concept of the economy as an interlocking system of markets that automatically adjusts supply and demand through price mechanisms . . . that, even with government interventions, remained in their view an equilibrating system of integrated markets."

To Polanyi, their concept of an economy implied that human social relations that arise out of human societies were just an adjunct to the economy, something embedded in the real economy—in this *equilibrating system of integrated markets*. To him this differed markedly from the reality of human societies throughout recorded history. Before the nineteenth century, human economies, Polanyi argued, were always embedded in human societies, subordinated to its politics, religions, and social relations—pretty much the way, one imagines, it might have evolved, and pretty much the way it would have been when our hunter-gatherer forebears roamed the planet.

But what is the boundary that delineates a modern human economy, the geographic perimeter enclosing the society whence it arose? Could Polanyi have missed the fact (or more likely felt no need to mention the obvious) that economies are not just the economic activities of Earth-life (or "societies" as he prefers) but are themselves further embedded in Earth's ecosystems and habitats whence life itself evolved? And could this failure to explicitly locate human economies within habitats and ecosystems be a reason why economists have failed to see the indispensable economic value and role these play as integral parts of society, and consequently, its economy? Polanyi rightly observed that "all types of societies are limited by economic factors," and to this one must add limitations that arise from the habitats and ecosystems in which those societies evolved and thrived.

Omitting the foundational components that underpin an economy—a society's habitats and ecosystems—means that economists overlook the ecological systems and services they provide. Yet that's precisely what economists do when discussing a human economy. They omit the economic value of the very foundations that enable life and human survival. And this omission paints a picture of human economies that are divorced from the very reality of life and from whence economies emerged.

Some foundational components found in habitats, ecosystems, and the biodiversity they house provide a stream of goods and services that underpin all economies and whose continued availability is essential to Earth-life species and human survival. Ecosystem goods include natural products that are harvested, such as wild fruit and nuts, forage, timber, game, natural fibers, and medicines. More importantly, ecosystem services support life by regulating essential processes such as air and water purification, pollination of crops, nutrient cycling, decomposition of wastes, and soil generation and renewal. These services also moderate environmental conditions, stabilize climate, reduce the risk of extreme weather events, mitigate droughts and floods, and protect soils from erosion. These are services that seemed to have been reliably delivered until the Industrial Revolution and fossil fuels came along.

What is the value of these and other ecological system services? According to a 1997 article by ecological economist Robert Costanza, "the services of ecological systems and the natural capital stocks that produce them are critical to the functioning of the Earth's life-support system. They contribute to human welfare, both directly and indirectly, and therefore represent part of the total economic value of the planet . . . At a time when the global gross national product total was estimated at US$18 trillion per year, some estimates of the possible economic value of the biosphere ranged from US$16–54 trillion per year, with an average of US$33 trillion per year."

In fact, the economies of the Earth would likely grind to a halt without these ecological life-support products and services. Viewed from that perspective, the total value contributed to human economies is arguably *infinite*. Notwithstanding such economic valuations, economists have yet to include them in any discussion and computation of human economies. In other words, the 2022 $101.225 trillion world GDP figure reported by the World Bank woefully underestimates the value of global ecosystem services.

Given the economic valuables stored away in habitats and ecosystems, it should come as no surprise that life would locate itself, and therefore the economies that emerge from life, within those habitats and ecosystems. Consider the value offered by habitats and ecosystems. For one thing, Earth-life economies came with batteries included. Pretty much everything life needed to evolve, survive, and thrive was already built in—food, water, fresh healthy air, and lots of places and materials in which to erect a tent or shack. Not only has Earth's biodiversity loved this arrangement, but our hunter-gatherer forebears did as well. And the Texans caught without power, water, food, and a warm, dry place to sleep during a one-of-a-kind blizzard in 2021, after being let down by their state's free-market electrical grid system, would have loved that too. Who wouldn't?

Think, too, of the Central Americans fleeing for survival only to be confronted by a border wall, or the forecasted one billion migrants who will flee climate change by 2050, and one begins to understand the purpose of the kind of Earth-life economy that evolved. And no, those seeming all-you-can-eat habitats and ecosystems weren't the Garden of Eden. That was just the way things were before *Homo sapiens* became farmers and eventually started basing economies on the free-market capitalism that is driving the destruction of those habitats and ecosystems and the biodiversity they support.

It should be clear, then, why Earth-life species and their economies might have located in habitats and ecosystems—they were survival-ready. Ensuring *life's survival* was the only outcome that mattered and the pre-eminent requirement that guided the design of Earth-life economies. There were no free-market imperatives here: no competition, wealth accumulation, profit maximation, or ways to exploit labor to improve productivity.

In Earth-life economies, there were no enclosures, no false choices between making a profit and honoring the right of self-subsistence or raising the minimum wage versus shuttering small businesses. Nor was there any concern that species would grow fat and lazy from free food and housing, and no direct coercion by religious, judicial, military, or political interventions. The goal was neither gain nor GDP maximization, but rather, the maximization of life's chances of survival. The operative economic principle was neither socialist, fascist, nor capitalist—just Earth's survival-driven-by-design economic approach. But why did survival become the overriding priority?

It would be strange indeed, wouldn't it, if one never noticed the way mothers in any species prepare for, protect, and hover over their offspring to ensure their birth, survival, and growth to maturity. Yet we typically fail to see the similarity between maternal behavior and the seeming obsession with the preparation for, emergence, and perseveration of life above all else. Might it be because one is not accustomed to thinking about evolution and life in quite such caretaking and nurturing terms?

Consider the 4.5 billion years' worth of care and feeding that has gone into the preparation of planet Earth, a planet seemingly so unique that it may be one of a kind in a galaxy of billions. Earth, a particular planet, orbiting around a particular star, on which a particular set of species was to evolve. There is, then, an investment in the evolution of life and its survival, a dedication we may not have considered, a commitment that a human economist can hardly begin to understand. This firm evolutionary stance has ensured that Earth-life species and their economies are designed for survival above all else. To appreciate this, one need only recall just how often life on Earth has been jump started, indeed after numerous mass extinctions, including the one when nearly all life died.

Adam Smith might have thought twice about excluding all nature from his theory of political economy had he understood that human economies, like other Earth-life economies, are embedded in and emerge out of species and their societies, which are themselves embedded in Earth's habitats and ecosystems and depend on their ecological services just to survive. Hence, Earth-life species economies were intended to be about those very "visible" economic activities that nurture and preserve life—not about the self-regulating market of producers and buyers, guided by that "invisible hand," that in Smith's mind generates endless growth and wealth as producers compete for profit. If a market were necessary, it's hard to imagine that nature would not have provided a market mechanism—it included everything else.

But one shouldn't be too hard on Adam Smith. Few people have given much thought to the level of preparation needed for humans to be alive on this planet, orbiting this star. Consider, for instance, the level of preparation that might have gone into the selection of the sun. According to Peter Ward and Donald Brownlee in their book *Rare Earth: Why Complex Life Is Uncommon in the Universe*, the home star of a potentially life-evolving and sustaining planet will preferably be a single star (not a binary or multiple star system—like Tatooine, the planet with two stars in Star Wars) and must be located in the galactic habitable zone. That zone does not pulse or rapidly change its energy output, or give off too much ultraviolet radiation, but emits a near-constant energy output for billions of years; is located in a safe region of the galaxy, far from the galactic center and from sources of gamma-ray bursts or supernovae; and is moving relatively slowly on its journey through its galaxy. That's our sun, and we have yet to find another exactly like it.

Consider, too, what may have gone into the selection of Earth as our home planet. To be a habitat for the evolution and sustainability of complex animal life, a planet must be terrestrial (rocky and with a hard surface); stable in a circular orbit (with a fixed spin rate—Earth's is once every twenty-four hours); and with a fixed tilt of its axis of rotation to give long-term surface temperature stability. (Aided by the gravitational effects of the sun and moon, Earth has had, for most of its recent geologic existence, a 23-degree tilt.) It must also be in a continuous habitable zone and far enough away from its home star to avoid being tidally locked by its gravitational force (where one side of the planet always faces the star and the other always faces the coldness and darkness of outer space, like our moon does), and it must be shielded from frequent comet and meteor bombardment by larger outer planets in its solar system, the way Jupiter shields Earth, as it did in July 1994 from the comet Shoemaker-Levy.

In addition, the planet must possess a stable climate, a range of temperatures (15°C–45°C) that allows complex animal life to evolve and survive, and liquid water to exist (0°C–100°C), and oceans with an average temperature of about 50°C and with a chemical composition conducive to complex animal life, including salinity and pH factors favorable to the formation and maintenance of proteins. The atmosphere must have the right mix of gases. The planet must be capable of supporting plate tectonics to help maintain suitable surface temperatures and formation of continents, thereby engendering biodiversity. It must also have a magnetic shield to protect the surface from cosmic, gamma, and UV ray bombardment. In addition, since it could take more than four billion years for an intelligent species to emerge (that's how long it took to get to *Homo sapiens*), the planet must do all the above and maintain these conditions for billions of years.

So yes, it must have been a lot of trouble to find and prepare a planet, and one can rest assured it was not about to come up with Earth-life economies, such as humans have, that would drive biodiversity to extinction and destroy the very habitats and ecosystems that are indispensable to the survival of life.

We have looked, ever so briefly, at how modern human economies may have come to differ from those early human economies: mobile economies that can remain within guardrails set by the trophic level and a sustainable population in an Earth-life ecosystem. And we have compared them with some Earth-life species economies and the economies of mobile hunter-gatherers. In subsequent chapters, we will see how the sheer force of mobility shaped participating species population and the resulting economy in ways seemingly unachievable in a sedentary agricultural and subsequent industrial economies. We will also see how mobility not only restrained the growth of hunter-gatherer human populations, but as a result, limited growth in the use of ecosystems and their services, thereby preventing the devastation that modern human economies now cause.

So, now it's time to dig deeper. But before continuing that search, it bears repeating that the most important and overriding principle that guides all Earth-life economies is *survival—survival* of all life participating in such an economy. Survival of Earth-life ecosystems and species and human survival is the only economic goal and outcome that matters in Earth's *survival-driven* Earth-life economies. Neither a growing GDP nor increases in shareholder or stakeholder value are adequate substitutes. And with survival as the goal of all Earth-life economic activity, and therefore our guide, we are ready to begin.

Our first question: What is an ecosystem and why should anyone care?

2.

Ecosystems: Foundations of Earth-life Economies

THE BIOSPHERE IS A GLOBAL ECOSYSTEM

"For the economy itself will die if our ecosystems collapse."
—Leonardo DiCaprio, climate speech at the United Nations

WHAT HAS LEONARDO DI CAPRIO LEARNED THAT economists apparently still won't? *It's the ecosystem, stupid.* Without Earth's ecosystems, there will be no life, and if there is no life, there can be no economies. But it isn't just DiCaprio making such claims. Two theoretical physicists specializing in complex systems conclude that global deforestation due to human activities is on track to trigger the "irreversible collapse" of human civilization within the next two to four decades. "If we continue destroying and degrading the world's forests," they claim in a peer-reviewed paper, "Earth will no longer be able to sustain a large human population."

Dinosaurs, like humans today, were once Earth's dominant species. Yet after walking the Earth for 180 million years, they and all but avian species went extinct. Not only because a massive meteorite slammed into Chicxulub, Mexico, 65 million years ago, but because that impact set off a chain of events that caused ecosystems around the world to collapse. Mr. DiCaprio's point? There'll be no economy to worry about if humans continue to destroy Earth's habitats, ecosystems, and the biodiversity they support because humans, too, will go extinct if enough ecosystems collapse.

By this time, you may well be wondering "What's with all this about ecosystems? I thought this was a book about economies and economics." Yes, but the question is best redirected to an Economics 101 professor. After all, it was economists, starting with Adam Smith, who chose to eliminate anything to do with nature from the study of economics, which he referred to as political economy. But as we have already seen, human economies emerge out of the activities of human societies, which are themselves embedded in, and dependent for their survival on, Earth's habitats and ecosystems.

Ecosystems, according to biologist Eugene P. Odum, are "living organisms and their nonliving (abiotic) environment are inseparably interrelated and interact with each other. An ecological system, or ecosystem, is any unit (a biosystem) that includes all the organisms (the biotic community) in a given area interacting with the physical environment so that a flow of energy leads to clearly defined biotic structures and cycling of materials between living and nonliving parts. An ecosystem then is more than a geographical unit (or ecoregion); it is a functional system unit with inputs and outputs, and with boundaries that can be either natural or arbitrary."

In fact, "Everyone in the world depends completely on Earth's ecosystems and the services they provide, such as food, water, disease management, climate regulation, spiritual fulfillment, and aesthetic enjoyment," according to the 2005 Millennium Ecosystem Assessment. Hence anything that lives, lives in an ecosystem and any study of human economies is *ipso facto* incomplete without an understanding of the evolutionary, biological, and ecological foundations upon which they're based—Earth-life ecosystems. And yet, one seldom thinks of where one lives as being within an ecosystem. Here, then, is where modern humans' troubled relationship with Earth-life species and ecosystems begins.

Ecosystems are not only the foundation of Earth-life species economies (whether human economies or those formed by other species). They are also the base of the entire biosphere and determine the health of the entire Earth system ranging from wet to dry and cold to hot. Ecosystems fall into one of two major categories, terrestrial and aquatic, which are further subdivided into biomes. Biomes are the largest unit of ecological classification after the world itself, and consist of large sections of land, sea, or atmosphere, including forests, such as temperate broadleaf forests or mountain grassland rainforest and boreal forest, ponds, reefs, tundra grasslands, savanna deserts, estuaries, taiga (biomes of the cold sub-arctic region), prairies, freshwater lakes, rivers, oceans, and swamps. Earth's surface is essentially a patchwork quilt of connected ecosystems grouped to form biomes. They're organized based on the types of plants and animals that live in them. Each forest, pond, or reef, and each section of tundra, for example, may contain many different ecosystems.

All living things—plants, animals (including humans) and organisms—that function as communities in a given area by interacting with one aother and with elements of the non-living environments such as weather, sunlight, soil, wind, water, chemicals, and the atmosphere, may occupy one or more ecosystems. Plants, animals, and other organisms comprise the biotic (living) parts while abiotic (non-living) elements include rocks, temperature, and humidity. National Geographic describes an ecosystem as a geographic area where plants, animals, and other organisms, as well as weather and landscape, work together to form a bubble of life—the key takeaways being "work together" and "bubble of life."

From this perspective, the entire biosphere forms a global ecosystem composed of biotic as well as abiotic parts all *working together* to form this *global bubble of life* that is planet Earth. Ecosystems, then, enable life and survival, and *Earth-life-species-economies* that emanate from *within* ecosystems are by default designed to preserve life and survival. Yet that has not been the pattern that characterizes post-hunter-gatherer human economies. This chapter explores why.

Everything in an ecosystem depends on everything else, directly or indirectly. A change in temperature can often determine which plants will grow. Animals that depend on plants for food and shelter must adapt to such changes, move to another ecosystem, or perish, as corals do in the Great Barrier Reef when surrounding waters become too acidic due to increased levels of carbon dioxide in the atmosphere. To survive in an Earth-life-species-economy, each species evolved to be codependent, a part of a community of species sharing common habitats and resources in those habitats.

This was and still is the prevailing subsistence method, the economic behavior of most, if not all Earth-life species, hunter-gatherers included. And it continues to be so for all other species except non-hunter-gatherer humans, who some 12,000 years ago chose to live *outside* of Earth's ecosystems. Yes, you read that right—*outside*. By adopting agriculture as their dominant method of subsistence, humans began living *outside* Earth-life ecosystems and began, slowly at first but now in a greatly accelerated way, the long, long journey that resulted in nearly 12,000 years of pillaging Earth-life ecosystems to build their human economies.

What "Continuous Habitable Zones" are to stars, ecosystems are to planets. These are zones and habitats, respectively, where conditions favorable to the evolution of life might exist and where life can evolve and thrive. Habitable zones lie within that range of distances from a star within which habitable planets could exist—not too far and therefore too cold, nor too close and therefore too hot, but just far enough away to allow water to remain in a liquid state on the surface of encircling planets. Similarly on Earth, ecosystems are those places where life can evolve, thrive, and survive, and where Earth-life species' economies, human economies, or both, might emerge.

Just as one is unlikely to find habitable planets capable of supporting complex animal and intelligent species life outside of habitable zones, so it is unlikely that human economies can survive *outside* of Earth's habitats and ecosystems. Yet, notwithstanding repeated environmentally driven economic and civilization collapse over the last 12,000 years, humans apparently did not connect this collapse with the ecosystems and biodiversity they were ravaging to build those economies, and perhaps never realized, either, that they were building their economies *outside* of Earth-life ecosystems and have continued doing so ever since.

Within Earth's ecosystems is everything an Earth-life species would need to survive. But unlike humans, who follow the money, other species simply follow the food. They experience neither food insecurity nor homelessness. Food, shelter, and water are freely available so neither food banks nor food stamps are necessary as ecosystems come stocked with the kinds of foods species inhabiting them might eat and all that food is local—one need only hunt. It's neither imported nor exported and hence neither Uber Eats nor container ships that can run aground are necessary. It follows, then, that there is also no need for wages, salaries, social security, unemployment checks, or charitable donations.

Free shelter comes in many forms such as caves, trees, nests, dens, and burrows. Once abandoned by one species a shelter can become home to another—there are no landlords, titles, transports of ownership or rental agreements to sign. No utility connections needed and hence no possibility of power failures nor blackouts as ecosystems also come equipped with built-in energy sources and waste recycling capabilities in the form of other species that share the ecosystem so that nothing goes to waste and hence there is no non-biodegradable pollution. What carnivores leave, scavengers devour, and what they leave, decomposers finish off. Then the cycle starts over again.

Unlike humans' buildings, cities, towns, and villages, ecosystems are designed for survival—an objective modern architects, city planners, and others often confuse with safety. Ecosystems are life-enabling environments designed to meet the survival needs of all species within them. Most of what plagues animal habitats today has been added or removed by humans. In ecosystems there are neither cages nor enclosures; all areas within them are accessible to and shared by all. And travel, of course, is free.

And, like getting around within and between EU countries, there are no border walls—not even for migrants. Inter-ecosystem wanderings require neither passports nor visas, nor vaccines nor anything else. In their pristine state, ecosystems have no highways to cross, hence there is no risk of being caught like a deer in the headlights of an eighteen-wheeler, nor would migrating birds risk getting sucked into Captain Sully's jet engines or colliding with the transparent glazed walls of a Chicago skyscraper.

Ecosystems also come with a built-in power source and a distributed energy grid system that functions regardless of weather conditions. Energy originates from the sun and flows through an ecosystem in the form of the food each species consumes, and hence through the bodies of species inhabiting an ecosystem. Plants, through photosynthesis, are primary producers of this energy, which is derived from the sun and stored as chemical bonds. Herbivores obtain the energy they need by feeding on plants, carnivores in turn feed on herbivores, and so on. In this way the bodies of these species are mobile bio-batteries and transmission grid components—a mobile energy storage grid and distribution system that functions regardless of weather! How clever!

Built into an ecosystem, therefore, are all an Earth-life species will ever need to survive and thrive. And that's precisely how hunter-gatherer humans survived and thrived for all but the last 12,000 of the 300,000 years of human existence on planet Earth—without a farm, a job, an employer, money, a car, a bike, or any of the myriad components that today make up the modern human lifeways, economy, and civilization. Imagine that! But how have modern humans used these Earth-life ecosystems?

The collapse of economies and civilizations over the last 12,000 years is due at least in part to the decimation of local ecosystems. If this taught humans any lessons, it is only relatively recently they have begun to associate the depletion of Earth-life ecosystems with the industrial-scale plundering of the natural resources being extracted to build human economies and civilizations. Indeed, not until relatively recently has there been much research, or care or concern, for ecosystems. Not until the *Millennium Ecosystem Assessment Report of 2005* emerged and laid bare the stark condition of Earth's ecosystems, warning of the potential for many to collapse unless the pillaging was substantially reduced or ceased, did humans begin to pay serious attention to the condition of Earth-life ecosystems across the planet.

Earth-life ecosystems and the services they provide were never meant just for humans and human well-being. But you would never know that given how humans have displaced or driven to extinction many other species, nor given the strong anthropocentric perspective taken by most research that calls attention to ecosystem destruction. Unsurprisingly, policies recommended to governments and business in ecosystem assessments are similarly characterized and presented in terms of the harm to human well-being caused by the loss of ecosystem services. And while harm to humans is certainly real, it does not begin to tell the real story.

The real issue humans must now confront is not just that we have devastated Earth-life ecosystems to the point of threatening our own extinction and that of all other species. Rather, we still don't have a clear understanding of what we have done and continue to do to cause this decimation. In fact, the real question is not *what* we have done but *why* we are destroying Earth-life ecosystems. Yes, think about it: Why? Is there a different way to build human economies? There is, and we will get to that in a bit.

Humans have always had a very cockeyed view of what Earth-life ecosystems are all about. Everyone knows from grade school, if not kindergarten, the city, town, or village where they live. But few could say, perhaps even at retirement, whether or not they live in an ecosystem, and if so what kind. Nor could they describe how the ecosystem services in their locale—as distinguished from services provided by the mayor, city council, or state government—increase their chances of survival.

Figure 2-1. Aerial view of the Suncor oil sands extraction facility on the banks of the Athabasca River near Fort McMurray in Alberta, Canada.

Not only is it difficult to connect polluters to specific harms, but there's also nothing illegal about extracting or burning fossil fuels. This carbon system has fueled human economies since the Industrial Revolution, and has not only been lawful, it's also been encouraged. (Credit: Mark Ralston/AFP via Getty Images)

Indeed, everyone recognizes numerous types of bird nests and understands their purpose, but not many appreciate that Earth-life ecosystems serve a similar purpose—they are a living, dynamic environment that enables one's daily survival, providing everything from food, water, and air to clothing, housing, and life itself, not just for the birds, but for humans and all other species. If humans truly understood what Earth-life ecosystems are, we would have realized that taking them apart to build our economies was akin to dismantling our houses to build our barns.

How did that which is so essential and integral to our very existence and survival become something with which we seem hardly familiar; whose purpose we so poorly understand and treat with such utter disregard?

This lack of appreciation for, or perhaps ignorance of, the purpose of Earth-life ecosystems prolongs a mistaken and dangerous view of ecosystems as economically nondescript, if picturesque, places: forests, deserts, mountains, and oceans, where humans go to get natural resources to build houses, roads, bridges, cities, and everything else we need. Generally, unless required by law and unless the law is enforced, no one is held responsible or accountable for any damage, waste, or harm that might result from resource extraction or when an action results in the degradation of an ecosystem, even if that action affects the entire world, such as the burning of the Amazon rain forest.

Figure 2-2. Aerial view of a chemically deforested area of the Amazon jungle caused by illegal mining activities in the river basin of the Madre de Dios region of southeast Peru.

(Credit: Cris Bouroncle/AFP via Getty Images)

Similarly, as I experienced in Singapore, no one is held accountable for the smoke from the clearing of forests in Sumatra, Indonesia, to establish palm oil plantations. While humans benefit from fresh air and good water quality, there is no market for fresh air and good water quality as such, and hence no market value. And if there is no value, then no person, company, or country has an incentive, or is compelled, to pay for such harm. Consider the illegally mined, chemically deforested area of the Amazon rain forest in Figure 2-2.

Oil companies, for instance, need only obtain a license to drill for fossil fuels, and until recently, bore little responsibility for any harm done to other species, native peoples, or the environment. And, what's true of oil is true of other extractive and most natural resource industries. Here are seven companies (Williams Energy, Northrop Grumman, General Electric, Dow Chemical, Rio Tinto, Koch Industries, and U.S. Steel) that pollute the world without consequences, according to Truthout.org. No one is charged for polluting the soil or atmosphere, nor for destroying pollinators or discharging chemicals into rivers and creating algae blooms and dead zones that destroy fish and other marine species in rivers and oceans.

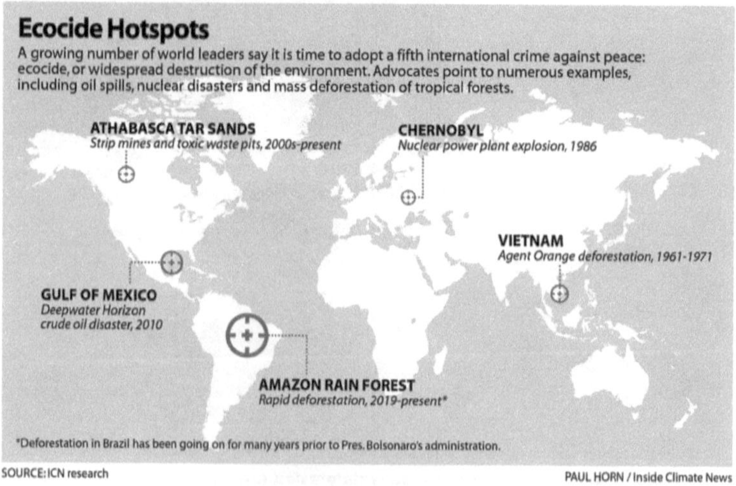

Figure 2-3. Ecocide Hotspots.

No one is being charged yet, but perhaps not for long. The International Criminal Court in 2023 deliberated defining a fifth international crime, ecocide, alongside war crimes, crimes against humanity, genocide, and the crime of aggression. Pope Francis describes ecocide as "the massive contamination of air, land and water," or "any action capable of producing an ecological disaster," and has proposed making such actions a sin for Catholics. International lawyers, environmentalists, and a growing number of world leaders say "ecocide"—widespread destruction of the environment as per examples Figure 2-3—would serve as a "moral red line" for the planet.

But if one ever stopped to wonder where humans get off thinking all those natural resources and species across the Earth belong to us, and are there for the taking, one need only look back a few centuries at what we began telling ourselves. We adopted beliefs, pulled out of thin air, that quickly permeated not only religions and politics but economics as well.

If one starts off believing, as Clive Ponting notes in *A New Green History of the World,* what the Christian Bible claims in Psalm 115—"The Heavens are the Lord's but the earth he has given to the sons of men"—or in Psalm 8—"Thou has given man dominion over the work of thy hands," it should come as no surprise that early and medieval Christians accepted that their God had given humans the right to exploit plants, animals, and the whole world for their benefit. In this view, Ponting writes, "Nature is not seen as sacred, but open to exploitation by humans without any moral qualms—indeed humans have the right to use nature in whatever way they think best . . . Interventions and modifications to the natural world such as by extending cultivated areas, deforestation, and driving species to extinction and appropriating the planet's resources were readily interpreted as taking part in God's plan to improve upon creation."

Ponting notes that this belief system "produced a highly anthropocentric view of the world and had an enduring impact on later European thought.

From such views it was easy to conclude that humans, the only creatures with a soul and a life after death (according to Christian belief), enjoyed a wholly different status from other animals and it was a small and logical step therefore to welcome greater control over the natural world and to believe that this would be pleasing to God." And it is fair to say that the fact that as a species we are now collectively worried about the state of Earth-life ecosystems, those inherited human views have had a profound effect and, today, might have hardly changed.

But Earth-life ecosystems are far more important than the philosophers, scientists, and religions of Western Civilization imagined. They are the very cradles that enable Earth-life species and humans to mature and build their economies and civilizations—and to survive. It was in "them-there" Earth-life ecosystems, long before there was ever a religion, politics, constitutions, kings, queens, governments, or economists, that our hunter-gatherer forebears lived and built their hunter-gatherer economies during most of those 300,000 years of our species' existence, and did so without destroying their economies, civilizations, or Earth-life ecosystems. What did they know about building survival-driven human economies that post-Neolithic Revolution humans seemingly forgot, willingly, and that twenty-first century humans may never have known?

While we seem hardly eager to care about Earth-life ecosystems right here on Earth, we seem to care a lot more about the potential for life on other planets, and one is awestruck by our efforts to explore them, such as with the amazing science and technologies that, for example, have made the International Space Station possible. We marvel that those astronauts routinely drink their "pee" and eat their "crap" and breathe a purified version of their "farts" and the air they exhale. But we seldom stop to think that those same functions, and many more, are routinely and unceremoniously performed by trees around us and the soil beneath our feet. These functions include production of atmospheric oxygen, soil formation and retention, nutrient cycling, water cycling, and the provisioning of habitats themselves, all without any of the fuss and muss of a SpaceX supply delivery—just plants, pollinators, soil, microbes, earthworms, and other Earth-life decomposers quietly going about the business of ensuring life in the ecosystem continues smoothly, neither NASA nor SpaceX included.

Indeed, we tend to forget that Earth-life ecosystems are also in space aboard "space station Earth," that third planet in the inner solar system, and that ecosystems are its indispensable life-support systems for all species, *including humans,* and have been performing such services for nearly 4.7 billion years without a hitch—and long, long, long before there was a space station.

As we get ready, then, to take a deeper look at what humans are doing to Earth-life ecosystems and what this means for our human economies, take time to consider the purpose of ecosystems and what they really are. Bear in mind that hidden beneath all those mouthwatering natural resources—or rather, if you prefer, the beauty and seeming simplicity of those gentle rolling hills, mysterious forests, warbling streams, rolling savannas, or soaring mountains, that were once filled with innumerable curious species scientists are still trying to identify and count before we drive them to extinction—are Earth-life ecosystems' life-support apparatus that keeps it all running smoothly, especially those systems beneath our feet. Be assured, they are every whit as amazing as those gizmos on the International Space Station—it's just that, well, they are biological and better hidden.

Even though everyone and all species in the world depend on the goods and services of Earth-life ecosystems and the services they provide for survival; and even though humans themselves physically exist in Earth-life ecosystems; except as needed, we built our economies and lived our lives entirely as if we were separate from, and independent of, all other species and from those ecosystems themselves—as if we were *outside* the community of life. Unlike all other Earth-life species that participate in ecosystem processes and cycles that make life possible (the flows of carbon, water, nitrogen, phosphorus, and energy, among others), humans pretty much managed to mostly ignore or marginally participate in them, then went on to create their own non-compatible and functionally unsustainable versions.

Humans essentially came up with an entirely different way to eke out a living, farming *outside ecosystems*—taking them apart to build our human economies while still managing to depend pretty much on all Earth-life's ecosystems' products and services. Unlike our pre-agriculture hunter-gatherer forebears, who collaborated with Earth-life's ecosystems and biodiversity to enable and sustain life, humans from the Neolithic Revolution to the present chose to rearrange ecosystems where possible to suit human purposes. And they came up with nonrenewable energy sources where they could not use the renewables of the ecosystem and have now come dangerously close to destroying them in the process.

It was only relatively recently that we noticed the impact of the changes we have been making to build our human economies on the *outside.* But for the likes of Darwin, they were neither monitored nor studied until about a hundred years ago. Most ecosystems were viewed as wildernesses awaiting scientific exploration, scenic landscapes to be discovered, or resource warehouses awaiting plunder by industries to build corporate wealth, the economic value of which, until recently, was not even seen as a contribution to the human economy.

Not until United Nations Secretary-General Kofi Annan commissioned a study of the state of the Earth's ecosystems did humans take a close look at the nature-economy nexus. And what was discovered turned out to be Earth-shattering: *Many life-sustaining ecosystems and the services we depend upon for survival and to build our economies are approaching a state of near-collapse. The Millennium Ecosystem Report of 2005*, the recent 2021 update, and other assessments lay out in stark detail these findings, some of which are highlighted and commented on below.

Scientists in these assessments refer to the benefits humans and all species obtain from Earth-life ecosystems as "ecosystem services" and describe them in terms of human well-being, depicting them as free services intended primarily for human benefit. They typically make only casual references to the innumerable Earth-life species that once occupied, and to a large extent still do, those Earth-life ecosystems for millions of years. This human-centric way of viewing Earth-life ecosystems, as Ponting noted above, has been, and continues to be, the root cause of the human pillage of Earth-life ecosystems. It would seem our scientists, with their human well-being perspective, are of a similar persuasion. Hence, whereas the primary goal for Earth-life ecosystems may well have been to enable the survival of Earth-life species and humans, the goal of humanity has been to take possession of all Earth's ecosystem resources as goods and services to be traded in our capitalist economy, whose goal is the pursuit of endless growth and gain rather than life and survival.

The current sorry state of Earth-life ecosystems is an indictment of the industrial-scale approach to exploiting these resources. Not unlike those humans who finally found their way to Easter Island then endangered their very survival by ravaging it, we too, geologically speaking, are relative Johnny-come-latelies to Earth-life ecosystems and have similarly set about ravaging them and endangering our survival as a species. Many species, like the dinosaurs, pre-dated *Homo sapiens'* existence. But, unlike humans who have chosen to build their economies *outside* of Earth-life's ecosystems and have eviscerated most of them in the process (just 3 percent are left in pristine form), surviving Earth-life species have remained where they can *within* surviving ecosystems and, like Orangutans in Borneo, leave only when they are driven out by humans. Or else they continue to hang on, dodging humans and building their economies within surviving Earth-life ecosystems wherever they can.

As noted above, one should never think of Earth-life ecosystems as places where extractive industries are free to plunder and pollute with impunity for a profit. Aboriginal humans, not just orangutans, live in them, too. Nor should they be seen as simply dynamic complexes of plants, animals, microbes, and physical environmental features that interact with one another any more than one would think of the complex ingenious machinery on the International Space Station as just racks of interacting electronic equipment. Just as the components on the station were carefully selected and engineered to enable scientists and astronauts to remain alive while performing numerous scientific experiments, so Earth-life ecosystems evolved to enable humans and all Earth-life species to survive as we go about the task of eking out a living aboard Spaceship Earth—even though, at times, it may seem unexciting.

Scientists have grouped ecosystems and ecosystem services as shown below.

Table 2-1. Earth-life ecosystems

Marine	Mountain	Urban
Coastal	Grasslands	Island
Inland Water	Mangroves	Forests
Ocean	Polar	Desert
Aquatic Shallow Spas	Cultivated	Taiga
Lake	Savanna	Dryland
Fresh Water	Tundra	Terrestrial

(Source: Millennium Ecosystem Assessment Report 2005, UN)

Ecosystems such as forests, grasslands, mangroves, and urban areas provide different types of services (Table 2-2) classified as provisioning, regulating, and cultural services. They also provide supporting services that support and maintain all other services. These serve all species, and affect all aspects of human well-being, including basic material needs such as food and shelter, personal health, security, good social relations, and freedom of choice and action. Ecosystem services, then, benefit all species, including people.

Table 2-2. Ecosystem services

Provisioning Services	Regulating Services	Cultural Services
Products obtained from ecosystems	*Benefits obtained from regulation of ecosystem processes*	*Nonmaterial benefits obtained from ecosystems*
■ Food	■ Climate regulation	■ Spiritual and religious
■ Fresh water	■ Disease regulation	■ Recreation and ecotourism
■ Fuelwood	■ Water regulation	■ Aesthetic
■ Fiber	■ Water purification	■ Inspirational
■ Biochemicals	■ Pollination	■ Educational
■ Genetic resources		■ Sense of place
		■ Cultural heritage

Supporting Services		
Services necessary for the production of all other ecosystem services		
■ Soil formation	■ Nutrient cycling	■ Primary production

(Source: Millennium Ecosystem Assessment Report 2005, UN)

Each ecosystem service is further detailed by type below, clarifying the many benefits derived from ecosystems.

Provisioning services

- ***Food and fiber.*** This includes the vast range of food products derived from plants, animals, and microbes, as well as materials such as wood, jute, hemp, silk, and many other products derived from ecosystems.
- ***Fuel.*** Wood, dung, and other biological materials serve as sources of energy.
- ***Genetic resources.*** These include the genes and genetic information used for animal and plant breeding and biotechnology.
- ***Biochemicals, natural medicines, and pharmaceuticals.*** Many medicines, biocides, food additives (such as alginates), and biological materials are derived from ecosystems.
- ***Ornamental resources.*** Animal products, such as skins and shells, and flowers are used as ornaments, although the value of these resources is often culturally determined. This is an example of linkages across categories of ecosystem services.

- ***Fresh water.*** Fresh water is another example of linkages between categories—in this case, between provisioning and regulating services.

Regulating services

- ***Air quality maintenance.*** Ecosystems contribute chemicals to and extract chemicals from the atmosphere, influencing many aspects of air quality.
- ***Climate regulation.*** Ecosystems influence climate locally and globally. For example, at a local scale, changes in land cover can affect temperature and precipitation. At the global scale, ecosystems play an important role in climate by sequestering or emitting greenhouse gases.
- ***Water regulation.*** The timing and magnitude of runoff, flooding, and aquifer recharge can be strongly influenced by changes in land cover, including alterations that change the water storage potential of the water system, such as the conversion of wetlands or the replacement of forests with croplands, or croplands with urban areas.
- ***Erosion control.*** Vegetative cover plays an important role in soil retention and the prevention of landslides.
- ***Water purification and waste treatment.*** Ecosystems can be a source of impurities in fresh water but also can help to filter out and decompose organic wastes introduced into inland waters and coastal and marine ecosystems.
- ***Regulating human diseases.*** Changes in ecosystems can directly change the abundance of human pathogens, such as cholera, and can alter the populations of disease vectors, such as mosquitoes.
- ***Biological control.*** Ecosystem changes affect the prevalence of crop and livestock pests and diseases.
- ***Pollination.*** Ecosystem changes affect the distribution, abundance, and effectiveness of pollinators.
- ***Storm protection.*** The presence of coastal ecosystems such as mangroves and coral reefs can dramatically reduce the damage caused by hurricanes or large waves.

Cultural services

These are the nonmaterial benefits people obtain from ecosystems through spiritual enrichment, cognitive development, reflection, recreation, and aesthetic experiences, including:

- ***Cultural diversity.*** The diversity of ecosystems is one factor influencing the diversity of cultures.
- ***Spiritual and religious values.*** Many religions attach spiritual and religious values to ecosystems or their components.
- ***Knowledge systems* (traditional and formal).** Ecosystems influence the types of knowledge systems developed by different cultures.
- ***Educational values.*** Ecosystems and their components and processes provide the basis for both formal and informal education in many societies.
- ***Inspiration.*** Ecosystems provide a rich source of inspiration for art, folklore, national symbols, architecture, and advertising.
- ***Aesthetic values.*** Many people find beauty or aesthetic value in various aspects of ecosystems, as reflected in the support for parks, "scenic drives," and the selection of housing locations.
- ***Social relations.*** Ecosystems influence the types of social relations established in cultures. Fishing societies, for example, differ in many respects in their social relations from nomadic herding or agricultural societies.
- ***Sense of place.*** Many people value the "sense of place" that is associated with recognized features of their environment, including aspects of the ecosystem.
- ***Cultural heritage values.*** Many societies place high value on the maintenance of either historically important landscapes ("cultural landscapes") or culturally significant species.
- ***Recreation and ecotourism.*** People often choose where to spend their leisure time based in part on the characteristics of the natural or cultivated landscapes in a particular area.

Cultural services are tightly bound to human values and behavior, as well as to human institutions and patterns of social, economic, and political organization. Thus, perceptions of cultural services are more likely to differ among individuals and communities than, say, perceptions of the importance of food production.

Supporting services

Supporting services are those that are necessary to produce all other ecosystem services. Examples of supporting services are primary production, production of atmospheric oxygen, soil formation and retention, nutrient cycling, water cycling, and provisioning of habitat. They differ from provisioning, regulating, and cultural services in that their impacts are either indirect or occur over a very long time, whereas changes in the other categories are relatively direct and short-term.

Different combinations of services are derived by Earth-life species and humans from ecosystems as shown in Figure 2-4. Their ability to deliver these services depends on complex biological, chemical, and physical interactions, which in turn are affected specifically mostly by human activities.

A Science Direct article notes that between 1960 and 2000, the human population doubled. Also, between 1960 and 2000 the global economy increased more than sixfold, and the world population doubled to six billion people, and with it the demand for ecosystem services grew significantly.

To meet this demand, food production increased by roughly two-and-a-half times, water use doubled, wood harvests for pulp and paper production tripled, installed hydropower capacity doubled, and timber production increased by more than half. These changes contributed to substantial net gains in human well-being and economic development and allowed the world to celebrate how many have been raised out of poverty.

According to the UN's 2015 Millennium Development Goals Report, extreme poverty declined significantly over the last two decades. In 1990, nearly half of the population in the developing world lived on less than $1.25 a day; that proportion dropped to 14 percent in 2015, and the number of people living in extreme poverty declined by more than half, falling from 1.9 billion in 1990 to 836 million in 2015. Most progress has occurred since 2000.

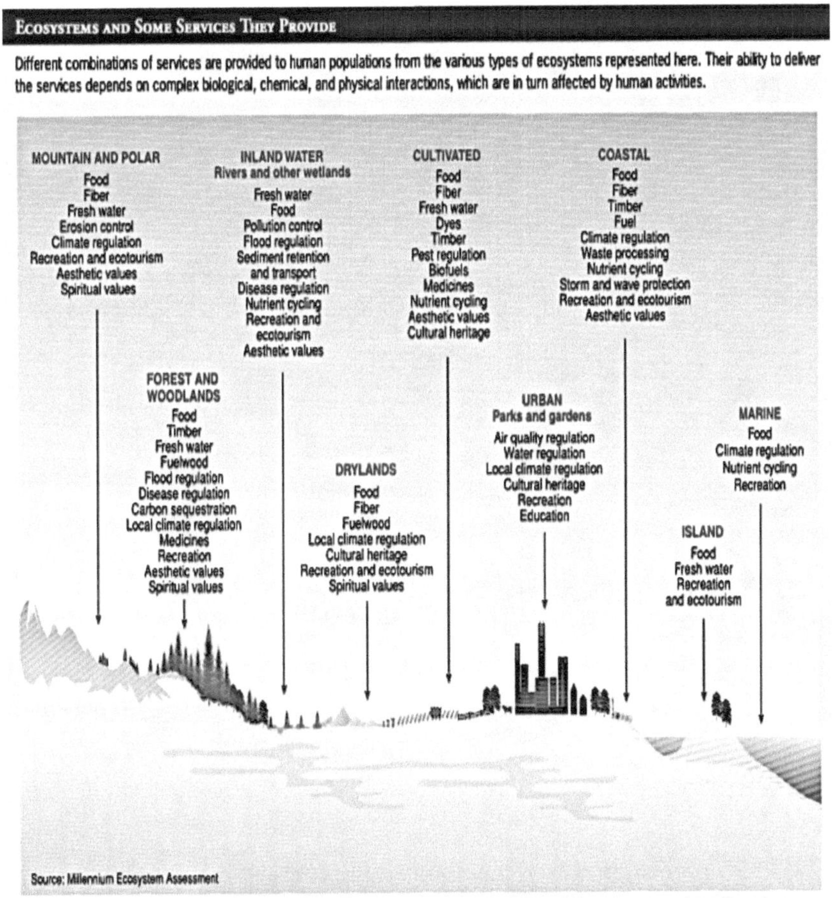

Figure 2-4. Ecosystems and selected services.

Different combinations of services are derived by Earth-life species and humans from ecosystems. Their ability to deliver these services depends on complex biological, chemical, and physical interactions, which are in turn affected specifically mostly by human activities. (Credit: Millennium Ecosystem Assessment)

Table 2-3. Key trends in ecosystems and their services

Status indicates whether the condition of the service globally has been enhanced (if the productive capacity of the service has been increased, for example) or degraded in the recent past. Definitions of "enhanced" and "degraded" are provided in the note below. A fourth category, supporting services, is not included here as they are not used directly by people.

Service	Sub-category	Status	Notes
Provisioning Services			
Food	crops	▲	substantial production increase
	livestock	▲	substantial production increase
	capture fisheries	▼	declining production due to overharvest
	aquaculture	▲	substantial production increase
	wild foods	▼	declining production
Fiber	timber	+/–	forest loss in some regions, growth in others
	cotton, hemp, silk	+/–	declining production of some fibers, growth in others
	wood fuel	▼	declining production
Genetic resources		▼	lost through extinction and crop genetic resource loss
Biochemicals, natural medicines, pharmaceuticals		▼	lost through extinction, overharvest
Fresh water		▼	unsustainable use for drinking, industry, and irrigation; amount of hydro energy unchanged, but dams increase ability to use that energy
Regulating Services			
Air quality regulation		▼	decline in ability of atmosphere to cleanse itself
Climate regulation	global	▲	net source of carbon sequestration since mid-century
	regional and local	▼	preponderance of negative impacts
Water regulation		+/–	varies depending on ecosystem change and location
Erosion regulation		▼	increased soil degradation
Water purification and waste treatment		▼	declining water quality
Disease regulation		+/–	varies depending on ecosystem change
Pest regulation		▼	natural control degraded through pesticide use
Pollination		▼[a]	apparent global decline in abundance of pollinators
Natural hazard regulation		▼	loss of natural buffers (wetlands, mangroves)
Cultural Services			
Spiritual and religious values		▼	rapid decline in sacred groves and species
Aesthetic values		▼	decline in quantity and quality of natural lands
Recreation and ecotourism		+/–	more areas accessible but many degraded

Note: For provisioning services, we define enhancement to mean increased production of the service through changes in area over which the service is provided (e.g., spread of agriculture) or increased production per unit area. We judge the production to be degraded if the current use exceeds sustainable levels. For regulating and supporting services, enhancement refers to a change in the service that leads to greater benefits for people (e.g., the service of disease regulation could be improved by eradication of a vector known to transmit a disease to people). Degradation of regulating and supporting services means a reduction in the benefits obtained from the service, either through a change in the service (e.g., mangrove loss reducing the storm protection benefits of an ecosystem) or through human pressures on the service exceeding its limits (e.g., excessive pollution exceeding the capability of ecosystems to maintain water quality). For cultural services, enhancement refers to a change in the ecosystem features that increase the cultural (recreational, aesthetic, spiritual, etc.) benefits provided by the ecosystem.

[a] Indicates *low to medium certainty*. All other trends are *medium to high certainty*.

(Source: World Resources Institute)

This progress, however, has come at the cost of degradation of many ecosystems, species, and their services (Table 2-3). This degradation has increased the risks of abrupt and harmful changes (the subject of these assessments) and harm to many species and some groups of people, especially if these ecosystems should collapse. In effect, instead of restraining human population growth (by far the major driver of ecosystem damage), thereby reducing demand for the world's ecosystems' services, the world, its nations, and their governments, together with international bodies and their programs designed to improve human well-being like the UN's Sustainable Development Goals, have opted to pillage Earth-life ecosystems, drive innumerable species extinct, and continue down the path of potentially destroying life as we know it.

Yes, yes, yes, but what exactly have humans changed, one is often asked somewhat exasperatedly, and what have these changes done to humans, other species, and Earth-life ecosystems? The referenced UN and other independent assessments provide answers in exhausting detail. Below are a few takeaways.

Many are just beginning to discover and are astonished to learn that human global changes to Earth-life ecosystems have been so vast that scientists believe that, like the dinosaurs, humans may have started a new geological epoch, a human epoch temporarily named the Anthropocene. Scientists have *proposed a new geological epoch to mark the start of significant human impact on Earth's geology and ecosystems.* This impact includes, but is hardly limited to, anthropogenic climate change.

Figure 2-5. Examples of Earth's biomes.

(Source: OpenStax.org Rice University)

How humans have changed the structure of Earth-life ecosystems. The ecosystems and biomes most significantly altered globally by human activity include marine and freshwater ecosystems, temperate broadleaf forests, temperate grasslands, Mediterranean forests, and tropical dry forests, some of which are shown in Figure 2-5. It's helpful to have some idea where these biomes and their ecosystems are located across the world, as seen in Figure 2-6.

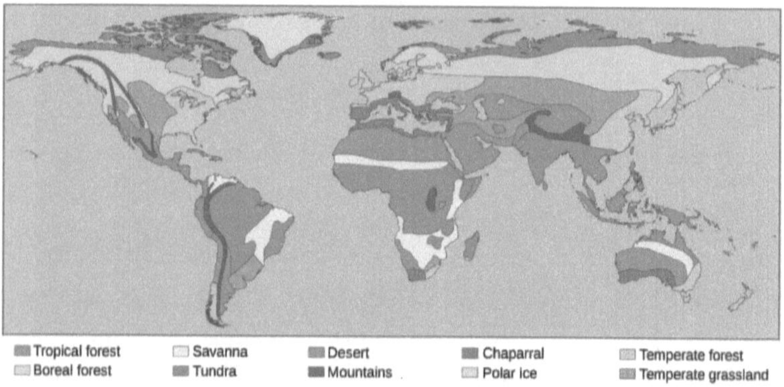

Figure 2-6. The world's eight major biomes are distinguished by characteristic temperatures and precipitation. Polar ice caps and mountains are also shown.
(Source: OpenStax)

Given humanity's massive population explosion, the demand for food, water, timber, fiber, and fuel has skyrocketed. So, it is not surprising that ecosystems have been heavily affected to meet that dramatic growth from two billion in 1927 to six billion in 1999 to eight billion on November 15, 2022 (as per the UN), and consequently, the demand for food, water, timber, fiber, and fuel has surged. More than half of the original area of many types of grasslands and forests had been converted to farmland by 1990. The only terrestrial ecosystems which have seen relatively little change are tundra and boreal forests but that is changing as climate change has begun to affect them.

This demand led to *the conversion of 33 percent of Earth's terrestrial surface to farms.*

Cultivated systems (areas where at least 30 percent of the landscape is in cropland, shifting cultivation, confined livestock production, or freshwater aquaculture) now cover one-quarter of Earth's terrestrial surface. In fact, more land was converted to cropland in the 30 years after 1950 than in the 150 years between 1700 and 1850. Consequently, further agricultural expansion is diminishing in many regions because most suitable land has already been converted.

In sum, the seizure of land for agriculture repurposed the Earth's ecosystems, displaced innumerable species and destroyed their habitats, and drove innumerable species to extinction, effectively ending the ecosystem services they had provided.

But who or what is driving this rapid conversion to agricultural land? Among the many ways Earth's ecosystems are being eaten up is through foreign investment. Affluence is driving the global displacement of land, according to research published in ScienceDirect. And in an article in takeapart.com, Erica Gies claims that foreign investors are increasingly buying or leasing large swaths of land in developing countries in pursuit of food, water, and profit, according to human rights groups and academics, putting people and the environment at risk. Since 2000, international investors have grabbed an estimated 93 million acres worldwide—an area the size of Japan—according to the Land Matrix, an international initiative that tracks the phenomenon. By the Land Matrix's reckoning, Indonesia has been the target of the largest number of deals, with 120, followed by Cambodia, Mozambique, Ethiopia, and Laos. Figure 2-7 shows a map of such investments across the globe.

Activists call these acquisitions "land grabs" and assert they violate human rights. The International Land Coalition, a group that includes Oxfam International and the United Nations Environment Program, defines land grabs as acquisitions completed "without prior consent of the preexisting land users, and with no consideration of the social and environmental impacts." Similar if not more extensive demand has been made of the world's marine ecosystems.

The environmental impacts of land grabs and other repurposing of primary forest and other terrestrial ecosystems are devasting to ecosystems and biodiversity, as well as to aboriginal human occupants. Those effects can include deforestation, human settlement in primary wildlife habitats, growth of crop and livestock production, and urbanization. Often, human health considerations are largely ignored in land grabs, land-use change, and destruction of habitat. Encroachment by humans and livestock into biodiverse habitats can provide new pathways for pathogens to spill over and increase transmission rates.

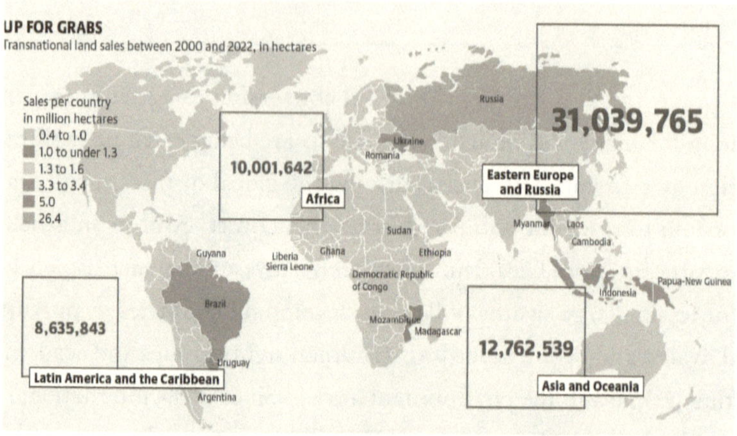

Figure. 2-7. Land grabbing: the race for hectares
(Source: Roman Herre ;Credit: Eimermacher/stockmarpluswalter)

It is also well known that land use change is a globally significant driver of pandemics and has caused the emergence of more than 30 percent of new diseases reported since 1960. In addition, such random repurposing of ecosystems has also been known to create effects with climate change (forest loss, heat island effects, and burning of forests to clear land) and biodiversity loss that in turn has led to important emerging diseases.

It's amazing that only 3 percent of the world's land remains ecologically intact with healthy populations of its original animals and undisturbed habitat. These fragments of undamaged wilderness are mainly in parts of the Amazon and Congo tropical forests, eastern Siberian and northern Canadian forests and tundra, and the Sahara. However, unchecked climate change will cause severe drying of the Amazon forest, possibly including the remaining fragments of pristine land.

And what's happening on land has begun to happen in Earth's marine ecosystems.

(1) ***Marine ecosystems – 'Oceans are in hot water and running out of fish.'***

Global demand for food and animal feed over the last 50 years has resulted in fishing pressure so strong that the biomass of both targeted species and those caught incidentally (the "bycatch") has been reduced in much of the world to one-tenth of the levels prior to the onset of industrial fishing operations, whose fishing grounds cover one-third of the planet. The degradation of fisheries is also reflected in the fact that fish harvested today are increasingly coming from less-valuable lower trophic levels as populations of higher trophic-level species are depleted.

Marine ecosystems are also facing many other threats. Since 1970, populations of more than 1,000 marine species have undergone declines of approximately 50 percent, and considerable habitat losses have been observed in key ecosystems including mangroves, sea grasses, and coral reefs. Fisheries are unmanaged or poorly managed across much of the world, and declines in these systems continue in most regions. Marine ecosystems are also much more intensively used today than in the past for purposes beyond fishing, including energy generation, transport, mining, and waste disposal. Even the deepest regions of the ocean are increasingly at risk from human activities.

Among marine ecosystems, coral reefs have been and will continue to be particularly affected by warming temperatures and the advance of ocean acidification. Coral bleaching events (in which corals expel the photosynthetic algae that live inside their tissues, leaving the coral white in appearance) have become increasingly common, largely because of temperature extremes.

(2) ***Freshwater ecosystems: the main source of drinking water***

Water covers about 70 percent of Earth's surface and houses a range of saltwater (marine) and freshwater ecosystems. Only about 2.5 percent of this water is fresh, and most of that is in the form of ice, leaving a relatively small amount—less than 1 percent—for freshwater ecosystems. However, this small fraction of liquid freshwater harbors about 10 percent of the planet's known animal species and supports critical ecosystem services, such as the production of a sustained clean drinking water supply. Both freshwater and marine systems are sources of food, transport, waste disposal, energy production, and protection for shorelines and coastal communities.

Freshwater ecosystems have been modified through the creation of dams and through the withdrawal of water for human use. The construction of dams and other structures along rivers has affected flows in 60 percent of the large river systems of the world. Water removal for human uses has reduced the flow of several major rivers, including the Nile, Yellow, and Colorado rivers, so much so that they do not always flow to the sea.

(3) ***Water use: 70 percent worldwide is used for agriculture.***

Groundwater is a key part of successful adaptation to periodic drought, which in turn is a key aspect of maintaining stable food supplies. In many cases it is unknown how long this groundwater depletion can continue without the supply reaching an end, possibly an abrupt end. The amount of water impounded behind dams has quadrupled since 1960, and three to six times as much water is held in reservoirs as in natural rivers. Water withdrawals from rivers and lakes have doubled since 1960.

Satellites measuring gravity now reveal that groundwater supplies have decreased rapidly around the world over the past decade, including from key aquifers in California, the High Plains, and the southeastern United States (Famiglietti et al., 2011). For example, aquifers are being depleted in many parts of the world, including the southeast of the United States. Groundwater is a critical "water savings account" that farmers can tap to ride out droughts; if that safety net reaches an abrupt end, the impact of droughts on the food supply will be even larger.

(4) ***Nitrogen and phosphorus in terrestrial ecosystems.***

Since 1960, flows of reactive (biologically available) nitrogen in terrestrial ecosystems have doubled and flows of phosphorus have tripled. Synthetic nitrogen fertilizer was first manufactured in 1913, but more than half of all the synthetic nitrogen fertilizer used since then has been used since 1985. This is just one of the many ways that demonstrate how humans have impacted the ecosystem.

(5) ***Climate change: Anthropogenic climate change will eventually become the strongest driver of ecosystem collapse.***

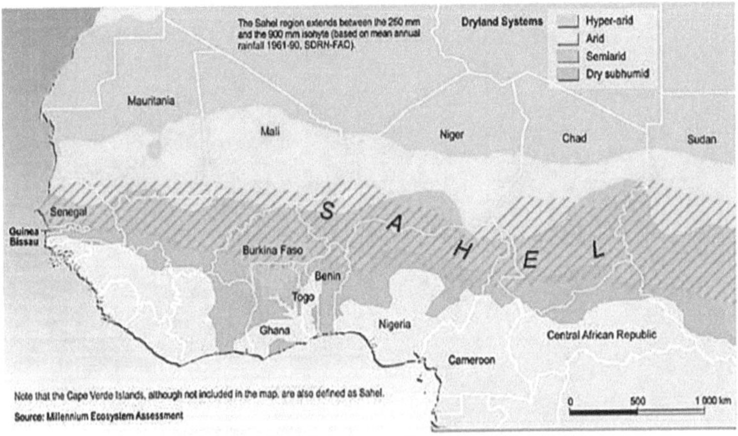

Figure 2-8. The Sahel is the semi-arid transition region.

(Photo credit: Ocean World)

Climate changes now underway will cause ecosystems to change noticeably and will include abrupt state changes within the next few decades.

Within five years of 1995, for example, cattle-supporting arable land in the Sahel region of Africa changed to an unproductive desert and caused widespread famine and an international crisis. The economies, agriculture, livestock, and human populations of much of Mauritania, Mali, Chad, Niger, and Burkina Faso were severely impacted. The Sahel (Figure 2-8) is a semi-arid transition region that comprises a dryland ecosystem between the Sahara Desert to the north and wetter regions of equatorial Africa to the south. It extends from the Atlantic in the west to the Indian ocean in the east. It has high variability of rainfall, and the land consists of stabilized ancient sand seas.

Similarly, the Amazon forest (Figure 2-9), which represents the world's largest terrestrial biome, is the tropical ecosystem potentially most vulnerable to abrupt shifts in response to climate change in concert with agricultural development. It has already begun to show signs of accelerating rather than reducing climate change. According to Phys.org it released nearly 20 percent more carbon dioxide into the atmosphere over the last decade than it absorbed. Moreover, transitions from forests to savanna and from savanna to grassland tend to be abrupt.

Figure 2-9. Deforestation in the Brazilian Amazon, one of the few fragments of wilderness undamaged by human activities.

(Photo credit: Florian Plaucheur/AFP/Getty Images)

CO_2 has always played a key role in the presence or absence of life on Earth. Some 12,000 years ago, as the last Ice Age receded, its increase may well have warmed the Earth sufficiently to allow some hunter-gatherer humans to abandon eking out a living *within* Earth-life ecosystems, and instead, find their way into farming. Now, 12,000 years later, it's twenty-first century humans that are driving the current anthropogenic CO_2 climate change. But this time around instead of helping humanity, CO_2 has become the source of multi-decade droughts and scorching heat waves and has begun to destroy the very farms we abandoned Earth-life ecosystems to cultivate. It may well destroy most Earth-life ecosystems and biodiversity before it's done.

Since 1750, the atmospheric concentration of carbon dioxide has increased by about 32 percent (from about 280 to 376 parts per million in 2003), primarily due to the combustion of fossil fuels and because of land-use changes. Approximately 60 percent of that increase (60 parts per million) has taken place since 1959. By the end of the century, climate change and its impacts may be the dominant direct driver of ecosystem and biodiversity loss and of changes in ecosystem services globally.

---

(6) ***Loss of biodiversity means loss of food, medicines, water, and energy.***

Humans are fundamentally, and to a significant extent irreversibly, changing the diversity of life on Earth, and most of these changes represent a loss of biodiversity. The number of species on the planet is declining. Genetic diversity has declined globally, particularly among cultivated species, and the distribution of species on Earth is becoming more homogenous. Across a range of taxonomic groups, the population size, range, or both, of the majority of species is currently declining. According to the Living Planet Report 2024, the most important direct driver of biodiversity loss in terrestrial systems in the last several decades has been land-use change, primarily the conversion of pristine native habitats into agricultural systems. Seventy-five percent of the Earth's ice-free land surface has already been significantly altered. Most of the oceans are polluted, and more than 85 percent of wetlands have been lost.

Reductions in biodiversity are detrimental to ecosystem functions.

Biodiversity plays a critical role in providing food, fiber, water, energy, medicines, and other genetic materials and is key to the regulation of climate, water quality, pollution, pollination services, flood control, and storm surges.

Scientists now have a good understanding of the importance of biodiversity. According to Cardinale et al. (2012), "Biodiversity loss and its impact on humanity":

- "There is mounting evidence that biodiversity increases the stability of ecosystem functions through time."
- "Reductions in the number of genres, species and functional groups of organisms reduce the efficiency by which whole communities capture biologically essential resources (nutrients, water, light, prey), and convert those resources into biomass."
- "The impact of biodiversity on any single ecosystem process is nonlinear and saturating, such that change accelerates as biodiversity loss increases." Therefore, as biodiversity loss increases, ecological systems are increasingly likely to suddenly hit a "tipping point."
- "Diverse communities are more productive because they contain key species that have a large influence on productivity."
- "Loss of diversity across trophic levels has the potential to influence ecosystem functions even more strongly than diversity loss within trophic levels."
- "Functional traits of organisms have large impacts on the magnitude of ecosystem functions, which give rise to a wide range of plausible impacts of extinction on ecosystem function." This means that removal of species with unique ecological attributes is especially disruptive to ecosystems.

The loss of biodiversity, then, is not only an environmental issue, but a self-preservation issue.

Freshwater biodiversity is declining far faster than biodiversity in oceans or forests. *The Global Ramsar Wetlands Outlook 2018* reports that almost 90 percent of global wetlands have been lost since 1700, and global mapping has recently revealed the extent to which humans have altered millions of kilometers of rivers. These changes have had a profound impact on freshwater biodiversity with population trends for monitored freshwater species falling steeply.

Soil biodiversity is often widely ignored, but critical to all life. *Life above depends on the life beneath.* Soil hosts one of the largest reservoirs of biodiversity on Earth: Up to 90 percent of living organisms in terrestrial ecosystems, including some pollinators, spend part of their life cycle in soil habitats. The variety of soil components, filled with air and water, creates an incredible diversity of habitats for myriad soil organisms that underpin our life on this planet. Without soil biodiversity, many terrestrial ecosystems would collapse. We now know that above and below ground, species are in constant collaboration. Improved understanding of this relationship will help to better predict the consequences of biodiversity change and loss.

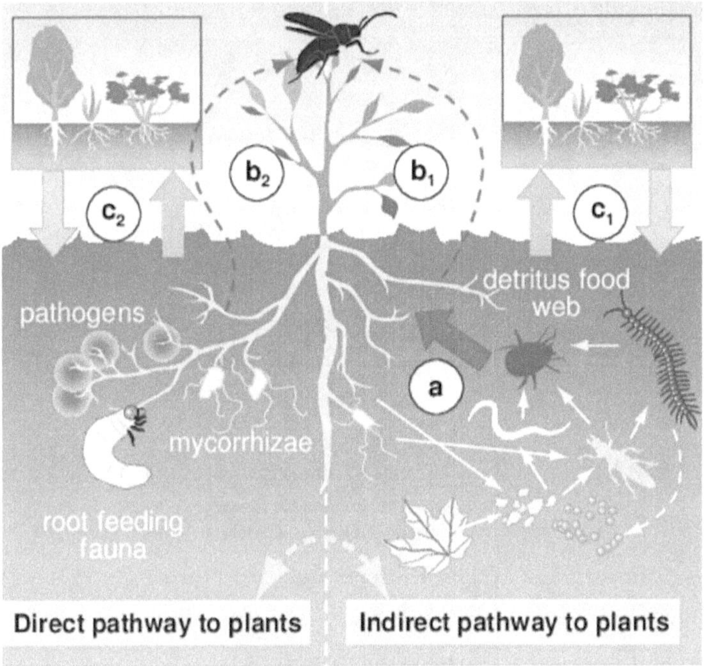

Figure 2-10. Soil biodiversity.
(Source: researchgate)

Insect biodiversity is rapidly diminishing. *National Geographic* claims there are about 1.4 billion insects for every human on Earth, and all of them play a crucial role in maintaining life in Earth-life terrestrial ecosystems. An October 2019 Forbes article reports that every season pollination from honeybees, native bees, and flies delivers billions of dollars in economic value. Between $235 billion and $577 billion worth of annual global food production relies on their contributions.

Beyond bees and flies, insects in general are indispensable to the human food chain and play a central role in a variety of processes, including pollination, herbivory, and nutrient cycling, and as food sources for higher trophic levels such as birds, mammals, and amphibians. Insects more than ever are experiencing a multicontinental crisis that is apparent as reductions in abundance, diversity, and biomass become evident. Driving this decline are habitat loss and degradation, pesticides, and climate change. Other factors include disease, invasive species, and light pollution.

Figure 2-11. Miscellaneous Insects.
(Source: Conservation Science and practice, a journal of the Society for Conservation Biology)

One can continue here but you get the idea. Humans have essentially rearranged and pushed Earth-life ecosystems to places they've not been before, and it is clear most are unlikely to return to their original state.

How humans changed the functions and cycles of Earth-life processes within ecosystems.

No one pulls up at an Exxon filling station expecting to recharge a Tesla at the gas pump or hails a taxi expecting it to take off and fly them to their destination city or country. Not yet, anyway, because everyone knows how these human inventions work. Yet, even after 12,000 years, and until relatively recently, humans had no idea that excavating or paving the Earth with endless stretches of asphalt roads would destroy the life below (i.e., soil bacteria). Those bacteria work with species above to sustain life, by, for example, providing services such as filtering groundwater. Nor had we understood that mining, extracting, processing, and burning fossil fuels would generate respiratory diseases, global climate change, and risk to all life on Earth. Still less did we understand that plowing the soil to plant crops and spraying plants with insecticides, pesticides, and herbicides would end up producing agricultural runoff that creates dead zones in the oceans, kills marine species, and destroys the very pollinators we depend on for food production.

As a species, humans still mostly and incorrectly continue to think of ourselves not as an integral component of our planet but as separate and apart from it. And we believe that everything else exists for our benefit. We have been very slow to realize that Earth-life species, their habitats, ecosystems, and biodiversity are but the components of a common Earth-life system that works together to evolve and maintain life, and that humans are just another of those component-species, albeit an intelligent one, but certainly not in charge of the planet as we like to believe. Instead, it turns out that the Earth-system has been self-managing from its beginning.

The Gaia theory posits that the Earth is a self-regulating complex system involving the biosphere, the atmosphere, the hydrosphere and the pedosphere, all tightly linked in an evolving system. The theory posits that this system, called Gaia, seeks a physical and chemical environment optimal for contemporary life. Scientists now view the Earth as a system containing a fixed amount of each stable atom or element. Each element can exist in several different chemical reservoirs. Each element on Earth moves among reservoirs in the solid earth, oceans, atmosphere, and organisms as part of geochemical cycles. Movement of matter between reservoirs is driven by the Earth's internal and external sources of energy. Humans wouldn't dream of re-arranging the cockpit or re-engineering the power system of the Apollo Space Shuttle built by NASA. But we hardly seem able to restrain ourselves from trying to re-engineer the components of Spaceship Earth and its life-sustaining components—Earth-life ecosystems and biodiversity.

Human modifications of Earth-life ecosystems, then, have changed not only the structure of these systems, such as what habitats or species are present in a particular location, but their processes and functioning as well. The capacity of ecosystems to provide services derives directly from the operation of natural biogeochemical cycles that in some cases have been significantly modified. Earth-life ecosystems, through their ecological and evolutionary processes (the cycles of water, carbon, nitrogen, phosphorus, and oxygen, along with energy and nutrient flows) sustains the quality of the air, fresh water, and soils on which all life, including human life, depends; distributes fresh water; regulates the climate; provides pollination and pest control; and reduces the impact of natural hazards.

More than 75 percent of global food crop types, including fruits and vegetables and some of the most important cash crops, such as coffee, cocoa, and almonds, rely on animal pollination. Moreover, marine and terrestrial ecosystems are the sole sinks for anthropogenic carbon emissions, with a gross sequestration of 5.6 gigatons of carbon per year (the equivalent of 60 percent of global anthropogenic emissions).

But humans have changed many of these ecosystems' cycles, bringing death and destruction to life on land, and to marine and freshwater ecosystems. According to the EPA, nutrient pollution is one of America's most widespread, costly, and challenging environmental problems, and is caused by excess nitrogen and phosphorus in the air and water. Nitrogen and phosphorus are nutrients that are natural parts of aquatic ecosystems, with nitrogen being the most abundant element in the air we breathe. Together, and in the right amounts, they support the growth of algae and aquatic plants, which provide food and habitat for fish, shellfish, and smaller organisms that live in water. This type of nutrient pollution has impacted many streams, rivers, lakes, bays, and coastal waters for the past several decades, resulting in serious environmental and human health issues, and impacting the economy. In amounts too great, the air and water get polluted as shown in Figure 2-12.

Figure. 2-12. Too much nitrogen and phosphorus in the water can have diverse and far-reaching impacts on public health, the environment, and the economy.

(Source: EPA; Photo credit: Bill Yates)

Too much nitrogen and phosphorus in the water accelerates growth faster than ecosystems can handle. It harms water quality, food, and habitats, and decreases the oxygen that fish and other aquatic life need to survive. Algal blooms severely reduce or eliminate oxygen, leading to sickness or death of large numbers of fish. Some produce elevated toxins and bacterial growth that can make people sick if they consume tainted fish or shellfish or drink contaminated water. Nutrient pollution in groundwater, which millions of people in the United States use for drinking water, can be harmful, even at low levels. Infants are vulnerable to a nitrogen-based compound called nitrates in drinking water. Excess nitrogen in the atmosphere can produce pollutants such as ammonia and ozone, which can impair the ability to breathe, limit visibility, and alter plant growth. When excess nitrogen comes back to Earth from the atmosphere, it can harm the health of forests, soils, and waterways.

Figure 2-13. Excess nitrogen in the air can impair our ability to breathe, limit visibility, and alter plant growth.
(Source: EPA; Shutterstock)

What's true of phosphorus and nitrogen is also true of numerous human-modified processes and cycles in Earth-life ecosystems, many of which can eventually succumb to abrupt and sudden ecosystem collapse and loss of the life-sustaining services they provide.

Given the dire state of the world's ecosystems, the question any normal person would ask is not unlike what Queen Elizabeth II asked in 2009 when confronted with the worst economic downturn since the Great Depression (1929–c.1939): *"Why did nobody see it coming?"* Included in that list of the nobodies were those who should have been in the best position to see it coming—economists at the Bank of England.

Similarly, if anyone were to ask almost any of the world's economists (almost, because there are some who get it) why the world's ecosystems and biodiversity were allowed to get to the state where a fifth of countries are at risk of ecosystem collapse, with almost no one knowing and caring (except perhaps scientists?), an honest answer would be something along the lines of, "Well, we know they are there, but economists generally do not, or cannot, or don't know how to"—take your pick—"assign a value or count the world's ecosystems and ecosystem services as part of or in addition to the world's GDP." In other words, GDP does not include food, fresh water, air, timber (aka, wildlife, fresh water, and trees), or any of the ecosystem services listed in Figure 2-4. Yet, the world's wealth is built on our planet's natural ecosystems, and if those collapse, so, too, would the global economy. Despite this fundamental truth, most economists still won't, or don't know how to, include them in GDP numbers.

One is probably already aware that most of the world's economists, those people who advise governments and companies regarding the best policies for ensuring the economic well-being of companies, nations, international institutions, and the world's peoples, do not include in their advice and accounting the value of those countries or of the world's ecosystems and their services. In fact, they were mostly taught to believe that nature and economics shouldn't mix. For centuries there was no accounting of human use, and misuse, of Earth-life ecosystems and their services.

But regardless of what some economists believe, their failure to recognize or assign a value to Earth-life's ecosystems and their services to the GDP of nations, and of the world, has turned out to be the biggest economic falsehood that has been foisted upon policymakers, business leaders, and peoples of the world, and may well have helped to create the notion that ecosystems lack economic value. Hence their use, or abuse, is not accounted for, neither in corporate nor government records, and consequently, their value is unrecognized in the eyes of citizens and is also diminished. It was not until the publication of Rachel Carson's *Silent Spring*, and the work of a retinue of her followers, that an awakening to the value ecosystems bring and the harm we have been doing to them and ourselves, prompted people, companies, and governments to begin taking notice.

Nevertheless, human economies are built from and depend entirely on the resources extracted from Earth-life ecosystems. *Nature is our most precious asset,* noted the Dasgupta Report on the Economics of Biodiversity. The omission of ecosystems' value is not just an exclusion from the accounting and financial records of the world. It's also a kind of economic erasure of the legacy of our hunter-gatherer forebears, part of the cancel culture that began with farming, a cancelling from the minds of humans of the fact that our very lives depend on these ecosystems and their services. This may well have created the impression that ecosystems are valueless and not part of the economic life of nations and their economies, and therefore that it hardly matters if they are treated as though they don't.

Thankfully, though—if it's not already too late—some nations have begun to right this wrong and have established a new kind of accounting that would ensure that natural capital—forests, wetlands, and other ecosystems—are recognized in economic reporting through a System of Environmental Economic Accounting. And others still seek to replace GDP as a measure of economic success, uniting instead around Alliance, a collaboration and movement to transform the economic system into one that delivers social justice on a healthy planet.

Twenty-first century humans have only now, for the first time, taken a close look at the global state of Earth-life ecosystems and the life support they provide for all. What have we learned? What is the state of the world's ecosystems? What have we done to them in our thirst for economic growth and in our efforts to build the world's economies? What does their current state portend for the planet, humans, and what's left of other species?

"*Humanity has reached a crossroads*" The Global Biodiversity Outlook Report (GBO) claims that humanity is at a crossroads. This, the flagship publication of the Convention on Biological Diversity (CBD), one of several global assessments of the state of the world's ecosystems, biodiversity, food webs, and soil, concluded that humanity had reached a crossroads.

Perhaps like me you have read one too many government and international organization climate and environment assessments, scientific research papers, or books and media updates about worsening climate change, plastic pollution, virus-infected bushmeat, and invasive species spreading pandemic-potential diseases such as Covid-19. It's easy to want to gloss over or ignore these emerging updated warnings about the serious state of Earth-life ecosystems and biodiversity and what these augur for a potential economic or civilizational collapse. Yes, it's easy to turn away, but this time too much is at stake, and, as the Queen discovered, one can't leave it to the experts. You want to get informed, and here is an example of why you should.

The entire world seemed to have been caught off-guard by the sudden emergence of shortages of consumer and industrial goods, and price increases, due to the Covid-19 pandemic and the war in Ukraine, of goods from semiconductor chips and oil, to various food items, none of which was anticipated—and that was only due to the impact of the Covid-19 pandemic, then the war in Ukraine, on national and global economies. Then the world discovered how little redundancy there was in the world's just-in-time supply chains, upon which local and global markets depend. Shortages suddenly appeared in supermarkets, on manufacturing floors, in gas stations, and in other venues. Yet should ecosystems and the services they provide begin to shrink or collapse, our Covid-Ukraine supply chain experience could turn out to have been just a practice run, so great will the economic disruptions likely be. That's the alarm these U.N. and other reports are raising. And no one appears to be planning, not even for the next major superstorm, let alone the disruption potential of one or more ecosystem collapses.

So, you might want to pay attention when most of your food, clothing, and essential goods and services that come from another city, state, or country begin to disappear without much notice, perhaps because the supplier region is confronting a climate change-driven shrinking water supply. All of a sudden farmers, producers, and suppliers can be hit with shrinking supplies due to droughts, other natural disasters, or production or supply chain disruptions, as when part of the world's oil supply was suddenly blocked in the Suez Canal or when Ukraine's ability to export grain was hampered by the war there. In such cases, and in contrast to the post-Covid-19 reality, should that become a thing, there probably won't be recovery from a post-ecosystem collapse for possibly scores of years.

The fact is, no one saw shortages coming and there was no warning, and even if anyone knew, most supplies would have vanished like toilet paper on supermarket shelves. But even more problematic, not even the world's economists, governments, industry mavens, politicians, or the press appeared to have known. And it is more than likely, once again, that no one in our twenty-first century efficiency-driven, lean, free-market capitalist economies will foresee a potential world economic, if not civilization, collapse coming before, like Covid-19, it shows up. And for this one, no bug-out bag will help. What then is the takeaway?

"If we can learn one thing from the past collapses of major civilizations, it is that all of those showed some (if not most) of the following symptoms during or immediately before their imminent collapse: environmental destruction, depletion of vital resources (such as water, arable soil and timber), famine, overpopulation, social and political unrest, inequality, invasion or other forms of devastating warfare, and disease" observed David B. Lauterwasser in a 2017 article entitled "The Collapse of Global Civilization Has Begun." The interesting thing is that those patterns of collapse seen in prior civilizations seem well underway in the twentieth-first century and these U.N. and other assessments and reports may well be a preview of them. They are the new Rachel Carson.

The UN's 2021 report on the state of nature, Global Biodiversity Outlook 5, observed, "The world has failed to meet a single target to stem the destruction of wildlife and life-sustaining ecosystems in the last decade." Natural habitats have continued to disappear, vast numbers of species remain threatened by extinction from human activities, and environmentally damaging government subsidies for energy suppliers, water services, road building, agriculture, fisheries and other activities that often have side effects that cost from $500 billion to $900 billion in environmental damage, have not been eliminated.

Under the 2010 Aichi targets agreed on in Japan, all signatories to the U.N. Convention on Biodiversity were supposed to draw up national biodiversity plans. Together, their voluntary actions were supposed to halt overfishing, control invasive species, reduce pollution, minimize the pressure on coral reefs from ocean acidification, and halt the loss of genetic diversity in agricultural ecosystems. But from tackling pollution to protecting coral reefs, the international community failed to slow the loss of the natural world.

This was not the first time. Governments had previously failed to meet targets set at the 2002 Convention on Biological Diversity, making the 2010s the second consecutive decade that the world's governments had failed. And as Lauterwasser noted: "Virtually every environmental crisis ever recognized as such in the last century has since worsened. All goals set by the Earth Summit in Rio de Janeiro (1992), its follow-up Rio+20 (2012), the Kyoto Protocol (1997), the Copenhagen Agreement COP15 (2009), and the Paris Agreement (2016) have failed to make a considerable difference." Did the 2021 G-7, COP27, or COP15 in Montreal save the planet's biodiversity? None turned out to be successful.

What you will learn from these assessments is not just the fact that:

- Forests all over the world continue to be destroyed in the name of economic growth,
- In 40 years, we lost half of the world's wildlife, and species extinctions proceed at an unprecedented rate—estimated at 10,000 species per year (WWF), or about one species per hour,
- The insect populations across Europe fell by over 70 percent, already engendering the label "Insectageddon," which is expected to have

disastrous impacts on crops and ecosystem stability in the coming decade, and,

- Humans logged over 75 percent of all forests in the 10,000-year history of our culture, and that logging continues (at a rate of 48 football fields per minute, while we concomitantly lose 30 football fields of topsoil per minute).

But even more important is what one won't learn in these assessments. They fail to identify and call out:

- *The real problem*. The foundational reason underpinning the collision between humans and Earth-life ecosystems and biodiversity has not been identified, and, if we can't name it, we won't fix it. Humans have been asking the wrong question. Here is the question nobody appears to be asking: Why are humans the only Earth-life species destroying Earth-life ecosystems and biodiversity? As Dr. Lanning said to Detective Spooner (Will Smith) in the movie *I Robot*, "That, lieutenant, is the right question."
- *Population growth as a primary driver*. Explosive human population growth has driven and is driving the destruction of Earth-life ecosystems and biodiversity. Human population growth in the last 50 years was not just an "Indirect Driver," as some of these assessments almost apologetically state, but in fact the driver and root cause of the depletion of all Earth-life ecosystems and their services.
- *Lack of action*. With few exceptions, there has been an astonishing absence of a robust global call and starter plan for re-educating current, next, and future generations of humans about their complete dependence on Earth-life ecosystems and biodiversity for their survival.

But now, as never before, humans may well have already passed the point of no return in key areas such as $CO_{2,}$ stratospheric ozone depletion, and biogeochemical flows, and may well have begun to pass tipping points that some scientists call "planetary boundaries." Crossing these ecological red lines would activate changes in the Earth system that could be beyond our ability to stop. We may already be barreling toward a "hothouse state" not seen in 50 million years, climate records show, and may have shifted the Earth system to a new steady-state, (Figure 2-14) a shift not seen since the time of the dinosaurs.

Table 2-4. Estimated human population worldwide

Estimated Human Population Worldwide	Year
200,000	c. 130,000 BCE
3 million	c. 10,000 BCE
10 million	c. 6,500 BCE
50 million	c. 2,000 BCE
200 million	c. 0 CE/BCE
1 billion	1804
2 billion	1927
3 billion	1959
4 billion	1974
5 billion	1987
6 billion	1999
7 billion	2012
8 billion	2022
9 billion	2050

(Source: World Atlas)

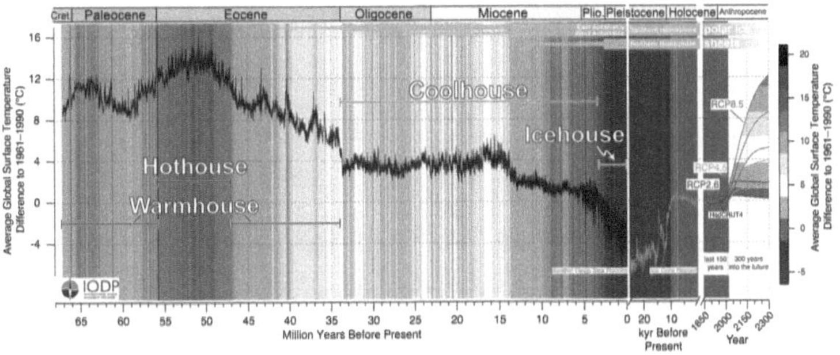

Figure 2-14. A climate map showing the last 66 million years of Earth's history. The next 300 could be unlike anything we've ever seen.

(Source: SciTech Daily; Image credit: Westerhold et al., CENOGRID)

"The Global Resources Outlook 2019 shows that we are ploughing through this planet's finite resources as if there is no tomorrow, causing climate change and biodiversity loss along the way," said Joyce Msuya, acting head of U.N. Environment. "Frankly, there will be no tomorrow for many people unless we stop," said Msuya of the agency formerly known as the U.N. Environment Programme (UNEP).

As one contemplates Earth's current plight, it helps to recall that for millions of years, Earth was mostly a lifeless watery orb being continuously pummeled by an endless stream of meteorites left over from the formation of the solar system. Early life forms may have repeatedly evolved and been sterilized. For most of the geologic eons known as the Proterozoic (2.5 billion–0.57 billion years ago), the Archean (4 billion–2.5 billion years ago), and the Hadean (4.54 billion-4.0 billion years ago) that together comprise the Precambrian geologic eon, Earth was populated by bacteria, only after which complex animals and intelligent species life began to appear with the advent of the Cambrian Explosion.

So, unlike the detritus on the surface of the moon and Mars, it is mostly accurate to say that much of Earth's crust, almost four billion years' worth of ecosystems, oceans, and early atmosphere, are partially the remains of these tiny bacterial life-forms. In fact, we live on a planet built by our bacterial ancestors, the remains of which are deeply integrated into the Earth and comprise the habitats and ecosystems we now treat with such utter disrespect. Yes, it took nearly 4.5 billion years to make possible what humans began destroying in just the last 10,000 years.

Given the alarming condition of Earth-life ecosystems, some are wistfully looking to Mars as NASA's Perseverance and China's Zhurong rovers begin their search for life there. But, unlike Mars (and Venus), Earth is alive. And, Earth is alive because Earth's species are alive, and Earth's species are alive because Earth's ecosystems are alive—but, as noted, it has not always been this way and will not remain this way if humans continue to destroy Earth's ecosystems and its species. If the growth of human economies continues to drive the elimination of Earth's ecosystems and its biodiversity—in other words, if we continue to live *outside* rather than *inside* Earth's ecosystems—Earth too would once again rejoin that short list of dead and lifeless rocky planets that make up the inner solar system now orbiting the sun.

One can understand, then, why Leonardo DiCaprio in his U.N. climate speech said: "For the economy itself will die if our ecosystems collapse." At this point, however, given the foregoing explanation of the known science, no one will be able to ask, as Queen Elizabeth II did of the 2008-2009 financial crash, "Why did nobody see it coming?" Well, at least Leonardo DiCaprio did. Nevertheless, there might still be a little time left to start living and building human economies *within* Earth-life ecosystems once more as our pre-agriculture hunter-gatherer forebears did for more than 290,000 years.

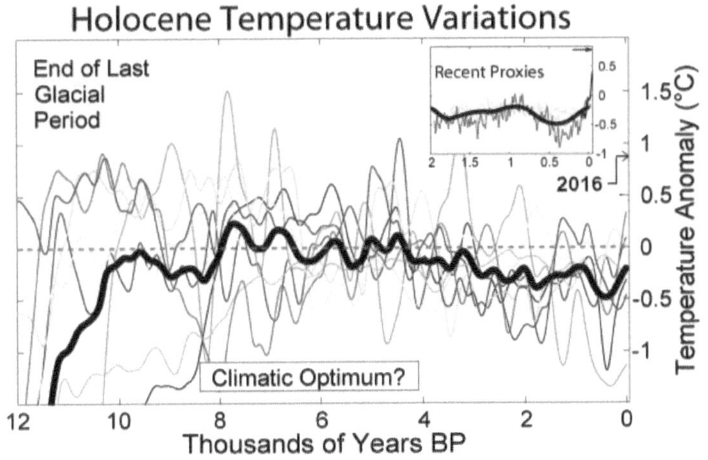

Figure 2-15. Holocene temperature variations.
(Source: Wikipedia; Credit: CC BY-SA 3.0)

But what does it mean to live and build human economies *inside versus outside* of Earth-life's ecosystems? Hunter-gatherer humans who evolved and lived during most of the Pleistocene, a very cold and climatically unstable 1.8-million-year epoch, knew what it meant to live *within* Earth-life ecosystems. They did so and experienced neither economic nor civilizational collapse for nearly all of the 300,000 years of *Homo sapiens'* existence—all but the last 12,000 years when the Pleistocene gave way to the Holocene, an increasingly warm and climatically more stable epoch. (Figure 2-16) This was when rising CO_2-driven climate change began warming the Earth, bringing the last ice age to an end, a time when the Earth's environment was more hospitable to growing crops.

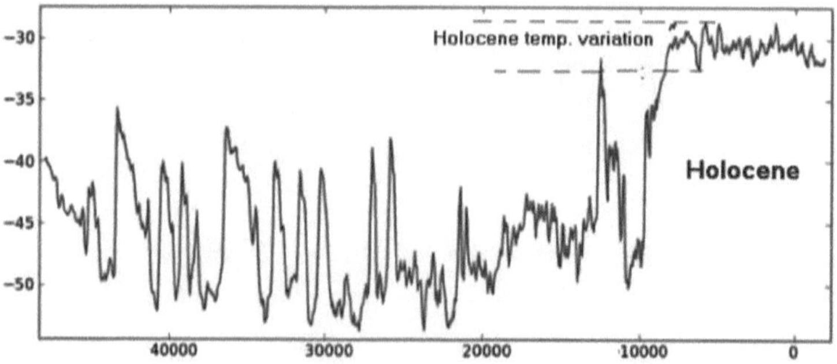

Figure 2-16. The Holocene cold and warm periods represent only small temperature changes compared to both the glaciation periods and the other interglacial periods.

This unique climatic stability made the development of agriculture possible; it created the basis for the development of civilizations and eventually enabled the industrial revolution and consequently the modern world. (Source: History of Earth's climate - Holocene Temp. Variation)

It was during the relative climatic calm of the succeeding 10,000 years of the Holocene epoch that human civilization as we have come to know it evolved. When our Neolithic Revolution human ancestors, perhaps emboldened by a warming fertile Earth and relatively stable climate, or perhaps driven by a food crisis some 5,000 to 6,000 years ago, began to abandon the hunter-gatherer way and their hunter-gatherer waterhole economies. They chose farming instead and thereby, knowingly or not, chose to begin to live and build their economies *outside* Earth-life's ecosystems. But, if the hunter-gatherer way of living and building economies *within* Earth-life ecosystems experienced neither economic nor civilization collapse for most of human existence, why did the human economies and civilizations that followed the Neolithic Revolution fail? What does it mean to live outside of

Earth-life ecosystems as they and all subsequent humans still do? Perhaps the following analogy might help.

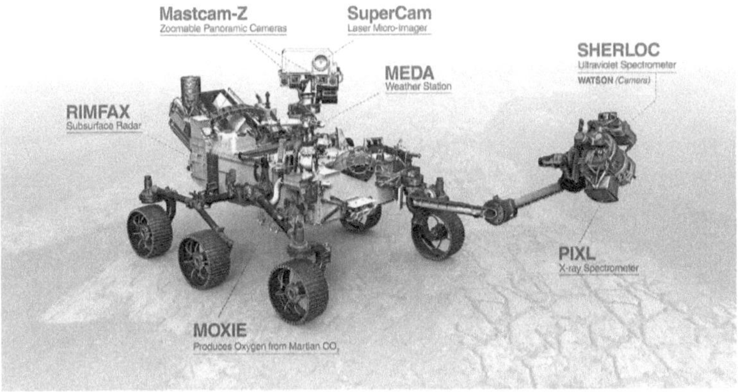

Figure 2-17. Science instruments on NASA's Mars 2020 Perseverance rover.
(Courtesy of NASA)

NASA's Jet Propulsion Lab had a single mission in mind for the Perseverance Mars Rover when it set out to design, build, and deploy it—to search for traces of life in an ancient river delta on Mars and collect samples for eventual return to Earth. That's all. But, until one sees the television special "Built for Mars: The Perseverance Rover" (2021) it's highly unlikely one could have imagined the complexity and special-purpose functionality of each unique built-to-fit component. The project required special-purpose dedicated teams, ultraclean rooms, and a lot of time and money to complete. And while the Perseverance Rover (Figure 2-17) was only designed to look for life on Mars, Earth-life's habitats and ecosystems evolved to enable and preserve life on Earth.

It may well be that only after contemplating efforts like what went into making that mission possible, and seeing how NASA so far has pulled this feat off, might one be ready, and perhaps be in the right frame of mind, to try to imagine what it might have taken to evolve Earth-life's habitats and ecosystems in the clean rooms of intergalactic space, and in the planet formation labs of the solar system, during the subsequent 4.5 billion years it took, using innumerable teams of often unique species of microbes, to be ready and fit for purpose, albeit a very different purpose—*the evolution and survival of complex animal and intelligent species life on planet Earth.*

Figure 2-18. NASA's new Mars rover landing successfully.
(Courtesy of NASA)

And one need not be a NASA Jet Propulsion Lab engineer to compare the Perseverance Rover, designed to look for life on Mars, nor an astrobiologist/geologist, to survey the terrain on Mars as shown (Figure 2-18), with the Earth-life ecosystem designed to evolve and sustain life on Earth, as in Tanzania where the Yaeda Valley is located, to see the difference in look and feel and in the design approach. It couldn't be starker. On Earth, the operative and prevailing life force is biological and that tells one all one needs to know—not a scrap of metal evolved in those four billion years—why?

The fact that modern Hadza hunter-gatherers (Figure 2-19) in Tanzania did not need an anti-bacterial suit, hazmat suit, or spacesuit to live within Earth-life's habitats and ecosystems demonstrates how unimaginably well its complexity is hidden from biological life. But that complexity, though only now being made a little visible by some emerging technologies, is there nonetheless and, like sticking one's finger in an electrical outlet, we encounter it when we ignore that simple yet visible rule all life must follow in order to survive—*to eke out one's living within Earth-life ecosystems* as modern Hadza hunter-gatherer women and children are seen doing in Figure 2-19, collecting tubers, a staple food, in the Yaeda Valley, Tanzania.

Figure 2-19. Modern Hadza hunter-gatherers collecting tubers, a staple food of the community, in the Yaeda Valley, Tanzania. The Hadza are a modern hunter-gatherer tribe.

(Source: National Geographic; Photograph by Matthieu Paley)

Humans left Earth-life ecosystems when we began eking out a living *outside* these ecosystems, when, among other things, we started growing our own food. Agriculture uses many processes alien to Earth-life ecosystems, as for example, tilling and irrigating the soil, spraying it with fertilizers, and sprouting plants engineered to contain hormone-disrupting insecticides (EDCs), fungicides, and pesticides that kill pollinators and cause lymphoma in humans, among other diseases—all processes alien to Earth-life ecosystems. We strayed from living within ecoystems again, millennia later, when we began pumping gigatons of CO_2 into the atmosphere, engendering global warming-driven climate change that drove ocean acidification, and a global economic expansion that for two-and-a-half centuries powered the industrial and subsequent revolutions, including an industrial scale destruction of myriad ecosystems and their supporting species that comprise the food web, and enable those same ecosystem services we rely on to build our economies and our lives.

And now, as we move further into the twenty-first century, we might just be getting started on yet another departure from living *within* Earth-life ecosystems: genetic engineering. This adventure might take us even further *outside* the ecosystem and into the swamp of who knows what new species.

Living *within* Earth-life ecosystems means following survival-driven rules that enable life *within* ecosystems. While humans have been willing to benefit from ecosystem services, we have been unwilling to follow those survival-driven rules. Humans went from hunting and gathering to agriculture; from relying on freely available food sources without destroying the ecosystems that provide them, as all other species still do, to plowing, planting, and growing our own. Paleontologist Niles Eldredge, curator-in-chief of the Hall of Biodiversity at the American Museum of Natural History, summarizes the transition to agriculture this way: "Converting land to produce one or two food crops, with all other native plant species all now classified as unwanted weeds, and all but a few domesticated species of animals now considered as pests—represented the single most profound ecological change in the entire 3.5-billion-year history of life. Indeed, to develop agriculture is essentially to declare war on ecosystems."

Abandoning life in the ecosystem to farm and grow our own food meant breaking out of Earth's biochemical-based, energy feedback network of animals, plants, water, air, soil, fungi, atmospheric and chemical cycles, as well as its built-in network of closed-loop waste recycling. These are survival-driven networks that have powered and sustained all Earth-life species and kept Earth alive for billions of years before Neolithic Revolution *Homo sapiens* showed up.

Earth and its complement of species evolved and survived because they shared and were codependent on a common food web, energy system, and biosphere—one could not exist without the others. Earth and the species within its habitats and ecosystems evolved to play specific contributing, reciprocating, and interdependent roles to maintain life and are thus integral and mutually indispensable components of its life-support systems. It is by no means random that trees give off oxygen and absorb carbon dioxide while humans and other animals do the reverse, but internal combustion engines do neither. In other words, Earth's biodiversity, which shares its ecosystems, is a *complementary biological species-set* whose components interoperate. It evolved to keep an equally matched set of Earth-life's ecosystems alive. If it can be contrasted with a highway designed for EVs only, then most if not all of what humans have done and are doing in Earth-life's ecosystems has been like showing up in supercharged Chevy V8s instead of in a Tesla.

If one prefers to reverse the metaphor, there are simply no outlets in Earth's network of ecosystems for humans to use from *outside of them*. We cannot hope to follow our own rules and expect stuff to work—or that nothing will go haywire when we randomly try to plug in our man-made, non-biological, gas-guzzling, CO_2-breathing mechanical species that criss-cross oceans, highways, and skies to keep the supply chains of our economies humming—any more successfully than imaginary Martians might be able take apart the Perseverance Rover for spare parts. This is what in Taipei are called "add-ons," illegal and unapproved additions to houses and apartments (usually for rental income) that can be unsafe. Similarly, the gases our human inventions spew to the atmosphere and to Earth-life ecosystems are like "add-ons," evolutionarily illegal, that have already proven to be hazardous to our health and may well drive us and other Earth-life species to extinction.

Yet not even humans are willing to tolerate other humans breaking the rules of eking out a living *outside* of their man-made schemes with impunity.

Recall what happened when Volkswagen and other automakers engineered a "Cheat Mode" to pass EPA's auto emissions tests. They succeeded for a few years but eventually got caught. Similarly, humans succeeded in ecological cheating for about 12,000 years after becoming farmers, but eventually got caught, too. By pumping, since the dawn of the Industrial Revolution in 1850, 2,400 gigatons of CO_2 into the atmosphere, with some absorbed by oceans and land, we have managed to trigger Earth's ecosystems with global warming and other detectors demonstrating that we have crossed what some scientists describe as "planetary boundaries." These boundaries include stratospheric ozone depletion; climate change; loss of biosphere integrity (biodiversity loss and extinctions); chemical pollution and the release of novel entities; ocean acidification; freshwater consumption and the global hydrological cycle; land system change; nitrogen and phosphorus flows to the biosphere and oceans; and atmospheric aerosol loading.

But unlike those comparatively lucky automakers whose cheating cost them a paltry few billion dollars in fines, the fine this time is for a crime against all Earth-life, paid with the lives of the millions of species, including humans, that died. They are still dying due to, first, leaded gasoline, then other auto exhaust and air pollution. The rest of the fine may well be paid in a lump sum in the potential extinction of the entire human race and of most, if not all, Earth-life species. What a price to pay for the coal, oil, gas, and other air polluting industries that powered the development of nineteenth- and twentieth-century human economies outside of Earth-life ecosystems! "How did 10 million annual air pollution deaths become normal?" asks David Wallace-Wells. Has it been worth it?

To the energy industry and their financial and political backers the price is still worth paying. But according to the 2021 International Energy Agency report, unless humans can get to "net zero" by 2050 it could well be almost game over for *Homo sapiens*. The report says that to limit warming to 1.5°C (2.7°F), the energy industry would have to essentially end oil and gas exploration and focus investment only on squeezing remaining resources out of existing fields, an achievable task, they determined. Yet, as unlikely as that might seem, if actions being taken against key oil majors like Chevron, Exxon, and Royal Dutch Shell are any indication, there might yet be reason to hope.

But even if humans do manage to stay within that limit (it now seems unlikely), the existing stock of CO_2 in the atmosphere could still turn out to have quite horrific consequences, according to research from the National Research Council in Understanding Earth's Deep Past: Lessons for Our Climate Future. If it took nearly 10,000 years for modern humans to begin to experience the full impact of the Neolithic Revolution—the transition from foraging renewable energy within ecosystems to farming and excavating nonrenewable energy sources without—imagine how the CO_2 released in the atmosphere by humans during the last two centuries will impact the climate system for future humans. That CO_2 will persist in the atmosphere for tens to hundreds of thousands of years because of the time scales over which the natural feedback in the climate system sweeps CO_2 from the atmosphere. Consider how hot it will get and what the chance of survival would be.

Humans have always had access to the energy emanating from the sun, the primary, if not the only, energy source in Earth-life ecosystems. And, to continue our NASA Rover design metaphor, one can be pretty sure that an awareness of the capabilities of fossil fuels and where to find them, was not unknown, yet that was not the energy source deployed in Earth-life ecosystems, and now we know why. But just as humans in the Neolithic Revolution left the ecosystem to grow their own food via agriculture, modern humans two to three centuries ago left the ecosystem to find their own sources of energy and thereby took yet another step away from the safety of the ecosystem and down the road to nonrenewable energy sources and potentially to Econocide, the death of human economies.

Have you noticed there are no mechanical or electrical species within Earth-life ecosystems? Naturally respirated gases comprising a planet's atmosphere are produced by the biological life forms inhabiting the planet.

Carl Sagan said it best, "What a marvelous cooperative arrangement—plants and animals each inhaling each other's exhalations, a kind of planet-wide mutual mouth-to-stoma resuscitation, the entire elegant cycle powered by a star 150 million kilometers away." The absence of an atmosphere on Mars and Venus may well be evidence of the absence of biological life. On Earth, the right amounts of these gases, including oxygen and carbon dioxide, are kept in balance by Earth's species, ecosystems, and biosphere, and must remain in balance for life as we know it to exist.

Ecosystems maintain this balance by cycling animal-, including human-, respirated CO_2, and other sources of carbon through long and short-term carbon cycles. However, the gigatons of carbon buried for billions of years, now being dredged up and pumped into Earth's atmosphere by the petroleum industry and human economies, is essentially short-circuiting Earth's long-term carbon cycle, resulting in a CO_2 build-up in the oceans, atmosphere, and soil much, much faster than Earth-life systems can recycle them, which in turn creates global warming-driven climate change.

While Earth-life systems routinely recycle naturally respirated gases from Earth-life species and processes within its ecosystems, it appears to have no way to recycle CO_2 emissions emanating at such rapid and voluminous rates and from non-biological sources. There may be simply no ecosystem process designed to absorb such volumes, which emanate from power station stacks, belching oil and gas rigs, autos, airplanes, ships, and other manmade inventions that function *outside* the energy and other cycles *within* ecosystems. Global warming-driven climate change, then, is the result and is a direct consequence of humans choosing to live *outside* of Earth-life ecosystems. Meanwhile, there are no unused outlets left in Earth-life ecosystems for humans to plug in their illegal "add-ons."

> *In sum, from an evolutionary perspective, life outside Earth's ecosystems is not only illegal, but undefined.*

Regardless of how humans may choose to build their economies—whether via free-market capitalism, command and control communism, or anything else in between—we inevitably end up breaking that *survival triad-of-life* we encountered earlier. This is because human economies of the past few centuries have increasingly razed Earth's forests; paved over its soils; polluted its atmosphere; boiled its oceans, killing phytoplankton that produce nearly 70 percent of Earth's oxygen; fished its oceans almost free of marine species; threatened most other species with extinction; eradicated most pollinators and insects; and chemically disrupted our human ability to reproduce. We inevitably end up breaking that *survival triad-of-life* we encountered earlier that embodies the complementarity and interoperability of Earth-life species, including humans, their economies, and Earth-life that must remain intact for life to survive. We have broken away from that Triad, initially for food (farming), then for energy (fossil fuels), and now we are doing so again for whatever benefits we hope to glean from genetic manipulation of the very foundations of life.

Despite how excellent these schemes may have seemed to humans when they were conceived, they were and are being done *outside* Earth-life's ecosystems. They are driven by socioeconomic models that place money and profit above life and wealth accumulation and GDP growth above survival, and that miss altogether the sole foundational goal and outcome for Earth-life economies: *life and survival*. Unlike NASA's Perseverance Rover, deployed on Mars in 2021 in search of life that may or may not have existed on Mars billions of years ago, Earth-life ecosystems were deployed on Earth billions of years earlier to evolve and preserve the life that came into existence then and that continues to exist even today.

> *There is only one way, then, to build human economies that can last the way pre-agriculture hunter-gatherer economies did and for Earth-life species to make a living and survive without committing econocide—and that is to build them within Earth-life's ecosystems and live in harmony with its biodiversity.*

Regardless of the brand of economics humans may choose, opting for agriculture, living and building our economies *outside* of Earth's ecosystems, and choosing fossil fuels over the sun, the renewable energy source already deployed in ecosystems, humans will end up destroying the very survival-driven elements of Earth-life's support systems—its atmosphere, water, soil, species, and food webs—that enable Earth-life species to survive. Humans then have not only been building economies that are driving global warming, ecosystem destruction, and biodiversity extinction, but essentially, we have been building economies that destroy life itself. By razing Earth-life ecosystems and biodiversity—the very foundational-survival-enabling-and-support systems that life must have to survive—humans have essentially been destroying the foundation upon which life is based.

In the words of Marco Lambertini, Director-General of WWF International, in the 2024 Living Planet Report, nature is declining globally at rates not seen in millions of years. The way we produce and consume food and energy, and the blatant disregard for the environment entrenched in our current economic model, has pushed the natural world to its limits. A deep cultural and systemic shift is urgently needed, one that so far, our civilization has failed to embrace: a transition to a society and economic system that values nature. Covid-19 was a clear manifestation of our broken relationship with nature and highlights the deep interconnection between the health of people and the planet.

We must rebalance our relationship with the planet to preserve the Earth's amazing diversity of life and enable a just, healthy, and prosperous society, and ultimately to ensure our own survival.

Like so many events in human history, the horrors we are unleashing on ourselves, subsequent generations, the planet, and its species cannot be undone, not even by scientists. Sadly, it becomes the burden of ensuing generations to live with the grief and consequences of our prior misadventures. It was a single shot, you may or may not have known, believed to be entirely preventable, and fired by Serbian extremists, that sparked World War I, costing the lives of more than 8,526,831 people. But while we might record and still recall such human misadventures of a hundred years or so ago, no one living would recall, and countably few might even connect the dots, showing that it was our Neolithic Revolution forebears who may well have begun to abandon that hunter-gatherer lifeway within Earth's ecosystems, and thereby, may have started our species down the road to farming, and managing the surplus that has morphed into the twenty-first century capitalist economies of today.

The events that have led us to climate change-driven global warming may well have had their beginning in that fateful choice to pursue agriculture, and it begs the question: What might human economies have been like if Neolithic Revolution humans had continued to build their economies within Earth-life ecosystems? One may never know, but one thing is for sure: Humans wouldn't be confronting a potential climate change-driven extinction due to the fossil fuel energy we dug up *outside* those ecosystems.

Notwithstanding, regardless of "who done it," humans became the first species, and as far as is known, the only species, to stop living *inside* Earth-life's ecosystems. All other species, including our hominin ancestors, all pre-agricultural humans, and remnant hunter-gatherer societies still extant, exist as semi-isolated populations playing specific roles (i.e., filling "niches") in local ecosystems. Unlike the way modern humans live, our pre-agriculture hunter-gatherer forebears lived in close harmony with other species that shared Earth's ecosystems and the Earth-life species waterhole economies they formed, and are believed to have counted themselves among, and as belonging to, one of the many species comprising Earth's biodiversity. But, as we have come to realize, abandoning Earth-life species ecosystems and adopting farming was no ordinary change in subsistence method and is one our species is still regretting.

But imagine for a moment, if instead of Neolithic Revolution humans starting to farm for the first time on Earth, it was twenty-first century humans starting over on Mars. How might things work out for these Mars migrants if they were to abandon NASA's proven, Mars-certified, food-and-life support systems and technologies, and instead, were to begin to replace these with ones they would improvise and terraform on Mars, adopting farming there? And yes, I know—as unimaginably crazy as this might sound today to anyone contemplating being among the first Mars migrants, choosing agriculture would not be unlike what Neolithic Revolution *Homo sapiens* had undertaken—except that back then, it wasn't NASA's rations or NASA's technology they had abandoned but Earth's four billion-year, operationally proven, planet-wide, biochemical life-support systems upon which all of Earth-life mechanisms ran and were dependent.

Essentially, to say it in the economic terms Andrew Yang might prefer, they chose to abandon Earth's universal basic income-like subsistence offerings—its rent-free luxury living quarters in ecosystems chock-full of all-you-can-eat buffets—and instead to toil and sweat, plant and reap, with the incessant risk of famine, of starvation, and of contracting numerous Covid-19-like zoonotic diseases that subsequently plagued collapsed human civilizations for millennia.

It took humans quite a while, about 12,000 years of experimentation, using various methods of growing food outside of Earth's ecosystems. At first, all food was organically grown in a way that supported ecosystems and the environment. But there was never enough food until, in the 1940s, humans hit upon what is known as the Green Revolution, which vastly increased the availability of the food supply. These were a set of agricultural technologies that eventually enabled humans to mostly leave behind the scourge of famine and starvation that plagued numerous civilizations until the twentieth century. This all changed, however, after the Green Revolution took hold and industrial, chemical-dependent factory-farming techniques became the norm. Use of pesticides and fertilizers on farms increased twenty-six-fold over the past fifty years, fueling increases in crop production globally—but, unfortunately, not without serious environmental consequences.

Indeed, as we have seen, many human technological advances and innovations that appeared to hold such promise to earlier generations often end up, in subsequent generations, creating greater problems than they had been invented to solve. In the case of agriculture, soon indiscriminate pesticide and fertilizer application polluted land and water, and chemicals often washed into streams, waterways, and groundwater when it rained. Pesticides also killed non-target organisms, including beneficial insects, soil bacteria, and fish. And while fertilizers may not be directly toxic, their presence can alter the nutrient system in freshwater and marine areas, where excess nutrients have resulted in an explosive growth of algae. As a result, water gets depleted of dissolved oxygen, creating dead zones (as in the Gulf of Mexico) causing fish and other aquatic life to die. But it wasn't just fish and aquatic life that died.

Hence, as we tore into the life support systems embedded in Earth's habitats and ecosystems to build our human economies, it never occurred to our forebears, and it's still not clear to some, that we were potentially setting up the very conditions and inventing the very chemicals and numerous innovations that could eventually lead to our extinction. So, oil, gas, and coal were economically amazing until they were not; plastics were magical until they too were not; palm oil was in everything until it was everywhere; and inter-city flying was convenient in France until it was not. Slowly but surely, we are now beginning to realize all those amazing, but *out-of-the ecosystem* wonders we had created are turning out to be nothing more than *'add-ons'—illegal and incompatible human add-ons* to Earth-life's ecosystems. These innovations seemed brilliant and worked for a while but soon came crashing down, putting at risk human life and survival.

Yes, it took a while for us to realize the magnitude of our errors, and even longer still to sense the time and season, as well as the danger it has brought. Twenty-first century humans, like our hunter-gatherer forebears, are in the midst of yet another transition in geologic time, accompanied by yet another CO_2-driven climate change. This time we are emerging from the relative climatic calm of the Holocene during 10,000 years of which humans built their economies and civilizations *outside* of Earth-life ecosystems, well into the Anthropocene. This is an epoch whose climate, which may have been started by anthropogenic-driven climate change, promises to look and feel more like the Pliocene Epoch (17 million–2.5 million years ago). Back then, *temperatures were 3°C–4°C warmer, trees were growing at the South Pole, and sea levels were 15 to 20 meters higher*—climatic conditions to which we might well be headed.

Nevertheless, it was not until Covid-19 struck like an evolutionary wake-up call that humans began to truly grasp the real choice, and one that was there all along and that had to be made—preserving life and ensuring survival, the intended socioeconomic goal and outcome of human economies—versus chasing profits, wealth accumulation, and endless GDP growth. Humans can choose life and survival by going back to living and building their economies *within* Earth-life ecosystems as our pre-agriculture hunter-gatherer forebears did and lived safely for hundreds of thousands of years; or we can take the risk of going extinct by continuing to follow our Neolithic Revolution ancestors by continuing to build our twenty-first century human economies *outside* Earth-life's ecosystems. Which will it be?

Sadly though, by all appearances, and contrary to what would seem to be in our best interest, humans, even in the face of intensifying global warming climate change, are showing no signs of letting up on our socioeconomic lifeways of the pursuit of profit, wealth, and endless GDP growth as goal and outcome of their economies. This has already left us facing these existential risks to begin with, but nevertheless, is beginning to double down by choosing to do to Earth's marine ecosystems what, over the last 400 generations, we have done to its terrestrial ecosystems: strip and mine them to near destruction to grow our economies. Yes, you heard that right. *Seabed mining* in search of minerals, riches—and alas, one fears, along with that, epic extinction of marine biodiversity—is coming to a marine waterway or ocean floor off a coast near you.

Mining the ocean floor could solve mineral shortages—but could also lead to epic extinctions in some of the most remote ecosystems on Earth. Plans are in the works, according to Olive Heffernan in a 2019 *Nature* article entitled "Seabed mining is coming," to harvest ores from the ocean floor even as scientists and conservationists warn of the devasting damage this will cause and urge caution given that so little is known, neither about these marine ecosystems and the species that would be destroyed in the process, nor about the potential ripple effects such changes might have across Earth's ecosystems. Mining companies, though, along with their investors and partnering nations, appear to be winning this struggle, and open season on the high seas, already in progress, is about to accelerate.

Humans are beginning to repeat the same mistakes, once again, that led to the destruction of all but 3 percent of Earth's terrestrial ecosystems and innumerable species of its biodiversity. Now humans are going after the remaining 70 percent of the Earth's surface covered by its oceans and waterways. This time around, though, the enticement to pillage these marine ecosystems is not to grow and produce its own food, as might have lured Neolithic Revolution humans to abandon foraging for farming, but rather, to secure access to the minerals needed to produce green energy, as shown in Figure 2-20.

According to a 2024 article in the *Economist*, "Scattered across the ocean floor are trillions of lumps of nickel, copper, cobalt, and manganese. Companies have long wanted to mine them; these "critical minerals" are needed in vast quantities to electrify the global economy and cut dependence on fossil fuels." But the International Seabed Authority (ISA), a U.N. body, is still figuring out how mining should be regulated. Some environmental groups want an outright ban. Supporters and critics of deep-sea mining hashed out these issues at an ISA meeting in Jamaica in the summer of 2023. Of the 160-odd countries participating, few have more interest in the outcome than China, which already controls 95 percent of the world's supply of rare-earth metals and produces three-quarters of

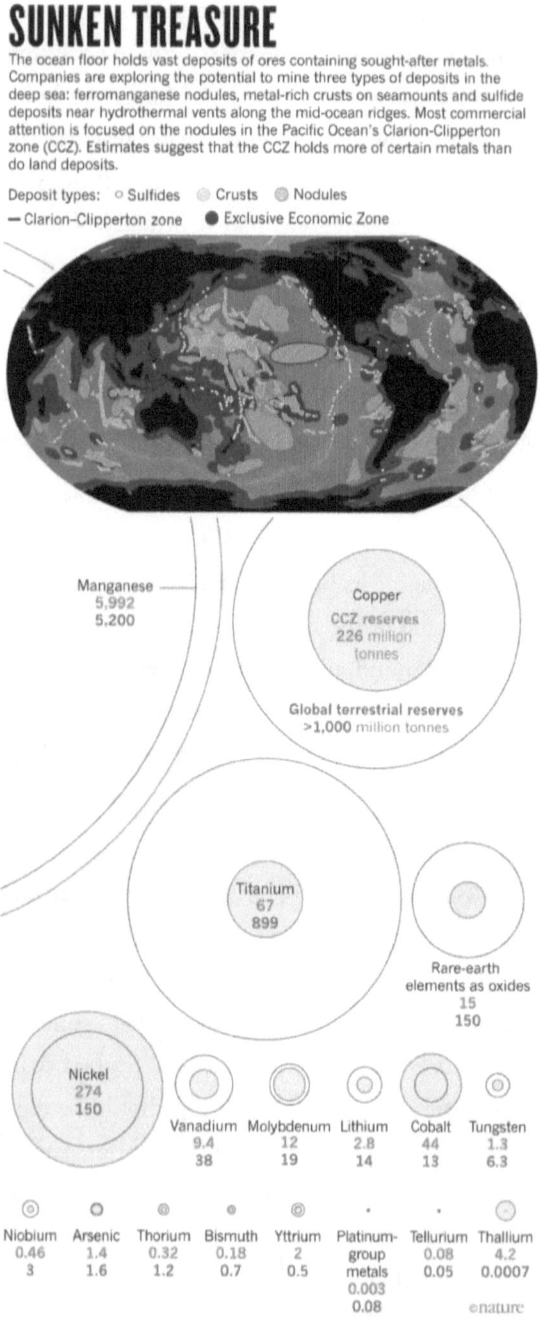
SUNKEN TREASURE
The ocean floor holds vast deposits of ores containing sought-after metals. Companies are exploring the potential to mine three types of deposits in the deep sea: ferromanganese nodules, metal-rich crusts on seamounts and sulfide deposits near hydrothermal vents along the mid-ocean ridges. Most commercial attention is focused on the nodules in the Pacific Ocean's Clarion-Clipperton zone (CCZ). Estimates suggest that the CCZ holds more of certain metals than do land deposits.
Deposit types: Sulfides Crusts Nodules
Clarion–Clipperton zone
Exclusive Economic Zone
Manganese
5,992
5,200
Copper
CCZ reserves
226 million tonnes
Global terrestrial reserves
>1,000 million tonnes
Titanium
67
899
Rare-earth elements as oxides
15
150
Nickel
274
150
Vanadium
9.4
38
Molybdenum
12
19
Lithium
2.8
14
Cobalt
44
13
Tungsten
1.3
6.3
Niobium
0.46
3
Arsenic
1.4
1.6
Thorium
0.32
1.2
Bismuth
0.18
0.7
Yttrium
2
0.5
Platinum-group metals
0.003
0.08
Tellurium
0.08
0.05
Thallium
4.2
0.0007
©nature

Figure 2-20. Sunken treasure.

all lithium-ion batteries. It is getting ready to extend its chokehold over emerging industries like clean energy.

These marine ecosystems are beyond the authority of any national jurisdiction and are beyond the 200-nautical-mile-exclusive-zones of any coastal nation, and, like so many of Earth's common resources (including the sun, the atmosphere, and the air we breathe) are intended to be equally available to all. They were never intended to be owned or to belong to anyone, and hence, from a human perspective, are defended by no one. And like so many vast terrestrial ecosystems (think the Amazon, the Congo, Indonesia, the Sahara, the Arctic); aboriginal peoples like Indigenous Brazilians fighting their former president Jair Bolsonaro to protect the Amazon; and until recently, when Brazil, Indonesia, and the Congo, home to more than half of the world's tropical rain forests, signed the Rainforest Protection Pact, no one was looking out for them.

So, if this investor-led open season on Earth's marine ecosystems is beginning to sound like something you may have heard or read about, you may be right—it's called "Land grabs" and may well mirror the way much open land across the Earth has been and is being seized and repurposed for agriculture, destroying vast terrestrial ecosystems, and displacing innumerable wildlife species in the process, all for profits, wealth accumulation, and GDP growth, the goal and outcome of modern human and legal-person economies.

Unlike Brazil's Indigenous peoples (Figure 2-21), marine species can't organize, and without protection, these marine ecosystems are now open to exploitation for commercial gain and, if land grabs and other forms of human exploitation of Earth's terrestrial ecosystems are any guide, one need not guess how this, too, would turn out. It took humans 12,000 years to reduce Earth's terrestrial ecosystems and biodiversity to their current unsustainable state, but given enhanced technologies, it's anybody's guess how quickly humans will destroy Earth's marine ecosystems.

The key takeaway here, then, is that humanity has not learned from the mistakes of its Neolithic Revolution ancestors who abandoned foraging for farming, nor from the mistakes it has subsequently made during the last 400 generations that saw the collapse of numerous civilizations. The key unlearned lesson is that human life and survival depend on economies that must be built in harmony with Earth's biodiversity and *within* its ecosystems, the practice followed by our pre-agriculture hunter-gatherer forebears, whose ecosystems survived for most of our species' existence.

This envisaged wanton destruction of Earth's marine ecosystems and biodiversity in search of minerals for green technologies, then, like the prior destruction of its terrestrial ecosystems and biodiversity to build its economies, would come at a severe cost. It would add to and intensify the global warming penalties from which humans are already reeling and may well shorten the time humans might yet have to mitigate the Earth-system's pushback against the destruction of its ecosystems and biodiversity—and would further increase the potential for human extinction.

Figure 2-21. Indigenous Brazilians sing while protesting outside the Supreme Court in Brasília, Brazil, on August 26, 2021, as they await an important ruling from the court. *They are among 6,000 people who came to the capital in opposition to measures that would dramatically roll back Indigenous territorial rights. (Photo credit: Andrew Fishman)*

In this regard, this 2024 study published in PNAS NEXUS entitled *Earth at risk: An urgent call to end the age of destruction and forge a just and sustainable future,* comes as a timely warning.

PART TWO

Rediscovering The Human Economy: Beginnings and Foundations

In Part One we saw that economies predated humanity and emerged out of the foraging activities of Earth-life species' within ecosystems. These were Earth-life species economies, and for those economies to exist and thrive, the species carrying out those foraging (economic) activities had first to exist and survive. And to eke out a living within ecosystems, these ecosystems too, must also exist and survive. We call this the *Evolutionary Triad of Life.*

Thus, economies are not a human invention that Adam Smith and his successors came up with but were an integral component of the evolving lifeways that enable life and survival. The original purpose of economies, then, was never about markets, surplus, profits, wealth accumulation, and endless GDP growth, but about enabling ecosystems, species (including humans), life, and survival.

In Chapter 3, we explore early *human economies* and will marvel at how these, and their egalitarian pre-agriculture hunter-gatherer societies, survived for 290,000 of our species' 300,000 years of existence, without economic or societal collapse. We explore what enabled pre-agriculture hunter-gatherer human economies to survive while the economies that followed the Neolithic Revolution, which gave rise to farming, sedentism, and civilization, collapsed one after another over the ensuing 400 generations.

What was so different, we asked, about these pre-agriculture hunter-gatherer societies and their waterhole economies that enabled them to survive? Far from being unique, they simply did what all other Earth-life species were doing to make a living. Like all other Earth-life species, societies, and economies, they too followed that foraging lifeway and eked out a living *within* Earth-life ecosystems, surviving for millennia without collapse. Their societies and economies, then, emerged from those foundational, survival-driven foraging lifeways and these became the foundations of their societies and economies.

In Chapter 4 we identify and explore what comprised these foundational, survival-driven foraging lifeways that became the foundations of pre-agriculture hunter-gatherer human societies and economies, which enabled them to survive for millennia without collapse. This suggests that there must have emerged over time very specific socioeconomic lifeways for all Earth-life species (including humans) to follow and thereby to successfully build societies and economies that would have endured, collapse-free, ensuring their life and survival—lifeways that post-agriculture human societies and economies apparently abandoned, which led to their collapse.

Modern human societies and economies, then, might well be in trouble because, like our Neolithic Revolution forebears, we too have abandoned those initial survival-driven lifeways that became the very foundations of all Earth-life societies and economies, and upon which their ability to survive and avoid collapse depended.

The fact that our modern human societies and economies might also be approaching collapse due to CO_2-driven global warming climate change brought on by our modern socioeconomic lifeways should be more than a hint from nature that our modern lifeways have taken us down the wrong path. By now, too, you are probably wondering, if there were indeed such *survival-driven lifeways* (and there must have been if only because our pre-agriculture hunter-gatherer forebears practiced them and survived for millennia), why haven't modern humans tried to rediscover them? How did those lifeways begin and what were their foundations? These are questions we will soon address.

In the rest of this book, we go on to identify, with a bit more specificity, how and why our modern socioeconomic lifeways have taken and continue to take us in the wrong direction. We will discover, for instance, that the foundational goal and purpose of Earth-life species economies, and hence human economies, was the enablement of life and survival of those species, humans, and the ecosystems wherein they foraged for a living.

We'll see, too, how Neolithic Revolution and modern humans replaced that original goal and outcome of life and survival with different ones: gathering surplus, making profits, accumulating wealth, and pursuing endless GDP growth—thereby changing the original goal and outcome of the human economy. And we will explore what humans might yet do to rediscover those survival-driven lifeways our pre-agriculture hunter-gatherer forebears practiced that enabled them to survive, and thereby, get back on the path of building human societies and economies that enable life and survival.

Rediscovering The Human Economy: Beginnings and Foundations

WHAT ENABLED PRE-AGRICULTURE HUNTER-GATHERER ECONOMIES AND SOCIETIES TO SURVIVE WITHOUT COLLAPSE FOR MOST OF HUMAN EXISTENCE WHILE NONE HAVE SINCE?

CHAPTER 3

Early Human Economies:
Beginnings

Economies That Preserved Life and Survival

CHAPTER 4

Rediscovering the Human Economy:
Foundations

3.

Early Human Economies Were Waterhole Economies

ECONOMIES THAT PRESERVED LIFE AND SURVIVAL

"All people known archaeologically lived in economies that relied upon hunting and gathering wild foods for subsistence."

—Bruce Winterhalder and Douglas J. Kennett, "Behavioral Ecology and the Transition from Hunting and Gathering to Agriculture"

Ninety-seven percent of the time *Homo sapiens* lived on Earth, or until about 12,000 years ago, all peoples were foragers of wild food, living a type of subsistence lifestyle in economies that relied on hunting and fishing animals, foraging for wild vegetation and other nutrients, and converging around waterholes to slake their thirst. Their economies required a daily pursuit and collection of wild foods to make a living, collecting numerous species over whose reproduction and sustenance they had no control.

Hunting and gathering was not just the only mode of human economic production, but the earliest as well, preceding the emergence of our species and persisting some 200,000 years after the appearance of anatomically modern humans. Hunting and gathering accompanied their spread across the Earth to the tropics, the coasts, and the deserts, and in the steppes, temperate zones, and even nearer the poles. It may have ultimately given rise to agriculture, according to Morgan et al. in "Hunter-Gatherer Economies in the Old World and New World."

But why should anyone today care about or want to discuss early human economies? Well, if only because they were the only human economies that persisted without collapse for 97 percent of our species' existence, and somehow managed to do so for those 290,000 years mostly without ravaging the planet's habitats and ecosystems and destroying its biodiversity, nor threatening the pre-agriculture hunter-gatherer societies that relied upon them to make a living, with risks of a potential extinction the way twenty-first century economies are threatening humans today. It bears asking (don't you think?): Is there something our forebears knew about how to make a living and survive on this Earth that humans from the Neolithic Revolution through the twenty-first century, notwithstanding all our accumulated knowledge, science, technologies, innovations, and supposed superiority, still don't get? Clearly, the answer must be yes. But what?

There is probably no single answer, but among the possible answers one is patently obvious. Those pre-agriculture hunter-gatherer societies and their economies that emerged soon after our species' origin, lasting until shortly after the adoption of agriculture, did so by building their economies inside Earth-life ecosystems and lived in harmony with its biodiversity. What changed was, starting about 12,000 years ago, Neolithic Revolution and soon subsequent humans would choose to become farmers. They began extracting ecosystem products and services to build their economies, and thereby, whether they knew it or not, had chosen to leave and eke out their living outside Earth-life ecosystems, an approach to economic development humans have followed into the twenty-first century. Economies and societies would grow from once-small 40- to-50-person bands to a few million and would eventually spread across the entire planet to become the eight billion-plus civilization of today.

But remarkably—and it would be negligent not to draw attention to this fact—since this change in economic approach, most major human civilizations and their economies have collapsed, our twenty-first century civilization being the last one standing. Why did they collapse? What was different? How did pre-agriculture societies and their economies survive while all that followed, so far, have collapsed? If the success of a civilization is measured by its longevity, then our pre-agriculture hunter-gatherer forebears were by far the most successful civilization in all human history.

And, for their civilization to last, their economies also had to last. Their choice to eke out a living inside Earth-life's ecosystems was obviously key to that longevity—their success then lay in their economic approach. In contrast, post-Neolithic Revolution human civilizations and all that followed collapsed because their economies collapsed and their economies collapsed because, unlike pre-agriculture hunter-gatherer economies, they were built outside of Earth-life ecosystems. Their collapse then lay in the failure of their economic approach—building economies outside Earth's ecosystems and out of harmony with its biodiversity.

Many historians correctly point to environmental destruction and climate change as key, if not principal, reasons for numerous post-Neolithic

Revolution civilization collapses. But there was something else, a more egregious though often overlooked reason of which environmental and climate damage are but consequences: that choice Neolithic Revolution humans made some 12,000 years ago. They chose to eke out a living and build their economies outside of Earth-life ecosystems and that choice to become farmers was the ultimate reason. There is simply no way to farm without destroying Earth-life ecosystems and its biodiversity while simultaneously remaining within these ecosystems and hoping to live in harmony with its biodiversity—the foundational prerequisite for life and survival.

Humans became the first and, so far, the only Earth-life species to abandon the foundational prerequisite for life and survival we encountered earlier—Earth-life species must eke out their living (aka build their economies) within Earth-life ecosystems and live in harmony with its biodiversity. It's amazing that despite our awareness of the reasons those civilizations failed, it bears emphasizing that twenty-first century human civilizations are still following that same failed economic development model—building human economies outside Earth-life ecosystems while destroying them, and the biodiversity upon which all life depends—and hence are subject to the same risks of economic and civilization collapse, and probably for similar reasons.

To further grasp why pre-agriculture hunter-gatherers' societies and their economies succeeded while agricultural, mainly sedentary societies and economies that followed the Neolithic Revolution failed, and continue to fail, one must begin with the economic definition inherent in their name—hunter-gatherers. It describes a people entirely dependent on, and that sought only, wild plants and animals for food; a people whose basic ways of making a living, whether by hunting, fishing, or foraging wild plants and animals, were deeply integrated and built around the pursuit and consumption of wild species; a people known as much for what they ate as for what they didn't—domesticated plants and animals. Notice in this description the conspicuous absence of the so-called factors of production:

land, labor, capital, and entrepreneurialism, the foundations of our modern economies.

Hunter-gatherer humans ate a vast variety of plants and likely numerous animal species, too, so no single species of plant or animal was hunted or gathered to extinction. Their impact on Earth-life ecosystems and its biodiversity was likely moderate, as their population densities were often very low. Moreover, because they were mobile, their impact on Earth-life ecosystems and the biodiversity that shared those ecosystems was likely diffused. Their food sources, as well as their fuels, fibers, and tools, were derived entirely from undomesticated, non-cultivated species. This implies they had no ownership or control over the sources upon which their livelihood depended—no ownership or control over how, whether, or how often such species reproduced, where such species might be found, or what quantities of plants or animal species they might find.

Nevertheless, according to James Suzman in his book *Affluence Without Abundance: What We Can Learn from the World's Most Successful Civilisation*, there was no lack of food sources derived by hunting, trapping, and fishing by men, mostly in northern temperate climates. And in tropical or semi-tropical climates, although meat was preferred, most of their food came mainly from plants gathered by women.

Was their impact on Earth-life ecosystems so slight or moderate, compared to post-agriculture humans, because they were mostly mobile with a dispersed footprint or because their population densities (band/group sizes of 20-50 people) were low? Or was it their inability or unwillingness to exert control over Earth-life ecosystems and biodiversity? Or perhaps it was simply a trust they had come to develop and thereby an expectation that Earth-life habitats, ecosystems, and biodiversity would continue to provide as always, a trust that enabled them and their economies to survive for those 290,000 years, whereas most subsequent sedentary agricultural societies and economies that took complete control of Earth-life ecosystems and biodiversity eventually collapsed, one after another, in just 12,000 years?

Hunter-gatherer societies eked out a living within Earth-life ecosystems and often, though not always, maintained a strong regard for nature, and being mostly egalitarian did not believe in a god that created nature to be used and dominated by humans. Nor did they pillage Earth-life ecosystems for their benefit as agriculture required and humans do today or drive innumerable species of biodiversity to extinction as humans have done since the dawn of agriculture. Simple population densities tell much of the story. A square kilometer could support one person in a hunter-gatherer economy but 1,000 people in an agricultural economy in Java. There were an estimated ten million humans in the world on the eve of food production; now over eight billion people live on the planet, an increase of 700 percent in only ten millennia and growing by 1.1 percent, or 83 million, per year.

It was only as humans became farmers and sedentary that they began caring for and controlling wild animals and plants for food, transportation, protection, production of valuable commodities (such as cotton, silk, or wool), warfare, and companionship. Animals that are commonplace today, including dogs, cats, sheep, geese, camels, cattle, pigs, and horses, started as wild animals but over time were domesticated ("Advances in Animal Biotechnology" by Zeder et al., 2006; Andersson, 2011). The level of control agriculturists chose to exert over Earth-life ecosystems and biodiversity our pre-agriculture hunter-gatherer forebears never wanted and clearly demonstrated for 97 percent of our species' existence was neither necessary to survive, nor a pre-requisite for a successful economy.

As post-agricultural human civilizations and their economies arose, thrived for a while, then collapsed (from the Akkadian and Egyptian civilizations to the Late Bronze Age societies in the eastern Mediterranean, the Mayan, the Tang Dynasty, the Tiwanaku, the Ancestral Puebloan Anasazi, the Khmer Empire, and the Ming Dynasty, to name a few), early hunter-gatherer societies and economies also varied substantially over time, according to their location on Earth, and relative to pre-human hunter-gatherer species. This hunter-gatherer way of making a living, and the economies that arose as noted earlier, are much, much older than *Homo sapiens*, our species, which has only been around for about 300,000 years. The behaviors and skills basic to hunter-gatherer adaptation depend not only on physical capabilities (e.g., their capacity for language) that certain of our more ancient predecessors (*Homo habilis,* 2.5 million years ago (Mya); *Homo egaster,* 200 Mya; and *Homo erectus,* 1.8 - 1.5 Mya) may have lacked, but as much on what geologic epoch (Pleistocene vs. Holocene) they lived in, where on Earth they were found, and in which biomes and at what latitudes they lived.

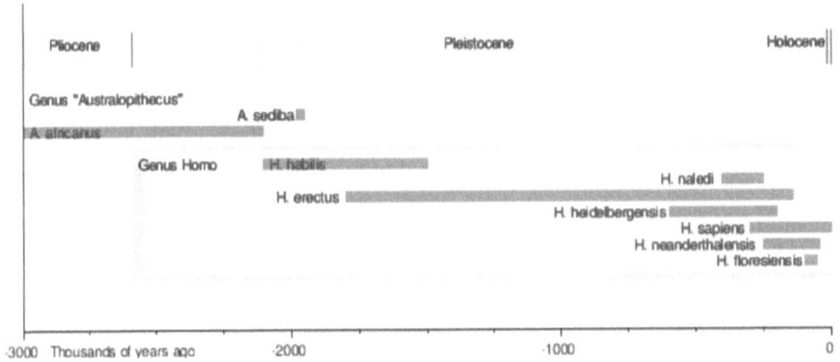

Figure 3-1. Human species during Pleistocene.
(Source: Wikipedia)

As modern humans across western North America, Canada, and the U.S., or across parts of Europe, experienced devastating but opposite climate disasters—scorching heat waves vs. torrential rainfall and floods, respectively—so hunter-gatherers during the Pleistocene (2.4 Mya - 11.8 Kya) faced dramatically different climate and environments from hunter-gatherers and farmers during the Holocene (11.8 Kya to today). All earlier species of the genus *Homo* evolved (and most went extinct) during the Pleistocene (2.6/2.4 Mya - 11.8 Kya years ago—known to us today as the Ice Age), including: *Homo habilis, Homo erectus, Homo heidelbergensis, Homo neanderthals*, Denisovans, *Homo floresiensis, Homo luzonensis, and Homo sapiens*. The Holocene, as noted earlier, though just the current or last inter-glacial after the Pleistocene so far, is rather special to humans as it was during this interglacial that all modern human economies and civilizations evolved, and during which all known human history has taken place and is still taking place. Climatically, it was much more stable and favorable to agriculture and has mostly remained that way until anthropogenic climate change began.

As humans today are beginning to experience the effects of rapid climate change and its economic impacts, can one imagine what economies might have been like during the much more frequent climate changes that occurred during the Pleistocene? Glacial periods during the Pleistocene, for instance, resulted in substantial decreases in sea level and shifted temperate biomes (think Ice Age) toward the equator. This would have resulted in resource redistributions for which there might have been no Holocene equivalent. Pleistocene climate was also wildly variable, marked by repeated cycles of rapid warming during interglacials, followed by several centuries of gradual cooling to glacial temperatures.

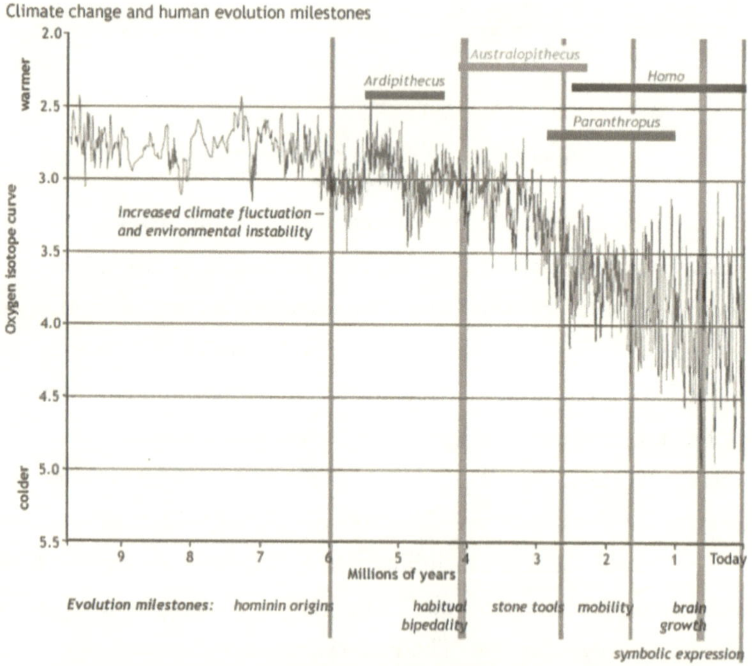

Figure 3-2. Milestones in human evolution correlated with climate variability.

This graph shows milestones in human evolution correlated with climate variability. Milestones indicated along the bottom of the graph show hominin origins; habitual bipedality; first stone toolmaking, eating meat/marrow from large animals; onset of long-endurance mobility; onset of rapid brain enlargement; and expansion of symbolic expression, innovation, and cultural diversity. (Adapted from Smithsonian Institution.)

Behaviors and innovations that were probably suited to cold conditions would likely have had limited application when the climate turned warm again. In addition, the Pleistocene atmosphere was carbon-dioxide-poor, thus inhospitable to plants, which, in combination with rapid climate change, might have prevented the development of technologies needed for the kind of intensive plant and animal agriculture, husbandry, and environmental manipulation that might first have enabled and later supported agriculture ("Was agriculture impossible during the Pleistocene but mandatory during the Holocene?" Richerson, Boyd, & Bettinger, 2001). (Figure 3-2).

Hunting and gathering societies and their economies expanded into a broad range of habitats during the Terminal Pleistocene and Early Holocene when approaches to foraging diversified (Steiner, "The Sociology of Economic Knowledge," 2001) in part due to the extinction of previously targeted, large-game species, but also because of the broad array of food resources that became available due to the warmer Holocene climates (Richerson et al., 2001). These societies and their economies persisted in various parts of the world (Lee and Daly, "Hunter-Gatherer Societies," SpringerLink, 1999) but starting after about 13,000 BP (before the present) most foragers evolved into or were subsumed or replaced by groups practicing mixed foraging and cultivation and, ultimately, agriculture (Diamond and Bellwood, "Farmers and Their Languages: The First Expansions," 2003).

This transition from societies relying predominantly on hunting and gathering to those dependent on food production through plant cultivation, animal husbandry, and the use of domesticated species embedded in systems of agriculture did not happen overnight. The fact that it took almost 4,000 years before abandoning their tried-and-true hunter-gatherer way of making a living suggests that they were in no hurry and must have thought long and hard before changing to agriculture—i.e., to a near-total reliance on domesticated plants and animals they would select and whose reproduction and subsistence they would manage. Nevertheless, that change eventually happened, and when it did it engendered an irrevocable split between humans and Earth-life ecosystems and biodiversity and marked the beginning of a separation that has been expanding ever since as humans began living *outside* Earth-life ecosystems and out of harmony with its biodiversity.

But while many have observed and noted the slow, gradual advance of the mother-of-all-changes in human history, few bother to explain what this split really meant for humanity; how it choreographed human economies and societies from ones that lasted collapse-free for most of human history, for 290,000 years, to ones that have collapsed numerous times within just the last 12,000; how it would enable rampant and unrelenting population growth, driving humans to take over and damage or destroy all but 3 percent of the Earth's ecosystems and drive most of its biodiversity to extinction; and how the transition would impact and greatly endanger human and Earth-life biodiversity and ecosystem survival. In the words of Erle C. Ellis, "Humans have significantly altered nearly all of Earth's systems, including its atmosphere, hydrosphere, lithosphere, and biosphere."

Beginning with agriculture, humans would go on to change not just the source and kinds of foods (from wild animals and plants to grains produced by agriculture and animals by husbandry) but how foods are obtained (from foraging to farming), and not just the sources and flow of energy and how they're conveyed within foods eaten by flora, fauna, and fungi across trophic levels within ecosystems, but the invention and addition of entirely new nonrenewable sources (especially fossil fuels: principally coal, gas and oil) not hitherto found nor used by flora or fauna within ecosystems.

And humans would go on to use not just biologic and natural materials found in ecosystems but would invent entirely new ones (concrete, steel, plastic, etc.) and produce new nonnatural processes and materials whose output includes hazardous waste that not only had no known natural purpose within ecosystems but was harmful to all forms of life. In fact, "taken together," Ellis continues, "over the past 300 years, these anthropogenic changes, especially in atmospheric chemistry and global climate, provide strong evidence that humans have altered the Earth system sufficiently to indicate the emergence of a new geological epoch."

Would 20-20 hindsight have stopped Neolithic Revolution humans from making these changes, and will it stop modern humans from continuing to make them? What motivated them back then and what's enticing us now? In this book this theme of post-agriculture humans choosing to make a living and build their economies outside of Earth-life ecosystems, and out of harmony with its biodiversity, and its consequences, is explored from multiple perspectives.

This transition to agriculture is thought by scientists to have been due to an expanding human population, cultural progress resulting from the perception that agricultural life was inherently superior to foraging, and changes in the environment brought on by climate change at the end of the Pleistocene Epoch. These environmental changes may have caused or accompanied the extinction of many game species that humans relied upon for food, forced migrations due to sea-level rise as the last ice age was ending and glaciers were melting, and rapidly warmed the climate due to increased CO_2 levels that enabled an expansion of agriculture not thought possible during the Pleistocene. This transition to the Holocene was accompanied by a significant increase in atmospheric CO_2 that may have improved the productivity of plants by 25-50 percent. But how did this all unfold?

Scientists believe crops preceded the earliest animal domestication by approximately 1,000 years. In East Asia, rice, millet, and soy were domesticated; in sub-Saharan Africa, it was millet, sorghum, and African rice; and in the Americas, potatoes, sweet potatoes, corn, squash, and beans. (Floros et al., "Feeding the World Today and Tomorrow: The Importance of Food Science . . . " 2010). By 10,000 BP, wheat and barley began to be domesticated in the Levant. Dogs and millet were first domesticated in northern China before 10,000 BP, pigs in western China before 9,000 BP, rice in southern China between 8,000 and 10,000 BP, and sheep and wheat in northern China around 5,500 BP. Domestication of cattle, sheep, and goats in China took place 8,000, 11,000, and 10,000 years ago, respectively, whereas buffalos, horses, asses, and camels were tamed approximately 5,000 years ago (Hirata, 2004, "Advances in Animal Biotechnology," University of Illinois Urbana-Champaign, 2004).

In time, a reciprocating pattern emerged of population growth on one hand, and on the other, a dependency on agriculture and animal domestication for sustenance. As population grew, so did agriculture and animal domestication, and as animal and plant domestication grew, so did surplus food, which in turn enabled further population growth. It was the emergence of this mutually reinforcing pattern that enabled the transition from mobile hunter-gatherer economies to settled-farming economies, and once established, it may well have become irreversible. It was this surplus grain, in particular (as per James C. Scott in *Against the Grain*) that enabled the rise of the state.

The domestication of plants and animals over the past 11,500 years to build post-Neolithic human economies has had a significant impact not just on the species domesticated but also on human evolution and the biosphere as a whole and was the start of the exploitation of Earth-life ecosystems and biodiversity extinction that is still in progress today. For the first time humans became landowners, owners of other humans (slaves), and owners of other Earth-life species. The ability to raise crops and livestock changed Neolithic humans' relationship with the land and Earth-life species to one that pre-agriculture hunter-gatherer humans had never had. This in turn encouraged the growth of permanent settlements that evolved into larger and more complex communities, societies, and economies, and eventually into states and civilizations. In addition, the sense of security that may have come with surplus food that became possible with agriculture may have further stimulated population growth, and that, in turn, may have necessitated a further expansion of agriculture. That's how agriculture may have hijacked civilization.

The domestication of plants and animals and the acquisition of land to build post-Neolithic human economies may also have had the unexpected effect of launching the initial buildup of atmospheric carbon dioxide (CO_2) and methane (CH_4) long before the first fossil fuels were extracted from the Earth, according to William F. Ruddiman in "The Anthropogenic Greenhouse Era Began Thousands of Years Ago." Anthropogenic greenhouse gas emissions are commonly but erroneously thought to have begun 150 to 200 years ago when the industrial revolution began producing large amounts of CO_2 and CH_4, but these first altered atmospheric concentrations thousands of years ago because of the discovery of agriculture and subsequent technological innovations in the practice of farming.

And if so, then as noted previously, it is remarkable that both ends of the Holocene epoch, during which most of human civilization occurred, may have been witness to an increase in CO_2. The beginning may have both given rise to, then accelerated, agricultural expansion, which in turn may well have launched the beginning of the threat of anthropogenic CO_2 buildup in the atmosphere and thereby climate change, potentially establishing a link between agriculture and anthropogenic climate change. And now at our end of the Holocene, fossil-fuel-driven CO_2 and CH_4 global climate change is threatening an even more radical change to human societies and economies 10,000 years after the Pleistocene-Holocene transition period.

While there have been older transformations of equal if not greater significance in hominin history, including bipedalism, encephalization, early stone tool manufacture, and the development of language, this transformation was and is particularly significant if only because it was a transformation away from the first and only way all hominins, including all humans, went about making a living *inside* Earth-life ecosystems for all of their existence. *It was an economic transformation*. The domestication of plants and animals and the acquisition of land to build post-Neolithic human societies and economies outside of Earth-life ecosystems not only led to the abandonment of those tried-and-true mobile waterhole hunter-gatherer economies they once knew but was arguably one of the most drastic lifeway changes in human history.

According to Katherine J. Latham in "Human Health and the Neolithic Revolution," "That transition from a hunter-gatherer lifestyle to dependence on agricultural production, often referred to as the Neolithic Revolution, is commonly considered one of the most important achievements of human history. It ushered in a variety of changes in human dietary intake, food processing and procurement methods, settlement patterns, and physical activity." It was a transition that included changes in diet, living conditions, and subsistence activities that had an enormous impact on human health, though effects varied from region to region. Skeletal analysis of early agricultural communities suggests that the transition to agriculture had an overall negative impact on human oral health; increased the incidence of infectious diseases that are still with us today, including zoonotic diseases such as Covid-19; increased the incidence of nutritional deficiencies; and contributed to an overall reduction in human stature.

What was it, we have asked, that enabled pre-agriculture hunter-gatherer societies and their economies to survive *within* Earth-life ecosystems without collapse for 97 percent of human existence, 290,000 years, while numerous succeeding post-agriculture human societies and their economies collapsed during the 12,000 years that followed? Along the way we have discovered two very different approaches to economic development, and we came away with a few lessons that might help twenty-first century humans and their economies make economic choices that can simultaneously enable the advance of Earth-life ecosystems, their biodiversity, and human economies, while enhancing the prospects of human survival.

Unlike Neolithic Revolution humans, pre-agriculture hunter-gatherer societies and economies eked out a living by remaining entirely *within* Earth-life ecosystems, lived in harmony with Earth-life biodiversity, and sought to control neither plant nor animal species from whence they derived a living, as domestication would have required. By being largely mobile and living in small bands, their ecosystem footprint was sustainable, if not invisible, according to archaeologists, and neither needed nor maintained an attachment to land in ways that later Neolithic human farmers required. They also remained largely egalitarian and believed in neither creator gods that direct the affairs of humans, nor in human kings, queens, presidents, ayatollahs, and other rulers, but made choices driven by the mutual need of their societies to survive.

According to James Suzman in "How Hunter- Gatherers May Hold the Key to our Economic Future," the twenty-first century descendants of the Kalahari's "Bushmen" peoples, the Ju/'hoansi, continue to hunt and gather into the twenty-first century: "...like their forebears they neither stored foods and only hunted and gathered to procure enough to meet their short term needs certain that there was always more to be had with a few hours of effort." They had no need to own, control, or acquire and accumulate wealth—theirs was indeed an "immediate return economy." And, given the way surviving hunter-gatherers continue to hunt and gather into the twenty-first century, one doubts that their and our pre-agriculture hunter-gatherer forebears, were they to last another 290,000 years, could have given rise to a Putin, Xi, Trump, or even a Biden. Neither would their economies have produced a Bezos, Musk, Zuckerberg, or Gates or the companies these men built. Nor would our forebears have created or tolerated the despicable inequality that distorts and is destroying modern human societies and their economies.

Their mobility is what got them out of Africa 70,000 years ago, and is why we are here today, and like all Earth-life species, mobility and migration enabled them not only to follow the food but also to avoid natural disasters and environment- and climate change-driven cataclysms. Mobility may have enabled them to avoid the vulnerability of environmental disasters, especially at times when climatic conditions were more variable such as during the Terminal Pleistocene Epoch. In other words, early complex, sedentary agricultural societies by comparison would have been more severely impacted than the simpler mobile societies of their pre-agriculture hunter-gatherer forebears.

And, while climate has been implicated among the ultimate causes of the collapse of most post-Neolithic Revolution societies and their economies in many parts of the world, the real hunter-gatherer advantage they gave up, in addition to mobility, smaller societal groups, and near-zero ecosystem footprint, was that for all those hundreds of thousands of years, pre-agriculture hunter-gatherers never built their economies *outside* of Earth-life ecosystems. Nor did they seek to domesticate, own, manage, or control other Earth-life species. And they did not need new sources of energy beyond what was available in ecosystems. Instead, they continued to eke out a living *inside* and in harmony with Earth's biodiversity.

Pre-agriculture hunter-gatherers and their economies survived, too, without collapse for all those hundreds of thousands of years and without even a fraction of the tools, technologies, science, and innovation that twenty-first century humans have and think they need to survive. Their survival across those many millennia enabled them to perfect a set of hunter-gatherer lifeways that neither Einstein, Adam Smith, nor any other great thinkers that followed had figured out. They wouldn't have known about the laws of gravity or how the universe works; who or what owns and controls the sun, the air, food and water; or whether their supply within Earth-life ecosystems would be enough to meet their demand as well as the demand of numerous species among whom they foraged—concerns that might have preoccupied the likes of Einstein and Smith but would have done precious little to enable their survival.

They did figure out, though, how to recognize and follow the wisdom of the waterhole, understanding that they need only eke out a living *inside* Earth-life ecosystems, not *outside* of them, and live in harmony with Earth-lfie biodiversity and not drive them to extinction. Only in this way would they, their societies, and economies survive—realizations that,

12,000 years later, modern economists and scientists, because of climate change, are just beginning to grasp. And since they didn't believe in a creator god, they may well have concluded, too, that something else had already done all the rest. Imagine that! One wonders whether twenty-first century scientists and economists would have understood the wisdom of the waterhole.

But what was the wisdom of the waterhole and how did observing and following the lessons it offered enable them to choreograph early human societies and economies, such that they would last for hundreds of millennia without collapse? What was so special about a waterhole?

To begin with, every species would have known where to find one or more within an ecosystem and how to get to it. And they needed no one's permission, nor did they have to pay, to slake their thirst. From the elephant to the dung beetle, the waterhole met the water needs of all species. Waterholes were often local, not subject to ups and downs of a supply chain and were available on demand any time of day or night. Except for seasonal variations of the weather or changes in the environment, there were no access or time-of-day limits. They were not controlled, modified, or owned by anyone, but were freely available to all.

No waterhole was dedicated to specific species. There were no elephant- or lion-only waterholes, nor waterholes only for species that dwelt in a particular region or part of an ecosystem. And by observing and imitating these accessibility principles and adding them to their societal and economic life-ways, they learned from their use of waterholes how to live in harmony with other species and within Earth-life ecosystems without destroying either. They learned how to see, organize, and plan these early human economies and societies from the perspective of the waterhole, and therefore, from a life preservation perspective. This was a way of seeing life, the Earth and use of its natural resources in ways that ensured survival for all, predator and prey alike—a way modern human societies and economies have yet to learn.

Figure 3-3. Animals around a waterhole in the Etosia salt pan.
(Source: Pinterest; Credit: Lucy Fielder)

Here are examples of how the wisdom of the waterhole may have shaped their societies and economies, organized by the principles that governed waterhole use and management:

(1) **Used within ecosystems only.** Note the location of waterholes. Hunter-gatherers learned from where these were located that life can only survive where there was water, and that was *inside* Earth-life ecosystems not *outside* of them, a clear pointer to where one should build one's economies and societies. By adopting agriculture, Neolithic Revolution humans began building their societies and economies *outside* of these ecosystems, which began destroying them and their biodiversity, thus threatening their own survival and that of all other species.

(2) **Ecosystem preservation and biodiversity survival ensure human survival.** This taught hunter-gatherers that their survival was codependent upon the survival of both ecosystems and other species. Modern humans have done just the opposite—we have built our societies and economies off the destruction of ecosystems and biodiversity extinction.

(3) **Coexistence.** As people sought out waterholes, they soon discovered that humans, carnivores, herbivores, and all other species must coexist and share common resources to survive. Personal or private ownership, partitions, apartheids, land grabs, and corporate or government ownership (all characteristic of modern human economies) are hardly a recognition of this wisdom.

(4) **Sharing.** To survive, humans had no choice but to share waterholes and most common resources with other species. Adopting this lifeway enabled them to survive without society or economic collapse for 97 percent of our species' existence. Only in the last 12,000 years have modern humans begun to abandon this lifeway, displacing and exterminating most other species and grabbing most of the Earth's resources for themselves, thus endangering their own survival.

(5) **No surplus and no hoarding.** Surplus accumulation became hoarding and was the very opposite of sharing. Early human economies were immediate-use economies. There was no ability to hoard water back then, and that translated to no hoarding of surplus food and other resources. Hoarding resulted from surplus accumulation and would become the foundation of profitmaking and wealth accumulation in subsequent human and twenty-first century market economies and societies. This in turn led to massive inequality and a society tiered by wealth—the type of society our pre-agriculture hunter-gatherer forebears would never have built.

(6) **No DOMC.** Don't Domesticate, Own, Manage, or Control. They would have observed, too, that for equal access of common resources to work, waterholes couldn't be owned, managed, or controlled, and the same applied to other common resources including land, food sources, and members of their own or other

species. Neolithic Revolution humans abandoned the wisdom inherent in this lifeway. They slashed and burned to clear and carve out land for agriculture, displacing species from their native habitats. Today agriculture occupies 30 percent of the Earth's arable land. No ownership and control also implied no opportunity for profit-making, rent collection, and wealth accumulation. No management implied no leverage over others. No control implied neither politics, rulers, kings, queens, nor presidents; and neither belief nor worship of creator gods nor religions. On the contrary their societies were egalitarian.

(7) **No access restrictions for any reason.** The waterhole is a common resource, and none should be able to control access to common resources of any kind or for any reason regarding who, when, where, why, and how a resource is needed or should be used. Russia's denial of natural gas to Poland, Bulgaria, and Finland, and of gas supplied under a contract with Shell to Germany and under a contract with Danish company Ørsted and Dutch company GasTerra BV, should help us understand the wisdom of the waterhole. So should Russia's blocking of the export of wheat and other agricultural products from ports in Ukraine, which threatened a worldwide food crisis.

(8) **Ease of Access.** Common resources must be easily accessible to all. Human economies and societies were local and it's beginning to look like they should have remained that way. In a waterhole economy, there could not have been a potential food crisis, a shortage of gasoline, lorry drivers, container ships and dock workers, baby formula, flour, and various grains due to climate change or wars disrupting supply chains.

(9) **Common resources must be free to all.** No charge or fee was exacted by anyone for the use of resources. One was unlikely to

go hungry or thirsty for lack of ability to pay, nor due to lack of sharing, nor because of hoarding, as all goods were free. Think of the economic and societal problems these socioeconomic lifeways would have prevented and can still solve in today's economies and societies if modern humans had learned or were to adopt this wisdom of the waterhole. Universal basic income, often proffered as a modern equivalent, is often seen as liberal EU-style overreach, but all resources for life, not just water, were free in these early human societies and economies and hence there was neither poverty, nor homelessness, nor any of the socioeconomic woes that plague the poor majority in the twenty-first century.

(10) **Mobility.** Willingness to be mobile and to migrate to find resources to survive was a prerequisite. Hunter-gatherer humans were nomadic, moved camp frequently, and eventually migrated out of Africa to the ends of the Earth to survive. Today's economic or climate migrants, unless they are Ukrainians, it would seem, would have been better off back then.

(11) **Common resources were often seasonal.** Dry waterholes made people aware of the seasonality of the ecosystem products and services upon which they relied. To survive, they would have followed the food as other species did. Humans today also experience and are aware of this seasonality but have chosen to be sedentary and rely on supply chains rather than follow the food.

(12) **Common resources were also exhaustible.** Waterholes that dried up and remained dry across seasons taught them that ecosystem products and services and biodiversity species were exhaustible resources—a lesson modern humans are finally beginning to understand as burgeoning human populations have pushed most ecosystems' services to their limits.

(13) **The benefit of group action.** Waterholes had to be shared with predators. This would have taught them the wisdom of foraging in bands and groups to enhance their safety.

It is not surprising, then, to find that the wisdom of the waterhole, while indispensable, was not unique to waterholes but rather was common to all essential Earth-life resources upon which all life depended. All life depends upon the unfailing existence of a set of common resources, including: the sun for energy, the rain to irrigate ecosystems, oxygen to breathe, land that comprises the Earth's surface upon which we walk, and oceans and numerous other resources that enable the life we take for granted. Common resources included food, clothing, and shelter, and together these became the foundation that supported early human economies.

The primary purpose, the economic and societal goal and outcome of these societies and economies, was life and survival for all. The only thing pre-agriculture hunter-gatherer humans needed to do to eke out a living, together with all other Earth-life species, was to hunt and gather within those ecosystems—and this they did for 290,000 years, until, that is, Neolithic Revolution humans thought it was smarter to produce and grow their own food and build their societies and economies *outside* of Earth-life's ecosystems.

Compared to modern human economies, it's hard not to notice how markedly different these early human economies and the societies they enabled must have been. It is probably well-nigh impossible today to imagine an economy that was not market-based; that did not include buying and selling; in which everything did not have a price tag but instead was freely shared. There was neither money, nor need for money; no ownership of property, land, or anything except personal use items (clothes) and things needed to make a living, like tools and bows and arrows. There was no industry, economic production, commerce, or trade.

There were also no rulers, governments, laws, police, or military. There were neither gods nor religions, and definitely no cities, towns, or villages—just small bands of fifty or fewer people. Everyone knew everyone else, and everything was local. Modern humans might consider this type of existence to be backward and might use a few other choice adjectives to describe it. Yet it was these apparently simple, backward, subsistence-based pre-agriculture hunter-gatherer societies and economies that survived without collapse for all but the last 12,000 years our species roamed the Earth.

Modern economies and societies, on the other hand, are based on modern capitalist free-market economic systems in which the *a priori* goal is to make a profit, accumulate surplus, and grow personal, business, or public wealth and the GDP. In such societies and economies, the survival of humanity, ecosystems, and biodiversity is no longer the priority it had been for most of our species' socioeconomic history. Modern societies and economies take pleasure in owning, controlling, and managing even the most basic resources and as much of the Earth's services as they can. From the food we eat to the clothes we wear and the homes we live in, at one point or another, all were or are owned and controlled by someone.

Utilities, roads, and most forms of transportation are owned and operated by private or public entities who provide service for a fee. We now know that in our modern socioeconomic system everything is for sale. And, when it's claimed that any common service or product, such as many digital services provided by Facebook and others, are free of charge, we now know that it is we humans who have become the product—one's personal information is relentlessly mined, packaged, and sold to the highest bidder for a fee. Alas! In these modern economies everything has a price, and everything is for sale—even humans. We have become targets of clickbait.

Given the wisdom of the waterhole discussed above, it is not surprising to find that the lifeways of pre-agriculture hunter-gatherer societies and economies tended to inculcate much, if not most, of this wisdom. Adapting all or some of this wisdom into their socioeconomic lifeways may have been what enabled them to survive without collapse for as long as they did. What is clear, though, is that modern economists, beginning with Adam Smith, apparently wanted nothing to do with the wisdom of the waterhole and wanted modern economics to be as far removed as possible from the laws of nature, and they said as much.

But given the state of our twenty-first century economies and societies, and what we have done to Earth-life ecosystems and biodiversity, it sure looks as though Smith and his successors succeeded overwhelmingly, as few if any of these early socioeconomic principles embodied in the lifeways of those pre-agriculture hunter-gatherers seem to have made it into our twenty-first century societies and economies. But if these waterhole economic principles worked out as well as they did for them, and for as long as they did, shouldn't Neolithic humans have taken a second look before becoming farmers? Isn't it time, too, for modern humans to rediscover how thier survival-driven lifeways and economic practices might have encoded the way modern human societies and economies were intended to work? Can modern human societies and economies benefit from adopting the wisdom of the waterhole?

In subsequent chapters we will have an opportunity to explore how modern human societies and economies would have changed and whether abandoning waterhole-inspired socioeconomic lifeways, *Waterhole Economics,* which shaped those early pre-agriculture hunter-gatherer economies and societies, would have been for better or for worse. But make no mistake, the outcome of this choice our species would subsequently make to farm *outside* rather than forage *inside* Earth-life ecosystems couldn't have been more consequential. The goal and outcome of the waterhole economy were life and survival above all else—the preservation of Earth-life ecosystems, its biodiversity, and humanity itself. This option enabled these societies and economies to survive 290,000 years without collapse.

But the goal and outcome of the other choice, farming, was surplus accumulation, hoarding, profit-making, and wealth accumulation that would eventually lead to the near-destruction of all but 3 percent of Earth's ecosystems, the continuing extinction of its biodiversity, and a potential risk of extinction for all species brought on by anthropogenic CO_2-driven climate change—and all of that after numerous civilization collapses in as little as 12,000 years. Given 12,000 years of economic hindsight, the correct choice, it would seem, couldn't have been clearer.

Above I hinted that hunter-gatherers relied upon very few, if any, human technologies to survive, and certainly had none of the technologies, science, and innovations that twenty-first century societies and economies possess and rely on. I will return in a later chapter to explore this in more detail. What they did have, though, were those *waterhole-inspired* socioeconomic lifeways we noted above, that may have been the principal reason they survived the Pleistocene-Holocene Transition, the last of the Ice Age, while other hominin species went extinct.

Modern humans, too, are approaching the end or may have just passed the end of the Holocene and the beginning of the Anthropocene geologic epochs, and are confronting, as pre-agriculture humans did, yet another global warming (but this time anthropogenic-driven) climate change, at the beginning of this new epoch. We must work out sooner rather than later whether our market-based, *surplus-driven* modern economies and the socioeconomic lifeways they engender are up to the tasks of enabling human survival this time around, or if we would have been better off adopting the wisdom of the waterhole, *Waterhole Economics.* One doubts pre-agriculture hunter-gatherer humans would have survived that transition if they had had to rely on our modern *market surplus-driven economics*. It might well have been the *wisdom of the waterhole* embodied in their socioeconomic lifeways, not their technologies, that enabled their survival.

In concluding this chapter, a few things about the way these early pre-agriculture hunter-gatherer societies and their economies were organized stand out, and they are markedly different from those that emerged after the Neolithic Revolution and through the twenty-first century.

Here are some; add your own:

- No markets, trade, or commerce.
- No hoarding; sharing was standard.
- No prices; nothing had a price. Nothing was bought nor sold.
- No profit making.
- No money. Some bartering for the occasional exchange.
- No trade or commerce, but sharing was standard.
- No property or land ownership; people and tribes were mobile.
- No ownership of most things needed to make a living. They were free and available to all species. One simply hunted and gathered.
- No government, laws, or rulers. No religion.
- No economic production or manufacturing.
- No indispensable technologies that people could not live without.
- No ownership of ecosystems, or their products and services.
- No domestication, ownership, management or control of biodiversty species.
- Group population and economy size was very small, 30-50 persons per camp.
- Everything needed to survive was biological and local; there were no supply chains.

Their pre-agriculture socioeconomic lifeways and waterhole economies were remarkable not for what they had but for what they lacked.

4.

Rediscovering The Human Economy *—Foundations*

ECONOMIES CAN EITHER ENABLE LIFE AND SURVIVAL OR CIVILIZATION COLLAPSE AND EXTINCTION. HUMANS HAVE TRIED THEM BOTH.

"Much of the work we do is aimed at keeping the wheels of commerce rolling rather than ensuring that our essential needs are met."

—James Suzman

There have been times in human history when our survival depended upon recognizing that things were not as they seem, when something felt different. We did not quite understand what was happening but felt sure that something had gone wrong or was going wrong. One such observation led to the discovery of a hole in the Earth's ozone layer and the story behind the discovery of this ozone hole in the stratosphere was one such occasion. In the 1980s, a team of scientists shocked the world when they detected this hole and in 1987 the world came together and agreed on a solution known as "The Montreal Protocol" that slowed and greatly reduced the expansion of this ozone hole above Antarctica and was later recognized as an environmental success story. If CFCs had not been detected and banned in the 1980s, by the end of the century it would have caused average global temperatures to rise by an additional 2.5°C on top of existing and ongoing warming. But above all, *without the ozone layer, complex animal and human life would not exist*.

It comes as a great surprise, therefore, but perhaps by now it shouldn't, that humans, somewhere, are still making this banned chemical (CFC-11) that destroys the ozone layer. Emissions have climbed 25 percent since 2012, despite being part of a group of ozone pollutants that were phased out under the 1987 Montreal Protocol. In a research paper published in *Nature* in May 2018 (Nature 557(7705): 413-417), scientists claim there was "an unexpected and persistent increase in global emissions of ozone-depleting CFC-11." Given what's at stake, the question is what is it humans desire so strongly that some are prepared to risk complex animal and human life extinction?

The answer we concluded previously is *the desire for surplus*, an appetite humans acquired with the dawn of agriculture. And, as we saw in previous chapters, given the actions of the tobacco and energy industries, to name a couple, this was neither the first nor the only time some humans knew their economic activities had the potential to cause great ecosystem harm and potentially drive humans and biodiversity to extinction, but continued nevertheless. Our history attests that human economies have driven life and survival, as well as civilization collapse and a potential for extinction, and humans have tried them both.

It is this otherwise inexplicable tendency to pursue economic activities—which drives human, Earth-life biodiversity and ecosystem destruction and potential extinction—that should alert all humans that something else is going radically wrong with our current methods of making a living. And the time may well have passed, but at least has come, to recognize that our survival is once more being put at risk, not just by the CFC-11 still being released into the atmosphere, nor by the fossil fuels we have chosen as energy sources, but by almost all the economic choices we have made as a species since the Neolithic Revolution and the start of agriculture.

The question all humans should be asking is: Is there a way to eke out a living and build human economies without destroying Earth-life ecosystems, biodiversity, and therefore life itself? The answer of course is yes, there is. As prior chapters have shown, early human economies were built exactly that way, and our pre-agriculture hunter-gatherer forebears eked out a living exactly that way and their economies lasted without collapse for more than 290,000 years of our 300,000 years on this Earth.

Human economies, then, emerged out of our pre-agriculture hunter-gatherer forebears' efforts to eke out a living *within* Earth-life ecosystems. Like all prior and extant Earth-life species and their economies, early human economies evolved and endured to fulfill a single purpose and meet a single need—the search for food and materials to enable life and survival. Today, just 1 percent of humans working in agriculture and a few other industries fulfill this need for the nearly eight-billion-plus humans spread across the Earth. And, as much again of the food we consume gets dumped into landfills.

Almost all the remaining 99 percent of human economic activity, in the words of James Suzman, stands apart from the task of survival: "Much of the work we do is aimed at keeping the wheels of commerce rolling rather than ensuring that our essential needs are met." Indeed, most of the economic activity in modern economies is not *survival-driven* but *"legal-persons"-driven*, or to borrow a phrase, is not *human-infrastructure-driven* but *corporate-infrastructure-driven*, and more than likely would find little to no counterpart in those early human economies. So, what economic activities would have comprised early human economies, and, without requiring humans to return to hunting and gathering, what in modern economies do humans need to preserve to survive, and what must we be prepared to ditch?

If indeed early human economies emerged out of the activities comprising their efforts to make a living, methods that enabled their survival and the longevity of their societies and economies for millennia, one takeaway must clearly be to ensure, at the very least, that our modern methods of economic production, whatever they might be, can similarly drive our survival and the longevity of modern human economies and societies. How alarming then it is to discover that the reverse is the case.

Over the last two to three centuries humans have been slowly growing in awareness, but have since become increasingly alarmed at discovering that the very ways we have chosen to eke out a living—our industries, technologies, natural resource extraction, construction, distribution, manufacture, production, transportation, consumption, disposal, and sometimes recycling, from beginning to end—are exactly the ways that are driving the very destruction of Earth-life ecosystems, biodiversity, and, though not currently recognized nearly as much as it should be, the very collapse of human economies they were intended to enable.

Rediscovering how those early human waterhole economies worked, then, and why they survived collapse-free for millennia while all subsequent human economies have collapsed and continue to collapse, should be among the most important and urgent topics humans, and in particular, economists, should ponder, and there are signs that some are beginning to explore these questions, and in some countries even attempting alternative economic approaches. The question, though, is what constitutes an alternative to twenty-first century capitalist market-driven economies? What kind of socioeconomic practices might humans adopt that would stop the continuing destruction of Earth-life ecosystems and biodiversity extinction while still enabling humanity to eke out a living? Where and how does one begin and is there still time? To answer these questions, one must go back to the very *foundations* that underpinned those early human economies. In this chapter we begin the exploration. What were those foundations?

What principles of economic production might one glean from those early human societies and their economies that enabled their longevity and survival? Without attempting a detailed comparison between these and their modern counterparts, it helps to examine at least a few key elements to understand how they differed and why those differences matter.

Pre-agriculture human economies were waterhole economies that emerged out of hunter-gatherer human societies organized near waterholes, in small, mostly mobile groups. *These groups pursued a single goal and outcome: life and survival.* They sought a living within Earth-life ecosystems and migrated when pickings grew sparse. They lived in harmony with other Earth-life species and, other than for food, sought neither to harm, farm, nor domesticate animal or plant species, nor to herd them. Culturally they were *egalitarian,* and they *shared rather than hoarded food* and other resources to ensure none would go hungry. In addition, when it came to Earth-life's ecosystems and biodiversity, they followed a kind of *DOMC* natural-resources-use principle—don't Domesticate, Own, Modify or Control natural resources. They sought neither to domesticate, own, significantly modify, or control natural resources within the ecosystem where they encamped and foraged. They were fiercely independent and obeyed neither king, nor queen, nor rulers of any kind, and believed neither in creator gods nor religion.

In contrast, modern human societies and their economies emerged out of the Neolithic Revolution that saw the transition from foraging to farming. These societies were entirely sedentary, comprised of local villages, towns, and cities that became mega-cities, states, counties, and geographic regions that eventually overspread entire countries; that paved vast parts of countless ecosystems, restructuring and/or destroying numerous wildlife habitats; and that dammed, displaced, or re-routed rivers, lakes, and wetland habitats for human use, blocking wildlife migration paths in the process. Modern humans hunt for jobs, not food, and maintain professions and farms rather than forage.

These became societies and economies where hoarding significant quantities of natural resources as furnishings and supplies was standard; where the norm is ownership, modification/destruction, and control of local ecosystems for agriculture, housing, roads, parks, corporate offices, and other human-designed infrastructure, as well as for domestication of numerous plant and animal species; and where resource sharing with the homeless and hungry is never a priority but relegating them to the care of humanitarian organizations, if to anyone, is the rule.

In these societies and economies today, animal farming and agriculture occupy more than 50 percent of the Earth's surface and consume more than 70 percent of its water. These societies are overtaken by cultures often riven by numerous philosophies, political ideologies, religions, and belief in numerous gods and deities that drive economies, where acquisition and accumulation of surplus is the goal even at the expense of human survival, and where the hoarding of wealth is preferred over the preservation of life.

But whereas those small, mobile, foraging societies and their waterhole economies resulted in restrained human population growth that in turn reduced the demand for ecosystem products and services and eliminated the possibility of ecosystem exhaustion and biodiversity extinction, agricultural societies with their animal and plant domestication and farming economies accelerated population growth that in turn would increase the demand for ecosystem products and services that, given enough time and people, could eventually engender ecosystem exhaustion and biodiversity extinction. *Thus, increased resource utilization due to population growth reduces the odds of survival by increasing the risk of ecosystem exhaustion and biodiversity extinction.*

Mobility rendered unnecessary, if not impossible, and thus discouraged, the acquisition and accumulation of stuff, and made it easier to flee or migrate to safer, less environmentally troubled regions to survive climate change or other natural disasters. By contrast, residents of those large sedentary farming villages, towns, and cities, being completely immobile, could not easily escape such disasters, thereby reducing their ability to survive. Moreover, their economics motivated them to do the very opposite of what seemed conducive to survival—it led them to increase their population to provide additional farmhands. *Thus, mobility makes it easier to flee or migrate to survive and reduces ecosystem exhaustion and biodiversity depletion.*

As agriculture-based economies kept growing so did their populations of domesticated farm animals and their possessions that would later grow to become city-states and eventually whole civilizations—but so too grew the risk to their survival should the ecosystems and biodiversity upon which that growth relied be exhausted. The threat of climate change and other natural disasters meant abandoning entire villages and towns, together with their houses, farms, crops, and entire sedentary lifestyles, including numerous accumulated belongings that in turn resulted in civilization collapse as history has repeatedly shown. *Thus, continued economic growth becomes inversely proportional to, and reduces, the chances of survival by increasing population growth and thereby risking exhaustion and collapse of ecosystems.*

So, what were the principles of economic production that enabled the longevity and survival of early human societies and their waterhole economies? Those small, non-complex, mobile, and what today might seem to some as atheistic, irreligious, independent, and freedom-loving peoples, with minimal-to-zero tolerance for political structures and human leadership of any kind, were indeed the most caring, egalitarian, ecosystem- and biodiversity-friendly societies and economies humanity may ever have seen, and they grew out of small, mobile, foraging, sharing, egalitarian societies that never collapsed but survived—and some are still around today. By contrast, most others that followed during the last 10,000 to 12,000 years, including our own, have collapsed or are in danger of collapse.

On the other hand, these agrarian, sedentary, often political- or religious-oriented and economically burdened economies grew out of socially and economically segregated farming societies that elevated the accumulation of *surplus* over *survival*. They brought peasants, kings, queens, priests, religions, and slavery. Many think they brought civilization, but instead they brought the state and the church, complete with their political and ecclesiastical hierarchies; human segregation and class structures; and above all, they brought us an agriculture-based economy that began the slow walk down the road to ecosystem destruction and biodiversity extinction—and today, to global climate change and the latest zoonotic-driven pandemic.

What can one glean from a review of these pre-agriculture, hunter-gatherer societies and their waterhole economies? In this section we identify eight takeaways.

> **—Takeaway #1: *Life and Survival were paramount.*** *The survival of ecosystems, biodiversity, and human life was the overarching goal and desired outcome of these early human economies.*

At a time when "Nobody Really Knows How the Economy Works," according to a recent Fed Paper shared by Neil Irwin in a 2021 *New York Times* article, if one were looking for takeaways on how best human societies might organize to survive, and how best to set up economies to achieve this original overarching goal, a summary comparison of the history of our species' economic past and present would provide a few object lessons across eight categories. The first category shown below, *Goal & Outcome,* occupies the first row of this table of eight categories comparing early vs. modern human societies and their economies.

It identifies the first takeaway, *"Life and Survival,"* including human survival, as the only goal and desired outcome that mattered to early human economies. To enable life and survival was and remains the original and ultimate reason human economies emerged and persisted for 290,000 of our species' 300,000 years of economic existence—an economic goal and outcome modern human economies, since the dawn of the Neolithic Revolution and the adoption of agriculture, have replaced with the pursuit of *"surplus"* (profit), wealth accumulation, and economic (GDP) growth.

Table 4-1. Takeaways on how human societies might organize to survive

	Takeaways Society & Economic		
	Categories	Early Human Economies & Societies	Modern Human Economies & Societies
1	Purpose & Goal	- Life & Survival - - Well-being -	- Profits/Wealth - - (Surplus)/Growth -

(Source: Samuel Layne)

But to understand these eight takeaways, one must first understand how they came together to expose a socioeconomic survival mechanism; how they interact to enable life and survival by supporting the longevity of early human societies and their economies on the one hand and, on the other, how by rearranging, and in some cases even omitting some of these categories or their interactions shown in Figure 4-1 and labeled (1)(2)(3) and (4), modern human societies and their economies have repeatedly collapsed. Why? What is their significance? What was so special about these categories and how they interacted?

In the "Foundations of Human Economies" diagram (Figure 4-1) locate the *human economy* label at the center and note the encircling chain of four smaller bean-shaped objects (that we will call circles) surrounding it. Note, too, that the first of these small circles, labelled "life," begins this chain, enclosing the human economy at its center and implying that the human economy is an emergent property of this inner chain of circles. Successful human economies then emerge out of the *a priori* successful existence and interactions of these smaller circles that comprise its very foundations, namely: (1) life, (2) Earth-life habitats, ecosystems, and biodiversity, (3) humans, and their ability to be (4) mobile to pursue changing ecosystem and biodiversity food sources, and their willingness to migrate to escape natural disasters and climate change to get to Survival, the outermost circle.

Foundations of human economies

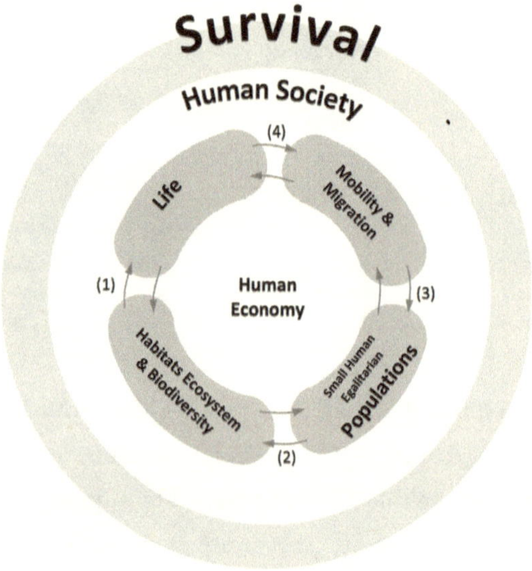

Figure 4-1. Foundations of human economies.
(Source: Samuel Layne)

Note next that the human economy and its supporting encircling foundations themselves form the center and emerge out of an even larger circle, human societies. The implication is that human economies can only emerge out of human societies as humans go about the task of eking out a living *within* Earth-life ecosystems and biodiversity. And finally, in the outer circle, survival. To survive, human societies themselves must remain mobile and must migrate.

For *life* to exist, it must evolve out of Earth-life habitats, ecosystems, and biodiversity, the *second circle,* and must support the continued existence of life. This two-way interaction is indicated by the arrow labelled (1). Note that humans do not evolve chronologically until one gets to *the third circle*. Humans, like all Earth-life species, evolved out of the *second circle*, Earth-life's ecosystems, and their biodiversity. The two-way interaction here too is shown by the arrows labelled (2) between the *circle of humans*, and the *circle of ecosystems and biodiversity*, the second and third circles, and emphasizes that their survival is dependent upon their mutual interactions—relationships humans have taken for granted. For humans to exist, life must first exist, and for life to evolve and exist, Earth-life ecosystems and biodiversity must first exist, and they must interact to maintain and reinforce each other's existence. But what roles does the fourth circle, mobility and migration, play in enabling the emergence of the human economy?

While life and therefore humans evolved and emerged out of and depend upon Earth-life habitats, ecosystems, and biodiversity to eke out a living, humans, like all Earth-life species, must in addition remain mobile to forage from ecosystem to ecosystem (hunt and gather) and be able and willing to migrate to escape natural disasters and climate change to survive. Though life might evolve and can be sustained in Earth-life ecosystems, these are not inexhaustible resources. Life can only remain alive if it remains mobile, foraging from ecosystem to ecosystem, and is willing and able to migrate to survive—hence mobility and migration are indispensable prerequisites to survival. Human economies then emerged out of the foraging activities of mobile human hunter-gatherer societies as they went from ecosystem to ecosystem eking out a living and were only able to survive for all those millennia because they were mobile and were willing and able to migrate.

But what does the above tell us about human economies? For a human economy to exist, *life* must exist; for life to exist, it must evolve and subsist within *Earth-life ecosystems* and in harmony with Earth-life biodiversity. Humans must also exist; and humans and all other species must be mobile to eke out a living across Earth-life ecosystems and must be willing to migrate to escape natural disasters and flee climate change to survive. Of course, nobody thinks of human economies without humans, but how many realize human mobility and migration are indispensable requirements for human survival, and therefore the survival of human economies? Modern humans, by contrast, and like their Neolithic Revolution forebears, have chosen to remain sedentary and to build supply chains, making their food mobile and growing increasingly hostile to human migration. But hopefully, pandemic lockdowns have by now shown us why it occured the other way around, with humans following the food.

—**Takeaway #2: Population size matters.** *Small populations facilitate mobility and migration and enhance survivability; are more sustainable; and reduce complexity and enable the ability to live within the carrying capacity of ecosystems and the Earth.*

Economists tend to worry more about the size of the labor force than about the size of the human population, but according to this second takeaway it would seem one might want to care at least as much, if not more, about the latter—because population size does matter. But how did population size contribute to the success of those early human societies and their economies? One of the terms used to characterize them by some historians is "small." Why were their populations small? Did they deliberately seek to restrain population growth, and if so, why? And if not, why after 290,000 years did their populations remain "small" (estimated to be about three million globally), while in a little more than 10,000 years, after the beginning of the Neolithic Revolution, human population exploded exponentially and now exceeds eight billion as per Figure 4-2? Why? What changed? Among the possible reasons one must consider is the fact that those early human societies and their economies were mobile. This brings us to:

—**Takeaway #3: *Mobility and migration matter.*** *Mobility and migration are indispensable to survival. Earth-life ecosystems and biodiversity and their productivity (plant and animal food sources, water, etc.) vary with location, seasons, weather, climate change, and natural disasters. Hence all Earth-life species must be mobile and prepared to migrate to find food and escape disasters to survive.*

Mobility served as a natural damper on population growth. In these mobile societies, mothers carried their young and that discouraged having more until existing children were old enough to walk and keep up. With nursing being the only food source, weaning was delayed and this in turn forced spacing of childbirth by as many as four years, reducing the number of children per mother and thereby slowing population growth. At about 10,000 BCE, close to the time when the Neolithic Revolution may have begun, the world's population was estimated to be about three million; then ten million by the year 6,500 BCE (largely because of the Agricultural Revolution); then three billion by 1959 and five billion by 1987. Today the human population has exceeded eight billion and is projected to surpass ten billion by the end of the century. When displayed on a graph as shown in Figure 4-2, the exponential nature of this growth is staggering. Yet, this exponential population growth appears to be of little concern to humanity.

But being mobile had another purpose. In addition to finding other ecosystems in which to forage, and slowing population growth, mobility also distributed and thereby reduced human depletion of ecosystems and biodiversity products and services. Pre-agriculture hunter-gatherers as we have seen neither domesticated, owned, significantly modified nor sought to control Earth-life ecosystems and its biodiversity—they followed that set of DOMC customs encountered earlier. Further, moving on to another campsite allowed ecosystems to recover. Given this pattern of resource use, it's not surprising therefore that not even after 290,000 years of hunter-gatherer foraging societies and economies, Earth-life ecosystems and biodiversity continued to thrive, whereas in less than 12,000 years its ecosystems have been pushed by rapidly growing sedentary societies and economies to the verge of collapse and much of its biodiversity to the edge of extinction.

If human life evolved out of Earth-life ecosystems and from among its biodiversity, and has depended upon their care and replenishment to survive, then this comparatively sudden and exponential growth of sedentary human populations and consequent exhaustion of its ecosystems and biodiversity resources by their agrarian, industrial, and technological economies may well have reached beyond the carrying capacity of these natural resources and is unlikely to continue to support human and other Earth-life species economies and ensure their survival.

Just as Earth-life ecosystems and biodiversity enabled the evolution and sustainment of life during those 290,000 years, their near-collapse and extinction will most likely bring the reverse—the end of life, of humans, their economies, biodiversity species, and the 3 percent of ecosystems that are said to be intact. In less than 12,000 years, humans and consequently human economies are on the verge of destroying the very foundations of life, all in the name of economic gain.

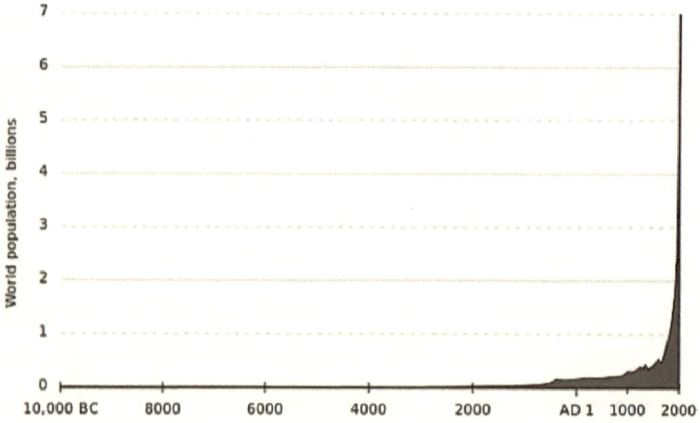

Figure 4-2. The sudden, exponential growth of sedentary human populations.
(Source: El T, Wikipedia)

—**Takeaway #4: Location matters.** *Species eke out a living inside Earth-life ecosystems (not outside), utilizing their natural processes in harmony with their biodiversity.*

Location, location, location is the real estate agent's mantra, but location has life-or-death importance when it comes to where humans choose to eke out a living. The choice is relatively simple: Like pre-agriculture hunter-gatherers, all subsequent humans had to do was continue to eke out a living *within* Earth-life ecosystems as they had done uneventfully for hundreds of millennia. Yet Neolithic Revolution humans got it wrong. They chose to eke out a living *outside* of Earth-life ecosystems and thereby led all subsequent humans to the farm. It doesn't matter that the farm may now be an apartment building with space for a garden and playground, or an expensive center-hall colonial estate for a tycoon as zoning permits. It's quite a different thing to *"eke-within"* than it is to *"eke-without"* an ecosystem. Consider the *takeaway* that follows.

—**Takeaway #5: Ecosystem and biodiversity care, or lack thereof, can drive survival or extinction.** *Obey the DOMC rules: Do not seek to Domesticate, Own, Modify and/or Control Earth-life's species, natural resources (land, soil, water/seas, wind, atmosphere, forests in ecosystems) and biodiversity species.*

Making a living *inside versus outside* Earth-life ecosystems takes a little more than getting an EPA approval, an Army Corps of Engineers sign-off, an accurate survey, or the right building permits. It takes understanding what it means to share Earth-life's ecosystem products and ecosystem services with its biodiversity without breaking anything, and as if your life depended on getting it right the first time, because it does—but not just yours. Our great-great-great-hunter-gatherer- Gramps followed a set of DOMC customs I call the "Do Not Rules" that enabled them to eke out a living safely on the *inside* without destroying Earth-life ecosystems, its products and services, nor the biodiversity with whom they shared these for more than 290,000 years.

These DOMC customs described earlier as comprising the wisdom of the waterhole are as follows: Don't seek to Domesticate, Own, Modify, or Control any natural resource in an ecosystem. There. It was that simple, but it kept their societies and economies going for hundreds of millennia. They also kept it all natural, and thereby avoided the chemical environmental pollution that now endangers humanity and drives biodiversity extinction.

> —**Takeaway #6: Natural Resources Only.** *Use only the natural, recyclable, biodegradable materials and renewable energy sources available within Earth-life ecosystems. By keeping it all natural, our forebears avoided the chemical and environmental pollution that now endangers human life and accelerates biodiversity extinction.*

Eking out a living outside Earth-life ecosystems means ignoring those hunter-gatherer "Do Not rules" and processes, and natural ecosystem cycles. It means not appropriating ecosystem products and services intended for the survival and well-being of all species and instead redirecting and dedicating them for mostly human well-being. To adapt agriculture was to declare war on ecosystems and Earth-life biodiversity species. It means to introduce into ecosystems, as modern humans subsequently would, the numerous agro-chemicals that pollute and harm Earth-life species and that can potentially drive human extinction.

Before buying, selling, and markets became the means of exchanging goods and services, sharing was the way hunter-gatherers met the needs of those who lacked.

> —**Takeaway #7: Share to survive, hoard to go extinct.** *Freely sharing food and other resources needed for life and survival prevents ecosystem resource exhaustion and biodiversity extinction, and thereby enables survival.*

It's likely quite difficult for modern humans in a market-driven capitalist economy whose supermarkets carry an abundance of goods and services or can easily procure them, to comprehend this society-wide socio-cultural economic-sharing system. The question is how did it come to be and why was it necessary? Why did it work? What were the economic incentives that drove it? And who benefited?

If sharing and survival were not well-known, essentially second-nature, expected behavior responses; and if these were not heavily socialized, well understood, and accepted individual and community goals and expectations that served an indispensable and preeminent societal purpose—one that was inculcated at all levels of the society of these early hunter-gatherer humans—it's not so obvious, nor even seemingly natural, that these early human societies and their economies would have come up with such self-sacrificing but "humane" and caring cultural and social practices, given that most post-Neolithic Revolution humans, and most cultures and civilizations that followed, apparently did not. Rather, they often chose the opposite: hoarding.

Its near, if not complete, uniqueness among human species prompts a desire to understand why and how they got to such a seemingly desirable culture, society, and economy, without which the longevity of their societies and economies over hundreds of millennia might not have occurred. The fact that they did and survived is an endorsement of a human socioeconomic system that really worked, one modern humans might want to adopt as many have begun to consider an alternative to the current winner-takes-all socioeconomic system, a potential replacement for modern twenty-first century market-driven capitalist societies and economies.

Fortunately, the supply chain shortages brought on by Covid-19 pandemic lockdowns, and further aggravated by growing demands from recovering economies across the world and the war in Ukraine, provide a helpful object lesson by offering a glimpse of a world economy struggling to overcome shortages of goods and services across numerous categories and countries. They might even partly explain why hunter-gatherer societies and economies simultaneously became sharing and survival-driven.

At a time when there were neither supermarkets nor supply chains; when breakfast, lunch, or dinner was always a hunt or foraging trip away, requiring hours or days and yielding perhaps nothing, a little, an abundance, or something in between, one can begin to understand what it meant when hunters and gatherers returned empty-handed or with not nearly enough. Even in a small group of between twenty and fifty persons, sharing scarce resources then becomes not just desirable but necessary, and in the longer term, even indispensable to survival.

This cultural sharing custom, this willingness—nay, obligation—some peoples feel to share is still practiced and can often still be heard in the form of a greeting in some countries and among some peoples. It is not unusual for one to be asked (although more out of politeness these days than necessity), "Have you eaten yet?" or "Is your belly full?" These are greetings I have since gotten accustomed to but initially thought strange and slightly amusing in Taiwan and on visits to China—(Chi bao le Ma?) in Pin Yin, or (吃飽了嗎) in traditional Chinese. These cultures and societies echo in their greetings a time when sharing was more than a greeting but a way of life that at times became a necessity for survival. Growing up in South America in the countryside where houses can sometimes be not so close, I can still recall my grandmother responding to the calls of a neighbor for a cup of rice or other food stuff and/or one of her chickens. Such a custom seemed not so uncommon back then.

But sharing did more than meet the immediate needs of members of their band unable to hunt, or those who were unsuccessful during the last hunt or foraging trip. They were also contributing to their own survival by ensuring that ecosystems and biodiversity species were not hunted to extinction or foraged to exhaustion. One has heard, no doubt, about supermarket shelves being cleared overnight, as it were, of toilet paper, milk, or other necessities, for instance, or seen the endless queues at gas stations, where some joined not out of immediate need but just in case. Well, hunter-gatherers might not have had to queue, but neither did they take more than they needed for the current and maybe next meal, thereby enabling those who might arrive later also to find food and other resources. They neither had nor wanted any of the tools and equipment humans use today to hoard (or as we prefer, to "store")—no pantries, cupboards, refrigerators, trunks, or other storage containers.

From their very inception, then, sharing was the default way of life among early human societies and a fundament component of their economies. It was a societal, cultural, and economic necessity. They shared to live and because they shared, they were able to survive for all those millennia. They survived, too, because sharing significantly reduced wear and tear on Earth-life ecosystems and significantly slowed biodiversity species use, allowing these in turn to be replenished and last longer, and to recover and be refreshed faster.

These early human economies, for example, wouldn't have depleted fish stocks and other marine species in lakes and rivers nor driven bison to near extinction on the American prairies. Hence, by sharing to live they ensured their survival by significantly reducing the overall need for ecosystem products and services, and thereby avoided the mistake all subsequent human societies and their economies have made—hoarding—which had the knock-on effect of driving Earth-life ecosystems to exhaustion and near collapse and its biodiversity to extinction.

The opposite unfortunately is also true. A society and economic system that thrives on hoarding surplus (profits, growth, and wealth accumulation) as in the City of London, among other havens, may escape paying income, capital gains, inheritance, and corporate taxes, and may also get away with refusing to share the fruits of their "economic hunts" with their fellow humans, or ignore the well-being or lack thereof of the less fortunate, but inevitably they will exhaust Earth-life ecosystems and drive its biodiversity to extinction, as all prior surplus hoarding human economies have done in countries and regions they inhabited. Unlike those early hunter-gatherer humans and their sharing economies that lasted for millennia, though, these surplus-hoarding humans, as history has shown, are unlikely to survive.

But there was another equally important takeaway one shouldn't lose sight of. Early human economies lasted as long as they did not only because they were mobile, sharing societies and economies—but also, of equal importance, because they were egalitarian. And, how interesting! Not only does no major human society or economy today follow the societal, cultural, and economic paths pursued by these, the most successful of human societies and economies to have ever arisen upon the Earth, but none has chosen to follow in its egalitarian societal and cultural ways of life. What was it like to live in an egalitarian society and economy? Perhaps Thomas Piketty or others may no doubt have more to say than I about what may comprise an egalitarian human economy.

> —**Takeaway #8: Egalitarian Culture.** *Hunter-gatherers created a culture that prioritized life and survival above surplus and profits with neither rulers, kings, queens, nor strongmen; gave no importance to politicians, their politics, or elections; and acknowledged neither gods nor religions but regarded with fervor the sanctity of life—including humans, ecosystems, and biodiversity.*

As one reflects on this socioeconomic survival mechanism underpinning their society and economy, one can't help but notice that all four foundations of their economy (*Life, Earth-life ecosystems and biodiversity, small egalitarian human populations, and mobility/migration*) seem to have been assigned a unique role yet interacted together to enable three unmistakable outcomes: 1) the emergence of the human economy, 2) the longevity of human society, and eventually, 3) human survival.

Pre-agriculture hunter-gatherer societies, we previously noted, used sharing and mobility to enable ecosystems and preserve biodiversity, thereby ensuring their mutual survival. But in addition to being mobile, sharing societies and economies, they played an additional key role, one that had less to do with how humans treated plants, amphibians, birds, fishes, insects, reptiles, and other animal species, but had everything to do with how humans treated other humans. They were (and apparently needed to remain) egalitarian as well as comparatively small in population size to survive.

The message seems to be that even if humans grew all green thumbs and became the best eco- and biodiversity-friendly species ever to walk the face of the Earth (and many would wish that were possible as it could put an end to global warming), to survive humans still needed to figure out how to treat their fellow humans right. But what is this really saying? It's in effect saying that nothing humans do is going to ensure their survival as a species if they don't, in addition, figure out how to put survival above surplus and life before profit.

I ceased being religious too many moons ago to remember, but one cannot be any more surprised than I was to discover that deep in the core of this *fundamental survival mechanism* was that old Sunday school Bible verse I learned too long ago to forget—"Love thy neighbor as thyself." There it was—except that this hunter-gatherer lifeway had nothing to do with religion.

In effect, in this *takeaway,* the life preserving process was in addition requiring humans to become, and to remain, well, *humane* if they wanted to survive. Figuring out how, against all odds, to remain human, then, was going to involve much, much more than learning to stand upright on two feet, grow a huge brain, and discover the use of fire, among other things, but this may well have been the whole purpose of having to build the human economy to begin with, itself a mere preamble to the ultimate objective: human maturity and survival.

By now one understands how mobility modulated and kept small the size of foraging hunter-gatherers' populations; how, when combined with sharing, the human impact upon ecosystems and biodiversity was further mitigated and thus enabled their longevity and preservation. Together, they made possible human society, economy longevity, and ultimately human survival for those 290,000 years—yet these weren't enough to guarantee human survival. There was still one more thing humanity needed to do, this time not for Earth's ecosystems and biodiversity, nor for the environment, but for humanity itself. The remaining question then is how did this last *takeaway*, being *egalitarian*, contribute to their survival, that ultimate outcome for all human societies and their economies? First, though, what was it like to be egalitarian?

The word "egalitarian" is derived from "égalité" and suggests an equality that's not neutral but a politically assertive equality of the French variety that carries with it echoes of revolution, of a fervor for equality in opposition to inequality, and implies a need for vigilance to maintain that equality as hunter-gatherer societal practices confirm. There are hunter-gatherer and non-hunter-gatherer societies that are both unequal and some that are egalitarian. But those in which inequalities have been known to be at their minimum tend to depend on hunting and gathering for their subsistence. Apparently, only the hunting and gathering way of life seemed to have permitted this great emphasis on equality.

Surviving hunter-gatherer peoples who are regarded as profoundly egalitarian practice various leveling mechanisms that ensure social equality, usually by shaming or humbling members of a group that attempts to put themselves above other members. Such peoples include the Mbuti Pygmies of Zaire, the !Kung Bushmen (San) of Botswana and Namibia, the Pandaram and Paliyan of South India, the Batek Negritos of Malaysia, and the Hadza of Tanzania.

If indeed our pre-agriculture hunter-gatherer forebears were mostly egalitarian in their lifeways, then they were the very opposite of the commonly accepted mantra that humans are inherently and universally selfish. Philosophers from Plato to the moral philosopher Arthur Schopenhauer, and even Adam Smith, the father of economics, shared this view. In his book, *The Wealth of Nations,* Smith claimed, "It is not from the benevolence of the butcher, the brewer, or the baker, that we expect our dinner, but from their regard to their own interest." (Smith, A. [1937]. *The Wealth of Nations* [1776].) Indeed, the very foundation of neoclassical economics is the concept that humans are selfish, rational decision-makers and need to be so to thrive and survive.

Such philosophical beliefs about our selfish human nature inspired many of the teachings we encounter in Christianity and in everyday life and runs counter to the egalitarian lifeways shared among our pre-agriculture hunter-gatherer forebears. But could these views of our selfish human nature be all wrong? Is it possible that the great thinkers of history were wrong? They were wrong about the lifeways of hunter-gatherers. For example, E.R. Service (1966), paraphrasing Thomas Hobbes, claimed that life before civilization was "solitary, poor, nasty, brutal and short!" yet it turned out their lives were comparably better than that of many modern humans and may even have been affluent, according to James Suzman in his book, *Affluence Without Abundance: What We Can Learn from the World's Most Successful Civilization.* We learned they were egalitarian and pursued caring and sharing socioeconomic lifeways.

But to be egalitarian would have required an extraordinary level of cooperation and mutual forgiveness in every aspect of their lives. They are the ones that taught us it takes a village to raise a child. Their sharing versus hoarding lifeways and the lessons they learned around waterholes would have taught them how to cooperate and coexist, not just with one another, but with prey and predator alike in order to survive—indeed, they must have been super-cooperators. They learned that they needed to cooperate, not compete—and not just with one another, but with Earth-life ecosystems and its biodiversity—to survive.

It is unlikely that these pre-agriculture hunter-gatherer societies and economies would have survived for as long as they did (most of human existence) without societal or economic collapse if they hadn't become and remained largely egalitarian. Would modern human societies and economies have been different had they, too, learned to be egalitarian rather than selfish competitors as we were taught? Let's examine how being egalitarian worked out for hunter-gatherer peoples.

Consider for example what is reported by scientists who have lived and worked among surviving hunter-gatherer peoples. Consider what is reported about the Hadza, one of the few remaining sources of valuable direct knowledge of how humans lived for most of their time on Earth.

They were societies with no fixed dwellings, yet experienced little if any homelessness. Unlike most sedentary societies, people lived in small camps containing two dozen or more people who moved fairly often. They had no fixed dwellings: no base camps, stores, hunting or fishing apparatus such as stockades or weirs, or fixed ritual sites to constrain movements. Socially, these societies tended to have the following basic characteristics: 1) social groupings were flexible and constantly changing in composition; 2) individuals had a choice of whom to associate with in residence, in the food quest, in trade and exchange, and in ritual contexts; 3) people were not dependent on specific others for access to basic requirements; and 4) relationships between people, whether relationships of kinship or other relationships, stressed sharing and mutuality but did not involve long-term binding commitments and dependencies of the sort that are common in agrarian societies.

Individuals are not bound to fixed areas like farms or places of work, to fixed assets, or to fixed resources. They could move away, without difficulty and at a moment's notice, from any constraint that others might seek to impose on them, without economic or other penalty. This possibility of movement is one of a few powerful levelling mechanisms, positively valued like other levelling mechanisms that are designed to ensure equality in these societies.

No social classes. Other than distinctions between the sexes, and unlike modern societies, egalitarian societies systematically eliminated distinctions of wealth, power, and status. There is here no disconnection between wealth, power, and status, no tolerance of inequalities in one of these dimensions any more than in the others. Formal relationships between men and women remain quite variable although in all of them women have far more independence than is usual in agrarian societies.

There are no rulers. No constitution, no law, nor rule of law and hence no law enforcement/police. Open carry was the norm. Imagine a society where "open carry" was the norm and yet in which crime was nearly non-existent and maintaining the peace was voluntary and everyone's business. Unlike most modern societies, all males had access to hunting weapons among hunter-gatherers as is still the case among the !Kung, Hadza, and Mbuti. All men possessed the means to hunt and therefore to kill anyone perceived as a threat to their own well-being.

There were no AK47s, but hunting weapons were nonetheless lethal, not just for game animals but when used against people as well. There was no constitution, no law, no police, no 911, and hence no law enforcement as modern people understand it. No one had authority over anyone else and least of all the right to arrest (citizen's arrest) anyone or take them into custody. Open carry not only limited crime, predation, and exploitation but also acted directly as a powerful restraint and is another of those egalitarian levelling mechanisms.

A guaranteed basic income. *Imagine a society and an economy wherein access to food, clothing, housing, and all other resources* was free. Imagine! No homeless, no poor, no destitute nor unemployed—how different would twenty-first century human societies and economies be?

The idea of a guaranteed basic income has been around for centuries, yet Sintia Radu, staff writer at USNEWS.com, saw fit to ask in 2018, "Will Universal Income Ever Work?" Western societies and economies debate the benefits or lack thereof of a guaranteed minimum income. The Alaska

Permanent Fund is one of the closest examples of functional universal basic income in place today. The concept of a government unconditionally transferring money to citizens is popular in European countries that often pay benefits to support children or families. Yet, according to the Organization for Economic Co-operation and Development (OECD), no country has yet implemented this as a "principal pillar of income support for the working age population."

But it might surprise the OECD to learn that universal (and not-so-basic) income was not only standard practice in early human societies and economies, but it was also the only source of income pre-agriculture hunter-gatherer humans had known for millennia. No, it was not paid by a government, as there were no governments, but was freely available through Earth-life's ecosystems and biodiversity products and services—those same products and services companies obtain for free from nature, then package and market as their own merchandise.

In these hunter-gatherer societies individuals have direct access, limited only by the division of labor between the sexes, to the ungarnered resources within the ecosystems wherein they camped. People have free and equal access to wild foods and water; to raw materials they need for making shelters, tools, weapons, and ornaments; and to whatever wild resources they use, processed or unprocessed, for trade. The direct and immediate access to food and to other resources which people enjoy is important in other ways.

Without seeking permission, obtaining instruction, or being recognized as qualified (except by sex), individuals in these societies can set about obtaining their own requirements as they think fit. They need considerable knowledge and skill, but this is freely available to all who are of the appropriate sex and is not, in general, transmitted by formal (or even informal) instruction: Rather, it is learned by participation and emulation. In most, but not all of these societies, neither kinship status nor age is used as a qualification to obtain access to hunting and gathering skills or equipment.

More important still, any person—man, woman, or child—who seeks to obtain food or other requirements either individually or in association with others can do so without entering into commitments to and dependencies on kin or contractual partners. Adults of either sex can, if they choose, readily obtain enough food to feed themselves adequately and are, despite the rules of the division of labor, potentially autonomous. What matters here is the lack of dependence on sharing or pooling of resources: A Hadza woman out gathering with other women will consume much of the proceeds on the spot and, out of what she brings back to camp, little, if any, may go to her husband. Similarly, a Hadza man out hunting will expect to feed himself by picking and eating berries and by consuming any small animal he may kill. Only food surpluses cross the sexual boundary.

Sharing vs. hoarding ; equality vs. inequality; and freedom to choose vs. control by others.

What hunters are to hunter-gatherer societies and economies, entrepreneurs and successful businesspeople (think Bill Gates, Mark Zuckerberg, Elon Musk, or Jeff Bezos to name a few) are to modern capitalist market-driven economies. Most of the hunting is done by men, and a high proportion of animals are killed by a small proportion of men (Lee 1979,242-4) — but that's where the similarity ends. The principal occasions in which individuals in these societies are brought into association with valued assets which could be accumulated or distributed to build status are when large game animals are killed. And it is then that the most elaborate formal egalitarian rules dissociating the hunter from his kill and denying him the privileges of ownership are brought to bear.

Levelling mechanisms come into operation precisely at the point where the potential for the development of inequalities of wealth, power and prestige is greatest. In hunter-gatherer societies and economies, then, there could never have been the inequality that plagues twenty-first century societies and economies that Piketty so ably describes in *Capital in the Twenty-First Century.* Neither the private nor corporate billionaires nor the public officials revealed in The Panama Papers and The Pandora Papers would have come into being. Nor could there have been places like London, which has become the hiding place for the world's stolen money.

But unlike our modern winner-take-all capitalist societies and economies, successful individual hunters are specifically denied the opportunity to make effective use of their kills to build wealth and prestige or to attract dependents. Instead of shareholder or stakeholder capital, imagine employee and citizenry capital; instead of Zuckerberg owning a majority of Facebook, its billions, along with those of every other multinational capitalist company, would be routinely distributed, like the hunter's kill, to meet the needs of the peoples of the world. There would be no need for the UN's SDGs, nor for the struggle to fund and execute COVAX (that worldwide initiative that was aimed at equitable access to Covid-19 vaccines); nor for the struggle President Joe Biden has had with Senators Manchin and Sinema (eventually resolved) to fund efforts to reduce climate change—as there might not have been climate change nor any rich to tax to begin with.

Indeed, many if not most of the issues that plague humanity and animate political progressives in the USA today might never have emerged if there were an equivalent egalitarian twenty-first century U.S. society and economy. Imagine that! What a different place the world would be if humans went back to being egalitarian again; if there were no capital, or distinction between public and private capital but instead only human infrastructure capital.

Lee has reported how !Kung are expected to be self-deprecating about their hunting successes; boasting is met with scorn. Turnbull tells us that "some [Mbuti] men, because of exceptional hunting skill, may come to resent it when their views are disregarded, but if they try to force those views they are very promptly subjected to ridicule." A Hadza returning to camp having shot a large animal is expected to exercise restraint. He sits down quietly with the other men and allows the blood on his arrow shaft to speak for him.

One effect of these rules is, certainly, to deny to the hunter praise which he might otherwise expect to receive. For the !Kung the owner of the first arrow to hit the animal effectively is the owner of the kill with the right to distribute it. Lee explains that meat distribution brings prestige, but it also brings the risk of accusations of stinginess or improper behavior if the distribution is not to everybody's liking. The society seems to want to extinguish in every way possible the concept of the meat belonging to the hunter according to director John Marshall in his 1974 film The Meat Fight.

What if, just as the meat of the kill is described as the people's meat, the earnings and accumulated wealth of companies were seen as belonging to the peoples of the Earth? What if, just as the meat was widely shared within the camp unit, the earnings of companies were widely distributed across the world? For the !Kung, equity begins at the kill site among those who had come to carry in the meat, is further practiced back at camp where the meat is distributed among those who remained behind, and then finally, when it is cooked, it is consumed by those who happen to be present and not simply by the person or the family grouping to whom the meat was allocated.

The hunter himself will often not be involved in dismembering the carcass and in distributing the meat but he and his wife's mother and father, if they are present, will receive substantial shares. Among the !Kung the meat is distributed and redistributed in waves of sharing through the camp: Everyone receives a share. But this sharing did not apply only to meat from the kill, but to all ecosystem products and services. Hence, the ecosystem products and services commandeered by corporations and governments today and resold for a profit, or licensed by governments for revenue, were instead intended to be used free of cost by humans and by Earth-life's biodiversity to meet their survival needs.

No one was permitted to accumulate wealth. Much of the financial services industry or its equivalent wouldn't exist in an egalitarian society. The financial services industry collapse that caused the 2008/9 recession couldn't have happened. Many of the industries that cater to wealth management and wealth accumulation simply would not exist, because everywhere in these egalitarian societies and economies there are sanctions against wealth accumulation. Imagine a society and economy in which no one is permitted to accumulate wealth—no for-profit firms, only nonprofits. No savings or other bank accounts. There were even *sanctions on the accumulation of personal possessions* that go far beyond what mobility concerns might suggest as these apply even to the lightest objects such as beads, arrowheads, or supplies of arrow poison. Imagine a country in which saving for retirement and/or to pass on to family is neither an individual, family, nor societal goal, nor a necessity.

No inheritance or transmission of possessions between people. Much wealth in modern societies is acquired through inheritance but not so in egalitarian hunter-gatherer societies and economies. Even today, among both the !Kung and the Hadza peoples, individuals with any objects for which they appear to have no immediate need are under the greatest pressure to give them up and many possessions are given away almost as soon as they are obtained. The Hadza use gambling as a method of distributing or transmitting personally owned objects between people, which has profound consequences for their relationships.

Gambling is the major means by which scarce, local objects are circulated throughout the country: Much intercamp visiting is stimulated by gambling, and winnings are constantly on the move. This circulation is accomplished not through some form of exchange which would bind participants to one another in potentially unequal relationships of kinship or contract. The transactions are neutralized and depersonalized by being passed through the game. Even close kin/relatives gamble with each other, and the game acts against any development of one-way flows and dependency in relationships between them.

Leadership and decision-making. Many of the conflicts and much of the division peoples and nations confront today are engendered by the struggle for power and leadership. From strongmen and would be strongmen in America, China, Turkey, Poland, and Russia, to name a few, to former mainstream political parties like some in the USA that seem willing these days to abandon the American Constitution just to have a chance of becoming the majority party again at any cost, one has yet to identify a form of government that can make choices and decisions on an individual's behalf better than hunter-gatherer groups can—at least that's how hunter-gatherers might have thought about governments and rulers; they lacked any and wanted none. Much of America's troubles today, for example, seem born of internal ideological and political struggles that identify with one political party or another. Such struggles have been known to tear nations apart. Who wouldn't wish nations did not have to endure the political struggles between their political parties; the cutthroat competition to be president, senator, governor, or congressperson at the federal, state, or local levels, or their equivalent positions outside the U.S.?

Western nations believe that democracy is the least bad of all the other forms of government, but most Western nations and their democratic systems of government couldn't hold a candle, as they say, to the peace and harmony made possible by the complete absence of governments, or pseudo-governments in the form of employers in the private sector, that hunter-gatherer societies and economies enjoyed for most of humanity's existence on Earth. In the absence of government, anarchy did not prevail, contrary to what one had no doubt been taught. Our hunter-gatherer forebears, their societies and economies lasted for hundreds of millennia without governments, legal systems, constitutions, or any of the control mechanisms and forms of authority democratic and other forms of governments have thought necessary to maintain the peace.

In these egalitarian societies, there are either no leaders or leaders who are very elaborately constrained to prevent them from exercising authority or using their influence to acquire wealth or prestige. Hadza decisions, for example, are essentially individual ones: Even when matters such as the timing of a camp move or the choice of a new site are to be decided, there are no leaders whose responsibility it is to take the decisions or to guide people toward some general agreement.

"None is arrogant, overbearing, boastful, or aloof. In !Kung terms these traits absolutely disqualify a person as a leader and may engender even stronger forms of ostracism . . . Another trait emphatically not found among traditional camp leaders is a desire for wealth or acquisitiveness . . . Whatever their personal influence over group decisions, they never translate this into more wealth or more leisure time than other group members have" (Leadership in an Egalitarian Society, 1979: 345). . . . "Their accumulation of material goods is never more, and is often much less, than the average accumulation of the other households in the camp" (The African Origins of Democracy, 1979: 457).

Leaders would ideally be "modest in demeanor, generous to a fault, and egalitarian (The African Origins of Democracy, 1979: 350). Leaders such as these pose no threat to egalitarian values and indeed could be said to display and reinforce egalitarianism. There is probably not a human today who might not prefer the true freedom to choose that came with hunter-gatherer egalitarian societies and economies over any form of government our modern world has to offer, be it communist, democratic, authoritarian, religious, or some other form.

Has it become any clearer why egalitarianism would have been a prerequisite to human survival? One only has to reflect on how, and upon what, our species employs its intelligence to appreciate the abundance of caution this takeaway may well have been designed to instill—the possibility that humans could well through their own self-extinction deny themselves the opportunity for survival. Our species has shown no lack of imagination nor creativity when it comes to destroying its fellow humans, and indeed we have had for decades the ability for one solitary human to destroy all humans.

Had modern humans followed DOMC rules the way hunter-gatherer humans did, they may well have afforded our species a bit more time to remain within the safety of Earth-life's ecosystems. Following these rules enabled our hunter-gatherer forebears to survive 290,000 years without coming up with weapons of mass destruction and other self-destroying technologies. Such rules would have prevented leaders like Putin, Trump and Xi from making their territorial claims against Ukraine, Canada and Greenland, Taiwan, and most of the South China Sea.

This may well have been the strongest argument in favor of continuing to eke out a living and build human economies *inside* Earth-life ecosystems as they did. Now that just in the last 12,000 years, however, humans have let the genie out of the ecosystem bottle, something our forebears managed to avoid, it is not clear that there is a way to put it back in, or for humans to either (1) accelerate its own maturity and morality enough to match and manage these new and growing capabilities it has unleashed, or (2) confront and come to terms with the distinct possibility that we may well have become the unsuspecting architects of our potential destruction. And if we do get there, it would have been all because we sought to eke out a living, and thereby build our human economies, *outside* of Earth-life ecosystems.

Reflecting upon these eight takeaways, then, a pattern begins to emerge—a *survival-driven pattern with mobility and migration at its very core*. One soon realizes that while each played a unique role, when combined they formed the foundations of pre-agriculture hunter-gatherer societies and economies. These foundations included the principles that:

(1) ***Life*** is indispensable to all Earth-life species economies, including human economies, and emerges out of Earth-life ecosystems and biodiversity. No life, no economy.

(2) ***Earth-life ecosystems and biodiversity*** are the source of all life yet are mutually dependent upon Earth-life species to survive.

(3) ***Small egalitarian human populations*** are needed. It won't be a human economy without humans. But these human populations must remain small, mobile, and egalitarian if they are going to rely on Earth-life ecosystems and biodiversity to survive, and vice versa.

(4) ***Mobility and Migration*** *are critical.* All life must be mobile to exist and must migrate to survive.

Having briefly reviewed some relevant aspects of early human societies and economies, possible takeaways, and implications, it's now time to compare these with a matching list of corresponding takeaways derived from modern human societies and economies. This comparison is shown in the eight-category *takeaway table in Table 4-2.* Which of these societies and their respective economies would you rather live in? Let's examine each of these comparisons.

If you have ever looked at any of those *best-countries-to-live-in-lists, with top selections* based on numerous criteria, the usual suspects always tend to pop to the top—but none of these would have appealed to our egalitarian hunter-gatherer forebears, and they shouldn't appeal to us, either, now that we know a bit more about what human societies and economies were intended to be and were once like. Some countries are trying to remake themselves into a new, caring, socioeconomic image, from a so-called Wellbeing Economy Alliance mold.

Table 4-2. Early versus modern human economies

	Takeaways Society & Economic		
	Categories	**Early Human Economies & Societies**	**Modern Human Economies & Societies**
1	Purpose & Goal	- Life & Survival - - Well-being -	- Profits/Wealth - - (Surplus)/Growth -
2	Population Size	- Small - (Self-Managing)	- Huge/MEGA - (Elected Government)
3	Societal Structure & Lifeways	- Mobile - - Migrations Friendly -	- Sedentary - - Migrations Hostile - (Fixed Locations)
4	Location of Economic Activity	- Inside - (Ecosystems)	- Outside - (Ecosystems)
5	Coexistence with Ecosystem & Biodiversity	- DOMC-Compliant {Don't Domesticate, Own, Modify or Control}	- DOMC Non-compliant • Ecosystem Destruction • Biodiversity Extinction
6	Natural Resource Use & Impact	- Light Usage - • Natural/Recyclable • Biodegradable • Renewable • From Within Ecosystems	- Heavy Usage - • Destructive • Regulated & Non-Regulated • Non-Renewal • Outside Ecosystems
7	Economic Lifeway & Culture (Share vs. Hoard)	- Sharing - (No Surplus/Profit) - Caring -	- Hoarding - {Surplus/Profit Wealth Accumulation} - Selfish -
8	Social-Political Lifeways	- Egalitarian - • No Political Systems • No Religion/GODs • Individual/Free • Humanitarian/Caring • Sharing/No Hoarding • DOMC compliant • Small Mobile	- Democratic/Market - • Authoritarian • Strongman/Dictator • Command & Control Economy
	Abbreviation: **DOMC** – Don't Domesticate, Own, Modify or Control		

(Source: Samuel Layne)

Unfortunately, though, these are comparing themselves with equally modern winner-take-all, market-driven, capitalist societies and economies—but unfortunately none of these would be among those our hunter-gatherer forebears would have found desirable. After one has learned how to see the world like an egalitarian hunter-gatherer, there are few, if any, modern human societies and economies one would find desirable. The real issue then is how does a people go about building one?

If one were truly serious, as some appear to be, about remaking modern human societies and economies to be somewhat survival-driven, as opposed to GDP-, wealth-, and profit/surplus-driven, then one could start by considering how some favorite modern human societies and economies, like those that seem to always end up at the top of those lists, might set out to transform themselves once they agreed to subject themselves to the economic and societal leveling mechanisms of egalitarianism.

Transitioning from one to the other won't be easy, though, as surviving remnant hunter-gatherer communities, such as the Central Kalahari San, traditional hunter-gatherers living in the ≠Kade area of the Central Kalahari Game Reserve, discovered when some were forced to adapt to the sedentism program of the Botswana government. It had a profound influence on the subsistence of the Central Kalahari San as they tried to adopt elements of our modern sedentary, hoarding, non-egalitarian socioeconomic customs. Note the difference, then and now, between these societies and economies as summarized by category.

Take some time to become familiar with this list of takeaways in Table 4-2 and note the first takeaway: *Early human societies and economies emerged to fulfill a single purpose and had a single goal and outcome—to ensure human life and survival.* Compare how today's economic purpose and goals have radically changed to begin to grasp the societal and economic chasm modern humans will have to cross to get back to the socioeconomic principles that enabled our pre-agriculture hunter-gatherer forebears to build societies and economies that lasted 290,000 years, or 97 percent, of our species existence. How did they do that?

If indeed the goal and purpose of human economies, as we have seen, is not to enable humans to become wealthy, drive economic and GDP growth, build startup companies, go to the moon or Mars and whatnot, but instead to map out and pursue a path to human survival, is the hunter-gatherer way the only way to get there? No one knows for sure, and modern humans aren't even trying to find out. Nonetheless their way remains the only way one is aware of that has worked since the evolution of anatomically modern humans—the survival-driven way faithfully followed by our pre-agriculture hunter-gatherer forebears.

Countries comprising the *Wellbeing Economy Alliance* may well imagine transforming their nations to ones whose societal and economic goals would one day no longer be GDP growth or wealth accumulation, nor focused on profiting off interactions with others in the name of commerce and building businesses, but instead would be motivated to ensure the well-being and survival not only of their fellow humans, but also the growth and replenishment of Earth-life ecosystems and the preservation of its biodiversity.

But whether supported by the Wellbeing Economy Alliance or not, there are no such modern societies and economies yet, nor are any likely to make this transformation until humans return to the foundational goal and outcome that led to the emergence of early human economies—*life and survival*—i.e., human, Earth-life ecosystems, and biodiversity life and survival. Life and survival set the direction and purpose for all subsequent societal and economic decisions and activity and did so, unfailingly, for our hunter-gatherer forebears. It was their true north and kept them on course for 290,000 years of human existence.

Unfortunately, Wellbeing Economy Alliance or not, life and survival is not the societal and economic goal and outcome modern humans have been pursuing or seem inclined to pursue. Ever since the Neolithic Revolution, humans pulled off that socioeconomic goal and outcome swap by replacing that original socioeconomic goal and outcome from foraging and sharing to farming, sedentary activity, and surplus accumulation, subsequent and modern humans have been following this misguided new goal and have been living with the resulting outcome.

Now in the twenty-first century, having followed this changed goal and outcome for almost 12,000 years, humans have found themselves confronting, as a consequence, global climate change, zoonotic pandemics, potential near-global ecosystems collapse, near-global biodiversity extinction, and a global increase in ocean temperature. Did that socioeconomic goal and outcome swap have anything to do with where we are today as a species? What do you think? Consider what James C. Scott thought in his book *Against the Grain: A Deep History of the Earliest States.*

Food surpluses, seized by local rulers from early communities formed in places like the Fertile Crescent, South China, the Indus River Valley of today's Western India and Pakistan, and Central America, enabled the establishment of the early empires that dominated the world. Surplus started as stored grain but soon morphed across time into numerous stores of value. Today it might even be stored as Bitcoins and NFTs (Non-Fungible Tokens). By abandoning the initial hunter-gatherer, mobile, sharing society's societal and economic goal and outcome of life and *survival*, surplus, profits, and wealth accumulation soon became the purpose and goal of Neolithic Revolution human societies and economies, with much of it managed and siphoned off by elites and rulers.

Today this siphoned grain has morphed into dollars, but these won't be found in grain elevators but in tax havens. According to the Pandora Papers the wealth held in tax havens is staggering. Estimates range from $6 trillion to $36 trillion and while the roster of tax evaders still consists of rulers and elites (the files expose some of the most powerful people in the world, including more than 330 politicians from 90 countries, according to the BBC), it now also includes oligarchs, criminals, and terrorists. Transactions are facilitated by global banks including Deutsche Bank, JP Morgan, Barclays, and Standard Chartered—with the latter still boasting they *are* "Here for Good," as reported in the FinCEN Files.

But wealth accumulation and attempts at concealment underscore an even bigger problem, inequality. This is precisely what those levelling mechanisms we briefly explored in early hunter-gatherer egalitarian societies and economies were designed to prevent. And yet, this is only part of what can go wrong when a society and its economy abandon those early, mobile, sharing, survival-driven egalitarian practices upon which pre-agriculture hunter-gatherer societies and economies were based and that enabled them to last as long as they did. Once a society and its economy elevate something else above human and nature's survival as its goal and outcome, the way the Neolithic Revolution and modern humans elevated farming and surplus, it essentially has turned its back on those survival-driven principles.

Then human life, Earth-life ecosystems, and its biodiversity all become fungible, interchangeable, exchangeable, replaceable, or all of the above. Life and survival become less important than surplus or economic gain, exactly the view apparently taken by many of the world's corporations who were aware their products and services were causing harm and death to humans and nature but nonetheless not only persisted but went on to persuade those in harm's way that their products and services were harmless.

At the beginning of this chapter, we drew attention to the Montreal Protocol that greatly reduced the expansion of the ozone hole that emerged above Antarctica. We noted that if CFCs had not been detected and banned in the 1980s, by the end of the century, it would have caused average global temperatutres to rise by an additional 2.5°C on top of existing and ongoing warming. But we also noted, above all, that *without the ozone layer, complex animal and human life on Earth would not exist,* yet scientists were still detecting a 25 percent increase in the ozone layer-busting CFC-11. Not even the threat of a potential elimination of all humans and all complex animal life on Earth was enough to deter these merchants, who preferred your money over your life. And yet they are not alone. Consider the following:

(1) **Cigarette manufacturers are racketeers.** In 2010, the U.S. Supreme Court upheld a verdict that tobacco companies conspired to deceive the American public and addict children. Cigarette manufacturers have been found guilty of engaging in a deadly fraud that is unprecedented in the nation's history.

(2) ***Exxon* misled the public on climate change.** Executives from BP and Royal Dutch Shell will testify before a House committee investigating allegations that oil giants misled the public about the role of fossil fuels in causing global warming.

> *"We are deeply concerned that the fossil fuel industry has reaped massive profits for decades while contributing to climate change that is devastating American communities, costing taxpayers billions of dollars, and ravaging the natural world," committee leaders wrote to company executives. "We are also concerned that to protect those profits, the industry has reportedly led a coordinated effort to spread disinformation to mislead the public and prevent crucial action to address climate change."*

(3) Monsanto has been ordered to pay $289 million U.S. **in damages** to a man who alleged the company's glyphosate-based weed killers caused him cancer. The U.S. Environmental Protection Agency in September 2017 concluded a decades-long assessment of glyphosate risks and found the chemical not likely carcinogenic to humans. But the World Health Organization's cancer arm in 2015 classified glyphosate as "probably carcinogenic to humans."

(4) **Perfluoroalkyl and polyfluoroalkyl compounds, or PFAS** refers to more than 4,000 man-made chemicals that are often called "forever chemicals" because they don't break down in the environment. This may no longer be true. Exposure to the chemicals

> has been linked to certain cancers, weakened immunity, thyroid disease, and other health effects.

A class-action lawsuit brought this issue to national attention in 2005. Workers at a Parkersburg, West Virginia, DuPont plant joined with residents to sue the company for releasing millions of pounds of one of these chemicals, known as PFOA, into the air and the Ohio River. Lawyers discovered that the company had known as far back as 1961 that PFOA could harm the liver.

The suit was ultimately settled in 2017 for US$670 million, after an eight-year study of tens of thousands of people who had been exposed. Based on multiple scientific studies, this review concluded that there was a probable link between exposure to PFOA and six categories of diseases: diagnosed high cholesterol, ulcerative colitis, thyroid disease, testicular cancer, kidney cancer, and pregnancy-induced hypertension.

Over the past two decades, hundreds of peer-reviewed scientific papers have shown that many PFAS are not only toxic, they also don't fully break down in the environment and have accumulated in the bodies of people and animals around the world. Some studies have detected PFAS in 99 percent of people tested. Others have found PFAS in wildlife, including polar bears, dolphins, and seals.

Replacing human life and survival, and the life and survival of Earth-life ecosystems and biodiversity, as the sole goal and outcome of human societies and economies, in that *socioeconomic goal and outcome swap* Neolithic Revolution humans made with the adoption of agriculture, was to start subsequent humans down a path that could eventually end in extinction. It was, probably, the greatest unintended harm—there would be others such as the adoption of fossil fuels—that any human generation would inflict upon subsequent generations.

Could succeeding generations have come to recognize this grave error and returned to eking out a living *inside* Earth-life ecosystems, instead of *outside,* which is destroying them in the process? There were many peoples who continued to eke out a living more in harmony with nature, but they were eventually overshadowed, outnumbered, and enslaved or marginalized, like surviving hunter-gatherer communities that, nevertheless, have persisted. Even after 12,000 years, however, mainstream human populations have not realized that they may have been shunted down a path that could eventually end in extinction, and that those who eventually did have been unable to free themselves from this snare.

Once modern human societies and economies, western ones, in particular, began to view other humans as being less than themselves, and believed in a creator god that endowed them with inalienable rights above both their fellow man and all nature, it became easy to elevate economic gain, surplus/profits, growth, and wealth accumulation even if doing so meant sacrificing the lives of those they viewed as lesser mortals. One only has to reflect on the whole sordid history, which the Portuguese are said to have initiated, of the more than 12 million-plus Africans enslaved by western nations to build their sugar plantations and other crop-based enterprises, and upon whose labor most of the western world was built, to understand how deeply the desire for surplus, profits, and wealth accumulation had enslaved the societies and economies that pursued the socioeconomic lifeways of the slave-trader.

According to Wikipedia, slavery in the twenty-first century continues, and generates $150 billion in annual profits; modern transportation has made human trafficking easier. In 2019 there were an estimated 40 million people worldwide subject to some form of slavery, 25 percent of them children. Sixty-one percent are used for forced labor, mostly in the private sector, while 38 percent live in forced marriages. Other types of modern slavery are child soldiers, sex trafficking, and sexual slavery.

Yet it was the forebears of some of those they enslaved, such as the Khoe-San or the Hadzabe (Hadza) hunter-gatherers of Tanzania who split off very early from the Khoe-San, pre-agriculture egalitarian hunter-gatherer humans, and their societies who neither knew of, nor believed in, a creator-God. Nor did they need the approval of any king, magna carta, or founding fathers' declaration of independence or constitution to tell them truths they instinctively knew, naturally understood, routinely practiced, and already held to be self-evident because they were egalitarian. Unlike Thomas Jefferson and the framers of the American Constitution, hunter-gatherer peoples kept no slaves and treated all men and women equally; and though they recognized neither God nor creator, their egalitarian socioeconomic practices enabled them to accord one another inalienable rights no god, magna carta, nor constitution could ever confer: Life, Liberty, and the pursuit of life and survival.

But population size really does matter when it comes to human survival. How interesting it is that modern humans seem unnerved by the exploding size of the human population—about eight billion and fast approaching the 11 billion believed to be the carrying capacity of the Earth. But you will note that while these so-called boundaries are being emphasized, human population growth and size, the real cause pushing most of those boundaries, if not all, is explicitly excluded from the "planetary boundaries" analysis depicted in Figure 4-3. In fact, it excludes any lifeform as if these are oblivious to the Earth-system.

How so? A key foundation that underpinned those early human survival-driven societies and economies was population size—back then population size really mattered, while most of the boundaries on this chart did not. If post-Neolithic Revolution humans had paid attention to population size as their hunter-gatherer forebears apparently did, humans today might never have gotten past any of these so-called boundaries.

Population mattered because small populations facilitated mobility and migration and thereby enhanced the chances of survival. Small populations were sustainable, less complex to manage, and easier to fit within the carrying capacity of ecosystems, biodiversity, and eventually the Earth. One can be quite sure the size of their foraging bands and overall population size were not an economic or societal policy decision any more than the population of the town or country in which one lives today becomes a subject for discussion at the local town council meetings. But then again, neither do town council meetings discuss the amount of energy the Earth derives from the sun, nor the current position of the Earth in its orbit around the sun.

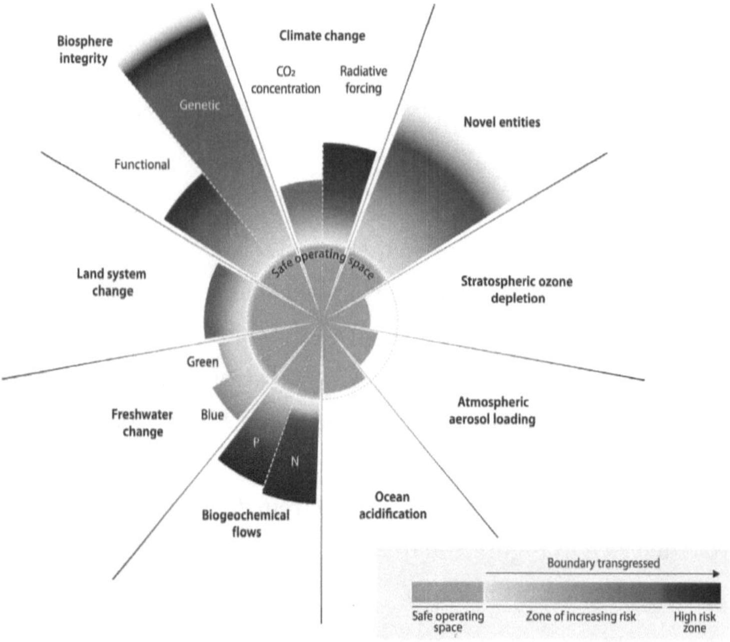

Figure 4-3. Planetary boundaries. The Earth System has passed six of nine planetary boundaries.

(Source: Stockholmresilience.org)

As long as what humans did fell within normal operating parameters of this survival-driven societal and economic Earth-system framework that enabled life, there wasn't anything to worry about—and for millennia no one knew or cared. Species population size was managed within and between trophic levels within Earth-life ecosystems. Humans unfortunately chose to eke out a living *outside* those ecosystems when they chose to become farmers and thence went down a path that was bound to collide with Earth-life ecosystem boundaries, as humans have in the twenty-first century.

Once humans abandoned that *life-preserving, egalitarian, survival-driven pattern* of mobility, hunting, gathering, sharing, and living *within* Earth-life ecosystems in harmony with its biodiversity, and once they began growing large sedentary populations that chose agriculture and lived with farm animals instead, the time eventually came when their populations began to outgrow the carrying capacity of the ecosystems in which they farmed. It took a few millennia, as it has taken 12 millennia to get to the present, but the time soon came when they farmed those ecosystems to near-exhaustion and hunted prey species to near extinction, resulting in repeated civilization collapse.

Today humans are once again, this time on a global scale, on the verge of possibly driving most Earth-life ecosystems to exhaustion and its biodiversity to extinction. This, in turn, has given rise to numerous successive zoonotic pandemics and global warming brought on by CO_2-driven global climate change that together may very likely turn out to be more than just another human civilization collapse but instead, potentially human extinction. This time, though, it's not just Leonardo Di Caprio, but theoretical physicists who are sounding the alarm that *"deforestation and rampant resource use is likely to trigger the 'irreversible collapse' of human civilization within the next two to four decades—unless we rapidly change course."*

The takeaway here is that as long as humans remained within the operating limits of the Earth's foundational *survival-driven architecture* all would have been fine, and indeed it remained fine for our pre-agriculture hunter-gatherer forebears for 290,000 years as they followed the economic *wisdom of the waterhole* that was built into their lifeways. They would not have known about that "*invisible hand,*" would neither have seen nor heard of "trickle-down economics" or "Doughnut economics." And until climate change and global warming began to invade human consciousness, there was nothing in the mighty mathematical models of modern socioeconomic thought that even imagined or cared that human population growth could drive ecosystem collapse and biodiversity extinction, or even imagined that human population growth could shoot past some unknown Earth-life survival boundaries. Oops!

And, by the way, our pre-agriculture hunter-gatherer gramps wouldn't have known of these boundaries, either. But because their populations were mobile and small, and because they shared within and amongst their bands the ecosystem products and services they foraged, they never drove Earth-life ecosystems to near-exhaustion, and hence, never encountered and didn't have to cross those ecosystem boundaries modern humans are suddenly realizing might really exist. Consequently, both their societies and economies survived millennia after millennia, whereas most since the dawn of agriculture have collapsed.

None of our hunter-gatherer forebears could have boasted a Nobel Prize in economics, nor would they have been aware of strange concepts like "inflation" and "unemployment"—but they knew the *wisdom of the waterhole*. They knew what it took to ensure the survival of those early human societies and economies. They knew how to keep their population comparatively small, and the need to share what they foraged with others in the band, even remaining mobile to avoid excessive wear and tear on Earth-life ecosystems and biodiversity.

In addition, they followed *DOMC* customs—they did not domesticate, own, manage, or control Earth-life ecosystems and biodiversity, nor pollute the Earth, the soil, its water sources, or its atmosphere—indeed, they eked out their living from *within* Earth-life ecosystems and in harmony with its biodiversity. These are socioeconomic lessons and a type of economics that modern humans and their economists might be finally starting to grasp—the *Waterhole Economics* of our pre-agriculture hunter-gatherer forebears.

Location, Mobility, and Migration also mattered to human survival. All life must be mobile to exist and must migrate to survive. Humans live on land, on the surface of a planet that is always moving, and within continents that are themselves on tectonic plates that are imperceptibly though incessantly re-organizing, and on a planet that tilts, wobbles, and rotates and changes the circumference of its orbit around the sun from near-circular to elliptical, changing the climate in the process and thereby impacting life and driving Earth-life species to remain mobile to eke out a living and migrate to escape climate change, all in service of survival.

All Earth-life species eked out a living *inside* Earth-life ecosystems (not *outside*), utilized its natural processes and remained in harmony with its biodiversity. In addition, all needed to be mobile and ready to migrate to survive. Earth-life ecosystems and biodiversity and their outputs (plant and animal food sources, water, etc.) changed with the seasons, weather, climate change, and natural disasters. Hence all Earth-life species, including humans, evolved to be mobile, to forage to find food, to keep pace with this moveable feast, even as they were ready to migrate to escape climate change and climate disasters, if need be, to survive.

Yet, though immersed in this sea of motion, post-Neolithic Revolution humans, in pursuit of eking out a living, perhaps unknowingly, chose to be sedentary on a planet that requires mobility and migration to survive. But twenty-first century humans can plead no such ignorance. It's plain for all to see that that historic *human-habitable-climate* band itself has begun migrating north even as global warming drives ecosystem products and services slowly but surely toward the poles.

The quintessential takeaway here is obvious: Humans will be forced to adapt by resorting to mobility and migration to survive. As during the Pleistocene, frequent glaciations drove pre-agriculture hunter-gatherers south of the equator, all the way down to South Africa where the forebears of all surviving humans barely hung on, while others that remained too far north, like Neanderthals, went extinct. Similarly, modern humans may well be forced on a reverse migration to survive; to abandon much of its sedentary lifestyle as temperatures soar, glaciers melt, and oceans rise potentially by 70 meters (230 feet) or more above current sea-levels. Eventually, increasing temperatures, approaching and exceeding 50°C, will render vast areas south of the 43rd parallel increasingly uninhabitable and will rearrange human society and the global economy. Unfortunately, living in densely packed, overpopulated mega-cities and urban areas will only compound this emerging disaster and may well be coming to an end.

Our hunter-gatherer forebears pursued a way of life that inherently regarded the sanctity of Earth-life's ecosystem and biodiversity and may or may not have understood how indispensable their chosen way of life was to their very survival. Did they understand how by remaining small, mobile, sharing, and egalitarian societies and economies, they would significantly reduce the wear and tear on Earth-life ecosystems and biodiversity? Did they understand, too, any more than modern humans do today, that by choosing not to Domesticate, Own, Modify and/or Control Earth-life's natural resources (land, soil, water/seas, wind, atmosphere, forests, and natural resources such as minerals and chemicals), they were thereby inadvertently enabling themselves to survive for millennia within the carrying capacity of those ecosystems and the Earth? How did they come up with such socioeconomic practices whereas subsequent and modern humans did not?

One thing they appeared to have had going for them that subsequent and modern humans still somehow have completely failed to grasp is that they had a clear-eyed understanding of their sole purpose as a species on this Earth. They seemingly understood that the only goal and outcome that mattered was life and survival—their life and survival, the life and survival of Earth-life ecosystems, and the life and survival of the species with whom they shared those habitats and ecosystems. They may have understood something that even twenty-first century societies and economies, notwithstanding their innumerable technologies, sciences, and innovations, still don't quite grasp, or even appear to recognize—that Earth-life *ecosystems and biodiversity life and survival were indispensable to their own life and survival.*

Nevertheless, their pursuit of life and *survival* as their goal and outcome versus our goals today of surplus, profits, and wealth accumulation—this seemingly insignificant and seemingly meaningless divergence in their respective socioeconomic lifeways, perhaps like a butterfly effect—had channeled their respective progeny down separate paths: one that would lead to survival for 290,000 years and the other that would lead to multiple civilization collapses in just 12,000 years and potentially, eventually to extinction. As the last ice age was ending, those pre-agriculture hunter-gatherer humans that made it through the Pleistocene-Holocene transition emerged into a world that turned out to be very different from the life they were leaving behind. Humans today, too, are about to embark on yet another geological transition, from the Holocene to the Anthropocene.

What is there about our modern socioeconomic cultures and economies one would be happy to commend to humans, who hopefully, might be lucky enough to survive during or beyond this emerging hothouse Earth? Would you recommend anything emerging from the domains of our religions? Politics? Science and technologies? Innovations? Economics? Or our ability to wage wars? What would you want to pass on? Perhaps the best advice would be that which modern humans so far have failed to follow, but I suspect with hindsight, before it's all over, would come to wish they had—to find a way to eke out a living, as our pre-agriculture hunter-gatherer forebears did and survived, within Earth-life ecosystems and in harmony with its biodiversity.

Share to survive; hoard to go extinct. Why would a people who had neither high-flying stocks nor 401(k)s; neither real estate nor riches left by a parent, or estates passed down from prior generations—why would they want to share? Hunter-gatherers had nothing beyond the current or perhaps the next day's meals, yet they, unlike our twenty-first century hoarding tax-dodgers as noted earlier, made sure every member of their band shared in the bounty of any successful hunt. Why? They shared to enable one another to survive, and by sharing they reduced the demand on ecosystem services and products, and that in turn enabled their mutual survival.

And given the Kunming-Montreal Global Biodiversity Framework (GBF)—that historic deal nations struck at COP15 in 2022 to end biodiversity loss by 2030 and to dedicate 30 percent of the Earth and its resources to biodiversity preservation—modern humans might just be beginning to realize that by living sustainably, and letting ecosystems and biodiversity live sustainably, they would ensure their own survival. But this sharing went far beyond not having a 401(k) or inheriting accumulated generational wealth. It spared hunter-gatherer societies and economies the social neglect and suffering that emerged in our world of haves and have-nots.

If the practice of food sharing had become a universal custom, built into the societies and economies of nations as it was into those that comprised hunter-gatherer bands, would the world be experiencing the current level of food insecurity? According to the FAO report "The State of Food Security and Nutrition in the World 2021," between 720 million and 811 million people in the world faced hunger in 2020 and as many as 660 million people may still face hunger in 2030. Regions of the world where people suffered hunger in 2020 include Africa (46 million people), Asia (almost 57 million), and Latin America and the Caribbean (about 14 million).

Beyond outright hunger, nearly one in three people in the world (2.37 billion) did not have access to adequate food in 2020, an increase of almost 320 million people in just one year. And for far too many, three billion people, healthy food is simply out of reach. Driving these trends are numerous conflicts (now aggravated by Russia's invasion of Ukraine, the Israel-Gaza and Iran conflict, Myanmar's military rule and ethnic conflict, and Sudan's paramilitary and army clash), climate variability and extremes, and economic slowdowns and downturns—all exacerbated by the underlying causes of poverty and very high and persistent levels of inequality—which are unlikely in an egalitarian hunter-gatherer society and economy.

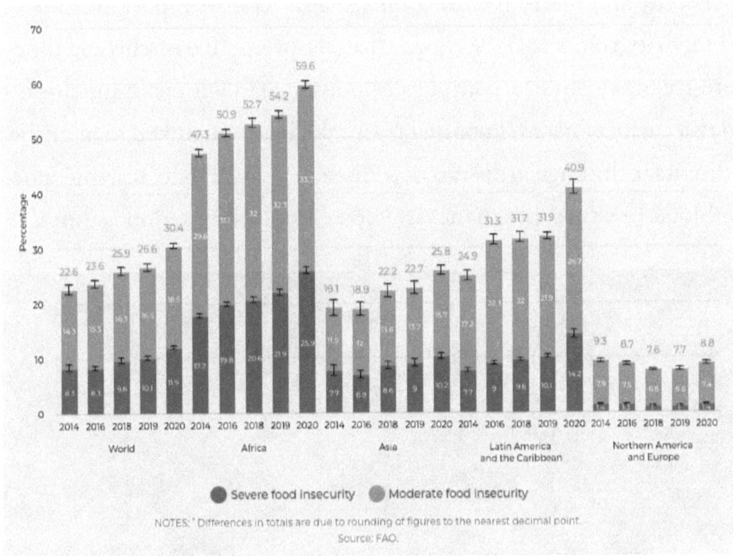

Figure 4-4. Moderate or severe food insecurity has been climbing slowly for six years and now affects more than 30 percent of the world population.
(Source: UNICEF Data)

Nevertheless, the UN Environment Program's Food Waste Index reports that 17 percent of the food available to consumers—in stores, households, and restaurants—is thrown away, and 60 percent of that waste is generated at home. Approximately 931 million tons of food go to waste every year with unconsumed produce accounting for 8-10 percent of global carbon emissions: Households account for 61 percent, food service accounts for 26 percent, and retail accounts for 13 percent. The United Nations Sustainable Development Goals aim to cut this waste in half by 2030.

But food insecurity unfortunately isn't only about lack of food, it is also a symptom of social diseases. Lack of food, or healthy food, is soon followed by health issues because hunger and health are inseparable. Food insecurity and insufficient access to healthy foods have been associated with negative health outcomes, including an increased vulnerability to micronutrient deficiencies and a higher probability of developing chronic diseases. While higher rates of chronic disease have been reported for both low-income and food-insecure adults, a 2017 USDA report indicated that food security status may be more strongly predictive of chronic illnesses. There are many physical complications associated with poor nutrition that food insecurity worsens. Poor dietary intake has been linked to many health conditions including cardiovascular disease, Type-2 diabetes, osteoporosis, high blood pressure, pregnancy-related complications, and asthma.

Figure 4-5. Global wastage of food and rise of food insecurity.

Seventeen percent of the food available to consumers–in stores, households, and restaurants–is thrown away, and 60 percent of that waste is generated at home. (Image source: BBC)

In addition to physical health risks associated with food insecurity, mental health risks are abundant as well. Depression, anxiety, behavioral problems in children, social issues, and stress are some of the mental health complications associated with food insecurity in adults as well as children. Going without this basic need will naturally stress the body, leading to mental health complications.

If the cycle of food insecurity and chronic disease begins with inadequate nutritious food, consider, then, how just by sharing food and ensuring that everyone within the band received a share of the take from foraging and hunting, hunter-gatherers may well have spared their societies and economies the individual and collective distress that a lack of food would otherwise have caused, perhaps just another of the quirky butterfly effects encountered earlier. Choosing food sharing led to healthier societies, while food hoarding that accompanied farming and sedentary communities and economies eventually led to widespread ill-health and the massive health-care issues that accompanied the rise of civilization. These ill effects are now aggravated by persistent inequality and continue to plague modern human societies and economies.

Imagine that! Not even with all the food waste described above and modern medical and healthcare know-how, can societies and economies see their way clear to ensure the poor and less fortunate are provided for in spite of the billions of dollars that make up the GDP of some countries. Fortunately, perhaps, or by choice, hunter-gatherers had just one socio-economic goal and outcome to shoot for—life and survival, and making sure none went hungry enabled that goal. What's our socioeconomic goal?

Imagine countries or nations that prioritized life and survival but eschewed surplus, profits, and wealth accumulation; that uphold and reward freedom and equality and emphasize human and Earth-life species' life and survival above all else. Imagine societies and economies that understand that Earth-life ecosystems and biodiversity well-being and survival are indispensable to their well-being and survival; that recognize neither rulers, kings, queens, nor strongmen, and have neither politics, politicians, nor elections—just equality and freedom for all to share, and to choose and foster an *Egalitarian Culture.*

Though it might read like it, the above is not a description of some new Apple TV flick you might have missed; a sequel to the Knights of the Round Table, or *the Chronicles of Narnia*, or Merlin, perhaps, or an update of the history of the Vikings, or even a new science fiction about a surviving post-global-warming, emergent human civilization—no, it's none of those.

But, as unreal as it might seem, it's a very brief overview of real-life lifeways and customs practiced by the societies and economies of our pre-agriculture hunter-gatherer forebears for most of humanity's history until sedentary societies replaced mobile ones, farming replaced foraging, hoarding replaced sharing, and collapsing human societies and economies began to replace ones that survived since anatomically modern humans began to walk the Earth, past the end of the last ice age and through the beginning of the Neolithic Revolution. And one no subsequent human society and economy seems to have adopted as their way of life. Why?

Had post-Neolithic Revolution humans chosen to follow the path of their forebears, would agriculture have become the foundation of our food source? Would the world have had to meet in Glasgow for COP26, or Egypt for COP27, or Montreal for COP15, to agree on a way forward and away from what began in Glasgow 200 years ago, to end further CO_2 build-up in the atmosphere, and cap global temperature rise at 1.5^{0}C or slightly above pre-industrial levels; or in Rome to hash out, among other issues, an equitable and fair way to expeditiously share vaccines with third-world countries for the fight against Covid-19? Without animal domestication would there have even been zoonotic diseases and pandemics?

There are many aspects of early human societies and economies, as seen in hunter-gatherer egalitarian societies and economies, that enabled their survival for most of human history and bear scant resemblance to our own, that one might wish were or could become commonplace within modern human societies and economies—and well-being societies and economies may well have started down this road. It's hard, though, not to admire our forebears' dedication to an individual's freedom to choose and, after a quick glance at the rulers of our world, their rejection of rulers of any kind, as well as their fierce allegiance to equality and society-wide dedication to sharing and their total rejection of hoarding, of wealth, and the inequality that comes from wealth accumulation.

And, given the blight that has accompanied a belief in creator gods and modern religions, one marvels at the foresight that enabled them to escape such societal spells. And given, too, how many nations today struggle under the thumb of governments, kings, queens, senators, congresspersons, strongmen, and dictators, one sure wishes that modern humans had at least managed to escape the greed, oppression and wars that often accompany political systems, as they did.

But if there was just one takeaway modern humans were able to glean and implement, which of those eight might that be? Looking back once more at the takeaway table (Table 4-2), the most important would no doubt be the first takeaway. Because it specifies that the only goal and outcome for all human societies and economies is to ensure the life and survival of all humans, and of Earth-life ecosystems and biodiversity. Comprehended in this first takeaway are the remaining seven. If modern humans were to begin to replace their current societal and economic goals of profit/surplus, economic growth, and wealth accumulation with human and nature's well-being, life and survival, they would have had to accomplish along the way the remaining seven takeaways to get there.

If academics, scientists, businesses, governments, and individuals were to begin to ask and answer in the affirmative, of themselves, of every effort, project and ambition, whether every possible outcome would ensure human and Earth-life ecosystems and biodiversity well-being, life and survival, they would eventually, individually and collectively, end up transforming humanity and its civilizations, and together, this would have started down a path back to the lifeways of our hunter-gatherer forebears that would eventually ensure the survival of our species—all without the effort and expense that would accompany weaning humanity not just off $C0_2$, but off of the many odious practices humanity has gotten itself addicted to during the last 12,000 years.

We set out in this chapter to rediscover the foundations that underpinned those early human economies. What comprised the human economy and what were its foundations? And we found that human economies emerged out of the activities they engaged in as they hunted and gathered for a living *within* Earth-life ecosystems in conjunction with its biodiversity. Their economies evolved around the daily need to get to a source of water, often a waterhole, and thus became imprinted by the prerequisites of the waterhole. Around these waterholes they learned that to survive they had to share. They learned to focus on sharing and on surviving and thus became sharing, survival-driven waterhole economies that prioritized sharing, life, and survival above all else. We also found out that as long as humans eked out their living *within* Earth-life ecosystems their societies and economies thrived and survived, so long as other Earth-life species and Earth's ecosystems were also able to thrive and survive.

We also found out that that threesome partnership of humans, biodiversity, and ecosystems worked well and lasted for 290,000 years and began to falter only after Neolithic Revolution humans chose instead to eke out their living *outside* those ecosystems by choosing to farm, hoard, and grow highly populated sedentary communities, and to herd, domesticate, displace, and destroy its biodiversity and ecosystems. It was only after the latter occurred that both ecosystems and biodiversity began to fail, and eventually, human societies and economies began to collapse.

The socioeconomic foundations that enabled pre-agriculture hunter-gatherer societies and economies to thrive and survive for as long as they did—maintaining small, mobile, foraging, and sharing egalitarian communities, living in harmony with Earth-life ecosystems and biodiversity, and remaining mobile, moving from place to place—meant that the wear and tear they exerted on Earth-life ecosystems and biodiversity was relatively light and may well have enabled rapid recovery. This way of eking out a living was eventually abandoned when Neolithic Revolution humans chose farming instead of foraging, hoarding instead of sharing, sedentary communities instead of mobile ones, and domestication and herding of biodiversity species instead of hunting.

By choosing to farm instead of forage, and to build large sedentary communities instead of small mobile ones, they not only chose to occupy vast areas of ecosystems but to extract ecosystem products and services over protracted periods, often only leaving when crop yields fell low enough to threaten future harvests. This slash and burn, plant, reap, and plant again routine soon exhausted the ecosystems on which they farmed, forcing them to find other ecosystems with areas suitable for farming.

This new way of eking out a living that no doubt wore heavily upon ecosystem products and services and over time would lead to their collapse, has been imitated up to the present by most human societies and economies that succeeded the Neolithic Revolution. Only a tiny fraction of the more than eight billion-plus extant humans follows this initial pre-agriculture hunter-gatherer way. Today, twenty-first century humans are finally having to confront the consequences of the last 400 generations of this way of eking out a living, including yet another zoonotic pandemic with more on the way as climate change accelerates viral spillovers and intensifies CO_2-driven global warming—both being a direct result of abusing Earth-life ecosystems and its biodiversity.

If anyone had told *The Bulletin of the Atomic Scientists* and other doomsday authors and organizations that warn humanity of a potential for human extinction, that that extinction was as likely to be caused by the human economy as by any nuclear bomb, AI, World War III, or any of the other nightmares our species has invented and is probably likely to unleash, they would more than likely stare in utter disbelief, speechless, wondering whether you had lost your mind. But global warming, and its potential to drive human extinction, is being driven not by any of those potential doomsday technologies or nightmares waiting to be unleashed, but instead by the economic sectors comprising the modern economy, our collective human effort to eke out a living by burning fossil fuels for energy. Through our economies, as currently designed, we are filling the atmosphere with more CO_2 than the Earth has seen in three million years and destroying, along the way, Earth-life ecosystems and biodiversity, and potentially all life—unless of course, we can find a way to defuse it first.

And if humans do manage to escape this self-inflicted threat, so long as greed, surplus/profits, growth, and wealth accumulation remain the driving goal and outcome for human societies and economies, there is no telling whether this, or something similar or worse won't happen again. This is not our first rodeo, you know—we were lucky to discover that hole in the ozone layer but this time around we will need more than luck and a lot more time to rid Earth's atmosphere of CO_2.

Given humans have had such a long and protracted proof period (97 percent of human existence) to observe which of these socioeconomic life-ways works best, how is it that economics, the so-called "dismal science" that undertakes to prescribe how humans should go about eking out a living and managing their economies, could end up prescribing instead what is beginning to look more like a path to collapse again, and this time, to human extinction as well? And, if economics got it so horribly wrong, the question all humans should be asking is this: "Is there a way to eke out a living and build human societies and economies without destroying ourselves, Earth-life ecosystems, biodiversity, and thereby life itself?" The answer, of course, is "Yes there is." But Neolithic Revolution humans and all that came thereafter, including us (twenty-first century humans) simply chose not to follow it. They, and we, chose instead to pursue surplus/profits, wealth accumulation, and endless GDP growth, and now it's our turn to reap the rewards of that choice.

Pre-agriculture human societies and economies, though, were built in an entirely different way—a way our hunter-gatherer forebears followed and survived collapse-free. A way that was based upon the survival-driven socioeconomic foundations identified in this chapter. Foundations that underpinned the lifeways of their societies and economies for most of human existence. They eked out a living *within* Earth-life ecosystems in harmony with its biodiversity, while simultaneously preserving them; consequently, their societies and waterhole economies lasted for more than 290,000 of the 300,000 years humans have walked the Earth. Why then aren't modern humans, and in particular economists, even trying to rediscover and imitate how they did it? As my Gen Z daughter would say, Go figure!

Economies, then, can either enable life and survival or, drive civilization collapse and extinction, and by the look of things, humans have tried both options. Our pre-agriculture hunter-gatherer forebears tried the first option and survived collapse-free for most of our species' existence. Our Neolithic Revolution forebears, on the other hand, tried the second option and human societies and economies have been collapsing ever since. Who could have imagined, though, that our technologies and innovations, fearsome though they might be, wouldn't be the things that would take humanity out? Instead, it's our efforts to eke out a living, our economies, that have been the cause of numerous civilizations' collapse and is set to become the cause of ours as well, and the most probable path to human extinction. Yes, it's the economy, stupid.

PART THREE

Modern Human Economies

Transitions

FROM MOBILITY, SHARING, LIFE, AND SURVIVAL TO SEDENTATION, SURPLUS HOARDING, AND ECONOMIC COLLAPSE

ECONOMIES, WE SAW, EMERGED OUT OF the foraging activities of Earth-life species (and eventually humans) *within* ecosystems and were and are integral and indispensable to how life thrives and survives on planet Earth, and became the third component in that *Evolutionary Triad of Life.* These early human societies and their economies, like all Earth-life species, followed the food, and by doing so became foragers that over time gave rise to a set of mobile "hunter-gatherer" lifeways for which they would become known.

And it was these mobile hunter-gatherer lifeways, forged over centuries of coexisting and eking out a living together with other species within Earth-life ecosystems, that became the foundations of early human economies and enabled them to thrive and survive for most of human existence.

These mobile hunter-gatherer lifeways, which became the socioeconomic foundations of their societies and economies, evolved to ensure and enhance the mutual survival of humans, ecosystems, and Earth-life species (biodiversity). By contrast, post-Neolithic Revolution societies and economies that eventually gave rise to agriculture and civilization; that grew to become massive farming communities; and that gave rise to sedentation, food production, and domesticated farm animals would collapse one after another and continue to collapse for the ensuing 400 generations, unlike their mobile hunter-gatherer forebears.

This difference in outcome is what drives Part Three—an investigation into the socioeconomic transitions that took place in the hunter-gatherer economies that enabled survival for millennia, versus those that took place in post-Neolithic Revolution economies that led to repeated social, economic, and civilization collapse. What were the social and economic transformations that aided the survival of the one but ensured the collapse of the other?

Chief among the transitions that forced transformations of these early human societies and economies was climatic change. They lived through the Pleistocene-Holocene Transition, from the freezing but waning centuries and decades of the last ice age of the Pleistocene to the concluding and increasingly warmer years of the Holocene, about 12,000 years, that may have only recently ended in the twentieth century with the dawn of a new geologic epoch that may or may not be called the Anthropocene.

A change in climate that saw a CO_2-driven 6°C increase in global temperature, from the freezing days of the last ice age to the warm and even hot days of the Holocene that would transform pretty much everything about how and where they lived. This change in climate drove massive habitat, biome, and ecosystem transformations; drove fauna and flora changes; and resulted in changes in human food sources, plant and animal food, and the methods and tools they would have needed to hunt and gather them.

While there were other factors driving socioeconomic change, this climate change backdrop was critical. Our pre- and post- Neolithic Revolution hunter-gatherer forebears spent this climatic transition adapting to a warming world that would eventually become more suitable for farming, and that may well have enabled the start of agriculture, even as many megafauna they hunted and crop varieties they gathered were driven to extinction while new, different, and in the case of animals, smaller species were beginning to emerge.

This planet-wide climate transformation would eventually drive humans to migrate out of Africa and across the entire Earth. This period would see numerous hominin species go extinct. Humans eventually began to abandon foraging for farming and animal husbandry and small, sharing, mobile, egalitarian, hunter-gatherer societies and economies for large sedentary, farming communities that produced their own food and grew to become villages, towns, cities, nations, and eventually civilization as we know it.

Today, about 12,000 years since that transition began, human societies and economies once again find themselves in the midst of yet another geologic epoch transition, from the Holocene to the Anthropocene. They are caught in the grip of yet another global CO_2-driven climate change, but this time anthropogenic, and have already begun to experience some of the socioeconomic disruptions a global warming climate change can cause. This time around, though, humans have the benefit of the example of how vast and complex such a socioeconomic transformation can become, and hopefully, can look back for clues as to what to expect. But just how vast and how complete was that transformation?

The change in climate took our early *Homo* forebears from the Pleistocene (2,580,000 to 11,700 years ago) to the Holocene, a period during which anatomically modern humans emerged 300,000 years ago and became hunters and gatherers by the time the Pleistocene ended; from hunters and gatherers, foragers, occupying a tiny fraction of the Earth in Africa when the Holocene began to an emergent, sedentary, agricultural civilization that began to spread across the Earth by the time it ended; from sedentary farmers dwelling with farm animals in villages, towns, and cities, to a human civilization that today overspreads the entire Earth; and from a species with limited knowledge of science and technologies to a comparatively advanced human civilization with space stations, spacemen, and spacewomen.

Before those geologic epochs and climate-change-driven socioeconomic changes and transformations would end, of the five or so coexisting hominin species, humans would be the only one left standing. But for how much longer? Modern humans have spent the last 400 generations of the Holocene building their societies and economies by destroying Earth's ecosystems and biodiversity, the very foundations that enabled life and survival for 97 percent of humanity's existence.

The question, then, is what will the current transformation just getting underway be like? How will climate change, this time around, transform the Earth, its remaining ecosystems, and surviving biodiversity species, human societies, and economies? What role will economies play? Will humans survive this next transition?

We have already seen how just by a seemingly simple change in the way humans went about eking out a living, from foraging to farming, we unintentionally managed to destroy most of the planet's ecosystems and biodiversity, the very foundations life needs to survive, and changed the global climate system from the cool and survivable temperatures of the Holocene to the increasingly warm and seemingly Hothouse Earth-like temperatures last seen in the Eocene epoch tens of millions of years earlier, long before humans appeared.

Among the many potential economic transformations that might lie ahead, none will be as indispensable to human survival as a return to the lifeways of our pre-agriculture hunter-gatherer forebears that prioritized life and survival above all other economic goals and outcomes. A return to maintaining Earth's ecosystems, biodiversity, and human life and survival must once again become the only goal and outcome of our next economic transition if we hope to survive.

Unfortunately, though, humans have instead doubled-down and enhanced our ability to gather profits and surplus, and to accelerate economic (GDP) growth by surrendering much of what used to be functions of the human economy to legal-person economies—an economic innovation that turns control of major functions of the human economy over to corporations. This surrender accelerated the industrialization and thereby the destruction of Earth's ecosystems and biodiversity species, further endangering human survival.

Modern Human Economies —Transitions

FROM ECONOMIES THAT EVOLVED TO
ENABLE LIFE AND SURVIVAL TO
ECONOMIES MODERN HUMANS REDESIGNED FOR SURPLUS,
PROFITS, WEALTH ACCUMULATION AND GDP GROWTH

CHAPTER 5

Modern Human Economies
—Transitions

From Mobile Foraging, Sharing, and Survival
To Farming Sedentation, Surplus, Hoarding, and
Economic Collapse

CHAPTER 6

From Modern Human Economies
To Legal-Person Economies

From Human Economies That Enabled Life and Survival
To Legal-Person Economies That's Driving
Growth, Economic and Societal Collapse

5.

Modern Human Economies —*Transitions*

FROM MOBILE, SHARING, SURVIVAL-DRIVEN, WATERHOLE ECONOMIES TO SEDENTARY, HOARDING, SURPLUS-DRIVEN, COLLAPSING ECONOMIES

"Much of the work we do is aimed at keeping the wheels of commerce rolling rather than ensuring that our essential needs are met."

—James Suzman

HUMAN ECONOMIES EMERGED OUT OF OUR PRE-agriculture hunter-gatherer forebears' efforts to eke out a living *within* Earth-life ecosystems. Like all prior and extant Earth-life species and their economies, human economies also had a single goal and sought to fulfill a single outcome—the search for food and materials to enable life and survival. Today, just 1 percent of humans working in agriculture fulfill this need for the more than eight billion humans spread across the Earth, and as much again as we consume gets dumped into landfills. How much of Earth-life's ecosystems now bordering on collapse, and biodiversity approaching extinction, might still be intact had modern human economies remained faithful to this initial goal and outcome?

It was that initial package of socioeconomic lifeway changes that came with the Neolithic Revolution: transitions to agriculture, animal husbandry and sedentation that became the new economic brief. This new economy is one that enabled post-hunter-gatherer humans to remake that initial, ever-so-simple method of economic production that had so successfully and demonstrably met their economic needs and enabled the survival of our species for 97 percent of its existence; that was gradually abandoned in exchange for farming, enabling the accumulation of surplus, the growth of cities, states, and nations; and that has generated today the wealth and GDP of modern post-industrial free-market capitalist "legal-person" economies that would destroy all but 3 percent of Earth's ecosystems and drive to extinction most of its biodiversity.

The Neolithic Revolution, you see, would not only mostly replace hunting and gathering with farming and agriculture, but, eventually, an economy built by and for humans with one built by and for "legal-persons." This was a transition not only away from a human society with its method of economic production embedded within it, as Polanyi, in his book *The Great Transformation: The Political and Economic Origins of Our Time,* understood it had always been and should continue to be, but instead, to a method of economic production with human societies embedded within it—the very opposite, and the very thing Polanyi feared.

This simple hunter-gatherer waterhole economy, millennia later, would become the modern market economy comprised of numerous sectors, some of which are shown in Table 5-1 and described afterward.

Table 5-1. Sectors of the modern economy

Sectors of the Economy	
Primary (raw materials)	Extraction of raw materials
	Farming/fishing
Secondary (finished goods)	Manufacturing
	Utilities - electricity, gas
	Construction
Tertiary (service sector)	Retail
	Financial services
	Communication
	Hospitality and leisure
	Real estate
	Information technology
Quaternary	Education
	Public sector
	Research and development
	www.economicshelp.org

(Source: www.economicshelp.org)

(1) **Primary sector** – refers to the extraction of raw materials: mining, fishing, and agriculture.

(2) **Secondary / Manufacturing sector** – comprises the production of finished goods; for example, construction manufacturing, and utilities such as electricity.

(3) **Tertiary / Service sector** – comprises intangible goods and services to consumers. This includes retail, tourism, banking, entertainment, and IT services.

(4) **Quaternary sector** – includes the knowledge economy, education, research and development.

How interesting, then, that apart from fishing, none of the other economic sectors above would come into existence until well after the Neolithic

Revolution some 12,000 years ago. For the preceding 290,000 years, all humans were hunter-gatherers, and their economies comprised the original, pre-agriculture, hunter-gatherer waterhole economies that nevertheless enabled humanity, biodiversity, and ecosystems to thrive and survive mostly in harmony and collapse-free for almost all of our species' existence.

Imagine that! No industries? No extraction of raw materials, nor agriculture and farming? No manufacturing, utilities (electric and gas), construction, retail, banking, and financial services? No communications, transportation, hospitality and leisure, real estate, information technology, education, or research & development? Moreover, there was neither surplus nor hoarding, no private or public sectors, no savings and wealth accumulation, and no economic or GDP growth. Except for hunting and gathering there was no other economic activity, neither employers nor jobs, full employment nor unemployment in these pre-agriculture hunter-gatherer societies and their waterhole economies. Yet they would sustain humanity for 97 percent of its existence without societal or economic collapse.

Emerging post-hunter-gatherer societies and their economies would eventually transform this original pre-agriculture hunter-gatherer waterhole economy into one made for "legal persons"—corporations—with human societies no longer calling the shots but rather reduced to human resources and embedded as a mere factor of production. Human economies, like the hunter-gatherer societies they once served, would be transformed and reduced to an economic island surrounded by a sea of legal-persons and their legal-person economies.

This change from hunting and gathering to farming, though gradual, was not merely a change in economic activity—how hunter-gatherers obtained their food—but along the way it turned out also to be a change in the way their society had been organized. According to North and Thomas (1977, p. 230) in an article entitled "The First Economic Revolution," published in *The Economic History Review*, "it is not the type of economic activity (such as foraging, herding, hunting and gathering) so much as the kind of property rights that were established that accounts for explaining the Neolithic revolution."

In pre-agriculture societies, few resources and few objects other than clothing, tools, weapons, smoking pipes, bead ornaments, and other similar items were personally held and owned or became personal property, and when they did, relations of property remained subject to relations among humans. But these societies, which were egalitarian and based on kinship, personal relations, and status, began to change, slowly at first, to ones based on property rights and relations, landownership (territory), and eventually contract, and when that happened, relations among humans were no longer the *a priori* basis of human relationships in society, but instead became a function of relations among items of property.

Hence, whereas in hunter-gatherer egalitarian societies property ownership would have been limited to personal property and would have been subject to the norms of human relationships, today in our twenty-first century capitalist economy, as was true during the Neolithic Revolution when it began, and in all human economies in between, human relationships in society have been subjugated and have become functions of relations among items of property. If farmers were going to protect crops from foraging, non-farming hunter-gatherers—who believed they had a right to eat and an obligation to share whatever they found, including planted crops—then farmland needed to be recognized as private property and carved out of the common foraging area.

Thus began a carve-out, a shift away from the equality that sharing demanded and made possible; from the expectation of and right to open sharing that came with the egalitarianism of hunting and gathering societies and economies. It was a shift that would have such a profound cultural impact that to this day it comprises some of the core components of human societies and economies, a change in the method of economic production that drove such vast societal and cultural changes that in the words of Jared Diamond it may have turned out to be "The Worst Mistake in the History of the Human Race."

So, land became personal property and a farmer's exclusive claim to its crops, and the hoarded surplus became exempt from the common expectation of sharing and thereby nullified the age-old hunter-gatherer right to a share of the produce of other hunter-gatherers. This was a whole new socioeconomic system in the making, born out of inequality and brought on by property rights. Along with it eventually came the rise of a relatively small elite that began profiting from the labor of the many (which turned out to be true during most of farming history). That elite grew and became the institutions of the state that enslaved the many and that in the twenty-first century has become the "one percent." This one percent are "the haves" and the rest of humanity "the have nots"; the super-rich versus the homeless and unemployed; humans, states, and countries that had the means to pay for Covid-19 vaccines versus the majority of the world that could not—"shithole countries" as one U.S. president described them.

If you ever wondered what some economists thought of the human condition in the global economy, I did too, until Aug 1, 2021, when I was left flabbergasted as I listened to the following dialogue between Paul Krugman, a Nobel Laureate, and Fareed Zakaria, host of the program "GPS" on CNN. This dialogue about the human condition in the modern global economy during the Covid-19 pandemic lays bare this inequality that began with a seemingly simple change from hunting and gathering to farming.

> *ZAKARIA: What about the global picture? Because, you know, we have—I mean, it's crazy thing in America is we have more than enough vaccines for everybody, you know, plus booster shots and everything, and yet you have 40 percent of the public that won't take it. Around the world people are begging for vaccines and quite literally dying.*
>
> *But will that slow down economic growth globally to have this kind of patchwork globalization where places like the United States, Europe and East Asia may be fine but lots of other places are not?*

> *KRUGMAN: Yes, let me say something that is extremely inhumane and brutal. The places that are not coping with this, that don't have sufficient vaccines, have enormous number of people but not a whole lot of money. If you actually ask me, it's not just if we take Western Europe, advanced East Asia, that's the bulk of the global economy. And then the places that are not managing to cope are places that are—the humanity is—the human cost is terrible, but it's a pretty small share of global GDP.*
>
> *Reminds me of some—there were some crazies, old enough to remember the East Asian financial crisis when the East Asian economy recovered but the East Asian people didn't, because Korea bounced back fast, and Indonesia did not. And, you know, it says there are not that many South Koreans, but they're relatively rich.*
>
> *So, this is one of those things where from an economics point of view, the fact that so much of the world are being left out of this is not such a big deal. Of course, from a human point of view, it's horrific.*

If one had any doubt there might be a disconnect between human well-being, survival, and the role and purpose of human economies today, this brief exchange could not be clearer. How was it possible that "the East Asian economy recovered but the East Asian people didn't"? What could that possibly mean except those economies are no longer a reflection of what they were intended to be—the results of humans eking out a living—but rather the activities of owners of surplus, "legal-persons" and multinationals, engaged in economic activities to multiply their surplus. And, while there are plenty of ordinary people eking out a living in East Asia, there just weren't enough owners of surplus in Indonesia compared to, say, South Korea—or as Krugman puts it, "there are not that many South Koreans, but they're relatively rich," and it was the rich in East Asian countries that enabled the East Asia economy to bounce back.

And what's true of the not-so-well-off in Indonesia is true of most of the world. According to Krugman, "If you actually ask me, it's not just if we take Western Europe, advanced East Asia, that's the bulk of the global economy . . . the human cost (of the pandemic) is terrible, but it's a pretty small share of global GDP." In other words, from an economic perspective, only the people and nations that comprise a significant component of the global economy—the owners of surplus—matter.

If our pre-agriculture hunter-gatherer forebears who started this whole notion of a human economy by eking out a living *within* Earth-life ecosystems had held this perspective of their economy, one doubts whether humanity could have survived those 290,000 years of hunting and gathering. One doubts, too, that hunter-gatherer economists would have on seeing masses of humans bereft of vaccines against a pandemic that had killed millions and had millions more in its sight, expressed the view that "from an economics point of view, the fact that so much of the world are being left out of this is not such a big deal."

As horrific a statement as Mr. Krugman himself, to his credit, admitted it was, it was nonetheless a true assessment of the relationship between humans today and the economies in which they live, and it gave the measure of most twenty-first century economies and what humans might expect from them. If ensuring human well-being and survival is not a big deal in a twenty-first century world economy, what is? If you guessed delayed unemployment checks, healthcare for all, aid to parents with dependent children, landlords blocked from executing evictions during a pandemic, an end to homelessness and hunger, the elimination of gun violence, an end to racial discrimination, a recognition of people of all genders as "persons," and more human well-being stuff—you would be dead wrong.

But if you guessed rising inflation; rising oil prices; collapse of the financial sector or the housing market; rising interest rates; proposals to tax the rich; failures of major banks such as Silicon Valley Bank (SVB), Sovereign Bank, or Credit Suisse; a stock market crash; or any of the many financial horrors that reduce surplus and give modern economists and politicians nightmares, you guessed right. You see, what's good for humans has become bad for the economy and vice versa—and that's because this modern economy is no longer a human economy, but a legal-person economy, a topic we'll discuss in the next chapter. And that's why, too, a strong jobs report is bad news for investors and inflation. So, in this upside-down economy, today's good economic news for humans (for example, an increase in jobs) could be bad economic news for the stock market.

Mr. Krugman was not the only one baring thoughts about human economies, and in particular the American economy, around this time. As it turned out, on September 16, 2021, President Joe Biden shared a few thoughts of his own and argued for support of his $3.5 trillion bill. He tore into surging wealth among billionaires even as the pandemic tore into poor and middle-class Americans.

It's rare that one gets a preview of the economic goals a world leader hoped to pursue like the ones Joe Biden outlined early in his term and summarized below—though several of these goals never quite became economic policy. Nevertheless, his speech offered an opportunity to imagine how our hunter-gatherer forebears might have seen these goals. They would have considered whether they were consistent with the *survival-driven* economic principles they practiced and would have drawn this contrast. They would have learned from his speech that modern economies were grossly unequal and hoarding in nature, driven by surplus rather than survival, and that they cared little for ecosystems and Earth-life species.

In his speech, Biden made several biting points:

- He condemned the widening inequality between the wealthiest Americans and everyone else, declaring "it's simply not fair" how wealthy Americans manage to evade taxes; how "billionaires have seen their wealth go up by $1.8 trillion. It's simply not fair." He was referring to a recent report from Americans for Tax Fairness and the Institute for Policy Studies.
- "How's it possible that the wealthiest billionaires in the country can entirely escape paying income taxes on what they make?" Biden asked. "For a long time, this economy has worked great for those at the very

top. Ordinary, hardworking Americans, the people who built this country, have been basically cut out of the deal."

- "They play by a different set of rules. They're often not employees themselves so the IRS can't see what they make and can't tell that they're cheating. That's how many of the top 1 percent pay virtually nothing," he said.
- "This is our moment to deal working people back into the economy. This is our moment to prove to the American people that their government works for them and not just big corporations and those at the very top."
- "We still have a long way to go to get the economy where it needs to be," he said. "These policies are what the science tells us we need to do, they're going to save lives, they'll protect our economic recovery as well and allow the economy to continue to grow," he added.
- "We can build an economy that gives people a fair shot this time," he said. "We can restore some sanity and fairness in our tax code. We can make investments that are long overdue in this nation."
- "I believe we're at an inflection point in this country—one of those moments where the decisions we're about to make can literally change the trajectory of our nation for years and possibly decades to come," Biden said.
- The President went on to argue for the inclusion of priorities like the expanded child tax credit, affordable childcare, and tuition-free community college in the bill Democrats were drafting to cut costs for families. He argued that those provisions were a way to tilt the economic scales toward middle-class Americans after four decades of safety net cuts and tax cuts centered on wealthier Americans.
- He also cited his proposal to beef up IRS enforcement, and his own Treasury Department's estimate that the wealthiest 1 percent of Americans dodge over $160 billion in taxes that they legally owe every year.

In the words of Senator Christopher Murphy of Connecticut, "There's no way to right the American economic ship if major corporations are paying nothing in taxes and plumbers in my state are paying a bigger percentage of income taxes than the bankers."

It's not clear where President Biden would have learned his *survival-driven economics*, but if Americans were to adopt his economic proposals, it would be making one small step toward implementing some of the economic principles that could begin to comprise a *survival-driven human economy*—one that's built to serve the needs of real, flesh-and-blood, anatomically modern humans instead of the 1 percent *surplus hoarders* and their "legal persons."

One must remember that none of the economic issues these goals set out to rectify would have haunted the dreams of hunter-gatherer economists (had there been such), nor threatened the well-being or survival of their fellow hunter-gatherers, because back then, there were no billionaires, one-percenters, or "legal persons," and above all, no economists. Back then, there was no such thing as infrastructure, but if there were, it would have meant *human infrastructure*, and human economies were only about ecosystems, biodiversity, and human life and survival, and as we have seen, nothing else. Theirs was an understanding of what a human economy once was and should be but one every subsequent post-Neolithic Revolution economy abandoned, leading to collapse. Yet it's one they must all return to if twenty-first century human economies are to avoid collapse and survive as pre-agriculture hunter-gatherer economies did.

Human societies and their economies have undoubtedly endured many transitions (Table 5-2) over their 300,000-year history, with most changes in subsistence method occurring only during the last 10,000 years of this long history, and with hunting and gathering being the only subsistence method during the preceding 290,000 years. One can think of these transitions as occurring in different geological epochs, from the Pleistocene (during which most of our hunter-gatherer forebears evolved) to the proposed Anthropocene, the name recommended but not yet adopted for the current or approaching epoch that modern humans have begun to carve out for themselves.

Another way, though, of thinking about when these early human economies existed is in terms of the prevailing climate that enshrouded the Earth—from the ice ages of the Pleistocene to the increasingly hot and hotter global warming occurring now in the Anthropocene. Or, one can also think of these transitions as occurring during intervals of time when Earth's known prior climate steady-states were changing—from "Icehouse Earth" to "Hothouse Earth."

Learning how those early human economies fared during their transitions might well inform humans today as we too begin to negotiate geologic time and climate change transitions of our own—from the Holocene to the Anthropocene—but one must first clarify what is meant by a human economy. Consider the "when, who, what, where, why and how" transitions in the Table 5-2.

What constitutes economic activity today and is passed off as human economic activity in a human economy has less and less to do with humans and human well-being and survival, and everything to do with the economic activities of a different type of person, a "legal person" or corporation—a new type of "person" designed to play in this new type of economy, and the focus of modern capitalist economies.

Haven't you noticed? Besides a few market reports and government statistics about the Civilian labor force participation rate and the like, most of what modern economics, market statistics and reporting seem to care about is the financial health and well-being of countries, states, and domestic, national, and multinational "legal persons" and their stock prices, bond issues, and futures values, whose very legal status as "persons" having the same rights as *anatomically modern humans* is reportedly based on a lie, according to Adam Winkler's March 6, 2018, article in *The Atlantic*.

Table 5-2. Human Economies - Transitions

Human Economies		
From	**—Transitions—**	**To**
When	**We Live**	**When**
We Existed **(Begin)**	The Pleistocene (Climate Change) to the Anthropocene (Climate Change)	We Still Exist But Will We?
Who	**Hunter-Gatherers**	**Who**
We Were	AMH (*Homo Erectus*) to *Homo Sapiens* aka *Homo Destroy-us*	We Have Become
What	**Technology**	**What**
Tools We Used Stone Age	Helped by Technology to Being. Replaced by Technology	Will Our Tools (AI) Replace Us?
Why	**Survival vs Extinction**	**Why**
We Exist to Survive	The Search for Food (Survival) to the Search for Wealth (Extinction)	Will We Continue to Exist?
Where	**Mobile groups**	**Where**
Small Mobile Groups	Freedom & Control (Live Everywhere) No Freedom, No Control to Live Nowhere	Sedentary Mega-Cities
Where	**Earth-life Ecosystems**	**Where**
In Earth-life Ecosystems Preservation	Inside Earth's Ecosystems Eking-out a-living Outside Earth's Ecosystems	Outside Ecosystems Destruction
How	**Economies**	**How**
Foraging & Sharing	Hunting & Gathering & Civilization Survival to Farming & Civilization Collapse	Farming & Hoarding
How	**Societies**	**How**
Hunting Gathering Sharing Egalitarian Economies & Societies	Open Egalitarian Sharing from Survival-Driven Economies to Closed Proprietary Surplus-Driven Economies	Surplus-Driven Hoarding Economies & Societies

(Source: Samuel Layne)

This inclination to rob real people, humans, of their true economic rights and freedoms did not begin with that series of events in the 1880s that Winkler wrote about but harkens all the way back to the true birth of peasantry, slavery, and economic hierarchy that came with the change to that now not-so-new economic brief—that change from hunting and gathering to farming, animal husbandry, and eventually agriculture. So, these modern capitalist economies are by no means "human economies," but rather, economies built of, by, and for the modern country or state and their population of "legal persons." Like operators of gargantuan pieces of industrial equipment or remote operators, the only role the overwhelming number of humans play in these economies (and not for long because the robots are coming) is as employees, or human resources, to create its products, and as consumers, to maintain demand for its endless streams of mostly dispensable, non-recyclable, and often non-biodegradable products and services.

When one thinks about human economies then, rather than economies built to serve countries, states, and their population of "legal persons," one must think first and foremost about what humans did to make a living across all those millennia of our species' existence because, back then, they were neither countries, states, nor "legal persons"—just real people. Humans have gone from the axe-carrying *Homo erectus* (among the first recognizable members of the genus *Homo* some 200 Mya during the Pleistocene)—braving the cold and ice across the frozen fields and ice-cold caves of Eurasia's ecosystems in search of food—to anatomically modern humans, *Homo sapiens* (which should probably be renamed *Homo destroy-us),* destroying Earth-life ecosystems and biodiversity in search not of food nor survival, but endless economic growth and surplus wealth.

Nearly all of *Homo destroy-us* ecosystem-destroying subsistence changes that began with farming occurred during the Holocene (that much warmer geologic epoch that began 11,500 years ago connecting the Pleistocene to the Anthropocene), during which most human economies and civilizations arose, thrived, and collapsed.

From hunters and gatherers to peasant workers or peasant farmers, to pastoralists herding animals, to vassals in a kingdom in a feudal economy, to employees or entrepreneurs of a company in a market economy, humans, their societies, and economies have seen more than their share of transitions. And when economies change, societies often change as well. With each transition came different ways of making a living, a shift from the mobility, freedom, and independence that came with hunting and gathering to the sedentation, monotony, bondage and lack of autonomy and independence of being a peasant on a farm or an at-will employee at the beck and call of an employer, from being completely free and responsible for one's own well-being to being dependent upon the surplus and resources of a farmer, employer, or state. Or, as Samuel Layne describes it in his book entitled *Survival: Evolutionary Rules for Intelligent Species Survival:*

> *Hunter-gatherers were free to do whatever they wanted, whenever they wanted, without getting anyone's permission. They chose to hunt and gather for a living and not to work for any boss (not that there were jobs then, but from what is known of surviving hunter-gatherer communities, given a choice, most will not). They did not work for any company or government, nor did they serve or fight for any ruler, king, queen, or country, God, or religion. That, by the way, is apparently how it was intended to be ,as all other species continue to live this way.*
>
> *Imagine what might have comprised a typical week, noting their absolute and complete freedom. They chose how, when, and where they would spend their time, and that only began to vanish when "working for the man" became de rigueur after the advent of agriculture and settled communities.*
>
> *They were completely self-directed and obtaining the food and materials they needed occupied only a small portion of their day, two to three days a week, and required less than half the group of fifty or less to engage in these activities, leaving huge amounts of time for leisure and ceremonial activities. . .*
>
> *There were no jobs, no employers, and for some the best part, no bosses, either. One might say they were self-employed when looked at in today's terms.*

> *Hunting and gathering to extract the necessary sustenance they needed from the ecosystems in which they lived was a highly stable, very long-lasting way to make a living. For hundreds of thousands of years, and until about 10,000 years ago, it was the only "profession" Homo sapiens had known. They independently chose how, when, and where to hunt and gather to sustain their lives.*

By far, then, the most significant change human societies and their economies might have undergone, and probably the first after 290,000 years, has been the change from an "immediate return economy" or, as one might say today, a kind of "just-in-time economy minus the lean manufacturing piece" that comprised hunting and gathering, to the "delayed return economy" of planting, watering, waiting, and reaping (and often weeping), that came with farming. In the former, individuals or small groups of individuals, hunters-and-gatherers responsible for their own livelihood, went out in search of their next meal, or next few meals, finding and sharing some of any catch with members of their small community, being ready to go again and again in search of more, once a prior bounty had been consumed, with the utmost confidence that they would find, every time, more of the sustenance they needed to survive.

They fervently and unwaveringly followed Earth's subsistence rules, a seemingly unwritten contract with nature that all other Earth-life species also followed, that post-agriculture humans may have lost since abandoning Earth-life ecosystems, and that nature had provided for the last 290,000 years and always will provide. Theirs was an economy that hoarded neither surplus nor sought to exert or maintain control over the wild animals and plant species they hunted or foraged for a living. It was an economy that caused neither disruption nor significant changes to ecosystems and biodiversity where humans foraged or in which they encamped or while they moved to another area within an ecosystem—a type of natural subsistence economy all Earth-life species have followed and have practiced since their evolution.

To understand early human economies, though, or economies during any geological epoch, one must consider the prevailing climate, and in this case, what it was like during those light-switch-like transitions from glacial to interglacial, during the ice ages of the Pleistocene, comparing its impact with the comparatively warming climate ushered in with the Holocene. Hunter-gatherers of the Pleistocene ice ages were confronted with a very different climate than those lucky enough to have lived through and after the Pleistocene-Holocene transition. Those twenty-four "light-switch-like" glacial-to-interglacial transitions that occurred between 110,000 and 15,000 BP, changing from full glacial to near interglacial conditions in just a few decades, raised temperatures by as much as 5°C to 8°C. And while similar transitions continued into the Holocene, they were an order of magnitude smaller and resulted in a comparatively peaceful climate regime.

Pleistocene hunter-gatherers would have needed to remain prepared for abrupt climate change. They must have been very mobile and kept aware of safe havens and must have developed the ability to survive in varying climates, during both full glacial and full interglacial conditions to keep pace with abrupt changes in climate; as it was, during the Pleistocene Neanderthals went extinct. By about 10,000 BP hunter–gatherers began to inherit a world that was becoming increasingly productive, stable, and very different from the one inhabited by their anatomically modern human predecessors. The Pleistocene climate ended around 11,200 BP but not before a change in CO_2 content in the atmosphere left plants more productive and resistant to cold and drought and may well have encouraged a greater reliance on plants as a food source. It may well, too, have set the conditions for the adoption of farming.

In addition, what was it like to live during what must have been wrenching societal and lifestyle changes that must have simultaneously begun during the climate shifts that drove the cultural and economic transformation from one type of human society and economy to another; from hunting and gathering during the Pleistocene to farming and animal husbandry and eventually agriculture that became possible during the

Holocene? What was it like during the waning days of the last ice age, as the temperature grew warmer and meltwater runoffs from ice sheets accumulated, forming new lakes where dry valleys once lay, where one was now able to fish in places where one once foraged?

Perhaps it might just be possible to get some sense of what those transitions must have felt like, and might have entailed, when one considers the current impacts from the two major challenges confronting twenty-first century humans. First, the rapid transition from a pre- to a post-Covid-19 world; from what was considered "normal" to a world that was going to be forever changed by the sudden outbreak of the Covid-19 pandemic to a yet-to-be-discovered new "normal." And second, climate change, the unanticipated fiery outburst of a rapid and seemingly unexpected increase in calamitous weather, from widespread wildfires raging across multiple continents to torrential rainfall driven by atmospheric rivers causing once-in-a-century floods brought on by human-induced climate change.

But first climate change, because without the relative calm of the Holocene, compared to the preceding Pleistocene Epoch, agriculture wouldn't have happened and the Neolithic Revolution with its agriculture, animal domestication, surplus, slavery, inequality, and city-states with their elites and subsequent civilizations, including the civilization we know today, might not have happened, or not in quite the same way. And given where we are today, that might not have been such a bad thing. Similarly, the civilization that will emerge over the next 1,000 years of global warming climate change will be nothing like we have experienced or can even imagine.

If one were to look back to the end of the last glacial period, 12,000 years ago, carbon-dioxide concentrations stood at about 240 ppm. As glaciers melted, concentrations rose to 270 ppm and fluctuated up to around 280 ppm for nearly 12 millennia, until the Industrial Revolution, the age of industrial hydrocarbon burning. During the last two centuries, atmospheric CO_2 concentration has risen from about 280 ppm to the modern record of

430.7+ ppm, a huge increase by anyone's reckoning. And according to Rex Weyler in a 2019 article for Greenpeace International, "That equates to an extra quadrillion molecules of CO_2 per cubic centimeter of atmosphere. Every one of those molecules serves as a tiny heat engine. This scale of carbon-dioxide heat absorption in the atmosphere is not only unprecedented in the Holocene, but also rare in Earth's History."

The CO_2-driven climate change that ushered in the Holocene warmed the Earth and made agriculture and civilization possible and may even, from some perverse perspective, have been a good thing for our hunter-gatherer forebears. But with CO_2 approaching nearly one and a half times (from 280 to 430.7 ppm) as much today, we, their twenty-first century descendants, are having quite the opposite experience, and few would doubt it's anything but a bad thing as it may well bring an end to at least agriculture if not life as we know it. But ending agriculture could turn out to be a really good thing. Imagine that! Human civilization thriving again as it once did, without agriculture. Yes, there was no agriculture for most of human existence.

The societal and economic disruptions unleashed by present-day climate change are becoming less and less uncertain and are beginning to look more like the disruptions of the Pleistocene, if not more ominous. What's becoming more and more uncertain, though, is how modern human societies and their economies will respond to these changes. "A Hotter Future is Certain, the IPCC Climate Panel Warns. But How Hot is up to Us," according to the Intergovernmental Panel on Climate Change's (IPCC) Sixth Assessment Report, "Climate Change 2021 – The Physical Science Basis."

And, for a look at how pre-agriculture humans and their economies negotiated previous climate change, it helps to look at how hunter-gatherers living through the end of the Pleistocene-Holocene transition responded, although, as we will see, the climate change they experienced would have been significantly milder going from a much colder to a warming world. And it was probably preferred, particularly since none of it was caused by anything they had done, unlike climate change today, which is shifting from an already hot to an even hotter world, the result of everything we have done and are doing.

They were living through a changing climate toward the end of the last ice age, going from a comparatively cold to a warming climate at the beginning of the Holocene Epoch; from the freezing and receding ice sheets of the Pleistocene, when the sea level stood about 20 meters higher (consider what that would mean for coastal cities today) and plant species were emerging while animal species were disappearing, to a warming world driven by rising CO_2 that enabled increased plant productivity that may well have facilitated an entirely new kind of economic production. It also meant a shift from hunting and gathering to a mix of foraging and farming and eventually to agriculture as the weather grew warmer; and from living in mobile societies, with small bands of family, friends, and close acquaintances to eventually sedentary, often packed, farming villages and towns and living among farm animals.

And, they were going from a time when, except for personal items, no one owned anything and instead shared most things, including food, to a society in which some people were beginning to own most everything but shared few things; from being free and beholden to none to being fixed on a farm and subject to the will of the farmer; from living among humans they knew and that were guided by interpersonal relationships within their small bands, to new kinds of relationships that became increasingly guided by property ownership, and one in which they themselves could become property; from a time when most people were healthy and ate a wide variety of nutritious food, to a time when animal diseases would begin to plague humans and food varieties would be reduced to a limited set of scarce, hoarded, harvested grain.

Their experience of climate change, featuring increasingly stable and comparatively warming temperatures, may well have enabled or accompanied a change in their method of economic production; one that would upend their tried-and-true hunting and gathering economic way of making a living that they and their forebears had practiced since humans first walked the Earth. And, while that change began independently in multiple places (the Middle East, South Asia, China, and Mesoamerica), and did not occur overnight, but may have taken as long as 4,000 years to become the de facto economic approach across the Earth, it was one that in turn would eventually lead to such vast cultural, societal, and personal lifeway changes, as well as changes in interactions with Earth-life ecosystems and biodiversity, that it would forever dictate the way they and all subsequent humans would make a living and interact with one another, other species, and the Earth itself.

It was a method of economic production so radically different that, 10,000 years later, it would drive the destruction of Earth-life ecosystems and much of its biodiversity to extinction; a change from foraging to farming that would both require much, much more labor, and through the surplus it would generate, enable human population growth from about ten million 10,000 years ago to more than eight billion today, with a forecast of ten billion by the end of this century.

And now, well into the twenty-first century, agriculture, this Pleistocene-Holocene climate change-enabled method of economic production and its surplus, has mutated like a virus across the centuries into monocrop industrial agriculture, and together with its surplus, into capitalism. This current, not-so-new form of economic activity has evolved into a global economic system comprising countries, states, and "legal persons," a global economy seemingly more suited to "legal persons" than to humans. It is to blame for the current rise in global temperatures such as Earth has not seen in 100,000 years.

This is a change in economic production that has hijacked that once simple human economy and its efficient human economic production system, hunting and gathering, that lasted for hundreds of millennia, changing it to one that barely 400 generations later could well lead to the extinction of humans and potentially all Earth-life species. This begs the question: Should twenty-first century humans somehow survive the effects of this Neolithic Revolution, what societal, cultural, and economic transitions might twenty-first century climate change engender?

If indeed it was climate change caused by Earth's orbital changes (the precession cycle that drove cyclic increases in carbon dioxide and methane, resulting in the warming climate during the Holocene, improved plant productivity that facilitated farming and agriculture, and massive human societal, cultural, and economic changes) how would twenty-first century human civilization, society, and economies change given the comparatively vast increases in anthropogenic greenhouse gases humans have already released into the atmosphere?

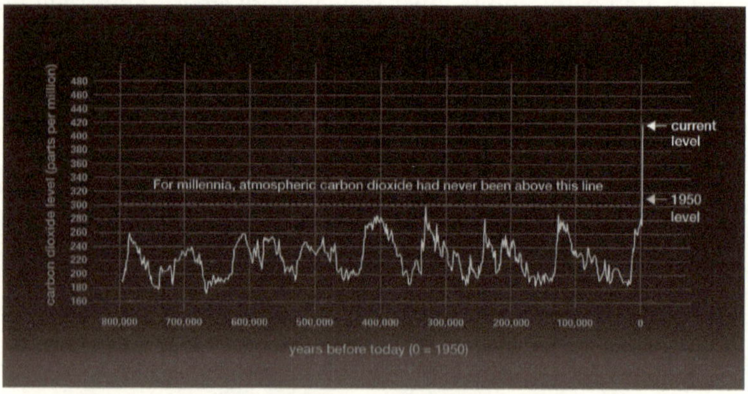

Figure 5-1. CO_2 levels from 800,000 years ago.

The concentration of carbon dioxide in the atmosphere today is well beyond past levels determined from ice cores. On March 14, 2021, the CO_2 level was about 417 ppm. The million-year time frame is important. (Image: NASA Jet Propulsion Laboratory)

Looking back at CO_2 levels 800,000 years before the present compared to the current level (Figure 5-1), one notes that it only rose above the 300-ppm level after 1950. Since then, it has risen steeply and today it tops the 430-ppm mark. What does that imply for twenty-first century humans, their economies, and civilization? If indeed it was global warming that facilitated the rise of agriculture and human civilizations, wouldn't it be ironic if it turns out that global warming is once again a changemaker? Only this time around, it seems set to do quite the opposite—facilitate a substantial change if not an end to agriculture and potentially to human civilization.

Unlike modern humans, our hunter-gatherer forebears probably hadn't a clue about what was causing the climate change that was enabling farming nor, except for farming itself, were they doing much else that would have increased global temperatures. Agriculture does contribute to CO_2 buildup, and along with fossil fuels and land use, has been one of the three largest producers of CO_2 the last 250 years. Modern humans, however, know quite a lot and we are doing even more to increase CO_2; nevertheless, we seem unable or unwilling to do what might still be possible to stop pumping $GtC0_2$ (gigatons of CO_2) into the atmosphere—but why? Because the main generators of CO_2 and CH_4 are the economic sectors of the economy and the primary generators of surplus, profits, wealth accumulation, and GDP growth.

Climate models indicate that the Earth could warm by 3°C to 4°C by the year 2100 and eventually by as much as 8°C or more. This would return the planet to those unstable, seesaw-like patterns of climate change that characterized the Pleistocene during which agriculture was more than likely impossible. So, it is not unlikely that climate change in the Anthropocene may well put paid to agriculture as we know it, if not to the civilization it enabled as well.

Which of the envisioned climate change trajectories (in Figure 5-3) is the world currently on? What do the future carbon dioxide and greenhouse gas emissions look like? For a 50 percent chance of remaining below 1.5°C degrees of global warming—that once-aspirational goal of the 2015 Paris agreement that since COP 27 is seen as unattainable—the world must not emit more than 580 gigatons of carbon dioxide before 2100. Environmental and energy economist Dan Welsby at University College London calculates (see Figure 5-2) that 89 percent of coal reserves, 58 percent of oil reserves and 59 percent of gas reserves must remain un-extracted, essentially leaving the majority of known economic fossil fuel reserves untapped.

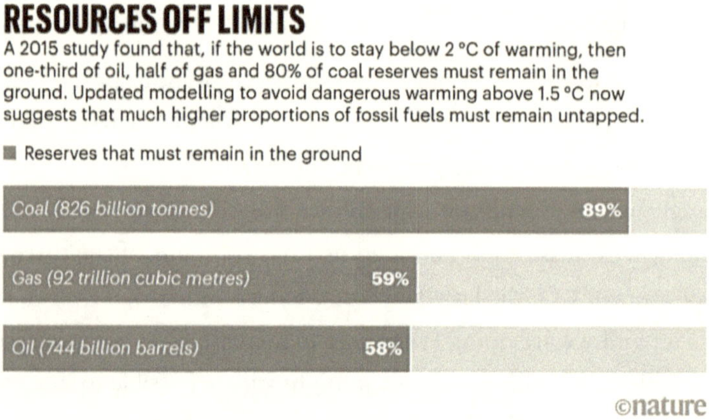
RESOURCES OFF LIMITS
A 2015 study found that, if the world is to stay below 2 °C of warming, then one-third of oil, half of gas and 80% of coal reserves must remain in the ground. Updated modelling to avoid dangerous warming above 1.5 °C now suggests that much higher proportions of fossil fuels must remain untapped.
Reserves that must remain in the ground
Coal (826 billion tonnes)
89%
Gas (92 trillion cubic metres)
59%
Oil (744 billion barrels)
58%
©nature

Figure 5-2. Resources that must remain off-limits.
(Source: Nature.com, DOI:10.1038/d41586-021-02444-3)

The visualization below (Figure 5-3) shows a range of potential future scenarios of global greenhouse gas emissions (measured in gigatons of carbon dioxide ($GtCO_2$) equivalents), and based on data from Climate Action Tracker. Here, five scenarios are shown:

- **No climate policies:** Projected future emissions if no climate policies were implemented; this would result in an estimated 4.1°C to 4.8°C warming by 2100 (relative to pre-industrial temperatures). This is beginning to look a bit more realistic but life across vast portions of the Earth will become unbearable, if not impossible.
- **Current climate policies:** Projected warming of 2.8°C to 3.2°C by 2100 based on currently implemented climate policies. This may be possible, but I won't bet on it.
- **National pledges:** If all countries achieve their current targets/pledges set within the Paris climate agreement, average warming by 2100 is estimated to be 2.5°C to 2.8°C. This will go well beyond the overall target

of the Paris Agreement to keep warming "well below 2°C," and though this is getting closer to what is needed, it too seems ambitious.

- **2°C-consistent:** A range of emissions pathways would be compatible with limiting average warming to 2°C by 2100. These would require a significant increase in ambition from the current pledges within the Paris Agreement. This too seems unlikely.
- **1.5°C-consistent:** A range of emissions pathways would be compatible with limiting average warming to 1.5°C by 2100. However, all would require an urgent, very rapid reduction in global greenhouse gas emissions. Unfortunately, that's not happening.

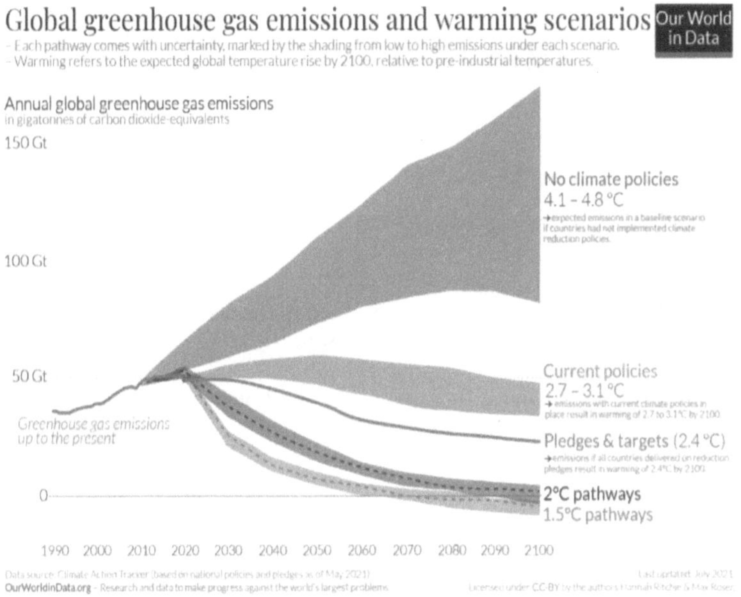

Figure 5-3. Global greenhouse gas emissions and warming scenarios.
(Source: Our World in Data)

But who gets to choose and why should you care which of these scenarios humans eventually achieve? That's a question for you. Let me tell you why I care. Hunter-gatherer humans, you see, may well have survived their last bout with global warming because they had nothing to do with why, how, or when it occurred. That 6°C increase in global warming that drove the Terminal Pleistocene ice age to an end, and the warming temperatures of the Holocene, occurred despite whatever humans were doing at the time. Today, however, it is the economic sectors that comprise the human economy that are driving the current CO_2 increase, and we have already driven it up 1°C (Figure 5-4) since the pre-industrial era (1880-1900). It is now up to us humans, if we can, to make it stop.

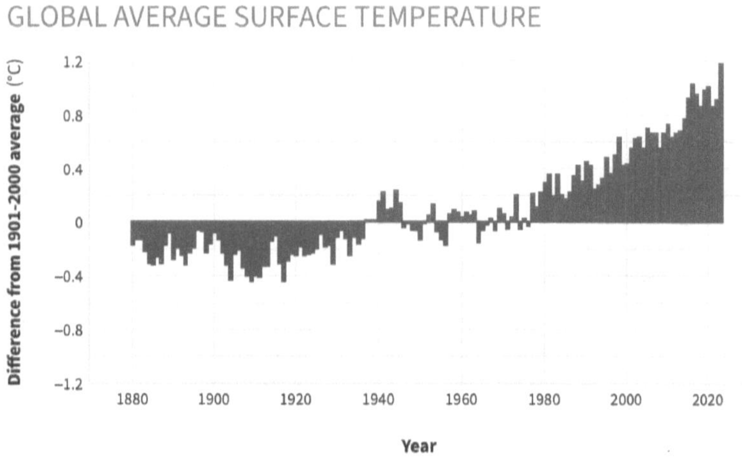

Figure 5-4. Global average surface temperature.
(Source: NOAA Climate.gov)

Which of us can make this growth in CO_2 stop? Which of us gets to choose—all of us? That would be great if we could and if that were possible. In fact, most humans won't even have a chance to choose because those choices are no longer up to us mere mortals, but rather are under the control of governments and, you guessed it, the world's energy, technology, and investment mega-corporations, those "legal persons" who have demonstrated over their history that human survival is not their priority.

A U.S. House of Representatives report on Big Oil profiteering and greenwashing makes it unmistakably clear that whatever companies may say about their climate policies, their investments show that they intend to continue producing and selling oil and gas deep into the future—and well beyond the life expectancies of the carbon budgets implied by any of the world's climate goals. The choice that now confronts humanity is between human survival and their profits and wealth. You already know what they have chosen. But that's just the beginning.

Most projections of global warming focus on either the year 2100 or the effects of a doubling of CO_2 (from the pre-industrial level of 275 ppm to 550 ppm). But, as noted in Chapter 2, apparently no country appears to be on track to meet their 1.5°C commitments made in the Paris Agreement (*New York Intelligencer*, Wallace-Wells, 2017), and because it seems unlikely that any of the policies required to keep warming at manageable levels can be implemented in time to avoid catastrophic climate change (Gowdy, J), that settles the question for me. We are running out of time.

The current lack of effective policies to deal realistically with climate change, even in the face of increasingly dire warnings, suggests that high emissions rates are our likely future, and high emissions projections provide the most accurate scenarios of climate change (Gabbatiss, 2017). Then there are the very long-term consequences of climate change, and these, too, have received relatively little attention (Bala, Caldeira, Mirin, Wickett, & Delire, 2005; Gowdy & Juliá, 2010; Kasting, 1998).

According to Gowdy, the lack of attention to the very long run is a serious shortcoming, since integrated carbon-climate models project that if CO_2 from current *in situ* fossil fuel resources are eventually released into the atmosphere, the peak concentration of atmospheric CO_2 could exceed 1400 ppm by the year 2300 and the average global temperature could warm by 8°C or more, according to Bala et al., 2005; Kasting, 1998, in "Our hunter-gatherer future: Climate change, agriculture and uncivilization." A CO_2 level of 1400 ppm would increase the risk of a rise in temperature as high as 20°C, which will certainly have catastrophic consequences for all life on Earth. It is sobering to consider that current levels of CO_2 are higher than at any time in the last 15 million years (World Bank, 2012 p. xiv).

Even if climate change mitigation policies reduce CO_2 emission rates, atmospheric CO_2 concentrations will continue to rise until emissions fall to the natural removal rate—and when is that? Much of the emitted CO_2 remains in the atmosphere centuries or even millennia after its release. Archer (2005, Fate of fossil fuel CO2 in geologic time) suggests that 300 years is a good average lifetime number for CO_2 and that 17–33 percent of the CO_2 will remain in the atmosphere 1,000 years after it is emitted. In "Long term fate of anthropogenic carbon," Montenegro, Brovkin, Eby, Archer, and Weaver (2007) suggest that released carbon may stay in the atmosphere an average of 1,800 years or longer. According to Archer & Brovkin (2008, p. 283), in "The millennial atmospheric lifetime of anthropogenic CO_2," "Ultimate recovery does take place but only in time scales of hundreds of thousands of years." The effects then of fossil fuel burning are irreversible on a time scale relevant to humans—and that, I am afraid, includes you and me and that's why I care. And now that you know what I know, do you care, too?

Given the above scenario, how might twenty-first century human societies, economies, and civilizations change under the pressures of an increasingly hot world? Fortunately, all prior and current human civilizations, including our own, arose during the last 10,000 years of the Holocene Epoch. And, while during those many centuries climate change bears scant resemblance to the growing intensity of climate change today, one still hopes to glean at least a few insights. Knowing what humans faced and how they adapted when comparatively not-so-bad climate change struck might help us prepare for what may lie ahead.

Compared to the Pleistocene and until the rise of anthropogenic fossil-fuel-driven climate change in the nineteenth century, the Holocene was indeed a relatively stable, warm, if a little wet, geologic period that enabled agriculture and the rise of civilization. But it was not without its own set of recurring climate change intervals that brought their share of nightmares upon human societies, economies, and civilizations and hint that there probably might never have been any time in Earth's history that would have been totally free of economic, societal, and civilization impacts of climate change. Indeed, most human economies and civilizations developed, thrived, and then collapsed, driven primarily by repeated, extended, and severe bouts of climate change and, in particular, by droughts (Layne, 2019). History shows that abrupt, intense, and persistent droughts occurred at the same time as societal collapse of the Akkadian, Maya, Mochica, and Tiwanaku civilizations.

The Holocene droughts referred to above caused extreme economic and societal responses and civilization collapse and were much more severe in duration and intensity than anything that has occurred since. According to Peter de Menocal, climate records show in detail major droughts in the last century, and the severity of rare multi-decadal to multi-century droughts recurring and widespread cooling events occurring every 1,500 years. Consider the "Great Drought" of the 1280s that occurred in the American Southwest, lasting 26 years (de Menocal). The Ancestral Pueblo (aka Anasazi) civilization rose from complete obscurity to build some of the largest towns in ancient North America about 1,000 years ago. Then, suddenly, they moved out of their great pueblos and vanished from history.

They simply dispersed from their homelands in the face of untenable environmental conditions during two major drought cycles identified from ancient tree rings: in 1130–1180 CE, and in the great drought of 1275–1299 CE. Their response to climate change lay in their ideology, in which the notion of movement played an important part. They inherited the cumulative knowledge of 10,000 years of foraging in an unrelenting landscape where survival depended on a close knowledge of alternative foods in times of hunger. They became farmers and developed water-conservation technology (Survival, S. Layne, 2019). Nevertheless, it was climate change in the form of droughts that brought their civilization to an end.

Another drought you might have missed or never heard about is the drought that ended the presence of English settlers in northern Virginia. Tree ring chronology from northeastern Virginia shows that drought periods from 1587 to 1589 CE and 1606 to 1612 CE were the driest in the last 700 years ("The Lost Colony and Jamestown Droughts," D.W. Stahle, et al.) and coincides with the arrival of the English colonists. They settled in Roanoke, Virginia, but had vanished by the time resupply ships arrived four years later. They are now thought to have died from disease and starvation caused by drought. In April 1607, a larger colony settled in Jamestown, Virginia, at the time of extreme drought and by 1632, 80 percent of that population had died from malnutrition associated with the arid climate. How different America's history, culture, and economy might have been had that second tranche of English settlers also died. Would Americans be speaking Spanish or French and English, or a little of both as in Canada?

One drought in particular that most people would have heard or read about is the Dust Bowl of the 1930s, which lasted six years, from 1933-1938. In terms of economic and societal impact, it's considered one of the most devastating ecological, sociological, agricultural, and economic disasters in U.S. history. This drought was caused by a lack of precipitation (climate change) across the northern Great Plains. It displaced millions of people and is believed to have been a possible cause of the subsequent economic collapse. Similar decadal droughts that repeatedly occurred in the American Southwest, long-term droughts, often meant failure of both summer and winter monsoon rains. New research shows that for the severe, multi-decadal droughts that occurred from 1539 to 2008, generally both winter and summer rains were sparse year after year.

Then there were the "Little Ice Age" (1300 to 1870 CE) and the preceding medieval warm period (800 to 1300 CE) believed to have been caused by solar irradiance variations and the effects of active volcanoes. These represent the most recent millennial-style Holocene climate cycle. While they did not terminate any human civilizations, they did manage to rearrange a few societies and economies. For instance, during this warming, the Norse, under Eric the Red, colonized southern Greenland in CE 985 because of the mild climate and stable ocean conditions (Sherwood and Idso, 2004).

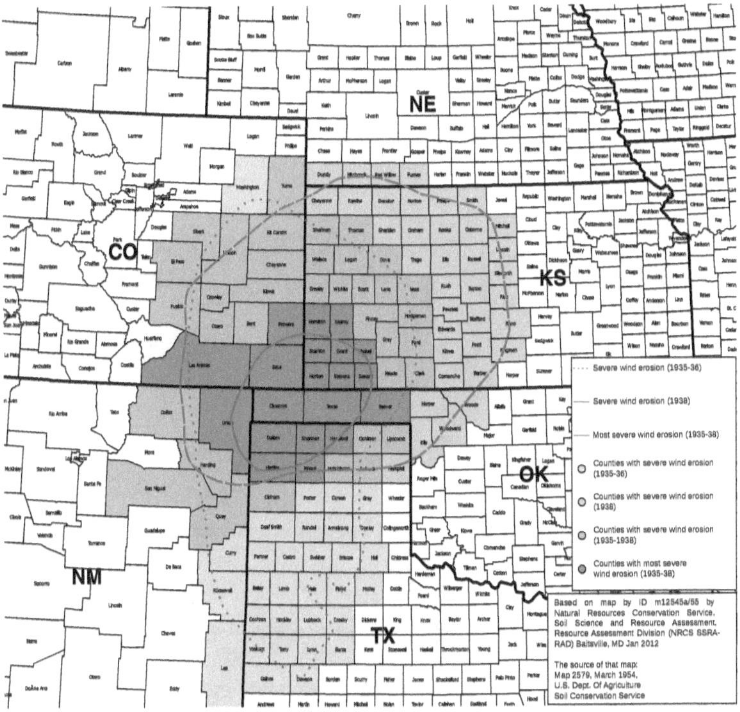

Figure 5-5. Map of states and counties affected by the Dust Bowl between 1935 and 1938.

The most severely affected counties during this period are colored. (Source: U.S. Dept. Of Agriculture Soil Conservation Service)

The arrival of the Norse occurred at the same time as the peak of medieval warming recorded in the Greenland Ice Sheet Project 2 (GISP2) ice core (Figure 5-6) from the summit region of central Greenland. This suggests the Norse took advantage of the peak medieval warm climate to establish settlements on the coast of Greenland. The demise of the Norse, after five centuries, may be attributed to onset of the Little Ice Age (also shown below). And according to D. Taylor, 2022, in "The original climate crisis – how the little ice age devastated early modern Europe," the increased winter sea ice closed off trade routes with mainland Europe that Norse settlements relied upon during the late fourteenth century. The collapse of Norse colonies involves many different complex sociological factors, but the Little Ice Age may have been a determining factor according to de Menocal in 'Cultural Responses to Climate Change During the Late Holocene.'

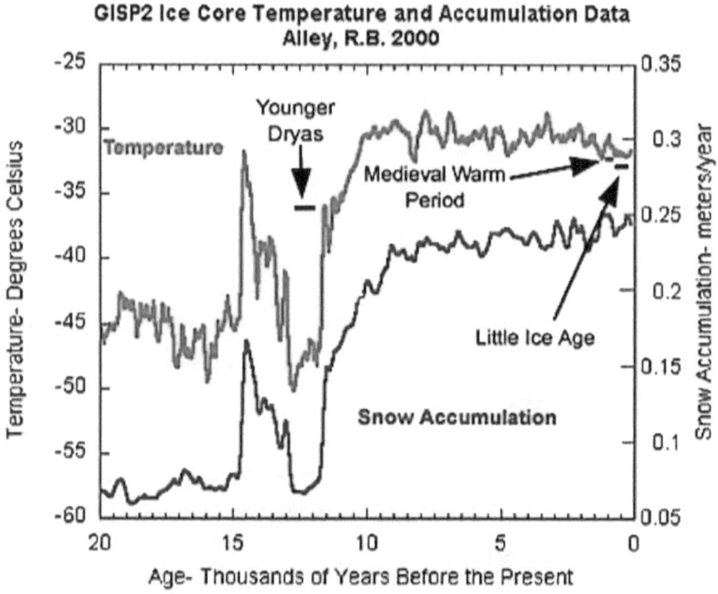

Figure 5-6. GISP2 ice core temperature and accumulation data.
The Younger Dryas is shown in this graph from the GISP2 ice core of Greenland at 11,500 BP. The peak Medieval Warm Period is shown at 985 CE, and the Little Ice Age at 1350 CE. (Source: Alley, 2000).

In addition, in northern Europe during the Little Ice Age, colder weather combined with changes in atmospheric circulation caused crops to fail, leading to famine, disease, and increased child mortality in the seventeenth to nineteenth centuries. However, in London the annual winter freezing of the Thames River was celebrated, and the colder climate inspired writers and painters. Charles Dickens wrote about the beautiful white Christmas, and Mary Shelley wrote the novel Frankenstein while snowed in.

Today, nearly 1,300 years since the medieval warm period began, warming across the Arctic that benefitted the Norse once again has begun to drive a repeat of history, this time by enabling the Russians to open routes that for centuries had been blocked by sea ice through which European explorers sought a navigable passage as a possible trade route to Asia. The advent of global climate change in the twenty-first century has brought about several different changes in the Arctic, including increased accessibility to Arctic ports as well as the opening of new Arctic shipping lanes and trans-Arctic routes, including the Northern Sea Route and the Northwest Passage, with geopolitical implications that are just beginning to emerge, according to The Arctic Institute.

These Holocene climate change events and their economic, societal, and civilization impacts are not intended to be exhaustive of all that occurred prior to the time humans began pumping CO_2 into the atmosphere. They were nonetheless devasting and, as we have seen, range from the collapse of entire civilizations to lesser but nonetheless distressing changes caused by decadal or multi-century droughts that have returned repeatedly and in the last 20 years have begun once more to stalk the North American continent as shown below in the U.S. Drought Monitor (Figure 5-7).

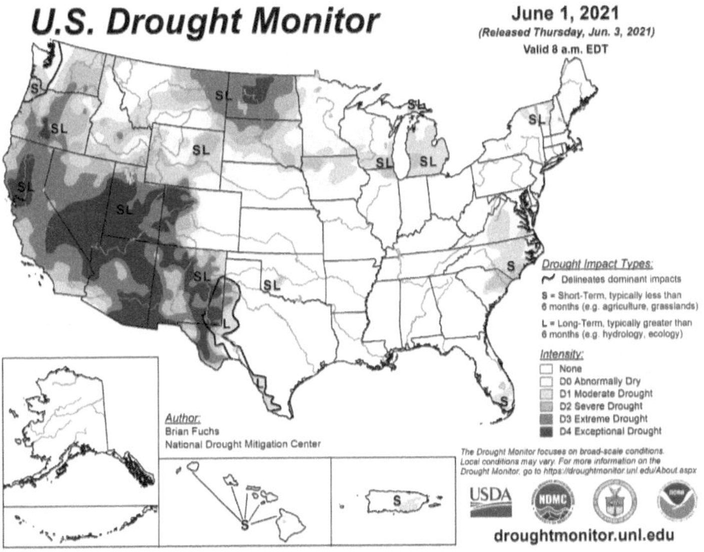

Figure 5-7. U.S. Drought Monitor.
(Source: US drought monitor - 2021 Map)

The economic impact of such droughts is severe. Depending on the severity of the drought and the size of the area affected, the local, regional, or national economy might experience a massive setback. Perhaps no other economic activity suffers more than agriculture during a drought. Water is also a major requirement of most industries. Low water levels due to reduced levels of precipitation translates to decreased production of hydroelectricity. The dry environmental conditions during droughts often serve as the ideal situation for the occurrence of wildfires. In locations where aqua tourism is a major attraction, the drying up of water bodies leads to a lower influx of tourists to the area. And worse, droughts often lead to famine and its ill effects on human health.

Unlike the droughts referenced above, however, this current drought is worldwide and is not confined to the North American continent, claims Physics.Org in a 2021 article. No continent except Antarctica has been spared, according to the SPEI Global Drought Monitor Index. Drought conditions like those now gripping the American West have occurred in different parts of the world including USA (California), Brazil, Australia, Madagascar and Taiwan, to name a few, and these do not even make the list of the world's most drought-prone countries. And, in an already water-stressed world as shown (Figure 5-8), the world should brace itself for more severe droughts as global warming intensifies.

These droughts have had and still have in most cases adverse consequences for people, businesses, and nature. Their impacts, though, are not evenly distributed, as Third World countries, and, or small and rural communities in developed countries—many of which have a greater proportion of low-income households and people of color, such as aborigines or native peoples like American Indians—often feel the worst effects. Freshwater ecosystems are at serious risk from low water flows and high water temperatures, and water quality issues are worsened by increased salt and contaminant concentrations and reduced oxygen levels.

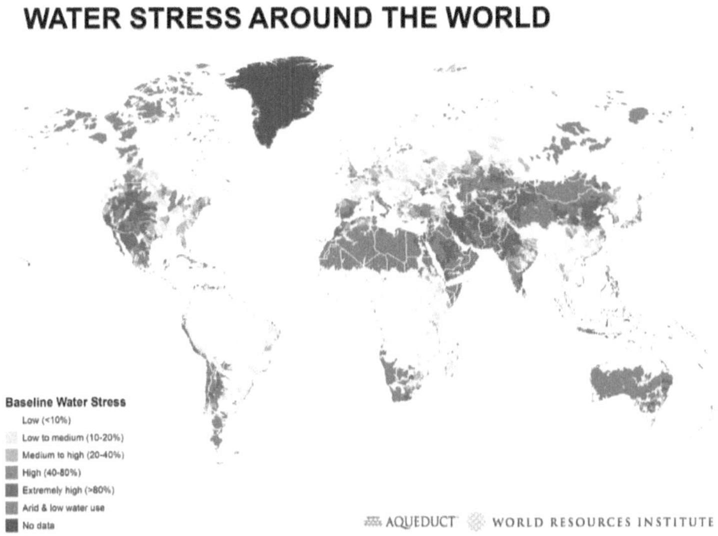

Figure 5-8. Water stress around the world.
(Source: World Resource Institute)

Surface water shortages for agriculture lead to more groundwater pumping, and continued overdraft causes land subsidence, property damage, drying of domestic wells, and a permanent loss in groundwater storage. In addition, fish and wildlife, wildfires, agriculture, and rural communities, as well as urban areas are all impacted, according to Cora Kammeyer, et al., in a 2021 article entitled "The 2021 Western Drought: What to Expect as Conditions Worsen" published by the Pacific Institute.

But in addition to droughts, there were other forms of climate change with potential economic impacts, as described above. If, for example, the societal and economic changes that occurred during the Little Ice Age (1300 to 1870 CE) and the preceding medieval warm period (800 to 1300 CE) could have been caused by climate-change-driven solar irradiance variations and the effects from active volcanoes, imagine what effects anthropogenic climate forcing, due to the gigatons of atmospheric CO_2 and CH_4 humans have since added to the atmosphere, might yet cause. And indeed, while we still don't know for sure just how bad it will ultimately get, we are already beginning to see and feel the kinds of impact not even those in a position to know might have envisioned.

One such impact must include the unprecedented outburst of heat waves and wildfires across the world during the summer of 2021, in Turkey, Greece, and North America, with wildfires in Siberia larger than in all other regions of the world combined. And probably for the first time, and for many people, global climate change had finally become real. It had finally caught on and began to leap from the pages of the IPCC AR6 2021 and prior annual reports to the world's streets, towns, cities, and countries, and onto iPhones and TV screens in a neighborhood near you.

For the first time, twenty-first century humans have begun to come to grips with real-time, full-motion video images of a world that appears to be on fire and have begun to digest what this new normal might well mean for us. For those immediately impacted, it has been anything but pleasant. Global climate change was now ready for prime time and humans, with cameras and iPhones ready, were going to record what might well turn out to be a worldwide documentary of the beginning of the end of an old normal and the start of the new—the reality of living with the effects of anthropogenic climate change as experienced by modern humans.

In describing the effects of what this new normal is going to feel like, Elizabeth Royte wrote in *National Geographic* in 2021 that it was simply becoming "Too hot to live: Millions worldwide will face unbearable temperatures," and the *Economist* in its August 28, 2021, edition added, "Climate change will alter where many crops are grown" and, in the words of Quirin Schiermeier in a July 8 article in Nature.com, "The record-breaking heatwave lasted from June 25th to July 1st, and affected large cities that rarely experience extreme heat, including Portland, Oregon; Seattle, Washington; and Vancouver, British Columbia."

More than 500 excess deaths and 180 wildfires were recorded in the western Canadian province of British Columbia. The region's peak temperature of 49.6°C, recorded on June 29 in the village of Lytton, was the highest ever reported in Canada. Lytton's inhabitants were evacuated before a devastating blaze almost completely destroyed the village. The devastating heat waves that struck parts of Canada and the United States recently would have been extremely unlikely without global warming, researchers have concluded. The chance of temperatures in the Pacific Northwest region coming close to 50°C has increased at least 150-fold since the end of the nineteenth century, according to a rapid analysis conducted in response to the heat wave.

By now it should be clear that climate change has shaped the evolution and survival of our species, is continuing to do so, and appears to act like the ultimate species survival chaperone (Layne 2019, Chapter 6). Keep in mind that all prior hominin species have gone extinct and not by choice. Human economies, societies, and civilizations, it would seem, existed only to the extent that local or global climate change permitted and nothing that we know of or have done hitherto, or have since invented, seems able to change this outcome—but if farming and fossil fuels are any indication, they may well have made the odds of survival much worse.

Even during the comparatively relative climate calm of the Holocene, when most human economies, societies, and civilizations evolved and flourished for a while, they eventually collapsed mostly due to climate change brought on by human destruction of the environment. Others, while avoiding complete collapse, have undergone severe economic, cultural and survival shocks, again due to climate change. Some, like the Mayans and the Ancestral Pueblo, dispersed, abandoning their cities and farms, and leaving deserted temples and monuments mere shadows of their former selves.

Anatomically modern humans exist today only because our hunter-gatherer forebears lived in small groups, were mobile, and were able to migrate out of Africa 70,000 years or so ago at a time of habitat loss due to climate change brought on by the last ice age, eventually migrating across the Earth. Since then, all subsequent human societies and their economies that have managed to survive have done so mainly because they did less harm to their environment, remained relatively mobile, or both, or at least were mobile enough to escape the ravages of local climate change as occurred during the summer of 2021, when droughts, floods, hurricanes, and wildfires occurred across China, Europe, North America, and Russia.

The urge to flee to safer climes to survive, to migrate from country to country, across oceans, from continent to continent across the planet, and eventually even to other habitable planets in the face of existential threats such as climate change, is a *survival trait* built into our species every bit as much as the compulsion to reproduce (Layne 2019, Chapter 11).

Modern societies, however, have become increasingly concentrated in mega-cities, and in many countries are stuffed to the hilt almost as much as the farming villages of our Neolithic Revolution ancestors. Efforts to survive won't be as easy and may well require intra-country, inter-country, inter-continental, or even global migrations to escape to parts of the planet that remain more livable. In a Proceedings of the National Academy of Sciences (PNAS) research paper first published May 4, 2020, entitled "Future of the human climate niche," the authors argue that "for most of human history, people have lived within a surprisingly narrow range of temperatures, in places where climate supported abundant food production but as the planet warms, those regions are shifting." Entire nations will lose their ability to farm grains and vegetables. Faced with starvation, those who can leave will have little other choice. But where will everyone go?

"Climate Change Will Force a New American Migration," argues Abraham Lustgarten in a Sept 15, 2020, article at Propublica.org. "Research shows that the most habitable climate niche in North America will shift northward, and the incidence of large fires will increase across the country and suggests that the climate crisis will profoundly interrupt the way we live and farm in the United States."

In the case of extreme warming, represented in the scientific literature as "Representative Concentration Pathway 8.5" (RCP 8.5), agriculture and temperate climates would be driven northward due to warming temperatures and changing rainfall patterns, even as coastlines are slowly submerged by sea-level rise and as dangerous levels of humidity swamp the Mississippi River Valley. These trends would effectively drive the habitability niche toward Canada as per Figure 5-9, leaving much of the lower half of the U.S. too hot or too dry and no longer the type of climate humans have historically lived in. Both scenarios suggest massive upheavals are in store for places where Americans currently live and grow food.

Figure 5-9. New climate maps show a transformed United States.

With extreme warming (represented as RCP 8.5), the niche moves sharply toward Canada, leaving much of the lower half of the U.S. too hot or dry for the type of climate humans historically have lived in. Both scenarios suggest massive upheavals in where Americans currently live and grow food. (Source: philstockworld.com)

According to the Rhodium Group, "The economic impact will be enormous. Rising energy costs, lower labor productivity, poor crop yields and increasing crime are among the climate-driven elements that will increasingly drag on the U.S. economy, eventually taking a financial toll that exceeds that from the Covid-19 pandemic in some regions." How much or how little benefit might those counties see, as a share of their GDP? Populous cities with expensive real estate, including Houston and Miami, will see damage tallied in the billions—losses worth several percentage points of GDP—largely driven by storms, sea-level rise, and deaths from high heat, Hannah Hess of the Rhodium Group said. "Climate will have a larger proportional impact in rural places like Gulf County, Florida, which might lose half its economy, and the human toll will likely be horrific."

Migrating to escape global or local climate change to survive is an "evolutionary survival pattern" (Layne 2019, Chapter 4) that has never been easy. It will be even less so for modern humans than it might have been for our mobile hunter-gatherer forebears because we traded our freedom and mobility to forage for farming. They needed no one's permission, nor passports, nor to be air-lifted, and were accustomed to moving at a moment's notice, carrying all their belongings, including minors, on their backs. They owned neither houses, cars, pets, nor jobs, nor did they have family and friends who weren't already members of their mobile band, or favorite neighborhood views they would have been loath to leave behind.

In the twenty-first century, migrating to escape climate change could be akin to trying to get out of Afghanistan; or escaping from the life-threatening economic deprivation or drug cartels in Central American countries; or hanging out on the coast of Calais, having spent two years trekking across the deserts of the Sahel in hope of leaving behind the drought-stricken villages of sub-Saharan Africa and finding a place in a refrigerated truck bound for the UK; or waiting to get into a smuggler's dinghy on the shores of Morocco to get across the Mediterranean Sea to Greece while aware of the risks of getting nabbed by local coast guards on either shore; or, at best, making a domestic or international house, job, or school move, with neither the reality of a real job nor the hope of relocation benefits.

It was climate change that led to the dispersal of hunter-gatherer humans across the face of the Earth; and it was climate change, again, during the Holocene that enabled the rearrangement of the economic and societal models of our hunter-gatherer forebears from foraging to farming that eventually enabled the emergence of agriculture and the rise of human civilizations. Today, it's becoming clear that climate change is again at work, globally this time, and has already begun to rearrange and redistribute human populations. The question is, how might it remake human economies, societies, and civilizations?

If the start of the Holocene accompanied by climate change in the form of rising CO_2 enabled a new economic order, a shift from foraging to farming, and a new societal order, from living in small mobile hunter-gatherer bands to densely populated, sedentary farming communities and the beginning of civilization, one need not be clairvoyant to envision how the start of the Anthropocene, also accompanied by climate change due to rising anthropogenic CO_2 forcing, can potentially offer humans a second chance to get it right. This second chance could give rise to a new economic order, one driven by population, crop, and species migration to cooler climes, marking a shift from destroying Earth-life ecosystems and biodiversity to one that can hopefully result in a new survival-driven economic order and a new civilization. But this time around, hopefully, the result will be a sustainable civilization, a change from civilization to *Ecolization* (Layne 2019, Chapter 16) because the alternative is too ghastly to contemplate.

A few pages back we wondered out loud, and later saw, what it might have been like for our hunter-gatherer forebears to simultaneously live through the Pleistocene-Holocene climate change; from a dry, arid, cold but thawing ice age, to an increasingly warm and wet world that may have facilitated the shift in their economic order from foraging to farming, as well as the change in their societal order from living in small, mobile, foraging bands, to densely populated, sedentary farm communities, sharing their living space with farm animals.

How might their experience living through those changes inform how twenty-first century humans navigate economic and societal transitions of their own, including global climate change and its potential impact on our economies, societies, and civilizations, and deadly killer pandemics such as Covid-19 that drove rapid economic and societal changes, from what was considered "normal" to a world that was going to be forever changed by the sudden outbreak of SARS-CoV-2, and the rapid spread of this mutating virus and its numerous and increasingly infectious variants—to a yet-to-be-discovered new normal.

It is important to note, however, that none of these transitions—economic, societal, and civilizational—that confronted our hunter-gatherer forebears and may have led to the dawn of human civilization, nor those confronting humans today in the twenty-first century, were planned or engineered economic or societal policy choices, nor were they the result of human ingenuity or innovation. Instead, they occurred in spite of any preferences either generation, theirs or ours, might have had, and were initiated if not orchestrated by climate change. And, while our foraging forebears might have done nothing to initiate the CO_2-driven warming that jump-started the climate change that drove the Pleistocene-Holocene transition, the emergence of agriculture, and the dawn of human civilization, modern humans have done and continue to do everything to drive the Earth-system from that near-steady-state climate regime of the Holocene to a potential increasingly hothouse Earth.

Both the hunter-gatherer and the modern human economies, societies, and civilizations seemed to be set on autopilot during most of the Holocene, with Earth's climate controls seemingly also set within that limited but habitable range, until, that is, modern humans discovered the industrial fossil fuel energy switch and its resulting CO_2; and they haven't stopped pressing it since the mid-eighteenth century. Humans may well now own the consequences, though apparently not the controls, of global climate change and the economic, societal, and civilizational consequences the world has just started to experience but has yet to endure. Similarly, it is important to note that prior to its encounter with humans, the SARS-CoV-2 virus existed in host animals (maybe bats?) and might only have exploded into a global pandemic because humans once again discovered and manipulated another of the planet's controls. This time, it might have decided to add a touch of variety to the wildlife selection on the menu or as another wildlife trade item at the Hunan wet market.

How interesting and yet how sad that modern humans still have not learned the pre-agriculture hunter-gatherer economics or the lessons from the failures of Neolithic Revolution humans' economies! It was animal domestication and husbandry that gave rise to the first zoonotic diseases that in turn led to numerous human diseases and pandemics, and it is once again the human desire to plunder what little wildlife remains that was appropriately rebuked by nature in the form of the SARS-CoV-2 virus and its variants.

In either case there is at least one lesson in economic production that post-Neolithic-Revolution humans failed to learn from their hunter-gatherer forebears, and as a result, nearly all their economies and civilizations have collapsed. Modern humans have also adopted this collapse-prone economic production approach and might well be headed for collapse, but we might yet have time to course-correct and learn how to eke out a *living within* Earth-life ecosystems in harmony with its biodiversity (as opposed to living *outside* and destroying them).

Living within is the method of economic production within Earth-life ecosystems that our hunter-gatherer forebears practiced for 290,000 years. *Living without* encompasses methods of economic production that operate outside of the processes of Earth-life ecosystems that Neolithic Revolution humans started when they chose to become farmers and adopted agriculture that, by default, requires the disruption and often destruction of Earth-life ecosystems. And as noted in an earlier chapter, by adopting farming and agriculture, humans had essentially declared war on nature and its ecosystems—a war that all humans have been fighting and losing, not just in the last 20 years as the Americans did in Afghanistan, but for most of the 10,000-plus years since Neolithic Revolution humans chose to farm rather than forage.

Prior human economic and societal behavior and activity have, apparently, tripped Earth-life "circuit breakers," so to speak, but the simultaneous occurrence of global climate change as well as a zoonotic-based pandemic is not only unusual but should be seen as two more such circuit breakers popping—but not just any two. Either one of these, a pandemic or climate change, has demonstrated in the past that it could derail even the best-run economy and society and has brought more than a few to an end.

The fact that these alarms are not only flashing simultaneously but announce identical lessons across two very different natural channels, global climate change and evolutionary biology, implies a level of urgency and intensity not hitherto seen. They are now converging at the juncture where global climate change and the Covid-19 pandemic intersect—human survival as embodied in their societies and their economies. And is it pure coincidence that both require a reduction in human economic activity to mount an effective response—a reduction of economic production activity driven by CO_2, on the one hand, and the collapse of industries that require close human interaction to avoid the spread of infection, on the other? But are humans hearing these alarms?

How differently might humans rally and respond if global climate change and the Covid-19 pandemic were seen as extraterrestrial attacks against Earth-life, comprising strike one and strike two with a third, even more ominous strike, seemingly yet to come? The first strike appears to target Earth-life ecosystems, our environment, and atmosphere, while the second has already wiped out much of Earth-life's biodiversity. And what if those recent scorching heat waves were perceived as a possible third strike—seemingly emanating from an invisible Dyson sphere orbiting near enough to the sun to concentrate some of its heat on parts of the Earth's surface? While this might well be the sort of science fiction some might envision, fortunately or unfortunately, none of this is science fiction but is all too real and the aliens attacking Earth are no less than surplus-crazed humans from the twenty-first century.

The takeaway from global climate change is really quite simple. Well, it's not, you say, yet in a manner of speaking it is. It is a lesson all prior human economies, societies, and civilizations that have collapsed to date have ignored or never learned—the need to return to preserving nature's assets, by sharing rather than surplus hoarding, while simultaneously eking out a living from *within* Earth-life ecosystems and in harmony with its biodiversity, as our hunter-gatherer forebears had done. But to many twenty-first century humans such an economic system and human society would seem unsustainable if not unrealistic, and most of us can't begin to imagine how one could possibly build a human economy, let alone a civilization, that way.

Yet, if the longevity of a human economy, society, or civilization is a measure of its success, then those built by our hunter-gatherer forebears who lasted 97 percent of the last 300,000 years of our species' existence must have been doing something post-Neolithic Revolution humans, including those living today, have long forgotten or never bothered to learn. Theirs was obviously a better way if only because they survived—over, and over, and over again. If we humans today have become so much smarter, why isn't anyone giving the hunter-gatherer method a try? Here is a hint—it does not generate surplus profit and GDP growth.

Hunter-gatherers didn't hunt and gather to accumulate surplus but to obtain enough to eat and freely share with others to survive. Living as they did within the seeming limits of Earth-life ecosystems would have steered humans away from surplus, rapid population growth and the civilizations these together enabled but which today are causing our economy to exceed the Earth's carrying capacity. Foraging wild animals and plant species while living in small mobile communities rather than in crowded, sedentary, agricultural villages with domesticated farm animals would have preserved Earth-life ecosystems and biodiversity and saved humans from a world of hurt that emanated from its civilizations and from zoonoses and would have preserved innumerable biodiversity species from extinction.

Living in those smaller mobile human communities, without the need for a source of energy beyond what was available in Earth-life ecosystems, prevented the turn to fossil fuels. The journey from foraging to farming to fossil fuels, with the former occurring 12,000 or so years ago and industrial use of the latter just in the last three centuries, tells the story.

How different would our world have been if neither farming nor the adoption of fossil fuels had happened? Will human survival require the abandonment of farming and fossil fuels? Like that hole in the ozone layer, the use of fossil fuels as an energy source must end, and since much of modern industrialized agriculture is powered by petroleum—and, in addition, the amount of fertile soil is likely going to decline significantly—global climate change, it would seem, is already hinting at that answer.

Earlier, when we looked for clues about how twenty-first century humans might navigate global climate change and the potential impact it might have on our economies, societies, and civilization, we looked at how our hunter-gatherer forebears simultaneously lived through the Pleistocene-Holocene climate change and its associated economic and societal changes as it transitioned from small mobile foraging bands to often large, packed, sedentary, agricultural communities. One thing they did not have to deal with was a simultaneous zoonotic-based pandemic and that's because they did none of what humans do today that engender zoonotic diseases and pandemics. It is worth noting that almost 100 percent of pandemics (for example, influenza, SARS, and Covid-19) have been caused by zoonoses.

Pre-Neolithic humans neither domesticated wild species, nor destroyed wildlife habitats via land grabs, nor cleared mega-hectares of forest for agriculture, nor traded in wildlife, nor displaced biodiversity with whom they shared ecosystems. But while they would not have been able to teach us how to deal with a deadly killer pandemic such as Covid-19, which drove rapid economic and societal changes and might well rearrange our world from a pre- to a possible post-Covid-19 reality, they do have a lot to teach us about how not to start a pandemic in the first place.

Zoonotic pandemics have their origins in diverse microbes carried by animal reservoirs, but their emergence is entirely driven by human activities. The most important reservoirs of pathogens with pandemic potential are mammals (in particular bats, rodents, and primates) and some birds (especially water birds), as well as livestock (for example, pigs, camels, and poultry). *The underlying causes of pandemics are the same global environmental changes that drive biodiversity loss and climate change.* They include land-use change, agricultural expansion and intensification, and wildlife trade and consumption. These are human activities that bring wildlife, livestock, and people into closer contact, allowing animal microbes to move into people and lead to infections, sometimes outbreaks, and more rarely into true pandemics that spread through road networks, urban centers and global travel and trade routes, according to an IPBES workshop report on biodiversity and pandemics.

According to this report, the risk of pandemics is increasing rapidly, with more than five new diseases emerging in people every year, any one of which has the potential to spread and become a pandemic. An estimated 1.7 million currently undiscovered viruses are thought to exist in mammal and avian hosts. Of these, 631,000-827,000 could have the ability to infect humans. The majority (70 percent) of emerging diseases (for example, Ebola, Zika, Nipah encephalitis), and almost all known pandemics (for example, influenza, HIV/AIDS, Covid-19) are zoonoses—i.e., are caused by microbes of animal origin. These microbes "spill over" due to contact among wildlife, livestock, and people.

The lesson humans might learn from Covid-19 and its increasingly lethal and contagious variants is also very clear and is not unlike what was observed when examining global climate change. Here, too, none is safe unless all are safe. It strikes at the very heart of a wildly uneven, discriminatory world economic system, whose tendency is to take care of those with surplus—the wealthy and the 1 percent—at the expense of the rest, as exemplified by the 2021 global vaccine distribution strategy shown in Table 5-3. The priority, in contrast, remains the same as that for global climate change and appears to be *survival*: the survival of Earth-life species, both human and biodiversity, and of Earth-life ecosystems. To survive, humans must make these elements—not economic surplus—its economic, societal, and civilizational priorities.

Table 5-3. List of epidemics and pandemics with at least one million deaths

Rank	Epidemics/ pandemics	Disease	Death toll	Global population lost	Regional population lost	Date	Location
1	Black Death	Bubonic plague	75–200 million	17–54%[Note 1]	30–60% of European population[4]	1346–1353	Europe, Asia, and North Africa
2	Spanish flu	Influenza A/H1N1	17–100 million	1–5.4%[5][6]	–	1918–1920	Worldwide
3	Plague of Justinian	Bubonic plague	15–100 million	7–56%[Note 1]	25–60% of European population[7]	541–549	Europe and West Asia
4	HIV/AIDS pandemic	HIV/AIDS	36.3 million (as of 2020)	[Note 2]	–	1981–present	Worldwide
5	Third plague pandemic	Bubonic Plague	12–15 million	[Note 2]	–	1855-1960	Worldwide
6	Cocoliztli epidemic of 1545–1548	Cocoliztli	5–15 million	1–3%[Note 1]	27–80% of Mexican population[8]	1545–1548	Mexico
7	Antonine Plague	Smallpox or measles	5–10 million	3–6%[3]	25–33% of Roman population[9]	165–180 (possibly up to 190)	Roman Empire
8	COVID-19 pandemic	COVID-19	4.6–10.2+ million (as of 11 September 2021)[Note 3]	0.06%–0.13% (estimated)[2]	–	2019[Note 4]–present	Worldwide

(Source: Wikipedia)

Prior pandemics (some shown in Table 5.3) have changed the trajectory of economies, societies, and the world. In general, as accounts of these have shown, economic life, societal life, or civilizations rarely go back to what they had been before a pandemic, and the changes that occurred because of Covid-19 also seem likely to be lasting and affect most areas of life.

From the very term Covid-19—the name the World Health Organization officially gave the disease on Feb. 11, 2020—renewed vocabulary emerged including the need to *"social distance,"* or stay six feet apart, so that we could *"flatten the curve,"* or slow the disease's spread and reduce the burden on the healthcare system.

Even epidemiological terms like the *"basic reproduction number"* (R0, pronounced R-naught), or the average number of people who catch the virus from a single infected person, quickly became required knowledge to follow official reports about the likelihood and rate of spread of the infection. Soon wardrobe changes began to appear, including the use of voluntary and mandated facial masks that, along with new nRNA vaccines—which turned out to be very effective in preventing serious illness and/or death—soon deteriorated into cultural wars, fake news, and the denial of science, dividing the U.S. by red and blue states, and perhaps forever changing the political landscape and marking the beginning of a "new normal."

School closures soon became part of this "new normal" and the cultural/political wars it provoked, as many schools across the U.S. and the world made the decision to close in 2020, and some through the beginning of the 2021 school year. Many would go on, but not without a fight in school boards and parent-teacher meetings focused on whether to require mandatory vaccination (once vaccines were approved) and facial masks of all school personnel, including teachers and children.

Soon the economy began to feel the impact as the pandemic forced individuals and businesses around the world to close, or where possible, to shift to working remotely to reduce the spread of the disease. This severely impacted businesses (restaurants, travel, tourism, and similar service industries) that require in-person customer presence, resulting in thousands of such businesses being unable to survive the Covid-19 pandemic despite state and federal support.

Business and office shutdowns in turn enabled the rise of multiple technologies, including telemedicine, and application services based on internet technologies such as Zoom, Skype, Slack, Microsoft Office Suite, and G-Suite, applications that enable remote communications and work, and may well have set the stage for a major transition in how, when, and where people work. Employers soon discovered that it was possible to run their businesses using employees working from home, and employees, too, confirmed what they always knew: that it was less stressful, less costly, and more convenient to manage and homeschool children while working from home. This transition forced companies to reevaluate their long-term office space and staffing needs, sending ripple effects across the office space real estate market.

But the pandemic laid bare numerous weaknesses across the "human-infrastructure" and social safety nets and led to action in the U.S. and other countries to address the gaps that were exposed including:

- Unemployment Insurance and Other Employee Protections.
- Added protections for gig and contract workers, with potential for adding to the safety net for these increasingly indispensable workers.
- Expansion of the child tax credit and family leave policies and a national paid family leave policy.
- A partial attempt at a Universal Basic Income. Economists credit the three rounds of direct stimulus payments authorized by Congress during the pandemic with sustaining elevated economic activity during the pandemic-induced recession and, along with concerted action by the Federal Reserve Bank of the United States, preventing a full-blown financial crisis. Many other countries implemented similar safety-net policies.

It has always been hard to truly grasp the horrors of living through prior pandemics, and while each has been different, nothing gives one that up-close and personal experience as actually living through Covid-19, which sent millions to the grave. Covid's death toll overwhelms the imagination, but even more stunning has been the deadly efficiency with which Black,

Latino, and American Indian and Alaska Native people in their 30s, 40s, and 50s seem targeted, even as it marked yet another grim milestone: At least one in 500 Americans died in this pandemic.

But an even more grim milestone had been reached when in a human economy and society humans were willing to callously trade the lives of other humans to score political points—as twice as many may have died in red (Republican leaning) states, as in "blue" (Democratic leaning) states (so called) due to undervaccination, according to the CDC statistics in Figure 5-10. In this new normal it's not just "your money or your life" but "your politics or where you live" that can prove deadly.

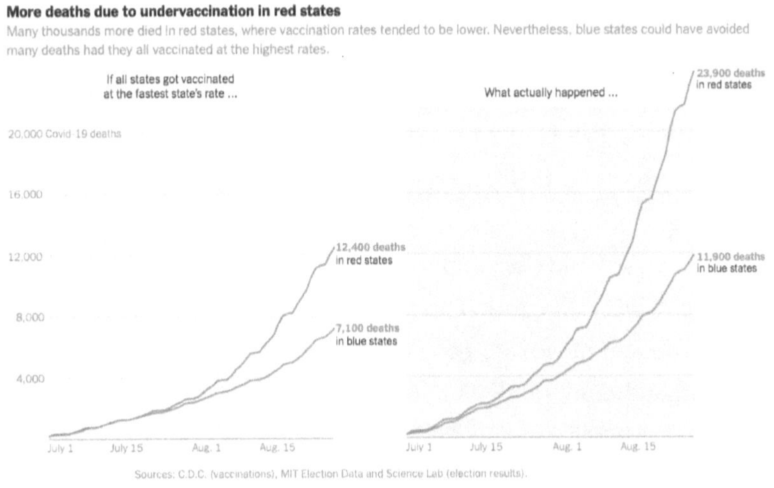

Figure 5-10. More deaths due to undervaccination in red states.

And while there is much to learn, there is probably little value in a historical recap of how prior pandemics have similarly savaged humans except to explore what has been done to prevent a reoccurrence, even if it were to take yet another hundred years before the next one occurs. And here is why—it wouldn't take that long, because pandemic frequency is increasing. At least six pandemics have occurred since the Great Influenza pandemic of 1918—three caused by influenza viruses, and HIV/AIDS, SARS, and

Covid-19. Yet, notwithstanding the huge loss of life, finding the cause and cure or discovering how to prevent pandemics has not turned out to be the human priority one would think it should be—but why?

The answer to this question not only explains why preventing pandemics has not been the moonshot it should have been, but it also answers an even larger question: Why are twenty-first century humans being confronted simultaneously with global climate change that, unlike a pandemic, can wipe out not only another few hundred million people, but potentially the entire human species? How are pandemics and global climate change related? Are they related? The fact that they occurred simultaneously hints at a relationship.

The fundamental underlying causes of pandemics are the same global environmental changes that drive biodiversity loss and climate change. While, as noted, pandemics have their origins in diverse microbes carried by animal reservoirs, their emergence is entirely driven by human activities such as land-use change, agricultural expansion and intensification, and wildlife trade and consumption. It is these human economic activities that bring wildlife, livestock, and people into closer contact, allowing animal microbes to move into people and lead to infections, sometimes to outbreaks, and more rarely to true pandemics that spread through road networks, urban centers, and global travel and trade routes. But why, you ask? Why have humans not taken action to end the ecosystem destruction, wildlife trade and consumption, and biodiversity extinction that result in widespread human death—to end these drivers of pandemics and global climate change and its potential for human extinction?

The short answer is the desire to accumulate *surplus*. Known today as profit, surplus drives the pursuit of wealth and endless economic growth as measured by GDP. When it comes down to a choice between making and keeping that money versus using it to save other people's lives, unlike those hunters in hunter-gatherer communities that allowed their kill to be shared with all in the community, humans today have consistently chosen hoarding over sharing, and money over life. This is an economic and societal change that took hold when Neolithic Revolution humans gave up foraging and sharing for farming and hoarding, opting to domesticate animals and practice agriculture and animal husbandry as their preferred method of economic production.

Figure 5-11. Wildlife Trade. Stop Wildlife Trade, Stop Wildlife Consumption, and Stop Destroying Nature, and We Will Stop Pandemics.
(Source: SCIENTIFIC AMERICAN)

Nearly 10,000 years ago, humans began razing forests; ploughing, irrigating, and fertilizing fields for crops; and destroying in the process Earth-life ecosystems, the soil and water table, to make room for agriculture, while domesticating Earth-life species and destroying its biodiversity. From that time forward humans began to abandon that foraging and sharing culture our pre-agriculture hunter-gatherer forebears practiced. Post-Neolithic humans rejected the method of economic production and a society that prioritized sharing what they foraged with all in their group rather than hoarding and accumulating a surplus; an economic system that prioritized the survival and the well-being of humans, Earth-life ecosystems, and its biodiversity, over surplus and the accumulation of wealth, one that as a result survived for most of human existence while all that arose thereafter collapsed.

In contrast, our twenty-first century capitalist economic system prioritizes profits over people; accumulation of wealth over human well-being; and endless GDP growth over preserving Earth-life ecosystems and biodiversity. According to the IPBES report "Escaping the 'Era of Pandemics'," the value of international *legal* wildlife trade in 2019 exceeded US$107 billion, a 500 percent increase in the last 15 years (since 2005), and 2,000 percent since the 1980s. In addition, the annual value of the world's *illegal* wildlife trade currently ranges from $7 billion to $23 billion.

This fight to stop wildlife consumption and trade that's driving pandemics and to stop ecosystem destruction and biodiversity extinction that drives global warming and among other things, threatens the human food chain, is essentially a proxy fight for human life and the survival of our species. It's a fight to value life and survival over profits, wealth accumulation, and GDP growth, a fight for humans to return to that sustainable economic system of their pre-agriculture hunter-gatherer forebears that prioritized Earth-life ecosystems and species life and survival over the surplus and profits that drives pandemics and global climate change.

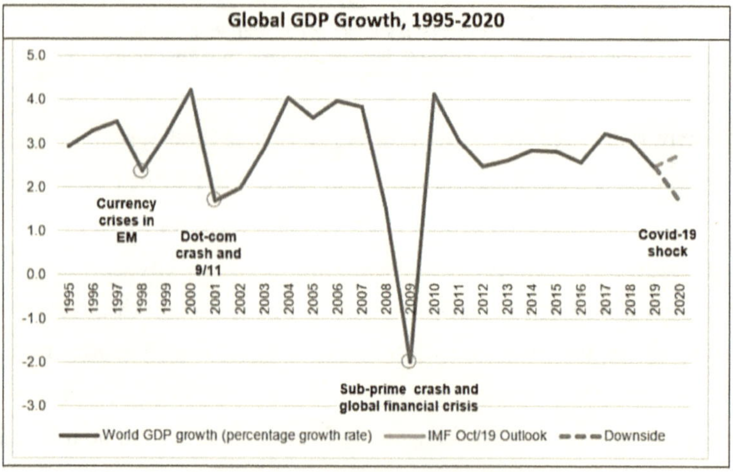

Figure 5-12. Global GDP growth, 1995-2020.
(source UNCTAD.org)

When modern humans talk about the economic impact of Covid-19, despite the feigned moaning and groaning, it's not so much the loss of human lives that seems to matter most but the fall in global GDP (Figure 5-12). In fact, for a while it was easier to get reasonable GDP estimates than even a remotely accurate count of lives lost due to Covid-19.

Although the official number of deaths caused by Covid-19 was estimated at 7.05 million people (as of April 2024), *The Economist*'s single best estimate is that the actual toll at that time was about 15.3 million, and that there was a 95 percent chance that the true value at that time may have been between 9.4 million and 18.2 million additional deaths. If worldwide news and images of the innumerable deceased—unceremoniously stacked and carted off in refrigerated trucks, or, even while dead, still queuing and waiting to be hurriedly buried—is any indication, it becomes simultaneously sad and clear that human death, as in life, is now accorded less ceremony than that given at the end of so-called "legal persons" that produce surplus. Our true humanity is best seen in our humane treatment of the deceased who can no longer attend to themselves and must always depend on the humanity of those who bid them adieu.

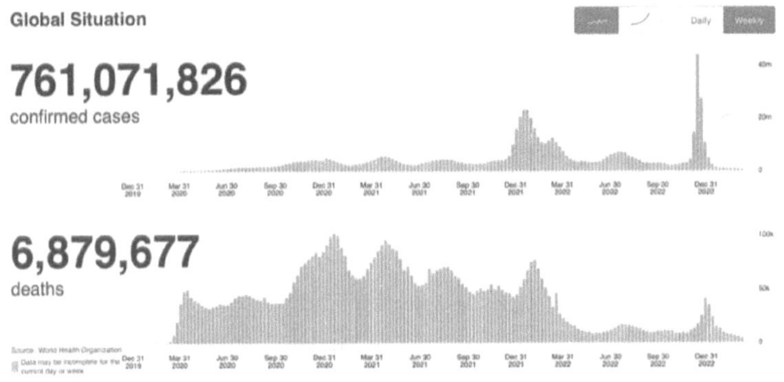

Figure 5-13. WHO Coronavirus (Covid-19) Dashboard.

Globally, as of 6:06pm CET, 21 March 2023, there had been 761,071,826 confirmed cases of Covid-19, including 6,879,677 deaths reported to WHO. As of 18 March 2023, a total of 13,244,177,602 vaccine doses have been administered. (Source: WHO)

The panic of Covid-19 has receded into the rearview mirror, but the statistics in the WHO Coronavirus (Covid-19) Dashboard (Figure 5-13), remind us of its grim toll. And while the number of cases and deaths has fallen substantially, the disease has by no means disappeared.

In this chapter we focused on human economies and societies and their transitions and the impact these have had on humanity and Earth-life ecosystem and biodiversity well-being and survival from the dawn of human existence. And while there have been numerous other transitions, the focus in this chapter has been limited to those economic and societal transitions that have had the potential to end human existence as a species. We listed these as follows:

- The transition from eking out a living by foraging wild animals and plant species—the only method of economic production practiced by humans for all but the last 10,000-12,000 years of our species' 300,000 years of existence—to farming, animal husbandry, and domesticated plant and animal species.
- The shift from living in small, mobile groups with little to no ecosystem and biodiversity impact to compact, sedentary, increasingly populated agricultural communities, villages, towns, and cities with increasing massive negative ecosystem and biodiversity impact.
- The transformation from sharing in open and egalitarian societies, where human relationships took precedence, to enclosed farms with little to no sharing, where ownership and property rights replaced or superseded mandatory sharing and human relationships.
- The abandonment of living in largely mobile, numerically small, and mostly fixed groups able to migrate to escape the effects of climate change and other natural disasters, in favor of increasingly large, numerically growing populations that became villages, towns, and cities, that were more vulnerable to climate change and environmental disasters.

It was those small, mobile, foraging, hunter-gatherer economies and egalitarian societies that survived for most of our species' existence and that ensured the well-being and survival of Earth-life ecosystems and biodiversity during all those millennia of their existence. By contrast, it was the sedentary, large, numerically growing populations of agricultural and animal husbandry communities that kept growing, dismembering Earth-life ecosystems, and destroying its biodiversity in order to grow, and from whence human civilization arose, that invariably collapsed after just a few thousand years, and largely because of what the World Economic Forum described as being the greatest risks confronting humans in the next ten years (Figure 5-14).

According to the World Economic Forum (Weforum.org), of the top five risks that will have the biggest impact in the next ten years (Figure 5-14), four—extreme weather, climate change, natural disasters, and water crises—are simply and sadly the consequences of human efforts to make a living, the economic production approach humans chose nearly 12,000 years ago when humanity abandoned foraging for farming and the consequent destruction of Earth-life ecosystems and biodiversity extinction that has caused. These five risks, shown below, and others like them, though important, are but twenty-first century derivatives of the main existential risk humanity faces. But to understand this risk, one must recap the foundations of what constitutes an economy.

Economies emerge because of the lifeways of species as they go about the tasks of making a living within Earth's habitats and ecosystems in harmony with its biodiversity. For economies to exist, life must first exist, and for life to exist, there must first be supportive habitats and ecosystems in which life evolves and survives. All three components must coexist for life itself to exist. Without Earth's ecosystems and habitats remaining intact, there will be no survival, and without survival, there will be no life, and without life, there can be neither human economies nor societies. Human economies must be thought of then as the third in that trio of interdependent components that comprise *the survival-driven triad of life*.

To assess the impact any activity might have on human economies, societies, or life itself, one must understand this trio of interdependent components that comprise the *survival-driven* triad of life—with the key phrase here being *survival-driven. Human economies fail because they are surplus-driven and because they operate outside of Earth-life ecosystem processes*. Earth-life species economies, like prior hunter-gatherer economies, succeeded because they were *survival-driven and operated inside Earth-life ecosystem processes.*

Their goal and outcome, it would seem, was to ensure the survival of all Earth-life species—not endless profit (surplus), wealth accumulation, and GDP growth. And as long as humans, their economies, and societies remain *surplus-driven,* rather than *survival-driven,* they will continue to collapse and potentially make extinction a possibility—*that's the real existential risk humanity faces and one nobody, not even the World Economic Forum, seems willing to name.*

Global Risks Report — The 5 risks that will have the biggest impact in the next 10 years

	rank
Weapons of mass destruction	1
Extreme weather events	2
Natural disasters	3
Failure of climate change mitigation & adaptation	4
Water crises	5

Source: Global Risks Perception Survey 2017-2018, World Economic Forum

Figure 5-14. The five risks that will have the biggest impact in the next ten years.

Surplus-driven economies, societies, and civilizations are the reason pandemics like Covid-19 exist, the reason global climate change exists, and the reason we face threats from weapons of mass destruction, world hunger, homelessness, slavery, human trafficking, and the innumerable ills that plague modern human societies, economies, and civilizations. Pursuit of surplus is what drove the tobacco industry, the oil industry, and every other human industry whose goal is to make a profit and grow shareholder wealth, and what led them to engage in deceptive practices and embark on false advertising and other means to defraud their fellow humans even when doing so was known to cost lives and could potentially have driven the extinction of our species.

If humans can get rid of that desire for surplus (profit, wealth, call it whatever you like) we might just stand a chance of rediscovering that original sharing economy that emerged as our pre-agriculture hunter-gatherer forebears foraged and shared, rather than farmed and hoarded, for a living.

The world was amazed when President Xi Jinping, unexpectedly, began emphasizing the idea of "common prosperity" over corporate profits as the country tried to address its growing "wealth gap," urging private education companies to become nonprofits while pushing other tech players to boost pay for low-skill workers—imagine that! And indeed, China, like the rest of the world, is not without its own set of economic and humanitarian issues. But, without seeming to take any geoeconomic or geopolitical stance, wouldn't it be wonderful if all countries of the G8 or G20, or all member countries of the U.N. were to begin adopting *survival-driven* economic policies?

President Biden, for example, might well have had an easier time getting corporations to pay their fair share of taxes (15 percent minimum was finally approved), securing that paltry $15 per hour minimum wage hike, or winning approval for his human infrastructure bills, as well as significant climate change funding. When it comes to human survival, the health of Earth-life ecosystems, and biodiversity preservation, the only economic policies that will ultimately matter are the *survival-driven economic goal and outcome upon which the first human economies, pre-agriculture hunter-gatherer waterhole economies, were built.*

Humans must eat to live, and our efforts to eke out a living are what comprise our economies. Human economies and human survival are therefore inseparable—one cannot exist without the other. Anything that can kill enough humans will eventually kill human economies, and vice versa, as Covid-19 has demonstrated. Global climate change, on the other hand, has demonstrated its ability to kill both humans and human economies. So, what are the things in our economies, societies, and civilization that enable pandemics and global climate change? And what's driving them? Humans know what needs to be done to stop both. But will we?

If *Homo sapiens'* survival were to come down to modern humans' willingness to abandon their post-Neolithic Revolution surplus-driven economic and societal policies, what chance do you think humans will have of survival? Would humans be willing to leave all remaining fossil fuels in the ground? Because that's what it will require. Will humans choose to stop destroying forests, the lungs of the Earth, and other Earth-life ecosystems and biodiversity through the production of palm oil and the mining of minerals and other natural and mineral resources? It may come down to this, too. Are we willing to reduce livestock husbandry and their discharge and agricultural runoff that's polluting Earth's water sources and oceans, creating dead zones, killing marine life, and putting at risk the millions whose livelihoods depend on seafood? We probably must do this as well.

Can we change to sustainable agriculture (if there can be such a thing)? And can we stop choking the planet with plastic and now Covid-19-related waste? Can we . . . ??? I think you know what some of the other questions are and you probably have some of your own, and the answers as well. But who gets to decide whether we do or we don't? And that's why the top five global risks listed by the World Economic Forum miss the mark.

Human economies, then, and legal-person economies in particular, have become the number one risk or threat to human life and survival. They have already demonstrated, during the preceding 400 generations, that they—more than weapons of mass destruction, extreme weather events, natural disasters, failure of climate change mitigation and adaptation, or water crises—are capable of driving human societies and civilization to collapse. As ominous and threatening to our survival as these might have been and still are, they are but a consequence of the socioeconomic surplus-driven choices humans have been making since the Neolithic Revolution. The real threat is that choice Neolithic Revolution humans made, and modern humans have since continued to make: to eke out a living *outside* ecosystems, and out of harmony with its biodiversity. That's what poses the greatest threat to human life and survival.

As we have seen, our pre-agriculture hunter-gatherer forebears have also endured global climate change during the Pleistocene-Holocene transition. They may not have had weapons of mass destruction, but they lived and survived megafauna-sized predators capable of mass destruction. They also faced numerous natural disasters as the ice age was coming to an end, as well as Pleistocene extreme weather events that drove at least five other hominin species to extinction. They also faced water crises such as modern humans have yet to face, though of a different kind, as valleys and plains in which they foraged became lakes and raging torrents as the ice melted and gave way to rising sea level and floods. Moreover, while they had no climate change mitigation and adaptation capabilities, they had something even better—they were mobile and were able to migrate to safer climes. But, alas, unlike modern humans, none of the troubles they endured were of their own making.

The problems modern humans confront today, and will confront tomorrow, are unlike those our hunter-gatherer forebears confronted and survived, and are due entirely to the way we have chosen to build our economies—*outside* Earth-life ecosystems and at war with its biodiversity. We have become so addicted to the surplus, profit making, wealth accumulation, and GDP growth we glean from eking out a living *outside* Earth-life ecosystems and thereby destroying those ecosystems and its biodiversity that we are unable to see the real reason for our plight.

Humans must give up our *surplus-driven* socioeconomic lifeways to enable ecosystem and biodiversity survival—a prerequisite to human survival.

Recall the *Evolutionary Triad of Life*. Without ecosystems and biodiversity remaining intact, there will be no survival, and without their survival there can be no life, and without life to eke out a living there can be no human economies—it's indeed really that simple.

6.

From Modern Human Economies to Legal-Person Economies

FROM HUMAN ECONOMIES THAT ENABLED LIFE AND SURVIVAL TO LEGAL-PERSON ECONOMIES THAT'S DRIVING GROWTH, ECONOMIC AND SOCIETAL COLLAPSE

> *"Economists forgot that the only legitimate purpose of an economy is to support households in making a living—not corporations in making a killing..."*
>
> *"Corporations have emerged as the dominant governance institutions on Earth, with the largest among them reaching into virtually every country of the world and exceeding most governments in size and power. Increasingly, it is the corporate interest rather than the human interest that defines the policy agendas of states and international bodies."*
>
> *—David C. Korten*

IT WAS ONLY RELATIVELY RECENTLY THAT HUMANS realized the pre-agriculture hunter-gatherer lifeways of making a living our forebears practiced for all but the last 12,000 years was not as bad as Thomas Hobbes (1650) and others like E.R. Service (1966) claimed—in Hobbes' case, that "Life before civilization was 'solitary, poor, nasty, brutal and short!"—but rather, was comparably better than that of many modern humans and may even have been affluent—according to James Suzman, in his book *Affluence Without Abundance: What We Can Learn from the World's Most Successful Civilisation*. But how could he know?

To know what it is like to live as people lived for most of human history, one would have had to live among them. And indeed, Suzman spent more than twenty years living among the Bushmen of the Kalahari, in southwest Africa. The San and the Khoekhoe peoples are aboriginal to southern Africa and are descendants of the first people who ever lived there. Archaeologists tend to agree that the San are the descendants of the original *Homo sapiens* (anatomically modern humans) who occupied South Africa for at least 150,000 years.

According to "A History of San People of South Africa," "Geneticists say that the oldest gene pattern amongst modern humans is that of the Khoe-San. It dates back to about 80,000 years ago. All other peoples on the planet—Europeans, Black Africans, Asians, North and South Americans, and Australians—are all descendants of this original gene type. The only possible exception is that of the Hadzabe hunter-gatherers of Tanzania who split off very early from the Khoe-San."

Nevertheless, until the 1960s, according to Svizzero et al., 2014, in "Hunter-Gatherer Societies: Their Diversity and Evolutionary Processes," hunter-gatherer societies were mainly seen from Hobbes' perspective and this vision was also adopted by other authors, the most famous among whom was E.R. Service. People were seen as poor. They roamed all the time to get food. Their deficient hunting and gathering technology resulted in low productivity, constrained them to a nomadic way of life to avoid starvation, and resulted in a method of food procurement that provided no surplus. As nomads, they couldn't have more than one child per family every four or five years and that resulted in a low population density which they organized in small egalitarian groups or bands consisting of at most 100 people.

Until the 1960s, Svizzero continues, most people agreed with this vision for many reasons. The main one probably was that it helped to reinforce the view that the Neolithic Revolution brought about a shift from societies of pre-agriculture hunter-gatherers (or primitive savages) to superior ones involving civilized agro-pastoralists, the type of societies in which these views were being propagated. It provided a basis for feelings of superiority of those agriculturally based commercial societies that had evolved in the seventeenth through the nineteenth centuries in Europe and developed further with the advent of the Industrial Revolution.

During the eighteenth and nineteenth centuries, many famous authors, economists (Turgot, 1750; Smith per Meek et al., 1978) and anthropologists (Morgan, 1877), adopted this vision to describe the evolution of human societies. For instance, Adam Smith (1776; Meek et al., 1978; and Turgot, 1750) described the economic development of human societies as a sequence of four stages: the age of hunting and gathering, of pastoralism, of agriculture, and finally of commerce, the latter involving among other things foreign trade and manufacturing.

For Hobbes, in the first type of human society laid out by Smith (that of hunter-gatherers), humans are little more than animals. Their only objective is to get food and to have children; the cultural dimension of human life is missing. Since they are not able to domesticate plants or animals, hunter-gatherers are dependent on the whims of nature. In other words, the survival of hunter-gatherers depended completely on the state of their natural environments. But had Hobbes, and others, lived long enough to attend the 2021 COP26 in Glasgow, they would no doubt have gotten a first-hand demonstration of just how those hunter-gatherers' progeny's survival, advanced modern human survival, is similarly completely dependent on the state of their natural environments.

Clearly, then, by choosing (and it must have been by choice—surviving hunter-gathers still make a living pretty much the same way) to remain completely dependent on Earth-life's ecosystems and biodiversity to survive, those hunter-gatherers recognized what Neolithic humans wouldn't, what those scientists and economists didn't, and what most modern humans to this day seemingly still miss—that all Earth-life species' survival would depend upon how they would treat Earth-life ecosystems and biodiversity.

One can't help but be amazed, though, at how Hobbes, Service, Smith, and others could have arrived at the conclusions they did about pre-agriculture hunter-gatherer economies and their societies. Why would they not have considered that, despite how comparably deficient those societies and economies might have seemed, those noble savages and their ilk, as they were viewed, must have been doing a few things right if, notwithstanding their seemingly obvious and numerous deficiencies, they yet somehow managed to survive for hundreds of millennia while most subsequent, comparatively advanced post-Neolithic Revolution societies and economies hardly lasted 400 generations? Asking and seeking an answer to this single question, if nothing else, might have led them and the world to an entirely different understanding about how human societies and economies should go about eking out a living within Earth-life ecosystems and biodiversity, so that, like their hunter-gatherer forebears, they too might survive.

Considering the available facts, could one have come to a somewhat different conclusion? Here were a people, "animals" as Hobbes preferred, whose ancestry likely went back to at least *Homo erectus*, believed to have existed 1.8 million to 300,000 years ago, about the time humans are thought to have emerged. Their ancient societies and economies likely practiced this hunter-gatherer subsistence economic model for all that time and without collapse. They survived to become forebears of anatomically modern humans—including Hobbes and friends.

Being animals was hardly a disadvantage as indeed humans are animals. But not even in the pejorative sense that Hobbes might have meant were they enabled to recognize that indeed humans were the only animals that had a problem with being, well, animals. It won't have taken a lot of science and economics to recognize that, besides being animals, there was indeed something very different about those pre-agriculture hunter-gatherer societies and their subsistence economies worthy of the best investigative scientific and economic minds.

Like all Earth-life terrestrial species, humans were indeed animals. They, too, were mobile and migrated (nomads), they hunted and gathered food, and, like most animals, they maintained no surplus but shared rather than hoarded to accumulate wealth. They developed neither spectacular "technologies" nor sought to domesticate, own, modify, or control Earth-life ecosystems and biodiversity. Accordingly, they confined their food sources to wild plants and animals and produced no food but depended entirely on Earth-life ecosystem products, services, and biodiversity from whence to eke out a living to survive. The fact that they had far, far, fewer offspring (low-density populations) and lived in small mobile bands compared to crowded, sedentary, Neolithic agrarian communities, enabled their survival for millennia, as these characteristics also redounded to the endurance of Earth-life ecosystems and biodiversity from whence they derived their food and shelter.

Indeed, all the components these scientists and economists were seeking as hallmarks of an economy, such as food production, trade, wealth accumulation, private property, political and social hierarchy, inequality, and a means of exchange were conspicuously absent from those simple egalitarian hunter-gatherer societies and economies. In the literature, and until the 1980s when so-called complex hunter-gatherers (Sassaman, 2004) were discovered, such socioeconomic traits were solely associated with Neolithic economies (C. Renfrew and P. Bahn, 2012). This conspicuous absence of what they thought were necessary components of a human society and economy certainly begs the question—were they even looking for the right markers?

Did they even understand what comprised an Earth-life species economy? Why wouldn't the longevity of these societies and their economies at least have hinted at the possibility of some socioeconomic survival pattern or system about which humans might have been yet unaware, and might be well advised to imitate, or at least delay judgment on—particularly since all other Earth-life species, except modern humans, pursued a similar subsistence pattern and survived? And yet with hindsight, there it was for all who had eyes to see it—an early human economy.

Embedded in those seemingly simple subsistence, non-hierarchical, egalitarian, non-surplus, non-hoarding, non-wealth accumulating, low-density, small, mobile, sharing pre-Neolithic Revolution human populations were societies and economies whose very existence comprised a living *survival-driven pattern*. It is one that showed how to make a living and still remain in harmony with Earth-life ecosystems and biodiversity, a survival pattern our pre-agriculture hunter-gatherer forbears, and all other animals, recognized, understood, and followed.

All, that is, except Neolithic through twenty-first century humans who were too blinded by their arrogance, greed, or religion to recognize and follow it. But what if they had recognized this survival pattern and had chosen to err on what today seems more like what would have been the safer bet? Would modern humans 400 generations later have found themselves ensnared in a rapidly warming world brought on by climate change—all a consequence of the way humans had chosen to build their societies and economies by destroying Earth-life ecosystems and driving its biodiversity to near-extinction in exchange for profits, wealth accumulation, and economic growth?

What, then, was in this survival-driven-pattern embedded in the socioeconomic lifeways of pre-agriculture hunter-gatherers that Neolithic Revolution humans and all subsequent humans failed to adopt? What were the kinds of societies and economies all Earth-life species, including modern humans, must adopt to successfully eke out a living in harmony with Earth-life ecosystems and biodiversity, as they had so successfully done? If nothing else, Hobbes, as well as others, may have identified elements of this survival-driven-pattern in his disparaging description of hunter-gatherer subsistence societies and economies, but because these lacked the Neolithic agrarian lifeways he knew, he might have missed their significance entirely.

Hobbes perhaps was expecting to encounter a broad-spectrum economy, burgeoning populations, and sedentary, hierarchical, farming, and livestock-rearing communities, rife with private property and inequality in their pursuit and distribution of surplus and wealth accumulation. These were communities that produced and traded rather than procured and shared food, and whose technologies enabled a division of labor and specialization but cared little for the well-being of Earth-life ecosystems and biodiversity. He must have thought he knew what a successful human society and economy should look like, saw none of that, and like so many who followed him and to this day still do, failed to see or understand the meaning of what was there and recoiled from the socioeconomic pattern that pre-agriculture hunter-gatherer lifeways exhibited.

It would have taken a lot of trouble, it would seem, to establish a planet with everything Earth-life needs to eke out a living to survive, including life's foundations within its atmosphere, lithospheres, and biosphere out of, upon which, and within which, all their societies and economies will emerge, but within which they must remain if they are to survive. Should one have been surprised, then, that it might also have included a survival-driven pattern, aka a user manual if you will? One that all Earth-life species, including humans, must follow to survive; one that encoded how all Earth-life species must go about eking out a living to remain alive?

And indeed, all Earth-life species for millennia, including humans, seem to have figured out and followed that survival-driven pattern—all, that is, until Neolithic humans came along. Haven't we noticed that except for the occasional extinction that occurred every few hundred million years over geologic time, and cyclical climate change driven by the planet's changing rotation on its axis as it orbits the sun, that everything Earth-life species needed to survive came built-in? Humans did not have to invent the sun, water, and the oceans, nor elements like oxygen, on which we are utterly dependent, as Covid-19 would not let us forget.

Habitats came provisioned with biomes that varied by region and climate; ecosystems came primed with products and services maintained by innumerable biodiversity species that together served up all that Earth-life species could eat and would need to make a living. There was no requirement for food production—food was already produced by nature. There was neither need, nor a requirement for animal and plant domestication, food hoarding, or private ownership of most things. Early hunter-gatherers lived like animals not only because they too were animals, even if some modern humans take issue with seeing themselves as animals. Yet it was animals, including pre-agriculture hunter-gatherers, that first figured out that survival-driven-pattern—how to live within Earth-life's ecosystems in harmony with its biodiversity, surviving for millennia while modern human societies and economies have since collapsed. Why?

Because modern humans were the only animals that abandoned that survival-driven-pattern and established instead what Hobbes might have been looking for but failed to find, an entirely new and different way to make a living that in time would destroy Earth-life ecosystems and drive its biodiversity to near-extinction. A way unfortunately that has since resulted in the collapse of nearly all human societies and economies and might well be on track to drive modern humans and all remaining Earth-life species to extinction.

If Neolithic humans did not envision, nor could envision, where their abandoning of the hunter-gatherer survival-driven way of eking out a living within Earth-life ecosystems and in harmony with its biodiversity was going to lead and potentially end up, modern humans now understand this path and have no such excuse and no obligation to continue down that path. Nor do the humans who punched that massive hole in the ozone layer that threatened all complex animal and human life late last century, those humans who have since started pumping CFC-11 once more into the atmosphere. If the British could not foresee that the use of fossil fuels as an industrial energy source, which they started nearly three hundred years ago, would lead to COP26 in Glasgow, hopefully, they can see that now.

And if the fossil fuel industry, and fossil fuel-based economies of the world, too, could not see as clearly where their profits and wealth-creating extraction business models were going to lead, although they knew but covered that up long before most humans had a clue, now they and all living humans know, and they also know that net zero does not equal zero CO_2—the level needed to keep global temperatures at or below 1.5°C. And, if investors, industries, businesses, and entrepreneurs whose business model continues to fund, develop, invent, and market fossil energy-driven products for profits, growth, and wealth—they too are just as guilty. Neolithic humans started humanity down this path, but there has been no lack of takers since then who wanted and went after their share of surplus and are still going after it.

It took 400 generations, but humans are now becoming aware of what those pre-agriculture hunter-gatherers did to survive for 290,000 years and it wasn't any of those agrarian societal and economic lifeways that Hobbes found missing. They were able to interpret and implement in their lifeways that survival-driven pattern and thereby found a way to live within Earth-life ecosystems and in harmony with its biodiversity without destroying either. They had one societal and economic goal and outcome—life and survival of Earth-life ecosystems, biodiversity, and themselves.

Is it still possible for modern humans to do the same? Perhaps we can if it's not already too late. But if we are going to make such a transition, it is up to all humans as individuals first, then as families and friends, to live the way those small pre-agriculture hunter-gatherer bands did—they followed no rulers, governments, or code of human laws but were guided by the single survival-driven goal of making a living within and in harmony with nature, thus ensuring mutual survival.

Humans made this socioeconomic transformation once and can do it again. There was neither ruler, king, nor queen, that initiated that change from foraging to farming; or came up with a COP26-like plan and led everyone to adopt agriculture, animal husbandry, and sedentation, leading eventually to what we call civilization. It all began with individuals, then small groups, then entire regions, across continents, over some four thousand years, who changed from foraging to farming, from sharing to hoarding, from the freedom of not owning private property to wealth accumulation.

Our species gradually changed from egalitarian to hierarchical communities, which grew into city-states, and nations that developed inequality, slavery, and warfare. Unfortunately, going back in the other direction won't be easy, nor can it be left to those who benefit from the status quo as all they would do is find yet another scheme, like net zero, to continue to make a profit under the guise of trying to rid the atmosphere of CO_2.

To get there, though, humans would have to change the current socioeconomic goal and purpose of their societies and economies from the acquisition of surplus/profit, growth, and wealth accumulation at any cost, and instead, return to human and Earth-life ecosystem and biodiversity life and survival at all costs. It was humans, not extraterrestrials, that once practiced this simple hunter-gatherer lifeway (and some humans still live this way), so we know it can be done. Humans made this socioeconomic transformation once and it led to civilization, but now we know it might potentially also be leading to our extinction and that of most Earth-life species. But to survive, if the way back is still open, we must find the courage and strength to make that transformation once again—but this time to benefit Earth-life species, its ecosystems, and human life and survival.

One would find it exceedingly difficult, if not impossible, to imagine with any degree of certainty what human societies and economies were like 10,000 years ago, yet the hunter-gatherers Hobbes described, if they were asked the same question, probably would have less of a problem getting close to a correct answer. Those pre-agriculture hunter-gatherer societies and the economies in which they lived were not just humanity's first, they were the only kind; a model, a survival pattern all humans followed, generation after generation, for 290,000 years—until Neolithic Revolution humans slowly replaced foraging with farming. And when they did, it was not long before humans would forget and eventually lose track of the only lifeways that would have enabled them to eke out a living *within* Earth's ecosystems while simultaneously remaining in harmony with it and its biodiversity.

They apparently never saw the big picture. They may not have understood, as humans today still don't, that foraging was never just about finding food but about a way to obtain food while simultaneously preserving Earth-life ecosystems and biodiversity. It was about survival—human, as well as Earth-life ecosystems and biodiversity survival. Do modern humans, even today, have the knowledge, the means, and the will to eke out a living without destroying Earth-life ecosystems and biodiversity and themselves? If it's not already too late, human survival may well depend upon our ability to do so.

Over multiple millennia of experimentation with numerous socioeconomic systems, humans would go on to expand upon what their Neolithic brethren started, with each new approach taking us further and further away from that survival-driven pattern pre-agriculture hunter-gatherers followed. Further and further away, too, from that harmony that was built into the pattern that would have enabled coexistence between humans, ecosystems, and biodiversity and thereby ensured their mutual survival. Now, 10,000-plus years later, we have ended up with what can only be described as a surplus-driven, legal-person, socioeconomic system almost completely divorced from Earth-life ecosystems and biodiversity.

This system has also completely displaced humans from being the center and reason for what used to be thought of as a "human economy," by a collection of business entities and corporations, all legal-persons, that have successfully relegated humans and their society to the unflattering peripheral role of being human resources and consumers-in-chief in a digital marketplace, wherein Earth-life ecosystems and biodiversity are mere materiel: natural resources to be extracted, finished, and sold for a profit in this new modern, international, free-market, global capitalist system seemingly designed more to serve legal-person economies.

What began, then, as a simple survival-driven human socioeconomic system intended to enable survival-driven interactions between humans and all Earth-life ecosystems and biodiversity species whose only goal and outcome was life and survival, has now degenerated into a surplus-driven, free-market, capitalist economic growth engine whose only goal and outcome is the economic growth of legal-persons and nations, a system that couldn't tell a vampire bat from the SARS-CoV-2 virus it may have helped to spread, so long as wildlife trade or wet markets make a profit. One wonders what Hobbes, Service, Smith, and others would think of today's socioeconomic systems whose sole purpose and goal is to enable these legal-persons to maximize shareholder/stakeholder profits, GDP growth, and wealth accumulation but couldn't care less about humans, ecosystem, and biodiversity harmony and their life and survival.

Suddenly, that simple hunter-gatherer socioeconomic system Hobbes took issue with, which enabled humans, ecosystems, and biodiversity survival for millennia, wasn't so bad after all. At least it kept humans alive, fed, healthy, and free of a population explosion that would have driven consumption of ecosystems and biodiversity products and services beyond Earth's limits, and caused global warming—and that's a hell of a lot more than one can say about its twenty-first century replacement. What made those pre-agriculture hunter-gatherer societies and economies work as well as they did while ours continues to struggle and, more often than not, fail?

Rediscovering what that early, simple, hunter-gatherer socioeconomic survival pattern of an economy was all about was discussed in the prior chapter. Eight characteristics that comprise this survival-driven-pattern were identified. They were referred to there as takeaways and bearing these in mind can help one understand why those societies and economies worked so well while ours failed, and why some humans, like Hobbes, got it so wrong. But Hobbes was not the first to wish survival patterns that became biodiversity and human lifeways would conform to some anthropocentric socioeconomic model preferred by humans, nor was he the last.

Human societies and economies are in the condition they are in today because we felt it necessary, as our Neolithic brethren did when they chose to abandon foraging for farming, to make a few adjustments that to us always seem better than the way things work naturally—until they are not. And it is our human adaptations as detailed by Layne (2019) that eventually led to the climate-change-driven global warming we now confront.

Many scholars believe social structures are determined by the nature of their underlying economies, and to this observation, one might ask, given the nature of our current economic system, what it says about the type of society twenty-first century humans are likely to end up with. What kind of society do humans want? And do we still retain the ability to shape our societies? If humans are mostly ceding control of their economies to legal-persons as suggested, what kind of socioeconomic system might one expect will emerge—will they still be human economies, or would they continue to be replaced by legal-person economies? On the contrary, the evolution of pre-agriculture human economies, it would seem, clearly wanted Earth-life species economies—human societies that would survive and be able to eke out a living within and in harmony with Earth-life ecosystems and biodiversity, in a way that would enable mutual survival. Can legal-person economies do that?

The socioeconomic system that was best able to satisfy those goals (human as well as ecosystem and biodiversity life and survival) turned out to be small, mobile, foraging, sharing, egalitarian, hunter-gatherer communities, and those formed by all other Earth-life species. It was a way for all species to make a living and survive; one that did the least harm to ecosystems and biodiversity species and thereby enabled them to survive as well. The survival of the one depended upon the survival of the other and the destruction of the one brought destruction of the other. And that's exactly what happened—it worked exactly as intended. Mutual survival continued for 290,000 years until Neolithic humans broke the pattern and chose to become farmers rather than remain foragers.

Why did the societies and economies that arose out of sedentary farming break this survival-driven pattern? How was it that pre-agriculture hunter-gatherer societies and economies managed to achieve these survival goals whereas most that followed the Neolithic Revolution and that were based on farming failed, and continue to fail? What was so different about foraging? What was so different about farming? Why did one succeed while the other failed?

Looking back at that list of takeaways in Chapter 5, it soon becomes clear what was different about hunting and gathering, and why foraging worked for hundreds of millennia without collapse while farming failed repeatedly in just a few. Here is what happened. If life and survival depended upon the preservation of all Earth-life habitats, ecosystems, and biodiversity species while allowing those same species, including humans, to simultaneously eke out a living within these ecosystems and in harmony with biodiversity species, it needed to find a way that would enable them to do that collaboratively and in harmony with one another so that all (humans, ecosystems and biodiversity species) might survive. That way turned out to be Earth-life species societies and economies built around the socioeconomic lifeways that emanated from those small, egalitarian, mobile, sharing, waterhole economies—aka pre-agriculture hunting-gatherer communities. And here is why.

From the *Foundations of Human Economies* diagram discussed in Chapter 5 and shown in Figure 6-1, recall that all life, including human life, evolved out of Earth's habitats and ecosystems, and their very survival depended on their ability to eke out a living *within* these habitats and ecosystems while doing so in harmony with the biodiversity species that also occupied them. Hence any species that inhibits the ability of ecosystems to function properly and survive, or that destroys the biodiversity species (e.g., pollinators—virtually all of the world's seed plants need to be pollinated) upon which ecosystems themselves depend, would potentially threaten the existence of all life. No ecosystems and no biodiversity means no life. No life means no survival. No survival means no human societies and no human societies means no human economies.

This hierarchy, interconnectedness, and interdependency is depicted by the four foundations (Figure 6-1) that underpin the human economy. They are shown as bidirectional, linked enclosures labeled Life; Habitats, Ecosystems and Biodiversity; Small Human Populations; and Mobility and Migration. Together, these encircle the human economy shown in the center of the diagram indicating its dependence upon them. Together too, the economy and its foundations are shown embedded within human society, the next larger circle.

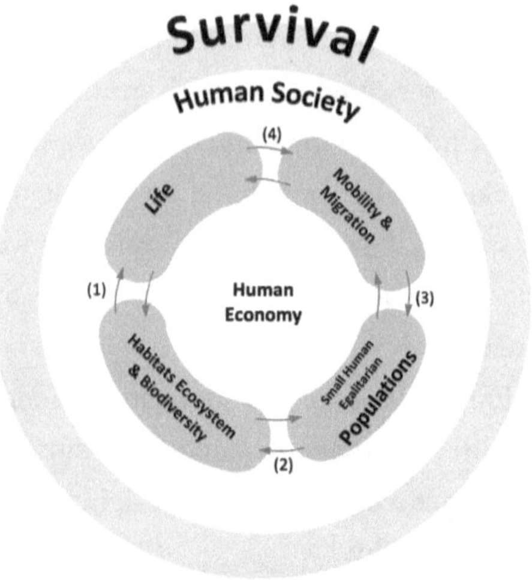

Figure 6-1. Foundations of human economies.
(Source: Samuel Layne)

If survival is the destination of life, then the goal and outcome of human societies and economies must also be life and survival—though you couldn't convince most economists of that. In fact, anything that inhibits survival must be seen as a limiting economic factor. Moreover, any economic system that inhibits Earth-life ecosystems and biodiversity species survival endangers life itself and thereby prevents survival and would be prohibited by a survival-driven socioeconomic system. Given the above, and what we now know of their lifeways, can one begin to see why foraging enabled pre-agriculture hunter-gatherer societies and economies to survive for hundreds of thousands of millennia while those built around sedentary farming communities failed?

In a universe wherein everything is in motion, mobile foraging societies turned out to be the lifeway that enabled humans to eke out a living and coexist with Earth-life ecosystems and biodiversity, enabling both to survive. But farming, while also enabling humans to eke out a living, damages the biodiversity species upon which all life depends. And doing so eventually drove repeated human civilization collapse. Because, once more, as we persist in continuing to make a living and building our economies by destroying Earth-life ecosystems and biodiversity, our twenty-first-century civilization has begun to be threatened with collapse as climate-change-driven global warming begins its devastation.

After 290,000 years of collapse-free human socioeconomic outcomes, there is no question which of these socioeconomic systems were survival-driven and succeeded in ensuring ecosystem, biodiversity, and human coexistence and survival. But now that we have some idea why human societies and economies as practiced by pre-agriculture hunter-gatherers survived while those practiced by Neolithic farmers failed and collapsed, let's examine which specific lifeways in these very different societies and economies drove survival and which drove collapse. How did their respective economic systems (foraging vs. farming and mobility vs. being sedentary) shape the human societies they underpinned?

We begin by paying particular attention to their respective lifeways and their impact on Earth-life habitats, ecosystems, biodiversity, human well-being, and their ability to survive versus collapse. The preferred outcome from a survival-driven socioeconomic system appears to have been mutual survival—a way for both humans and all other species to eke out a living simultaneously and harmoniously *within* Earth-life habitats and ecosystems, without destroying them or one another. Breaking this socioeconomic goal into its component parts we have:

(1) A way for both humans and all other Earth-life species to eke out a living to survive.

(2) A way for all to do so continually, simultaneously, and harmoniously, *within* Earth-life habitats and ecosystems, thus enabling mutual survival.

Given the socioeconomic goal, purpose, and outcome described above, which of these two rather disparate socioeconomic systems was best suited to enable humans to accomplish this goal and outcome of life and survival?

Let's begin with the hunter-gatherer way.

Foraging, sharing, and mobility that led to low population growth as well as ecosystem and biodiversity survival.

These are uniquely hunter-gatherer socioeconomic lifeways that interoperate to significantly reduce human use of ecosystem products and services and thereby wear and tear, thus enabling their sustainability and survival.

Foraging enabled the hunter-gatherer *DOMC lifeways* of not *Domesticating, Owning, Modifying, or Controlling ecosystem products and services and biodiversity species.* Their food was not produced by farming but produced by nature and obtained by foraging. They ate wild plants and fruits, seeds, and wild honey, and hunted wild animals, fish, and birds. They domesticated neither Earth-life species nor plants, and did not disturb the soil, in which 90 percent of all land-based species live.

Sharing resulted in mutual care for one another and ensured that no one was denied sustenance because they were unable to hunt or forage, thus attending to their mutual well-being. It also had the effect of reducing the demand for ecosystem and biodiversity products and services because the results of a day's foraging or hunting were shared with all in the band.

Mobility minimized the use of trees and other ecosystem products that erecting permanent housing would require. It also minimized the accumulation of non-portable personal belongings as everything they owned had to be carried from campsite to campsite. And being nomadic meant they would not remain in any one area indefinitely but would move multiple times a year. This mobile lifeway had the combined effect of significantly reducing any lasting impact on the ecosystem in which they camped and on the wildlife species they hunted, and thus enabled these areas and species populations to rapidly recover. This way of life would have made no significant and lasting impact on ecosystems and biodiversity that would have threatened their sustainability and survival.

Mobility & Population. Mobility had the additional effect of modulating human population growth. Children needed to be old enough to trek long distances and carry stuff or had to be carried by their mothers. They were completely dependent on breast milk for food and this dependence drove a hormonal response that prevented pregnancy and thus served as natural birth control. Together, protracted treks and protracted nursing had the effect of spacing childbirth as much as four to five years apart, and thereby reduced child rearing and population growth.

It's easy to see, then, how with such significant population control designed into the very socioeconomic lifeways of pre-agriculture hunter-gatherers, their populations remained small even after hundreds of thousands of millennia and how this, in turn, minimized their impact as a species on Earth-life ecosystems and biodiversity, enabling their mutual survival. Unlike farmers, hunter-gatherers would have had less use for the extra hands an agriculture community might need for food production.

Besides the sustainable lifestyle designed into the foraging lifeways, there was also a strong population-size control mechanism, and had hunting and gathering remained the socioeconomic lifeway it is estimated the human population would have been about ten million today rather than today's eight-plus billion. Given the current threatened collapse of Earth-life ecosystems and approaching extinction of its biodiversity it's clear to see why built into the pre-agriculture hunter-gatherer socioeconomic lifeways was a clear population limiting mechanism. But following the Neolithic Revolution, humanity's socioeconomic systems became agrarian and sedentary, this built-in population control mechanism was eliminated, and population growth took off.

In fact, "around 130,000 years BCE, the number of humans on earth was estimated to be around 200,000 and largely concentrated on what is now the African continent. Fast-forward to the year 10,000 BCE, the world population was significantly higher than those early estimates. During these years, the earth housed around three million people," according to "Worldwide Population Throughout Human History." It was not until the year 6500 BCE that the population reached ten million, and this was largely due to the first Agricultural Revolution.

The world population soon reached two billion in 1927, then three billion by 1959 and five billion by 1987. Today, the human population has surpassed eight billion while Earth-life ecosystems and biodiversity have witnessed a corresponding decline in growth and are approaching collapse. It is this population growth, turbocharged by the surplus-driven socioeconomic lifeways of modern human economies, that has resulted in less than 3 percent of the Earth's ecosystems remaining intact and accounts for the human-driven biodiversity extinction in progress today.

It should be clear, then, why Earth's survival-driven socioeconomic pattern, practiced by pre-agriculture hunter-gatherers and surviving without collapse for nearly 97 percent of human existence, came with built-in population control mechanisms. This pattern was broken when farming replaced foraging, surplus and hoarding replaced sharing, and sedentary societies replaced mobile ones. Humans have not stopped breaking Earth-life survival patterns—the most recent of which is resulting in global warming.

No surplus/no hoarding is the next group of hunter-gatherers' socioeconomic lifeways. No surplus and no hoarding implied they made less use of Earth-life ecosystem products and services and only when and as needed. Thus, in addition to the human well-being these lifeways enabled, they also had the additional effect of reducing ecosystem wear and tear as it complemented the *immediate-reward economic system* enabled by foraging. Obtaining a surplus and hoarding it would mean obtaining more than one would need or can share and that would result in greater use of ecosystem products and services and, if practiced by large populations, would have led to resource depletion and even threatened their exhaustion as they do in the twenty-first century.

The remaining lifeways of the hunter-gatherer socioeconomic system are:

Freedom, Independence, Fiercely Egalitarian, and No Rulers. The impact of these final lifeways on Earth-life ecosystems and biodiversity is not immediately obvious, but they wield an unmistakable impact nevertheless. Their fierce individualism and personal freedom, when combined with their fierce egalitarianism, made it less likely for:

(1) Crimes against the environment to be committed in their name, as is often done today by an elected government or by rulers such as Jair Bolsonaro, former President of Brazil, who is now sued at the ICC for "genocide" and "ecocide." They wouldn't, therefore, for example, belong to or subscribe to political systems of any kind, or support any economic process that would result in the dismembering of Earth-life ecosystems and biodiversity such as, for example, extraction of Canada's tar sands (which is by no means unique). This is the world's most destructive oil operation, and it's growing, according to a 2019 article in *National Geographic*. Here oil and gas companies like ExxonMobil and the Canadian giant Suncor have transformed Alberta's tar sands, also called oil sands, into one of the world's largest industrial developments in the name of economic development and corporate profit.

(2) The oceans to be fished to exhaustion to make a profit.

(3) The deforestation of Earth's forests in the name of economic growth, as documented in "Trees Fell Faster than in 2014, the Year Since Companies and Governments Promised to Stop Cutting Them Down" in a 2021 issue of Inside Climate News,

> and in a Global Forest Watch article that claimed Primary Rain Forests destruction increased 12 percent from 2019 to 2020.

It's unlikely, too, they would have been part of a socioeconomic system in which non-egalitarian practices were the norm. Given that mobility led families to space childbirth four to five years apart, infant mortality or abortions would not have been an option and Texas-style laws as well as the U.S. Supreme Court ruling that made abortions more difficult could not have happened—there wasn't a legal system. The very idea of dictating whether a foraging mother already carrying a one-year-old would have had to carry a pregnancy to term would have been unthinkable and potentially a death sentence.

Those pre-agriculture hunter-gatherers whom Hobbes considered animals that were only interested in making babies would also have considered anti-abortion laws and human trafficking unthinkable. And they would also have been alarmed at modern humans' inhumanity, as seen in the turning back of boats laden with migrants, building border walls, patrolling borders, and other forms of migrant deterrents causing hundreds to die or encamp in sub-freezing temperatures in the hope of being granted access.

And a society and economy where sharing food and resources was the norm, one that kept few personal possessions—instead of storing and hoarding while others were in need—would have been equally alarmed by the glaring inequality and inhumanity, high levels of poverty, homelessness, and food insecurity that could have engendered. In a society where open carry was the norm, as every hunter packed deadly weapons, modern gun violence as in the USA would have been unimaginable.

Table 6-1. Comparison of the socioeconomic lifeways of foraging versus farming and their respective impact on Earth-life ecosystems and biodiversity

Human Socioeconomic Ecosystem & Biodiversity Impact				
	Hunting & Gathering		Agrarian	
	Socioeconomic Lifeways	*Ecosystem Biodiversity Impact*	**Socioeconomic Lifeways**	*Ecosystem Biodiversity Impact*
1	**Mobile/Sedentary** **Mobile** (nomadic)	*Impact* *Light – rapid recovery*	**Mobile/Sedentary** **Sedentary** (stationary)	*Impact* *Massive and destructive*
2	**Food** **Procurement:** **Foraging:** Hunting and gathering wild fruits, vegetables	*Impact* *Little to none Hunter -Gatherer DOMC [1] Rules apply*	**Food** **Production:** Farming Agriculture	*Impact* *Plowing Sowing seeds Reaping crops Owning land Enclosing land*
3	**Surplus** No	*Impact* *Little to none*	**Surplus** **Yes** Accumulated	*Impact* *Ecosystem depletion*
4	**Equality/Inequality** Egalitarian Liberty and equality	*Impact* *Little to no inequality*	**Equality/Inequality** **Hierarchical** Very unequal	*Impact* Inequality
5	**Sharing/Hoarding** Sharing	*Impact* *Substantially reduces food needed*	**Sharing/Hoarding** Hoarding surplus to feed non-farmers	*Impact* *Huge - Increases the food planted and animal husbandry*
6	**Population** Tiny - bounded Small group 20-50 Offspring - few 1 every 4-5 years	*Impact* *Mobile Nomadic Light foot traffic and temporary living spaces*	**Population** Large - unbounded Sedentary Towns, villages, cities Many children	*Impact* *Widespread Intense, and continually increasing driving exhaustion and extinction*
7	Rulers No Rulers: Free & equal social status	*Impact* *None No increased consumption due to rulers*	**Rulers** Rulers, Kings, Queens: Unfree & unequal social status	*Impact* *Legal-person, State-driven consumption of ecosystem prod & services*

1. DOMC Rules: Don't Own, Modify or Control ecosystems and biodiversity

(Source: Samuel Layne)

Similarly, they would probably have rejected an economic system that is as hopelessly unequal, and a political system as inherently racist, or one that is also as inherently and systemically unjust as are most human societies today. In other words, the simple socioeconomic system practiced by hunter-gatherers about whom Hobbes had nothing nice to say, was unlikely to tolerate or become as comfortable as modern humans seem to have become with our current socioeconomic systems. What would Hobbes have written about twenty-first century human lifeways? For a summary, consider the comparisons in Table 6-1.

Earth's life support systems and their mechanisms are encoded in the lifeways of all species, including humans. From what we have seen so far, these mechanisms work best when they are left to work on their own and as designed. Whether or not hunter-gatherers and all other foraging Earth-life species instinctively felt this need, none hitherto has tampered with them as Neolithic farmers subsequently did with the choice to farm instead of forage for a living. Earth came equipped with everything any species, including humans, would need to survive—including food. Food production was *a priori* builtin, as all other species except Neolithic Revolution humans figured out.

As long as species confined their search for food *within* the operating boundaries of its ecosystems, and in harmony with its biodiversity, they apparently were able to go about the task of eking out a living for millennia—as indeed our hunter-gatherer forebears were able to do for most of our species' existence. Earth-life systems and mechanisms operated in a self-maintenance mode and did so mostly without any human help for thousands of millennia, and if left alone, might yet enable life for the next five billion years or before the sun begins to change its operating parameters and thereby Earth's.

On the other hand, how did those sedentary, agrarian socioeconomic lifeways that followed the Neolithic Revolution impact Earth-life ecosystems and biodiversity, given the same goal and outcome pursued by pre-agriculture hunter-gatherers—a way for humans and all other species to eke out a living simultaneously and harmoniously *within* Earth-life habitats, ecosystems, and biodiversity without destroying them or one another?

While it is easy to see how pre-agriculture hunter-gatherer socioeconomic lifeways enabled them to satisfy the life and survival requirements for ecosystems, biodiversity, and humanity, with hindsight, given the Neolithic agrarian socioeconomic lifeways' impact upon Earth-life ecosystems and biodiversity, attaining that goal via the agrarian lifeways was never going to be possible. They could not have known the outcome back then, as we who are living its consequences do today, nor where their choice would eventually lead. As farmers and herders, they went about modifying Earth's life support systems and their mechanisms, and that led to the inevitable outcome of the collapse of many subsequent human civilizations.

Neolithic humans were not just giving up foraging for farming, however. They were abandoning the built-in socioeconomic constraints that came with foraging: mobility, sharing, small community bands, low-population density, sharing instead of hoarding, and an egalitarian lifeway instead of the inequality and sociopolitical nightmare human governments would become, and which would soon change the survival-driven lifeways their pre-agriculture hunter-gatherer forebears, and ours, had practiced for millennia.

Were their sedentary, hoarding, agrarian socioeconomic lifeways just a collapse away, waiting to happen—as indeed they did? Or was there a sustainable way to farm, as many today think possible, that just wasn't known back then? No need to wonder though, as history has shown that any human socioeconomic lifeway that needs to modify Earth's support systems—the soil, the atmosphere, water, and other elements—and eliminates most of its biodiversity, to build its economy as humans have done and continue to do, will result in the collapse of those Earth-life support systems and eventually of civilization, if not of the human species.

For much of human history, most of the world's land was a wilderness: forests, grasslands, and shrubbery dominated its landscapes. But as per the "Global land use for food production" diagram below, over the last few centuries, this has changed dramatically. Wild habitats have been turned into agricultural land. The expansion of agriculture has been one of humanity's largest impacts on the environment. It has transformed habitats and exerts the greatest pressures on biodiversity species.

Of the 28,000 species threatened with extinction, agriculture is listed as a threat for 24,000 of them on the IUCN Red List (*The International Union for the Conservation of Nature's Red List of Threatened Species*), a critical indicator of the health of the world's biodiversity. There is also an IUCN Red List of Ecosystems Categories and Criteria, a global standard for how the conservation status of ecosystems, applicable at local, national, regional, and global levels, is assessed.

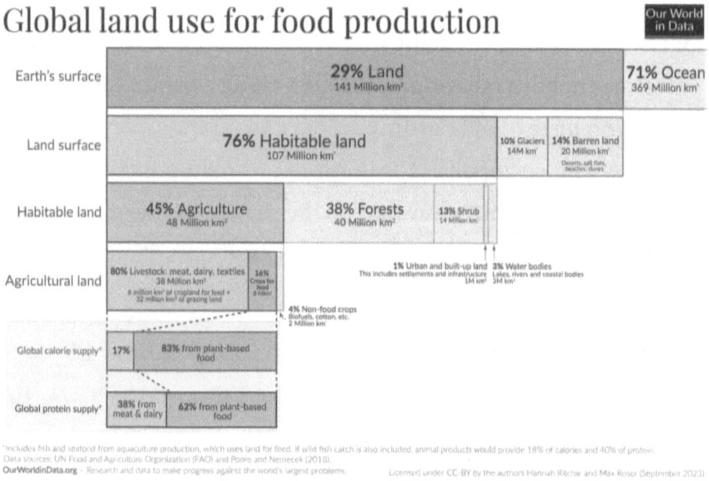

Figure 6-2. Global land use for food production.

(Source: Our World in data)

Today, though, modern humans know a few things about the consequences of their choices that post-Neolithic Revolution humans couldn't have known. Figure 6-2 shows the impact of global land use for food production, while Table 6-2 lists just some of the many ways farming and agriculture impacts Earth-life habitats, ecosystems, and biodiversity, and their consequences—including their effects on soil, water, biodiversity, and air/climate (EPAR Brief No. 65 of the Bill & Melinda Gates Foundation). And we now know, too, there are planetary boundaries that humanity might cross to its eventual peril.

Modern humans, not unlike Neolithic Revolution humans, are similarly confronted with socioeconomic issues, potential solutions to which carry harmful ecosystem and biodiversity impacts that are not always obvious. The economic challenge post-Neolithic Revolution humans confronted was how to continuously produce enough food for their ever-expanding populations—a challenge hunter-gatherers may have rarely encountered even after 290,000 years—and a challenge modern humans still face even now, when agriculture occupies over 50 percent of the world's habitable land, as explored in a 2019 issue of *National Geographic.* Post-Neolithic Revolution humans naturally turned to more intense farming, surplus generation, and hoarding. Modern humans, too, have been there and done that and today have already exhausted those options and more, and consequently are now confronted by global warming, the mother of all consequences, and an impact we, too, never expected.

> *Agriculture already uses almost half of the world's vegetated land. It consumes 90 percent of all the water used by humanity and generates one-quarter of the annual global emissions that are causing global warming. And yet, of the eight billion people living today, 820 million are undernourished because they don't have access to—or can't afford—an adequate diet.*
>
> *We have to produce 30 percent more food on the same land area, stop deforestation, [and] cut carbon emissions for food production by two-thirds.*
>
> *All of that must be done while reducing poverty levels and the loss of natural habitat, preventing freshwater depletion, and cutting pollution as well as other environmental impacts of farming.*

Unfortunately, modern humans, like their Neolithic Revolution brethren who began this problem in the first place, are failing to even recognize or address the elephant in the human food pantry: a continuously growing human population, even if the rate of growth has recently slowed.

Table 6-2. Overview of agricultural technologies and impacts on ecosystem services

Technology	Impacts on Soils	Impacts on Water	Impacts on Biodiversity	Impacts on Air/Climate	Case Example
Monoculture			Reduces habitat for insects and wildlife, leading to increased need for pesticides		Reduced bird populations in monocropped coffee fields in Colombia and Mexico
Continuous Cropping	Soil fertility declines due to nutrient mining		Reduces farmers' ability to use natural pest cycles, leading to increased need for pesticides		Nutrient offtake in reduced fallow cassava farms in Kenya and Uganda
Conventional Tillage	Reduces soil organic matter, leading to increased erosion			Contributes to CO_2 emissions due to decomposition of soil organic matter	Soil compaction due to tillage in maize fields in Nigeria
Intensive Hillside Cultivation	Increases erosion, leading to soil degradation				Significant soil loss rates due to erosion in Ethiopian highlands
Intensive Livestock Systems	Increases erosion and soil compaction due to overgrazing and hoof action	Untreated livestock waste degrades water quality; water usage competes with other needs	Degrades grassland habitat due to overgrazing	Contributes to CH_4 and N_2O emissions due to enteric fermentation and manure management	Soil degradation and erosion caused by overgrazing in the Irangi Hills in Tanzania
Inorganic Fertilizers	Increases soil acidification due to nitrate leaching	Reduces oxygen levels due to runoff, harming aquatic ecosystems; impairs water for human uses		Contributes to smog, ozone, acid rain, and N_2O emissions	Eutrophic dead zones in the Baltic Sea, Black Sea, and west coast of India

Pesticides			Harms animal and human health by accumulating in soils and leaching into water bodies		Use of unauthorized pesticide recipes in maize fields in Ethiopia
Irrigation Systems	Inadequate drainage and over-irrigation causes waterlogging and salinization	Degrades downstream ecosystems due to polluted run-off and over-extraction of water			Shrinking of Aral Sea due to over-extraction for irrigation, particularly for cotton cultivation
New Seed Varieties	May increase need for inputs that negatively impact soils	May increase need for inputs that negatively impact water quality and quantity	Reduces maintenance of genetic diversity in landrace varieties	May increase need for fertilizer, leading to increased greenhouse gas emissions	
Intensive Rice Production	Inadequate drainage and continuous flooding causes waterlogging, salinization, and nutrient problems	Degrades downstream ecosystems due to polluted run-off and over-extraction of water		Contributes to CH4 emissions due to anaerobic conditions in paddy fields	Over-extraction for rice irrigation in Tamil Nadu, India
Industrial Crop Processing		Degrades downstream ecosystems due to water requirements and discharge of untreated wastewater		Contributes to CO2 emissions due to energy requirements of machinery	Water pollution near coffee processing plants in Mexico

(Source: Compiled by Killebrew, 2012)

It probably never occurred to Neolithic humans, as they transitioned from foraging to farming, that they were signing up for more than a potential increase in their food supply, just as it might not have occurred to modern humans that with fossil fuels, we, too, signed up for more than just an increase in energy. Neolithic humans also apparently had no idea they were abandoning that built-in population control mechanism that came with being mobile as opposed to being sedentary, and, while more people might have been a benefit to farming back then, today, having more people is the problem.

They probably thought, too, that it made more economic sense to hoard than to share as modern economists also seem to think; that they should settle down in one place instead of being nomadic; that the increase in birth rate enabled by being sedentary was a decided economic advantage they couldn't afford to forgo; and, no doubt, that animal milk and meat that came with animal husbandry outweighed the zoonoses that getting up close and personal with feral species would also unleash upon humanity.

But again, they completely missed the fact that by enabling the human population expansion to meet their farm labor needs, they would simultaneously be fusing a human population time bomb that is now getting ready to explode in the twenty-first century just as modern humans also missed the fact that by replacing the renewable energy of the ecosystem with fossil fuels, though it yielded more energy, they, too, were lighting a global warming fuse that now threatens to incinerate civilization.

Neolithic humans also apparently never saw the ecosystem collapse nor biodiversity extinction that farming would eventually cause; nor the zoonotic diseases like Covid-19, malnutrition, and the transformation of their societies, from being egalitarian, caring, sharing, human-well-being-centered, and survival-driven, to becoming unfree, subject to kings, queens, and other rulers whose surplus and property ownership-driven economic ways would morph into a global free-market capitalist system by the twenty-first century.

Nor could they have foreseen the societal consequences their foraging-to-farming economic transition would eventually cause. It would bring the rise of unequal social classes—a ruling class, slaves, warriors, and religions. It also brought other socioeconomic consequences that agricultural food production and surplus hoarding would enable. Moreover, they had no way of knowing back then that agriculture would become one of the three main causes of the increase in greenhouse gases observed over the past 250 years—right up there with land use and fossil fuels.

Unfortunately, modern humans were no more clairvoyant than their Neolithic brethren. Did we fail to see, or just didn't bother to do anything to restrain, this explosive human population growth, and the consequent ecosystem collapse and biodiversity extinction in progress that provisioning for the billions of new mouths would have caused—even though prior human civilizations have collapsed for similar reasons, and even though all human life depends upon the preservation of those ecosystems and biodiversity? Did we envisage the consequences some of our proposed modern solutions to these and similar problems would cause?

The technology solutions we thought would solve one agricultural problem have caused others (Table 6-2). And it is likely, too, that many of those we envisage as potential solutions to global warming, such as carbon capture and storage or solar radiation management, though seemingly attractive solutions today, might well turn out tomorrow to have an unexpected social, economic, and environmental sting. Inorganic fertilizers were good until we discovered they cause eutrophic dead zones in numerous seas across the planet and contribute to smog, ozone, acid rain, and N_2O emissions; similarly, pesticides were the greatest until we realized that these harm animal and human health by accumulating in soils and leaching into water bodies. Our solution to one problem often became the origin of another—and it has been that way since the dawn of agriculture.

Have you ever wondered why humans, Neolithic or modern, seem disinclined to acknowledge a seemingly obvious fact: that already in place are all the life support mechanisms required to survive, and that tampering with them could well lead to collapse—or worse, our extinction? Our pre-agriculture hunter-gatherer forebears, and all other Earth-life species (notwithstanding their lack of human-like intelligence), survived on Earth for millennia but changed practically nothing about how the Earth-system works, and, for as long as they remained the extant or dominant species on the planet, managed to avoid bringing down environmental hell upon themselves.

But then came the *Huu-mans*, Neolithic through modern humans, and oh well, all hell broke loose. But as crazy as humans have behaved since abandoning hunting and gathering, not many would try sticking the battery recharging plug of a Tesla into an extra can of gasoline should the Tesla battery run low. Yet humans seem unable to recognize that this Earth-life system we share remains as novel to humans today as perhaps an EV would be to a Formula-1 pit-stop mechanic. Hopefully, there's still time to try discovering how this all may have been intended to work instead of attempting yet another suicidal socioeconomic, scientific, or technology-based solution we might yet conjure up—because it didn't go so well for Neolithic humans, and despite our ingenuity thus far, it's still not going well for us either, as we appear to be heading for a collision with nature.

Erle C. Ellis noted in a research paper entitled "Anthropogenic Transformation of the Terrestrial Biosphere," "Human populations and their use of land have transformed most of the terrestrial biosphere. Current anthropogenic rates of climate change may exceed any experienced by most extant terrestrial species and might therefore cause a mass extinction. We humans have significantly altered nearly all of Earth's systems, including its atmosphere, hydrosphere, lithosphere, and biosphere. Taken together over the past 300 years, these anthropogenic changes, especially in atmospheric chemistry and global climate, provide strong evidence that humans have altered the Earth system sufficiently to indicate the emergence of a new geological epoch: the Anthropocene."

And yet, humans didn't engage in all this Earth-life ecosystems makeover and biodiversity annihilation just to name the next geologic epoch after itself, but believe it or not, we were simply trying to eke out a living to survive. How different, though, the last few years would have been, temperature-wise, had we followed the *survival-driven-pattern*—yes, those pre-agriculture hunter-gatherer lifeways were all it would have taken.

But if Neolithic humans, individually or collectively, could somehow have foreseen the horrific consequences their choice to abandon foraging for farming would have entailed for all subsequent humans, would they have done so anyway? Would we have done so if we were in their place? And if late eighteenth and nineteenth century humans, who began the widespread adoption of fossil fuels as an abundant energy source during the Industrial Revolution, had known what is known now about their climate impact, would they have done so anyway? Would we? But these are questions mostly about what others might or might not have done.

How about what you or I as individuals, or in our collective identity, have done or might yet do? Knowing what we now know about the impact of CH_4 and CO_2 on global temperatures, would we have chosen fossil fuels to power the Industrial Revolution? Knowing too, what we now know about just how long CO_2 and other GHGs emitted to the atmosphere might last, and how hot the planet will potentially get, would its impact on subsequent generations drive us to abandon our individual or collective fossil fuel use, our so-called collective carbon footprint, as soon as possible? What can you or I do, or what can humans do, to stop the continued use of fossil fuels?

While pre-agriculture hunter-gatherers retained the freedom to choose, and chose to remain as individuals in small egalitarian foraging bands, and did more or less as they very well pleased, including remaining or leaving the band they were a part of if they so desired, Neolithic humans as individual farmers or workers on a farm, would, for the most part, have lost much of that rugged individualism and freedom and were more likely than not subjected to choices made by a farmer, or the collective decisions of a workgroup on a farm of which they became a part.

Any decision for any reason not to farm was essentially a decision to leave the farm and return to a life of foraging. Essentially then, it was highly likely Neolithic humans would have lost the individual ability to choose that they once had as pre-agriculture hunter-gatherers. Moreover, those who remained on a farm, and that was probably most, were essentially choosing to make their living by farming regardless of the known or unknown consequences to subsequent humans.

Similarly, in a rather uncanny sort of way, humans today would have to essentially drop out of modern civilization to avoid any use of fossil fuels altogether, whether one is aware or not of its current or long-term consequences on subsequent generations. Few would have had any say in whether they were going to continue to ride a horse and buggy or drive a Ford Model T. Like Neolithic humans, we, too, are now bound by the economic and societal decisions others would have made and the outcome over which we, as individuals, were never going to have much, if any, control. But who are those others that are making choices on behalf of most everyone else? Today these choices are not being made by simple farmers as they began back then, not even by governments as some would have us believe, but mostly by managers and executives in boardrooms of a new type of *person—a legal person*—the multinational corporation.

Whereas Neolithic humans began to lose their freedom to choose to farmers and then to rulers, kings, and religious leaders, modern humans, in addition, have had and are having theirs preempted by their employers, the modern multinational corporation. And notwithstanding what politicians or Western governments may have to say about freedom and democracy, Neolithic humans lost their freedom to choose when they began to cede control of their human economy to the farm, just as modern humans lose theirs once they sign on as an employee and begin "Working for the Man", or owner of a corporation.

When they traded their individual ability to forage for the collective ability to farm, they were giving up more than just their personal freedoms. In fact, they had begun the process of abandoning their human waterhole *economies* for what would eventually become *legal-person economies*.

Economies comprised mostly *of legal-persons, by legal-persons*, and *for legal-persons* with humans serving as mere employees and consumers. Today one no longer works for the "man" but rather for a legal-person corporation in the legal-person economy.

An economy would come to exist for legal-persons that, according to David Korten in his book *When Corporations Rule the World*, "would emerge as the dominant governance institutions on Earth, with the largest among them reaching into virtually every country of the world and exceeding most governments in size and power." And just as early Neolithic human societies and economies were eventually replaced by those that came with the rise of governments, the state, and civilization, similarly, modern human societies and their economies are now being replaced by legal-person economies and legal-person societies.

Human societies have now been mostly taken over and are run by *legal-person societies*. One shouldn't be surprised then, says Korten, "it is corporate interest rather than human interest that defines the policy agendas of states and international bodies." Alas! Modern humans, like Neolithic humans, have now lost both their freedom and control of their human societies and economies to legal-person societies and economies that are led and operated by global multinational corporations.

If you work or operate a small business via the internet, manage your social life via Facebook, have Alexa monitor your conversations and keep your diary, search the internet or obtain directions via Google, use an Apple device or store your content on iCloud, shop via Amazon or have your dinner delivered by Uber Eats or Food Panda, or work in the so-called gig economy, then you have become a resident in the legal-person society and that *main street human economy* you were once a part of has been subsumed, like your local bookstore and grocery, into Amazon.

Thus, Main street is rapidly being replaced by Wall Street and members of the legal-person economy that are owned and operated by multinational corporations worldwide. And whether modern humans choose to acknowledge it or not, most aspects of our lives are now managed and run by legal-persons in a legal-persons society and minutely monitored and managed by legal-persons in that legal-persons economy. But what is it that's driving these changes?

What was it that drove the transformation from foraging to farming and thereby to the Neolithic Revolution, and eventually, the Industrial Revolution? And what is it, too, that's now driving the transformation of our once-human societies and economies to legal-person societies and economies? In a word: the human desire for hoarding, surplus/profits, and economic growth.

We sometimes kid ourselves into thinking these transformations were the result of changing technologies and innovations but those were only enablers of that original goal and purpose of surplus accumulation our Neolithic brethren adopted way back then. As different as those transformations have been, they were all driven by the same human failing—the desire to organize human economies to be surplus-driven at all costs even if that cost included sacrificing their fellow humans and Earth's ecosystems and biodiversity.

And we have done exactly that. We chose to abandon the encoded *survival-driven-pattern* in the socioeconomic lifeways of pre-agriculture hunter-gatherers, as well as all other Earth-life species, for a socioeconomic lifeway whose only goal and purpose was the maximization of surplus, aka profits, wealth accumulation, and unending GDP growth—better known by its modern name, Global Capitalism.

Survival-driven economies have as their only goal and outcome human, ecosystem, and biodiversity life and survival. That translated into sharing food and other resources rather than hoarding; food procurement (foraging) rather than food production (farming and animal husbandry); living in small mobile bands and thereby spreading and reducing human ecosystem and biodiversity impact rather than living in large sedentary farming communities and thereby protracting a concentrated impact. It also meant remaining free, socially and economically equal, and egalitarian, rather than unfree, unequal, and subject to rulers.

On the other hand, agrarian economies (farming and animal husbandry) necessitated interrupting and destroying Earth's natural ecosystem processes and lifeways; disturbing or destroying wildlife habitats; clearing and taking possession of fields and domesticating wild animals for food production and wealth accumulation; being surplus-driven and organizing an economy to maximize and hoard food surplus; acquiring and enclosing land as private property for economic growth and wealth creation; and owning, managing, and controlling farmland and biodiversity species. This translated into opportunities to accumulate wealth; gave rise to inequality, surplus accumulation, and hoarding rather than sharing; stimulated the emergence of rulers and different social classes; and prioritized a focus on the self, with little care for others, Earth-life ecosystems, or its biodiversity.

There was, however, one requirement that both socioeconomic systems, foraging and farming, had an obligation to satisfy: the need to ensure life and survival—a requirement to eke out a living simultaneously and harmoniously *within* an Earth-life ecosystem and with its biodiversity; and to do so without destroying either, or oneself, thus enabling mutual survival.

But, as we have seen above, there seems to have been no way to satisfy this goal and outcome of life and survival while simultaneously trying to satisfy a socioeconomic imperative to maximize surplus from crop and animal farming. It was not going to be easy, if at all possible, to get there from a social lifeway that chose to hoard rather than share with fellow humans in need any more than that's possible today; nor from an economy that chose food production rather than food procurement; from a society that remained sedentary in an ecosystem and erected permanent housing, regardless of impact, rather than temporary dwellings; and one that needed to till and disrupt the soil, wherein more than 90 percent of land species live, rather than just tread on it and move on.

Post-Neolithic Revolution humans who chose those options may have seen little economic value in the pre-agriculture hunter-gatherer socioeconomic lifeways they were getting ready to leave behind, just as modern humans that spent the last 400 generations destroying them still can't or won't. They may never have quite grasped any more than modern humans have, or have but totally ignored, the survival-driven component they needed to satisfy as they went about the task of eking out a living, just as modern humans have done and are doing today. There was not much built into the farming socioeconomic lifeways they chose that evinced much care for their fellow humans or Earth-life ecosystems and biodiversity, nor for the civilizations that eventually arose therefrom and collapsed multiple times, reflecting this sad deficiency.

It's difficult to grasp just how strong and irresistible a hold this urge to acquire and hoard surplus/profits, drive growth, and accumulate wealth has come to have on humans and just how far away our species has drifted from the *survival-driven* lifeways of our hunter-gatherer forebears. This chase after surplus and wealth has completely distorted the socioeconomic goals from being a survival-driven, human socioeconomic lifeway to a "Who wants to be on the Forbes billionaires list of legal-persons?" socioeconomic lifeway; from one that at least for a while pretended to be survival-driven, that tried to show mutual caring and sharing, and that showed some concern for Earth-life ecosystems and biodiversity species as some wellbeing economies hope to do, to one that today takes pleasure in maximizing earnings and wealth through the destruction of natural assets, and one that revels in a level of inequality that is now beyond obscene.

Compared to the *survival-driven* lifeway goals for humanity, does it matter that 26 billionaires own the same wealth as the poorest 3.8 billion people? Or that just 162 billionaires have the same wealth as half of humanity? Whose goals are these and how did they contribute to our species, ecosystem, and biodiversity survival? The goal for human socioeconomic lifeways on planet Earth was and is mutual life and survival with Earth-life species—it never was and never could have been about anyone, not even a few, becoming billionaires.

Human survival and the survival of Earth-life ecosystems and biodiversity have always been inseparable. Can these billionaires, and modern humans, in general, abandon these Neolithic goals of surplus and wealth accumulation we adopted 400 generations ago, goals that have already led to the collapse of numerous human civilizations during this geologically brief interval and are currently threatening ours, and return to the *survival-driven pattern* as lived out in the lifeways of pre-agriculture hunter-gatherers? Lifeways that enabled them to survive for most of our species' existence—290,000 of the 300,000 years of human existence? Lifeways we humans once knew. How do we turn ourselves around?

It won't be easy, but shouldn't we give it a try? The survival of our species depends on all humans making this about-face. It won't be the first time humans have realized the path they were on was leading to a dead end and made a U-turn. We are here talking about this because 70,000 years ago, a small group of our hunter-gatherer forebears, confronted by climate change, chose to migrate out of Africa to survive. They are the ancestors of all existing humans. Imagine where our species would be today if they hadn't. Here are a couple more examples of how some humans (as opposed to legal persons; we will get to those later), made this about-turn, but none so far has had the survival of our entire species dependent upon the choice they made. Here is how one man made that U-turn.

"F.W. de Klerk had to abandon what his ancestors had believed in," the *Economist* reported. But just how does one do that? It's no small task to turn one's back and walk away from life, customs, community, and a belief system in which one had been raised, though he wouldn't have been the first. Ten thousand years ago, Neolithic humans turned their backs on

290,000 years of their ancestral pre-agriculture hunter-gatherer foraging lifeways for farming, and today, humans are still farming. But today, too, thanks to F.W. de Klerk, Nelson Mandela, and Archbishop Desmond Tutu, South Africa is no longer an apartheid state. What they did for South Africa modern humans must now find the courage to do for humanity—it's time to take down this whole *surplus-driven socioeconomic lifeway* our Neolithic brethren started, the way de Klerk, Mandela, and Archbishop Desmond Tutu took down apartheid, and return humanity to the survival-driven lifeways our hunter-gatherer forebears followed.

De Klerk's life and role have given rise to numerous detractors but some supporters as well and according to his obituary in *The Economist,* "F.W. de Klerk, Builder and dismantler," "his uncle became South Africa's prime minister in the 1950s, and his father also served in government. Both men built up the National Party, which in 1948 introduced apartheid. Under this system, it was illegal for different races to marry, socialize, own property, or work without permission across much of the country. In 1970 black South Africans were barred from citizenship and expected to move from the cities to 'Bantustans,' distinct tribal states, leaving whites as the majority."

Of course, "whites never thought they did anything wrong with apartheid, and quite a number of them were racists and still are. So, he was no exception from the rest of the white community, it's just that in his case he was their leader," de Klerk said. "He grew up and studied behind the walls of his own culture, and this seemed how things should be. God, having created the different races from Adam, also allotted the boundaries where each race should live. Apartheid was Scripture, to the letter. But then in 1993, as president, he took the whole system down. June 16, 1976, is remembered as "The Day Apartheid Died."

He had been part of, and served under, the brutal apartheid regime until he worked his way up to the presidency in 1989 when he replaced P.W. Botha. The next year he took the decision to unban liberation movements, paving the way for the release of political prisoners, including Nelson

Mandela, and negotiation for a democratic South Africa. He was the last president of apartheid South Africa. He ruled over the final years of apartheid between 1989 and 1994 and died in his Cape Town home on November 11th, 2021, at age 85. Considered the last white ruler of South Africa, de Klerk shared the Nobel Peace Prize in 1993 with Nelson Mandela "for their work for the peaceful termination of the apartheid regime, and for laying the foundations for a new democratic South Africa."

In a final message to South Africa, former apartheid president F.W. de Klerk apologized for his role in apartheid. "I am often accused by critics that I in some way or another continued to justify apartheid or separate development, as we later preferred to call it. It is true that in my younger years I defended separate development, but afterward, on many occasions, I apologized to the South African public for the pain and indignity that apartheid has brought to people of color in SA. Many believed me but others didn't." De Klerk says that he is apologizing once more as the leader of the National Party and in his personal capacity. He said in a video released soon after his death, "I without qualification apologize for the pain and hurt and the indignity and the damage that apartheid has done to black, brown, and Indians in South Africa."

But one must not be too hard on de Klerk as he was not the only colonial-era ruler that brought grave pain and indignity to the people of Africa—he at least apologized, if that is actually possible, and tried to undo what he, his father, uncle, and others began in 1948. For other leaders, though, one must turn to the nations of the global north, and unless I am mistaken, I have yet to hear any of them come close to offering an apology to the African peoples they enslaved. King Charles came as close as I have heard any Brit get to anything resembling an apology. He said slavery was an "appalling atrocity," but did it require 400 years to realize that? Yet even then his speech seemed more about how slavery would stain British history—never mind the lives of the Africans they enslaved, for example, on the sugar plantations in Barbados.

In a speech, Prince Charles (now King Charles) delivered a message from his mother, conveying her "warmest good wishes," in November, 2021, on the occasion when Barbados swore in its first president, on what would have been their second attempt to end, by then, nearly 400 years of British rule, and 55 years after the island nation of some 300,000 people had gained independence from Britain. In the speech, he congratulated Barbadians and said, "From the darkest days of our past, and the appalling atrocity of slavery, which forever stains our history, the people of this island forged their path with extraordinary fortitude . . . Tonight, you write the next chapter of your nation's story," he added. "You are the guardians of your heritage."

Figure 6-3. De Klerk shared the Nobel Peace Prize with Nelson Mandela.
A prominent Afrikaner, he defended the separation of the races before helping to dismantle that system, leading to his sharing the Nobel Peace Prize with Nelson Mandela.
(Source: N.Y. Times.com)

And indeed, the time had come, and Barbados finally cast off the Queen as the Head of State to become the fourth Caribbean country to cut ties with the monarchy. It has now joined Guyana, which gained independence in

1966 and became a republic in 1970; Trinidad and Tobago, which became independent in 1962 and a republic in 1976; and Dominica, which gained full independence as a republic in 1978.

While de Klerk will be forever remembered for his and his family's role in architecting apartheid, and rightly so, it was the Portuguese that began the slave trade. The transatlantic slave trade began during the fifteenth century when Portugal, and subsequently other European kingdoms, were finally able to expand overseas and reach Africa. According to PortCities Bristol, it was the Portuguese that started the European slave trade with Africa. The Portuguese first began to kidnap people from the west coast of Africa and to take those they enslaved back to Europe. The Portuguese explorations of Africa have been identified as the origin of the modern plantation system, based on large-scale commercial agriculture and the wholesale exploitation of slave labor. Today, Portugal proudly claims to be one of the first countries to abolish slavery following a 1761 decree that only applied to Portugal.

Full abolition didn't come until more than a century later. Meanwhile, Portuguese slave traders simply diverted the slave traffic to the colonies in Brazil. One only has to look at the favelas of Brazil (some of the first settlements were called "barrios africanos," African neighborhoods), or the issues African Americans continue to face in the U.S., to grasp the devastation the slave trade brought upon these enslaved people of Africa. Across the world one can find stories of African peoples enslaved and their long and sad journey to a freedom that still eludes them. Their labor built the riches of the Global North, yet they count among the poorest of mankind.

Today, Portugal is marketed as one of the best countries in which to retire or obtain EU citizenship on the cheap. But alas! Whatever one may call it in the twenty-first century, Portugal is still in the business of enticing humans to leave their countries of origin, only this time, instead of being bought or kidnapped and bundled onto a slaver and taken across the Atlantic to Brazil to labor on a sugar plantation, for a more fungible alternative such as a tidy sum of Euros, one gets to live in Portugal—yes, unfortunately, it's still about trading humans for wealth; about obtaining that surplus our Neolithic brethren went after and that got humanity where it is today.

Portugal is now a respected nation, but it is unlikely that António Guterres, the ex-Prime Minister of Portugal and current Secretary-General of the UN, would feel obliged to apologize for the slave trade the Portuguese launched in 1441; or for the pain and indignity that the slave trade they pioneered brought upon the peoples of Africa who ended up as slaves in nations the world over, the way de Klerk did for Afrikaners who caused the pain and indignity that apartheid brought to people of color in South Africa. But again, Portugal wasn't the only country to pillage Africa as any map of the nationalities comprising the nations on the continent of Africa illustrates.

The above brief snippet of this aspect of human history shows, then, why being egalitarian was a fundamental component of that *survival-driven pattern*, discussed earlier, that became the socioeconomic lifeways pre-agriculture hunter-gatherers followed for nearly all of human existence. Being egalitarian meant, among other things, being socially, economically, and politically equal and hence excluded slavery. And, whereas sharing was an indispensable requirement of all, and was encouraged, ownership of private property, surplus hoarding, and wealth accumulation were not. And, whereas individual freedom was fundamental and fiercely protected and a prerequisite to being a member of a hunter-gatherer society, neither rulers, kings, nor queens were tolerated; nor did they acknowledge or worship creator gods or practice any religions.

It requires neither political nor economic genius, then, to recognize just how very different human history would have been had Neolithic humans stuck with the socioeconomic lifeways of their, and our, simple hunter-gatherer forebears and continued foraging instead of farming. Then, in that case, neither a de Klerk, nor a King Charles could have existed, nor would there have been any need for apologies. But alas! They do and who is going to apologize for *the pain, hurt, indignity, and harm* that Neolithic and all subsequent humans have wreaked upon humanity, upon Earth-life ecosystems now approaching collapse, and upon its biodiversity species potentially on the verge of extinction?

Who is going to save humans from themselves? Are there any more like de Klerk, Mandela, and Tutu out there? Is it too much to hope for the leaders of China, America, Russia, EU nations, and nations of the world to come together once more, but this time not to foster more economic growth, debate territorial borders, spheres of economic influence, or political and military dominance, but human survival?

Are any of you willing to put your personal, political, and national ambitions aside for the cause of our entire species? Are you intending, Chairman Xi, to deep-six the world by invading Taiwan? And are you willing too, President Putin, to do the same to Ukraine? Are you willing, President Trump, Prime Minister Keir Starmer, President Macron, Chancellor Merz, Prime Minister Anthony Albanese, Prime Minister Carney, Prime Minister Takaichi, President Lee Jae-myung, and Prime Minister Modi—is there a leader among you willing to lead the world away from being surplus-driven back to being survival-driven?

Are all leaders of the world intent on continuing down this mistaken path that Neolithic humans carved out for humanity, or are you willing to do what de Klerk, Mandela, and Archbishop Desmond Tutu began, and help not just South Africa, but all humanity find its way back to what began in Africa, back to the socioeconomic lifeways that enabled our species to survive for more than 290,000 years?

If we hope to survive, humans need to return to that *survival-first and survival-only socioeconomic* lifeway goal and outcome that our pre-agriculture hunter-gatherer ancestors followed. But at a time when a new generation of legal-person societies and economies has begun to replace human societies and economies, do humans still retain the right and ability to put human and nature's well-being above profits and to choose life and survival over wealth accumulation and endless economic growth?

Will human leaders, nations, and states be willing to abandon this *surplus-driven socioeconomic lifeway* that Neolithic humans chose, and modern humans still blindly follow? Is destroying Earth-life ecosystems and biodiversity, and potentially our entire species, the best humans are capable of? Global warming, climate change, and numerous Covid-19 pandemic variants are making it clear and hopefully helping us realize even as they are killing us, that to survive, humans have got to return to those *simple, hunter-gatherer, survival-driven, socioeconomic lifeways*. The time is now to replace our current profit-chasing, surplus-driven, wealth accumulation, and GDP-growth-first economic focus with the *survival-driven-pattern* and lifeways that enabled all Earth-life species, including our hunter-gatherer forebears, to survive for millennia.

We have seen how hard it has been for prior human leaders to acknowledge the harm they have caused and are causing, and to change course. Can one expect any better from those who have secured most of the Earth's resources and wealth for themselves, the 1 percent, and those who sit atop this new legal-person society and legal-person economy that has now almost replaced our once-human socioeconomic system? Why did the car and gas industry, which knew about the health risks of leaded fuel, sell it for 100 years anyway? Over the century, the product took millions of lives and to this day leaves the soil in many cities from New Orleans to London toxic.

Why? Because of the surplus it generated. Leaded gasoline enabled engines to run quietly and put out more power, and that meant selling more cars and making vast profits, but it also marked a century of tragedy, according to Bill Kovarik, Professor of Communication, Radford University, in an article published in The Conversation in 2021. After numerous public safety struggles, in 1996, the U.S. officially banned the sale of leaded gasoline for public health reasons. Europe was next in the 2000s and was followed by developing nations. In August 2021, the last country in the world to sell leaded gas, Algeria, banned it. The leaded gasoline story provides a practical example of how the industry's profit-driven decisions can cause serious and long-term harm.

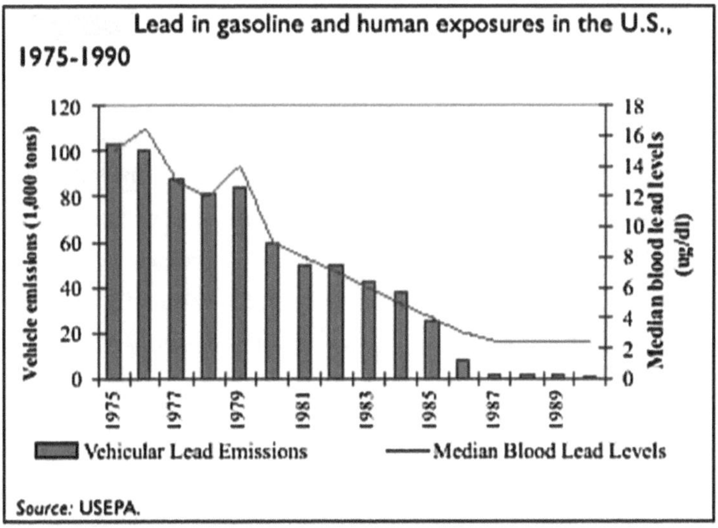

Figure 6-4. Lead in gasoline and human exposures in the U.S.

As leaded gasoline fell out of use, lead levels in people's blood fell as well. (Source: US EPA)

The oil industry was aware of the risks of CO_2-driven climate change decades ago. Consider what Big Oil knew about climate change, in the words of renowned physicist Edward Teller.

On its 100th birthday in 1959, Edward Teller warned the oil industry about global warming. He was asked to "summarize briefly the danger from increased carbon dioxide content in the atmosphere in this century." The physicist, as if considering a numerical estimation problem, responded:

At present, the carbon dioxide in the atmosphere has risen by 2 percent over normal. By 1970, it will be perhaps 4 percent, by 1980, 8 percent, by 1990, 16 percent [about 360 parts per million, by Teller's accounting], if we keep on with our exponential rise in the use of purely conventional fuels. By that time, there will be a serious additional impediment for the radiation leaving the earth. Our planet will get a little warmer. It is hard to say whether it will be 2 degrees Fahrenheit or only one or five. But when the temperature does rise by a few degrees over the whole globe, there is a possibility that the icecaps will start melting and the level of the oceans will begin to rise. Well, I don't know whether they will cover the Empire State Building or not, but anyone can calculate it by looking at the map and noting that the icecaps over Greenland and over Antarctica are perhaps five thousand feet thick.

What Exxon Mobil Didn't Say About Climate Change: The question dominating multiple court cases is whether the company misled consumers, shareholders, or the public about the environmental or business risks of climate change or about the risk that oil and gas reserves might become stranded assets that won't be developed, affecting shareholder value, according to Geoffrey Supran and Naomi Oreskes in a 2017 *New York Times* article. And, oh yeah, shareholder value! —that's the important thing!

American oil's awareness of global warming—and its conspiracy of silence, deceit, and obstruction—goes further than any one company. It extends beyond (though includes) ExxonMobil. The industry is implicated to its core by the history of its largest representative, the American Petroleum Institute.

At a House Oversight and Reform Committee hearing in Washington, D.C., in October of 2021, Rep. Carolyn Maloney (D-N.Y.), the chairwoman, said:

"Exxon and other big oil companies had the opportunity to tell the truth and lead the way to find alternative energy sources," she said, "but instead doubled down on fossil fuels and worked through a network of think tanks to play up scientific uncertainties and undermine national and global efforts to limit emissions."

It is now too late to stop a great deal of change to our planet's climate and its global payload of disease, destruction, and death. But we can fight to halt climate change as quickly as possible, and we can uncover the history of how we got here. There are lessons to be learned, and there is justice to be served, says Benjamin Franta, who holds a Ph.D. in applied physics from Harvard University. Other oil firms were also aware.

> *What Did Shell Know? Internal Shell Climate Documents Revealed - Climate Investigations Center on April 5, 2018.*

A 1988 document marked "CONFIDENTIAL" and titled "The Greenhouse Effect" details Shell's extensive knowledge of climate change impacts and implications. It also reveals an internal Shell climate science program dating back to 1981, well before the U.N. Intergovernmental Panel on Climate Change (IPCC) was founded. There were also other firms that supported this deception.

The Firms That Help Keep Oil Flowing. Secret investment funds put billions into fossil fuel projects, buying up offshore platforms and building new pipelines. According to new research, private equity firms have invested at least $1.1 trillion into the energy sector since 2010. Only about 12 percent of investment in the energy sector by private equity firms went into renewables, like solar or wind, since 2010, though those investments have grown at a faster rate. This matters as sales to private equity investors transfer those assets, and their emissions and other environmental hazards, away from the public eye so that they would not get counted in total CO_2, according to Jim Wilson of the *New York Times*.

When public companies sell high-emitting assets to smaller public or private companies that "face less operational scrutiny and investor pressure on climate issues," the "transfer in ownership potentially worsens real-world emission outcomes." But for asset managers that invest on behalf of these asset owners in private markets, hiding in the shadows will no longer be an option as asset owners representing more than $11 trillion are warning private equity firms and other alternative managers handling unlisted assets to make sure they don't fall behind the rest of the investment industry in reducing financed emissions.

A new report reveals coal knew, too. It wasn't just big oil that knew about climate change decades ago. The coal industry knew about the danger of rising greenhouse gas emissions as early as 1966. It looks like rather than just a few big oil giants, it's the whole fossil fuel industry that was aware of climate change as far back as the 1960s. An article by James R. Garvey, president of the now-defunct research firm Bituminous Coal Research, Inc., even goes on to say, "Such changes in temperature will cause melting of the polar icecaps, which, in turn, would result in the inundation of many coastal cities, including New York and London."

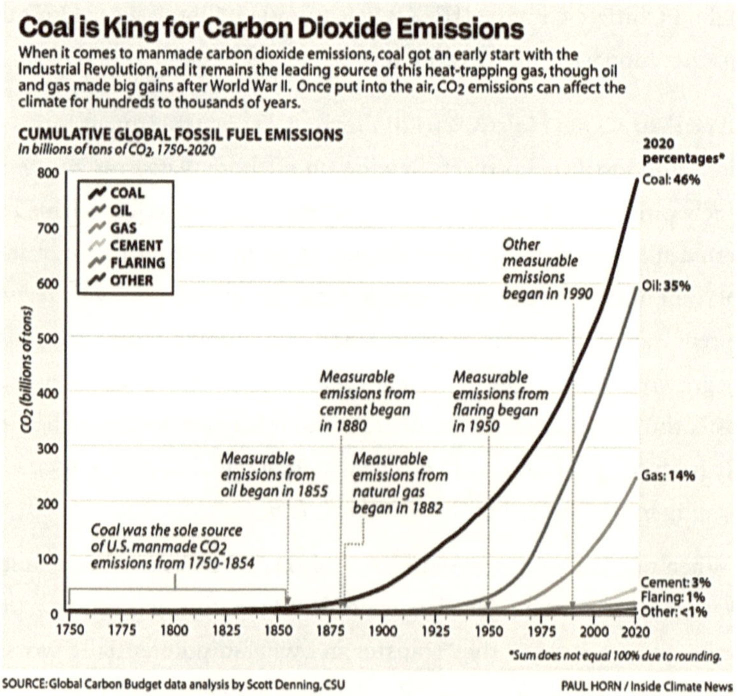

Figure 6-5. Coal is king for carbon dioxide emissions.

And although Coal Powered the Industrial Revolution, it left behind an "absolutely massive" environmental catastrophe. China and India burn two-thirds of the world's coal, and getting beyond coal will be an enormous challenge. Nevertheless, "Accelerating the global phaseout of coal is the single most important step" toward meeting the Paris Agreement's goal of keeping global warming to 1.5 degrees Celsius, according to U.N. Secretary-General António Guterres. This is a goal that may no longer be achievable.

At this point humans should be asking themselves, how is it that an intelligent species like us has managed to drive ourselves and all other species to the brink of what could well turn out to be an existential threat to our survival? How is it that humans, the lone surviving intelligent species on planet Earth, in its effort to eke out a living, have managed in the process to destroy innumerable Earth-life ecosystems and biodiversity, something our pre-agriculture hunter-gatherer forebears and all other not-so-intelligent Earth-life species since the Cambrian Explosion, including the dinosaurs, avoided for 290,000 years, safeguarding the survival of themselves and other species, and not driving the planet to the brink of what might well turn out to be a *Homo sapiens*-driven mass extinction? Why did Neolithic and modern humans get it so wrong?

With apparently not much prior knowledge of how the Earth-life systems work, why did Neolithic Revolution humans think they could have come up with such a new, novel, and non-obvious way to eke out a living without incurring risks of unknown negative consequences; a way no other Earth-life species, not even other hominins, attempted in half a billion years; a way that early members of our species, *Homo sapiens*, never tried? Why?

Here's why. The task to eke out a living was given to biological species with bio-instincts, emotions, and sensitivities needed to interact with other living biological species to mutually, interdependently, and successfully perform this task to survive—the goal and outcome of Earth-life species economies was life and survival, not surplus/profits generation, wealth accumulation, or GDP growth. It was never intended for mechanical nor electrical programmable robots, AI, or any other human invention lacking the means to understand, and biology to intelligently interact with, Earth-life processes that formed the very foundations of ecosystems and their biodiversity—and certainly not for legal-persons that would eventually wrest this task away from humans.

These human socioeconomic tasks of eking out a living *within* Earth-life ecosystems were the job of a biological species, such as humans, in harmony with other biodiversity and in a way that would ensure their mutual survival, and that of Earth-life ecosystems as well.

Doing so required following a particular set of *survival-driven patterns* as lived out in the lifeways of pre-agriculture hunter-gatherers. This was a socioeconomic approach characterized and choreographed by foraging, sharing, living in small mobile bands, and following a survival-driven pattern of neither owning, manipulating, nor destroying Earth-life ecosystems nor biodiversity species; a lifeway that they and all Earth-life species followed as they eked out a living successfully for hundreds of millennia. Neolithic humans, though, chose instead to farm rather than forage for a living and from that point onward humans began to pursue a new and different socioeconomic lifeway—one that is *surplus-driven instead of survival-driven*, and that has resulted in, and is continuing, the destruction of Earth-life ecosystems and biodiversity.

Modern humans would go on to adopt and enhance the surplus-driven lifeways of Neolithic humans, and, in an effort to maximize surplus, delegated this task of eking out a living to numerous innovations, and in particular legal-persons in the form of multinational corporations, such as those that comprise the oil, gas, auto, and coal industries; legal-persons that have none of the life-aware sensitivity of biological species, nor desire to ensure their survival; and neither the ability nor desire to do so without destroying all they encounter—including most human socioeconomic lifeways and Earth-life ecosystems and biodiversity.

Consequently, human survival today is imperiled by the economic pursuits of these human-enabled legal-persons, multinational corporations, that humans taught to be surplus-driven and surplus-driven only, with absolutely no built-in awareness of what it means to be alive and survival-driven and to hold life and survival above surplus accumulation and profit generation, which, in the twenty-first century, is resulting in global ecocide and is placing all biological life at risk.

One can continue to list these atrocities by industry of innumerable legal-persons, multinational corporations, that have relentlessly transformed and mostly destroyed Earth's habitats, biomes, human socioeconomic lifeways, and Earth-life ecosystems and biodiversity in pursuit of that *Neolithic surplus,* or as we prefer today, profits, shareholder wealth accumulation, and GDP growth. Today every area of modern human society and economy has been transformed, dominated, or supplanted and is currently run by these entities that are essentially replacing once-human societies and economies with legal-person societies and legal-person economies, and *human survival-driven lifeways* with new, non-biological surplus-driven lifeways of their own.

These legal-persons economies see humans as *financial beings* rather than *living beings.* They ignore critical distinctions between the accumulated financial assets of individuals and the health and well-being of living communities. They are incapable of grasping that the only legitimate purpose of an economy is to support and enable biological species' life and survival—of households in the case of humans—in making a living, not corporations in making a killing.

According to David Korten in his book *When Corporations Rule the World,* the company has now replaced the household as the defining unit of economic organization and analysis and money has become the measure of well-being. The modern home has become little more than a place to sleep and watch television. For many, food is delivered, movies and entertainment are streamed, clothing is laundered, and childcare is left to daycare or after-school tutoring or care. Few people find time to participate in community activities and services that once made neighborhoods more than a physical address—and fewer and fewer even know their neighbors.

The money and market economy has transformed our human lifeways into a socioeconomic system of individuals. Activities that were once done in the social (non-money) economy have now shifted to the money economy, increasing the dependence of the working class on money and therefore on those who own assets, provide professional services, and control access to jobs and the creation and allocation of money. Our once-dense fabric of relationships based on long-term sharing and cooperation that began with simple hunter-gatherer economies, and that subsequent human economies once maintained, has been unraveled.

How did our non-waged, non-monetized, and non-market, local-in-scope, sharing economies, that were by nature energized more by love than by money—how did these once socioeconomic lifeways shift from a human economy to a money economy and now, once more, to a legal-person economy? How did our activities shift from the non-money social economy of household and community; from a time when people met their basic needs for food, shelter, clothing, childcare, health care, care of the elderly, housekeeping, education, physical security, and entertainment, locally—to a money economy, and with it, the consequent erosion of our human socioeconomic lifeways?

Humans are now left dependent on global supply chains, harmful toxins, an automobile-dependent infrastructure, destabilizing carbon energy sources, and the pillage of nature's bounty at a rate far faster than nature can regenerate. There were human economies, non-waged, non-monetized, and non-market, local in scope, and by nature energized more by love than by money. (Korten, David C. (2015-06-28T22:58:59). But how did *legal-persons* and their surplus-driven lifeways come to dominate what was once human socioeconomic lifeways? Did humans abandon those once-caring human socioeconomic systems? If so, why?

With hindsight, having seen what kings, queens, presidents, dictators, and various rulers, whether democratic, communist, or fascist, or, whether religious, atheistic, benign, or despotic, have done to their own nations and countries throughout our brief history as a species, beginning with our Neolithic Revolution history, it can't be too hard to see why the socioeconomic lifeways practiced by pre-agriculture hunter-gatherers deliberately and forcefully precluded any societal or economic role for any such ruler, and why our early human ancestors were so fiercely egalitarian.

And yet, probably the only thing worse than having to live under one such ruler is living under one of those endowed with the power, resources, and reach of a global multinational corporation at their disposal. So, if you think Adolf Hitler, for example, was bad for Germans and the world, or Mao was bad news for the Chinese, or Putin for the Russians, to name a few, think of what such rulers would have been like combined with the power, economic and technological resources, and reach of, say, Apple, Google, or Facebook.

This is what happens when one combines the economic reach and power of a global multinational corporation with the political power of the state. This unholy alliance used to be called fascism, but many would recognize it better today as Big Oil, Big Pharma, Big Agriculture, Big Food, and . . . Big Tech. So how did these multinational corporations come to wield so much of the power of the state? In a word, because it was given to them by the state when corporations came to be seen as legal-persons, having the same rights and privileges accorded to human individuals under the U.S. Constitution.

According to Korten,

> *It is instructive to recall that the modern corporation is a direct descendant of the great merchant companies of the fifteenth, sixteenth-century England and Holland. These were limited-liability joint-stock companies to*

which the Crown granted charters that conferred on them the power to act as virtual states in dealing with vast foreign territories. The corporate charter represented a grant from the Crown that limited an investor's liability for losses of the corporation to the amount of his or her investment in it - a right not extended to individual citizens. Each charter set forth the specific rights and obligations of a particular corporation, including the share of profits that would go to the Crown in return for the special privileges extended. This essentially was a grant of royal power for a fee that today continues to be paid in the form political contributions.

Such charters were bestowed at the pleasure of the Crown and could be withdrawn at any time. Not surprisingly, the history of corporate-government relations since that day has been one of continuing pressure by corporate interests to expand corporate rights and to limit corporate obligations.

In 1602 for example, the Dutch Crown chartered The United East India Company, giving it a monopoly over Dutch trade in the lands and waters between the Cape of Good Hope at the southern tip of Africa and the Strait of Magellan at the tip of South America. Similarly, as if not to be left behind, the British established The British East India Company that became the primary instrument of Britain's colonization of India, a country it ruled until 1784 much as if it were a private estate. The company continued to administer India under British supervision until 1858 when the British government assumed direct control.

British Crown corporations also played an important role in the colonization of North America. The London Company founded the Virginia colony and for a time ruled it as company property. The Massachusetts Bay Company held rights to trade and colonization in the New England region. The Hudson's Bay Company, which was founded to establish British control over the fur trade in the Hudson's Bay watershed area of North America, was an important player in the British colonization of what is now Canada.

Corporations, then, having first come into being as the instruments of colonial extraction, have emerged as instruments of natural resources extraction, as well as the dominant institutions on Earth with the largest among them reaching into virtually every country in the world and exceeding most governments in size and power. It was President Abraham

Lincoln who observed just before his death: "Corporations have been enthroned . . . An era of corruption in high places will follow and the money power will endeavor to prolong its reign by working on the prejudices of the people . . . until wealth aggregated in a few hands and the Republic is destroyed." (See John Young, "Mining the Earth" in *State of the World 1992*, New York, W.W. Norton, 1992).

Similarly, President Rutherford B. Hayes, the eventual winner of those corporate-dominated negotiations, subsequently complained, "This is a government of the people, by the people, and for the people no longer. It is a government of corporations, by corporations, and for corporations."

Indeed, in 1886, in a stunning victory for the proponents of corporate power, the chief justice of the United States declared in Santa Clara County vs. Southern Pacific Railroad that *a private corporation is a natural person under the U.S. Constitution*—although the Constitution makes no mention of corporations. Subsequent court decisions interpreted this to mean that corporations are entitled to the full protection of the Bill of Rights, including the right of free speech and other constitutional protections extended to individuals in the Bill of Rights.

Thus, corporations came to claim the full rights enjoyed by individuals while being exempted from many of the responsibilities and liabilities of citizenship. In being guaranteed the same right to free speech as individual citizens, they achieved, in the words of Paul Hawken, "precisely what The Bill of Rights was intended to prevent: domination of public thought and discourse." The subsequent claim by corporations that they have the same right as an individual to influence the government in their own interest pits the individual citizen against the vast financial and communications resources of the corporation and mocks the constitutional intent that all citizens have an equal voice in the political debates surrounding important issues. (Korten, David C. (2015-06-28T22:58:59). Hence the rise of K Street, home to many lobbying firms that advance the interests of corporations.

In commenting on this takeover of human economies by *legal-person economies*, Korten observed that "Human societies have long faced the question of whether the power to rule will reside only with the rich or will be shared by all. Will the power to rule reside with people, no matter their financial circumstance, or will it reside with the artificial persona of the corporation?" But while twenty-first century humans must resolve these questions to survive, historically, these were not issues humans have ever faced as almost all of human history has been devoid of both governments and legal-person corporations.

Moreover, returning control to human governments will offer little or no improvement, as it was Neolithic humans in pursuit of economic surplus that started the handover of control to those humans with the means and ability to generate this surplus—farmers. Today, surplus generation is no longer just in the hands of farmers, but mostly in the hands of corporations, and twenty-first century governments are often manipulated by these corporations.

When one considers that being ruled by other humans, or by anything whatsoever, has for humans been more the exception than the rule; that for 290,000 years of pre-Neolithic Revolution existence, human societies and economies were more egalitarian than not and had neither rulers, religions, nor gods of any stripe; one soon realizes that the real difficulty humans face today is much deeper than just deciding whether any human or corporation should rule or have authority over humans but rather, how to return to those socioeconomic lifeways that needed no rulers whatsoever to survive—the survival-driven lifeways of our pre-agriculture hunter-gatherer forebears.

Ten thousand years ago, humans had to decide for the first time in their 290,000-year existence whether they would continue their foraging socioeconomic lifeways and thereby retain their individual freedom-to-choose and continue to control their individual destiny, and thereby, too, enable human society to remain egalitarian, or whether they would become farmers and thereby give up the freedom of their foraging lifeways, abandoning their foraging bands to farm as members of an agrarian community instead, in exchange for the economic surplus that farming promised.

This was the choice they had to make, and it is the same choice humans confront today. But back then it was not a democratic-style referendum, nor was it going to be easy. It was a choice made by humans all over the world independently, and sometimes collectively. They voted with their pocketbooks as people still do today—they chose farming over foraging or may have had that choice forced upon them. The fact that only a smattering of hunter-gatherers exists today tells us how that vote, or lack thereof, went. Perhaps this time around, though, having seen the outcome of voting for one's pocketbook, or having had the choices of others forced on them, if given another chance, humans might well be ready to vote for their survival.

Indeed, it took the better part of 4,000 years before that transition became commonplace among what became agrarian communities, cities, nations, and eventually civilization. In making this socioeconomic transition, and likely unrecognized by them, by deciding how they were going to eke out a living, as foragers or farmers, they were choosing on behalf of all subsequent humans, and deciding, among other things, whether humans would remain free and egalitarian (foraging), or work as peasants on a farm, and whether subsequent generations would end up ruling or being ruled by other humans. Embedded in this choice were numerous socioeconomic lifeway changes that they couldn't have seen.

They may have been choosing a method for procuring food (foraging vs. farming), but they were also deciding, among other things, whether humans were going to rule other humans; whether the power to rule would reside only with the rich as it did for subsequent millennia and mostly still does; or whether it would be shared by all. And they most certainly would not have realized, too, that they were choosing new and different lifeways that subsequent humans would inherit. They were giving up their hunter-gatherer freedom to choose the lifeways of the farm and would become peasants, subject to rulers, immersed in religions, and in time, would become slaves and eventually employees of a legal-person corporation.

Today, though, the question is no longer just whether that power to rule should or should not reside with people, no matter their financial circumstance, or with the artificial persona of the corporation, but eventually, whether this power to rule would abandon humans altogether to reside in the artificial intelligence of a machine. But as we have seen above, to truly get rid of this scourge altogether, in whatever form it might manifest itself, whether it be as human, *legal-person,* or superhuman machine AIs, *humans must abandon* the surplus-driven socioeconomic lifeways that Neolithic Revolution humans started and return to the *survival-driven lifeways* as lived by humans for most of our species' existence—a return to being fiercely egalitarian and free to live in harmony with its biodiversity *within* Earth-life ecosystems.

Now there is a corporation for almost everything and companies like Y Combinator, a technology startup accelerator, has launched more than 3,000 of them. The combined valuation of the top YC companies was more than $300 billion and counting as of January 2021, with the goal of creating even more "successful"—yes, *surplus-driven*—companies. But no one so far, it seems, thinks it would be worth humanity's socioeconomic while to establish *survival-driven startup companies* instead of the *surplus-driven* ones that Y Combinator churns out. Why is that so? Because corporations exist to pursue a single purpose and fulfill a single goal—to maximize shareholder profit and market growth, not ecosystem, biodiversity and human life and survival, nor the collective aspirations of human society. The closest modern economies have come to the latter is the so-called not-for-profit corporation.

And one should be suspicious, too, of the Jan Piotrowski(s) of this world, business editor of *The Economist*, who in a Jan 15, 2022, special report entitled, "Business and the State: The new interventionism," declares that more government interference would be counterproductive, and is even more troubled with the notion of a return of control of human economies back to humans. Human control of their economies is their evolutionarily assigned role—to eke out a living within Earth-life ecosystems in harmony with its biodiversity. These are tasks that, economic history demonstrates, neither governments nor corporations have had even a clue how to manage without committing ecocide—consider climate change-driven global warming and numerous zoonotic diseases—and running the risk of global "Econocide."

Economists and government regulators today continue to miss the obvious purpose of human societies and economies. They still tend to talk of key corporations as national champions. Corporations, on the other hand, view government economists and regulators and their industrial policies and tax and anti-trust regulations as meddlesome and a return to big government. Today, too, economists and government regulators like Margrethe Vestager, former EU competition commissioner, who is far from being a champion of human, ecosystem, and biodiversity survival, meekly mutters feeble aspirations like "We need to push for a broader notion of consumer harm." Others see some of the same corporations from whom consumer well-being needs to be protected as national champions and are wary of reliance on corporations controlled by adversaries for critical resources, and dependence on increasingly shaky supply chains for goods ranging from semiconductors to fossil fuels to pharmaceuticals.

Still others like Mariana Mazzucato, in her book *The Entrepreneurial State*, blame what's seen as an innovation drought on governments abandoning their role as chaperones to technological breakthroughs, as they were for the internet and biotechnology, while some proponents of industrial policy doubt that the goals of boosting innovation and creating lots of well-paying jobs complement each other. But the one thing on which they all seem to be in alignment is that neither economists, nor governments and their regulators, nor corporations see human, ecosystem, and biodiversity survival and well-being, as their principal goal and outcome for being and the only role of a human economy.

Why, then, would humans choose to relegate their task of eking out a living among Earth-life's ecosystems and biodiversity to corporations? Corporations have no awareness of biological life nor any obligation to ensure human or Earth-life species' well-being and survival when executing their profit maximization tasks. They are commanded by a hierarchy of managers that, operating like robots, are compelled to fulfill their business objectives and obligation regardless of the consequences, whether those cause damage to Earth-life ecosystems (97 percent to date) or drive most of their biodiversity to extinction.

And in case of doubt, one need only remember that this corporate economic behavior is why humans are confronted by zoonotic diseases like Covid-19 and climate-change-driven global warming, which threatens our very survival. From a corporate perspective, Earth's habitats, biodiversity, and even humans, generate services that are mere commodities to be bought and sold in this free, open, global corporate capitalist market economy. Why, then, did humans relinquish to them the task of eking out a living? And why are modern humans still doing so?

Corporations, according to Layne (2019), behave like a kind of artificial intelligence. While not autonomous, they are mostly unaware of and insensitive to the impact their financial and trade inputs and outputs have on humans, ecosystems, and biodiversity. But like an AI actor, a corporation knows no way to account for the ecosystem services provided by Earth's habitats, ecosystems, and biodiversity. It is choreographed by market movements, thinks in dollars, and communicates in market growth and profits.

It has no capacity to care about the harm this growth is doing to humans, the environment, Earth's habitats, biodiversity, or the buildup of CO_2 in the atmosphere and consequent global warming. It never eats, sleeps, breathes, or drinks, so it couldn't care less about the integrity of the human food chain, clean drinking water, or clean air, nor the health systems that are under siege by the chemical, biochemical, biotechnology, and agricultural businesses that are high on profits and low on species survival and the health of *Homo sapiens*.

Corporations are unaware of the disappearing pollinators and the damage being done to the oceans, including dead zones created by agricultural runoffs; dying coral reefs and the aquatic ecosystems they enable; and islands of plastic forming from the 18 million tons dumped into them each year. Corporations wouldn't know that plastics emit methane and ethylene, greenhouse gases, when they are exposed to sunlight and degrade; nor could they care less that microplastics are toxic to phytoplankton, which supplies 50 to 70 percent of the oxygen we breathe.

Corporations wouldn't know, either, that phytoplankton take carbon dioxide from the atmosphere and ocean to produce carbohydrates via photosynthesis and zooplankton; neither do they care that microplastics eaten by plankton may impair oceans' ability to trap and transport CO_2 to the seafloor, instead enabling it to escape back into the atmosphere, thereby creating a positive feedback loop that can accelerate global warming and warming seas, which, in turn, further threatens our atmospheric oxygen supply with a potential phytoplankton die-off.

Their algorithms do not enable them to recognize whether that dollar comes from the sale of an endangered species, an illegally harvested human organ, humans sold for sex, or from an auction for human slaves. And finally, they have no ability to stop until and unless the market-driving natural resources, Earth-life ecosystems, and biodiversity are exhausted; until humans stop buying what they produce and stop feeding them their skills, labor, innovations, and technologies; or until what's left of human societies and economies collapses.

Among the ways to avoid an extinction a potential legal-person-driven economy might well cause, humans must decide whether to return to the freedom and rulerless lifeways of our hunter-gatherer forebears; or continue to allow the power to govern to remain in the hands of human governments as is ostensibly mostly the case, and which has gotten us into this socioeconomic mess, or worse, will allow that power to continue to transition to corporate entities guided by *surplus-driven* agendas that care neither for humanity's nor nature's survival.

But until then, at this critical historical moment, while our species faces the fundamental challenge of freeing itself from the risk of a new global zoonotic disease outbreak while simultaneously wrestling with how it's going to contain global warming to within or close to 1.5^{0}C; humans must simultaneously consider how to go about re-igniting that survival-driven purpose and goal of all life, that original goal and outcome for human societies and economies—life and survival. Are modern humans going to step up to the challenge of undoing the false choice that Neolithic humans made? Are we ready to wrest control of our choices from governments and legal-persons (corporations) and choose the lifeways of our pre-agriculture hunter-gatherer forebears—to choose sharing over surplus hoarding and life and survival over wealth accumulation?

In this chapter, we have seen just what happens when, on a planet demonstrably capable of evolving and sustaining life for billions of years as Earth has, a species attempts to build its societies and economies and, in the process, begins to destroy the planet's life-sustaining mechanisms, habitats, ecosystems, and biodiversity that co-evolved to enable their survival. In abandoning the lifeways followed by all other species of how to eke out a living and build a sustainable society and economy, humans have turned out to be an unwitting example of just what could go wrong when a species becomes intelligent enough and develops the hubris to think it knows better than nature and chooses to re-engineer those life-sustaining mechanisms.

But humans may not have been the first intelligent species to make this mistake on their home planet and maybe that's one reason we have not encountered E.T. If such species did evolve and made mistakes similar to the ones humans are currently making, they may well have already driven themselves to extinction.

During the last 10,000 years, we have seen, too, what began and continues to happen to such species, and in this case, our species, *Homo sapiens*, believed to be the last surviving intelligent species on planet Earth. How, after successfully eking out a living within Earth-life ecosystems and in harmony with its biodiversity for 290,000 years, Neolithic Revolution humans began to abandon those *survival-driven lifeways* that sustained their human hunter-gatherer forebears, in exchange for a new *surplus-driven lifeway* with little regard for ecosystems or biodiversity; one that had little understanding of their purpose, but rather regarded them simply as materiel for human consumption.

We have seen, too, how humans, from the emergence of the Neolithic Revolution, began to destroy ecosystems and biodiversity, and thereby began to bring destruction upon themselves and upon those life-enabling ecosystems and biodiversity that hitherto enabled human survival. To survive and possibly have a chance at fulfilling any potential and yet-unexplored or unknown galactic roles that may yet await intelligent species, humans have a lot of correcting to do to recover from our current plight. The following are a few of the actions we might consider.

First, we must stop thinking and acting as though all life that evolved billions of years before humans did has little value, that everything on Earth is here primarily for human benefit. *Second,* we must rediscover and readopt those survival-driven lifeways that all other species follow if we hope to survive. *Third*, we must regain control of what's left of our future and bring human societies and economies into harmony and alignment with Earth-life ecosystems and biodiversity. *Fourth,* we must reclaim the power we have yielded to *surplus-driven* human economies, governments, and legal-person multinational corporations and rediscover the egalitarian lifeways that kept our hunter-gatherer forebears going for most of our species' existence. *Fifth*, we urgently need a return to humility.

While Hobbes and others might take exception to being characterized as animals, humans are nonetheless nothing more than one of the many animal species (albeit an intelligent one) that evolved on this planet and represent just 0.01 percent of all life. Hence, we must adjust our view and understanding of our place among the other life forms that share this planet. *Sixth*, we must immediately find a way to reduce and restrain human population growth to a level such that it does not encroach upon biodiversity's share of 30 percent of the carrying capacity of the Earth as per COP15. And *seventh,* we must redirect the goal and outcome of all human societies and economies to follow that original goal and outcome: Earth-life ecosystems, biodiversity, and human life and survival. Why these prerequisites, you ask?

Because only after humans have learned how to thrive and survive in harmony with other Earth-Life species on one planet without destroying the *foundations* for life and survival on that planet, and only after understanding the role ecosystems and biodiversity serve on Earth, perhaps then and only then will humans have attained the *maturity* required to continue to survive on Earth, and potentially, be ready to take on the challenge of spreading mature human lifeways on an Earth 2.0.

PART FOUR

Technology and Human Economies

NEITHER TECHNOLOGIES NOR INNOVATIONS ENABLED HUMAN SURVIVAL DURING THE LAST GLOBAL CLIMATE CHANGE AND MIGRATION, AND CHANCES ARE THEY WON'T THIS TIME, EITHER

TECHNOLOGIES AND INNOVATIONS HAVE become so pervasive across most aspects of modern human societies and economies that it is hard to imagine there was actually a time when there were almost none. And it comes as a surprise to learn that they emerged, originally, from within Earth-life species economies, and eventually out of human economies driven by the same need to eke out a living within ecosystems in harmony with its biodiversity.

In fact, the first Stone Age foraging tools, the earliest known technologies and innovations, though adopted and refined by humans, weren't initially developed by early modern humans but by earlier hominin species to forage for food and to avoid becoming food. In short, to ensure life and survival. Here, then, were the purpose and need technologies and innovations may have emerged to fulfill. Note, too, where they emerged—within early economies that evolved within ecosystems.

And if ensuring life and survival is the goal and outcome technologies and innovations emerged to enable, how does this compare with the goals and outcomes modern technologies and innovations are designed to serve—to drive profits, market share, economic growth, and competitive advantage? Which of these disparate sets of goals and outcomes has been more successful at enabling ecosystem, biodiversity, and human life and survival? By pursuing the former, pre-agriculture hunter-gatherer humans thrived and survived for most of humanity's existence, whereas pursuit of the latter over just the last 12,000 years has driven the collapse of numerous human societies, economies, and civilizations.

One would think that given that hunter-gatherers lived collapse-free for 290,000 years compared to the widespread economic and civilization collapses of the last 12,000 years, modern humans by now would have abandoned their failing socioeconomic lifeways of the last 400 generations and returned to the proven economic goal and outcome of our hunter-gatherer forebears. But that clearly has not happened. Instead, humanity has doubled down on this failed misuse of its technologies and innovation capabilities, which has intensified the likelihood it would instead use these to engineer its own destruction.

Today, the locus and focus of technologies and innovations are no longer exclusively within the human economy, nor has their main purpose remained helping humans eke out a living within ecosystems or ensuring ecosystem, biodiversity, and human life and survival. In fact, the reverse is now the case. Today these are developed and deployed primarily in profit-making ventures and often result in the destruction of Earth-life ecosystems, numerous biodiversity species extinctions, and activities that threaten human life and survival.

Modern human technologies and innovations have now expanded beyond ensuring human life and survival from within human societies and economies. In fact, they have been hijacked by legal-person economies that began replacing human economies, and their growth accelerated. Once meant for enabling human life and survival, they have become instruments of ecosystem destruction and biodiversity extinction and are threatening human life and survival with a potential global warming climate change-driven extinction.

Their purpose has changed to helping corporations make a killing rather than allowing humans to make a living. And that initial purpose, the enablement of economies to support human, biodiversity, and ecosystem life and survival, has been hijacked, reversed, and redeployed within legal-person economies by legal-persons that exist mainly to generate surplus, profits, shareholder and stakeholder wealth, and GDP growth.

Humans become mesmerized and are often misguided by the promise of emerging technologies and innovations while their true impact remains unknown, as with AI today. But when their effects are seen from the perspective of the preceding 10,000 years, it's clear their net effect has often been more harmful than beneficial, and they have contributed more to ecosystem, biodiversity, and human harm than to life and survival. Often what was hailed and celebrated as life changing and possessing great promise has turned out to be the scourge of subsequent generations.

Chemical fertilizers, herbicides, pesticides, and insecticides, for example, were once seen as great innovations. They became the foundations of the Green Revolution and enabled humanity to provide enough food to solve another of its problems—the need to increase food production and reduce poverty and hunger in developing countries—until it was discovered that these also led to environmental degradation, killed numerous pollinators (bees, insects, and bird species) and threatened parts of the human food chain that rely on the ecosystem services these species provide, such as pollination. These also enable agricultural runoff charged with phosphorus, nitrogen, and carbon that may make a cornfield or a lawn grow faster, but that promote algae growth as well, often creating algae blooms that kill numerous marine life species, and impair human health, aquatic ecosystems, and consequently the economy.

Similarly, gasoline-powered internal combustion engines were great until, one hundred years after their invention, we reluctantly admitted that the carbon monoxide they emitted was a major cause of disease and death, and the CO_2-spewing automobiles and industrial equipment were just the beginning installments on the gigatons that would follow from the adoption of fossil fuels as our main energy source, having mostly abandoned the renewable energy sources of the ecosystem.

Few might have understood their impact back then. But from the beginning of the Industrial Revolution, humanity began a rapid buildup of CO_2 in the atmosphere that three hundred years later has brought us face to face with what is threatening to become a potential greenhouse-gas-driven global warming self-extinction.

Now, after centuries spent grooming the powers and capacities of legal persons (national and multinational corporations), and legal-person economies, to become generators of profit, wealth, and GDP; and of coming up with even more wealth-creating innovations and technologies that have continued to threaten ecosystems, biodiversity, and human survival, some humans, perhaps awakened by the threat of climate change, have finally begun to rethink humanity's reasons for creating technologies and innovations and their approach to deploying them, as well as their purpose, and how to safely deploy them instead to build sustainable human societies and economies.

Finally, too, others have begun to research, discover and imitate nature's bio-inspired-eco-friendly solutions and have even begun to consider and pursue a new kind of economy—so called wellbeing economies. So today "biomimicry" has become a thing, and "technology for good" is going mainstream. Imagine that! Humanity might be just beginning to rediscover the initial goal and purpose innovations and technologies might have evolved to serve—to enable humans to sustainably eke out a living within Earth's ecosystems in harmony with its biodiversity.

But what was so different about the technologies and innovations our pre-agriculture hunter-gatherer forebears came up with and used during those 290,000 years that enabled their societies and economies to survive and grow without destroying themselves and almost everything around them, as our use of many modern technologies and innovations seem incapable of avoiding today?

And why, too, if indeed early humans survived and thrived without collapse for all those millennia, did they only come up with what would seem like less than 1 percent of all the technologies and innovations humanity has invented during its entire 300,000-year existence? Here's a hint! Inventing and innovating was not a goal in itself—life and survival was! They invented and innovated only what was necessary to preserve life and survival, not for profit, wealth creation, and GDP growth.

It has been more than 10,000 years since that period ended and given the direction, or rather lack thereof, of modern technologies and innovations, it's clear that humans still have not figured out the goal and purpose these capabilities were intended to fulfill. Yet one thing is clear: The survival of those hunter-gatherer societies and economies did not require an incessant flow of new, novel, and non-obvious technologies and innovations like the ones deemed so indispensable today.

It would seem that early humans were not interested in technologies and innovations for their own sake, whether these were technologies to explore the universe, discover the secrets of nature, increase food production, or manipulate human societies and human choices. Nor were they seeking to prey on humanity to generate a profit as, for example, social media companies like Facebook, Instagram, Google, Microsoft, Tik Tok and others do. Nor were they seeking to wage wars but rather, simply to enable life and survival.

And indeed, though the pre-Stone Age and Stone Age technologies they came up with weren't the kind that would have inspired a Nobel Prize, they nonetheless may have enabled their life and survival for millennia—and that, it would seem, was the point and all they ever wanted. Theirs were technologies and innovations that were inspired by the *survival-driven lifeways* they followed.

These lifeways prioritized life and survival above all else, and that socioeconomic philosophy guided and shaped what technologies and innovations they did, but mostly did not, come up with. It ensured the building of societies and economies that preserved the ecosystems, biodiversity, and life itself, which lasted for most of human existence.

The fact that they sought neither to domesticate, own, manage, nor control (DOMC) Earth-life species or ecosystems, but followed the *wisdom of the waterhole* in their economies, enabled them to come up with technologies and innovations that helped them eke out a living *within* those ecosystems in harmony with its biodiversity, without collapse, for most of our species' existence. This, then, must be the only goal and outcome that modern human technologies and innovations imitate if we, too, wish to build societies and economies that last for millennia without destroying ecosystems, biodiversity, and humanity itself.

In contrast, today our technologies and innovations are funded and developed to explore our R&D curiosity; to enable profit and wealth generation; and for economic growth rather than ecosystem, biodiversity, and human survival. We use them to help us domesticate, own, manage, and control all Earth-life species and exploit ecosystem resources and our fellow humans. They are often wielded more like instruments of death than of life and survival.

To change the goal and outcome of our technologies and innovations, humans must first change the socioeconomic lifeways that drive their creation. Only by adopting those survival-driven, waterhole-inspired socioeconomic lifeways that guided our forebears and inspired their survival-driven approach to technologies and innovations, can modern humans hope to develop technologies and innovations that would ensure humans build societies and economies that prioritize life and survival and can last for millennia as theirs did, without destroying Earth-life species, ecosystems, and humanity in the process.

In Chapter 1 we learned that economies were an emergent property of the existence of life, and that economies emerged first from the foraging activities of Earth-life species (Earth-life species economies), and eventually from humans (human economies), as humans, too, went about the task of eking out a living *within* Earth's ecosystems. Economies emerged as the third component of a survival-driven *Triad of Life*, which posits that without intact ecosystems, there can be no survival; without survival, there can be no life; and without life foraging for a living *within* Earth's ecosystems, there can be no economies.

In this chapter we now see that human technologies and innovations were also emergent. They emerged to serve a survival-driven purpose—that without life's *survival-driven* technologies and innovations that helped life forage for a living within those ecosystems, there would be neither life nor economies.

It may not have occurred to humanity that, as with many other aspects of the Earth system, there might have been a *survival-driven* role intended for human technologies and innovations, but clearly there is, and modern humans getting this role right may well determine whether these become instruments that enable life and survival or death and extinction.

Technology and innovation applied with a survival-driven touch, as our pre-agriculture hunter-gatherer forebears did for most of our species' existence, ensures life and survival. But when applied as our Neolithic Revolution forebears did, and as subsequent humans have imitated, ecosystems get destroyed, biodiversity is driven to extinction, entire civilizations collapse, and humanity itself is left at risk of extinction. Yet, for human technologies and innovations, the survival-driven role, purpose, and outcome remain the same as they were 300,000 years ago when humans emerged—to enable humanity to eke out a living *within* Earth's ecosystems in harmony with its biodiversity, destroying neither them nor ourselves in the process.

One can't help but wonder, though, just how many start-ups, and how many academic-, corporate-, or government-driven innovation and scientific research efforts, have adopted humanity's life and survival as the overarching goal and outcome underpinning their technology and innovation efforts. Unless and until this becomes the overarching goal and outcome of all innovation, research, and technology efforts, life and survival will always remain at risk of a technology-enabled extinction—as it is at present by a technology-enabled, fossil fuel-driven climate change, and as it potentially could be at the hands of a superhuman artificial machine intelligence.

Technology and Human Economies

NEITHER TECHNOLOGIES NOR INNOVATIONS ENABLED HUMAN SURVIVAL DURING THE LAST GLOBAL CLIMATE CHANGE AND MIGRATION, AND CHANCES ARE THEY WON'T THIS TIME, EITHER

CHAPTER 7

Technology
and
Human Economies

7.

Technology and Human Economies

"Our intelligence is responsible for our civilization. With access to greater intelligence, we could have a greater and perhaps better civilization."
—Stuart Russell, Human Compatible

IS IT TRUE THAT EVERYTHING CIVILIZATION HAS TO offer has been the product of human intelligence and that gaining access to considerably greater intelligence, as in superhuman artificial machine intelligence (Superhuman AI), would be the biggest event in human history? There are many who believe human intelligence is responsible for our civilization and that achieving a higher level of intelligence would not only be our greatest technological achievement but the greatest event in human history. Others, though, think that such a technological breakthrough, if achieved, might well be the last in human history, and they might well have a point, not necessarily because of potential human annihilation by a rogue super-intelligent machine AI (although that's probably possible), but more likely, by a power-crazed rogue human in control of one.

While pursuing such innovations and technologies, humans may not have bothered to notice that none of the powers or capabilities that enable the entire planet to function and sustain life, are under the control of humans or any other species. Was that intentional? Among these forces and mechanisms is the planet's climate, and as far as we know humanity has exhibited little to no ability to manipulate or safely control Earth's climate. Except, perhaps inadvertently, by applying one of its not-so-recent innovations—the burning of fossil fuels and other greenhouse gases as energy sources to power our economies—thereby engendering the global warming climate change extinction risk that humanity now confronts.

Noting what can result, it's more likely that denying humans, as well as other Earth-life species, access to the Earth's control mechanisms may well have been deliberate. And that's probably because no Earth-life species has yet attained that level of maturity that would restrain it from using such powers in ways that would bring about its own extinction and potentially that of all life on the planet. This is a level of maturity an intelligent species attains when it matures past the point of self-extinction. It is also known as "evolutionary maturity" as described by Layne (2019). Perhaps humans, too, should apply the same maturity test to its AI and similar innovations before surrendering the keys to its societies and economies.

One often hears that humans are hardwired to respond to short-term problems—to follow the path of least resistance, to help one another, to behave in a socially caring manner that some call biological altruism—more than to maximize personal gain, although it would be hard to convince the world's deprived 99 percent of this. But this biological wiring, if indeed it exists, would have had 290,000 years of anatomically modern human evolution, the evolution of hunter-gatherers, and may well have prepared early humans for the Stone Age more than it prepared modern humans for this complex world that we, their progeny, have built just 10,000 years later.

While humans have yet to attain that level of maturity, our ability to adopt and innovate new technologies has accelerated since the Neolithic Revolution, and these are being used more for harm than for good, highlighting a strong correlation between our ability to innovate and invent new technologies and our inclination to use these to choose harm over good. Without this level of maturity, humans have experienced numerous examples of the devasting effect to which its technologies and innovations have been and could be put. After all, it was President Vladimir Putin, who is wont to threaten the use of nuclear weapons to settle international disputes, who remarked in September 2017, "whoever reaches a breakthrough in developing artificial intelligence will come to dominate the world."

And while Putin won't be the first or the only human to use such technological innovations to dominate or destroy others, if the February 24, 2022, unprovoked invasion of Ukraine is any indication, he would no doubt be among those who would have few qualms about doing so. For the world's sole surviving intelligent hominin species, humanity's biggest and most urgent challenge, then, is not how to invent a superhuman intelligent machine (AI), or some other astonishing scientific or technological marvel, but rather, how to advance as an intelligent species to that level of maturity and thereby get past this seemingly growing inclination to use our intelligence and the technologies we produce to drive our own extinction.

But lest one forget, when it comes to either dominating the world or destroying life by nefarious use of human innovations and technologies, if the climate change-driven global warming that now threatens our survival is any indication, humans won't have to await the invention of a superhuman machine artificial intelligence to do either, as the invention of farming and fossil fuels has already gotten us to that precipice. The invention of agriculture at the dawn of the Holocene facilitated the transition from foraging to farming as a way to eke out a living and build human societies and economies. When combined with other technologies now enabled and energized by the fossil fuels discovered some 250 years ago, agriculture became industrialized. Thus, agriculture together with fossil fuels truly became the "Destroyer of Worlds," long before Oppenheimer would invent the atomic bomb, and thus became all that would be necessary to dominate the world and destroy all life.

With just these two sets of innovations, farming and fossil fuels, humans have not only transformed the Earth but have become the most dominant and dangerous species to roam it, and we've gone on to use these inventions to put at risk not only our own survival but that of all Earth-life species and ecosystems as well. Yet, who would have imagined, or foreseen, that it would be farming, not AI, and fossil fuels, not nuclear bombs—invented to feed, mechanize, and turbocharge human economies and societies, or so we thought—that could become the built-in destroyers of both? Imagine that!

Today we're awash in innumerable technological innovations that have fundamentally changed the lifeways in which modern societies and economies work and play, so much so that we have come to think of them as though they are indeed indispensable and impossible to live without. But clearly, they are not. Our pre-agriculture hunter-gatherer forebears built their societies and economies and survived for 290,000 years with neither need of, nor use for, any of the innovations or technologies we have conjured up in the last 10,000; and survived without engendering any of the existential threats to themselves, other species, and the Earth as modern humans have done through our inventions and innovations. It should be clear, then, that human survival, and therefore the success of our economies and societies, was once independent of twenty-first century technologies and innovations and can become so once more should humans choose to abandon them as we are choosing to abandon the use of GHG-generating fossil fuels as an energy source.

It begs this question, though, doesn't it: If most of our modern innovations and technologies do not enable human life and survival, what then is the real purpose driving so much scientific research, modern technology innovation and development? And what indispensable roles, if any, do they play that without them our species would cease to exist? If humanity survived without these for most of our species' existence, what makes them so indispensable now? For 97 percent of our species' existence, stone tools were not just all, but the only technologies and innovations anatomic modern humans possessed. They were adopted from earlier hominin forebears and enhanced by our pre-agriculture hunter-gatherer forebears to hunt for food and to prevent themselves from becoming food. Their sole purpose was to ensure their life and survival.

Many can and will point to innumerable scientific discoveries and inventions that have proven beneficial, and that have saved lives, such as penicillin or the more recent Covid-19 mRNA vaccines. But we seldom stop to connect the dots and recognize that it was our so-called Neolithic Revolution that may have started it all. It was mainly after early humans began herding and dwelling with farm animals that most common infections, in this case zoonotic viruses, might have jumped to humans. If humans had not encroached on their habitats as we continue to do today for illegal wildlife trade, land grabs, and wildlife habitats seized for agricultural products expansion, penicillin would not be needed today. In addition, some such infections could well have been the result of scientific research, such as bioweapons research. What human survival purpose is served by enhancing already deadly zoonotic viruses by such research?

If the history of our species is any guide, our forebears also invented and used numerous stone tools, technologies, and innovations but primarily, it would seem, to eke out a living in ways that simultaneously preserved Earth's ecosystems, biodiversity, and their own lives. As discussed, early humans looked to the goal and outcome, *life and survival*, as their true north—it appears to have informed many of their societal and economic lifeway choices and decisions. Modern humans, though, pursue scientific research, new technologies, and innovations for entirely different reasons; seldom is the driving reason shaped by a desire to preserve Earth's ecosystems, biodiversity, and human life and survival.

Scientific research and development may well begin with noble academic, scientific goals and for altruistic purposes (which is purportedly the rationale for the International Space Station) but invariably morph into other goals, including military goals devoted to creating weapons of war as Neil deGrasse Tyson and Avis Lang relate in their book *Accessory to War*. Or R&D is devoted to technology products and services that drive surplus, profits, wealth, shareholder and stakeholder benefits, economic development, and GDP growth—often with little regard, if any, for the preservation of Earth-life ecosystems, biodiversity, and human life.

And it is this change in the purpose of some, if not most, scientific research and development, technologies, and innovations to achieve societal, economic, and military goals, unrestrained by the need to preserve Earth's ecosystems, biodiversity, and human survival, that has led to outcomes that drive more harm than good and that have now placed our very survival as a species at risk. There will always be a good reason for conducting scientific research, or the pursuit of sundry technologies and innovations, but there will never be a good reason to pursue or use such in ways that destroy the very foundations of life. That, unfortunately, is where the purpose and results of much of humanity's research and development of technologies and innovations are headed, or often end up.

Given how much modern humans revel in technology, one would think we were its originators. But if you thought so, you would be wrong. Evidence of the existence and use of technology predates *Homo sapiens* and can be traced as far back as 3.3 million years ago as evidenced by what looks like stone tools (Figure 7-1), knives, hammers, and anvils uncovered at Lake Turkana in Kenya. And that would take us back to the time of the genus *Australopithecus*, and *Lucy,* a famous member of this species who lived some 4.4 million to 1.4 million years ago in southern Africa. They predated even the best-known forebear of our species, *Homo erectus*,who dates to 1.5 million years ago, and with whom the first controlled use of fire is associated. These all lived during the Pliocene and Pleistocene epochs (which lasted from 5.3 million to 11,700 years ago) and emerged well before our species evolved.

Figure 7-1. A stone tool revolution occurred some 300,000 years ago.

The two objects on the right are pigments used between 320,000 and 500,000 years ago in East Africa. All other objects are stone tools used during the same time period in the same area. (Source: Smithsonian Institution - Human Origins Program, NMNH)

But as we have seen in an earlier chapter, anatomically modern humans emerged just some 300,000 years ago and lived 290,000 of that during the

Pleistocene, through the end of the last ice age, and into the Holocene. This most recent ice age peaked between 24,000 and 21,000 years ago, when vast ice sheets covered North America and northern Europe, and mountains like Africa's Mount Kilimanjaro and ranges like South America's Andes were encased in glaciers. The last ice age corresponds with the period archaeologists call the Upper Paleolithic period (40,000 to 10,000 years ago), the last subdivision of the Paleolithic or Old Stone Age, in which humans made great leaps forward in toolmaking and weaponry, including the first tools used exclusively for making other tools. It lasted through the Neolithic Revolution and the beginning of agriculture some 10,000 to 12,000 years ago.

During this period, the only technologies and innovations these pre-agriculture hunter-gatherers possessed were made of stone (Figure 7-1). They were foraging, pre-agriculture hunter-gatherers using stone tools and packing stone weapons when a global warming change in climate began driving the migration of numerous species, enabling new technologies and innovations, including agriculture, and may well have facilitated their eventual transition from foraging to farming.

And yes, these pre-agriculture hunter-gatherers also had an encounter with global warming climate change and survived to build a civilization. But that change in the Earth's climate would not have been a consequence of any of their stone-age technologies and innovations. Now 12,000 years later, we, their progeny, have also found ourselves confronting a far worse encounter—yet another global warming climate change. But this one is a consequence of our use of GHGs, an energy innovation we came up with in the nineteenth century to power the growth of our economies. They survived to build a civilization—but will our fossil-fuels energy technologies prevent us from surviving to build the next one?

As the Pleistocene - Holocene transition progressed, the Last Glacial Maximum, the last ice age, was coming to an end. Humans and other surviving *Homo* species were forced to adopt new societal and economic lifeways and more generalized stone tools (Figure 7-1) to exploit and survive a changing environment, fauna and flora, and other resources. As the temperature grew warmer, many species, including megafauna that dominated the last ice age, went extinct, including all other Hominin species—only *Homo* sapiens survived. Such changes would, no doubt, have been pronounced. Not only was this a transition through an ice age that comprised numerous rapid climate fluctuations from less cold to very cold, and eventually, to temperate and slowly warming weather, it was also one that resulted in a global remodeling of Earth's habitats (particularly in East Africa), biomes, and ecosystems, with significant changes in the biodiversity, fauna, and flora that occupied them—and hence, the food sources and lifeways of all surviving species.

But also occurring at this time was not just a transition of Earth's climate but of its geology and topography, continuing a process that had begun some 20 million years earlier when the Indian and Asian continental plates clashed and elevated the massive Tibetan plateau. According to Mark Maslin, in a 2013 article in Scientific American, "as the peaks of Tibet were thrusting upwards a rifting process began in Ethiopia that ran south all the way to Mozambique that produced a deep, wide hanging valley half a mile above sea level with two-mile-high mountain ranges on either side."

The effects on local climate of this Rift Valley formation, as it became known, were dramatic. Maslin continues, "it not only prevented moist air from the Indian Ocean from passing over East Africa, but completely changed its topography from a homogeneous flat region covered in moist forests to a mountainous landscape with plateaus and deep rift valleys, resulting in fragmented vegetation where it varied from cloud forest to desert scrub." The development of this East Africa Rift Valley fragmented the landscape and formed many separate deep lakes that, over time, disappeared and reappeared, causing fundamental environmental changes during the Pleistocene, around 2.6 million, 1.8 million, and 1.1 million years ago—all key dates in human history, and a period that records the highest diversity of hominin species in human history, and that may well have pushed early humans out of Africa. Was it, then, the powerful forces of plate tectonics and climate variability that ultimately led to our hominin ancestors' development and their dispersal from Africa to the Caucasus, the Fertile Crescent, and ultimately the rest of the world?

It is worth interjecting a comment here to draw attention to some similarities between their dilemma and ours, and to the limitations of human technologies and innovations. As early Africans were confronted by great seismic and geologic transformations in addition to climate change, it's likely that none of their Stone-Age technologies and innovations would have made a difference or could have changed how the Earth was being transformed. Fortunately, they were able to migrate. It is unlikely, too, that any of our technologies and innovations in the twenty-first century will make enough of a difference either, as global warming climate change continues to bellow out heat across the world like an angry dragon, enshrouding the planet in a blanket of heat in response to the gigatons of GHGs we continue to discharge into the atmosphere.

But for them there was more, as meltwater from receding glaciers carved out huge valleys and created numerous lakes, and as patchy boreal forests gave way to broadleaf tropical forests and grasslands. And it was this change in topography and climate that accompanied the Terminal Pleistocene-Holocene transition that choreographed a remaking of our species (Layne, 2019). It may have driven numerous adaptations and a survival-driven technology and innovation explosion that changed for good not only where and how they would forage but their socioeconomic lifeways as well.

Humans, perhaps for the first time, began to live in a stable climate made possible by the dawn of the Holocene; they became sedentary. They began to stay in one place and take advantage of emerging new crops that eventually may well have enabled the emergence of farming, the Neolithic Revolution, agriculture, and eventually, the birth of civilization. Indeed, scientists are continuing to assemble a coherent picture of how the changing East African landscape and its climate drove human evolution.

Climate change and plate tectonics, then, played a significant role in the inter-epoch transition our species endured. It engendered a burst in adaptation-driven Stone Age technologies and innovations at the dawn of the Holocene that is believed to have driven the cumulative culture that became the foundation for future human technology expansion. Note, however, there were no mitigation-based technologies as, unlike modern humans, no one back then would have imagined or thought their Stone-Age technologies could have stopped the seismic, topographic, geographic, and geological changes that were occurring, or the global warming they were experiencing.

Now, some 12,000 years later, humans find themselves once again at the start of yet another geologic epoch transition, from the Holocene to (what may or may not be called) the Anthropocene, and at the start of yet another global climate change—this time, though, a global climate change spurred by human innovation and technology. And it's beginning to appear, too, that this time around climate change, also in the form of global warming, seems set—not with plate tectonics but with the help of rising and overheating oceans—to not only re-architect Earth's habitats, biomes, ecosystems, and biodiversity, but once again to choreograph the societal and economic lifeways of our species, perhaps in ways no modern human would have ever encountered.

Having learned, during the last 12,000 years, how to navigate the change from eking out a living during an ice age to doing so in the increasingly warm and even temperatures of the Holocene, humans must once again figure out just how to do that. This time, though, we exit the mostly even temperatures of the Holocene that enabled agriculture and civilization and enter the increasingly hot temperatures of the Anthropocene that may well bring an end to both. Like our hunter-gatherer forebears, we too will be forced to resort to new mitigations and adaptations, and new technologies, in the hope they will enable us to survive the increasingly hot temperatures that will accompany the rest of the twenty-first and succeeding centuries.

Humans barely survived the last geologic and climate transitions from the ice age of the Pleistocene to the moderate temperatures of the Holocene, and it remains unclear whether humanity can survive this next transition, one that it has triggered via its energy technologies and innovations. In this way, it has launched societies into the great geologic unknown, from the mostly level temperatures of the Holocene to what's beginning to look more like the Hothouse Earth of the Eocene.

"Humanity has a 'brief and rapidly closing window' to avoid a hotter, deadly future," says the latest report from the IPCC, the Intergovernmental Panel on Climate Change. "It foresees an escalating toll and warns that many of the impacts of global warming are now irreversible, and humans and nature are being pushed beyond their abilities to adapt." In this increasingly hot world, parts of the planet will become uninhabitable in the not-so-distant future, and if unchecked, rising CO_2 levels will increase ocean temperatures and thereby raise sea levels several feet, swallowing small island nations and overwhelming even the world's wealthiest coastal regions.

Drought, heat, hunger, and disaster may force millions of people from their homes and countries and drive a level of climate migration that would dwarf the migration of Ukrainians driven from their land by an unprovoked Russian invasion. Coral reefs could vanish, along with a growing number of animal species. Disease-carrying insects, and potentially more deadly pandemics, could proliferate. Deaths—from malnutrition, extreme heat, and pollution—will surge.

These are some of the grim projections detailed by the IPCC. And yet there is still hope, top scientists say. The world can still choose a less catastrophic path—yet it has not, even after 30 years of IPCC sounding the alarm. For a more in-depth review of the impact global warming-driven climate change will have on Earth's habitats, ecosystems, biodiversity, human societies, and economies, be sure to review the "IPCC Climate Change 2022 Impacts Report: Why it matters." And look here: "Unfccc (2006) Technologies for adaptation to climate change" for some of the types of lifeways adaptations, technologies, and innovations scientists think might yet enable our survival.

But don't pin too much hope on all that talk of new technologies that could fight climate change and overcome sea-level rise; nor on our species' much-vaunted ability to innovate and develop such technologies. As seen earlier, this won't be the first time humans have encountered the ravages of a global change in climate, or the socioeconomic impact that results from a rearrangement of the Earth's surface within ecosystems.

History shows that notwithstanding the adaptations, technologies, and innovations of humans and numerous other extant *Homo* species, including *Homo habilis, Homo ergaster, Homo erectus, Homo floresiensis*, The Denisovans, and *Homo Neanderthals*, they all went extinct. Apparently, none of their adaptations, innovations, or technologies enabled their survival. *Homo sapiens* apparently barely made it, and not because of our technologies but because of where some of our species were located—"humans appeared to have held on as it were by a thread" (Layne, 2019).

The good news back then was that, unlike twenty-first century humans, our hunter-gatherer forebears, despite what may seem to us a meager set of technological abilities, survived numerous bouts of global climate change (glacials and interglacials). Their survival, though, wouldn't have depended on their Stone-Age mitigations and adaptations—as foundational to subsequent human technology and innovation development as these turned out to be—nor, fortunately, did it require them to sprout superhuman abilities such as stopping the natural rotational processes of the Earth system that drove the ice ages of the Pleistocene. Back then, too, the human population was less than ten million.

They lived in small foraging bands, were highly mobile, and those who survived were already in, or mostly able to migrate to, less frozen parts of the planet. Humans were just lucky to be where the ravages of the last ice age were less extreme and survived, which is believed to be in coastal regions and in caves in South Africa. Not even the Neanderthals, who may have once shared caves with humans in Europe and were thought to be better adapted to the ice age, survived.

This time around, though, unlike the climate change that accompanied the Pleistocene-Holocene transition, which may eventually have enabled agriculture and civilization, and which was entirely natural and engendered by the Earth system, twenty-first century global warming climate change is not natural, but instead, is entirely anthropogenic and is rapidly increasing. In addition, the human population is also increasing, approaching ten-plus billion by mid-century, and it remains mostly sedentary, dwelling mostly in mega-cities with neither a desire nor room for climate migrants. And, the bad news is, absent the level of migration practiced by the relatively small, mobile populations of our hunter-gatherer forebears, who were able to escape extinction by migrating to more hospitable parts of the planet, modern human survival may depend more on human innovations and technologies to slow, if not stop, the growth of warming and population.

But despite knowing for decades about the increasing existential threats that a growing population and continued CO_2 emissions would have on ecosystems and biodiversity, and potentially our survival, there hasn't been, nor does there now seem to be, the kind of alarm, shock, or call to action for R&D capabilities and other resources—such as that which drove the Manhattan Project, or the race to land a man on the moon—to identify meaningful, timely solutions, if they could be such, to slow or stop either.

And, yes, we do know what it will take to slow or perhaps even stop this CO_2 buildup. The Covid-19 pandemic-driven worldwide economic slowdown, though short-lived, revealed the direct causal relationship between, on one hand, human economic growth, societal lifeways, and CO_2 increase, and on the other, global warming. The choice has become clear—and seems ultimately to be either CO_2-enabled economic growth or human survival. But this seeming revelation, unfortunately, has yet to inspire much effort to halt or slow economic growth, and therefore the generation and use of CO_2. Some economists believe the world can perhaps have both. They point to a few developed economies that for a while have managed to do both. Meanwhile there has been no clear resolution. Rather, we seem to have just picked ourselves up, dusted ourselves off, and kept going—perhaps hoping this choice will somehow turn out to be one humanity won't have to make.

Indeed, one sees a relaxed, business-as-usual political and economic approach with a continued focus on innovation and R&D for unrelated scientific explorations, economic development, products and services for economic growth and wealth creation, and wars. There are even creative attempts to turn the greenhouse gases that are driving global warming into yet another commercial for-profit product for wealth generation. Much of the climate R&D and innovation efforts to find technologies that can slow or stop global warming is market-driven—i.e., there is no effort put forth unless a clear return on investment has been identified.

There are no known or proven planet-wide technologies, nor globally focused efforts to develop such, that can reverse the probable inevitable Earth-system lurch toward its probable next steady state—a Hothouse Earth. In the words of the U.N. Secretary-General, António Guterres, "the world is 'sleepwalking to climate catastrophe,' as the ongoing pandemic, the war in Ukraine, and a lack of political willpower undermine humanity's efforts to slow the warming of the planet."

Will any of the twenty-first century mitigations, adaptations, technologies, and innovations identified in the latest IPCC report, or yet to be discovered, turn out to be enough to nudge the Earth system back a few degrees centigrade, back to its pre-anthropogenic global warming state the way humans managed to stop and shrink that hole in the ozone layer that also threatened survival? Can we at least force a pause, or is it too late for that? Because that's what it might well take. Given the level of effort being poured into advanced computing technologies, is there some application of quantum computing or better still, a human level, or superhuman intelligent machine AI effort, that is focused on finding a way to turn the Earth's thermostat back to pre-Industrial Revolution temperatures? Can any offer a guarantee or enable our survival—or would that be pinning too much hope on technology?

What if this time around, as was true for our hunter-gatherer forebears until 12,000 years ago, human survival once again depended not on human technologies but on our individual and collective choices and actions? What can each of the more than eight billion humans do each day to stop CO_2 buildup? Unlike us, they didn't have to, and they weren't even trying to stop the global warming-driven climate change they were experiencing. After all, how bad would it have been to feel a bit of warmth for a change after enduring an ice age for millennia? They couldn't have known it would continue to increase by another 6°C before the global temperature would stabilize and would remain at some new high for another 10,000 years before modern humans would come along and raise it even higher—any more than we know today just how hot the planet will become before its temperature stabilizes, and how long the transition to a new climate state will take.

Nevertheless, they did what they could. They migrated out of Africa and across the Earth to survive and ran into the ice that enshrouded most of Europe and North and South America. Today, though, migrating humans fleeing climate change would face a very different problem—the population density of many countries and a deep opposition to migrants in general and in particular, ironically, to migrants from Africa. Would climate migrants be as welcome as Ukrainians appear to have been? What other solutions did our hunter-gatherer forebears consider? How did their lifeways enable them to survive? How would ours?

They couldn't have known how the Terminal Pleistocene-Holocene climate change they were living through would rearrange their daily lives—the goals, aspirations, and priorities of their societies and economies—as the cold of that last seemingly endless winter began to slowly give way to the warmth of the Holocene, as that last ice age was ending? How did this global warming-driven climate change end for many? In a word: worldwide extinctions. Extinction of numerous megafauna and flora and numerous hominin species. There were at least four other hominin species during the end of the last ice age, the Pleistocene–Holocene Transition, but humans were the only one to survive by the time it was over. Are modern humans contemplating, or can we even imagine, that such a level of extinctions is possible, maybe even likely, by the time humans emerge, if we do emerge, from the current global warming-driven climate change we have caused? What else changed? How will our civilization change? How did their society, economies, and lifeways change?

They were foragers when it began but farmers when it ended. They were mobile, sharing-oriented hunter-gatherers living in small bands but became hoarding, sedentary villagers and city dwellers living among domesticated animals before it ended. They were egalitarian, knew neither rulers nor religions, yet became subjects of and were often enslaved by rulers, kings, and devotees of religions. They became the first subjects, slaves, and peasants of what became known as human civilization. And yes, they were healthy, living in harmony with other Earth-life species within its ecosystems, from which they eked out a living. Later they would start farming and dwelling with farm animals in densely populated farming villages and towns and become afflicted by numerous zoonotic diseases that would plague subsequent humans for generations.

They went on to develop agriculture, irrigation, and numerous technologies, but also became destroyers of the environment, ecosystems, and biodiversity that millennia later would become a major cause of the twenty-first century global climate change that now plagues us, their progeny. By the time this transition was over, they had traded their pre-agriculture hunter-gatherer forebears' survival-driven lifeways within ecosystems for the sedentary, farming, hoarding, non-egalitarian lifeways outside these ecosystems.

So, if that's what happened to their way of life, how might twenty-first century man-made climate change rearrange ours? What will human civilization look and feel like 50, 100, 1,000, or 10,000 years from now because of how we choose to respond to climate change-driven global warming this century—assuming there can be an adequate response? Where our forebears ended up seems to have had more to do with the way they chose to interact with Earth's ecosystems, biodiversity, and their fellow humans and less to do with their technology. After all, their Stone Age technologies (Figure 7-1) would not have been of much help against the climate change that drove the last ice age. And it is quite likely our twenty-first century collection of anti-climate change technologies may well turn out to be no more effective than theirs might have been.

Yet as seen earlier, the controlled use of fire and the history of technology predate our species. And though human Stone Age technologies at the time were unlikely to have been responsible for the survival of our species, it was humans that survived the extinction of that Last Glacial Maximum (LGM), the last ice age, that occurred roughly between 26,000 and 19,000 years ago, while most megafauna and all other hominin species went extinct. Pre-agriculture humans lived through the Stone Age to launch the Neolithic Revolution, during which they developed agriculture and irrigation, built civilizations, created innovations in the Bronze and Iron ages, and advanced to the beginning of the Industrial Revolution in the mid-eighteenth century. Rapid acceleration in innovations and technologies drove massive human lifeway changes that vastly rearranged human societies and economies. Changes in the sources of energy from renewable (water, steam, solar, and wind) to nonrenewable (fossil fuels and nuclear) have enabled human population to grow so rapidly that it could potentially exceed ten billion at the global level by 2050.

But while our scientific advances, technologies, and innovations have added computing, transistors, spaceflight, space stations, the internet, social media, personal computing, communications devices like iPhones, breakthrough bio-medical techniques like CRISPR, AI, and more recently mRNA vaccines to the toolbox, these wonderful capabilities have enabled humans to also invent the technologies that now threaten our very survival.

The impacts range from the not-so-startling Neolithic Revolution innovation of farming and agriculture, which feeds our species but also destroys Earth-life ecosystems and biodiversity, to fossil fuels that power even more innovations that came with the Industrial Revolution. They also range from weapons of mass destruction designed to annihilate members of our species—which Russia's president seems willing to use on Ukraine, and the Israelis on the Palestinians and Iranians—to our capitalist economic systems and legal-person economies that we seem unable to stop from accelerating the demand for and production of the very greenhouse gases that are driving global warming and endangering human survival.

Whereas, though, it was natural climate change that accompanied the terminal-Pleistocene-Holocene transition that drove Stone Age technologies and cumulative learning and became the foundations of all subsequent human technological advances, it is anthropogenic climate change, a product of this cumulative learning, that is now accompanying the Holocene-Anthropocene transition and that is set to re-architect the look and feel of human lifeways, societies, and economies as the once-mostly even temperatures of the Holocene that enabled agriculture and saw the emergence of human civilization has begun to give way to temperatures that potentially could undo both.

These temperatures may well come to resemble an earlier geologic epoch—the Eocene. This was a time when, according to the New World Encyclopedia, the planet heated up in one of the most rapid (in geologic terms) and extreme global warming events recorded in geologic history, called the Paleocene-Eocene Thermal Maximum (PETM) or Initial Eocene

Thermal Maximum (IETM). This was an episode of rapid and intense warming (up to 7°C at high latitudes) that lasted less than 100,000 years. Sea surface temperatures rose between 5°C and 8°C over a period of a few thousand years. Is there a takeaway here, then, for twenty-first century humans? Yes, at least two.

First, until relatively recently, the forces that drove our modern human technologies, societies, and economies were largely market-driven, economic, and focused on profit-making, wealth accumulation, and GDP growth. They are about to undergo the equivalent of a seismic shift more drastic than the Russian invasion of Ukraine that was forced upon Europe and Western democracies. Perhaps not since the ravages of the last ice age that ended some 10,000 years ago have human societies and economies been driven to focus on human survival as they are once again about to be.

We might not only be living at the intersection of two geologic epochs, but also at the intersection of separate global climate change regimes—one that emerged naturally and one driven by humans. The world in which modern humans emerged during the Holocene changed naturally due to natural climate change. But the world we're leaving behind will undergo as unprecedented a change as any that humans have ever experienced, a change that could turn out to be as different and as drastic, if not more so, than the one our pre-agriculture hunter-gatherer forebears endured when the terminal Pleistocene-Holocene transition was ending. And that emerging change could be as existential for coming generations as the prior global climate change eventually turned out to be for all those non-human hominins and megafauna species that were driven to extinction during that transition.

When we think of the last ice age we probably still think of woolly mammoths, mastodons, and saber-tooth tigers roaming miles of icy glaciers that stretched across Europe and North and South America. But we forget that humans, too, evolved during those same icy times and are children of that last ice age that began during the Pleistocene some 2.5 million years ago. Our species evolved at a time when Earth's global temperature was nearly 6°C cooler than it is today and when atmospheric CO_2 ranged between 180 and 280 ppm during those ice ages compared to nearly 427 ppm on May 16, 2024. It took a global temperature increase of about 6°C to rid the Earth of those glaciers and by the look of things it may take another bump in CO_2 and global temperature to get rid of the remaining polar caps and take the planet back to an even warmer geological epoch—the Eocene, when CO_2 rose between 400 and 500 ppm.

Humans survived that last geologic and global climate change transition, yes, but not because we were smarter or had better technologies, and not for any of the many explanations we use to misguide ourselves. Humans survived because of where they might have been located, nearer the southern, eastern, and northern coasts of Africa, and far, far away from the worst of the ravages of the last ice age. But don't count on going to some very, very cold place to escape the heat, like New Zealand, where some billionaires are said to be setting up camp, because if an Eocene-like climate eventually overtakes the Earth, there could be crocodiles and palm trees on the South Pole. But you're probably thinking that if alligators made it, chances are humans might, too. Perhaps, but not so fast, as the Eocene ended in extinction, and the fauna that emerged on the other side of that extinction was unlike those that entered.

Now for the second takeaway. Many of the survival challenges our pre-agriculture hunter-gatherer forebears would encounter were beyond any scientific, technological, or innovative capabilities they might have possessed during the Pleistocene-Holocene transition, just as our survival challenges are likely to be beyond the capabilities of modern humans as we confront the climatic, topographic, and Earth-system changes already in progress, which threaten the Holocene-Anthropocene transition that, in turn, threatens human survival today. Even though their technologies and innovations, or as some might say, the near-absence thereof, couldn't and indeed didn't save them, modern humans still tend to overestimate the human ability to invent and innovate, and miss the real purpose these capabilities may have evolved to serve.

Innovation did contribute to their survival but not by undertaking the kinds of mitigations and innovations modern humans might have imagined and would have wanted to try. These might include attempting somehow to change the freezing ice age weather they no doubt confronted the way some are hoping to reverse or stop the global warming we engendered. Or trying to reclaim habitable land that had been submerged by those massive lakes carved out in the African Rift Valley because of plate tectonics and melting glaciers, the way some humans hope to prevent or reclaim submerged island nations and coastal cities around the world. Nor by enabling them to embark on conservation efforts to save the flora, fauna, and funga they came to rely upon for food but that were rapidly going extinct, due to no fault of their own but due to climate and topographical transformations within ecosystems over which they had no control.

Their early technologies would have at best enabled them to eke out a living in harmony with Earth's equally challenged biodiversity, and together with some species, might have managed to migrate to survive notwithstanding the climatic and topographic changes ecosystems in the Rift Valley were undergoing. It helps to recall that humans at this time were engaged in an intense climate-change-driven migration out of Africa that began during and toward the end of the Late Pleistocene 125,000-12,000 years ago. They would have been engrossed in cultural and ecological adaptations as they migrated from continent to continent to become the last hominins on the planet.

Pre-agriculture hunter-gatherer humans would have had to learn to live in every biome—including terrestrial grasslands, and ranging from caves in South Africa and tropical forests in western and central Africa, to the Sahara, Kalahari, and Namib deserts—and to adapt to relatively cold and ecologically patchy high-altitude environments in Ethiopia. The environments of eastern Africa, from whence anatomically modern humans are thought to have migrated, ranged from arid grassland inhabited by mesic coastal tropical forests to coastal adaptations that may have stimulated a rapid dispersal that enabled humans to reach as far as Australia via a Southern Coastal Route (Figure 7-2).

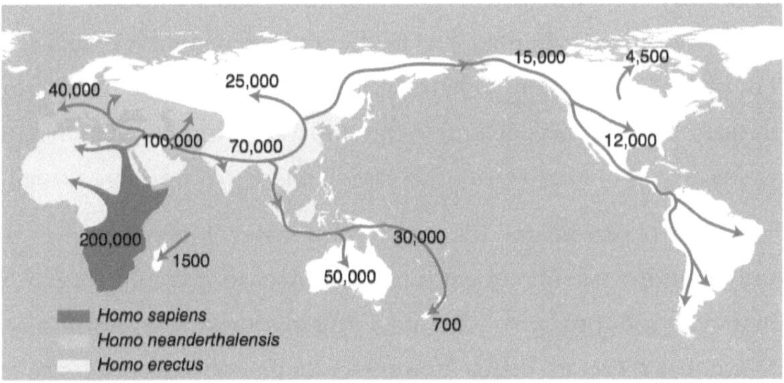

Figure 7-2. Human migration out of Africa via the Southern coastal route.

(Source: Early Human Migration, World History Encyclopedia)

Being driven by climate and topographical changes that occurred during that last glacial led to abrupt changes that may have rendered large portions of North, East, and West Africa unsuitable for hominin habitation and may have compelled *Homo sapiens* to migrate out of Africa. But climate change was global, so while they migrated out of Africa, they ended up facing an ice age in Europe and elsewhere. And to help early humans survive and overcome these challenges may well have been the real purpose of whatever innovative and technological capabilities they may have had ("Out of Africa and into an ice age . . ." (Carto et al., 2008). How did these massive disruptions in the ecology and climate within ecosystems shape the lifeways, societies, and economies of our pre-agriculture hunter-gatherer forebears? What new technologies and innovations emerged as a result?

Was this why they were hunter-gatherers and not farmers; why they were mobile and not sedentary; why they shared food and natural resources among themselves instead of hoarding while others starved; why they raised small families and dwelt in small bands rather than in overpopulated sedentary villages, towns, and cities; why they owned neither land nor a multitude of personal items; why they neither farmed nor herded animals; why even after 290,000 years the human population may have hardly reached a half-million; and why they were able to exist within the carrying capacity of the Earth even during an ice age? Perhaps so, and it would have helped, too, that they were egalitarian, had neither governments nor religions, and did not build civilizations. Theirs were lifeways that were preoccupied with just one goal and outcome—the survival of human life, of Earth's ecosystems, and of biodiversity. This is what they relentlessly pursued.

These were reasons and lifeways Neolithic Revolution humans would abandon, and most subsequent human civilizations would forget. And humanity is about to be rudely forced to rediscover, if not relearn some of them: that there are better lifeways and a greater purpose for human existence than surplus-driven economic development, wealth accumulation, and GDP growth; and that there was once and still is an a priori goal and outcome that drove the existence and survival of all Earth-life species, one we not only may never have learned, but by our very preoccupation with economic growth and advanced technologically-enabled lifeways, are working hard to ensure we just might not survive long enough to rediscover. It takes just one look at the map of human migration across the entire planet (Figure 7-2) to realize what humanity accomplished when survival was its only goal. Today their modern migrant descendants are lucky to make it out of Africa alive.

Today scientists are immersed in new particle physics research trying to figure out better ways to understand how the universe works, even as others are trying, perhaps just as hard, to create superhuman machine artificial intelligence and other technologies that might one day, among other things, enable human migration to Mars and other planets, while we have yet to figure out, and are not even seriously trying to figure out, how to coexist with other Earth-life species on this one. We are also exploring new and more powerful forms of energy that could help end our addiction to fossil-fuels, a resource that seemed so appealing two-and-a-half centuries ago. And we are working on numerous other technologies and innovations that aim to drive economic growth faster and to greater heights, rather than learning what enabled our pre-agriculture hunter-gatherer forebears' economies and societies to survive without any existential threats for 97 percent of our species existence, until 10,000 years ago.

How did their lifeways, economies, societies, and meager technologies enable a co-existence with Earth-life's biodiversity and within its ecosystems? How—given that they had comparatively little technology, perhaps less than 1 percent of what exists today; orders of magnitude smaller human population, perhaps fewer than 10,000 across the globe; almost no carbon footprint; and a tiny fraction of the biomass that overspread the Earth—were they able to survive while subsequent human societies and economies collapsed? The question is critical, given that humans, with superior technological capabilities by multiple orders of magnitude, could well be confronting a potential global warming climate change self-extinction.

For our pre-agriculture hunter-gatherer forebears, the pursuit of technologies and innovations wasn't a destination in itself but a boost to their ability to make a living—their destination was life and survival as a species. They didn't develop new technologies and innovate to build the next mega-technology startup, or to garner proprietary positions via patents, and thereby gain market dominance—they innovated only as needed to survive. Haven't you noticed, too, that although they survived and prospered without collapse for 290,000 years, and were able to migrate across the entire planet, they developed none of the science, technologies, or innovations modern humans have in just the last 10,000 years?

Indeed, they left us neither technologies nor innovations that modern humans would have been excited to write home about, nor for that matter, weapons of mass destruction. But what they did leave us was their pre-agriculture hunter-gatherer lifeways—the survival-driven wisdom they gleaned around the waterhole. They modeled how to grow a human economy and society that enabled them to survive and thrive within Earth's ecosystems in harmony with its biodiversity without destroying them or themselves. Is anyone working on a Ph.D. on how they did it? Are there any academic majors focused on how they might have done it? Any courses in our modern universities' curricula that teach how to ensure the survival of Earth's ecosystems, biodiversity, and human life? Where are the professors of these subjects? When will economists realize that the human economy evolved not to drive economic growth but to enable human life and survival?

What drives human innovation and technologies today? Why do we develop new technologies? What is the motivation of that new startup? Who wants to be an entrepreneur? Why does it often turn out that what begin as great ideas often end up becoming such colossal disappointments and often cause great harm? Why did the Neolithic Revolution that gave us agriculture, and the Industrial Revolution that came with fossil fuels and subsequent innovations, keep getting it so wrong, while our pre-agriculture hunter-gatherer forebears got it right, time after time after time—for 290,000 years?

The answer by now should be obvious. Humans today innovate and invent mainly for profit, to create the next unicorn, and to create wealth rather than to ensure Earth's biodiversity, ecosystems, and human life and survival. Even where scientific research is the initial driver of new knowledge that leads to new technologies and innovations, sooner or later we manage to find a way to measure and evaluate even such by their potential economic outcome. Yes, eventually everything we do as a species has to be tailored to serve a profitable economic purpose—else it wouldn't get done. But could making that seemingly simple change away from this economic obsession—away from the surplus accumulation and hoarding our Neolithic Revolution forebears adopted and all subsequent humans imitated—and instead, return to those sharing and caring economic lifeways our pre-agriculture hunter-gatherer forebears practiced have made a difference?

Can humans redirect their economies, societies, and civilizations back to that initial goal and outcome of life and survival? Given how twenty-first century migrants fare, if humans were to embark on that fateful out-of Africa migration across the planet (Figure 7-2), would our species even exist? Would humans, 70,000 years ago, have made it even past Saudi Arabia, given the reported mass killings of migrants at the Yemen border and systematic abuses of Ethiopians; given too, their struggle to get across the Sahel only to become *personae non gratae* in the countries of northern Africa; and given the risk, taken by so many migrants, of dying in the jungles of Central America or drowning in the waters of the Mediterranean or the English Channel? But somehow, it's beginning to look like we may not even have a choice. We either return to the survival-driven economic lifeways of our pre-agriculture hunter-gatherer forebears, or risk yet another civilization collapse and potential extinction.

Try Googling the 243 antonyms for entrepreneur and see what comes up. Here are a few examples: couch potato, slug, loser, laggard, idler, slob, slacker, bum. Perhaps then one would understand why nobody grows up wanting to be whatever Google says that is. The challenge today should no longer be who wants to be an entrepreneur, a billionaire, or both, but rather, who wants to help save humanity from, potentially, an anthropogenic climate-change-driven extinction? It's the greatest risk of extinction humanity has ever faced and one that has a good chance of succeeding. Who wants to save humanity? The answer of course should be everyone—but haven't you noticed, no one is breaking down doors to fund such people, not even the new Bezos Earth Fund, nor even McKenzie $cott.

By the time humans emerged from the last ice age into the warmer temperatures of the Holocene, their socioeconomic lifeways, and their relationships with Earth's other species, habitats and ecosystems that enabled mutual survival for 290,000 years, were changing fundamentally. The mostly egalitarian societies of our pre-agriculture hunter-gatherer, foraging forebears were in the process of being replaced by non-egalitarian, sedentary, burgeoning farming societies that followed the Neolithic Revolution. Life as they once knew it was disappearing and would never be the same again.

For the first time humans would produce rather than forage for food; herd and live with farm animals in crowded, sedentary villages, towns, and cities rather than small mobile communities; hoard rather than share; accumulate possessions and acquire and enclose land; acquire and possess personal property and domesticate other species to garner and accumulate profits; and enslave other humans to grow their economies and societies.

And although the world had seen how, generation after generation after generation, humans would use their technologies and innovations to destroy Earth's ecosystems and environments, displace and destroy countless biodiversity species, and decimate countless generations of their fellow humans, often in pursuit of wealth, we nonetheless would continue the pursuit of innovation after innovation, and technology after technology, some increasingly deadly, in the process continuing down these unequal socioeconomic- and technology-enabled lifeways until Feb. 24, 2022, when the world came face-to-face with Vladimir Putin.

One human seemed prepared to threaten the use of humanity's deadliest technologies, nuclear weapons, for a land grab: to add Ukraine to Russia, already the largest country on Earth. On that day, Vladimir Putin reminded the world that it was still living in an age of existential uncertainty and would continue to for as long as such technologies and weapons exist and humans continue to reject the *lifeways that had enabled our species survival for most of its existence on Earth.*

He was neither the first nor the only human, and probably won't be the last, who would wish to use humanity's best/worst and latest technologies to blackmail or destroy his fellow humans to secure his corner of the Earth—President Xi by his own words might be planning something similar for Taiwan and the South China Sea. Yet throughout our history, post-Neolithic Revolution humans have not learned, but continue to innovate apace to create the world's first superhuman machine artificial intelligence which some of its would-be creators hope will be humanity's greatest achievement and would, hopefully, be subject to human control. But so, too, are nuclear weapons. Putin's threat to the West should remind such scientists what human control ultimately means.

Control of WMDs, if nothing else, shows us that by inventing and retaining the right of control to any such technology, humans are also choosing to retain the right to self-extinction—a choice most humans would perhaps never make, but that once made, can never be undone. So, who or what should oversee and control such capabilities? From an evolutionary perspective, apparently, no one yet—no Earth-life species and definitely not humans. "Humans must first mature beyond the point of self-extinction; must reach and scale that survival plateau before they can be trusted and can trust one another with such planetary or solar-system-wide capabilities" (Layne, 2019).

In pursuit of such innovations and technologies humans may not have bothered to note that none of the powers or capabilities that manage and enable the entire planet to function, and upon which all Earth-life depends, are in the control of humans or any other species. Was that deliberate or purely accidental? Earth has seen numerous near-total extinctions, but none were biodiversity-driven. Today, humans are smart enough to understand the role of key elements and the planet's natural components that enable life—including the Earth, sea, air, sun, biosphere, and atmosphere, among others. None, however, are controlled by any single species yet all exist and can only survive because of the involuntary, though joint, simultaneous, and independent interactions of all species. Programmed into this Earth-system is no setting for human control, but rather, just one for human survival. Survival of the one eventually comes down to survival of the many—a lesson, apparently, modern humans have yet to learn.

One has only to take note of Putin's complete cut-off of natural gas to Poland, Bulgaria, and other nations—and, for a while, his obstruction of Ukraine's ability to export its grain, thereby causing a potential worldwide food crisis; and further, his threat to use nuclear weapons against any nation that would intervene—to understand what evolutionarily immature humans would eventually do if they could control elements such as the sun, moon, oceans, and the atmosphere. The very thought is absurd, yet acquiring such capabilities features prominently in the science fiction of our species and on the technology wish lists and fantasies of Nobel Prize-aspirants, if not yet the to-do lists of some scientists.

But who today thinks humans are ready and would want our species to gain such powers? And if not, why would human control of a superhuman machine artificial intelligence be any different from having yet another Putin possessing such intelligence as a weapon? "Attaining evolutionary maturity first, not scientific and technological invincibility, is the only path forward to attaining such planetary, solar system, or galactic capabilities—to avoid the risk that such powers will be used by humans to drive extinction of itself and all Earth-life species" (Layne, 2019).

It is clear, at least to some, that humans are not yet ready and indeed, may never be ready. Our marvelous abilities in science and technologies, unless seen through the lens of "Evolutionary Maturity", only deceive us into thinking we can trust humans with nuclear weapons, and superhuman machine AIs, too, whereas our post-Neolithic Revolution history demonstrates we can't even trust humans with agriculture and fossil fuels without the risk of destroying ourselves and the planet.

By the look of things, since humans abandoned those hunting and gathering socioeconomic lifeways that enabled our species' survival for nearly 97 percent of our history, our ability to ensure our survival after that time seems to have weakened and slowed even as our numerous technological advances and scientific achievements that could be used, often inadvertently, to ensure our extinction have strengthened and accelerated. After 12,000 years of trying and failing, it is clear that unless human societies and economies begin to prioritize life and survival above all else, even above R&D and the endless pursuit of technologies and innovations, our accomplishments may well turn out to be nothing more than advance reservations on the train to self-extinction.

Absent the will to prioritize life and survival over economic growth as the only goal and outcome for human economies and societies, and, forgetting for the moment, if one can, the horrors a rogue superhuman intelligent machine AI could cause, or what leaders like Putin might do with the world's worst weapons, how far can technology go to, say, stave off climate change? With carbon dioxide emissions continuing to rise, scientists believe major technological breakthroughs, such as CO_2 capture, will be necessary to slow global warming.

But can even the best technologies be enough without the human will to decarbonize? In a world with thousands of coal-fired power plants, more than two billion cars and trucks, and billions of tons of coal, oil, and natural gas mined and combusted, is it any surprise that more than 40 billion tons of CO_2 are still being discharged into the atmosphere annually, setting off changes from a meltdown in the Artic to thawing glaciers worldwide to unprecedented global warming and rising seas? Indeed, the atmosphere has now accumulated enough CO_2 to stave off the next ice age for millennia.

Where is the economic incentive to preserve human life and survival? It still costs nothing to continue to spew CO_2 into the atmosphere and there are still no financial incentives nor mandates to stop dumping let alone to clean up the air, while fossil fuel companies like Exxon still continue to acquire and expand, betting that U.S. and perhaps global energy policy will continue not to move against fossil fuels in a major way. If the goal is to limit global warming to 2°C—and better still to 1.5°C—above pre-industrial levels, already-emitted carbon will have to be sucked back out of the atmosphere. What's causing and intensifying global warming is the total volume of CO_2 already in the atmosphere plus the volume that's still being dumped into it, and not even our most ambitious mitigation plans so far appear able to achieve the goal of removing it.

There are two main ways to remove CO_2 from the atmosphere: nature-based, through ecosystem restoration, afforestation, and sustainable land management over lots of time, and technological, including carbon capture and storage (CCS) and some kinds of carbon capture and use, like locking carbon away into concrete-like building materials. However, there are almost no business cases for carbon removal right now that will get us down to 2°C or 1.5°C above pre-industrial levels.

What could happen, and likely will, if we fail to come up with technologies that can get this excess global warming carbon out of the atmosphere? As noted earlier, even if climate change mitigation policies reduce CO_2 emission rates, atmospheric CO_2 concentrations will continue to rise until emissions fall to *the natural removal rate*.That means that much of the emitted CO_2 will remain in the atmosphere centuries or even millennia after its release. "Fate of fossil fuel CO_2 in geologic time" (Archer, 2005) suggests that 300 years is a good average lifetime number for CO_2 and that 17–33 percent of the CO_2 will remain in the atmosphere 1,000 years after it is emitted. Montenegro, Brovkin, Eby, Archer, and Weaver, in "Long term fate of anthropogenic carbon" (2007) suggest that released carbon may stay in the atmosphere an average of 1,800 years or longer. According to Archer & Brovkin (2008), "Ultimate recovery does take place but only in time scales of hundreds of thousands of years." The effects then of fossil fuel burning are irreversible on a time scale relevant to humans. Unless humanity can extract CO_2 out of the atmosphere, then, why would other technologies and innovations that cannot neutralize this global warming threat continue to matter?

Today, the real and present threat our species faces is not a rogue superhuman intelligent machine AI, perhaps not even a global thermonuclear war, but rather, an anthropogenic CO_2-driven global warming climate change extinction driven by the GHGs we use to power our economies. It is the sectors of our economies that are the primary producers and users of the GHGs that now threaten our extinction. The real and present danger threatening humanity is not AI, but the humble human economy.

So again, one must ask, how far can technology go to stave off climate change? Given our current trajectory, can humans avoid this potential for a technology-enabled, greenhouse gas-driven self-extinction? Perhaps, but that would require us to realize that hitherto, our pursuit of bigger and better science and technology for answers has not always worked. Rather, given enough time, more often than not they end up putting us at greater risk. The answers we sought and those we seek are not, nor will be, found outside but must come from within us—not from the things we create but from what's already evolved within us.

It will be found in the awakening of that dormant yet far more powerful urge than the one that currently drives our pursuit of scientific and technological achievements—the urge to survive. It requires the reawakening of that latent but far more powerful urge that 70,000 years ago drove humanity out of Africa and across the planet in pursuit of life and survival, that shaped their lifeways, societies, and economies: the tenacious pursuit of life and survival above all else that we once followed for most of our existence.

Reawakening this dormant survival urge will at the very least require a rediscovery and return to those seemingly humble lifeways of our pre-agriculture hunter-gatherer forebears. It demands a return to the wisdom of those early human societies and their waterhole economies that understood why *sharing* and *caring* would outlast *hoarding* and *owning*; that chose to eke out a living *inside (foraging)* rather than *outside (farming) Earth's* ecosystems; that *chose, too, coexistence* with, rather than *displacement and near-extinction* of, Earth-life's biodiversity; and, in a universe wherein everything is mobile, chose as well to *remain mobile rather than sedentary*.

They understood how *mobility and migration kept their populations small*, *reduced their ecosystem impact*, and enabled them to *remain within the carrying capacity of ecosystems and of the Earth,* even during an ice age, and without exceeding any of its planetary boundaries. We now know that it was those lifeways, those socioeconomic practices, that enabled their collapse-free survival for 290,000 of the 300,000 years of our species existence—and without any of the lifeways of our modern economics, technologies, and innovations.

For 290,000 of the 300,000 years humanity existed, pre-agriculture hunter-gatherer humans managed to do so without any of the technologies and innovations that followed the Industrial Revolution. Like them, modern humans, too, can also survive but will need to abandon our current economic and societal obsession with surplus, profits, wealth accumulation, and GDP growth; its equally misplaced near-exclusive reliance upon profit-driven scientific, technological, and innovation-based answers to everything for creating even more planetary economic opportunity; and a return instead to that unwavering *survival-driven* principle that elevates survival and the preservation of life above all else—the protection of human life and that of all Earth-life species, habitats, and ecosystems.

PART FIVE

Energy and Human Economies: From Renewables to Renewables

THE JOURNEY FROM RENEWABLES BACK TO RENEWABLES

AT A TIME WHEN HUMANS LOOK TO A diverse range of energy sources, including biomass, coal, oil, gas, nuclear, and a range of renewables including hydropower, solar, and wind, it may come as a surprise to learn that for most of our species' 300,000-year history, and until about 200 years ago, humans relied entirely on a single, free, renewable energy source, the sun—in the form of solar energy stored within the biomass of Earth-life's flora, fauna and funga, and in its habitats and ecosystems that overspread the planet.

By the time 2020 came around, however, this single reliable renewable energy source had morphed into a global energy mix that, according to *Our World in Data,* was displaced by coal, with 27.6 percent of total global energy use; oil, with 31.6 percent; gas, 25 percent; nuclear, 4.4 percent; hydropower, 7 percent; wind, 2.6 percent; solar, 1.4 percent; and other renewables, 0.5 percent. This means that just 16 percent of the energy in use today comes from low-carbon sources: nuclear accounts for about 4 percent, with the remaining 12 percent coming from renewable technologies.

It would take humans a little more than 297,000 of their 300,000 years of existence before it would embark on a journey that would replace Earth's single unlimited renewable energy source that powered all Earth life with a fossil-fuel-dominated energy mix, use of which has now placed all life at risk of a potential global warming extinction. To survive, humanity must now, in a small fraction of that time, embark upon and complete a reverse energy journey—from nonrenewable back to renewables. Will we make it?

In a little less than 300 years, humans would come up with an energy architecture of our own. One that would transform that once 100 percent renewable energy world that enabled human survival for 97 percent of its existence, to one that is now dependent upon *a nonrenewable energy mix* for 88 percent of its energy needs; and one that now threatens our very survival.

Given the many energy sources humans would subsequently discover, there must have been a very good reason for this single energy source, the sun, that drove all Earth life for millennia. Why just one? Why was it renewable? Among the numerous takeaways that stand in bold contrast to humanity's discovery and use of other forms of energy, is the sun's architecture:

(1) It is entirely renewable. There are no nonrenewable components to this initial *survival-driven energy architecture.*

(2) With the sun 93 million miles away at its source and with ecosystems and biodiversity its last-mile distribution and Earth-side storage grids, this energy is mostly found within the biomass comprising Earth-life's ecosystems and biodiversity—with each species being its own energy terminus.

(3) It is an energy mechanism that is built into and inseparable from life itself as it is stored and distributed within and by each individual species that comprises life—the funga, fauna, and flora that comprise Earth-life species.

(4) It is controlled by no one. Except for the energy that is within and energizes an individual member of a species, no individual owns, manages, or controls the generation, storage, or distribution of solar energy. No one has the ability or power to dominate its supply, or block or refuse access to other species as

is now possible in modern human energy architectures—as Russia and other natural resource-rich nations now do.

(5) It is only accessible and transferable as a live, mostly above-ground food source, and does not need to be farmed, husbanded, produced, or mined.

(6) It is not confined to a specific location but available globally.

(7) Unlike fossil fuels, this renewable energy source is omnipresent, mobile, and can migrate as part of the biomass that comprises the flora and mobile fauna that occupy Earth's habitats and ecosystems.

What was Earth-life's original energy architecture and supply chain? In brief, it was a renewable energy source derived from the sun to energize life, and Earth's ecosystems and biodiversity in support of life—a *survival-driven energy architecture* that evolved to energize *biological* life. Energy is indispensable to all life and, like all other Earth-life common resources such as water and air, is indispensable to survival, and therefore free.

And, unlike access to nonrenewable energy sources, Earth's renewable energy is everywhere and obtainable directly by each individual species across and within all biomes, ecosystems, and geographies. Neither supply chains nor distribution mechanisms are necessary. Each individual species determines its own energy needs and can meet those needs by simply hunting and gathering to eke out a living in harmony with other species *within*

Earth-life ecosystems, which double as an energy storage source and last-mile distribution point.

How is it, then, that for 4.7 billion years of Earth's existence, all Earth-life species, flora, and fauna relied without fail, and without the threat of an energy-driven extinction, on Earth's single source of renewable energy? One that only in the last 300 or so years, humans have determined to be inadequate. But we have also discovered that the preferred energy substitutes, fossil fuels, are simultaneously nonrenewable and a potential source of extinction.

During all of humanity's time on Earth, and until less than 300 years ago, humans were unlikely to experience an energy shortage, nor would they have had to confront a global energy distribution crisis such as is occurring at present, nor face the real risk of a potential *nonrenewable energy-driven extinction*. To satisfy their energy needs, all an Earth-life species had to do was simply to feed—to hunt and gather to eat, *within* Earth-life ecosystems where these renewable energy sources were to be found.

And indeed, that was exactly what our pre-agriculture hunter-gatherer forebears did for those 290,000 years that preceded the Neolithic Revolution. And, if this renewable energy source of the ecosystem was sufficient for all Earth-life species and humans for all but the last dozen millennia of humanity's existence, how and why did it become inadequate for modern humans? How and why did humanity get here?

One can't help but notice the frenzy, the urgency, and the hustle to find and develop new renewable energy technologies and energy sources. But not many apparently seem equally keen to explain to the world what originally drove humanity to its current nonrenewable energy mix. If no other Earth-life species, hitherto, has experienced such an energy transition emergency, nor has encountered such an urgent need to abandon nonrenewables and find and return to renewable energy sources, what is it that's driving humanity's rapid about-turn from the dominant nonrenewables that energize its economies and societies, back to the renewables of the ecosystem—from renewables, and now back to renewables?

Modern humans for the most part, then, not only abandoned Earth-life ecosystems and biodiversity and thereby have put all Earth-life at risk, but by so doing, have until recently, abandoned and failed to build upon that *free solar renewable survival-driven energy architecture* that enabled human survival for most of its existence. By destroying Earth-life's ecosystems and biodiversity, humans were also destroying Earth's primary renewable energy, last-mile distribution and storage mechanisms—its biomass.

And because these were primarily designed to energize biological life, humans finally resorted to nonrenewable energy sources that can energize the non-biobased innovations they would invent to construct new for-profit and GDP growth-driven socioeconomic lifeways *outside* those ecosystems. These nonrenewable fossil fuel energy sources have now become humanity's main sources of energy, but, unlike renewable energy sources that enable life, these man-made nonrenewable sources dug out of the Earth have become harbingers of a potential Earth-life species extinction that now threatens human existence, and potentially all life.

While Earth has seen many a mass extinction, none (except perhaps that Great Oxygenation Event thought to have been driven by the rise of cyanobacteria) has been caused by the actions of a single species. Humans could be the exception. Cyanobacteria filled the atmosphere with oxygen that enabled life, but humans are filling it with CO_2 that over geological time, has mostly driven death and extinction.

Can humans survive this third energy transition?

Energy and Human Economies: From Renewables to Renewables

THE FRAUGHT HUMAN ENERGY JOURNEY
FROM RENEWABLES TO RENEWABLES

CHAPTER 8

Energy
and Human Economies:

From Renewables to Renewables

A Common Though Indispensable Resource Within Ecosystems That Enabled Human and Biodiversity Survival

8.

Energy and Human Economies:

From Renewables to Renewables

HOW HUMANITY ABANDONED THIS COMMON AND INDISPENSABLE ENERGY SOURCE WITHIN ECOSYSTEMS THAT ENABLED HUMAN AND BIODIVERSITY LIFE AND SURVIVAL FOR MILLENNIA

"Few socioeconomic lifeway changes confirm the folly of human attempts at eking out a living outside Earth-life ecosystems as its search, adoption and now rapid abandonment of fossil fuels, and equally rapid retreat to Renewables."

—*Samuel Layne*

EVERY LIFE FORM NEEDS ENERGY TO SURVIVE AND ON Earth that energy comes from the sun: Solar energy is converted to biochemical energy, stored in the biomass of plants and animal life, and made available to all Earth-life species in the food they consume to survive. This was and ultimately is the only source of energy within Earth-life ecosystems; it was and still is renewable; and for 290,000 years, all hominins including pre-agriculture hunter-gatherer humans, and all Earth-life species, apparently needed no additional energy source to eke out a living to survive within Earth-life ecosystems. In fact, modern humans not only survived but successfully migrated across the entire Earth using nothing more than this single renewable energy source. Earth-life's fauna and flora comprised both energy storage and a distribution grid with each species a self-contained mobile, renewable energy storage source. Thus, solar energy has a distributed architecture that assumed and enabled mobility and migration while remaining a built-in component of life itself.

Energy, like waterholes, is one of those fundamental ecosystem resources that is indispensable to the survival of all Earth-life; is centrally generated by the sun and locally stored and distributed in biomass that comprise Earth-life flora, fauna and funga; and is freely available to all species, yet owned and controlled by none. Although it is the only available energy source, it is nonetheless renewable and therefore inexhaustible and can only be obtained by eating the biomass available as food at a trophic level within Earth-life ecosystems.

It is simultaneously local as well as global (available in all biomes everywhere); built-in as well as external; mobile and migratory as well as sedentary. It is a resource available mainly *within* ecosystems and in an energy architecture designed to support Earth-life species' life and survival; one that is not accessible *outside* the energy cycles that flow within Earth-life ecosystems, nor can be interfaced with human energy generation systems or sources (coal, gas, oil, nuclear and more) *outside* Earth-life ecosystems. Moreover, it is one that bears scant resemblance to the for-profit nonrenewable energy sources and generating systems that humans would go on to invent to enhance their efforts to eke out a living *outside* those ecosystems.

Notwithstanding subsequent human energy sources, related inventions, and innovations, it was this single renewable energy source found in ecosystems that energized all life for the 4.7 billion years of Earth's evolution and existence. It was what energized all human life from the emergence of anatomically modern humans and for most of humanity's 290,000 years of existence as hunters and gatherers, as well as for most of the last 12,000 years, from the time Neolithic Revolution humans began abandoning foraging for farming. It was this single renewable energy source that enabled all life and that currently drives nearly 12 percent of worldwide energy use.

Today, though, while energy remains indispensable to all life, human societies, and economies, that energy is mostly nonrenewable and anything but free. Unlike the universally distributed and freely available renewable energy provided in Earth-life ecosystems, humans, just to be able to develop their societies and economies *outside* those ecosystems, sought and found new energy sources that can function *outside* those ecosystems that, to this day, remain separate and apart from the biogeochemical energy flows within Earth-life species and ecosystems.

Until the Industrial Revolution, humans relied on the annual cycle of plant photosynthesis for both heat and mechanical energy. And while this energy source supported all pre-agriculture hunter-gatherer human societies and economies for the 290,000 years of their existence, as well as the energy needs of all Earth-life species for the 4.7 billion years of Earth's existence, once humans began building their societies and economies *outside* Earth's ecosystems, this inexhaustible and renewable source of energy seemed inadequate. Neolithic Revolution humans apparently could not deploy this renewable energy found within ecosystems to support the economic growth they sought to deploy *outside* those ecosystems.

Indeed, for nearly all our species' history, humanity did whatever it wanted and however it wanted all within Earth-life ecosystems and its biodiversity. Yet it turned out, from their perspective, that additional energy sources had to be found if economic growth was to continue. And eventually, new energy sources they found, indeed. But while they continued to depend on the energy derived from plant photosynthesis, they would do so in a new form—fossil fuels—specifically coal that had formed out of biomass over geologic time. And with the emergence of the Industrial Revolution, the fossil fuel age had arrived.

But while it may seem pre-industrial societies and economies had access to a rather limited energy supply, few have realized that a low energy architecture may well have been intentional and was not a design flaw. While mechanical energy came principally from human or animal muscle, and heat energy from wood; and while the resulting maximum attainable level of productivity was by today's standards relatively low, that may well have been all the energy and productivity that was necessary to survive—again, apparently by design. Indeed, it was this same, seemingly low-energy Earth-system that energized all Earth-life species, flora, fauna, and funga, for the billions of years they hunted and gathered, and was enough to energize their societies, economies, life, and survival. Apparently, then, that was all the energy Earth-life ecosystems, biodiversity, and humans needed to fulfill that fundamental goal and outcome expected of Earth-life societies and economies—life and survival.

It was only after humans started building their societies and economies *outside* Earth-life ecosystems, destroying many of these in the process, and only after they stopped living in harmony with its biodiversity, driving numerous species to extinction, that humans encountered a need for more energy than appeared to have been available, in the form needed, *within* ecosystems. By abandoning the lifeways of their pre-agriculture hunter-gatherer forebears, Neolithic and subsequent humans also abandoned those *DOMC* and *Waterhole* socioeconomic lifeways that enabled life and survival within the low-energy levels that may have been extant *within* ecosystems. From a modern human energy perspective then, the Earth-life energy system architecture must have been by intent a low-energy system. Yet it energized all Earth-life species, including humans, for all Earth's existence. But if, until then, this seemingly *low-energy Earth-system* was adequate for all life, what drove this Neolithic and subsequent human thirst for more and more energy than appears to have been available to Earth-life species *within* ecosystems?

Over the last 400 generations, humanity learned that energy consumption increased as populations grew bigger and people grew richer, a process that apparently began to accelerate with the Neolithic Revolution. As we will soon see, humanity was not just starting a transition from foraging to farming, and from sharing to hoarding, but essentially, humans were changing the way they obtained the energy they would need for economic growth. Perhaps this was the first human energy transition: from foraging, a method of obtaining food that required comparatively little expenditure of energy, to one that was decidedly energy intensive, farming. And the more they farmed and hoarded, the more their population and "economic wealth" grew and their demand for energy increased.

For most of human existence, and until the beginning of the Neolithic Revolution—when humans began to abandon their foraging lifeways for farming, and to turn from dwelling in small, mobile, sharing, hunter-gatherer bands of about fifty, to large, sedentary farming communities that lived with farm animals—estimates of human population, even after 290,000 years of existence, were less than four million and the world GDP at that time would have been infinitesimally tiny. It wouldn't even have made it onto any of those lists that appear on sites like Wikipedia's "List of Countries by GDP" that compare countries by GDP and numerous other economic criteria. Today, though, what began with the Neolithic Revolution has morphed exponentially by 2024 into a world GDP of over $113.23 trillion and a population of over eight billion. But how different the world's population, economy, and society might have been if humanity hadn't sought to increase its access to energy outside Earth's ecosystems?

Thus began the great human energy journey from renewables back to renewables shown in Figure 8-1. This is a journey away from the renewables of the ecosystem that enabled all Earth-life for 4.7-plus billion years, including all pre-agriculture hunter-gatherer human societies and economies, until nearly 10,000 years ago. And today, forced by the threat of a global warming extinction that can potentially be brought on by nonrenewable fossil fuel use adopted nearly 300 years ago, humans are now racing to abandon these nonrenewables to get back to the renewables of the ecosystem that energized all Earth-life for most of the planet's existence.

Hence the human energy journey, so far, has been a movement away from renewables and now back to renewables as illustrated in Figure 8-1. Humanity's energy journey that began with the renewables within ecosystems through the nonrenewables that began in the last two-and-a-half centuries may never have begun had humanity stuck with the renewables supply found within those ecosystems.

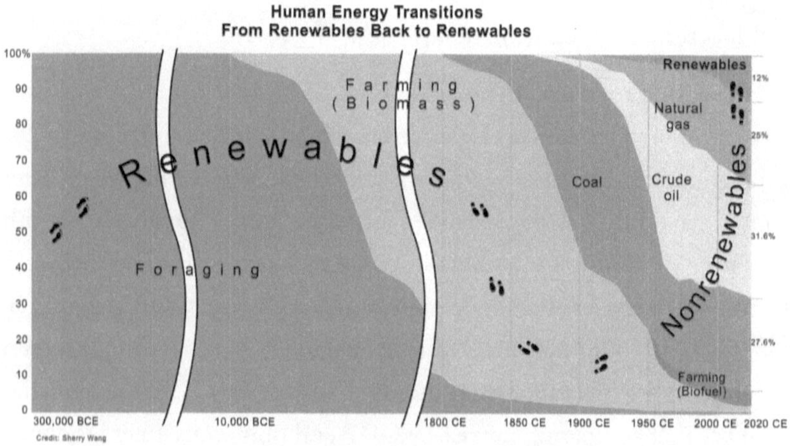

Figure 8-1. Human energy transitions: From renewables back to renewables.

(Source: Samuel Layne)

Nothing since the Neolithic Revolution—and notwithstanding all the changes humanity has made to Earth-life systems in search of energy to grow its societies and economies *outside* its ecosystems, even severely damaging all but 3 percent of its ecosystems and driving to extinction innumerable quantities of its biodiversity in the process—has hitherto triggered the kind of life-threatening global warming response that burning fossil fuels to generate energy has provoked. And, in response, as Ayn Rand might have said, "*Atlas Shrugged.*" Nature for the first time began to push back. Humans are being forced to abandon their pursuit and use of life-destroying nonrenewable energy sources like coal, oil, and gas—fossil fuels—and to promptly return to the renewables of the ecosystem in an effort to survive.

Human societies and economies have been left no choice—although you won't hear this from most scientists, politicians, or economists—regarding precisely what energy sources are henceforth possible, and will be acceptable, economically, scientifically, politically, collectively, and individually. Humans must now promptly abandon the use of all nonrenewable fossil fuel energy sources and must return to the safety of the renewables of the ecosystem if they wish to survive.

And—WOW! Humanity has finally found itself in an energy tug-of-war with nature, one it can only lose—unless . . . Yes, we know how humanity got to this energy impasse and how it will end unless we beat a hasty retreat to the renewables of the ecosystems, which we began to abandon 12,000 years ago. "What are our options?" someone asks, seemingly in a mild panic. Another asks, "What about fire?" Fire has been around seemingly almost forever; is fire even an alternative option?

Fire was first used some 200,000 years ago and no doubt played a huge role in our species' evolution and because of this some have come to regard it as a source of energy. But fire, it must be noted, is not itself a source of energy but a chemical reaction of rapidly oxidating fuel such as wood or coal. The energy isn't the fire itself, but rather the heat and light that fire gives off. This heat and light enabled early humans to gain control of caves that were dominated by predators; to see and ward off predators at night; and to clear vast areas for agriculture. The energy used in these instances is in the fuel being burned, stored within as chemical potential energy, that would have come from the sun and been stored in the biomass the fire consumes.

Nevertheless, even when humans started using fire for protection and warmth and to clear land for farming; and even after Neolithic Revolution humans emerged and began building their sedentary agricultural societies and economies *outside* Earth-life ecosystems—not even then did an additional source of renewable energy emerge. It was going to take several millennia before a new, but in this case, nonrenewable energy source, coal, appeared in China, where mining is believed to have begun about 2000 BP.

Driven by the desire to hoard and to grow wealth while having to feed an ever growing population, humans would go on to discover and invent numerous other sources of energy: petroleum, hydrocarbon liquid gas, natural gas, and nuclear energy, all nonrenewable, that came with consequences they may not have fully understood, or were content to ignore. And it is these consequences, now mostly in the form of a population explosion and a massive CO_2 buildup (Figures 8-2 and 8-3), and the global warming climate change this caused (Figure 8-4) that was now forcing a hasty retreat toward the renewable sources of the ecosystem.

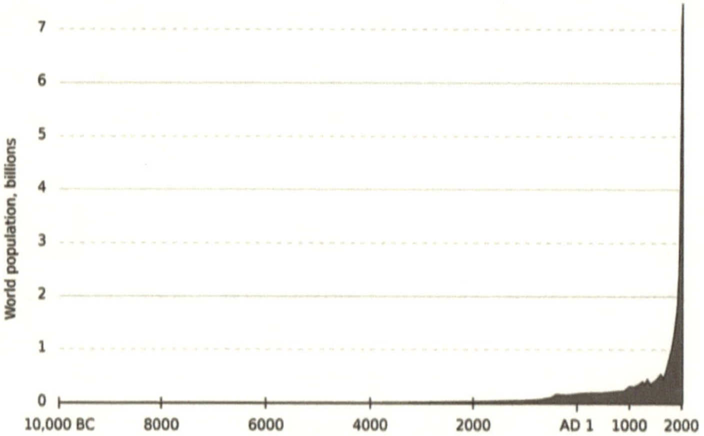

Figure 8-2. World human population (est.) 10,000 BCE–2000 CE.

(Source: Wikipedia)

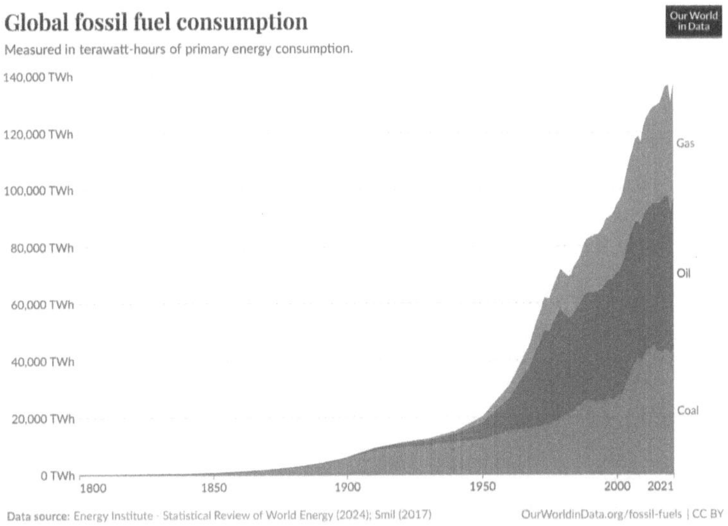

Figure 8-3. Global fossil fuel consumption through 2021.

(Source: Our World in Data based on Vaclav Smil [2017] and BP Statistical Review of World Energy)

With nothing more than 0.05 percent of the radiant energy emanating from the sun, this tiny percentage of the solar radiation was all that drove the photosynthetic, biochemical, renewable energy process that was absorbed by the biomass within ecosystems, and that would energize all life on Earth. And, with neither knowledge nor access to any of the other sources of energy Neolithic Revolution and subsequent humans would later discover and use *outside* ecosystems, having just this seemingly tiny amount of energy did not prevent pre-agriculture hunter-gatherer humans from building their societies and economies. On the contrary, they successfully eked out a living *within* Earth-life ecosystems and lived in harmony with its biodiversity for most of humanity's existence.

Indeed, they survived and thrived for 97 percent of our species' existence, and along the way, survived numerous glacial and interglacial climate changes including the Last Glacial Maximum, as well as that warming climate change that accompanied the Pleistocene-Holocene Transition, and that may well have facilitated agriculture and eventually civilization.

Here then were early human societies and economies that survived without societal or economic collapse for 290,000 years of our species' 300,000-year existence using nothing more than that minimal energy (0.05 percent) of the sun's radiation found in ecosystems. Neolithic Revolution and subsequent humans would find this modest amount of energy inadequate and would eventually strike out in search of greater energy sources.

The charts shown in Figure 8-2, "World Human Population," Figure 8-3, "Global Fossil Fuel Consumption," and Figure 8-4, "The relentless rise of carbon dioxide," show just where abandoning foraging, which had enabled access to the meager but adequate energy source *within* ecosystems, for farming, which engendered the need for greater energy sources *outside* those ecosystems, has landed us. This may not have been the intent of modern humans, who were worried about having insufficient energy to grow their societies and economies, but this may well have been the result. Humans apparently have never lost this hunger for more energy, this pursuit of more and more economic growth and the consequent population growth that came in tow.

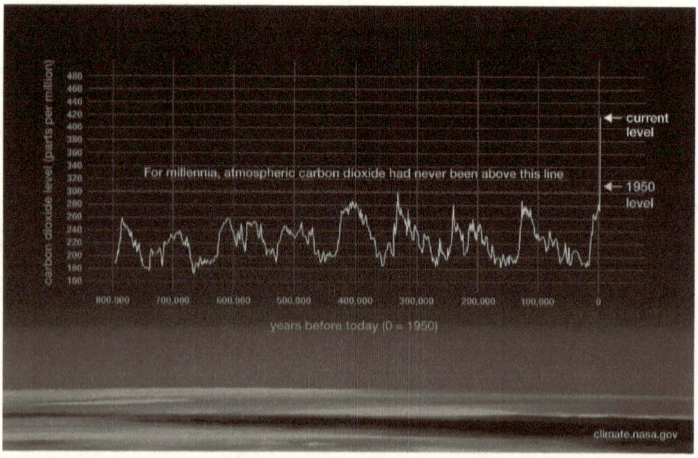

Figure 8-4. The relentless rise of carbon dioxide.

Carbon dioxide (CO_2) is higher than at any time in the past 400,000 years. During ice ages, CO_2 levels were around 200 parts per million (ppm), and during the warmer interglacial periods, they hovered around 280 ppm (see fluctuations in the graph). (Source: NASA.GOV)

Four hundred generations later, modern humans have the energy they craved, but it came with a devastating penalty. We got what we wanted but now, it seems, we don't want what we got. Today humans are becoming apoplectic from fear of the population explosion and accelerating global warming due to the CO_2 rise that accompanied unending economic growth and increased energy use. These charts, when viewed as the consequences of this search for energy, demonstrate the correlation between population, economic growth, and the corresponding increase in energy consumption, as evidenced by global warming.

The above charts show the cumulative consequences of the last 12,000 years of humanity's pursuit of unending economic growth, the search for more and more energy, and the resulting population explosion. This outcome should drive modern humans back to the socioeconomic lifeways of their pre-agriculture hunter-gatherer forebears who survived for most of our species' 300,000-year existence without collapse, and free from energy-driven existential threats.

In the preceding chapter we noted that our pre-agriculture hunter-gatherer forebears had nothing remotely resembling the level of technology and innovation modern humans possess, and now we note in addition that they did not develop any of their nonrenewable energy sources, either. Their only source of energy across all our species' existence was nothing more than the energy found in the biomass that comprised the flora, fauna, and funga they hunted and gathered for a living.

The picture that is beginning to emerge here is of how this comparatively tiny energy source within ecosystems—just food—was all humans had and used to take over the entire Earth. And as seen in the prior chapter, it was unlikely, too, that the technologies and innovations they did have were indispensable to their survival. Their survival, then, was independent of both the exotic technologies and added nonrenewable energy sources that modern human societies and economies, until recently, had come to regard as indispensable.

These two observations seem to suggest that pre-agriculture hunter-gatherer human survival, and the survival of their societies and economies, were never dependent on their ability to develop advanced technologies, nor upon gaining access to additional energy sources not already available *within* ecosystems. Neither, presumably, might these technologies and nonrenewable energy sources even have been necessary as life existed for hundreds of millennia for all Earth-life species without them.

The takeaway here seems to be that if Neolithic and modern humans had limited their resource demand to the comparatively meager necessities required to build survival-driven socioeconomic lifeways *within* Earth-life ecosystems, as our pre-agriculture hunter-gatherer forebears had done, the need for ecosystem services and biodiversity would have been substantially less, leaving healthier ecosystems to modern humans. Even now, of the purportedly 3 percent of ecosystems still intact and the comparatively little that may still remain of Earth's biodiversity, chances of their restoration may well become a possibility, and who knows, human survival may yet be achievable.

When humans chose farming over foraging as their means of eking out a living, whether they knew it or not, they were simultaneously choosing to do so *outside* Earth-life ecosystems and out of harmony with its biodiversity. And few things humans have done since confirm as clearly that we had moved our socioeconomic existence *outside* Earth-life ecosystems as did our search for and adoption of new energy sources. There was no need to search for energy sources *within* ecosystems because energy was already freely available to all biotic species via the food they ate. Like waterholes, energy is one of those common ecosystem resources, perhaps the most important one, and is accessible to all living species—but only from within the ecosystem.

And, just as we drink water to quench our thirst, availing ourselves of this energy source requires that we are biotic and that we consume as food the biomass in which energy is stored. There is and was no other way to access this energy source other than as a biotic species within an ecosystem. And that energy can only be replenished by eating the food sources found *within* Earth-life ecosystems. Is there a way to connect non-biotic mechanisms to the biotic energy source that drives life? Think about a defective pacemaker whose failing battery has to be replaced. Is there no way to recharge it from the energy coursing through the human body?

However, humans soon learned how to use the energy present in other Earth-life species to perform numerous energy-intensive tasks that farming necessitated and without the need for a biotic-to-abiotic energy interface. No physical connection was needed, as species were domesticated and used as draft animals. Humans next set out to find entirely new, novel, non-biotic sources, and stores of energy to power the many innovations and technologies we would eventually invent to help build and power our societies and economies *outside* Earth-life ecosystems. And indeed, unlike the renewable energy sources found only *within* Earth-life ecosystems, most human-engineered energy sources are nonrenewable, exist *outside* these ecosystems, and have no way to interface, connect with or fit naturally *within* the energy cycles that flow through these ecosystems such as the biogeochemical cycles—or pathways by which chemical elements move through the biotic (biosphere) and the abiotic compartments of Earth (the atmosphere, hydrosphere, and lithosphere).

Energy flows directionally through ecosystems, entering as sunlight (or inorganic molecules for chemoautotrophs) and leaving as heat during the transfers between trophic levels. Rather than flowing through an ecosystem, the matter that makes up living organisms is conserved and recycled. The six most common elements associated with organic molecules—carbon, nitrogen, hydrogen, oxygen, phosphorus, and sulfur—take a variety of chemical forms and may exist for long periods in the atmosphere, on land, in water, or beneath Earth's surface. These elemental components are cycled through the biosphere in interconnected processes that scientists call the water cycle, the carbon cycle, the biological carbon cycle, the biogeochemical carbon cycle, the nitrogen cycle, the phosphorus cycle, and the sulfur cycle.

The cyclings of these elements, as noted, are interconnected—but not using man-made energy sources. For example, the movement of water is critical for the leaching of nitrogen and phosphate into rivers, lakes, and oceans. The ocean is also a major reservoir for carbon. Thus, mineral nutrients are cycled, rapidly or slowly, through the entire biosphere between the biotic and abiotic world and from one living organism to another. Most man-made energy sources, however, do not interconnect or fit naturally within these cycles and result in numerous waste products and deleterious effects, including harmful impacts on ecosystems, biodiversity species and humans, often due to the way these are extracted, processed, used, and disposed of. The effects also vary depending on the type of nonrenewable energy source being used, and there are at least five ways nonrenewable energy sources cause harmful impacts:

(1) **Greenhouse gas emissions.** Perhaps the most well-known impact of using nonrenewable energy sources is the emission of greenhouse gases. Nonrenewable energy sources are not just altering Earth's atmosphere by increasing the amount of greenhouse gas emissions, they also emit a variety of pollutants that affect Earth's ecosystems, biodiversity, and human health. For example, coal-fired power plants are the single largest source of mercury emissions in the U.S.

(2) **Air pollution.** Greenhouse gas emissions also emit a variety of pollutants that affect people's health and the environment and according to the Harvard T.H. Chan School of Public Health, is now responsible for one in five deaths worldwide. Perhaps as many as ten million people worldwide die each year from the acute and cumulative effects of air pollution, and as many as eight million of those deaths are linked to the particulate matter produced from the burning of fossil fuels.

(3) **Acid rain and water pollution.** Acid rain is corrosive to machinery and disrupts local ecosystems. It also changes the acidity of lakes and streams which can be very harmful to fish and other aquatic organisms; it is also damaging to trees, thereby weakening forest ecosystems.

(4) **Land pollution and waste generation** often occur during extraction of nonrenewable resources or the disposal of the waste they generate.

(5) **Oil spills and other accidents** are extremely damaging to nearby shores and ecosystems.

But as humanity sought to meet its growing energy needs *outside Earth-life* ecosystems, all or most of what it came up with turned out to be nonrenewables with expiration dates and with hints of death or species extinction attached. All are incompatible with most Earth-life processes and result in harm to the environment, the atmosphere, and the entire biosphere. And, if CO_2 is any indication of their side effects, given enough time these nonrenewable energy sources may all be on a path to destroying life itself. Given this evolving outcome to the human search for new energy sources to power its attempt at eking out a living *outside* Earth-life ecosystems, and given their potential for harm, is there a message or warning here for humans? Perhaps it is to quit our foolish quest for ever more energy and return to eking out a living within Earth-life ecosystems with renewable-only energy, while there may still be time? But is there still time?

In 2021, according to an International Energy Agency (IEA) press release, humans pumped 36.3 billion tons of planet-warming gases into the atmosphere, more than in any previous year, which helped to lift the CO_2 level 50 percent above the average for the pre-industrial era, when humans had not yet begun widespread burning of oil, coal, and gas in the late nineteenth century. May 2024 saw CO_2 reach its highest level in human history, moving the needle up to just over 426 ppm. And you would no doubt have noticed our species' current rapid, global-warming-driven retreat to renewable energy sources of every description. But not many have recognized this retreat for what it really is—that humans are in fact being driven back and might have begun beating a retreat to the renewable energy sources that were always available within ecosystems, and therefore, back to the compatibility with the biosphere early humans once enjoyed while eking out a living *within* Earth-life ecosystems.

Humans hold grandiose views of ourselves and our twenty-first century civilization given how advanced we have become in science, technology, innovation, and quality of life compared to prior civilizations. But given the collapse of numerous civilizations throughout the Holocene, notwithstanding their achievements, there is no other way to call it but to say that humans have paid a great price for continuing to build their socioeconomic lifeways *outside* of Earth-life ecosystems. And even now as we continue into the Anthropocene, humans may end up paying an even greater price—perhaps even extinction, a not-so-implausible outcome given the rapid onset of anthropogenic climate change-driven global warming and our equally rapidly faltering remedial efforts to halt it so far.

Unfortunately, there may be only one sure way to end this dilemma and it's unlikely to come from our economies, technologies, science, and innovations, or from our global or local politics as these have all been major contributors to prior civilization collapse. That way goes something like this: Regardless of whatever new energy sources might yet emerge, unless humans recognize the need for, then prioritize, an accelerated return to eking out a living *within* Earth-life ecosystems and in harmony with its biodiversity, there is no way to tell with any degree of certainty how this may all play out for our species. And, while it may always turn out to be a bad idea to bet against humanity, the odds today don't look so great for humanity and may well favor extinction—the potential cost for having destroyed most of the very foundations of all life on Earth.

By attempting to eke out a living during the last 400 generations *outside* Earth-life ecosystems and out of harmony with its biodiversity, humans have destroyed all but 3 percent of ecosystems and innumerable species of its biodiversity. Moreover, by growing its population from a few hundred million 400 generations ago to eight billion-plus just recently, and with a projected population of 10-plus billion by the end of the twenty-first century, humans may well exceed the carrying capacity of a planet being simultaneously ravaged by climate change.

It is unlikely one would find such reasoning coming from the pundits, or from the many analysts that have undertaken or would undertake to explain away the circumstances in which humans now find themselves and the consequences we have begun to face, the worst of which we might have yet to endure. Few if any would see our global warming dilemma as having begun with that colossal mistake our Neolithic Revolution human ancestors made, choosing to farm rather than forage, a choice that all subsequent humans inherited and adopted and largely for the same reasons—to gain surplus, profits, wealth accumulation, and GDP growth.

Nevertheless, that's where this all began, and while many think the way forward, the way out of this dilemma, is through our scientific and technological innovations, unfortunately, it's more likely that only a return, if still possible, to the *survival-driven-principles* inherent in those pre-agriculture hunter-gatherer socioeconomic lifeways offers a viable strategy for survival.

It's fast becoming clear that humans have found themselves in the midst of a global, civilization-wide, energy-driven transformation and must hastily abandon and replace nearly all of the energy sources it has relied upon to power the growth of its societies, economies, and indeed entire civilizations for most of the last 300-plus years. This is a transformation it must complete within fixed time limits or as soon as possible, to avoid known and unknown dire consequences, including the increasingly worsening hazards of fossil fuel-driven CO_2 global warming climate change.

This transition, however, is not voluntary and is by no means the first energy-driven transformation humans have undertaken. Humans once relied entirely on renewable energy sources within Earth's ecosystems. Renewables are the only form of energy within these ecosystems, and for our species' entire existence, they have been the only known energy source used by all hominin species, including humans. It was only long after the Neolithic Revolution and subsequent humans chose to become farmers rather than remain foragers that their need for new and non-biotic energy sources seemingly became a necessity, at least to them. They needed a source of energy that could perform work on farms they were planting *outside* Earth-life ecosystems. They may not have thought of it this way, but effectively, they were looking to break free from the constraints of the organic bio-based economy within ecosystems.

Humans were able to meet this growing energy need for a while by harnessing the wind, water, and numerous Earth-life species, such as draft animals, to perform the arduous energy-intensive agricultural work, including plowing, planting, and reaping, that came with farming. But this method of obtaining additional energy soon proved inadequate and new abiotic sources of energy were sought and eventually discovered. They were looking for and found an escape from the constraints of the organic economy energy sources based on: solar energy, muscle power, and biomass, found within ecosystems.

These new abiotic sources of energy would turn out to be the nonrenewable energy sources we know and use today. But first, during the millennia that separated the Neolithic Revolution and the Industrial Revolution, humans began a long and slow but voluntary transition to eking out a living *outside* ecosystems. Great civilizations would emerge in China, India, Egypt, the Indus Valley, the Tigris and Euphrates region, Greece, and Rome, and eventually, their efforts would be accelerated by innovations that came with the Industrial Revolution.

By inventing numerous machines capable of using these nonrenewable energy sources such as diesel-powered engines, diesel locomotives, coal-powered machinery, and eventually, automobiles, airplanes, and numerous others, humans were able to perform work and increase economic growth not hitherto possible. But, as it would turn out, not without bringing great harm and risk upon humanity.

Could they have known that these alternative nonrenewable energy sources, so eagerly adopted, would come at so great a cost; that, 300 years later, these nonrenewable fossil fuels would turn out to be the foundations of a potential fossil fuel-driven global warming extinction? As seen earlier, many knew of the harm CO_2 could inflict while it was still safe to abandon them but chose instead the profits, wealth accumulation, and GDP growth they were enabling. This was especially true of those who led the legal-person corporations that populated the legal-person economy they were erecting.

Figure 8-5. The relentless extraction of fossil fuels.

Fossil fuels are the primary source of energy in the world today. But people started using fossil fuels long before the first steam engine running on coal or the first commercially drilled oil well. (Source: Tom Kool for Oilprice.com)

Unlike this current non-voluntary, global-warming-driven, back-to-renewables energy transformation that now grips the world, this earlier transition to nonrenewables has its roots in the eventual emergence of Neolithic Revolution humans' desire to leave the ecosystems in search of more energy than apparently was available *within*. This voluntary search continued throughout the Holocene until about 300 years ago, when coal began to be used as an industrial energy source in Great Britain. The transition to coal as an alternative energy source and its rapid replacement of wood in the U.S. from 1776 to the present is clearly shown in Figure 8-6 and wouldn't have been the first time humans would discover and use fossil fuels—see "The Complete History of Fossil Fuels" by Tom Kool at Oilprice.com.

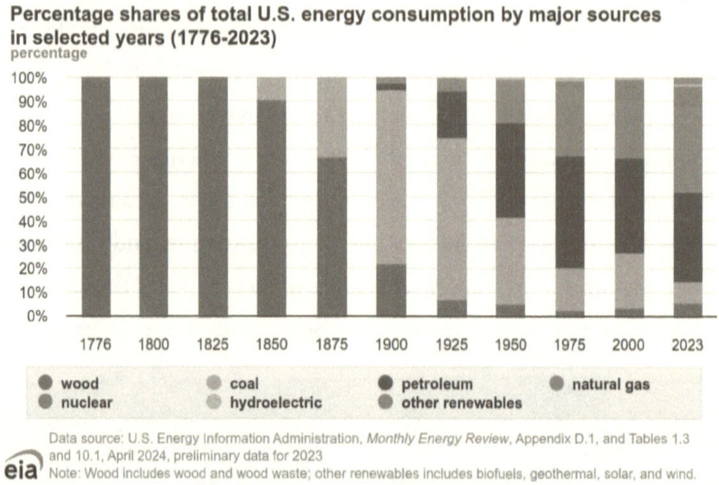

Figure 8-6. Shares of total U.S. energy consumption by major sources, selected years (1776-2023).

(Data source: U.S. Energy Information Administration)

In the U.S., wood was and remained the only source of energy—100 percent wood—until 1825. Then wood's share of energy use dropped to 90 percent in 1850 as coal was adopted; then to 60 percent in 1875 and 20 percent by 1900 as use of coal accelerated. The rest of this chart shows how the use of coal shrank as it began to be supplemented and partly replaced by petroleum, and petroleum by natural gas, then by nuclear, and eventually by a few renewable sources like hydroelectric and others. These were all energy transitions away from wood, a renewable energy source, a form of biomass, to mainly a variety of nonrenewables in the form of coal, petroleum, and natural gas—all fossil fuels.

This transition to nonrenewables, as noted, was driven and still is, not by a human survival threat such as the current global warming-driven climate change now being caused by use of these nonrenewables. Instead, it was caused by the socioeconomic lifeways' need and desire for surplus that accompanied the unending desire for economic expansion, increased profits, wealth accumulation, and endless GDP growth. These were made possible, according to Ellen Meiksins Wood in *The Origin of Capitalism: A Longer View,* by an increase in energy that began to emerge in Great Britain in the form of coal during those early days of what would become capitalism.

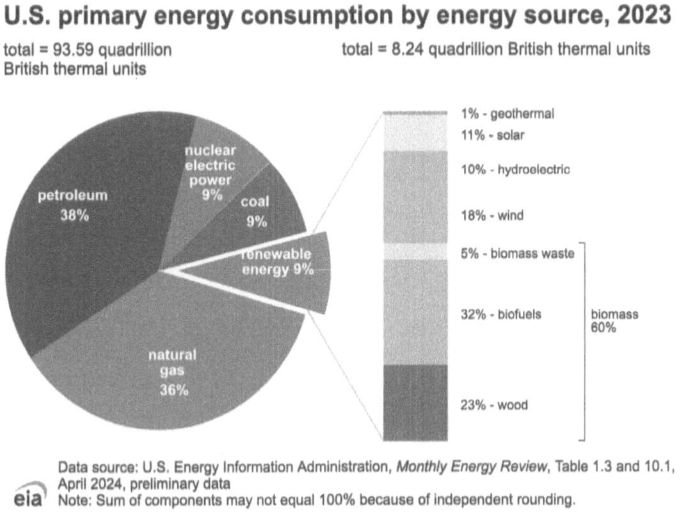

Figure 8-7. U.S. primary energy consumption by energy source, 2023.

(Data source: U.S. Energy Information Administration)

In fact, this transition to nonrenewable, fossil fuel-based energy sources would be so complete that by 2021 renewable sources of energy in the U.S. had fallen to a mere 12 percent from 100 percent in 1825 (in just 200 years) with fossil fuels assuming the ascendency to become the primary sources of U.S. energy consumption as shown in Figure 8-7. And what became true for the U.S. is now mostly true for most of the rest of the world. It should be clear, then, that humanity's transition back to a carbon-neutral economy based on renewables has a rather long way to go, I am afraid.

If 2023 was any indication, humans may not reach there in time to avoid even worse global warming climate change-driven catastrophes, signs of which became increasingly apparent due to the fire and floods that descended upon the Earth in 2023. Whereas that first human energy transition, from foraging to farming and agriculture, is believed to have taken humans 4,000 years, this second energy transition, from renewables *inside* the ecosystem to nonrenewables *outside*, from wood to coal, oil, and gas, would take a mere 200 years (at least in the USA).

But as noted, this was more than a transition to new sources of energy, but rather was simultaneously, first if not foremost, a bold-faced economic choice to enhance the human ability to eke out a living *outside* Earth-life ecosystems and out of harmony with its biodiversity, just as Neolithic Revolution humans began to do some 10,000 years earlier when they became the first humans to choose to farm *outside* rather than forage *inside* Earth-life ecosystems for a living. This, then, was a choice to augment, if not replace, the sole renewable energy source available *within* ecosystems and that could only be used mostly *within* ecosystems, with new energy sources that can be used *outside* those ecosystems.

Farming, however, needed energy sources capable of performing work *outside* Earth-life ecosystems where humans had begun to build their societies and economies. *Hence, it would turn out, these sources couldn't and wouldn't be integrated with the existing biogeochemical energy cycles within ecosystems*. Earth's evolution, it would seem, provided no external energy solutions, much less one that would have enabled eking out a living *outside* Earth-life ecosystems and that would be compatible with the sole renewable energy source *within*. Hence, humans had to hoe their own.

The evolutionary process would, no doubt, have been aware of the existence of nonrenewable energy sources, such as fossil fuels, yet offered pre-agriculture hunter-gatherer humans a single renewable energy source—the solar energy bound up in chemical bonds in the food they would hunt and gather and eat to release that energy. Would knowledge of the harm that use of nonrenewables would eventually bring to all Earth-life ecosystems, and life in general, have prevented them from being made available together with the renewables of the ecosystem?

Awareness of the death and destruction that nonrenewables would end up causing may have prevented making them simultaneously available along with renewables. But that knowledge and awareness, as we saw earlier, did not stop humans from pursuing socioeconomic lifeways, enabled by their fossil-fuel-driven multinational legal-person economies that exploited nonrenewables for economic surplus, profits, wealth accumulation, and GDP growth.

So, it begs the question: Is this fossil-fuel-driven global-warming climate change that's forcing humans to return to renewables to survive an implied message—nay, a rebuke? You see, ecosystems evolved to enable species survival, but it is we humans in pursuit of new energy sources that could enable profits and wealth accumulation, who seem intent on turning these instead into a raging inferno. Can anyone think of a similar event or time when a natural process appeared to have stepped up to say to a species, "Stop! No can do, or you will go extinct!"

To survive, twenty-first century humans are now being driven by nature and have no choice but to abandon their fossil fuel and other nonrenewable energy sources, including nuclear power. Humans now, perhaps for the first time, have no choice but to replace these, if possible, with renewables—the only kind of energy source in Earth-life ecosystems. To survive, humans must now make this transformation, however reluctantly, from nonrenewables back to renewable energy sources; from coal, oil, gas, and nuclear, all nonrenewables, to renewable sources of energy: solar energy, wind energy, geothermal energy from the heat inside the earth, hydropower from flowing water, ocean energy in the form of wave, tidal, and current energy, ocean thermal energy, and biomass from plants—and maybe eventually even fusion, the energy of the sun.

With hindsight, this energy transition would no doubt be counted among the few that have driven humanity's great transformations and it's right up there with the Neolithic Revolution transition from foraging to farming that occurred soon after the beginning of the Holocene some 12,000 years ago. That transformation, too, though not often recognized as such, was also an energy-driven transformation. Neolithic humans were changing how they were going to obtain food, their only source of energy, from simply foraging for food to producing their own food through agriculture and animal husbandry—a decidedly more energy-intensive way to eke out a living. Indeed, they soon found out that food production required lots more energy than foraging did. And it was this choice to produce their own food *outside* Earth-life ecosystems that may have eventually driven their search for additional energy sources that could be used *outside* ecosystems, and thus could support their choice to eke out a living *outside* ecosystems.

Thus began what may well have been the first human energy transition, a change in how humans would obtain energy, from foraging to farming, a voluntary transition. But farming soon led to a second energy transition, from renewables already available *within* the ecosystem to nonrenewables *outside* the ecosystem. And now, 10,000 years later, humans have embarked upon yet another energy transformation, this time an involuntary one driven by nature—forcing humans to abandon nonrenewables and return to renewable energy sources.

And, whereas the prior transition to nonrenewables was driven by what would later be seen as, and indeed was, a desire for economic expansion, profits, wealth accumulation, and unending GDP growth, this third energy transition now occurring some 10,000 years later, from nonrenewables back to renewables, is just beginning, and, is being forced upon humans because of a CO_2-driven global warming climate change—a direct consequence of the prior transition to nonrenewables outside the ecosystem.

But will this choice, though involuntary, awaken a new human survival awareness and preference? Has humanity's latent but emerging desire to survive begun to assert itself over its desire for endless economic growth? Will humanity finally begin to prioritize life and survival above wealth accumulation and economic growth? In just 400 generations, humanity has found itself, once again, embarking upon yet another energy transition: voluntarily at first, from foraging to farming, then *from renewables to nonrenewables, and now, 10,000 years later, from nonrenewables back to renewables.* This will be an energy transition that will drive a transformation of twenty-first century human socioeconomic lifeways as dramatic as, if not more than, the earlier transition from foraging to farming.

Seen from the perspective of our civilization's seemingly renewed and emerging desire to survive, will this latter emerging energy transformation be accompanied by a reawakening, one that would drive modern humans to return to some modern equivalent of eking out its living, once more, as pre-agriculture hunter-gatherer humans did, within what's left of Earth-life ecosystems and in harmony with what's left of its biodiversity?

Given that renewable energy in ecosystems comes from the sun and comprises the sole energy source available to all life, how did modern humans get started on nonrenewables? And as long as we are asking, how did Neolithic Revolution humans get started on farming? Whereas the latter energy transition ended up leading humans down a path that today has led to the destruction of all but 3 percent of Earth-life's ecosystems, and by all accounts, is not too far from decimating its biodiversity species and its oceans as well, the former now confronts us with the potential existential risk of our species' extinction that could well be due to a CO_2-driven global warming climate change.

Here, then, are two of humanity's major socioeconomic lifeway transformations, both due to energy transitions that occurred during the Holocene. The former, from foraging to farming, was voluntary and occurred near the beginning of the Holocene and continues to this day, and the latter, from the renewables *inside* the ecosystem to nonrenewables *outside*, was also voluntary, beginning near its end, some 300 years ago. Each bookended the Holocene geologic epoch that saw the development and expansion as well as the collapse of most human civilizations. Neither transition, it would seem, has been great for our species.

Humans, reluctantly, have now embarked upon yet a third energy transition. This one, though, is involuntary. We are moving away from the life-threatening global warming being generated by the nonrenewable fossil fuels we adopted some 300 years ago that turbocharged the second energy transition, and back to the renewable energy of the ecosystem.

Could humanity have lived the last 10,000 years of the Holocene differently? The answer is a resounding yes. Did the numerous human civilizations that emerged during the last 10,000 years need to collapse the way they did? No, not at all, according to some historians. And could twenty-first century human civilization—which has just emerged from the throes of a global pandemic, and which faces wars in Africa, Europe, the Middle East, and potentially Southeast Asia that could engulf the world, the global food supply, and efforts to arrest global CO_2 growth and the worst of climate change so far—turn out differently? Absolutely. As different as these transitions may have been, each caused numerous major human socioeconomic lifeway changes that seem to have been driven by a common cause—the Neolithic Revolution-driven socioeconomic lifeway desire for surplus, profits, wealth accumulation, and endless GDP growth that subsequent humans adopted.

Humans chose these Neolithic Revolution socioeconomic lifeway goals and outcomes over the original survival-driven socioeconomic lifeway goal and outcome that had enabled them to endure collapse-free for most of our species existence—that of ensuring Earth-life ecosystems, biodiversity, and human life and survival above all else. The implication is that except for the Neolithic Revolution and the socioeconomic lifeway changes it enabled, human history might have turned out very differently—and indeed, minus these lifeway changes, it once did. Pre-agriculture hunter-gatherer human economies and societies survived collapse-free for all but the last 400 generations that began with the start of the Holocene.

How did foraging societies and economies survive while farming ones didn't? Foragers, as seen in earlier chapters, followed very different socioeconomic lifeways that were *survival-driven*, that ensured they eked out their living *inside* Earth-life ecosystems and did so in harmony with its biodiversity rather than drive them to extinction as Neolithic humans began to and as subsequent humans continued to do. Their survival, and the survival of Earth-life's ecosystems and biodiversity for all those millennia, was a direct consequence of those *survival-driven lifeways* they practiced. This is proof that human societies and economies had survived without collapse once and could have done so again during the last 10,000 years of the Holocene had Neolithic Revolution humans continued, rather than abandoned, the survival-driven lifeways that ensured our species' survival for most of our existence.

Today, one may or may not have noticed how this need to rapidly abandon nonrenewables is often nonchalantly discussed, and as dispassionately as one might a minor technology inconvenience. It's as though humans are just opting to go down a different energy path, with little if any acknowledgement being voiced, and little or no postmortem of what drove the initial choices to begin with. Why is this, though, given that one can easily find oneself in a heated debate on almost any topic in our polarized twenty-first century social media-obsessed societies?

Few people, especially not the world leaders who finance fossil energy, the politicians who benefited from it, and least of all, the legal-person multinational corporations who dredge up fossil fuels, seem interested in revisiting the choice to tap nonrenewable energy, which has always been suspected of being harmful, but which is now turning out to be a colossal and potentially existential mistake. Why aren't those choices and their consequences being debated and examined for lessons learned? Why are twenty-first century humans (except perhaps for generation Z) being so reticent about discussing earlier human socioeconomic lifeway choices that have now placed our entire species in jeopardy?

As noted, in just the preceding 400 generations our species made two momentous, species-changing socioeconomic lifeway choices—to farm and to adopt nonrenewable energy—neither of which seemed to have included an impact assessment of minor topics like the possibility that the very foundations upon which all life is based, including the survival of Earthlife ecosystems, its biodiversity species and human survival itself, might be destroyed. Instead, as a society we seem driven and led, as Neolithic Revolution humans seemed to have been, by elites with an insatiable desire for surplus, profit, wealth accumulation, and GDP growth at any cost.

Beginning with the Neolithic Revolution and the choice to farm rather than forage 10,000 years earlier, and again just 300 years ago, with the adoption of nonrenewable energy sources driven by the Industrial Revolution, it is unfortunate how these two sets of choices have now left our species near total ecosystem destruction and biodiversity extinction on the one hand, and the fossil fuel-driven climate change predicament on the other. What was the socioeconomic reasoning that underpinned these choices? How was it that the choices of a few have left so many in harm's way?

But there is a small problem here. Four hundred-plus generations later, twenty-first century human civilization is still making these same socioeconomic lifeway choices (surplus, profits, wealth accumulation, and GDP growth) and is still committed to the same socioeconomic lifeways that got us here to begin with. Not only are we not debating these past choices to learn what went wrong and what we must change, but unfortunately, the problems these choices have already caused leave us little time and no other choice but to focus on taking corrective action sooner rather than later. Hence the rush back to renewable energy sources in which we now find ourselves. But can humans really make the rapid lifeway changes that this involuntary energy about-turn will require?

Prior energy transitions (from foraging to farming, then from farming with renewables to farming with nonrenewables) were both voluntary and ended, more-or-less happily, with the continuation of the human species, though not especially because of something humans did or did not do but, more likely, because humans had not yet pushed past boundaries that could trigger a planetary response such as a global change in climate. But in this third and ongoing transition from nonrenewables back to renewables, it should be unequivocally stated, it is increasingly unclear whether humans will also have a happily-ever-after ending.

The first energy transitions began when early humans chose to change how they would obtain their food and thereby energy, from hunting and gathering initially to farming, agriculture, and animal husbandry. This in turn transformed human socioeconomic lifeways from those once free, small, sharing, mobile, egalitarian, hunter-gatherer bands, societies, and economies, to large, sedentary, hoarding, farming, agricultural, towns, cities, and eventually civilizations, ruled and often enslaved by kings and misguided by religions. This transition marked the first time ever that humans would choose to eke out a living *outside* Earth-life ecosystems and the beginning of the search for new energy sources that would enable them to do so.

The new energy sources they would find turned out to be nonrenewables and became the beginning of the transition away from the renewables *inside* the ecosystem to nonrenewable sources *outside*. First came the switch from wood to coal that enabled industrialization and the rise of Great Britain. This transition, though, unlike the switch from foraging to farming, would not only upend social structures and human relationships, particularly in Britain and Europe and eventually worldwide, but would also engender the birth of the *legal-person* and enable the emergence of the *legal-person economy*. Coal was followed by oil, which similarly transformed geopolitics, and with the aid of the Crown and these *legal-persons* that would become *multinational corporations,* turned some countries, like the U.S., into energy superpowers. Eventually gas, both natural and liquefied, along with nuclear power, would in turn be added to this mix of nonrenewable energy sources that would vie to meet modern human energy needs.

How nations would use these fossil fuel resources should remind us of the reason all ecosystem resources, such as waterholes and energy, were neither owned nor controlled in early human societies and economies by any species but remained free and available to all. The world would be a different place today if modern humans were to adopt those *survival-driven lifeways* our hunter-gatherer forebears practiced within Earth-life ecosystems for millennia, enabling them to survive for 97 percent of our species' history.

And it is history that would show us how, on the contrary, ownership of energy, access to energy, and control of energy processing endowed nations and their legal-person corporations with the ability to shape geopolitics, as Russia is currently doing across Europe with fossil fuels, and China is, worldwide, with rare-earth minerals. Nations endowed with fossil fuels have used them to blackmail and force other nations to pander to their geopolitical will as the OPEC oil cartel did back in the 1970s. Today, it is Russia that is using its vast fossil fuel sources of oil and gas to force nations like Germany, Poland, and the Baltic states to comply with its geopolitical preferences by cutting off, or threatening to cut off, supply, thus starting a mad rush by the EU to find other sources. Now, once again, in the twenty-first century, it is a new and expanded OPEC that threatens the energy supply by withholding production.

Economists, politicians, and various scientists dryly and often clinically characterize this rapid return to renewables in terms of an energy transition, but they've had little if anything to say about the transformation of human and Earth-life species lifeways this transition will cause, nor are the consequences nearly as well understood or being explored and explained in layman's terms as one might have hoped. It took about 4,000 years for hunter-gatherer humans to transition from foraging to mostly farming societies and economies, but I doubt humanity would have more than a tiny fraction of that time to return to renewables.

Today humans must make perhaps an even bigger energy transition (at least numerically) from nonrenewables back to renewables, and we must do so in a real hurry if we hope to survive. The fact that this rapid abandonment of fossil fuel energy sources is not by choice, but rather one that is being forced upon humanity—and one that must occur within narrow time intervals whose lengths humans have no say in, except to comply to survive—is also hardly being seen and emphasized as the ultimatum it is.

Instead, one hears plenty about these matters: the science and technologies humans must come up with to decarbonize; the economics and inflation; the geopolitics; the supply chain; the knock-on effects on the world food supply; and more. But as important as these aspects of the energy transition story may have hitherto been, and no doubt are, the real story here is not just about an energy transition, though energy is what grabs our attention. The real story here, nay, the big story not getting nearly the emphasis it should, is the human story—*human life and survival*. Humans may have survived the prior two energy transitions, from foraging to farming and from renewables *inside* the ecosystem to nonrenewables *outside*, but neither was bookended by a ticking potential global warming extinction event.

So, issue one for humanity then must be "Can humans survive this third energy transition?" Why? What's so special about this transition that can't be overcome with emerging modern technologies? Time, which is perhaps the one thing humans don't have and can't innovate. *Because this may well be the first time in human history the Earth system has begun to push back, and push back hard, visibly and globally, against something humans have done and are still doing—a response that some euphemistically describe as planetary boundaries.*

Nevertheless, humans are being forced to make yet another energy transition, not by choice this time but by nature. A transition to an energy system based predominantly on non-fossil fuel energy resources that is in its earliest phase; one I seriously doubt humans have 4,000 years, this time around, to complete; and one that must unfold in only one direction—*from nonrenewables back to renewables.* And renewable energy, you will recall, is the energy source of the ecosystem and was in fact the only energy source all Earth-life species, including our hunter-gatherer forebears, had ever known.

Our societies and economies are being told this time, not in so many words and not by its scientists, politicians, or economists, but by nature, what must be done energy-wise. We must get back to renewables and if necessary, the renewables of the ecosystem. What must be done economically, scientifically, politically, collectively, and individually if we hope to survive? Hopefully, humans will begin to listen before it is too late.

But getting back to the renewable energy that prevailed and enabled human life within ecosystems for 290,000 years of our species' existence is not necessarily the same as what modern humans mean by a return to renewables, decarbonization, or green energy. Modern humans talk about "renewable energy," "decarbonizing the economy," and switching to "green energy"—apparently only for human economies, though—as if there is going to be one renewable energy source and infrastructure for humans and a separate one for biodiversity and everything else. And, by the way, there already exist two separate energy grids. The renewable energy grid within ecosystems that's powered by the sun through photosynthesis, energizing all life, and the mostly nonrenewable man-made energy grid that powers humanity's non-life human inventions.

Life has always run on an energy grid separate and apart from that on which all human inventions, technologies, and energy sources that power the economies humans built *outside* Earth-life ecosystems run. And this life grid is powered by the renewable energy we obtain from our food that is derived from *within* ecosystems and remains separate from the fossil-fuel-powered energy grid that powers all else in human societies and economies. So, can going to a green human economy enable a sharing with the renewable energy that flows within Earth-life ecosystems?

Can the renewable energy flows envisaged for the economic sectors of modern human societies and economies—including power, oil and gas, automotive, aviation and shipping, steel, cement, mining, agriculture and food, and forestry and land use—in any way connect to or integrate into the renewable energy that flows through Earth-life ecosystems and biodiversity? Here, then, is an energy disconnect problem that arose in the last 300 years that only modern humans have had to live with.

Can this renewable energy that enabled all Earth-life for nearly 4.7 billion years, and energized all human existence for nearly 300,000 years—and, by the way, still does—ever be connected to the man-made, geographically stationary, fossil-fuel-driven energy generating systems that energize modern human societies and economies? So far—no. Hence, getting to a green economy will in no way resemble the renewable energy flows that enabled life nor the energy environment our pre-agriculture hunter-gatherer forbears experienced and enjoyed.

By building human economies *outside* Earth-life ecosystems, humans have essentially ended up with two separate energy systems. One that relies on the sun, which is omnipresent and energizes all Earth-life species, including humans, and is radiated across space into the biogeochemical systems, cycles, and flows *within* ecosystems. The other is built by humans and embedded within its societies and economies at fixed geographic locations to energize its for-profit industries and is disconnected from and operates *outside* Earth-life ecosystems. It's the latter that's broken and must be fixed—if not entirely abandoned.

Hunter-gatherer access to renewable energy did not require our forebears to dig up vast stretches of those ecosystems in search of rare-earth minerals and conflict minerals including cobalt, nickel, lithium, and graphite as shown in Figure 8-8 and Figure 8-9; nor did it require a rapid deployment of clean energy technologies that demand these minerals; nor was there a need to decarbonize the lifeways of early human societies and economies within those ecosystems. In fact, carbon in ecosystems is an essential and indispensable component of the biomass of Earth-life's flora, fauna, and funga and participates in one of those major ecosystem cycles, the carbon cycle. There was not one energy source and infrastructure for humans and a separate one for everything else but, today, that's where humans have ended up. Today, because Neolithic and modern humans chose to eke out a living *outside* Earth-life ecosystems and needed to find an energy source that can work *outside* those ecosystems, we have ended up with nonrenewables that we must now work hard to leave in the Earth. Will we make it? I hope we do.

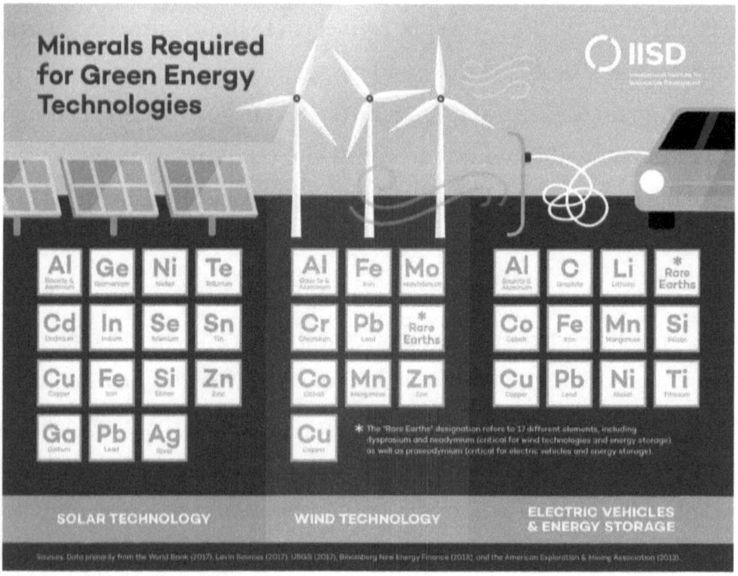

Figure 8-8. Minerals required for green energy technologies.
(Source: IEA)

But is beating a path back to renewables, decarbonizing economies, and converting to green energy the right way forward, and will it prevent a potential human extinction? That will depend on two outcomes: how quickly, and why, humans might choose to do so if they still have a choice. If the sole reason to decarbonize, to get back to renewables and meet all our energy needs using green energy is to ensure Earth-life ecosystems, biodiversity, and human survival, then humanity might well have a chance of pulling this off if the heat in the atmosphere has not already surpassed an amount that would prevent life, as we know it, from continuing. If, however, the global increase in temperature were to surpass levels that allow human survival (the last time CO_2 was this high, humans didn't exist), then regardless of what we do all bets will be off.

Modern humans must never forget that it was the false goals of surplus, profits, and wealth accumulation that enticed our Neolithic Revolution forebears to abandon foraging for farming; to eke out a living *outside* Earth-life ecosystems rather than *inside;* and to find new energy sources that turned out to be nonrenewable to help build that life *outside* those ecosystems; and thereby away from the renewable energy that once met, and would have continued to meet, all their energy needs had they remained *inside*. The real problem humanity faces therefore is not just an energy transition problem but a human survival problem, and the only way to solve that problem, as we have seen, is to prioritize and protect the things that keep life alive—Earth-life's ecosystems, biodiversity, and human survival over and above everything else.

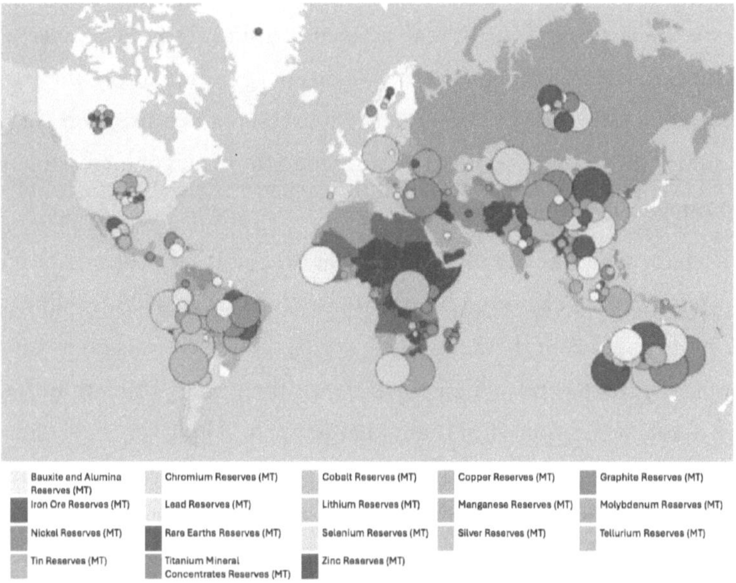

Figure 8-9. Global reserves of minerals required for green energy technologies, overlaid with fragility and corruption measures.

(Source: Fund for Peace, 2018; Transparency International, 2017; USGS)

The real goal of this third energy transition, then, shouldn't be just to decarbonize the economy, transition to green energy, or both, because decarbonization would require a rapid deployment of *clean energy technologies* as part of this energy transition. That in turn would engender a significant increase in demand for minerals like lithium, graphite, and cobalt, and obtaining these would drive an equally massive increase in the mining and extraction of these minerals that are to be found mostly in some of the Earth's few remaining intact ecosystems (Figure 8-9). And that will result, once again, in yet another round of humans destroying that remaining 3 percent of Earth's ecosystems that might still be intact, and of what remains of its biodiversity. It also potentially risks eliminating any chance of survival humans as well might yet have had.

Humanity survived two prior energy transitions, and unsurprisingly, didn't even recognize those as energy transitions. Their focus wasn't on finding and navigating a transition to new sources of energy but rather on finding *new sources of food* and ways to increase food (food production) using those new sources. The first transition was from foraging to farming, and the second was from animal-assisted farming (renewable energy) to machine-assisted farming (nonrenewable energy). In making these transitions, they came up with new energy sources, not because their survival was under threat, but because they wanted to find ways of increasing their economic output.

Perhaps what they really wanted was an ability heretofore not possible—an ability to eke out a living *outside* Earth's ecosystems while continuing to live *within* them. In other words, their focus was on continued economic growth and not particularly on the energy transition that, it turned out, was required to make that happen. Along the way, they did manage to meet the increased energy needs required for food production by farming. By using fossil fuels from outside the ecosystem—a nonrenewable source of energy—together with the animal and biomass renewable sources they already had within the ecosystem, they were able to meet the increased energy needs farming required.

Unfortunately, though, it is no longer going to be possible to survive if humans continue to use nonrenewable fossil fuel energy sources to eke out a living *outside* Earth-life ecosystems. And one seriously doubts whether, minus the urgency of a CO_2 climate-change-driven existential threat, modern humans would even be interested in, or, be motivated to carry out, this global nonrenewable to renewable energy transition currently in progress. Legal-person economies as well as what remains of human economies certainly won't be doing so just to accelerate green growth. Humans then are being forced to make a choice—return to the renewables *inside* ecosystems in order to survive or continue to use the nonrenewables *outside* at their peril. Who or what will make this choice?

It is clear what most humans prefer, but as noted earlier, modern economies are no longer just human economies but have become, in addition, *legal-person economies* run by or manipulated by global multinational corporations (aka legal-persons), and Exxon et al. aren't being harmed by the global warming their fossil fuels have caused. In fact, left to their own devices, they would continue their extraction business and indeed, are abandoning their commitments to transition to a carbon free future.

How different, then, would solutions to this third energy transition be if humans were able to wrest control of modern economies away from multinational legal-persons, and rather than focus on profits and economic growth, return to that economic goal of ecosystems, biodiversity, and human survival? Decarbonization and transitioning to green energy would no doubt still occur, but without the industrial-scale environmental, biodiversity, and human destruction that inevitably would otherwise also occur. In addition, if survival were to once again become and remain the goal for human economies as it was for most of our species' existence, many socioeconomic lifeway strands that have traditionally fallen between the profit-making cracks and were thereby neglected would fit naturally within the overarching purview of a *survival first, survival-driven economy and society.*

It is important to remember, too, that prior and current searches for new, more powerful sources of energy indicate that humanity has failed to recognize and accept the low-energy design of the Earth-system architecture. Neolithic through modern humans assumed a need for more energy to accelerate human progress and enable its survival, but as we have seen, pre-agriculture hunter-gatherer humans survived for most of humanity's existence with no need for new or additional sources of energy beyond what was already available within ecosystems. So, too, did all Earth-life species that eked out a living and survived during the preceding 4.7 billion years of Earth's existence, using just the energy that was available *within* ecosystems.

This search for additional energy, then, only started when our Neolithic Revolution forebears began the socioeconomic transition from foraging to farming. And now, 12,000 years later, as humanity embarks on its third energy transition, it is important to recognize, too, that neither of the prior two energy transitions (from foraging to farming, and from the renewables *within* ecosystems to nonrenewables *without*) was essential to human survival. This current "nonrenewable back to renewable" transition, however, is absolutely essential to human survival because it seeks to undo the harm to humanity, biodiversity, and ecosystem survival that the preceding two energy transitions enabled. It would seem that use of nonrenewable energy sources might well have been one of those so-called planetary boundaries humanity should never have crossed.

For humanity to survive, then, life and survival must become the *raison d' etre* that guides and justifies all subsequent human choices and actions. Because that's the only way, if there is still a way, humanity will survive—and survival, as we have seen from the very inception, is the goal and outcome for human societies and economies.

The takeaway from this energy misadventure in which our species has found itself might well have been a long-overdue lesson humans have hitherto failed to learn: that to survive on planet Earth modern humans must follow the *survival-driven* rules that guided all Earth-life species. These are rules pre-agriculture hunter-gatherer humans learned and followed but Neolithic Revolution through modern humans may once have known but abandoned. Those *DOMC* rules—don't Domesticate, Own, Manage, or Control Earth's ecosystems and biodiversity species—were learned by our pre-agriculture hunter-gatherer forebears, their societies, and economies around the waterholes in the ecosystems they shared with other Earth-life species. These became engrained in their socioeconomic lifeways, lifeways that enabled mutual life and survival of all species within those same low-energy levels that pervaded ecosystems.

These lifeways, lived within ecosystems, depended on a renewable and low-level energy system that, nevertheless, enabled humanity to survive collapse-free for all but the last dozen millennia, and for most of humanity's existence, without risk of kindling a mass extinction like the one modern humans have generated in our search for new sources of energy *outside* those ecosystems. By simply following these same lifeways that enabled the survival of all prior Earth-life species for billions of years, and by following the wisdom of the waterhole in building their economies, modern human societies and economies can survive as well.

PART SIX

Climate Change, Migration, and Human Economies

THERE'S NOT MUCH THAT CLIMATE change, migration, and human economies have in common except that 70,000 years ago they came together and drove early humans out of Africa and across the Earth. And by the look of things, in the twenty-first century, these elements might just be getting ready to start all over again. This fearsome trio choreographed the evolution of the *Homo* species and shaped Earth's habitats, ecosystems, and therefore the lifeways of Earth-life species, including its biodiversity, with whom humans evolved and would share the Earth. This time around, though, modern sedentary humans appear to be far less ready than their mobile, hunter-gatherer forebears might have been back then.

Many of those events occurred prior to and during the mid-to-late Pleistocene Epoch (2.6 million-11,700 years ago) when our *Homo* species evolved. Many would go extinct due to frequent changes in the Earth's climate, from glacials to interglacials over eleven ice ages that shaped the lifeways, and therefore the economies, of all extant *Homo* and megafauna species, and drove the extinction of most. Now, once again, this trio has begun to raise its ugly head. Climate change and migration, and what these would do to the human economy, are coming together to choreograph and cap what could well be the end of the human saga—or the beginning of the next chapter.

During this epoch, all species migrated and foraged to survive, and all humans were hunter-gatherers. They foraged within Earth's habitats and ecosystems and learned to live in harmony with other Earth-life species. Their economies were mobile, hunter-gatherer, waterhole economies and emerged out of the foraging lifeways they developed. Around waterholes they would have learned to share with prey and predator alike and to survive. They sought neither to domesticate, own, manage, nor control any species but lived in small bands, migrated to new campsites, and foraged for food. They would live free of politics, religions, and philosophies that polarized the subsequent sedentary human communities that would succeed them.

Even though they and their waterhole economies survived for most of our species' history with neither economic nor civilizational collapse, they did so with little to no need for any of the technologies, innovations, and new sources of energy that would come to dominate the lifeways of post-Neolithic and modern humans during the succeeding 10,000 years of the Holocene epoch. Yet, somehow, they managed to survive in harmony with Earth's biodiversity, within its habitats and ecosystems, destroying neither, nor putting the survival of humanity at risk.

By dwelling in small, mobile, sharing communities, they were already predisposed and better able to respond rapidly to climate change and climate-driven migration than modern overpopulated, sedentary human societies and economies would. And their ability to migrate out of Africa across a largely unpopulated planet finds little parallel in our twenty-first century overpopulated world, now divided among ideologically different, warring nation-states, whose technologies and innovations have engendered the climate change that humans and the planet now face.

For the preceding three million years, Earth's climate had been in an Icehouse state. Our hunter-gatherer forebears and their mobile economies survived through naturally forced glacials and interglacials of the last ice age of the Pleistocene epoch. And yes, they too experienced global warming climate change (due to no fault of their own), as the planet grew less cold and as the last ice age came to an end, transitioning into a Warmhouse state that would last most of the Holocene epoch during which most of what is known as human civilization occurred.

But now, seemingly, it is modern humans' turn to figure out how to migrate and survive, given their sedentary societies and economies, as Earth's climate has begun to transition yet again into what's beginning to look and feel like a Hothouse state not seen since the Eocene Epoch 50 plus million years ago and, more than likely, is being brought on this time by anthropogenic-driven global warming. This is a consequence of humanity's energy transition away from the renewable energy sources *within* the ecosystem our hunter-gatherer forebears used for most of humanity's existence, to the nonrenewables being generated by our modern economies *outside* the ecosystem.

Today, too, humans rightfully fret about the potential loss of the Amazon and remaining dense forested regions of the Central African Republic of the Congo—all due to human economic activity—but may not realize that our hunter-gatherer forebears also had to survive the colossal reshaping of numerous parts of the Earth's surface. This reshaping included the massive changes in geological features such as the transition from dense forests to savannas and the formation of the Great Rift Valley that tore through the African continent; the formation of multiple massive lakes as glaciers melted; and the uplifting of the Tibetan plateau and numerous such changes that plate tectonics and this global thaw and other geological changes would have caused (but once again, due to no fault of their own).

Imagine the consternation and fear as ocean levels rose from generation to generation as glaciers across a third of the planet began to melt and continental land bridges began to disappear, cutting off access to known food sources, forcing separation between families, and stranding a diversity of species. Imagine their fear as species after megafauna species and many of their food sources slowly began to go extinct along with several members of other *Homo* species they would have known.

Unlike today's migrants, who must abandon jobs, homes, family members, and numerous other material possessions and relationships they spent a lifetime accumulating, at least pre-agriculture hunter-gatherers were able to take with them their mobile economies and everything they might have owned (which wasn't much, by design) along with the skills they needed to survive. By contrast, modern sedentary humans have no such choice but must abandon their sedentary economies and mostly all their personal possessions and begin to migrate (a novel experience for most) with at most a backpack.

Post-Neolithic and modern humans changed the survival-driven foundations of the original human, sharing, hunter-gatherer, waterhole economy from being mobile to being sedentary; from foraging to farming; and from storing and hoarding nothing, to storing and hoarding a surplus. Early humans had sought neither to own, modify, nor control ecosystems or biodiversity species but practiced sharing and co-existing with them; dwelling in small mobile camps of fifty or fewer rather than congregating in massive, often overcrowded, sedentary towns and cities; and living in harmony with Earth's biodiversity within ecosystems rather than destroying these species and the ecosystems that support all Earth-life. In sum, post-Neolithic Revolution and modern humans negated the very economic attributes that enabled ecosystems, Earth-life species, and humanity to survive for millennia.

When Neolithic Revolution and subsequent humans abandoned those hunting-gathering, foraging, mobile waterhole economies to become sedentary farming economies and communities, dwelling with farm animals, they also abandoned the flexibility and freedom to flee while still maintaining the primary productive capabilities of their mobile economies—their ability to forage, to hunt and gather all they needed to survive even while migrating.

As they migrated, they also wouldn't have had to confront, as migrants do today, a planet stuffed to the gills with humans, whose numbers now exceed eight billion, that now not only block access to other parts of the planet with border guards and walls, but are also prepared to imprison, murder, or repatriate migrants to their countries of origin or to other countries that would have them, for a fee—a forced reverse migration.

But the most important and fundamental change humanity would make to those once-mobile, foraging, sharing, waterhole economies is the reason they came into being to begin with. These economies evolved for one purpose and one purpose only—to enable human, biodiversity, and ecosystem life and survival above all else. That was their only goal and outcome. How ironic, then, that it's our modern human economies and their legal-person counterparts that have become the primary producers of the GHG emissions that are enabling the global warming that might well be on the way to destroying both us and them.

So, how is it that those once-mobile, hunter-gatherer, egalitarian societies and their waterhole economies emerged in and migrated out of Africa 70,000 years ago, out of the ravages of climate change and migration, establishing life and survival across the planet for most of our species' existence—undoubtedly the greatest human achievement? And how is it that modern humans, in contrast, in just the 10,000 years of the Holocene, have transformed those mobile, hunter-gatherer, waterhole economies not only into sedentary producers of surplus, profits, wealth accumulation, and endless GDP growth, but also into industrial-scale destroyers of Earth's ecosystems and biodiversity—and might well be establishing the conditions for humanity's extinction?

Climate Change, Migration, and Human Economies

CLIMATE CHANGE DROVE HUMAN MIGRATION, SHAPED HUMAN ECONOMIES, AND NOW THREATENS HUMAN SURVIVAL

CHAPTER 9

Climate Change, Migration,
and
Human Economies

How Climate Change Choreographed Human Evolution, Forcing Migration, Foraging, and the Formation of Mobile Human Economies

9.

Climate Change, Migration, and Human Economies

HOW CLIMATE CHANGE CHOREOGRAPHED HUMAN EVOLUTION, FORCING MIGRATION, FORAGING, AND THE FORMATION OF MOBILE HUMAN WATERHOLE ECONOMIES.

THAT CLIMATE CHANGE AND ORBITAL-SCALE-DRIVEN changes in temperature, precipitation, and net primary productivity played a major role in the evolution of our genus *Homo* during the last two million years is a well-established fact. Orbital-scale changes are changes in Earth systems brought on by changes in the Earth's orbit. But they may have also been the reason all other *Homo* species went extinct. This fact and possibility must be kept in mind as Earth, and therefore humanity, confronts yet another shift in the planet's climate mechanisms, only this time one of our own making. Here we note how prior climate change, by shaping Earth's geography and fashioning its ecosystems, drove human and biodiversity evolution, speciation, and diversity, as well as their migration and dispersal across the planet, and thereby shaped the kinds of societies, lifeways, and economies that emerged.

To understand how twenty-first century man-made climate will change Earth's ecosystems and Earth-life species, including humanity, one must understand the connection between our species and Earth's ecological environment and the impact prior periods of climate change have had. Post-Neolithic humans adapted and developed preferences for specific vegetation types and have developed a tolerance to changes in biotic and climate conditions that emerged during the last 11,600 years of the Holocene epoch when what is generally regarded as human civilization emerged. What will happen when climate forcing becomes man-made and exceeds the boundaries that framed the ecological environments in which our species, and more recently, modern human civilization, evolved?

How would our use of adaptations to and specialization in different types of ecosystems that emerged have changed? Confronted with such vast changes, all other hominin species eventually went extinct largely due to changes in biomes and ecosystems, flora and fauna engendered by climate variations. One can't say for sure, but one has already begun to see how humans, the last remaining *Homo* species, might respond to the inevitable mass migration, dispersal, and billion-dollar disruptions climate change has already caused across the planet.

Earth's history showed what happened, and what could happen again, when climate change, seasonal or non-seasonal, natural or anthropogenic, begins to reshape Earth's geography and environment, and therefore the ecosystem products and services all Earth-life need to survive. One should expect it will again choreograph the lifeways, survival, and extinction of numerous Earth-life species, including members of our own species, as it has previously done. And because ecosystem products and services vary with the natural change of seasons, which vary with the natural climate cycles, which in turn vary by location and geography, all Earth-life species and their economies that rely on these resources had to adjust their lifeways accordingly, to be mobile. Therefore, they built mobile economies to survive.

This, of course, is why hunter-gatherers were foragers rather than farmers and the reason pre-agriculture hunter-gatherer economies were mobile economies. They followed the seasonal and geographic availability of these ecosystem products and services by migrating to wherever they were available. Hence the seasonal migration of Earth-life species we have come to know.

But what will happen when that seasonal order that Earth's natural rotation imposes, and to which during most of the last 10,000 years of the Holocene our species has acclimated, is disrupted or arbitrarily intensified or rearranged? What happens when the globally aggregated vegetation characteristics that are controlled mainly by global mean temperature variations, that relationship between orbital-scale forcings (Milankovitch cycles, greenhouse gases, and ice sheet effects) and vegetation, becomes arbitrarily unpredictable and increasingly more complex due to an anthropogenic-driven greenhouse gas climate change in the planet's global temperature?

Unlike what humanity experienced during the Holocene and most of the twentieth century, our planet's history has known numerous geological epochs during which natural climate disruptions have occurred that have choreographed the evolution of our species. Researchers have proposed a variety of prior environmental drivers of human evolutionary change, including climatic cooling, persistent warmth, pulses of aridity that included the spread of C4 grasses, phases of high rainfall and humidity, and variability itself as causal forces that shaped the evolution of Earth-life species, including humans, according to Richard Potts in "Hominin evolution in settings of strong environmental variability." How might this bout of global anthropogenic climate change further choreograph human evolution?

These environmental patterns included trends or oscillations in hydrology, landscape, and vegetation, and it is these shifts in resources and ecological setting that may have led to, for example, the expansion of grasslands in northern Africa, and the expansion and contraction of the Sahara Desert. They may also have played a keen role in creating green corridors which supported multiple transcontinental migration events of archaic humans. Migrations from Africa into Eurasia exposed ancient humans such as *Homo erectus, Homo heidelbergensis* and early *Homo sapiens* to new environmental conditions and ecosystems and enabled the eastern African forests to gradually turn into grasslands during the early-to-mid Pleistocene that are thought to have contributed to human evolution, according to Timmermann and Friedrich in "Late Pleistocene climate drivers of early human migration" (*Nature*, 2016).

Natural changes in temperature, rainfall, and droughts drove dispersal of our species to live in various types of biomes, including tropical forests, tundras, savannas, and deserts that came with specific combinations of climatic factors, soil properties, and atmospheric CO_2 concentrations. Hominins who, during the early Pleistocene, may have settled in areas with little climate variability and would become global wanderers by the end of the mid-Pleistocene transition and would have experienced a wide range of climate change, adapted as they migrated to areas with higher landscape diversity.

But, unlike modern humans who during the Holocene would cause a massive decline in global ecosystem diversity due to land use practices, monocultures, and by abandoning integrated agriculture, hunter-gatherers utilized a vast variety of natural resources from various biomes, and this diversity of natural resources may well have enabled their survival. In fact, during the last five million years, climate conditions gradually changed from the warm and wet weather of the Pliocene (5.3 million to 2.6 million years ago) and would become cold and dry during the ice ages of the Pleistocene (2.6 million to 0.011 million years ago) before eventually settling down into the warmer, wetter, and more stable climate of the Holocene Epoch, the most recent 11,700 years, during which all that is known of modern human history occurred.

Yet, as seen earlier, this transition, which occurred approximately 11,000 years ago, also had some of the worst impacts on early humans as it occurred even as the ice age was ending. It was a time of drastic climate fluctuations, which in turn had a great impact on the environment, atmosphere, ecology, and human populations. Humans, their settlement numbers, and locations, as well as their subsistence patterns, were greatly affected. Archaeological indicators of the Pleistocene-Holocene transition's climate were punctuated by repeated glacial cycles. Their mass glaciation and de-glaciation effects were vast, intense, and felt globally, according to Lawrence Barham and Peter Mitchell in a chapter entitled "Transitions: From the Pleistocene into the Holocene" in their book, *The First Africans.*

Today, humanity is about to enter, or may have already entered, another geological time and climate transition, from the Holocene to the Anthropocene, and from a time when all climate change, as described by the Milankovitch cycles, were naturally forced into what is becoming an entirely new climate paradigm driven by anthropogenic global warming. But picture for a moment what it must have been like living at a time when, at its peak during those prior global climate transitions, approximately 30 percent of the Earth's surface was covered by glacial ice sheets with sea levels having dropped 100 meters or more across the entire surface of the Earth, due to the large volumes of water contained in those glacial sheets.

The world would not only have looked very different than it does today, but it would also have felt different, too. Compared to the global average temperature of 14°C today, the average annual temperature near these glacial regions was just 6°C. And compared to the 427.6 ppm atmospheric carbon dioxide level as of June 10, 2024, back then it was just 180 ppm and only rose to 280 ppm just before the Industrial Revolution, which began around 1740 CE.

There were major climatic events spanning the Pleistocene-Holocene transition that included (1) the Last Glacial Maximum, (2) Heinrich 1 event, (3) the Bølling-Allerød, (4) the Younger Dryas, (5) the Preboreal, and (6) the 8.2 ka event. Each of these events had extreme effects on the environment, as temperatures oscillated between warm wet periods and dry arid ones. How twenty-first century anthropogenic climate change would transform the once mostly calm and temperate climate of the Holocene that enabled the rise of human civilization is yet to be seen. But if the increased temperature during 2023 was any indication, humanity might well be going from the Coolhouse Earth of the Holocene to what may well turn out to be the Hothouse Earth of the Anthropocene.

Yet through all those prior global climate transitions *Homo sapiens* survived and continued to evolve, but only just, and in a world that then differed markedly from that of their ancestors. According to Richard Potts, "from the Pliocene through Pleistocene, the major features of African hominin evolution include the first appearances of three genera—*Australopithecus, Paranthropus*, and *Homo*—and the emergence of three major stone tool industries, the Oldowan, Acheulean, and Middle Stone Age. The two largest biogeographic events were the Plio-Pleistocene dispersal of the genus *Homo* and the late Pleistocene dispersal of *Homo sapiens* out of Africa. It was during these times that tropical savannas and open grasslands expanded in central and eastern Africa. These contributed to the evolution of our early ancestors and enabled the formation of multiple migration corridors from sub-Saharan Africa into northern Africa, the Arabian Peninsula, Europe, and Asia."

But before that warmer, calmer climate of the Holocene epoch arrived some 11,700 years ago, our species would have lived through numerous biogeographical climate upheavals during the Pleistocene epoch. These became environmental drivers of hominin evolution. They drove not only the extinction of at least five other *Homo* species but would choreograph the development of many of the attributes of our species we identify today as being uniquely human, attributes that with hindsight may well have been adaptive responses to those intense habitat upheavals and environmental instability.

They couldn't have known ahead of time, for example—and it wasn't because they were desperate to see the rest of the world—that those climate-driven biogeographical changes sweeping across their encampments on the grassy savannas of sub-Saharan Africa would have driven them to embark upon a migratory journey that would eventually take them across the planet and to the very ends of the Earth.

Today, as the Anthropocene (a temporary name for the next geological epoch) gets underway, humanity finds itself yet again at the beginning of another epochal change in the climate mechanisms of the Earth system only this time, it will be one we have caused. It will be a change from the mostly calm and comparatively stable climate of the Holocene that enabled the rise of human civilization during the last 10,000 years of our history, to what has begun to look and feel like yet another Earth-system environment and climate shift that remodeled the planet and our species during the Pleistocene-Holocene transition, one that has already begun and seems set on driving humanity off on yet another planet-wide migration. Only this time there is not much left of the world that hasn't been seen. Except for the remaining 70 percent of Earth's surface covered by its oceans, not much *terra firma* remains that is not already claimed and occupied by humans, most of whom seem unwilling to share.

Built into the lifeways and economies of all Earth-life species was a need and compulsion to migrate, to follow the food, to dodge any untoward effects due to climate variations that accompany this annual rotation of the Earth system, and to ensure continued access to the ecosystem products and services that also migrated with those seasons. This cyclical rotation of the Earth system implies a cyclical and seasonal rotation of its ecosystem products and services and thereby required migratory and mobile lifeways. Hence, their economies, too, would have been mobile, a phenomenon that almost all Earth-life species appear to have followed, including our pre-agriculture hunter-gatherer forebears until the Neolithic Revolution. Thereafter most humans would gradually abandon and replace these mobile lifeways and mobile economies for the sedentary lifeways and sedentary economies still in vogue today. Nevertheless, hunter-gatherers still exist.

Given how markedly the lifeways and economies of prior *Homo* genera changed, including via extinctions due to the last major shifts in the Earth's climate system, among the questions that should loom large in the minds of humans is this: How would twenty-first century humanity and their world fare and change given the emerging climate-driven disruptions already in progress, as those that occurred in 2023 so ably demonstrated? The neat separation we have imposed upon the rest of Earth's biodiversity, cloistering ourselves in cities, towns, and villages while relegating all other species to what little wilderness we haven't yet terraformed, is about to be disrupted as fauna and flora, in search of food and places to nest, begin to migrate into cities and towns as the climate, and therefore their habitats, begin to change.

But if our evolutionary past can be prologue to our evolutionary future, then we, too, should expect climate change-driven biome and ecosystem changes to be accompanied by a corresponding human and biodiversity survival-driven migration. This has already begun and should be expected to intensify and therefore planned for, rather than blocked and disparaged as many nations are currently doing. At least 11,600 years have passed since the end of the Pleistocene-Holocene Transition, and the Holocene Epoch, during which humans built their civilizations, has already ended or is about to end. The next transition in geological time, from the Holocene to the

Anthropocene, may have already begun. But unlike how that first transition ended, going from the ice age of the Pleistocene to the comparatively warmer, calmer, and stabler climate of the Holocene, modern humans seem headed, climate-wise, in a reverse chronological direction, from the relative climate calm of the Holocene to what might well turn out to be a potential repeat of the climate of the early Eocene 52 million-56 million years ago when palm trees grew as far north as Alaska.

During this transition, climate-driven biome, ecosystem, and biodiversity disruptions are going to change life on Earth as we know it, as they did for our *Homo* and early *Homo sapien* ancestors during the early Pleistocene, and the Pleistocene-Holocene Transition. They were foragers when it began but farmers when it ended. They and their economies were mobile when it began but sedentary when it ended. As climate change re-architected biomes and ecosystems and drove our forebears out of Africa, we should expect the world of agriculture and food webs today to be rearranged and to gradually migrate within a corridor of survivability that will move north with the change of climate. The network of industries, and the economies within countries they support, would also be forced to migrate even as human and biodiversity lifeways and communities are rearranged and upended as theirs were.

But how does one move a sedentary economy? Spoiler alert—one can't. Our forebears, though, wouldn't have had to, as their economies were mobile, built into their foraging lifeways. It's now 11,600 years later and humanity is at the beginning of yet another geological epoch, the Anthropocene, and finds itself staring at the start of yet another worldwide climate change-driven migration in as many geologic epochs. A level of migration our foraging hunter-gatherer forebears would no doubt have known, and no doubt would have been up to, but that few of us, their modern sedentary progeny, would have experienced, leaving us unprepared.

Nevertheless, modern humans, perhaps with increasing clarity enabled by the climate disasters of 2023, may have only just begun to pay attention. But scientists on the Intergovernmental Panel on Climate Change have been issuing warnings for years. In a report entitled "Human Migration in the Era of Climate Change" (IPCC, 2018) they warned that in the coming decades, hundreds of millions, if not billions, of people will be exposed to the impacts of anthropogenic climate change. Those impacts, including the increase in average temperature, changes in precipitation patterns, rising sea levels, and extreme weather events, such as heat waves, droughts, and floods, will increasingly become the norm. These trends, the report claimed, will have serious impacts on water supply, crop production, health, and economic growth, with some parts of the world much more affected than others.

Figure 9-1. Fleeing Hurricane Harvey.

(Source: Stamford Advocate)

People will try to adapt to these events and their impacts by, among other solutions, migration, a process that has already begun. In both the ancient and more recent history of extreme weather conditions, humanity has responded, as our hunter-gatherer forebears did, by moving from one region into another. But this time around, this climate-driven worldwide human migration won't be the same, but rather, orders of magnitude more complicated and perhaps one not even our forebears that survived that last great out-of-Africa human migration would have been able to endure, let alone survive. Humanity needs to prepare for the possibility that we just might not make it through this second time around.

Table 9-1. Global weather mega-disasters costing $20+ billion, 1980-2021

Rank	Disaster	Location	Year	Damage	Deaths
1	Hurricane Katrina	U.S. (LA/MS/AL/FL)	2005	$182 billion	>1,085
2	Hurricane Harvey	U.S. (TX/LA)	2017	$141 billion	89
3	Hurricane Maria	U.S. (PR/VI)	2017	$102 billion	2,981
4	Hurricane Sandy	U.S. (NY/NJ/CT)	2012	$80 billion	159
5	Hurricane Ida	U.S. (LA/MS/NJ/NY/CT)	2021	$75 billion	96
6	Hurricane Irma	U.S. (FL/GA/SC/PR)	2017	$56 billion	97
7	Hurricane Andrew	U.S. (FL/LA)	1992	$54 billion	62
8	Flooding	China	1998	$51 billion	3,656
9	Flooding	Thailand	2011	$49 billion	813
10	Drought/Heat Wave	U.S. (Midwest/East)	1988	$48 billion	454
11	Flooding	U.S. (Mississippi River)	1993	$41 billion	48
12	Hurricane Ike	U.S. (TX/LA/MS)	2008	$40 billion	112
13	Drought/Heat Wave	U.S. (Midwest/East)	2012	$37 billion	123
14	Hurricane Wilma	U.S. (FL), Mexico, Cuba	2005	$36 billion	35
14	Drought/Heat Wave	U.S. (Midwest/East)	1980	$36 billion	1,260
16	Hurricane Ivan	U.S. (AL/FL)	2004	$31 billion	57
17	Flooding	China	2021	$30 billion	347
18	Hurricane Michael	U.S. (FL/GA)	2018	$28 billion	49
19	Winter Weather	China	2008	$27 billion	145
19	Flooding	North Korea	1995	$27 billion	68
19	Hurricane Rita	U.S. (LA/TX)	2005	$27 billion	119
22	Hurricane Florence	U.S. (NC/SC)	2018	$26 billion	53
22	Wildfires	U.S. (Western)	2018	$26 billion	106
22	Drought/Heat Wave	China	1994	$26 billion	104
22	Flooding	China	2016	$26 billion	475
26	Winter Weather	U.S. (South and Central)	2021	$24 billion	226
26	Hurricane Charley	U.S. (FL)	2004	$24 billion	35
28	Flooding	China	2010	$23 billion	1,691
29	Flooding	Germany/Belgium	2021	$22 billion	240
29	Flooding	China	1996	$22 billion	2,775
31	Hurricane Laura	U.S. (LA/TX/MS/AR)	2020	$20 billion	42
31	Wildfires	U.S. (Western)	2017	$20 billion	54

All damages are in 2021 USD. Numbers for the U.S. are from NOAA, EM-DAT for the rest of the world.

(Source: Yale Climate Connections)

It's possible to imagine one has seen and experienced at least some of the hassles that accompany migration and that we need not worry too much about what a climate-change-driven migration might entail, especially if as a student, one may have moved for college across a state, to another country, or thereafter, for an international assignment or for the military. And it is unlikely any of those non-military moves would have been life threatening. But for a more accurate assessment consider instead the experiences of people who were forced to flee the effects of climate change-driven disasters, such as those who fled before Hurricane Harvey (Figure 9-1) or who experienced what it felt like to have to flee from the effects of a climate change-driven disaster such as the Lahaina, Maui fires of 2023. Such extreme weather has displaced more than a million people from their homes in just a year. One need only review the list of climate-driven disasters (Table 9-1) that has wracked the world in 2022 and 2023 to gain a more accurate idea of what could lie ahead.

Unlike our forebears who migrated across a world largely free of humans, what's different this time around, and 65,000 years later, is that the Earth is fully peopled and modern migrants are finding all those places where they would like to have sought refuge already taken. Many lost their lives (see Figure 9-2) just trying to get to their desired destinations—not at the hands of other extant *Homo* species (*Homo heidelbergensis; Homo neanderthalensis*, and others), nor because of savage encounters with saber-toothed tigers, mastodons, or any of the many now-extinct species our migrating hunter-gatherer forebears might have encountered 65,000 years ago, but rather, at the hands of their fellow humans.

DEATHS DURING MIGRATION
RECORDED SINCE 2014, BY REGION OF INCIDENT

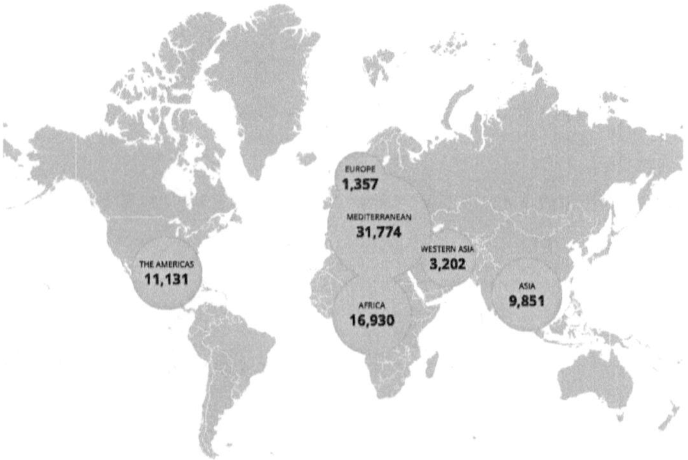

Disclaimer: The boundaries and names shown and the designations used on this map do not imply official endorsement or acceptance by the International Organization for Migration. Data represent minimum estimates and locations are approximate. The latest incident recorded occurred on 03 April 2025.

Figure 9-2. Missing Migrants Project.

(Source: The International Organization of Migration (IOM)'s Council on Foreign Relations.)

Unfortunately, the people modern migrants encounter along the way, at border crossings and at their destinations, are not too keen to grant them entry to their countries. Indeed, regions and countries like the EU and the

U.S. are going to great lengths to build border walls or, in the case of the UK, to fly them back to their countries of origin, or to other countries who would take them in for a fee.

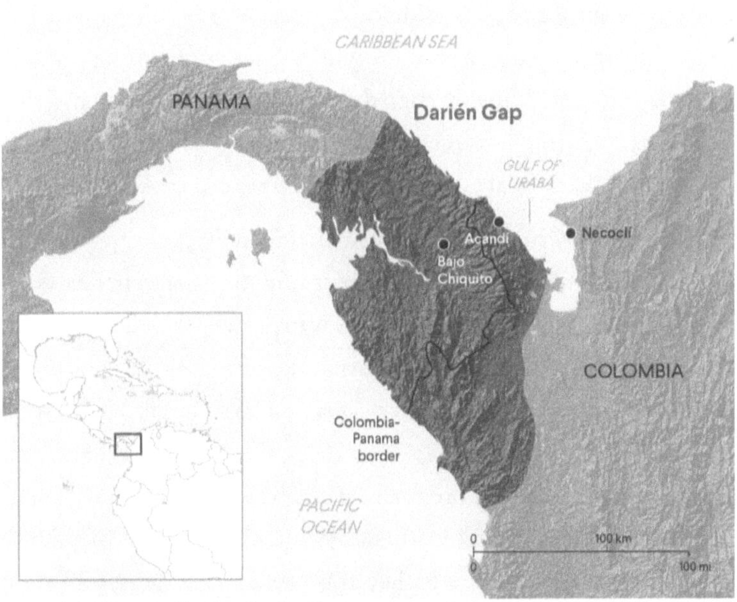

Figure 9-3. Migrants flock to the Darién Gap, a remote jungle region bridging Central and South America.

(Source: Voice of America; NASA, Council on Foreign Relations)

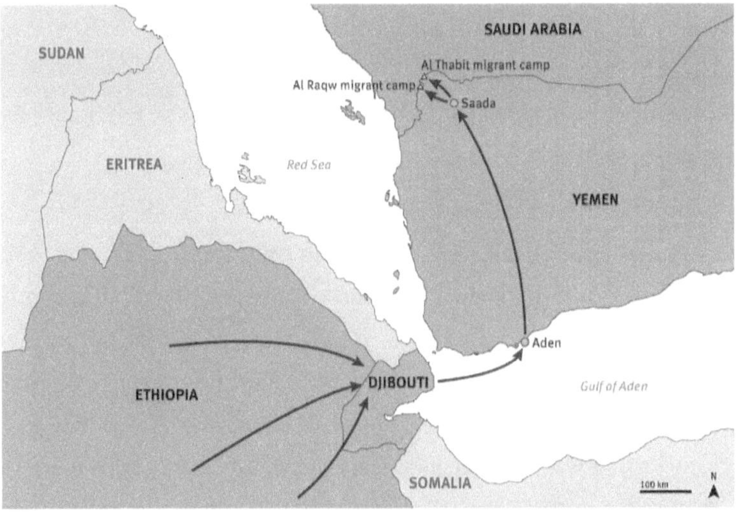

Figure 9-4. Map of the migration route from Ethiopia to Saudi Arabia through Yemen.

Graphic © 2023 Human Rights Watch. (Source: Human Rights Watch. https://www.hrw.org/)

According to the Missing Migrants Project, many have lost their lives just trying to get to their country of choice, and a record number of migrants risked their lives in 2022 to cross the treacherous Darién Gap (Figure 9-3), a remote jungle region bridging Central and South America. And there are numerous routes across the world where humans have died just trying to migrate, including through the now infamous route from Ethiopia to Saudi Arabia through Yemen shown in Figure 9-4. How many of our forebears died 65,000 years ago trying to migrate out of Africa?

More than 8,500 migrants died worldwide in 2023, a record since the U.N. started counting in 2014. And, according to a *Guardian* analysis, EU member states have used illegal operations to push back at least 40,000 asylum seekers from Europe's borders during the pandemic. It's one thing for migrants to die due to accidents, like capsizing boats in the Mediterranean (3,129 deaths in 2024, up from 2,411 in 2022), the Aegean Sea, or by crossing the English Channel (more than 200 deaths over the past decade), but it's an entirely different matter when they are killed in cold blood by citizens of countries whose borders they approach. The Saudis, for example, were accused of murder in a 2023 Human Rights Watch report entitled "Mass Killings of Ethiopian Migrants at the Yemen-Saudi Border," and of "systematic Abuses of Ethiopians that May Amount to Crimes Against Humanity." The report noted that "Saudi Guards have been accused of live explosives use and of shooting at migrants like rain." The Saudis are by no means the only nation guilty of such crimes against migrants.

According to the Human Rights Watch report, "Saudi border guards have killed at least hundreds of Ethiopian migrants and asylum seekers who tried to cross the Yemen-Saudi border between March 2022 and June 2023" (Figure 9-5). Human Rights Watch research indicates that, at the time of the report's writing (summer of 2023), the killings were continuing. Saudi border guards have used explosive weapons and shot people at close range, including women and children, in a pattern that is widespread and systematic. If committed as part of a Saudi government policy to murder migrants, these killings would be a crime against humanity. In some instances, Saudi border guards asked survivors in which limb of their body they preferred to be shot, before shooting them at close range. Saudi border guards also fired explosive weapons at migrants who had just been released from temporary Saudi detention and were attempting to flee back to Yemen.

Figure 9-5. Saudi Arabia: Mass killings of migrants at Yemen border.

(Source: Human Rights Watch)

But, as deadly as the Ethiopia to Yemen to Saudi Arabia route has proven, it's not the world's most dangerous migrant route, as per the list in Figure 9-6. That distinction is reserved for the "Central Mediterranean Route" running through the deserts of Niger to conflict-ridden Libya and across the Mediterranean to Italy, which is even more deadly, according to an August 2020 article published by the International Rescue Committee. It was once the world's most dangerous migrant route—dangerous at every step, according to its July 2020 article entitled, "These Illustrations Reveal the Human Stories of the World's Most Dangerous Migration Route."

The article drew attention to the plight of migrants who found themselves on this route. Economic hardship, climate change, conflict, and political instability are among the reasons millions more people are forced to leave their homes. At all those places shown on the map (Figure 9-6) and more, migrants die in transportation accidents, shipwrecks, violent attacks, or due to medical complications during their journeys.

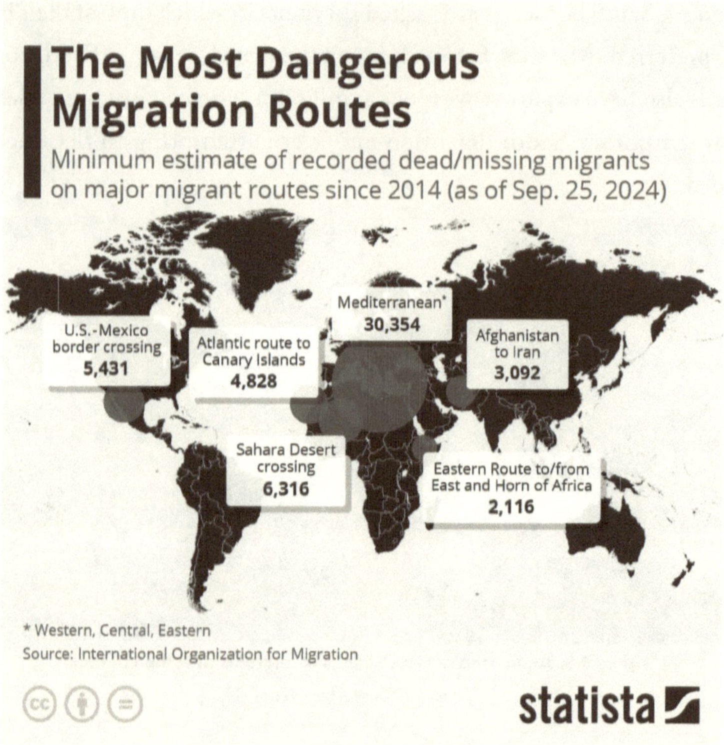

Figure 9-6. The most dangerous migration routes: Eastern, western, and central.
(Source: International Organization for Migration)

It is sobering to note that the world's most dangerous migrant route originates on the same continent, Africa, and largely from some of the same regions from which, 65,000 years ago, our hunter-gatherer forebears may well have begun their out-of-Africa journey across the Earth, and for some of the same reasons—climate change-driven economic and survival threats. The earliest migrants were ancient humans who originated on the African continent. Their spread to Eurasia and elsewhere remains a matter of significant scientific controversy. The earliest fossils of recognizable *Homo sapiens* were found in Ethiopia and are approximately 200,000 years old.

Comparing the route shown of modern migrants leaving Africa in Figure 9-4 and that used by hunter-gatherer migrants approximately 65,000 years earlier (Figure 9-7), one can't help but note their similarity (from Ethiopia through what is now Yemen into what is now Saudi Arabia). It makes one wonder whether humanity would have survived had those hunter-gatherer migrants been confronted with the same murder, mayhem, and death by members of their own species their twenty-first century migrating descendants faced at the Saudi border on their out-of-Africa journey. What's even more alarming is that among those migrating hunter-gatherers had to have been a particular female migrant, "Mitochondrial Eve," from whom all living humans descended. She would have been among those who crossed a land bridge at what is now the Bab-el-Mandeb Strait (Figure 9-7) which separates Djibouti from the Arabian Peninsula at the southern end of the Red Sea. Imagine that! A good thing she made that crossing 65,000 years ago and there weren't Saudis back then.

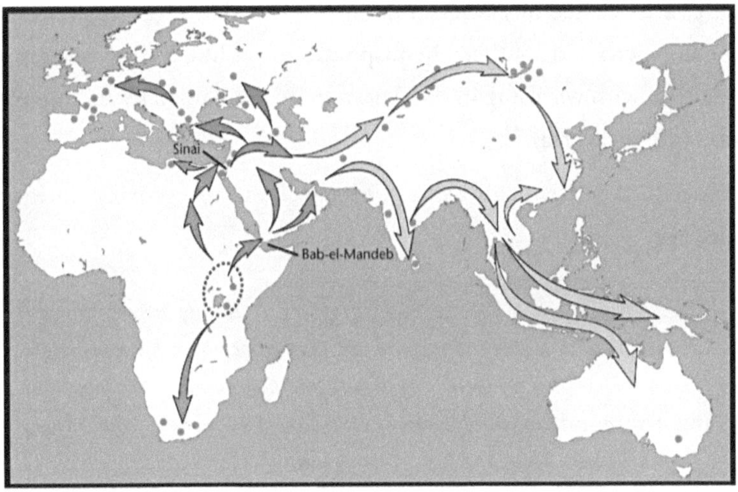

Figure 9-7. Possible migration routes taken by ancient humans starting from Africa.

(Source: Geoff Chambers.)

But while our out-of-Africa hunter-gatherer forebears wouldn't have been confronted with national boundaries and protected borders, they were nonetheless driven out of Africa by very severe bouts of climate change along the way. "Ancient humans left Africa to avoid drying climate," claims Jessica E. Tierney et al., of the University of Arizona in an article published in October 2017 in *Science Daily*. "Humans migrated out of Africa as the climate shifted from wet to very dry about 60,000 years ago." This new research shows that around 70,000 years ago, climate in the Horn of Africa shifted from a wet phase called a "Green Sahara" to an even drier and colder phase than it is today.

And in the *Journal of Human Evolution*, in their paper entitled "Out of Africa and into an ice age: on the role of global climate change in the late Pleistocene migration of early modern humans out of Africa," Shannon L. Carto and Andrew J. Weaver et al., wrote: "Although the fossil record is still too fragmentary to establish precise correlations with paleoclimate records, our results support the notion that Africa experienced profound and abrupt (over several decades) shifts in climate associated with the episodic occurrence of Heinrich events (episodes during which large numbers of icebergs are released by glaciers into the North Atlantic causing the oceans of the northern and southern hemispheres to act like a climate seesaw or pendulum, with warming in the Antarctic accompanied by cooling in the Arctic and vice versa)."

Indeed, more than half a dozen Heinrich events occurred during the last ice age.

> *These changes would have been superimposed on steadily increasing aridity associated with global cooling and the onset of northern hemisphere glaciation. Nevertheless, increasing aridity and desiccation of biogeographic resources associated with Heinrich events could have rapidly rendered large parts of North, West, and East Africa unsuitable for hominin habitation, thereby potentially prompting them to migrate to more hospitable areas.*

How somber it is, then, that now, approximately 65,000 years after early humans began migrating out of Africa, a similar human migration is just getting started, and seemingly for mostly similar reasons—climate change and climate change-driven geographic, environmental, and economic changes—only this time it's humans, not Heinrich events, that are driving this climate change. But unlike migrants leaving Africa today, their challenge migrating out of Africa back then wasn't an encounter with an overpopulated planet, nor a border confrontation with members of their own species blocking their out-of-Africa escape from climate change, but rather, the geographic and ecological changes resulting from the powerful forces of plate tectonics and climate variability that was reshaping the African continent at that time and forcing them to leave. And leave they did.

But modern humans are not so ready. Most haven't seen or experienced enough of these devastations to be sufficiently motivated to take the kind of decisive actions our hunter-gatherer forebears did. So, while many hear of ongoing and impending sea-level rise, ocean warming and acidification, extreme weather, and desertification of vast portions of the planet, this has all been occurring so slowly and out of sight that many are still finding it hard to imagine just how their twenty-first century life and landscapes would be altered. But our hunter-gatherer forebears had no such hesitancy. They and their *Homo* forebears lived through a climate and environmental transformation that was both unprecedented and existential. It's just as well that they left before it was over because by the time it had ended it had re-architected and altered the East African landscape beyond all recognition.

Indeed, from being flat and forested this landscape was transformed to one filled with spectacular, two-mile-high mountains, savannas, tropical forests, and deep lakes that formed along the length of the Great Rift Valley, from Somalia and Ethiopia down to the coast of Mozambique. Extreme climate pulses of alternately arid and wet periods occurred and had a profound effect on them and all living species in East Africa. These geographic and environmental upheavals ultimately would lead to our hominin forebears' development and their dispersal out of Africa, to the Caucasus, the Fertile Crescent, and ultimately the rest of the world.

That first great human out-of-Africa migration across the Earth is said to have lasted for millennia. But for how long will the current climate change-driven migration now on its way last, and how might humanity and the planet fare? There were at least five other *Homo* species when that first great out-of-Africa migration across the planet began. Most are believed to have been driven to extinction by climate change—only *Homo sapiens* survived. Indeed, past extinctions of *Homo* species coincided with increased vulnerability to climatic change.

Homo sapiens made it through that Pleistocene-Holocene transition that ended 11,000 years ago, but will we make it through this Holocene-Anthropocene transition? Yes, humanity survived global climate change once while all other *Homo* species went extinct. It was also the end of the ice age, and back then climate change was naturally forced, and was controlled by the Earth system. This one, however, is mostly not; it's anthropogenic, and is controlled by human greed. Neither humanity nor the Earth system seems willing or able to control it. Will humans survive global climate change again? Will we even be around when it ends, and if so, where and in what form? How different will life be when anthropogenic climate change finally ends or eases? How will the planet change? Ancient humans fled Africa to survive. Will modern humans also have to flee to survive, and if so where to this time? Will modern humans have to flee the Earth?

"There is a shocking, unreported, fundamental change coming to the habitability of many parts of the planet, including the U.S.A.," claims Peter Gleick, co-founder of the Pacific Institute. "To understand the magnitude of this change one must revisit the reasons why humans left their African homeland 80,000 years ago to colonize the world—that great human migration out of Africa to the ends of the Earth. It was climate that re-arranged their world, and it is climate that has begun to re-arrange our world. And as it did for them, it will change not just where we live but how we live." To gain some idea of the extent, kind, and magnitude of the changes that await humanity, one need only reflect upon how our hunter-gatherer forebears and their world changed during the Pleistocene-Holocene transition.

Recall, they were hunter-gatherers when it began but mostly sedentary farmers when it ended.

> *According to Bob Kopp, a climate scientist at Rutgers University, "We quite possibly are already living in a climate that no human has lived through before and we are certainly living in a climate that no human has lived in, prior to the emergence of agriculture." "Should global temperatures rise by a further 1°C or more, which is widely predicted to happen by the end of the century barring a drastic reduction in emissions", said Matthew Huber, an expert in paleoclimatology at Purdue University. Huber said, "the world will be plunged into the sort of warmth not seen since 1-3 million years ago, a period called the Pliocene (5.3 – 2.6 million years ago), which is outside the realm of human experience. And this is such a massive change that most things on Earth haven't had to deal with it. It's basically an experiment on humans and ecosystems to see how they respond. Nothing is adapted to this."*

Figure 9-8. The countryside in Samangan Province in north-central Afghanistan, where water for agriculture and even drinking is scarce.

(Source: New York Times; Credit: Lynsey Addario)

One recent study in the journal *Nature Climate Change* predicts that by 2050, as much as 30 percent of the world's land surface could face desert-like conditions (Figure 9-8), including large swaths of Asia, Europe, Africa, and southern Australia. More than 1.5 billion people currently live in these regions. In the U.S., a recent study by Mathew Hauer, a demographer at the University of Georgia, estimates that 13 million people will be displaced by sea-level rise alone by the year 2100. In Hauer's study, about 2.5 million will flee the region that includes Miami, Fort Lauderdale, and West Palm Beach. Greater New Orleans is projected to lose up to 500,000 people; the New York City area, 50,000.

In addition, if climate change were to progress unchecked, by 2070, more than three billion people may live outside that corridor of survivability, the "Human Climate Niche," areas on "Earth where humans have historically lived due to favorable climate conditions related to temperature and precipitation." For thousands of years, humans have concentrated in a surprisingly narrow subset of Earth's available climates, characterized by mean annual temperatures of around 13°C. According to the researchers who developed this dataset, "The bottom line is that over the coming decades, the human climate niche is projected to move to higher latitudes in unprecedented ways. At the same time, populations are projected to expand predominantly at lower latitudes, amplifying the mismatch between the expected distribution of humans and the climate."

These researchers estimate that roughly 30 percent of the projected global population would have to move toward the poles if they hoped to remain in the human climate niche. Such a reduction in livable space would no doubt further increase human vulnerability to climate change. More than 25 percent of the Earth will experience serious drought and desertification by the year 2050 if global warming is not curbed, according to a new study by the journal *Nature Climate Change*.

Notwithstanding increased pledges and targets to tackle climate change, current policies still leave the world on course for around 2.7°C of global warming above pre-industrial levels by end-of-century—far from the ambitious aim of the Paris Agreement to limit global warming to 1.5°C. Even if all 2030 nationally determined contributions, long-term pledges, and net-zero targets were fully implemented, nearly 2°C global warming is expected later this century. Yet, temperatures of more than 2°C above pre-industrial values have not been sustained on Earth's surface prior to the Pleistocene Epoch more than 2.6 million years ago. And temperature rise is crucially dependent on the overall dynamics of the Earth system, not just the anthropogenic emissions trajectory.

If humans don't act now to curb climate change, humanity may be faced with a climate-driven migration of a third of the world's future population, and maybe more. Humans would not have evolved, let alone been able to live on Earth, if the conditions suitable for life had not become possible, and we may well cease to exist if those life-enabling conditions continue to move poleward.

Earth evolved and supported the life-forms, flora, fauna, and funga that evolved on it. Such life-forms are native to the planet, its gravity, atmosphere, and biosphere, and they thrive on the products and services that emerge within its biomes and ecosystems. The biological species that evolve on Earth come "Earth-ready." They are fully adapted to its biosphere, atmospheric pressures, chemistry, and temperature variations, and that's why humans don't need pressurized space suits on Earth but couldn't survive on Mars, the moon, or on any other planet inside or outside our solar system without them. Hence, to survive on a particular planet, life must not only be local but must be indigenous to that planet and must be able to live within its survival niche.

Among the things that have made Earth different from other planets is this ability to support life. This difference has always existed but has varied over time. Anthropogenic climate change has now begun to shrink the survivability niche that enabled the life that the Earth system supported since the Cambrian Revolution. And that raises the very distinct possibility that humanity, by giving rise to anthropogenic climate change, may well have begun to shrink Earth's survival-enabling temperature niche. But just how far poleward can this human temperature niche migrate? All the way to the poles, apparently. It must have gotten there at least once before as not only were there no ice caps during the Eocene Epoch (56-33.9 million years ago), but crocodiles and palm trees were at the poles about 53 million years ago.

Indeed, note how "The Tropics too are getting bigger at 30 miles a decade" (Figure 9-9), according to Nicola Jones in "Redrawing the Map: How the World's Climate Zones Are Shifting." Similarly, she continues, "the plant hardiness zones" in the U.S. (a USDA metric that farmers use to determine which plants are most likely to thrive at a location; see USDA hardiness map) are moving north at 13 miles per decade. So too, the wheat belt is pushing poleward at up to 160 miles per decade.

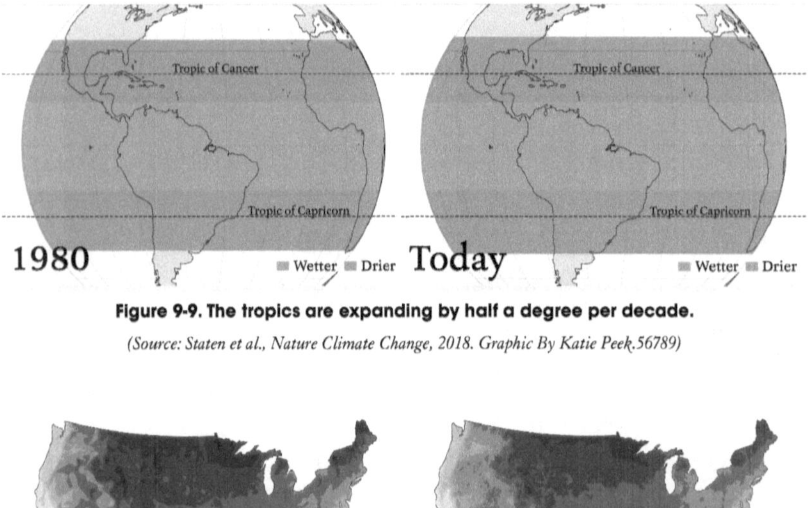

Figure 9-9. The tropics are expanding by half a degree per decade.

(Source: Staten et al., Nature Climate Change, 2018. Graphic By Katie Peek.56789)

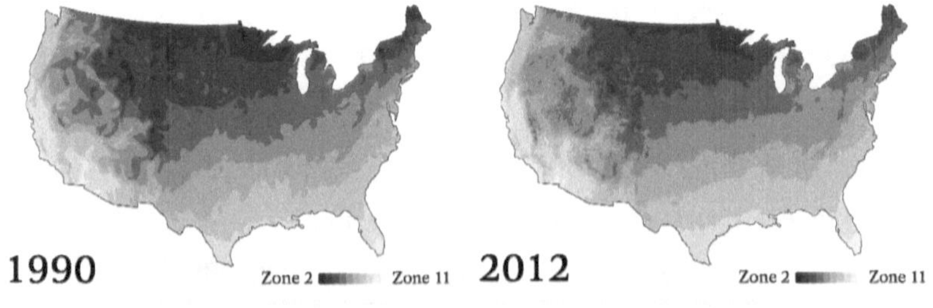

Figure 9-10. Hardiness zones in the U.S., which track average low temperatures in winter, have all shifted northward by half a zone warmer since 1990.

(Source: United States Department of Agriculture. Graphic by Katie Peek.)

Temperatures in the northern regions are rising at twice the global average and the permafrost—ground that typically remains frozen all year round—is thawing rapidly. The permafrost line has moved 80 miles north in just 50 years in parts of Canada. Studies in boreholes have revealed frightening rates of change. Nicola Jones explains: "In northern Russia, buildings are tilting, cracking, and must be condemned. In Bethel, Alaska, roads are buckling, homes are collapsing and as the ground thaws, buildings and infrastructure collapse."

Thus, by shifting that climate niche just a few more degrees too far north, or south, life as we know it may no longer be able to exist. The Earth may no longer be able to support a survivability niche large enough to enable all Earth's flora and fauna and a human population that is expected to exceed 11 billion by century's end, according to the U.N., as we are reminded in that October 23, 2020, article in *One Earth* entitled, "Past Extinctions of Homo Species Coincided with Increased Vulnerability to Climatic Change."

This shrinking of the climate niche is among the reasons scientists Luke Kemp, Chi Xu, et al., explore catastrophic climate change scenarios and publish research papers like the one entitled, "Climate Endgame: Exploring catastrophic climate change scenarios." People are beginning to worry that anthropogenic climate change could well turn out to be the end of humanity and have started to ask questions such as:

(1) What is the potential for climate change to drive mass extinction events?

(2) What are the mechanisms that could result in human mass mortality and morbidity?

(3) What are human societies' vulnerabilities to climate-triggered risk cascades, such as from conflict, political instability, and systemic financial risk?

(4) How can these multiple strands of evidence—together with other global dangers—be usefully synthesized into an "integrated catastrophe assessment" to seriously consider whether anthropogenic climate change could result in worldwide societal collapse or even eventual human extinction?

To some, these questions might seem somewhat alarmist, but the authors offer "four key reasons to be concerned over the potential of a global climate catastrophe."

First, there are warnings from history. Climate change (either regional or global) has played a role in the collapse or transformation of numerous previous societies (Antiq. 85, 2020, 627–651) and in each of the five mass extinction events in Phanerozoic Earth history (Brannen, 2017). The current carbon pulse is occurring at an unprecedented geological speed and, by the end of the century, may surpass thresholds that triggered previous mass extinctions (Rothman, 2019, 14813–14822). The worst-case scenarios in the IPCC report project temperatures by the twenty-second century like those that prevailed in the Early Eocene, reversing 50 million years of cooler climates in the space of two centuries (Burke et al., 2018).

And this, the authors thought, was "particularly alarming, since all Earth-life, including human societies, as seen earlier, are locally adapted to a specific climatic niche. The rise of large-scale, urbanized agrarian societies began with the shift to the stable climate of the Holocene approximately 12,000 years ago (Richerson et al., 2017). Since then, human population density peaked within a narrow climatic envelope with a mean annual average temperature of approximately 13°C. Even today, the most economically productive centers of human activity are concentrated in those areas (Xu et al., 2020). Thus, the cumulative impacts of such warming may well overwhelm the capacity of humanity to adapt."

Second, "Climate change could directly trigger other catastrophic risks, such as international conflict, or exacerbate infectious disease spread, and spillover risk. These could be potent extreme threat multipliers."

Third, "Climate change could exacerbate vulnerabilities and cause multiple, indirect stresses (such as economic damage, loss of land, and water and food insecurity) that coalesce into system-wide synchronous failures. This is the path of systemic risk. Global crises tend to occur through such reinforcing 'synchronous failures' that spread across countries and systems, as with the 2007-2008 global financial crisis. It is plausible that a sudden shift in climate could trigger systems failures that unravel societies across the globe."

The potential for systemic climate risk is marked. Extreme temperatures combined with high humidity can negatively affect outdoor worker productivity and yields of major cereal crops. These deadly heat conditions could significantly affect populated areas in South and Southwest Asia.

Fourth, and finally, climate change could irrevocably undermine humanity's ability to recover from another cataclysm, such as another global pandemic, like Covid-19, or a nuclear war. That is, it could create significant latent risks. Disasters that may be manageable during times of stability could become dire when responding to and simultaneously recovering from a catastrophe. These different causes for catastrophic concern are interrelated and must be examined together, and yet, though highly likely, human social, economic and political systems rarely consider or prepare for such scenarios.

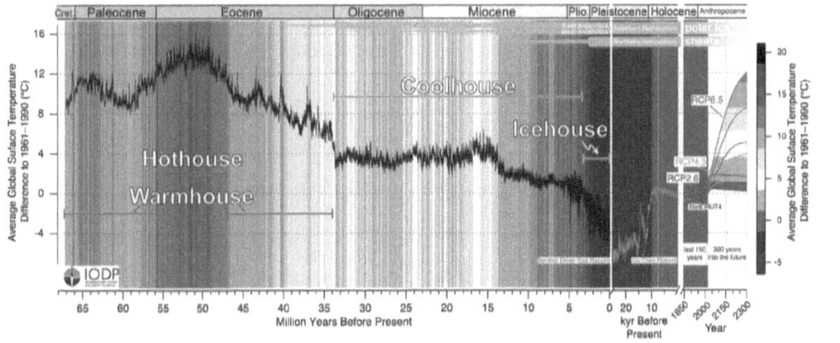

Figure 9-11. Past and future trends in global mean temperature spanning the last 67 million years.

(Source: SciTech Daily; Image credit: Westerhold et al., CENOGRID)

The alarming nature of this current anthropogenic greenhouse gas-driven climate change is better understood when viewed from the perspective of Earth's climate history over the last six geologic epochs (Paleocene, Eocene, Oligocene, Miocene, Pilo-Pleistocene, and Holocene), during the last 66 million years as shown in (Figure 9-11). This continuous record shows that natural climate variability due to natural changes in Earth's orbit around the sun is much smaller than projected future warming due to anthropogenic greenhouse gas emissions.

This history reveals that the Earth's climate system has been slowly cooling over the last 50 million years, from the Hothouse Earth of the Paleocene to the Icehouse Earth of the Pleistocene and into the Coolhouse Earth of the Holocene, the last 11,200 years during which most modern human history and civilization occurred. Now, as it begins to warm again, the Earth system will move toward increasingly warm climate states as shown during the Paleocene, Eocene, Oligocene, and Miocene epochs, climates for which humans have no lived experience.

The *Homo* genera from whom hominins and hence *Homo sapiens* evolved appeared during the Pleistocene, during the ice age, and therefore would not have had to adapt to the much, much warmer climates of the preceding epochs. Hence IPCC's calls to keep the Earth's climate within a safe and familiar operating space, within the range of temperatures experienced during the Holocene that saw the emergence of agriculture, civilization, and our complex global economy.

Much of what humans know and do today is based on assumptions and recent baselines about a Holocene-like climate that will disappear as the Earth begins to return to those prior Warmhouse and Hothouse states. According to the IPCC's own scenarios, by the end of this century, Earth's mean global surface temperature is expected to rise to 4.8°C. Understanding and preparing for this level of climate change will be challenged by the emergence of Earth system states far outside our individual, societal, and species experience. Under IPCC's Representative Concentration Pathway

8.5 (RCP8.5)—the so-called worst-case business-as-usual emission scenario—by 2030, future climates will most closely resemble Mid-Pliocene climates, and by 2150, they will most closely resemble Eocene climates. However, if we can slow GHG emissions, as under RCP4.5, Earth's climate stabilizes at Pliocene-like conditions by 2040 CE.

But can we? According to the IPCC's 2023 Emissions Gap Report we are finding out, discovery by discovery, that climate change is already worse than previously estimated. For example, scientists have discovered that higher CO_2 levels will cause the atmosphere to heat up more quickly than previously estimated by the IPCC. Scientists are now saying it might already be too late to avoid a temperature rise of up to 7.36°C (13.25°F) above pre-industrial levels by 2100. That's way above the upper limit of 4.8°C (8.6°F) predicted by the IPCC in 2014 as shown in Figure 9-12.

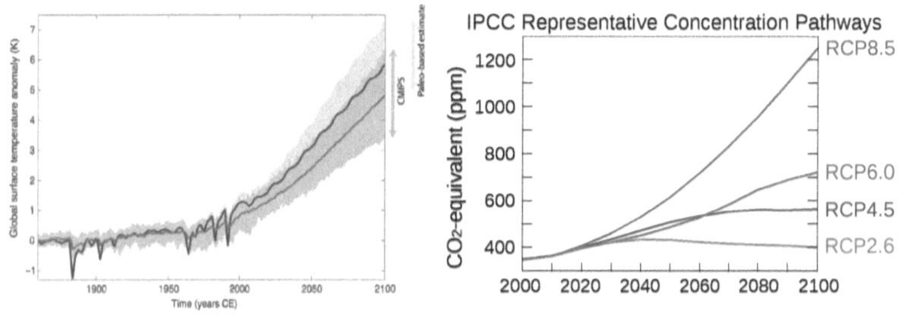

Figure 9-12. IPCC CO2 and temperature projections.

The new models show the chance of a rise above 7°C by 2100.

((Left) Source: Science Advences, Credit: Tobias Friedrich et al.; (Right) Source: IPCC, Credit: Efbrazil, CC BY-SA 4.0)

To make matters worse, a new study suggests that doubling of atmospheric carbon dioxide would heat the world more than many climate models suggest; and that we have been underestimating just how sensitive Earth is to greenhouse gases. In fact they claim that at 7.3°C "it could already be 'Game Over' for Climate Change"—and for the planet as we know it."

Perhaps equally disturbing are the numerous known unknowns, such as the parts of the Earth climate system we don't quite understand. Then there are the unknown unknowns, the parts of the Earth climate system we do not even regard as problems, or thought we understood, such as our prior imperfect understanding of how sensitive the Earth climate system is to additional GHG buildup in the atmosphere. Both types of unknowns contribute to the increase of GHG escaping into the atmosphere, increasing that uncertainty.

Particularly worrying, too, is the fact that humanity may never really know the true quantity of GHGs escaping into the atmosphere and therefore may never be able to truly forecast just how hot the Earth could become—though, should the planet grow increasingly warm, knowing exactly how warm may well be irrelevant. For example, the petroleum and gas industries have left millions of so-called "zombie wells" across the world (Figure 9-13), both on land and in the oceans, where oil and gas continue to ooze into the atmosphere, mostly unknown, and onto land where they are creating environmental disaster zones. According to a 2022 article in the Guardian, 'Thousands of abandoned oil wells dot the Permian Basin in west Texas and New Mexico, endangering humans and wildlife." And what's true of Texas is also undoubtedly true of Canada's tar sands, and of every oil- and gas-producing state and country across the globe.

Figure 9-13. Texas's zombie oil wells are creating an environmental disaster zone.
Texas oil wells are leaking toxic waste, and no one wants to pay to clean it up. (Source: Houston Chronicle)

Every year companies around the United States capture around 18 million metric tons of carbon dioxide from natural gas processing plants, oil refineries, and power plants. As long as that CO_2—equivalent to the emissions of around 4 million cars on the road for a year—is buried somewhere deep underground, it won't be available to contribute to global warming. But only as long as it remains buried. Or so one thought, but thawing permafrost is a warning that burying CO_2 is no guarantee that it will be sequestered forever. Indeed, companies are poised to inject millions of tons of carbon underground. But will it stay put? asks Nicholas Kusnetz in a March 2024 *Inside Climate News* article.

Among the unknowns is the amount of GHG (CO_2 but mostly methane (CH_4) in this case) that began escaping across the permafrost in countries like Canada and Russia. Permanently frozen permafrost soils cover large areas of the northern hemisphere, especially in northern Asia and North America. If they thaw in a warming world, this can pose dangers, because CO_2 and methane are released during thawing—and they amplify the anthropogenic greenhouse gas effect. "Methane is particularly dangerous here because its warming potential is many times greater (approximately 25 times higher over a 100-year period) than that of CO_2," explains Nikolaus Froitzheim et al., in a PNAS (Earth, Atmospherics, and Planetary Sciences) paper entitled, "Methane release from carbonate rock formations in the Siberian permafrost area during and after the 2020 heat wave."

And, what's occurring on land apparently is also occurring beneath the seas as Charles Paull et al. explain in another PNAS paper, "Rapid seafloor changes associated with the degradation of Arctic submarine permafrost." Temperature increases in Arctic regions have focused attention on permafrost degradation on land, but little is known about the dynamics of extensive glacial-age permafrost bodies now submerged under the vast Arctic continental shelves. How this contributes to GHG and its effect on global warming is indeed an unknown.

Then there are unknown unknowns—threats we don't even know exist, threats that can potentially exist but have yet to be identified. Just recently, one such unknown unknown suddenly became known when a deeply troubling discovery was recently made. According to a February 2024 Physics.Org article entitled, "Earth may have already passed the crucial 1.5°C warming limit" we thought was still ahead of us. This worrying finding, based on temperature records contained in sea sponge skeletons, suggests global climate change has progressed much further than previously thought. In fact, Earth may already have reached at least 1.7°C warming since pre-industrial times.

Another alarming finding is that since the late twentieth century, land-air temperatures have been increasing at almost twice the rate of surface oceans and are now more than 2°C above pre-industrial levels. It appears then that until a few weeks ago, humanity did not even know it had long missed its chance to limit global warming to 1.5°C and now has a very challenging task to keep warming below 2°C. This underscores the urgent need to halve global emissions by 2030. But according to that Emissions Gap Report referenced above, this seems unlikely. To get there, the world will have to cut 2030 emissions by 28 percent to get on a Least Cost Pathway for the 2°C of the Paris Agreement and by 42 percent for the 1.5°C goal.

Also, many of the strategies being developed by governments and corporations to address climate change rely on plants and forests to draw down planet-warming CO_2 and lock it away in the ecosystem. But according to a 2024 study led by Dr. Heather Graven from Imperial College London, current climate models significantly underestimate how much CO_2 is absorbed by vegetation annually and overestimate the duration it is retained, suggesting that carbon is released back into the atmosphere sooner than expected. The global carbon stored by plants is more short-lived and susceptible to climate change than previously believed.

These findings have significant implications for our understanding of nature's role in mitigating climate change, particularly for nature-based carbon removal projects like mass tree-planting initiatives. The findings also mean that while carbon is taken up by plants quicker than thought, the carbon is locked up for a shorter time, meaning carbon from human activities will be released back into the atmosphere sooner than previously predicted. This finding challenges the effectiveness of nature-based carbon removal strategies and underscores the urgency to cut fossil fuel emissions to combat climate change. It also has huge implications for the accuracy of estimates of the quantity of CO_2 in the atmosphere.

Again, while one hears about GHG increasing rapidly in the Earth's atmosphere, not nearly as much is heard about CO_2 driving up temperatures and acidity in Earth's oceans and the harm that entails. But just how hot is too hot? According to an Inside Climate News article from January 2023, "Oceans cover 71 percent of Earth's surface and have absorbed more than 90 percent of the heat energy trapped by greenhouse gases since the start of the industrial age, dominating the global climate system." Climate change brings with it the increasing risk of extinction across species within ecosystems. Marine species in particular face risks related to warming water and oxygen depletion.

In an April 2022 *Science* article, scientists found that under business-as-usual global temperature—RCP8.5, an IPCC warming scenario—marine systems are likely to experience mass extinctions on par with past great extinctions based on eco-physiological limits alone. The unknown unknown here is: How can humanity avoid an ocean-driven mass extinction due to the oceans overheating as they did 252 million years ago, driving Earth's greatest mass extinction—the "Great Dying"? In fact, the evidence compiled by scientific research on today's pace of change is ominous to say the least. Carbon dioxide in the atmosphere is increasing at a pace 100 times faster than it naturally should. Our planet is warming 10 times faster than it has in 65 million years. Our oceans are acidifying 100 times faster than they have in at least 20 million years, and oxygen dead zones in our oceans have increased tenfold since 1950.

"Right now, emissions are 10 to 20 times higher than at the end of the Permian mass extinction, which was the largest and biggest mass extinction," according to Professor Uwe Brand. "Earth is amid what science says is an unprecedented rate of change, unlike anything seen in tens of millions of years. Overconsumption, unsustainable practices, and the release of immense amounts of greenhouse gases from the burning of fossil fuels are altering Earth's life-sustaining climate at a dangerous pace, oceans are acidifying and losing oxygen, and species are dying off."

Bill Laurance in August 2015 wrote in *The Conversation*, "The scariest part of climate change isn't what we know, but what we don't." One wonders how much more scared he would be today. Nevertheless, some remain relatively confident that humanity will invent numerous technologies to beat back the effects of these unrelenting discoveries of one source of GHG after another. But among those innovations had better be quick and effective ways to remove most of the post-Industrial Revolution GHG already lofted into the atmosphere and dissolved in the oceans that seemingly threatens to take the temperature of the planet back to, and probably beyond, levels that prevailed during the Eocene Epoch (56-33.9 million years ago). Why? Because it could take from months to millennia for GHGs to naturally dissolve.

By now, if you haven't already come to this conclusion, you probably aren't too far off from realizing that humanity, by burning GHGs as an energy source, may well have triggered a shift in the Earth climate system over which humans have no control, except to aggravate it, and about which our understanding appears woefully inadequate and immature. And our tools and technologies are orders of magnitude less than might be needed to turn things around, assuming that's even possible, and at present, are certainly not yet up to such geo-engineering tasks.

Even if humans were to cease pumping GHG into the atmosphere and were to get to net zero (and that's not guaranteed), global warming, and whatever ills it would have unleashed upon the Earth by then, will still be around for millennia, and could still trigger numerous known and unknown "tipping points." In other words, it may already be "game over for life as we have known it on Earth and hence for humanity"—and that, dear reader, is the most troubling unknown unknown because it means it may already be too late.

Unless, of course, modern humans were to migrate as our hunter-gatherer forebears who, 65,000 years ago, survived climate change by migrating out of Africa. And, no doubt, many will continue to try—but migrate to where? This time around the cause of climate change is different. It's anthropogenic and it's global, and neither humans nor the Earth has had any prior experience of how the Earth climate system will react when subjected to the normal Milankovitch cycles in addition to unprecedented and rapid anthropogenic GHG forcing. One thing is becoming clearer—it might well leave humans very few safe havens.

We will do well, then, to take what may be a message in that climate change bottle and heed the advice of Stephen Hawking, who said that to survive, "I Am Convinced That Humans Need to Leave Earth," and that "Humans Have 100 Years to Move to Another Planet." And if this turns out to be so, according to Hawking, humanity may well require a rather different kind of migration—humans will have to leave the Earth. But is anyone, besides Elon Musk, taking his advice or thinking that humans should give it serious consideration?

How uncanny it seems, then, that humanity is confronted yet again by another climate change-driven existential threat, and that it must migrate to survive. That out-of-Africa-to-the-ends-of-the-Earth climate change-driven migration would no doubt have been the greatest challenge any hominin species would have faced and all but one—*Homo sapiens*—survived. But to survive this second time around this migration may well require *Homo sapiens* not just to leave Africa and overspread the Earth. We've already done that. But rather, to leave the Earth and extend across the solar system, and eventually perhaps, the galaxy. Unthinkable! Yes, this may seem impossible, but life has done these seemingly impossible inter-element migrations at least once before when it migrated from living in water to living on dry land. Could living in space, learning to survive away from the Earth, be life's next great survival leap?

Yet once again we find, for the second time in our species existence, that humans are about to be chaperoned by climate change to begin another species-wide migration that will end either in survival or extinction—as discussed in *Survival*, Book 1, Chapter 6: "The role of climate change in the making of an Intelligent Species." Minimally, this time around, humans will migrate from increasingly hotter to cooler regions of the planet—away from the equator and toward the poles.

But what do you imagine would become of all those sedentary twenty-first century human economies and legal-person economies (at the local, regional, national, and global levels, in addition to multinational corporations) built during the closing centuries of the Holocene? Many will be abandoned, and most in hotter regions of the planet, sooner rather than later. And it won't be the only time during the Holocene that climate change would have driven modern humans to abandon their sedentary, agricultural economies and lifeways.

Figure 9-14. Migrants from Venezuela making their way through the Darién Gap between Colombia and Panama last year.
(Credit: Federico Rios for The New York Times)

Unlike our hunter-gatherer forebears who were able to migrate along with their mobile economies, the modern migrants shown navigating the Darién Gap Forest in Figure 9-14 are clearly not carrying much apart from their children and personal necessities. In that particular region of the Americas, the ancient Maya, whose early settlements date back to about 2,000 BCE, lived in present-day southern Mexico and northern Central America.

They were celebrated for their stunning architecture, realistic artistic expressions, and for advancing human understanding of astronomy and mathematics. For hundreds of years, the ancient Maya flourished in cities located in and around present-day Guatemala. Then, according to Elizabeth Nix in an updated 2023 article in *History Magazine*, "around CE 250, the Maya entered what's now known as the Classic Period, an era in which they built flourishing cities with temples and palaces, and when population size peaked."

However, by the end of the Classic Period, around CE 900, almost all the major cities in what was then the heart of Maya civilization—the southern lowlands region, in present-day northern Guatemala and neighboring portions of Mexico, Belize and Honduras—had been abandoned. In an August 6, 2021, article in *Discover Magazine*, Carina Woudenberg wrote, "The Maya dispersed throughout the region, generally heading north and west. Many settled in Mexico's Yucatán Peninsula, where they built the city of Chichén Itzá, famous for its Temple of Kukulcán.

Others spread throughout Central America, landing in Honduras, El Salvador, and Belize, among other places. Archeologists often refer to this civilization's "collapse" in quotes, because much of the population continued life elsewhere—though sometimes in smaller, less conspicuous settlements through the countryside. There are more than six million Maya people living throughout the region today.

Like the Anasazi people, the Ancient Pueblo peoples who lived in cliff dwellings and pueblos, another civilization that arose as early as 1500 BCE in southwest America then collapsed, the Maya in Central America also abandoned their farms, livestock, houses, temples, villages, towns, and cities filled with possessions—including their entire agrarian economy. And, what was true of the Maya and the Anasazi was mostly true of numerous prior human civilizations that arose and collapsed during the Holocene.

Peoples of numerous prior collapsed civilizations chose to migrate, leaving the foundations and once indispensable parts of their sedentary economies behind. They spread out across mostly uninhabited or sparsely populated regions of the Earth but would not have encountered the widespread, organized, nation-state anti-immigrant pushback modern migrants now face. And though it's never easy, it may have been easier to start over back then. Back then, too, none of the climate change that contributed to bringing, or that brought, their civilizations and economies to an end was global.

Unfortunately, twenty-first century migrants fleeing collapsing economies and failing nation-states may have no such choice as the planet is now mostly fully populated with little to no unclaimed regions left, and the climate change that's driving modern migration is not only anthropogenic but global. What's pretty clear, too, from the foregoing is that once humans began to abandon their belongings and to migrate, none of their sedentary economies survived. And once their economies began to collapse it was only a matter of time before their civilizations and nation-states collapsed. So, given the above, what should one expect to become of our modern sedentary economies as climate change intensifies, and millions begin to migrate?

Consider, then, the various sectors of modern human and legal-person economies. They constitute the source of all GHG emissions driving global climate change. Note the percentage of greenhouse gas emissions being generated by each sector of the modern economies as shown in Figure 9-15. Now compare the GHG share associated with these modern economic sectors with what might have been generated by the sectors of a pre-agriculture, hunter-gatherer mobile economy (i.e., hunting, gathering, sharing, and recreation) also shown in Figure 9-15. Unsurprisingly, little to no GHGs would have been produced by any of these economic sectors that comprised those mobile, pre-agriculture, hunter-gatherer economies.

We know that not only because there were no fossil fuels back then, but because it was only after the beginning of the Industrial Revolution that anthropogenic greenhouse gas emissions began to significantly and continuously build up (especially CO_2) in the atmosphere, resulting in the global warming we now confront.

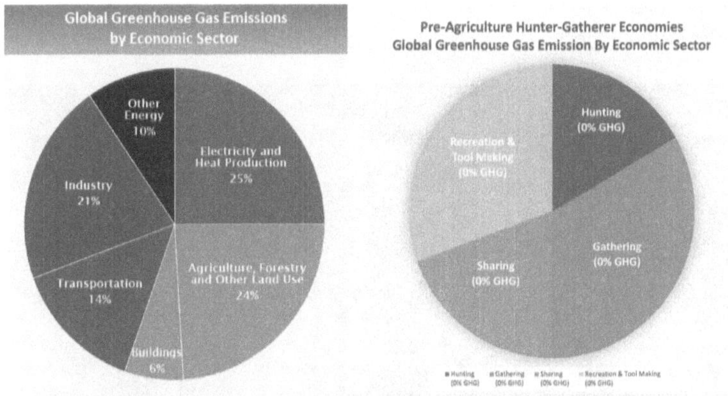

Modern-human economies
Source: IPCC (EPA's website. Based on global emissions from 2010.)

Hunter-gatherer mobile economies
Source: Samuel Layne

Figure 9-15. GHG output by sector of modern human economies compared with pre-agriculture hunter-gatherer mobile economies.

Pre-agriculture hunter-gatherer economies, as noted in the chapter "Energy and Human Economies," neither sought nor needed additional sources of energy to survive comfortably beyond what was available in ecosystems. Post-Neolithic Revolution humans, who chose to become farmers and herders, eventually discovered that to grow, produce, and store their food surplus, and to husband and feed livestock rather than hunt and gather, required much more energy than they had available in ecosystems. Hence, they began the search for new sources of energy that would take centuries but would eventually lead to the discovery and use of fossil fuels—the sources of all GHG emissions now overheating the planet.

Humans tend to view such scientific breakthroughs as a mark of their ingenuity, societal and scientific progress, and as being good both for the economy and for humanity. Discovering new sources of energy no doubt would have been seen as a good thing back then—but clearly it was not. It took humanity nearly three centuries to become convinced that burning fossil fuels as their new source of energy was a bad idea—bad for humanity, bad for all other life on Earth, and bad for the planet. How many more seemingly good ideas we've invented since might yet turn out to be to our undoing? Yet now, once again, the search for new energy rages anew. This time, though, the search is only for so-called "green energy"—humans have finally learned.

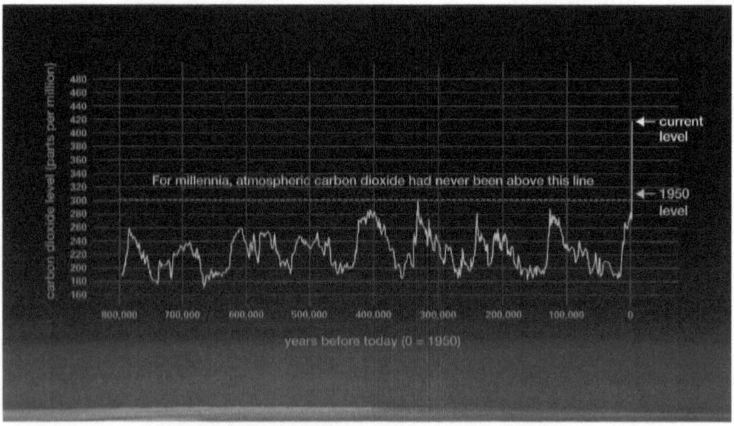

Figure 9-16. The relentless rise of carbon dioxide.

CO_2 levels were around 200 ppm, and during the warmer interglacial periods, they hovered around 280 ppm (see fluctuations in the graph).(Source:NASA.GOV)

For 290,000 years, then, 97 percent of our species' existence, those pre-agriculture hunter-gatherers and their mobile economies left little to no impact on the Earth system. It was only in the last 10,000-plus years of the Holocene, during which Neolithic Revolution human civilizations with their agricultural-based sedentary economies gained traction, that human economies begin to contribute to the buildup of GHG in the atmosphere. Agriculture may well have made the earliest contributions, but this buildup only really took off after the rise of legal-person economies (aka national economies and multinational corporations) that accompanied the Industrial Revolution. The history of this relentless rise of CO_2 is shown in Figure 9-16.

Carbon dioxide levels in the atmosphere are higher now than they have been at any time in the past 400,000 years—all due to the pursuit of new energy sources that humanity had managed to live without for all but the last 300 years. Alas! And now we can't get rid of them fast enough. Now, once again, even as we struggle to get rid of fossil fuels, humanity has embarked upon yet another hunt for new energy sources, and hopefully this time around, this energy hunt won't be driven by profits, wealth accumulation, and economic growth—except that that's precisely what's happening. As much as one would wish for a change, unfortunately, ecosystems, biodiversity, and human life and survival still remain consolation prizes of modern economies.

Sometimes it's good to stop and take stock of where, as a species, we have been, and where else we might, with hindsight, wish we had not gone. How can humans avoid similar survival-threatening mistakes going forward? Clearly our great science and innovations have not helped us but rather were the source of the GHG emissions we now confront. When one realizes that the sources of all our GHG-driven climate change problems are the same economic sectors upon which we built our modern human and legal-person economies and lifeways (Figure 9-15), and upon which our civilizations depend, one soon realizes, as John L. Swigert, Jr., command module pilot and commander of Apollo 13, aboard the Odyssey cried out: "Okay Houston, we've had a problem here." The problem humans have discovered is that the very economic sectors that build our economies are the same ones churning out the GHG emissions that are heating the planet.

The problem he was reporting was the explosion of the oxygen tanks that Mission Commander Jim Lovell confirmed as "a main B bus undervolt," according to a 2020 article by Marco Margaritoff. Lovell, Swigert, and Haise (the third member of the crew) not only heard the explosion "which sounded like a thunderclap"—but saw it firsthand. The gas they saw venting into space was "their oxygen supply rapidly escaping from their ship." With their spacecraft now crippled by the explosion, the crew was left with one resource to get back to Earth, the undamaged Aquarius lunar lander. However, it wasn't supposed to be used until Apollo 13 was ready to land on the moon, nor was it kitted-out for the trip back to Earth—but this crew had no choice. And neither does humanity. They had a crippled ship, and humans now have a crippled planet.

In more ways than one, this updated Apollo 13 disaster description is not too far off from being a description of the global warming dilemma humanity is now experiencing aboard a similarly seriously damaged craft, Spaceship Earth. The problem humans have discovered is that the very economic sectors that build our economies are the same ones pumping into the atmosphere the GHG emissions that are heating the planet. In fact, humanity might be in an even worse situation and hopefully, like NASA, we will find a way to turn this global warming disaster into a "successful failure" for our species.

Humanity, though, has no lunar lander, no Houston to ask for help, nor crew experienced with flying back to Earth in a craft that was designed specifically to land on the moon. Like that lunar lander, Earth is not kitted-out to enable ecosystems, biodiversity, and human survival given a seriously overheating climate system. Humanity must solve its GHG-driven global warming problem or begin to incinerate itself and much of Earth-life species aboard Spaceship Earth upon re-entry.

Like those expended oxygen tanks, the oceans—Earth's oxygen tanks—are being rapidly depleted. And accelerating the buildup of GHGs in the atmosphere is driving up global temperatures to match and exceed the temperatures that drove the "Great Dying," when 97 percent of life in the oceans died. We, too, may well be trapped on Spaceship Earth, aboard a planet humanity may have unintentionally sabotaged by switching to fossil fuels as our main energy source, thereby causing the planet to rapidly overheat as CO_2, methane, nitrous oxide, and other greenhouse gases trap solar radiation in the atmosphere, causing the planet's temperature to begin to increase soon after the beginning of the Industrial Revolution.

The stunning differences and similarities of these two situations are indeed amazing. Both involve delivering humans from certain death on the one hand, and a potential for extinction by incineration on the other. Whereas Houston worked feverishly with the trapped and endangered astronauts to get them back safely to Earth, one can hardly identify the equivalent of a Houston in this looming tragedy. Rather than working to safely rid the Earth's atmosphere of GHG emissions, we are confronted by leaders of the industries responsible for their generation and distribution who continue to invest huge sums they know would only increase fossil fuel availability. Indeed, according to a FORBES Dec 11, 2024 article entitled: "What Energy Transition? ExxonMobil Plans 18% Production Boost By 2030 ... more than 50% higher than in 2024," the company notes.

In fact, "Big Oil executives are pushing back against calls for fast energy transition," according to a March 19, 2024, Reuters report from a major energy conference in Houston, Texas, by Marianna Parraga. "The world's top oil and gas executives criticized global efforts to rapidly move away from fossil fuels at an industry conference in Texas, claiming, 'We should abandon the fantasy of phasing out oil and gas and instead invest in them adequately,' said Amin Nasser, CEO of Saudi Aramco, the world's biggest oil company, to applause." Moreover, according to the International Monetary Fund's January 2024 World Economic Outlook Update, all other countries and their legal-persons (aka multinationals) comprising the remaining economic sectors are just as intent on economic growth, despite knowing that growth, in the short to intermediate term, would increase, rather than decrease, humanity's dependence on fossil fuels, the GHG emissions which are the root cause of global warming.

Worse still, nations are undercounting emissions, putting the U.N. 1.5°C goal at risk. Because of lax rules, national inventories reported to the United Nations grossly underestimate many countries' greenhouse gas emissions. The result, analysts say, is that the world cannot verify compliance with agreed emissions targets, jeopardizing global climate agreements. According to a March 21, 2024, Yale Environment 360 report by Fred Pearce of the Yale School of the Environment, "The data supplied to the UNFCCC (United Nations Framework Convention on Climate Change), and published on its website, are typically out of date, inconsistent, and incomplete." For most countries, "I would not put much value, if any, on the submissions," says Glen Peters of the Center for International Climate Research in Norway, a longtime analyst of emissions trends. So, what exactly is the world's current temperature and where exactly is humanity in its struggle to restrain it?

What's bizarre about this seemingly unreal, though quite real drama in which we are active participants is that humans appear to be tacitly engaged, as it were, in the economic equivalent of some kind of cult-like "mass-murder-suicide-pact." We "permit" these companies to continue to extract fossil fuels even as we continue to use them to keep our lifeways running, and our economies growing, knowing full well that by so doing we mutually continue to produce and use the GHGs that are generating the emissions overheating the planet. One is not sure which of these roles one would choose if one had to.

Like Houston, humanity is seemingly so resourceful, yet our ability to mount a rescue seems so hapless, on the one hand, while on the other, the desperate crew whose initial actions might have imperiled their own lives remains, sadly, in peril. Together these characters may well represent the many facets of the global warming dilemma humanity has found itself in. All of humanity uses fossil fuels in one form or another and we have simultaneously depended upon them and been enabled by them in all aspects of our existence, perhaps some more than others.

But now that one knows what the consequences could be, shouldn't humans jointly, as well as individually, work feverishly, as NASA and the Apollo 13 crew did, to stop the production and use of yet more fossil fuels? Sadly, if the continued growth in the level of CO_2—compared to efforts to stop adding, or start removing, GHG emissions from the atmosphere—is any indication of humanity's relative success as shown in Figure 9-17, there doesn't appear to be much evidence we are going to get there fast enough to avoid a climate calamity. To date, none of the world's efforts to reduce CO_2 and stop or slow climate change has been effective. In fact, most climate policies flop. Only 63 of the 1,500 policy interventions evaluated by Stechemesser et al. actually produced an appreciable reduction in carbon emissions, as reported in a 2024 Science.Org article.

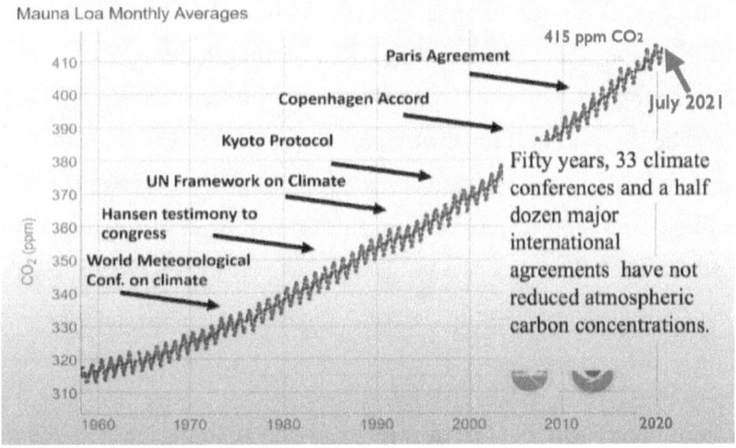

Figure 9-17. Mauna Loa CO_2 annual averages versus humanity's efforts to restrain or remove GHGs.

(Source: NOAA Earth System Research Laboratories.)

As discussed in Chapter 5, "Modern Human Economies—Transitions," this won't be the first time our species has had to confront such vast economic and lifeway changes. When seen from the perspective of geologic time they are not an entirely new phenomenon. However, the experience would have been entirely new for the generations that got caught up in any of these multi-century, multi-millennia transitions as humans are at present. What's unique about this current transition is that it need not have happened. It's entirely of humanity's making and probably is unlike any preceding transition, and because of that, one can't be sure lessons gleaned from prior transitions can serve as guides to navigating this one. Indeed, one can't even be sure humanity will be able to mount an adequate economic and lifeways decarbonization transformation of offending economic sectors sufficient to make a meaningful difference in the time global warming will allow.

Humans would need to undo what took most of the Holocene to become, especially in the last few centuries, our modern twenty-first century global economy and civilization. It will require changes across all aspects of life: individual, national, local, as well as global. These have been of such magnitude and variety that it is difficult to imagine fully the extent of the transformations that must be undertaken without looking back at earlier climate change-driven transformations early humans endured—such as during the Pleistocene-Holocene transition as the last ice age was coming to an end. Because no prior transformation has been quite like this one, it is unlikely one can grasp or fathom this oncoming transformation fully, not even after reflecting upon some of the events and changes those prior transformations engendered.

Revisit for a moment, but this time in greater detail in Figure 9-18, the global GHG emissions being generated by each economic sector and compare these, again, with what might have been the economic sectors of pre-agriculture hunter-gatherer mobile economies. Note that none of those GHG-producing sectors in our modern human and legal-person economies are to be found among the sectors comprising their mobile economies. Somehow, they managed to survive without electricity, transport, manufacturing and construction, agriculture, industry, buildings, waste, land use change and forestry, aviation and shipping, and other fuel combustion economic activities—and in addition, *without economic growth*. This wasn't simply a case of hunter-gatherer societies and economies not being advanced enough. In fact, as discussed in Chapter 3, "Early Human Economies," they may well have been "the original affluent society" as per James Suzman in his book *Affluence Without Abundance: What We Can Learn from the World's Most Successful Civilisation."*

Their lifeways and economies were able to survive quite well using the energy flows within the Earth's ecosystems for all their existence with neither economic nor societal collapse, and without bringing upon themselves and the planet the disasters, diseases, and existential threats our technologically advanced societies and growth-driven modern economies have brought in just the last three centuries. These early human economies and societies obviously weren't preoccupied with becoming scientifically advanced, technologically brilliant, or uniquely innovative, nor did they seek unending economic surplus, growth, and abundance.

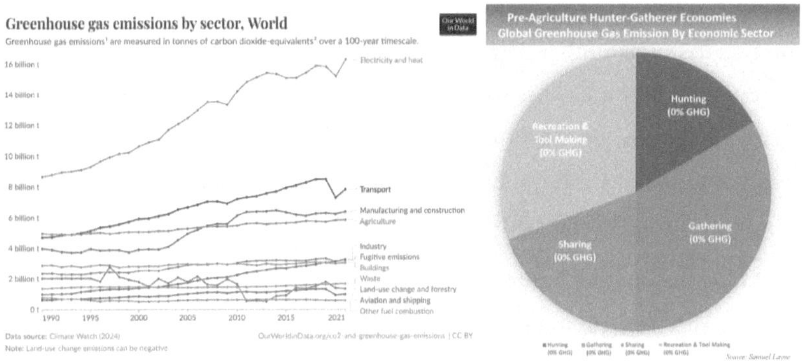

Figure 9-18. Global GHG output by economic sectors: Modern sedentary human economies versus pre-agriculture hunter-gatherer mobile economies.

After all, they had nearly 300 millennia to figure that one out and give it a try, but they didn't. Even today remnant hunter-gatherers continue to reject our modern sedentary growth-driven economic approach. Instead, they chose and continue to choose to pursue that singular but powerful original goal and outcome of *life and survival for all*—ecosystems, all Earth-life species, and humanity.

And, as discussed in Chapter 3, "Early Human Economies," they needed no additional energy source, and sought none, neither inside nor outside ecosystems during the 290,000 years of their existence. Modern humans, meanwhile, in just the last 300 or so years, have invented lifeways that cannot be sustained without finding even more energy sources, including taking on the risks of deep-sea mining of ocean and seabed ecosystems.

Today, scientists write, and economists opine, about how climate change will affect the world economy, conveniently forgetting, it seems, that it was and still is the world's economy, by the GHGs emissions it generates, that is creating climate change. This tight link between climate change and economic activity has given rise to a search for methods to decouple one from the other. But despite the need to reduce GHG emissions, according to IMF's world economic growth projections, 2023-2025 (See IMF GDP Growth Table 2) growth is still assumed, nay required to continue, giving rise to terms such as "green growth" (growth that is environmentally sustainable) and concepts such as "net zero" (net-zero emissions by 2050, meaning that by 2050 human economic activity releases and removes the same amount of GHGs). Both of these are dependent on some form of "decoupling" of GHG emissions growth from economic growth.

Many debate too, how to decouple growth of the modern human economy and accompanying legal-person economies from the need to combust fossil fuels to grow the economy. In effect, decoupling is driven by the need to replace GHGs with new energy sources (hence the search for renewable energy) and by the desire to grow the economy without generating GHG emissions.

But decoupling, though shown to be possible in some developed economies (such as France, Sweden, and Germany, for limited periods), has not been possible overall, according to a 2024 GIST article entitled "How to 'decouple' emissions from economic growth? These economists say you can't" by Akielly Hu and Joseph Winters. Only countries experiencing an economic crisis were able to reduce their emissions, they claim. The hope for an inverse relationship—GDP growth up and CO_2 emissions down—has seldom been found even where decoupling has been shown to occur in some countries.

According to Jefim Vogel and Jason Hickel, researchers at the University of Leeds and the Autonomous University of Barcelona, respectively, it will take economies that are able to decouple more than 220 years to cut emissions by 95 percent—making it impossible to achieve net zero by 2050. The Lancet Planetary Health study shows this, too. Thus, decoupling is inadequate for meeting the climate commitments of the Paris Agreement—and hence, as a strategy for reducing GHG, decoupling will fail to avoid a climate calamity.

However, as we have seen in Figure 9-18, pre-agriculture hunter-gatherer economies not only had nothing to do with economic growth, let alone the generation of GHG emissions, but on the contrary, had everything to do with how humans and biodiversity species would mutually eke out a living within ecosystems, destroying neither these nor one another—a feat modern humans, despite all our science, technologies and innovations, have failed at, or have no desire to accomplish.

Today economists talk about degrowth (shrinking rather than growing economies, to use less of the world's dwindling resources), and post-growth (seeking to freeze new growth and to identify and build on what is already working, rather than focusing on what is not) and numerous other terms to describe their brand of growth. But here I wish to emphasize that the only growth, if any, our pre-agriculture hunter-gatherer, waterhole-inspired, mobile economies appeared to have practiced was "no growth." They would have been humanity's first and only true no-growth economies. Imagine that!

They had no use for any of the so-called factors of production—land, labor, capital, and entrepreneurship. Rather, they hunted and gathered and shared the results among themselves, then as resources ran low, moved their camps to another location, always within reach of a waterhole, leaving nature, in the form of Earth's ecosystems and biodiversity (flora, fauna and funga), to replenish the socio-ecosystem services they consumed. It was nature that did any production, and it was nature that preserved any surplus.

Hence, as discussed in chapter 3 "Early Human Economies," they prospered without the need for any form of "economic growth" as modern economists would define growth. Their socioeconomic unit, the camp, consisted of about 30-50 individuals. They were small, mobile, egalitarian groups that organized around a set of waterhole economy sharing principles that required mutual sharing. They practiced "No DOMC" no-growth economic principles, meaning they didn't Domesticate, Own, Modify, or Control ecosystems or biodiversity species or resources, and encamped within reach of a waterhole—with hardly a thought given to growth.

These were some of the lifeway differences (socioeconomic principles) between their mobile waterhole economies and our modern, sedentary, capitalist, GDP growth-driven ones. Their lifeways enabled them to survive for most of our species' existence without collapse or destroying Earth's ecosystems, biodiversity, and environments, whereas, in considerably less than 10,000 years, numerous modern human civilizations and economies, like the Anasazi and Maya, arose, thrived for a while, then collapsed.

Indeed, those socioeconomic lifeways of our pre-agriculture hunter-gatherer forebears comprised a radically different economic system and way of living that enabled them to survive and prosper for 297,000 years with neither economic nor civilization collapse. Their mobile waterhole economies required nothing more from the planet beyond the ecosystem and biodiversity products and services it already offered. Their small mobile units avoided many of the ills that accompanied our considerably larger sedentary populations. Their mobility restrained not only population growth but prevented the level of ecosystem modification and biodiversity destruction that are inevitable in much larger sedentary societies and surplus-hoarding, growth-driven economies.

And, in a universe and on a planet where most things move, their mobility predisposed them to respond by migrating to where seasonal shifting of flora and fauna, and ecosystem products and services, would themselves have moved with the natural change of seasons brought on by rotation of the planet. Mobility also equipped them to be always prepared to move in response to climate change-driven disasters such as occurred frequently during the Pleistocene ice age epoch during which they evolved.

Theirs may well have been the original lifeways intended and maybe even required to enable life and survival on a mobile planet. Mobile lifeways are what most Earth-life species appear to follow, and they appear to be more consistent with the original life and survival goal and objective for all Earth-life species, ecosystems, and *Homo sapiens* themselves. They also managed to live within the energy, water, food, and other natural resource budgets of the ecosystem, and needed neither surplus hoarding nor "growth"—the latter thought to be a relatively recent phenomenon of industrial capitalism that economists first measured in the 1930s, and whose pursuit only became universal from the 1950s.

But pre-agriculture hunter-gatherers and their mobile no-growth waterhole economies not only predated what twenty-first century humanity regarded as the dawn of civilization and the Industrial Revolution but had flourished for hundreds of millennia without knowing or caring about "growth," even before the Neolithic Revolution that would lead to the rise of agriculture and jump-start modern global sedentary societies and economies. Not only did their mobile economies lack any concept of growth, they also lacked the concept and practice of surplus hoarding—the prerequisite for growth. Instead, they practiced societal sharing, the very antithesis of surplus hoarding and therefore of growth. Sharing was foundational to their mobile lifeways and mobile waterhole economies and to the conservation of ecosystem and biodiversity products and services.

Moreover, because they were primarily egalitarian, and formed neither nations nor states nor dwelt in very large communities, they escaped the frailties that accompany densely populated or overpopulated cities and states and that comprise modern sedentary economies and societies. They also avoided much of the politics, class structures, and warfare that accompanied rulers, kings, queens, and governments. And they managed to escape the spells of priests, and the formation of competing sects that accompany systems of religions, and belief in creator gods.

Their practice of sharing may well have prevented the growth of inequality and economic class structures that hoarding would have encouraged, while serving as a bulwark against poverty and neglect of the homeless, sick, and needy. Their DOMC lifeways steered them clear of the inclination toward possessiveness regarding land, people, property, money, and the hoarding of surplus, that among more recent human societies would eventually enable wealth accumulation, capitalism, and the pursuit of endless GDP growth.

The pursuit of growth of any kind (including degrowth, post-growth, green growth, no growth) and endless GDP growth would become the scourge of post-agriculture human economies and civilizations and would lead to the destruction of most of the planet's ecosystems and biodiversity species that form the very foundations of all Earth-life. Indeed, this obsession with growth would eventually become the cause of environmental destruction, economic collapse, and the demise of civilization after civilization as human history during the Holocene demonstrated.

If anthropogenic climate change were to eventually drive humanity to seek new and improved lifeways and economic systems, none come more highly credentialled than the well-tested, no-growth, mobile, egalitarian, sharing economic system, equipped with the DOMC guardrails of the pre-agriculture, hunter-gatherer waterhole economies of our forebears. It not only enabled their life and survival for 97 percent of our species' existence without destroying the planet's ecosystems and biodiversity species, but also obviated the need for additional energy sources and unproven profit-driven technologies and innovations that often conceal their potential for harm and the risks they pose. That harm and those risks—like anthropogenic GHGs whose generation began three or so centuries ago—threaten to grow until it's too late to avoid bringing upon humanity, and all Earth-life species, economic and civilization collapse—or worse, as humans now face: the risk of a potential GHG emission-driven mass extinction.

PART SEVEN

Human Economies and Human Survival

THE ECONOMIES THAT EVOLVED TO ENABLE LIFE AND SURVIVAL

FOR AN ECONOMY TO EXIST, LIFE MUST FIRST EXIST. AND FOR LIFE TO EXIST, EARTH'S HABITATS, ECOSYSTEMS AND BIODIVERSITY MUST ALSO EXIST.

IT'S ALWAYS MORE THAN A LITTLE DISCONcerting when major concepts one understood to be settled science turn out to be anything but. Imagine the surprise on discovering that human economies were anything but what one understood an economy to be or what one learned in Economics 101. One's only consolation in this case is that not even Adam Smith, it would seem, nor perhaps any of those Nobel Prize-winning economists, might have known what an economy *really* is, either.

And it was surprising, too, to discover that economies—Earth-life species economies, that is—existed long before humans evolved, and came into existence when these species began foraging—the task of eking out a living *within* Earth's ecosystems, a way of making a living early humans would imitate, and from which the human economy would emerge. But the surprise didn't end here.

It was even more surprising to discover that those Earth-life species economies and early human economies that imitated them evolved to perform a very specific function— to form the bond that would enable Earth's biodiversity, ecosystems and humans to coexist and collaborate in a way that would ensure their mutual life and survival. One soon realizes that without Earth's habitats and ecosystems, there can be no life; and without life, humans, or biodiversity eking out a living within those ecosystems, there would be no economies.

Economies, it would seem, are an emergent property that came into existence as Earth-life species, including biodiversity as well as humans, went about the task of foraging for a living within ecosystems. As Earth's flora depends on its fauna to spread pollen, so its fauna depends on its flora for the food they derive in return and upon which their lives depend. So, bees, for example, need flowers as much as flowers need bees, while humans need them both to survive.

There exists, then, a mutual life-survival codependency between Earth's ecosystems, its biodiversity, and humans, such that none could exist without the simultaneous existence of the others. The seeming magic that holds this all together and enables this mutual coexistence is *the economy—Earth-life species economies and human economies—which is the process of eking out a living within Earth's ecosystems without destroying them and doing so in harmony with its biodiversity.*

Economies, then, comprise that set of processes species would execute to eke out a living; processes that would with time become socioeconomic lifeway bonds that evolved to enable their mutual life and survival. These bonds would bind Earth's biodiversity and humanity around shared resources, as around a waterhole, as they eke out a living *within* ecosystems, enabling their mutual survival. Over time, these processes would become the definitive set of socioeconomic lifeways pre-agriculture hunter-gatherer humans would adopt and follow for all but the last 12,000 years of human existence.

This goal and outcome for Earth-life species economies, and human economies in particular, seems intended to enable Earth's biodiversity, ecosystems, and human life and survival. They guided humanity's socioeconomic lifeways for most of our species' existence but were gradually replaced over the last 12,000 years by Neolithic Revolution humans and modern humans. These lifeways stand in stark contrast to the surplus/profit generation, wealth accumulation, and endless GDP growth lifeways that became the socioeconomic goals and outcomes of modern human economies and their competitors, the legal-person-economies also known as multinational corporate economies.

If the longevity of those pre-agriculture hunter-gatherer economies can be taken as an indicator of their socioeconomic success, how different modern human economies might have turned out had Adam Smith and his followers understood the role human economies were intended to serve. They, apparently, never understood that the initial goal and outcome for the economy was life and survival, not profits, wealth accumulation, and endless GDP growth. This change in direction and purpose of the economy today is what has led to near-total biodiversity extinction, continuing ecosystem destruction and the potential for an anthropogenic global warming-driven extinction.

Today, though, one need not imagine the consequences of abandoning the hunter-gatherer economic model. One can clearly see the bio-socioeconomic consequences that have ensued since humans began destroying Earth's ecosystems and its biodiversity, the very foundations that enable life and survival. Humans would go on to build their economies *outside* Earth's ecosystems and would resort to nonrenewable energy sources to power their socioeconomic growth—energy sources that were neither found nor used within Earth-life ecosystems, and that are now driving global warming climate change.

It was Neolithic Revolution humans that began this transition. They abandoned the socioeconomic lifeways of our pre-agriculture hunter-gatherer human forebears that enabled their survival for all but the most recent 12,000 years of our species' existence.

This concluding chapter on "Human Survival and Human Economies" seeks to remind us of the original purpose human economies might have evolved to serve. It draws the contrast between the collapse-free life and survival of pre-agriculture hunter-gatherer societies and economies during the first 290,000 years of our species' existence, versus the collapse-prone existence of subsequent human economies and civilizations during the succeeding 12,000 years; and makes the connection between this collapse and humanity's destruction of the very foundations Earth-life economies must have to survive—Earth's biodiversity and ecosystems.

Finally, it explains why the goal and outcome of human economies was never about the creation of surplus/profits, wealth accumulation, and endless economic growth, nor about the development of new, novel, and non-obvious technologies and innovations that contributed to their collapse; but rather about what drove the life and survival of all Earth-life: humans, biodiversity, and ecosystems. This is an economic goal and outcome modern humans have yet to adopt for their modern human economies.

Too bad, then, for humanity that its economists and numerous leaders still haven't figured out that *Life and Survival* are the only goal and outcome human economies evolved to fulfill.

Human Economies and Human Survival

THE ECONOMIES THAT EVOLVED TO ENABLE LIFE AND SURVIVAL

CHAPTER 10

Survival-Driven Economies
Were Waterhole Economies

The Economies That Enabled Life and Survival

10.

Survival-Driven Economies

Were Waterhole Economies

THE ECONOMIES THAT ENABLED LIFE AND SURVIVAL

For an economy to exist, life must first exist; and for life to exist, Earth's habitats, ecosystems, and biodiversity must also exist.

BY NOW SOME HUMANS ARE BEGINNING TO REALIZE that pre-agriculture hunter-gatherer human economies were quite different from what modern economic thought, theory, and practice have imagined and defined human economies to be; and are far less complex than the systems of interrelated production, consumption, and exchange activities that today ultimately determine how resources are allocated. As seen earlier, they included neither production, growth, exchange, nor market allocation of resources. On the contrary, Earth-life species economies emerged out of simultaneous foraging, hunting, and gathering activities as species independently engaged in the tasks of eking out a living within Earth's habitats and ecosystems.

These Earth-life species economies, as we saw, not only predated human evolution, and would have come into existence from the time Earth-life species began foraging for a living, creating socioeconomic lifeways that hunter-gatherer humans would adopt millennia later, but also served the indispensable function of enabling the survival of both humans and Earth-life species and the ecosystems *within* which they evolved. Modern humans apparently still have trouble grasping that without Earth's ecosystems remaining intact, there would be no Earth-life species, and that without these species foraging for a living *within* those ecosystems, there would be no Earth-life species economies and consequently, no human economies, either.

It is difficult not to notice just how intertwined with and mutually dependent human survival is on the survival of Earth's biodiversity and its ecosystems; how human survival is utterly dependent on Earth-life species' survival; and how these in turn are dependent on Earth's ecosystems' survival. Yet, as we have seen, when choosing to build their economies, Neolithic through modern humans built them *outside* of these ecosystems and out of harmony with its biodiversity, and thereby began to unravel this foundational and primary role of enabling life and survival that economies may well have evolved to fulfill.

Humans ignored or may never have grasped this survival-enabling role Earth-life economies played in sustaining ecosystems, biodiversity, and human life, and indeed except where precluded, continue to play for all other Earth-life species except Neolithic Revolution and subsequent humans. Instead of the survival-driven goals that guided the existence of all Earth-life species, including all pre-agriculture hunter-gatherer humans for most of our species' existence, Neolithic Revolution and subsequent humans would choose entirely different socioeconomic lifeways.

They chose to farm *outside,* instead of forage *inside* these ecosystems, and would go on to develop what would turn out to be a system of socioeconomic lifeways that would start out as surplus-driven but would eventually become profit-, wealth accumulation-, and eventually GDP growth-driven; that would see the eventual transition from human economies to legal-person economies; and that consequently, to date, would leave only 3 percent of Earth's ecosystems intact and drive most of its biodiversity to extinction.

The socioeconomic lifeway changes that Neolithic Revolution humans began to adopt approximately 10,000 to 12,000 years ago would be subsequently expanded by emerging generations of human thinkers, chief among whom was Adam Smith, the so-called father of economics. Smith was a Scottish moral philosopher whose arguments in *An Inquiry into the Nature and Causes of the Wealth of Nations*, published in 1776, implied that societies benefited not from the foraging and sharing socioeconomic lifeways of pre-agriculture hunter-gatherer humans, but from the individual's need to fulfill his or her own self-interest, that the human tendency to look out for "number one" benefited all society and would result in prosperity for all, that our individual choices would ultimately satisfy the interests of all, and that responding to our individual profit motives would promote the socioeconomic welfare of all.

Except that's not the way things worked out for most of humanity. In fact, nearly all subsequent economies, spanning the last 12,000 years, and in contrast to the 290,000 years during which our pre-agriculture hunter-gatherer human forebears survived collapse-free, adopted the newly adapted Neolithic Revolution socioeconomic lifeways, with most such economies going on to destroy the ecosystems they occupied and driving to extinction much of the biodiversity with whom they once shared those ecosystems.

The only humans who benefited were those who owned or controlled the factors of production. Those, more often than not, turned out to be royalty—the ecclesiastically, politically, and militarily powerful that over time turned out to be a tiny fraction of humanity. In fact, according to a 2020 Oxfam report, the world's 2,153 billionaires had more wealth than the 4.6 billion people who make up 60 percent of the world's population. Too bad Smith, and several who followed and enhanced his ideas, are not around to see how their ideas have worked out. Today this tome would be more appropriately renamed *The Wealth of the Billionaire Class, and their Legal-Persons, aka Multinational Corporations*.

By changing this primary and foundational role of the human economy from one of preserving ecosystem, biodiversity, and human life and survival, to one that would exploit them, ditching life and survival for surplus, profits, growth, and wealth accumulation, ensured that there was nothing even remotely survival-driven left about these modern human economies that emerged and the surplus-driven legal-person economies that are replacing them. But to understand what a socioeconomic makeover this has been and its consequences for all Earth-life, including humans, one must first grasp what a survival-driven economy must have been like. So, what is a survival-driven economy?

Unlike the kinds of socioeconomic systems Smith et al. would promote, survival-driven economies had just one goal and one outcome—life and survival, specifically, the survival of Earth's ecosystems, biodiversity, and human life. This socioeconomic goal was neither new, novel, nor non-obvious as early hunter-gatherer human economies knew no other goal and experienced no other outcome for most of our species' existence. It was only after Neolithic Revolution humans abandoned foraging for farming, sharing for hoarding, and small mobile bands for large, sedentary farming towns and cities, thereby changing the socioeconomic lifeways of our species, that this socioeconomic goal and outcome of life and survival was eventually replaced with what is best described as a new socioeconomic goal of acquisition and consumption. Thereafter, human societies and economies would begin to experience a new and different outcome—socioeconomic collapse.

Thereafter, and for the next 400 generations through the present, humans would pursue and expand upon these changed socioeconomic goals and consequently have continued to experience this changed and expanding socioeconomic outcome—socioeconomic and civilization collapse. They collapsed because modern human lifeways and socioeconomic goals were no longer survival-driven but driven instead by pursuit of surplus, profits, wealth accumulation, and GDP growth. But now, in addition, this collapse has begun to be accompanied by a growing risk of self-extinction. Can modern humans return to the socioeconomic survival-driven lifeways their pre-agriculture hunter-gatherer forebears once practiced and survived on for most of human existence?

To do so modern humans will need to rediscover what those Earth-life species economies and early human economies were like and why they survived while modern human economies seem headed for collapse. One must understand the survival-driven socioeconomic foundations and survival-driven architecture that evolved to make this survival possible. And for as long as these species and early humans remained within this architecture and continued to build their economies upon those foundations, they continued to survive, as most Earth-life species still do, and as pre-agriculture hunter-gatherer humans did for 290,000 of the 300,000 years of human existence. Then Neolithic Revolution humans came along, and for humans, everything changed.

Going back, then, to those initial foundations, that Evolutionary Triad of Life discussed earlier, we saw how both biodiversity species' survival and human survival were not only dependent upon each other's survival but upon Earth's ecosystems' survival as well. Without ecosystem survival, there could be no Earth-life species survival; and without their mutual survival, there would be no human life; and without human life and human survival, there would be no human economies. In this triad of life their survival was based as much on their interconnectedness as upon their mutual dependency; and was one of many foundational inter-relationships essential to life and survival that, when building modern economies, humans have ignored at their peril.

Survival-driven economies, then, are an emergent component of this survival-driven architecture that emanates from the interaction of Earth's ecosystems and Earth-life species as the latter go about the task of eking out a living *within* those ecosystems. By eking out a living within ecosystems, species create a mutual dependency not unlike how bees seeking nectar also end up gathering and spreading pollen, or how Earth-life flora rely on oxygen from their fauna and these in turn rely on the CO_2 exhaled by Earth's flora. This mutual interdependency forms an indispensable survival bond that would enable their mutual survival.

These economies emerged out of Earth-life species eking out a living within a survival-driven, mostly pre-evolved and pre-built Earth-life planetary infrastructure. They consisted of habitats and ecosystems and were inhabited by Earth-life species including hominins and eventually humans; and were provisioned with all the resources essential for life and survival. These include air, water, food sources, raw materials, minerals, places to live, natural resources and medicines, and a free, extant, no-fuss, ubiquitous renewable energy source that was easily accessible by all species and that without fail energized all life on Earth for billions of years.

There were also survival-driven rules that govern these interactions that were equally simple but fundamental to survival. No one owned or controlled this survival-driven architecture, nor its infrastructure and built-in common resources essential to all life and survival. While numerous species may dwell within or use them as they do waterholes and savannas, no one species owned, developed, invented, or could modify them in ways that would make them no longer capable of serving their intended survival-based functions. Nothing was owned nor could anything become the property of any species, anyone, or anything. No one individual, people, or nation (when such would emerge) could own land, mountains, continents, islands, forests, oceans, rivers, or air space, for any purpose, nor deny their use to other Earth-life species that might dwell within or access them.

No one could acquire an exclusive right to any feature or component of the infrastructure comprising this architecture, such as the sun, the moon, a river, a forest, the atmosphere, the biosphere, a sea, or an ocean. Neither could anyone rule, govern, or control geographic areas and regions, nor other species or individuals within those areas. All species and individuals evolved following an instinctive path or, in the case of "intelligent" species, were free to choose a way to eke out a living if that way, except as a source of food, did not endanger the survival of other individuals or species within, say, a food web. Food and resources, individually or collectively acquired, were shared, not hoarded or sold.

Inherent in this pre-architected, pre-evolved, custom-built, survival-driven, Earth-life enabling planetary infrastructure comprised of habitats, ecosystems, and a biosphere, and maintained by innumerable Earth-life species, was also a set of survival-driven-rules (that humans now know may have been included among planetary boundaries) that were designed to enable Earth-life ecosystems, biodiversity species, and human survival. Most species, including pre-agriculture hunter-gatherer humans, came to know and instinctively followed these survival-driven rules, and as a result, survived collapse-free for millennia—except Neolithic Revolution humans. Like beavers, these post-agriculture humans chose to come up with an architecture of their own, built economies on foundations *outside* ecosystems and of their own making, and developed socioeconomic lifeway rules they may have thought were better than the survival-driven lifeway rules all other Earth-life species appear to have followed.

Humans, for example, would choose a subset of seeds, clear land, plant, water, and grow their food instead of forage for food as all Earth-life species had done since "the beginning" and continue to do to this day. Choosing a specific subset of seeds to farm meant regarding all others as unwanted weeds; clearing land meant displacing other Earth-life species above and below ground; and waiting for crops to grow meant eventually abandoning the mobility that enabled foraging and instead adopting a sedentary lifestyle. Soon small mobile hunter-gatherer bands were being replaced with large sedentary populations that would till the soil and harvest the crops. Instead of mobile tent-erecting foragers gathered in small encampments, houses were built; villages, towns and cities were erected with space enough to house farm animals; and hectares of land were cordoned off to grow grain.

What might have appeared as progress, innovation, and economic development to humans was, in fact, a declaration of war against nature. Soon that sedentary lifeway would engender population growth, and those small foraging bands that kept population small would soon become villages; villages would become towns, towns would become cities, and these would eventually merge to become nations. Those villages, towns, and cities would require clearing more land to plant crops, raise farm animals, build homes, roads, and public spaces, and in the process displace innumerable Earth-life species that in time would lead to the annihilation of countless species and the destruction of numerous hectares of wildlife habitats and ecosystems. Hence, to grow their economies, humans would destroy Earth-life species' economies.

By abandoning the survival-driven lifeways that included living in small, mobile, foraging, sharing, egalitarian bands, and the built-in population growth restraint that mobility enabled, humans would eventually overspread the Earth. Their population would grow from a few million during the time of pre-agriculture hunter-gatherers to more than eight billion today, which is perhaps approaching the carrying capacity of the planet. Soon, the process of provisioning for this ever-increasing horde would threaten with extinction Earth-life species that range from megafauna to dung beetles to earthworms.

Today humans have destroyed or rearranged all but 3 percent of ecosystems and have driven to extinction innumerable quantities of Earth-life species whose interworkings and interdependent relationships were meant to enable their mutual life and survival. By wantonly destroying Earth-life species and ecosystems, humans essentially destroyed two-thirds of Earth-life components that were meant to collaborate with humanity in emergent economies that, in turn, would have become the foundation of their mutual life and survival. By destroying Earth-life species and ecosystems, humans may have essentially destroyed much of the means of their own survival.

In place of this relationship, modern humans would come up with rules of their own. These include economic principles that would exclude and discount any relationship or role nature played in human economies; religious rules and beliefs in creator gods that had left humans in charge of Earth, its ecosystems, and its biodiversity to use and treat as they would see fit; political rules and practices that would give rise to numerous rulers, kings, queens, and dictators with their armies and modern-day slaves in political systems that have served mostly to deepen the misery and confusion of our species and its peoples; rules and laws of science, math, and numerous topics that may have managed to push back the frontiers of human ignorance a bit, often flouting survival-driven rules whenever and wherever they could, with impunity, but offered little to help humans recognize Earth-life's survival-driven architecture and survival-driven rules that would have taught humanity how they were meant to survive on planet Earth.

Instead, Neolithic Revolution through modern humans would go on to build their economies *outside* rather than *inside* Earth-life ecosystems. They would abandon or fail to recognize that Earth-life species and ecosystems are as codependent on each other as bees are on flowers and vice versa, an interdependence that would be indispensable to their mutual survival, and a biological bond that would underpin the economy that would emerge from eking out a living within those ecosystems.

Now, 400 generations later, with most ecosystems laid bare or repurposed, and innumerable biodiversity species driven to extinction, humans are just beginning to realize—perhaps a little too late—that unlike the gods they once imagined and may still imagine gave rise to their existence, their evolution, it would seem, required neither obedience, nor disobedience, nor sought scholarship, technical brilliance or wealth, but simply their life and survival.

The evolution of life resulted in simple rules and a path to human survival no more difficult than the survival-driven rules and laws of eking out a living *within* ecosystems that our pre-agriculture hunter-gatherer human forebears followed for millennia. Had we followed these lifeways as all other species had done and continue to do, humans might have avoided having to resort to nonrenewable energy sources *outside* ecosystems and going down a path that has resulted in the CO_2-driven global warming that now threatens not only humanity but perhaps what might be left of Earth's biodiversity and ecosystems as well.

Humans have known for a while that there had to have been a survival-driven architecture that underpins all Earth-life infrastructure, with survival-driven foundations upon which all Earth-life habitats, ecosystems, Earth-life species, and economies are based. These foundations support survival-driven lifeways that would inform and enable life to survive, if only because Earth, and its ability to sustain life, appears to be so different from the numerous other planets that scientists so far have managed to peer at, if only because there is life on Earth.

Peter Ward and Donald Brownlee, in their book *Rare Earth: Why Complex Life Is Uncommon in the Universe* (quoted earlier in a different context but worth mentioning again here) claimed, "Most of the Universe is too cold, too hot, too dense, too vacuous, too dark, too bright, or not composed of the right elements to support life. Only planets and moons with solid surface materials provide plausible oases for life as we know it." Such a planet must include certain items we take for granted such as an oxygen-based breathable atmosphere; a suitable temperature range; shielding on the surface from ultraviolet and gamma-ray bombardment from space and from the home star; running water on the surface; food of any kind; fertile soil; animals, birds, reptiles, insects, and marine life; oceans, rivers, and lakes; and of course, plants of any kind. Without plants there'd be no photosynthesis, and without photosynthesis there wouldn't be enough oxygen in the atmosphere to support complex animal life.

According to Ward and Brownlee, "The home star of a potentially life-evolving and sustaining planet will preferably be a single star (not a binary or multiple star system) in the galactic habitable zone: one that does not pulse or rapidly change its energy output, or give off too much ultraviolet radiation, but emits a near-constant energy output for billions of years; one that is located in a safe region of the galaxy, far from the galactic center and from sources of gamma-ray bursts or supernovae; and one that is moving relatively slowly on its journey through its galaxy."

To be a habitat for the evolution and sustainability of complex animal life, a planet must also be terrestrial (rocky and with a hard surface), stable in a circular orbit (with a fixed spin rate—Earth has a twenty-four-hour spin rate), and with a fixed tilt of its axis of rotation (aided by the gravitational effects of the sun and moon, Earth has had, for most of its recent geologic existence, a 23-degree tilt angle that drives long-term stability of its surface temperature). It must also be in a continuous habitable zone and far enough away from its home star to avoid being tidally locked by its gravitational force (where one side of the planet always faces the star and the other always faces the coldness and darkness of outer space, as our moon does when it orbits the Earth), and it must be shielded from frequent comet and meteor bombardment by larger outer planets in its solar system, the way Jupiter shields Earth, as it did in July 1994 from the comet Shoemaker-Levy.

So, if a prerequisite for life is such a survival-driven architecture, built on survival-driven foundations in which species are guided by survival-driven rules upon which Earth-life habitats, ecosystems, species, and economies are based, could life on Earth have even existed let alone survived for billions of years without them? We know what happened when these Earth-life prerequisites were thrown out of whack: Earth has seen numerous extinctions including a few major ones, such as was caused by that massive asteroid collision some 65 million years ago that led to the extinction of all non-avian dinosaurs and the ascent of mammals; and earlier still, what came to be known as "The Great Dying," when this survival-driven architecture and its foundations became so seriously impaired that 252 million years ago life nearly died.

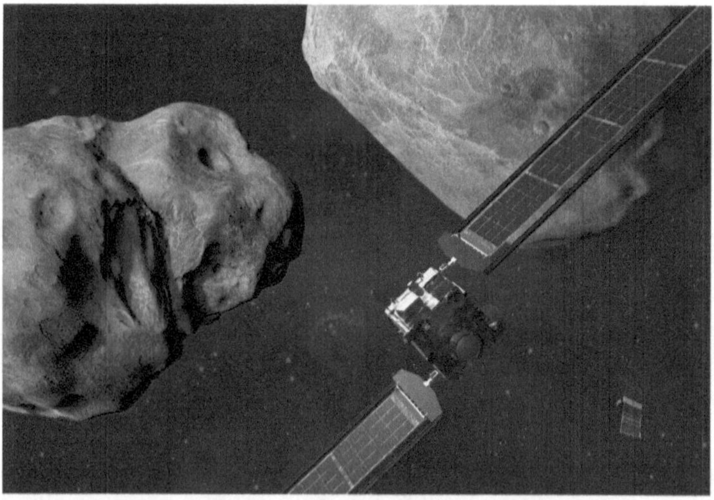

Figure 10-1. DART spacecraft near the two asteroids, Didymos and Dimorphos.
(Credit: NASA/Johns Hopkins APL/Steve Gribben.)

The chances that yet another civilization-ending or Earth-life-destroying asteroid with Earth in its crosshairs might even now be hurtling through space—not impossible, scientists say, but unlikely at least for now—have not stopped NASA's DART spacecraft (Figure 10-1) from getting ready for such a possibility. Yet the undeniable fact that it was greenhouse gas emissions that drove eleven of Earth's dozen mass extinctions, including Earth's worst 252 million years ago, does not seem to have stirred a corresponding global effort to save humanity from the real and potential threat of a fossil fuel-driven mass extinction.

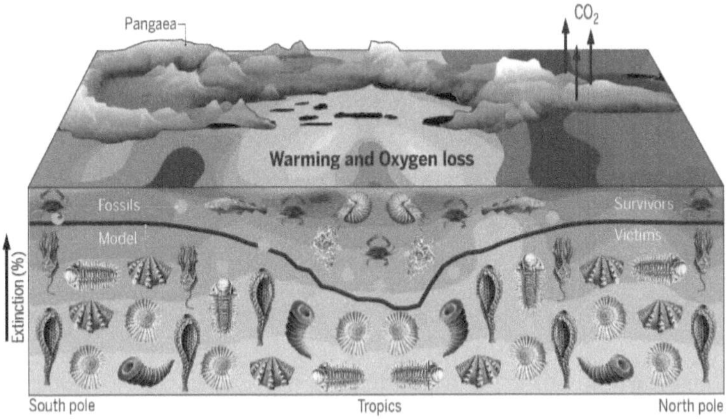

Figure 10-2. Fossilized crinoids, marine invertebrates that lived during the Permian Period.
Scientists say The Great Dying, which wiped out 96 percent of all life in the oceans, was caused by global warming, which deprived the oceans of oxygen. (Source: Science.org ;Credit: Illustration- J. Penn, et al, Fossil Drawings - E. Haeckel, et al, Photos-W. Kaveney et al)

What's happening right now reveals some marked similarities between the fossil fuel-driven global warming that's driving global climate change today and what may well have caused this great dying 252 million years ago, and it demonstrates what an unplanned and unscheduled change to the planet's climate architecture can do to life on Earth. Even though for about one million years, in what today is Siberia, volcanoes spewed enough magma and lava to overspread an area about the size of America, it wasn't the volcanism as much as it was the ancient fossil fuels burned by the magma that drove this extinction. In just tens of thousands of years, 96 percent of all ocean life and about 70 percent of all land life perished (Figure 10-2). Today, with sea-surface temperatures on the rise, oceans acidifying, some shelled animals already showing signs of bleaching, and modern human economies belching carbon 14 times faster per year than emanated from those Siberian traps that drove the largest mass extinction Earth had ever known, the question is, might not Earth be on its way, once again, to yet another (but this time anthropogenically devised) fossil fuel-driven mass extinction?

Today, though, it is modern humans, not Siberian traps, that are causing the spewing of carbon dioxide and doing so fourteen times faster per year; that are changing the survival-enabling climate architecture that came with and hung around during much of the Holocene and witnessed the rise of human civilizations; and that are changing the survival-driven architecture, and its survival-driven foundations and rules that had underpinned Earth-life for most of human existence. Could life as we know it survive going forward given that life nearly ended back then with fourteen times less CO_2 per year being disgorged by those Siberian traps than humans spew today?

How much of this underpinning architectural infrastructure, foundations, and rules can humans rearrange without endangering life as we know it? Is there anything our species can do now that might possibly undo the harm already done? There are those who think so. But if the death and devastation Hurricane Ian hurled across parts of Florida in September 2022 or, the unprecedented rainfall across parts of Spain in 2024, serves as an object lesson, there comes a time when starting over might well be the only option left. Humanity may well need to rethink its economic approach.

Why and from when did humans begin to change Earth's atmosphere and thereby its temperature? Was it to enhance science, technology, and innovative capabilities, or perhaps to facilitate the operation of weapons of war? Apparently, it was none of the above. In fact, neither Neolithic Revolution humans nor modern humans realized the atmospheric changes their socioeconomic efforts to eke out a living *outside* Earth's ecosystems caused. For the former it was farming and animal husbandry, aka agriculture, that became the initial source of anthropogenic CO_2 content changes to Earth atmosphere; and for the latter, it was an intensive form of agriculture and a society and economy powered by novel nonrenewable energy sources in the form of fossil fuels that as of May 2025 had driven atmospheric CO_2 concentrations to 430.7 ppm—the highest level since pre-industrial times.

What brought humans to this survival-threatening impasse, then, was nothing as sinister as the Cuban Missile Crisis, nor Putin's threat of the use of tactical nuclear weapons in Ukraine, but simply our efforts to eke out a living which we insist on doing *outside* Earth's ecosystems. The threat comes from humanity's effort to develop an economy whose goal was surplus, profits, and wealth accumulation, and whose outcome was GDP growth, rather than the initial goal of preserving ecosystems, biodiversity, and human life and their mutual survival as outcome.

It was our misguided efforts, too, that drove our species down a path that turned out to be diametrically opposed to the survival-driven lifeways our pre-agriculture, renewable-energy-using, hunter-gatherer forebears had pursued for all but the last 12,000 years of our species' existence. It was only a matter of time, then, before humanity's preferred socioeconomic approach, built on the exploitation of fellow humans, biodiversity extinction, and ecosystem destruction, would come crashing down as it did repeatedly over the last 400 generations, as nation after nation and empire after empire that comprised human civilization collapsed. But how did human economies change after adopting this new way to eke out a living *outside* Earth-life ecosystems?

For many the answer to that question is an "I don't care" or is still an unknown, and it still manages to escape some of the greatest minds and intellects to whom our species once looked or still looks for guidance. Hobbes, the English philosopher, and similar thinkers, for example, took a close look at these early human hunter-gatherer societies and their economies and came away unimpressed. He concluded life before civilization was "solitary, poor, nasty, brutish, and short." Yet, pre-agriculture hunter-gatherer humans managed to survive for most of our species' existence, some 290,000 years, without societal or economic collapse, without any of the societal and economic enhancements he might have considered essential, and before the dawn of governments or "civilization."

Regardless of what seventeenth-century or modern humans like Hobbes may have thought about pre-agriculture hunter-gatherer humans or their economies, our species might not have too long to wait or too far to go to find out because humans have earned the distinction of becoming the first Earth-life species intelligent or foolish enough (have your pick) to make the mistake of changing the initial *goal and outcome* of an Earth-life species society and economy, and then compounded this error by choosing to build their economies *outside* Earth-life ecosystems.

Considering what's known about the *outcome* of human societies and economies over the last 12,000 years, one would have thought given it was only after those Neolithic Revolution socioeconomic lifeways became *de rigueur* that most human societies and economies begun to collapse, that this would have been reason enough to start a socioeconomic stampede back to the survival-driven lifeways of our pre-agriculture hunter-gatherer forebears—after all, they survived collapse-free for 290,000 years. Yet that's not what happened during the last 400 generations to the present. Assuming humans do survive this potential fossil fuel-driven climate change extinction, can one imagine, 400 generations later, a return to fossil fuels as an energy source? I can and here's why.

Notwithstanding the 1987 Montreal Protocol to stop CFC-11 type substances from depleting the ozone layer, in 2018 researchers reported that levels of this banned chemical had been rising since 2012, and that's despite human understanding that without the ozone layer complex animal and human life would eventually cease to exist. Similarly, the threat of a fossil fuel-driven global warming extinction has not stopped fossil fuel-peddling multinational corporations, aka legal-persons, and their private equity and public relations buddies, from misrepresenting scientific facts and findings, and funding devious ways to continue mining and profiting from fossil fuels.

Fossil fuel companies may well have made the modern world, but the challenge they face now is to remake themselves. Can Big Oil be part of a post-carbon world? In both of these threats to human survival, it is pursuit, at all costs, of the profit-, wealth-, and GDP-growth-driven socioeconomic lifeway goal and outcome, rather than the original pre-agriculture hunter-gatherer socioeconomic goal and outcome of life and survival humans replaced, that makes these companies unable or unwilling to stop.

Fossil fuel companies, for example, have access to an obscure legal tool that could jeopardize worldwide efforts to protect Earth's climate, and they're starting to use it. Over the past 50 years, countries have signed thousands of treaties that protect foreign investors from government actions—a colonial-era leftover. These treaties are like contracts between national governments, meant to entice investors to bring in projects with the promise of local jobs and access to new technologies. But now, as countries try to phase out fossil fuels to slow climate change, these agreements leave them facing overwhelming legal and financial risks.

The result could cost countries that press ahead with those efforts billions of dollars and jeopardize the global effort to save humanity from the devasting effects of fossil fuel-driven global warming climate change, according to an October 2022 article in *The Conversation* entitled, "A secretive legal system lets fossil fuel investors sue countries over policies to keep oil and gas in the ground."

These treaties allow fossil fuel investors to sue governments for compensation in a process called investor-state dispute settlement, or ISDS. In short, investors could use ISDS clauses to demand compensation in response to government actions to limit fossil fuels, such as canceling pipelines and denying drilling permits as TC Energy, a Canadian company, has done in seeking more than US$15 billion in compensation for U.S. President Joe Biden's cancellation of the Keystone XL Pipeline. In a 2022 study in the journal *Science*, it's estimated that countries would face up to $340 billion in legal and financial risks for canceling fossil fuel projects that are subject to treaties with ISDS clauses and severely threaten the global green energy transition.

That's more than countries worldwide put into climate adaptation and mitigation measures combined in fiscal year 2019, and it doesn't include the risks of phasing out coal investments or canceling fossil-fuel infrastructure projects like pipelines and liquefied natural gas terminals. This means that money countries might otherwise spend to build a low-carbon future could instead go to the very legal-persons within industries that have knowingly been fueling climate change, severely jeopardizing countries' capacity to propel their green energy transition and thereby putting human survival in jeopardy.

And as bad as the above is, it gets even worse. "We've subsidized oil companies for a century. That's long enough," said President Obama, in his 2012 State of the Union address. Governments have routinely subsidized fossil fuel corporations. Globally, according to the IMF in a 2023 update, fossil fuel subsidies were $7 trillion in 2022, or 7.1 percent of GDP. The U.S. government, for example, has subsidized coal, oil, and gas for decades and gives away $20 billion in public money every year to fossil-fuel corporations. These subsidies come in the form of tax breaks, low-interest loans, and the failure to account for the true cost of fossil-fuel pollution.

According to Greenpeace, subsidies make it easier for fossil-fuel corporations to invest in lobbying operations that block efforts to tackle the climate crisis. Between 2000 and 2016, fossil-fuel interests spent nearly $2 billion to derail climate legislation. Think about that. Some of the largest and most profitable corporations in the world receive billions of dollars from the federal government, which allows them to go and spend billions of dollars influencing federal policy that aims to abandon fossil fuels.

How, then, can these and similar profit-seeking companies that comprise the engines of modern legal-person economies ever stop, if it is good for business to burn a hole in the ozone layer, or pump gigatons of greenhouse gases into the atmosphere—then sue countries that wish to stop doing so for billions of dollars, thus jeopardizing the transition to a carbon-free economy? Some ask, Can profit-seeking companies really help save the planet or rather, humanity? Others suggest this is possible only when doing so is rendered unprofitable and thus not good for business.

But from the perspective of that *initial, survival-driven human economy*, the type we have been discussing in this book, the correct economic goal and outcome should be neither profitability nor unprofitability but rather life and survival. Saving the planet, or rather humanity, will be possible only when, at a minimum, economic growth and profit-making of any kind ceases to be part of the goal and outcome of modern human or legal-person economies. Yet these seem to be the only kinds of economies modern humans apparently know how to build.

But it's important to remember that human economies haven't always been this way, nor did they pursue economic goals and outcomes such as surplus, profits, wealth accumulation, and GDP growth. It was Neolithic Revolution humans that changed Earth-life species and those early human economies from being a set of interwoven survival-driven lifeways that enabled eking out a living harmoniously with other Earth-life species *within* ecosystems. They abandoned those lifeways that evolved over time to preserve life and enable human, biodiversity, and ecosystem survival; that engendered economies that enabled our pre-agriculture hunter-gatherer forebears to survive for most of our species' existence.

They chose instead to build surplus- and wealth-creating economies *outside* Earth-life ecosystems that drove biodiversity extinction and destroyed all but a paltry 3 percent of its ecosystems. Returning the *goal and outcome* of a human economy to what it once was for most of human existence is one way humans now know certainly enabled life and survival—and it may well be the only way. Yet these are hardly the socioeconomic lifeways modern human economies and their substitutes, or replacements legal-person economies, are pursuing.

It was these initial changes in human socioeconomic lifeways, likely begun with Neolithic Revolution humans, that today not only generate massive surplus, profits, wealth accumulation and GDP growth but in the process have also triggered what's beginning to look like an unscheduled change in the planet's temperature, to what may well turn out to be a potential climate transition to another steady-state phase in Earth's temperature cycles—from a Coolhouse Earth to, potentially, a Hothouse Earth with all of human history sandwiched in between.

By now, humans shouldn't still be asking, they should know, what aspects of those pre-agriculture hunter-gatherer human economies were changed when Neolithic Revolution humans abandoned that initial *survival-driven* socioeconomic *goal* and *outcome* that may well have been the way human economies were intended to function—a goal and outcome that ensured their life and survival. Nor should humans still claim to not know the difference between *eking out a living inside rather than outside* Earth-life ecosystems. Nor should we fail to understand the consequences that have resulted from driving most Earth-life species to extinction and 97 percent of their ecosystems to destruction, versus coexisting with them as pre-agriculture hunter-gatherer humans did, surviving for millennia.

By now, too, modern humans should understand they will not survive unless they grasp why and how human life and survival are intertwined with and codependent upon the life and survival of Earth's biodiversity and ecosystems, and that humanity will cease to exist if we continue to succeed in driving the residue of Earth-life species to extinction and the remainder of its ecosystems to destruction.

Some nations and world organizations are at least beginning to get it. Some nations are talking about abandoning the GDP growth-driven economy for wellbeing economies, which argues that a new way of developing economies around the well-being of people and planet is not only possible but is our most urgent task. Some global organizations, too, the United Nations in particular, support the pursuit of Sustainable Development Goals, a universal call to action to end poverty, protect the planet, and ensure that by 2030 all people enjoy peace and prosperity.

But these stated socioeconomic goals and intended outcomes, though noteworthy, are hardly what is required and are hardly anything like the goal and outcome of those early survival-driven human economies that enabled pre-agriculture humans to survive collapse-free for most of humanity's existence. That goal and that outcome, you recall, was life and survival, respectively. The goal was simply to facilitate and ensure Earth-species life and human life as they mutually and co-dependently went about the tasks of eking out a living and thereby building economies *within* ecosystems; and doing so in a way that would result in their mutual survival—the desired outcome.

In either case, those urging these new types of economies or socioeconomic lifeways likely hope their approach will at least improve the quality of life and even enable humanity to survive and thus slow, if not stop, the current rapid slide toward a potential global warming-driven socioeconomic collapse, or worse, a global warming-driven mass extinction. But to solve the problems modern human economies, and the legal-person economies that are replacing them, have created, they should at least know the initial goal and outcome hunter-gatherer human economies pursued, and why, how, and what changed after Neolithic humans went from foraging to farming; from sharing to hoarding; from eking out a living *inside* to doing so *outside* those ecosystems; and from living in small mobile bands to dwelling with farm animals in large and often overpopulated, sedentary, towns and cities that eventually followed the Neolithic Revolution.

But given their goal and purpose, it's clear that neither approach grasps what it might take to return to anything resembling that initial survival-driven goal and outcome human economies seem to have evolved to fulfill. They were clearly a deliberate effort to ensure that these early economies, whether human or Earth-life species, would result in a bond of mutual preservation and coexistence. A bond that would enable both life and the survival of ecosystems, biodiversity, and humanity.

These emerging versions of modern human and legal-person economies must therefore choose one of these two very different economic goals and outcomes for humanity—there is simply nothing in between. There is just no way to maintain economies whose goal is not life but surplus and profits, and whose outcome is not human, biodiversity, and ecosystem survival, but wealth accumulation. This is true even if more of that surplus/profit and wealth will be dedicated to human, biodiversity, and ecosystem preservation, even if endless GDP growth would no longer be the desired outcome, and even if advocates hope thereby to attain anything resembling that original goal and outcome of pre-agriculture human economies—i.e., ecosystem, biodiversity, and human life and survival. There is simply no way to ensure life and survival as goal and outcome, respectively, from economies whose actual goal remains surplus and profits and whose actual outcome remains wealth accumulation, regardless of how one rebrands them—whether as wellbeing economies or Sustainable Development Goals.

Going from modern economies back to survival-driven economies, if that were possible, would mean a reversal of most of the damage humans have done to Earth's ecosystems, with now just 3 percent left intact; a restoration of Earth's biodiversity, most of which has already been driven to extinction; and a return to the egalitarian, sharing and caring socioeconomic lifeways of our pre-agriculture hunter-gatherer forebears, or something like it. But even if any of this was possible, given that it took humans 400 generations to get from hunter-gatherer waterhole economies to modern ones, it is doubtful, given the rapid increase in global warming climate change, and the devastation it has already begun to unleash upon humanity, that there would be enough time for such efforts to begin to bear fruit even if it were possible to unwind some or all of the damage humans have done in the last 12,000 years.

Humans will essentially be starting afresh. Moreover, even if any of that were possible, modern humans will have to become acquainted with those survival-driven socioeconomic lifeways we encountered earlier, or develop something similar, that enabled those pre-agriculture human economies to last, collapse-free, for most of our species' existence. But alas! None of that seems to be of interest today, let alone in sight.

Unfortunately, though, notwithstanding the misleading views held of these early human economies by Hobbes and friends, referred to earlier, there are some who understand that history differently, including James Suzman's *Affluence Without Abundance*: *The Disappearing World of the Bushmen,*" Marshall Sahlins' "Stone Age Economics," and Richard Manning's *Against the Grain,* to name a few. Most, though, just don't seem to have much interest in really understanding and learning from what enabled those early human economies. Nor in discovering what they must have been like, given they were able to survive for most of human existence. Nor do they seem interested in understanding the survival-driven Earth-life architecture, foundations, and lifeway customs they apparently followed, to begin to grasp just how much modern human economies and accompanying legal-person economies would need to change. There seems to be little interest, even if it were possible, in starting all over in the hope modern humans might just get it right a second time.

There are some, though, who have concluded that to survive, humans will need an opportunity to start over. They envision and advocate for human migration to an Earth 2.0. But does the re-start humanity needs require migrating to a new planet, or instead, a return to the pre-agriculture economic goals and outcome of life and survival on planet Earth? After all, if humans successfully lived this way for most of our existence, might there not be the latent ability to do so once again?

But omitting for the moment how humans might get there, if there were an Earth 2.0, some, such as the late Stephen Hawking, assert that "humans must colonize another planet in 100 years or face extinction." Others think an Earth 2.0, perhaps such as Kepler-452b, once regarded as the most Earth-like planet ever discovered, or Kepler 186f—and there will be others—might well offer humans another shot at getting this right.

But suppose for a moment that human migration to an Earth 2.0 were possible. Given current economic thinking, the goal and outcome that would be needed to finance such a venture, and the payback that will be sought from any envisioned extraterrestrial economic development, such as mining asteroids, the moon, Mars, and other planets for rare minerals and related resources, it is doubtful that any surviving human civilization would turn out differently without an *a priori* major change in its socio-economic goals and outcome. Ultimately, humans will have to abandon surplus, profits, wealth accumulation, and GDP growth, and re-adopt the survival-driven goals of life and survival it once knew, if humanity and any native life-forms and their ecosystems are to have a chance of surviving.

Yet there seems to exist a tacit assumption that somehow everything will turn out all right; that modern humans are somehow different, and with our current and emerging technologies we would be able to survive the worst, perhaps even a potential anthropogenic mass extinction. Why? Because unlike the dinosaurs, humans are already preparing to shoot down or deflect errant asteroids. Humans are an innovative species, we say, and will adapt and remediate as needed to survive. But those who think this way are ignoring an essential fact—Earth is not a human innovation. And, while humans have discovered plenty about the planet, much of the functioning of its mechanisms (like how GHG emissions have changed global climate) remains mostly unknown and beyond humans' ability to control.

Not only did humans not invent the Earth, but clearly, we have learned very little about its survival-driven Earth-life-system architecture; its life-enabling foundations; the lifeway rules that evolved to establish Earth-life and human economies with their built-in interdependence, and mutually codependent goal of life with an outcome of survival. Despite our much-acclaimed ingenuity and intelligence, humans know of no way to change Earth's architecture, its foundations, or its survival-driven rules that enabled all Earth-life, including humanity, to survive for millennia.

And yes, pre-agriculture, hunter-gatherer humans survived the Pleistocene-Holocene ice age transition while numerous other human species went extinct, not because of any Stone Age technology or invention, but mainly because some were in the right place at the right time, such as the southern tip of Africa. And, until recently, humans have managed to, or have been fortunate enough to, remain just barely within seemingly key operating planetary boundaries that enable and sustain life, and have apparently benefitted from seemingly very generous zones of safety even when we have inadvertently ventured beyond these rules and boundaries.

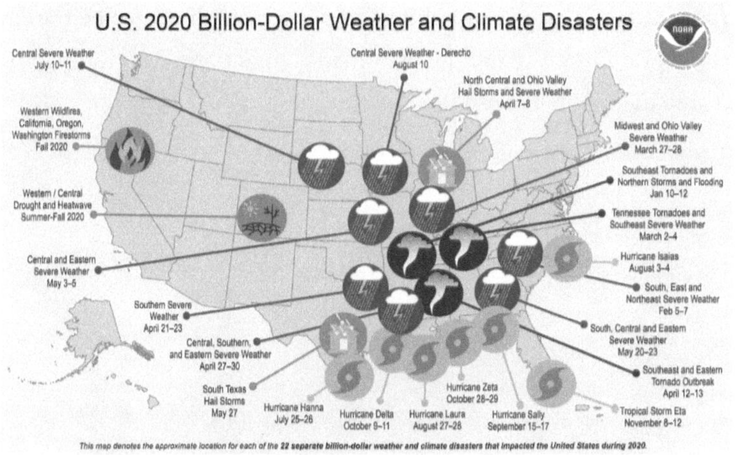

Figure 10-3. U.S. 2020 billion-dollar weather and climate disasters.

This map denotes the approximate location for each of the 22 separate billion-dollar weather and climate disasters that impacted the United States during 2020. (Source: NOAA's National Centers for NCEI)

It would seem that only after our determined effort to fill the Earth well-nigh beyond its carrying capacity with innumerable numbers of our species—having ravaged most of its ecosystems to feed them, driven innumerable numbers of its biodiversity to extinction to make room for yet more agricultural and industrial expansion, and filled its atmosphere with excessive volumes of fossil fuels for hundreds of years—that humans began to experience noticeably visible and increasingly life-threatening responses from the planet in the form of rapidly increasing global warming fossil-fuel-driven climate change, which has begun to engender a noticeable increase in billion-dollar disasters (Figure 10-3).

"Humans have just now begun to realize," according to the United Nations and the Red Cross, "that by the year 2100, extreme heat events will make parts of Asia and Africa uninhabitable for up to 600 million people." And by mid-century, nearly "two-thirds of Americans will experience perilous heat waves, (Figure 10-4) with some regions in the South expected to endure more than 70 consecutive days over 100 degrees," according to an August 2022 *Washington Post* article. Humans are just beginning to realize, too, that some Earth-life systems appear to no longer function the way they did for centuries during most of the Holocene, which witnessed the emergence of agriculture and the rise of human civilizations. And humans don't seem able to do much about it.

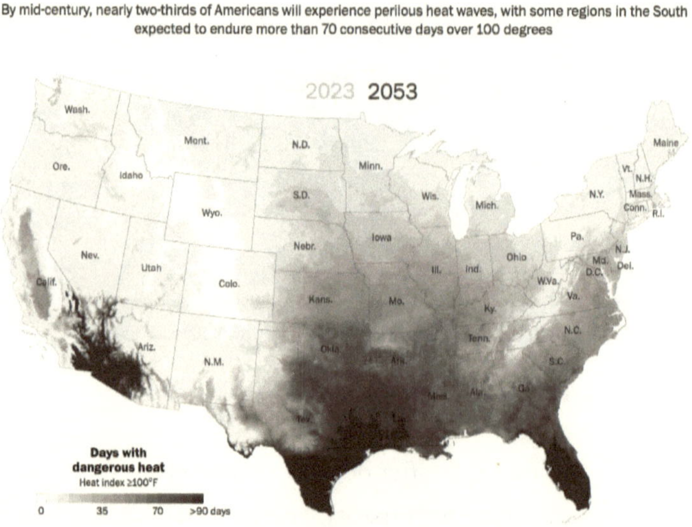

Figure 10-4. More dangerous heat waves are on the way. See the impact by state.
(Source: Washington Post*)*

Because of changes made to Earth's ecosystems, biodiversity, biosphere, oceans, and atmosphere, it would seem this once-survival-driven architecture, its foundations, and lifeway-choreographing rules that enabled human socioeconomic survival for millennia have begun to unravel in ways and at a pace few would have anticipated. In just 400 generations spent building new socioeconomic systems and civilizations outside Earth-life ecosystems in pursuit of surplus/profits, wealth accumulation, and endless GDP growth, humans appear to have harmed Earth-life's enabling and support mechanisms to such an extent that they may no longer be capable of supporting ecosystems, biodiversity, and human economies the way they once did.

Yet these changes don't seem to stir the level of worldwide awareness and alarm one might have expected given the resulting calamities these caused and are still causing—not nearly the level of alarm that talk of a potential nuclear Armageddon appears to have stirred up. Indeed, humans seem more scared of a potential nuclear Armageddon than the potential for a repeat of a Great Dying fossil fuel-driven mass extinction.

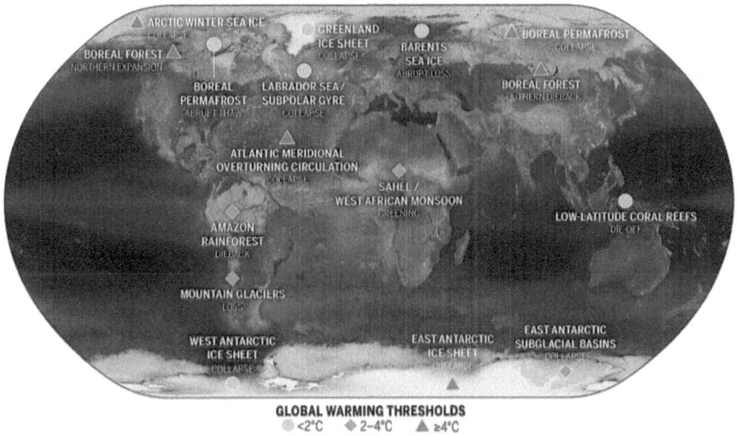

Figure 10-5. Exceeding 1.5°C global warming could trigger multiple climate tipping points.

The location of climate tipping elements in the cryosphere (blue), biosphere (green), and ocean/atmosphere (orange), and global warming levels at which their tipping points will likely be triggered. Pins are colored according to the central global warming threshold estimate being below 2°C, i.e., within the Paris Agreement range (light orange, circles); between 2 and 4°C, i.e., accessible with current policies (orange, diamonds); and 4°C and above (red, triangles). (Source: Science & AAAS

The fact that the United Nations Secretary-General called global temperatures back in 2021 "the make it or break it year" for climate action, and that the past seven years have been the hottest in recorded history and were among the highest ever observed—with 25 countries setting new annual records, according to scientists from NASA, NOAA, and Berkeley Earth—didn't seem to have stirred nearly the level of alarm as when President Biden said that for the "first time since the Cuban Missile Crisis, we have the direct threat of the use of a nuclear weapon if in fact things continue down the path they are going" (Reuters, 2022). Nor did the fact that, scientists say, human failure to slow warming will set off climate "tipping points" that occur when change in large parts of the climate system—known as tipping elements—become self-perpetuating beyond a warming threshold and may lead to abrupt, irreversible, and dangerous impacts with serious implications for humanity—yet, this too is being sloughed off just as cavalierly.

But again, when Biden went on to say: "We have not faced the prospect of Armageddon since Kennedy and the Cuban Missile Crisis (AP, 2022) and "I don't think there's any such thing as the ability to easily (use) a tactical nuclear weapon and not end up with Armageddon" (AP, 2022), *those* statements got some attention. He was referring to the potential global destruction that can result from a global nuclear war. And, as bad and scary and awful as that could no doubt become, global warming is an existential threat humans must doubtless fear even more but are doing not nearly enough to confront. It is a threat humans should worry about even more, one that could turn out to be even worse, if that is possible, than the nuclear Armageddon we also fear. It is a greenhouse gas-driven global warming climate change mass extinction—perhaps worse than the "Great Dying."

This time around, though, should there be another fossil fuel-driven mass extinction, it wouldn't have been caused by those Siberian Traps that 252 million years ago drove that global warming mass extinction—The Great Dying—though it may well once again be caused by fossil fuels, and may yet become the mother of all Armageddons. Nor would it have been caused by Putin, nor Siberian Traps, but by all humanity—an anthropogenic climate change-driven mass extinction. So, while many worry about Putin's potential Armageddon, and rightly so, not nearly as many seem as worried that it is each one of us, including Putin, that may well be individually contributing to something even worse than Armageddon—to yet another mass extinction—and we won't even need a war or nuclear weapons to do so, just our carbon footprint. Yes, but can you believe it?

It is building our human and legal-person economies, not nuclear weapons, that has landed humanity in this fossil fuel-driven global warming predicament. Indeed, all GHG emissions are produced within some sector of the economy. As James Carville, a U.S. political consultant, is known to have said in 1992, "It's the economy, stupid." And climate change might just be getting ready to destroy both us and our economies.

Unfortunately, none of the socioeconomic lifeways and methods humans developed during the millennia that spanned the Holocene Epoch, during which most of human civilization arose, would be able to extricate humanity from where it has now landed in the twenty-first century, 12,000 years later. Many have begun to realize, too, that regardless of our technologies, innovations, and scientific abilities, the damage we have done to the Earth system might be so great that few if any of these would likely be capable of undoing that damage to the planet, its ecosystems and biodiversity, or would be able to do so in time to make a difference. Time, unfortunately, is not on our side.

Yes, indeed, humans might finally get around to inventing or discovering new and novel renewable energy sources such as wind and solar, and perhaps even get around to building a carbon neutral or carbon-free economy with fusion energy. But it's entirely possible that by the time we get there, the intensifying global warming-driven social, economic, and political issues that would have arisen in the interim from the GHGs we had already hoisted into the atmosphere would have rendered them too little, too late.

Scientists warn that climate change has already destabilized the Earth's poles, putting the rest of the planet in peril. New research shows how rising temperatures have irreversibly altered both the Arctic and Antarctic, and the ripple effects will be felt around the globe. Some scientists think the Arctic may well be a way to look into the future of how climate will change the planet. According to the Arctic Report Card, "Temperatures in the Arctic are rising twice as fast as the global average and small changes in temperature can have huge effects in a region that is dominated by ice." According to a study published in *Nature Geoscience*, the Thwaites ice shelf is among glaciers in Antarctica that are now shedding ice faster than they have at any point in the past 5,500 years and may well collapse within the next three to five years, unleashing a river of ice that could raise sea levels initially by 2-3 feet, a dramatic rise.

By the time humans would have stopped pumping even more gigatons of GHGs into the atmosphere, managed to stop the destruction of Earth's remaining ecosystems, and halted the extinction of what's left of its biodiversity, the remaining habitable surface of the planet would have begun to become uninhabitable or incapable of supporting life to the extent it does now. Humans may soon become perplexed by inflation, failing supply chains, shrinking food availability and costly supplies, and may be besieged by drought and dwindling water supplies even as remaining habitable regions begin to be overwhelmed by millions of climate change and economic refugees.

Imagine how different life on Earth would have played out for humanity had that Neolithic Revolution not happened. How different would life be today, if instead of abandoning foraging for farming—and adopting agriculture that would begin and for millennia continue to enable the destruction of most of Earth's ecosystems and biodiversity, the very foundations of all Earth-life and human economies—humans had chosen instead to continue those survival-driven lifeways that enabled human societies and economies to survive without collapse for all but the last 12,000 years of our species' existence? Now, in the twenty-first century, instead of having to contemplate a potential anthropogenic fossil-fuel-driven mass extinction, the last 400 generations could well have been the most productive of our species' history. We could have invented and innovated ways that support life and survival rather than what we have today, that with hindsight, appear more capable of enabling our extinction than our survival.

What may have been the purpose of foraging, for example, that foundational survival-driven lifeway that all Earth-life species, except most humans, still follow? Can you imagine a mobile economy? This pure hunter-gatherer way of life is now largely extinguished, pushed out by agriculture, industry, and modern lifeways generally. But throughout much of the last half of the twentieth century, anthropologists could find and study hunter-gatherers who had been very little affected by modern ways. As descendants of our hunter-gatherer forebears, these humans still live mostly that way.

Examples of such groups include the Ju/'hoansi (also called the !Kung, of Africa's Kalahari Desert), Hadza (Tanzanian rain forest), Mbuti (Congo's Ituri Forest), Aka (rain forests in Central African Republic and Congo), Efé (Congo's Ituri Forest), Batek (Peninsular Malaysia), Agta (Luzon, Philippines), Nayaka (South India), Aché (Eastern Paraguay), Parakanã (Brazil's Amazon basin), and Yiwara (the Australian desert).

But just how did becoming sedentary food-producing societies and economies change the way humans economies have evolved? What impact did this have on ecosystems, biodiversity, humanity, and the desired economic goal and outcome of life and survival for all? Foraging societies and economies are mobile and for 290,000 years, foraging was *de rigueur*. Such societies and their economies would have borne scant resemblance to what societies and economies look and feel like today. Mobility brought with it numerous constraints that would have rendered modern sedentary lifeways impossible. Modern societies and economies have evolved around fixed locations to which humans have assigned specific meanings that could engender different actions. Homes, for example, are not thought of as schools or offices, even though during the Covid-19 pandemic home schooling and working from home became commonplace.

The fundamental concept of a fixed geographic location, around which so many aspects of modern life are organized and based or might be associated—a particular person, address, place, village, town, city, state, or nation—might not have become the default way around which modern human societies and economies are organized. There might have been no such place as the White House, or the Empire State Building. Without sedentary societies, the concept of getting driving directions to a particular address would probably not make sense or would mean something else entirely. Going home, to work, or to school would have meant going to a different geolocation most times as the concept of a street address may not have developed or may have meant something else entirely.

The concept of property and business address associated with a particular plot of land—which is so fundamental to how humans locate and find one another and how we associate real estate ownership and therefore a particular form of generational wealth—might not have happened, and certainly not by accident. Real estate tycoons such as Donald Trump, now president of the USA, would never have existed in an egalitarian socioeconomic system to begin with. In fact, as noted previously, no one Domesticated, Owned, Managed, or Controlled anything.

Here, then, was one of those foundational survival-driven lifeways early humans practiced that enabled Earth-life species, ecosystems, and human survival for millennia. Hunter-gatherer humans were never owned, nor did they control locations or assets, particularly such as might be needed by other species and other humans such as waterholes, the sun, a mountain range, or particularly fertile corners of a savanna, sources of food that could have been found by other foraging species. Hence there was no food production—just sharing ecosystem resources that were meant to be freely available to all. Every Earth-life species had the right of access to any food source or resource if it was not being used by another species—such as a den or nest. Imagine how little inequality would exist among humans if the means for life and survival could not be owned, commandeered, and controlled by others. For example, the concept of NIMBY (not in my backyard) would not have existed—there would have been, of course, no backyards.

Imagine too, if foraging and sharing rather than owning and hoarding those things fundamental to life and survival were the default socioeconomic lifeway to earn a living. Would homelessness and poverty be the socioeconomic problems they are across the world and in many wealthy U.S. cities? About 9.2 percent of the world, or 689 million people, lives in extreme poverty on less than $1.90 a day, according to the World Bank. By forbidding ownership and the exclusivity that comes with it, those early human economies would not have encountered the numerous issues that arise due to inequality and that pervade and plague modern human societies and economies.

If humans could no longer own and hoard but must instead share the necessities for life and survival, the world would indeed be a very different place, and humanity would once more begin to experience some of the quality of life that enabled the societies and economies of our hunter-gatherer forebears to survive collapse-free for millennia. Instead, today, most humans are living in poverty, according to World Vision, and poverty means not being able to afford a doctor or medical treatment. It means no electricity, limited shelter, and often little or no food on the table. For young children, improper nutrition can mean stunting and wasting that permanently impact their development. In impoverished countries where many people lack access to clean water and sanitation, poverty means the spread of preventable diseases and the unnecessary death of children.

But there was more to mobility than simply not living in a fixed location for very long periods as Neolithic humans did and human still do today. Mobile hunter-gatherers, as we have seen, foraged rather than farmed. That means they would not have cleared and disturbed the soil or felled trees to plant crops and displace or destroy the biodiversity species with habitats in the area. Thus, humans began the destruction of Earth's ecosystems and the extinction of innumerable Earth-life species. Humanity has used 50 percent of the world's habitable land and one-third of the world's forests for agriculture. Today only 3 percent of the Earth's ecosystems are left intact.

Mobility, then, was essential to both foraging and to the preservation of Earth's ecosystems and biodiversity species. It rendered unnecessary the clearing of land to farm, grow food, graze cattle, build roads, and thereby destroy two of the key components of that *Evolutionary Triad of Life* upon which Earth-life species economies and human economies would depend for life and survival. Earlier, we saw how both biodiversity survival and human survival were not only dependent on each other's survival but together depended on the survival of ecosystems as well. By destroying all but 3 percent of Earth's ecosystems and most of its biodiversity, then, modern humans may have essentially placed in jeopardy any hope we might have had of survival.

Besides enabling foraging and preventing the destruction of Earth's ecosystems and biodiversity—as indispensable as these are to human survival—there was more to those hunter-gatherer mobile socioeconomic lifeways. Being mobile served as a control mechanism and restraint on human population growth. The reason why for the first 290,000 years of human existence human population until about 10,000 BCE hovered around one million and never exceeded 15 million (Our World in Data - Population Growth), was mainly due to low birth rates caused by mobility-driven-delayed weaning that did not occur until children were about four years old. This had the impact, as seen earlier, of keeping those early hunter-gatherer populations relatively low and stable. This small near-constant population also had the effect of reducing the number of mouths to be fed and thereby provided the added benefit of reducing ecosystem and biodiversity wear and tear.

Table 10-1. Planetary boundaries, 2025

Earth-system process	Control variable[1][9]	Boundary value in 2025	"Current" value (i.e. for the year provided in the source)	Boundary now exceeded beyond the 2025 values? (based on "current" value)	Preindustrial Holocene base value
1. Climate Change	Atmospheric carbon dioxide concentration (ppm by volume)[12] *See also: Tipping point (climatology)*	350 ppm	423 ppm	yes	280
	Total anthropogenic radiative forcing at top-of-atmosphere (W/m^2) since the start of the industrial revolution (~1750)	+1 Wm^{-2}	+2.97 Wm-2	yes	0
2. Change in Biosphere Integrity[9]	*Genetic diversity:* Extinction rate measured as E/MSY (extinctions per million species-years)	<10 E/MSY but with an aspirational goal of ca. 1 E/MSY (assumed background rate of extinction loss)	>100 E/MSY	yes	1 E/MSY
	Functional diversity: energy available to ecosystems (NPP[a 1]) (% HANPP[a 2])	HANPP (in billion tonnes of C year−1) <10% of preindustrial Holocene NPP, i.e., >90% remaining for supporting biosphere function	30% HANPP	yes	1.9% (2σ variability of preindustrial Holocene century-mean NPP)
3. Land System Change	Part of forests rested intact (percent)[7]	*75 % from all forests including 85 % from* Boreal forest and Tropical forests, 50 % from Temperate forests	*Global:* 59%	yes	0
4. Freshwater Change	Blue water: human induced disturbance of blue water flow	Upper limit (95th percentile) of global land area with deviations greater than during preindustrial, Blue water: 12.9%	22.6%	yes	9.4%
	Green water: human induced disturbance of water available to plants (% land area with deviations from preindustrial variability)	12.4%	22.0%	yes	9.8%
5. Modification of Biogeochemical Flows	Phosphate global: P flow from freshwater systems into the ocean; regional: P flow from fertilizers to erodible soils (Tg of P year^{-1})	*Global:* 11 Tg of P year^{-1}; *regional:* 6.2 Tg of P year^{-1} mined and applied to erodible (agricultural) soils.	*Global:* 4.4 Tg of P year^{-1}; *regional:* 18.2 Tg of P year^{-1}	yes	0
	Nitrogen global: industrial and intentional fixation of N (Tg of N year^{-1})	62 Tg year^{-1}	165 Tg year-1	yes	0
6. Ocean Acidification	Global mean saturation state of calcium carbonate in surface seawater (omega units)	2.86	2.84	yes	3.44
7. Increase in Atmospheric Aerosol Loading	Interhemispheric difference in AOD (Aerosol Optical Depth)	0.1 (mean annual interhemispheric difference)	0.063	no	0.03
8. Stratospheric Ozone Depletion	Stratospheric ozone concentration (Dobson units)	277	285.7	no	290
9. Introduction of Novel Entities	Percentage of synthetic chemicals released to the environment without adequate safety testing	0	>0 (transgressed)	yes	0

1. ^ Natural Primary Production
2. ^ Human Appropriation of Natural Primary Production

(Source: Stockholm Resilience Centre; Credit: Johan Rockström et al - Wikipedia)

But as soon as humans began to become sedentary starting some 12,000 years ago, that built-in population growth control mechanism began to vanish. Human population thereafter grew rapidly, and in about 10,000 years has surpassed eight billion, and is approaching ten billion, the estimated carrying capacity of the Earth. It is this rapid population growth that occurred over the last 10,000 years, and the effort to grow its economies to keep up with this growth, that has driven humanity beyond six of those nine (so far) key Planetary Boundaries shown in Table 10-1. These are areas vital to life, such as the amount of GHGs humans have emitted into the atmosphere and the global warming-driven climate change we have begun to experience in response.

Was there an *a priori* biological way humans were expected to organize themselves to survive? Were humans intended to live in huge sedentary agricultural communities? Doesn't surviving collapse-free for more than 97 percent of its existence in small, mobile, foraging, sharing groups that preserved and shared Earth's ecosystems with all other Earth-life species suggest an answer? Now, becoming the most populous nation in the world has become "a thing"—India just overcame China to become the most populous nation on Earth. Is such population growth really a *cause célèbre*?

As sedentation and agricultural-based socioeconomic lifeways became the norm, humans began dwelling in increasingly large communities—towns, cities, and eventually nations—and these gradually began to replace those survival-driven, pre-agriculture, socioeconomic lifeways, those small, mobile, foraging, hunter-gatherer bands, the only known way humanity organized and lived as a species for 290,000 years of its existence within Earth's ecosystems, and in harmony with its biodiversity before the Neolithic Revolution.

This transition must have been as disruptive, disconcerting, and dysfunctional as the reshuffling of the mobile hunter-gathering lifeways of our species. Yet not many humans today seem to see this socioeconomic transition humans have endured, and are still enduring, as not only biologically strange and disruptive but perhaps even unnatural to the lifeways of any species, particularly after 290,000 years of living and organizing to survive in a very different way: that mobile, foraging, sharing, living-in-small-bands way, the hunter-gatherer way. Indeed, if there is a way for humanity to organize itself that best enables its survival, pre-agriculture hunter-gatherer humans may well have found it.

Yet not many humans appear to ponder or consider just how disruptive this socioeconomic lifeway change from mobile foraging in small egalitarian bands to living with farm animals in cramped quarters within large sedentary populations in farming towns and cities had to have been—this was a lot more than a mere reorganization to produce food. Humans might never have been intended to live and survive in highly populated sedentary towns and cities as we do today. This was a transition that humanity, but for its intelligence, might not have endured nor emerged from intact.

How much does the way a species is organized to eke out a living within ecosystems impact its ability to survive? What are the consequences that result from the kinds of transitions such as humanity has experienced from the Neolithic Revolution through today? Consider, for example, the sociopolitical issues that have arisen from the use of the internet and social media technologies as means of communicating among known small groups as well as across and between vast unknown populations. It is well-nigh impossible to spread false news and/or manipulate communications within small bands of 20-50 people where everyone knows everyone else.

There are socioeconomic and political problems that are unique to and emerge within large populations that would never have occurred within those small egalitarian bands. Would the U.S. have experienced the spread of fake news and propagation of hate speech it often experiences? But for misinformation would the riots that occurred in the UK over the death of three small girls have happened? These are just a couple of examples. When one thinks about what else would have been different one can begin to see, perhaps, why our pre-agriculture hunter-gatherer forebears survived without collapse for most of our species' existence.

There was yet, however, another aspect to those survival-driven socioeconomic lifeways our pre-agriculture hunter-gatherer forebears followed that Neolithic and modern humans abandoned—their socioeconomic lifeways were egalitarian. While mobility constrained their population growth, and foraging and sharing in harmony with biodiversity within ecosystems minimized their overuse, thereby enabling their preservation and mutual survival, it was their egalitarian lifeways that kept them on the survival straight and narrow to a collapse-free civilization for most of humanity's existence.

According to Dr. Peter Gray in his paper, "How Hunter-Gatherers Maintained Their Egalitarian Ways,"

> *During the 20th century, anthropologists discovered and studied dozens of different hunter-gatherer societies, in various remote parts of the world, who had been nearly untouched by modern influences. Wherever they were found—in Africa, Asia, South America, or elsewhere; in deserts or in jungles—these societies had many characteristics in common. They lived in small bands, of about 20 to 50 persons (including children) per band, who moved from camp to camp within a relatively circumscribed area to follow the available game and edible vegetation. The people had friends and relatives in neighboring bands and maintained peaceful relationships with neighboring bands. Warfare was unknown to most of these societies, and where it was known it was the result of interactions with warlike groups of people who were not hunter-gatherers. In each of these societies, the dominant cultural ethos was one that emphasized individual autonomy, non-directive childrearing methods, nonviolence, sharing, cooperation, and consensual decision-making. Their core value, which underlay all of the rest, was that of the equality of individuals.*

Continuing, Dr. Gray claimed:

> *Hunter-Gatherers also practiced a system of "reverse dominance" that prevented anyone from assuming power over others. These so-called 'leveling mechanisms' were used to keep the high and mighty from getting too, well, high and mighty or to pull them back down when they nonetheless manage to scale untenable heights. They also maintained equality by nurturing the playful side of their human nature, and play promotes equality; and maintained their ethos of equality through their childrearing practices, which engendered feelings of trust and acceptance in each new generation.*

Egalitarianism, according to the Encyclopedia Britannica, is often contrasted with hierarchy, the classification of people according to ability, economic power, social status, or other factors. While early human societies were often quite egalitarian, some scholars have proposed that the advent of agriculture and the consequent accumulation of wealth may have encouraged the development of hierarchical societies. In an egalitarian society, all are considered equal, regardless of gender, race, religion, or age. There are no hierarchies in an egalitarian society as all are relatively equal and have equal access to income and wealth or their equivalents.

Being egalitarian, then, enabled them to restrain the ambition and greed that would accompany the transition from foraging to farming that has wrecked most subsequent agrarian-based social, economic, and political systems to this day. But how was humanity going to maintain those egalitarian lifeways so essential to their survival when those small bands were being replaced by hordes of people that soon crowded those agrarian towns and cities? They obviously couldn't and didn't. It's clear, and the record shows, that these pre-agriculture egalitarian hunter-gatherer socioeconomic lifeways survived mostly when and where humans continued to organize their communities as small, mobile, foraging, and sharing bands—and some, as noted above, still do today. The egalitarian lifeways soon disappeared as the socioeconomic lifeways of farming, hoarding, and sedentarism took root, and with them, humanity's chance of returning to lifeways that once enabled our species to thrive and survive collapse-free.

What, then, were those survival-driven lifeways upon which pre-agriculture hunter-gatherer societies and economies were built; that enabled their survival for 290,000 years with neither economic nor civilization collapse; and that did not provoke an extinction-threatening Earth-system response like climate change? These were lifeways those Neolithic and subsequent human societies and economies abandoned, and consequently collapsed innumerable times in less than 12,000 years. By now you no doubt know the answer, and yes, it's as James Carville famously said: "It's the economy, stupid."

One resource our pre-agriculture hunter-gatherer forbears ensured was in the vicinity of every camp was a source of water, often a waterhole.

This was an indispensable resource they had to share with predator and prey alike and they thereby learned to build economies that catered to the needs of all within the camp. Their economies were informed by such lifeways that taught them how to coexist and share Earth's resources even as they eked out a living within its ecosystems; how to live in harmony with its biodiversity whether predator or prey; and how to build together their economies and societies without destroying themselves or Earth's ecosystems. And that's what enabled ecosystems, biodiversity, and human survival for most of the 300,000 years of humanity's existence. Could the example of a socioeconomic path to life and survival our forebears shared with Neolithic and subsequent humans have been any simpler?

Their Waterhole Economies were survival-driven economies and turned out to be the only human economies that never collapsed, nor placed humanity at risk of extinction. Imagine that!

AFTERWORD

When humans began abandoning their mobile foraging waterhole economies for sedentary farming ones 10-12Kyrs ago, they had no idea they would end up changing not only their economies but Earth's biogeochemical cycles as well. Changes that would drive a slow buildup of GHGs (global greenhouse gases: CO_2, CH_4) that, over millennia, would level-off around 280 ppm. Then with the discovery and use of fossil fuels, GHG buildup would accelerate past 423.93 ppm, forcing a continuous increase in global temperature.

But what happens when GHGs build up faster than Earth can recycle? Mass extinctions are what happens. Indeed, all but one of Earth's mass extinctions were greenhouse gas mass extinctions and were driven by millennial buildup of GHGs in the planet's atmosphere. Humans then, may well become the first Earth-life species to cause a greenhouse gas mass extinction. By using fossil fuels to power its economies, humanity is disrupting Earth's biogeochemical cycles that enable the planet's survival. Modern human economies then, may well have become drivers of Earth's next mass extinction.

GLOSSARY

Adaptation

The changes Earth-life species or humans might make to devices or mechanisms because of new applications or situations. Evolutionary species often adapt to changing habitats or migrate to survive. Failure to adapt or migrate in the face of life-threatening conditions will result in extinction. Evolutionary survival-driven adaptations emerge to preserve habitats and biodiversity survival.

AI (Artificial Intelligence)

An umbrella term for a vast array of technologies—AI has no single definition. According to Google, "AI is a field of science concerned with building computers and machines that can reason, learn, and act in such a way that would normally require human intelligence or that involves data whose scale exceeds what humans can analyze. AI is a broad field that encompasses many different disciplines, including computer science, data analytics and statistics, hardware and software engineering, linguistics, neuroscience, and even philosophy and psychology."

Artificial intelligence is already altering the world and raising important questions for society, the economy, governance, and even human survival. Humanity is rightly concerned about whether there can be "human control" of "Super-Human Intelligent Machine AI" that could eventually emerge and replace humans.

Anthropocene

A proposed epoch that defines Earth's most recent geologic period as being human-influenced (anthropogenic), based on overwhelming global evidence that atmospheric, geologic, hydrologic, biosphere and other Earth system processes are now altered by humans.

Anthropogenic

Consequences caused by humans or their activities, e.g., anthropogenic climate change, which refers to human-caused global warming.

Anthropogenic CO_2

Carbon dioxide that is generated from human activities. CO_2 (aka carbon dioxide) is a greenhouse gas. Carbon dioxide is the most abundant anthropogenic greenhouse gas and is the greatest contributor to global warming. Major greenhouse gases include carbon dioxide, methane, nitrous oxide, and various synthetic chemicals. Among the sources of greenhouse gases are power generation, transportation, and numerous industrial sources such as chemical production, petroleum production, and agricultural processes. Many of these sources burn fossil fuels (coal, oil, and natural gas), with CO_2 emissions as a byproduct.

Anthropogenic fossil-fuel-driven climate change

The change to Earth's climate caused by burning fossil fuels such as coal, oil, and natural gas. The overwhelming majority of climate studies indicate that human activity is causing rapid changes to the climate, which will cause severe environmental damage.

Biodiversity

The enormous variety of life on Earth. The term refers to every living thing, including plants, bacteria, animals, and humans. Biodiversity is often used more specifically to refer to all the species in one region or ecosystem.

Biodiversity hotspots

A biogeographic region with significant levels of biodiversity that is threatened with destruction. Thirty-five areas around the world qualify as hotspots, and while they represent just 2.3 percent of the Earth's surface, they support more than half of the world's plant species that are found no place else and nearly 43 percent of bird, mammal, reptile, and amphibian species that are also found no place else on the planet.

Biogeochemical cycles

Cycles of natural elements that are important to living organisms. They include the water, carbon, nitrogen, phosphorus, and sulfur cycles. The ways in which these compounds move between living and nonliving forms and locations in the biosphere are referred to as biogeochemical cycles.

Biomass

Renewable organic material that comes from plants and animals and is often used as an energy source. Wood is the largest biomass energy resource today. Other sources include food crops, grassy and woody plants, residues from agriculture or forestry, and oil-rich algae.

Biosphere

A thin life-supporting layer of Earth's surface comprising a complex community of living and nonliving things, across multiple ecosystems, that functions as a single unit and that can be regarded as one large ecosystem. It is made up of the parts of the Earth-system where life exists. The Earth-system consists of the lithosphere or solid surface; the atmosphere or layer of air surrounding the Earth; the hydrosphere or the water on Earth's surface, below the ground and in the atmosphere, and the biosphere. More often, however, the biosphere is described as having many ecosystems.

Carbon cycle

The movement of carbon molecules in various forms through elements of the Earth-system. Carbon is a constituent of all organic compounds, many of which are essential to life on Earth. The source of the carbon found in living matter is carbon dioxide (CO_2) in the air or dissolved in water. The carbon cycle describes how carbon transfers between different reservoirs located on Earth and includes a short- and long-term cycle. These cycles are important for maintaining a stable climate and carbon balance on Earth. According to NASA, over the long term, the carbon cycle seems to maintain a balance that prevents all of Earth's carbon from entering the atmosphere (as is the case on Venus) or from being stored entirely in rocks. This balance helps keep Earth's temperature relatively stable, like a thermostat.

By mining and using fossil fuels as their source of energy to power their economies, humans have changed Earth's thermostat by upsetting this short-term, long-term, carbon balance. By adding to Earth's atmosphere long-term carbon, contained in fossil fuels, humans have changed this carbon balance. This increase in carbon is what is now driving global warming.

Civilization

The process and structure by which *Homo sapiens* organized themselves beginning 12,000 years ago to sustain their lives outside of the Earth's ecosystems. That process so far has resulted in the destruction of numerous Earth habitats and the extinction of more than half the planet's species, as well as putting at risk the survival of the *Homo sapiens* species itself. Civilizations replaced nearly all hunter-gatherer communities. This began with a transition to agriculture, which involved enclosing the land for farming, domesticating animals, and adopting the practices of forced labor and slavery. The latter created the world's first poor population, depriving them of the native economic freedom and independence from which they evolved.

Climate change

Long-term shifts in temperatures and weather patterns. These shifts may be natural, such as through variations in the solar cycle. But since the 1800s, human activities have been the main driver of climate change, primarily due to the burning of fossil fuels like coal, oil and gas.

Climate change-driven human extinction

The elimination of humans from the planet because of changes to the climate. The rapid transition from the cool and moist Late Glacial to the warm, dry Holocene-like climatic conditions was likely unfavorable to many species of Pleistocene mammals. A climate-induced extinction implies that this last glacial cycle and its termination were more extreme than previous glacial cycles and/or glacial terminations. Climate change likely drove early human species to extinction. Of the six or more different species of early humans, all belonging to the genus *Homo*, only *Homo sapiens* has managed to survive. Now, a study combining climate modeling and the fossil record in search of the cause of the earlier extinctions suggests that climate change—the inability to adapt to either warming or cooling temperatures—likely played a major role in sealing their fate.

Climate change's role in hominin evolution

The influence of climate change in the evolution of hominins. Climate change appears to be a tool to prod species on to greater maturity or to extinction. It acts like the ultimate species survival chaperone, prompting what can turn out to be extinction or adaptation events and thereby a growth in maturity from the time a species evolves to the time it either goes extinct or reaches a higher level of adaptation and maturity and thereby survives.

Climate engine, climate machinery

Earth systems that contribute to climate change, such as El Niño, La Niña, and the ENSO (El Niño-Southern Oscillation). According to the United States Geological Survey, El Niño ("young boy" in Spanish) is an irregularly occurring and complex series of climatic changes that affects the equatorial

Pacific region and beyond every few years. It is characterized by the appearance of unusually warm, nutrient-poor water off northern Peru and Ecuador, typically in late December. El Niños often mean droughts, famines, forest fires, and floods, and the world has seen many devastating El Niños that resulted in millions of deaths and destruction.

El Niño and La Niña ("little girl" in Spanish) are opposite phases of what is known as the El Niño-Southern Oscillation (ENSO) cycle. The ENSO cycle is a scientific term that describes the fluctuations in temperature between the ocean and atmosphere in the east-central equatorial Pacific (approximately between the International Date Line and 120° west).

La Niña is sometimes referred to as the *cold phase* of ENSO, and El Niño as the *warm phase* of ENSO.

Corporations, aka legal persons
Entities that act as a single, fictional person. Much like an actual person, a corporation may sue, be sued, lend, and borrow. Additionally, a company which has been incorporated can easily transfer ownership through stock sales and exist indefinitely. National and multinational corporations are de facto legal persons.

CRISPR
CRISPR (short for "clustered regularly interspaced short palindromic repeats") is a technology that research scientists use to selectively modify the DNA of living organisms. CRISPR was adapted for use in the laboratory from naturally occurring genome editing systems found in bacteria.

Cuban Missile Crisis
The event in October 1962 that pitted U.S. President John Kennedy against Soviet statesman Nikita Khrushchev, America against Russia, with the fate of our entire species dangling from the finger of either man. For the first time, as far as is known, *Homo sapiens'* existence as a species was subject to the whim of a single man. Precisely at that point in time (October 16-28, 1962) *Homo sapiens'* evolving maturity caught up and intersected with *Homo*

sapiens' innovation and seemed inexorably headed in opposite directions. *Homo sapiens'* ability to innovate had finally surpassed its ability to mature, and with devastating consequences.

Dead zones
Oxygen-depleted areas in the oceans that are becoming commonplace across the Earth. In some places, the oxygen content of marine areas is so low that fish and other animals cannot survive. They can either leave the oxygen-free waters or die. The Louisiana Universities Marine Consortium reported that this year's dead zone in water along the Gulf of Mexico shoreline covers 7,722 square miles. There are now more than 400 coastal dead zones around the world.

Decarbonization, Decarbonization of the economy
The economic shift from carbon-based energy to renewable energy. There are two aspects to decarbonization: stopping the burning of fossil fuels and spewing of CO_2 into the atmosphere and, if possible, removing greenhouse gases from the atmosphere (carbon capture) to get to net zero. Humans might have a better chance of accomplishing the former. The carbon dioxide and methane emissions that are warming the planet come largely from the power generation, industry, transport, buildings, agriculture, and land-use sectors of the global economy and must be transformed. Decarbonization of the economy means that all these aspects of the economy must change, from how energy is generated and produced, to how goods and services are delivered, to how lands are managed. Humans must essentially transition their economies from a reliance on nonrenewable to reliance on and return to renewables.

Doomsday Clock
A symbol that represents the likelihood of a human-made global catastrophe, determined by the Bulletin of the Atomic Scientists. Maintained since 1947, the clock is a metaphor for threats to humanity from unchecked scientific and technological advances. The Doomsday Clock was created

by the board of the Bulletin of the Atomic Scientists in 1947 as a response to nuclear threats.

Drought
An extended period of lower-than-average rainfall in a region. Droughts over extended periods deprive a population of food and water and can cause the collapse of cities and civilizations and the migration of entire populations.

Early human economies, Pre-agriculture human economies
Economies that arose out of the foraging activities of pre-agriculture hunter-gatherers going about the task of eking out a living within Earth's ecosystems.

Earth-life economies aka Earth-life species economies
The sum of activities that arise out of Earth's biodiversity's eking out a living within Earth's ecosystems. The term encompasses both human economies and biodiversity economies.

Earth-life species economies
The set of customs and lifeways that arise out of Earth-life species going about the task of eking out a living (foraging) within Earth's ecosystems.

Ecocide
The extensive damage to, destruction of, or loss of ecosystem(s) of a given territory, whether by human agency or by other means, to such an extent that peaceful enjoyment by the inhabitants of that territory has been or will be severely diminished.

Ecolization
Describes how *Homo sapiens* organized themselves and lived for most of the three million years that preceded agriculture and civilization. Mimicking the term "civilization," "ecolization" is the set of processes by which pre-agriculture hunter-gatherer humans, as well as all other Earth-life species, coexisted and survived within the Earth's ecosystems without destroying themselves and those ecosystems.

Economics

A social science that focuses on the production, distribution, and consumption of goods and services, and analyzes the choices that individuals, businesses, governments, and nations make to allocate resources. Economics focuses on this behavior, the interactions of economic agents, and how economies work.

Economies

The system of interrelated production, consumption, and exchange activities that ultimately determine how resources are allocated among all the participants. It is the system of trade and industry by which the wealth of a country is made and used. As a social science, economies are concerned with description and analysis of the production, distribution, and consumption of goods and services.

Ecosystem services, aka Earth-life ecosystem services

The direct and indirect contributions of ecosystems to human well-being. Ecosystem services have an impact on our survival and quality of life.

Ecosystems, Earth-life ecosystems

The organisms and a defined physical environment with which they interact. These biotic and abiotic components are linked together through nutrient cycles and energy flows. Energy enters the system through photosynthesis and is incorporated into plant tissue.

On Earth, ecosystems are those places where life can evolve, thrive, and survive and where Earth-life species' economies, and/or human economies, might emerge.

Einstein's static universe

Einstein's model of a homogenous, static, spatially curved universe. However, this interpretation, which emerged from his theory of general relativity, has one major problem: If gravitation were the only active force, the universe would collapse—an issue Einstein addressed by introducing the cosmological constant. Einstein fiercely resisted the view that the universe was expanding, despite his contemporaries' suggestions that this was the case. He eventually accepted the modern cosmological view that the universe is expanding, long after his contemporaries.

Eking out a living *inside* Earth-life ecosystems, Eking out a living *outside* Earth-life ecosystems

Describes living and making a living *inside* versus *outside* Earth's ecosystems, where all Earth-life species obtained a living and survived—by foraging *within* the biogeochemical boundaries of Earth's ecosystems. Post-agriculture humans eked out their living by farming, which entailed making a living mostly *outside* those biogeochemical boundaries of Earth's ecosystems.

Eking out a living *within* Earth's ecosystems enabled pre-agriculture hunter-gatherer humans to survive collapse-free for 290,000 of the humanity's 300,000-year existence on planet Earth. By contrast, doing so *outside* Earth's ecosystems, which accompanied the adoption of agriculture, saw the continual collapse of human civilizations over the last 12,000 years.

Endocrine-disrupting chemicals (EDCs)

Synthetic chemicals that interfere with human endocrine (or hormone) systems at certain doses. Any system in the body controlled by hormones can be derailed by hormone disruptors. They mimic or partly mimic naturally occurring hormones in the body like estrogens (the female sex hormone), androgens (the male sex hormone), and thyroid hormones, potentially producing overstimulation. They bind to a receptor within a cell and block the endogenous hormone from binding. These disruptions can cause cancerous tumors, birth defects, and other developmental disorders.

Evolutionary and foundational role of human economies - See Economies.
Evolutionary goal and outcome of early human economies - See Economies.

Evolutionary maturity

A measure of a species' ability to survive. The maturity scale ranges from the zero or near-zero maturity level, indicating the near-certainty of its self-extinction, to the fully matured level, the point at which it surpasses the ability to drive itself to extinction. When a species has matured beyond the likelihood, and perhaps even the possibility, of self-extinction, it is said to have reached a Survival Plateau.

Evolutionary survival-driven goal and outcome - See Economies.

Evolutionary survival-driven goals - See Economies.

Evolutionary survival-driven human economies - See Economies.

Evolutionary survival-driven lifeways (See also Lifeways.)

The why and how of early human strategies for survival covering the first 290,000 years of humanity's 300,000 years of existence. Much attention is paid to how early humans lived during the Paleolithic period (roughly 2.5 million years ago to 10,000 BCE); especially that they lived in caves or simple huts or tepees and were hunters and gatherers; used basic stone and bone tools as well as crude stone axes for hunting birds and wild animals; cooked their prey, including woolly mammoths, deer, and bison, using controlled fire; and fished and collected berries, fruit, and nuts. But little has been found that explains the why, what, and how of their lifeways that enabled them to build societies and economies that lasted until 12,000 years ago without collapse, nor to explain most of the ills that have plagued human civilizations thereafter and caused their collapse.

Evolutionary survival-driven socioeconomic goal and outcome - See Economies.

Evolutionary sustainability

The care and feeding of a habitat by an intelligent species to ensure mutual survival, even during climate change cycles, and for as long as it takes to attain evolutionary maturity.

Evolutionary Triad-of-Life

The economies, species, and ecosystems that are indispensable to life and survival. Economies evolved to enable that indispensable collaboration among Earth-life species, ecosystems, and humans that would result in their mutual life and survival. Life on Earth is a result of this triad of conditions that must co-exist for life to exist. All Earth-life species, including humans, evolved and emerged out of Earth's ecosystems. So, for life to exist and survive, ecosystems must first exist. And for humans to survive, human economies must emerge to enable them to eke out a living within those ecosystems.

Genus *Homo*

The genus *Homo* belongs to the Hominidae family, which includes the great apes and humans. Genus *Homo* and the hominins that followed, including *Homo sapiens*, may well have comprised a nascent breed of intelligent species.

Glacials, Interglacials

Major ice ages (glacials) and warm periods in between (interglacial) are associated with Earth's orbit around the sun (which depends on its "eccentricity," or the flatness of its orbit, and which occurs once every 100,000 years).

Goal and outcome of early human economies vs. modern human economies

The purpose and result of economies of various types. The goal and outcome of early human economies (aka pre-agriculture hunter-gatherer human economies) differs fundamentally from the goal and outcome of post-agriculture human economies and the legal-person economies that are replacing them today. The goal and outcome of the former was life and survival whereas that of the latter was surplus, profit-generation, wealth accumulation, and eventually, GDP growth.

Early human economies eked out a living within Earth's ecosystems in harmony with its biodiversity in a way that ensured their mutual life and survival and that of Earth's ecosystems. Post-agriculture human economies, including modern human economies, have replaced this initial goal and outcome with the pursuit of surplus, profit generation, wealth accumulation, and eventually, GDP growth.

Goal and outcome of modern human and legal-person economies

Today, the goals of these two types of economies are almost the same: surplus generation, wealth accumulation, and GDP growth.

(The) Great Dying

The episode, roughly 250 million years ago, when a massive number of species of plants and animals—both aquatic and terrestrial—winked out of existence as entire ecosystems struggled to thrive. Also known as the Permian-Triassic extinction event or end-Permian extinction, it unfolded over roughly 100,000 years or more. By the time it was over, all but a handful of species had dwindled away to nothing.

Greenhouse mass extinctions

Extinctions emerging in the Devonian, Permo-Triassic (or Permian-Triassic), and Triassic-Jurassic periods, and multiple times during the Jurassic and Cretaceous periods, ending with the last known greenhouse extinction at the end of the Paleocene Epoch some 60 million years ago.

These greenhouse extinctions occurred over a vast expanse of time, 400 million to 100 million years ago, and shared common characteristics of high temperatures, high CO_2 levels, and low oxygen levels. Research now shows that each occurred in a world of quickly rising CO_2 (and perhaps methane as well, based on another line of evidence).

Habitable zones, continuous habitable zones

The habitable zone is the range of distances from a star where liquid water might pool on the surface of an orbiting planet. If a planet is too close to its parent star, it will be too hot and water will evaporate. If a planet is too far from a star, it is too cold, and water is frozen. Stars come in a wide variety of sizes, masses, and temperatures. Stars that are smaller, cooler, and with lower mass than the sun (M-dwarfs) have their habitable zone much closer to the star than is the case with our sun (G-dwarf). Stars that are larger, hotter, and more massive than the sun (A-dwarfs) have their habitable zone much farther out from the star.

Habitats and sustainable-capable habitats

A habitat with the array of resources, physical and biotic, needed to enable a species' survival. A species habitat can be seen as the physical manifestation of its ecological niche. Earth comprises a survival-capable habitat for humanity while, for example, Mars does not. A sustainable-capable habitat is one that self-resuscitates or can be revived notwithstanding multiple climate events. The Earth consists of multiple sustainable-capable habitats.

Herbivore

An animal that feeds chiefly on plants.

Holocene-Anthropocene transition

The shift from the Holocene Epoch to the Anthropocene Epoch. The Anthropocene Epoch is an unofficial unit of geologic time, used to describe the most recent period in Earth's history when human activity started to have a significant impact on the planet's climate and ecosystems. Scientists still debate whether the Anthropocene is different from the Holocene, and the term has not been formally adopted by the International Union of Geological Sciences (IUGS), the international organization that names and defines epochs. The primary question that the IUGS needs to answer before declaring the Anthropocene an epoch is if humans have changed the Earth system to the point that it is reflected in the rock strata.

Hominidae family

The family of species that includes the great apes and humans. There are seven extant species in four genera: orangutans (two species in genus *Pongo*), gorillas (two species in genus *Gorilla*), chimpanzees (two species in genus *Pan*) and humans (genus *Homo*).

Hominins

A class of primates, which are a type ofmammal. Hominins are primates that share characteristics such as bipedalism, smaller canine size, and increased brain size. Hominins are part of a larger group of primates called hominids, which include orangutans, gorillas, chimpanzees, and human beings. All hominins are hominids, but very few hominids are hominins.

The only hominins alive today are human beings. There are many, many, extinct hominins, a fraction of which are represented here. Fossilized remains of extinct hominin species have been found in parts of Africa, Europe, and Asia, many dating back millions of years.

Hubble, Edwin

A twentieth century astronomer. In the 1920s, Hubble made history by looking through a 100-inch telescope at Mount Wilson in Southern California. Training his gaze on the Andromeda Nebula, he saw stars like ones in our galaxy, only dimmer. One of those stars was a Cepheid variable, which astronomers could use to measure distances. The discovery of the Cepheid variable allowed Hubble to deduce that the Andromeda Nebula was not a nearby cluster of stars, but an entirely different galaxy. By the 1930s, most astronomers had been convinced that the Milky Way galaxy was but one of millions in the universe. The very notion that there was more than one galaxy in the universe was revolutionary and earned Hubble the title as the greatest astronomer since Galileo.

Hubble's Law of Redshift of cosmological redshift expansion

The observation in physical cosmology that galaxies are moving away from Earth at speeds proportional to their distance. In other words, the farther they are, the faster they are moving away from Earth.

Hubble's Law of cosmological expansion was first formulated by Edwin Hubble in 1929. Hubble compared the distances to galaxies to their redshift and found a linear relationship. He interpreted the redshift as being caused by the receding velocity of the galaxies. The recession-distance relationship is interpreted as an overall expansion of the universe. As light travels toward us from the distant galaxies, it is stretched over time by the ever-expanding space it is travelling through. The longer it travels, the more the wavelengths are increased (reddened). This shift is different from the doppler effect, which is caused by the motion of the light source itself. It is like drawing an image on a piece of rubber or latex and then distorting the image by stretching.

Human energy transitions

A shift in the sources of energy that satisfy energy demand. The current energy transition—from fossil fuels to low-carbon energy—is not the first energy transition the world has experienced.

It is commonly held that this is the fourth major transition to different energy sources. The first (1830-1950) was the shift from traditional biofuels (primarily wood) to coal; the second (1950-1980) consisted of the development and adoption of refined oil products; and the third (1980-2020) involved an increased reliance on natural gas.

This accounting of human energy transitions, however, omits the Earth's initial and fundamental energy source, the sun—the very first source of energy and *a renewable energy source* that predated humans and human discovery and use of fire and hence of biofuels. So, long before humans learned to use biofuels, they were using the energy from the sun that was stored as chemical energy in the flora, fauna, and funga they consumed as food within Earth's ecosystems. Therefore, the first human energy transition must be the transition from hunting and gathering to farming, which would have occurred about 10,000 years ago shortly after the dawn of the Neolithic Revolution.

Humans are now engaged in their fifth energy transition—from nonrenewables back to renewables. From a long-term historical perspective, the fifth transition can be framed as the shift away from renewable sources of food and use of the fauna and flora available to all species in Earth's ecosystems—which satisfied all of humanity's energy needs for most of our species' existence—to the transition to fossil fuels some 200-300 years ago. Now, this fifth transition is from the nonrenewables (coal, oil, gas, etc.) found outside Earth's ecosystem, back to the renewables of the ecosystem.

Humans, modern humans, anatomically modern humans

Early modern human (EMH) or anatomically modern human (AMH) are terms used to distinguish *Homo sapiens* (the only extant hominin species) that are anatomically consistent with the range of phenotypes seen in contemporary humans from extinct archaic human species. Some of the oldest remains of modern humans in the world are much older than scientists thought. There is uncertainty as to when modern humans appeared on Earth. Fossils found in the Sahara Desert in 2017 were more than 300,000 years old, but these fossils lack some of the key morphological features that define humans, so there are questions whether they are linked to modern humans, or another species related to humans.

Hunter-gatherer economies - See Early human economies.

Hunter-gatherer humans socioeconomic lifeways - See Lifeways.

Hunter-gatherers, hunter-gatherer humans

Humans who practiced a highly stable, very long-lasting way of life for hundreds of thousands of years, until about 10,000 years ago, when their subsistence method of living began to change in several locations across the globe. Hunting and gathering was the only way in which *Homo sapiens* were able to extract the necessary sustenance from the environment.

Industrial fishing

The taking of fish and other seafood and resources from oceans, rivers, and lakes for the purpose of marketing them. In the early twenty-first century about 250 million people were directly employed by the commercial fishing industry, and an estimated one billion people depended on fish as their primary source of animal protein.

The rise of industrial fishing has led to the harvesting of wildlife at rates too high for species to replace themselves. Decades of harvesting the seas have disrupted the delicate balance of marine ecosystems—despite global efforts to mitigate the damage. Commercial fishing is a $150 billion global industry—and just 2 percent of the fleet captures over 50 percent of the catch. Most of the wild fish catch comes from industrial fishing operations whose practices are depleting wild fish populations across marine ecosystems. Fish populations around the globe are in serious trouble, thanks to the modern fishing industry. Instead of simply using poles and intuition, factory ships employ radar, sonar, helicopters, and even spotter planes to hunt down schools of fish, which they catch using massive nets and lines studded with hundreds of hooks. These technologies allow us to snare all kinds of deep-water delicacies—but they come at an ecological cost.

Invisible hand

A metaphor, introduced by the 18th-century Scottish philosopher and economist Adam Smith, that characterizes the mechanisms through which beneficial social and economic outcomes may arise from the accumulated self-interested actions of individuals, none of whom intends to bring about such outcomes. It describes the unseen forces of self-interest that impact the free market.

IPCC – Intergovernmental Panel on Climate Change

The United Nations body for assessing the science related to climate change.

ISDS – Investor State Dispute Settlement

A provision in Bilateral Investment Treaties (BITs) and other international investment agreements that allows investors to enter arbitration with states over treaty breaches. It is a mechanism that enables foreign investors to resolve disputes with the government of the country where their investment was made (the host state) in a neutral forum through binding international arbitration.

Just-in-time supply chains

A management strategy that aligns raw material orders from suppliers directly with production schedules to minimize the need to stockpile supplies. Just-in-time supply chains took a lot of heat during the pandemic after empty shelves laid bare the pitfalls of ordering as little inventory as possible in the name of efficiency.

Keystone XL Pipeline
A planned 1,179-mile (1,897km) pipeline running from the oil sands of Alberta, Canada, to Steele City, Nebraska, where it would join an existing pipeline. It could carry 830,000 barrels of oil each day.

Owned by North American company TC Energy, the Keystone XL Pipeline is the fourth phase of the Keystone Pipeline System, an existing 2,687-mile pipeline whose Canadian portion runs from Hardisty, Alberta, east into Manitoba where it turns south and crosses the border into North Dakota, according to the company's website.

Oil spills along the Keystone pipeline that runs from Canada to Texas have become more frequent and severe, prompting stricter regulations for a 1,200-mile stretch of the pipeline. The pipeline was shuttered in January 2021 after President Joe Biden canceled the pipeline's border-crossing permit.

Legal-person economies (See also Legal-persons.)
Economies comprised of legal-persons, operated by legal-persons, and for the benefit of legal-persons.

Legal-person economies, multinational corporation economies
Human economies that have been taken over and are run by corporate interests. The policies, preferences, and economic benefits become slanted to the goals and outcomes of these legal-persons—economic surplus, profits, wealth accumulation, and GDP growth—while the human economic goals and outcome of life and survival are abandoned. Legal-Person Economies are National and Multinational Corporations Economies.

Legal-persons (See Multinational corporations.)
Lifeways, human socioeconomic lifeways, surplus-driven lifeways

The socioeconomic lifeways, hunting and gathering vs. farming, that humans chose to make a living. Farming needed to be surplus-driven to succeed.

Manhattan Project

A U.S. government research project (1942-45) that produced the first atomic bombs. It was started in response to fears that German scientists had been working on a weapon using nuclear technology since the 1930s and that Adolf Hitler was prepared to use it.

Market-driven economies

Post-agriculture human economies that have adopted the market as the principal means of organizing how goods and services are produced and distributed. A market economy, or a free-market or free-enterprise economy, is one in which economic decisions relating to things such as the prices of goods and services are determined by supply and demand.

Megafauna

A term used to describe animals with an adult body weight of over 44 kg (97 lbs). Megafauna can be found on every continent and in every country. For every living species of megafauna, there are a large number of extinct megafauna. Pleistocene megafauna is the set of large animals that lived on Earth during the Pleistocene Epoch and became extinct during the Quaternary extinction event.

Metabolic rate of animals

The pace at which oxygen is used by an organism. As temperatures rise, metabolic rate goes up, and as metabolic rate rises, so, too, does the need for oxygen, as the chemical reactions of life are oxygen-dependent. Research shows that metabolic rate doubles to triples with each 10-degree rise in temperature. The consequences of this in a low-oxygen world would be major and life impacting.

Migration

A built-in survival response that appears to be independent of a species' innovative and technological prowess.

Mobile, mobile hunter-gatherer bands (small)
Hunter-gatherers lived in small bands of 50 or less and foraged for a living. Hence they were mobile.

Mobile economies, aka mobile hunter-gatherer economies
Economies characterized by regular movement of communities to follow available food supplies. All Earth-life species, including pre-agriculture hunter-gatherer human economies, were mobile economies. While mobile economies still exist for all other Earth-life species, human mobile economies ceased to exist soon after humans abandoned foraging in favor of sedentary farming economies.

Montreal Protocol (1987)
The landmark multilateral environmental agreement that regulates the production and consumption of nearly 100 man-made chemicals referred to as ozone-depleting substances (ODS).

NASA DART spacecraft
The first-ever mission dedicated to investigating and demonstrating one method of asteroid deflection by changing an asteroid's motion in space through kinetic impact. On September 26, 2022, DART impacted the asteroid moonlet Dimorphos, a small body just 530 feet (160 meters) in diameter.

NASA Mars Reconnaissance Orbiter
The second-longest lived spacecraft to orbit Mars, after 2001 Mars Odyssey. It has been studying the Red Planet since March 2006.

Neanderthals
Neanderthals (*Homo neanderthalensis* or *Homo sapiens neanderthalensis*) is an extinct species or subspecies of archaic humans in the genus *Homo*, who lived within Eurasia from circa 400,000 until 40,000 years ago.

Neolithic humans, Neolithic Revolution humans
Humans who lived after the Neolithic Revolution and derived a living based on farming and animal husbandry.

Neolithic Revolution

The wide-scale transition of many human cultures during the Neolithic period from a lifestyle of hunting and gathering to one of agriculture and settlement, making an increasingly large population possible.

Neolithic Revolution, Neolithic Revolution humans

The wide-scale transition of many human cultures during the Neolithic period from a lifestyle of hunting and gathering to one of agriculture and settlement, making an increasingly large population possible. Neolithic Revolution Humans lived during the Neolithic Revolution.

Neolithic Revolution humans' socioeconomic lifeways - See Lifeways.

Neolithic Revolution socioeconomic lifeway changes

Neolithic Revolution humans abandoned the foraging, sharing, egalitarian lifeways of their hunter-gatherer forebears and adopted new practices. They replaced foraging with farming, sharing with hoarding, and small mobile bands with large, sedentary populations that dwelt with farm animals in towns and villages.

NIMBY

An abbreviation for the phrase "not in my backyard," referring to the position that something unpleasant but necessary should not be built or done near one's home. An example of NIMBYism is campaigns against a wind farm because of the noise it might generate.

Ozone layer - See Montreal Protocol.

PFAS (Per- and polyfluoroalkyl substances)

A group of synthetic chemicals that have been in wide use since the 1940s. They are known as "forever chemicals" because the molecular bonds that form them can take thousands of years to degrade, meaning that they accumulate both in the environment and in our bodies. PFASs make carpets stain-resistant and fast-food packaging able to repel grease and water. They're also used in fire-fighting foams and give nonstick cookware its non-stickiness.

Phthalates
A group of chemicals used in hundreds of products such as toys, vinyl flooring and wall coverings, detergents, lubricating oils, food packaging, pharmaceuticals, blood bags, tubing, and personal care products such as nail polish, hair sprays, aftershave lotions, soaps, shampoos, perfumes, and others.

Phytoplankton, Plankton
Organisms at the base of what scientists refer to as oceanic biological productivity, the ability of a body of water to support life such as plants, fish, and wildlife. Plankton are the foundation of the oceanic food chain. Some 50 percent to two-thirds of the planet's total atmospheric oxygen is produced by ocean phytoplankton; therefore, a loss of phytoplankton would result in the depletion of atmospheric oxygen on a global scale. This would likely result in the mass mortality of animals and humans.

Planetary Boundaries
A scientific framework introduced in 2009 that aims to define the environmental limits within which humanity can safely operate. It has proven influential in global sustainability policy development.

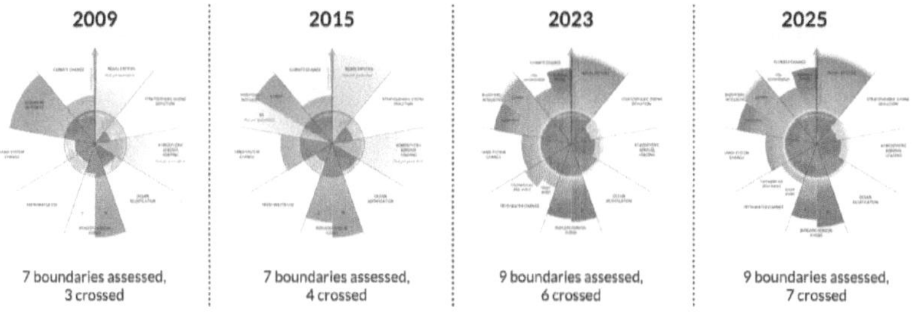

Figure G-1. Planetary boundaries that have been breached (in orange), 2009-2025.

(Source: Stockholm Resilience Centre; Licenced under CC BY-NC-ND 3.0; Credit: Azote for Stockholm Resilience Centre, Stockholm University. Based on Sakschewski and Caesar et al. 2025, Richardson et al. 2023, Steffen et al. 2015, and Rockström et al. 2009)

In January 2022, 14 scientists concluded in the scientific journal *Environmental Science and Technology* that humanity has exceeded a planetary boundary related to environmental pollutants and other "novel entities," including plastics. The progression of boundary breaches back to 2009 is shown in Figure G-1.

Pleistocene-Eocene Thermal Maximum (PETM)
A time period with a more than 5-8°C global average temperature rise. It is also known as the "Eocene Thermal Maximum 1" (ETM1) and was formerly known as the "Initial Eocene" or "Late Paleocene Thermal Maximum."

Pleistocene-Holocene climate change
The change in climate from the Pleistocene to the Holocene. The rapid transition from cool moist Late Glacial to warm dry Holocene-like climatic conditions was likely unfavorable to many species of Pleistocene mammals in the southwestern USA. A climate-induced extinction implies that this last glacial cycle and its termination were more extreme than previous glacial cycles and/or glacial terminations.

Pleistocene-Holocene climate change, Terminal Pleistocene-Holocene transition climate change
The change of climate that occurred during this transition was among the major changes, if not the major change, that marked the emergence of the warming temperatures of the Holocene and the spread of humans across the Earth.

The Holocene would see the rapid proliferation, growth, and impacts of the human species worldwide, including all its written history, technological revolutions, development of major civilizations, and overall significant transition toward urban living in the present.

Pleistocene-Holocene Transition, Terminal Pleistocene-Holocene
The transition from the Pleistocene epoch to the Holocene. The Pleistocene ended 11,700 years ago. It was preceded by the Pliocene Epoch of the Neogene Period and is followed by the Holocene Epoch. The Pleistocene Epoch is best known as a time during which extensive ice sheets and other glaciers formed repeatedly on the landmasses and has been informally referred to as the "Great Ice Age." A radical change of environments

occurred at the Late Pleistocene-Holocene boundary (10,300-9300 BP, or 11,500-9500 cal. yr BP) and marked the end of the ice age. This transition was a period of dramatic warming and ecosystem change marked by a shift from non-domesticated to domesticated foods.

Pliocene, Pleistocene, Holocene, and Anthropocene Epochs

Eons are a long span of geologic time. The geologic/geological time scale, a system of chronological dating, is a representation of time based on Earth's rock record and is divided into eons, eras, and periods. Eons are the longest portions of geologic time (eras are the second-longest). Three eons are recognized: the Phanerozoic Eon (dating from the present back to the beginning of the Cambrian Period), the Proterozoic Eon, and the Archean Eon. Eons, eras, periods, and their epochs are shown below.

Table G-1. Geological time scale

Eon	Era	Period		Epoch	
Phanerozoic	Cenozoic	Quaternary		Holocene	Today / 11.8 Ka
				Pleistocene	
		Neogene		Pliocene	
				Miocene	
		Paleogene		Oligocene	
				Eocene	
				Paleocene	66 Ma
	Mesozoic	Cretaceous		~	
		Jurassic		~	
		Triassic		~	252 Ma
	Paleozoic	Permian		~	
		Carboni-ferous	Pennsylvanian	~	
			Mississippian	~	
		Devonian		~	
		Silurian		~	
		Ordovician		~	
		Cambrian		~	541 Ma
Proterozoic	~	~		~	2.5 Ga
Archean	~	~		~	4.0 Ga
Hadean	~	~		~	4.54 Ga

(Younger ↑ … ↓ Older)

(Source: La Cooltura)

Periods and epochs of interest—the Pliocene, the Pleistocene, and the Holocene—are shown in table G-1. Not shown is the Anthropocene—the possible name of the epoch expected to follow the Holocene. It was and is during the Holocene Epoch that human civilization as we have come to know it developed.

Pre-agriculture hunter-gatherer human forebears
Hunter-gatherer species that lived prior to the emergence of agriculture as a way of making a living.

Pre-agriculture hunter-gatherer humans, Pre-agriculture hunter-gatherer human forebears
Hunter-gatherer humans that eked out a living within Earth's ecosystems as foragers before the emergence of farming.

Pre-agriculture egalitarian hunter-gatherer socioeconomic lifeways - See Early human economies.

Quaternary glaciation
The pattern of glacial and interglacial periods that began about 2,588,000 years ago and continues today. The "Ice Age," the most recent glacial period, occurred from around 110,000 to 11,700 years ago.

Renewable vs. nonrenewable energy
Renewable energy comprises energy that is derived from renewable sources like the sun

Rules - See Survival-driven rules.

Sapiens—Techno sapiens
Homo sapiens who are known for being particularly capable in the fields of inventions, technologies, and innovations and whose contributions enable them to be seen as leaders in the techno sphere.

Sapiens—Moneyed sapiens
Homo sapiens who have managed to amass enormous wealth and are known as being among the 1 percent that controls most of the wealth in the world.

Sedentary lifeways
The way post-Neolithic Revolution humans began to live after they abandoned foraging for farming, hoarding for sharing, and a mobile lifestyle for crowded sedentary villages and towns, dwelling with farm animals instead

of in the small, mobile camps and socioeconomic practices that arose out of the foraging lifeways of pre-agriculture hunter-gatherer humans.

Siberian Traps

Massive volcanic activity that is the prime suspect behind the mass extinction that ended the Paleozoic Era about 250 million years ago. Scientists suspect that this volcanic activity, in a large igneous province called the Siberian Traps, may have had a role in the global die-off, raising air and sea temperatures and releasing toxic amounts of greenhouse gases into the atmosphere over a very short period. Scientists now believe that just one year of spewing Siberian lava could have put 1.5 billion tons of sulfur dioxide into the Earth's atmosphere—and the eruption continued for one million years. This death-fest dwarfs the one that would later kill the dinosaurs; even fish and insects were hard hit. Scientists guess that 96 percent of marine species and 70 percent of land species were completely wiped out. If you haven't seen a trilobite lately, blame Siberia.

Smithian stage

A million-year time interval around 247 million years ago that had the highest of all known temperatures since the time when animals first occurred.

Socioeconomic goal and outcome

Describes the purpose and destination that all Earth-life species, including human societies and economies, evolved to pursue. Inherent in the pursuit of this purpose and destination were the foundational goal and outcome of life and survival.

Socioeconomic goals

The social and economic goals a society might develop and pursue. The socioeconomic goals developed and pursued by pre-agriculture hunter-gatherer humans were markedly different from those that followed the adoption of agriculture. Whereas the goal and outcome sought by the former was life and survival, those pursued by the latter were surplus, profit-seeking, wealth accumulation, and economic growth.

This change in their respective socioeconomic goals led to socioeconomic lifeways that ultimately enabled the longevity of the societies and economies built by pre-agriculture humans and frequent socioeconomic collapse of those that arose after the change from foragers to farmers.

Socioeconomic survival-driven lifeways

The road of life as indigenous people see it. From the mid-19th century, the word "lifeways" was used with the meaning "way through life" or "way of life." Such a perspective can be associated with the concept "worldview," a distinct way of thinking about the cosmos and of evaluating life's actions in terms of those views and focuses on "an interpretive effort to express indigenous understandings of human-earth relations as an interactive and pervasive context that outsiders might label religion. Recent explanations of the term in the field of Native American and other indigenous studies suggest a tight interplay between worldview and economy in societies that are small in scale.

In this book, lifeways refers to the mobile, foraging, sharing, and egalitarian socioeconomic practices of pre-agriculture hunter-gatherer humans that enabled them to build societies and economies that survived collapse-free for most of humanity's existence.

Surplus-driven human economies and surplus-driven legal-person economies

Human economies and legal-person economies whose economic goal and outcome is generation of surplus and profits, wealth accumulation, and GDP growth.

Surplus-driven lifeways, goal and outcome consist of profits, wealth accumulation, and GDP growth.

Survival-driven

A term indicating an overarching goal and outcome that embraces the preservation of life and survival—human, biodiversity, and ecosystems life and survival. Survival-driven outcomes have to date turned out to be foundational.

Survival-driven architecture, Survival-driven Earth-life architecture, foundations and lifeway rules

Architectures whose overarching goal and outcome is the preservation of the life and survival of all species that are subject to the workings of such architectures.

Survival-driven economies

A term used to characterize pre-agriculture human economies whose socioeconomic lifeways resulted in the preservation, life, and survival of Earth's ecosystems, biodiversity, and human societies and economies for 290,000 of humanity's 300,000 years of existence.

Survival-driven lifeways

Ways of making a living on the Earth that ensure above all else the mutual survival of Earth's ecosystems, biodiversity, and humanity.

Survival-driven lifeway rules

Rules designed to ensure the life and survival of species that follow or are impacted by these rules. **(See also Lifeways.)**

Survival-driven rules

The rules that drive the ways of making a living on the Earth that ensure above all else the mutual survival of Earth's ecosystems, biodiversity, and humanity

Survival-driven, survival-driven economies, survival-driven architecture, survival-driven socioeconomic foundations

Terms for the lifeways of a species that embrace the pursuit of life and survival as its only goal and outcome. This happens when the economic systems and architectures that shape how these systems function are founded upon and pursue a single goal and outcome—the life and survival of all species that adopt and follow these lifeways.

Survival-driven Triad-of-Life - See Evolutionary Triad-of-Life.

Sustainable-capable habitat

A habitat that self-resuscitates or can be revived notwithstanding multiple climate events. The Earth consists of multiple sustainable-capable habitats.

Terminal Pleistocene-Holocene Transition climate change

Climate change at the end of the Pleistocene was both rapid and global in extent, with important consequences for the human environment. More and more we become aware of the impact of climate change on our natural environment, as it became increasingly warmer and wetter, expanding plant ranges and sea level rise. The fossil record shows how extensive that impact had been to human groups.

"The few"

"The few" refers to that small fraction of *Homo sapiens* (rulers, governments, kings, queens, priests, elites, bureaucrats, craftsmen, and traders) who managed to seize control of economies and societies starting some 10,000 years ago and have hung onto it, becoming the architects and overlords of the civilization we see today. Ever since farming drove hunter-gatherers off the land, "the few" in control began appropriating for themselves the produce, labor, and freedoms of "the rest" while relegating "the rest" to the basement of civilization.

The kings and queens, some of whom still exist, mostly became nation-state governments, dictators, and military strongmen; priestly castes morphed into organized religions with offshoots that became institutions of learning like universities; the elite and bureaucrats soon became the wealthy; traders became the business class, companies, and multinationals; money changers are now our financial institutions; and craftsmen became the technology builders. What these all had and still have in common is a transfer of the freedom of the individual to institutions and organizations headed by "the few."

Trophic levels

The group of organisms within an ecosystem that occupy the same level in a food chain. There are five main trophic levels within a food chain, each of which differs in its nutritional relationship with the primary energy source. The primary energy source in any ecosystem is the sun (although there are exceptions in deep-sea ecosystems).

The rest of the trophic levels are made up of consumers, also known as heterotrophs; heterotrophs cannot produce their own food, so must consume other organisms to acquire nutrition.

The second trophic level consists of herbivores. These organisms gain energy by eating primary producers and are called primary consumers.

Trophic levels three, four, and five consist of carnivores and omnivores. Carnivores are animals that survive only by eating other animals, whereas omnivores eat animals and plant material.

Trophic level three consists of carnivores and omnivores that eat herbivores; these are the secondary consumers.

Trophic level four includes carnivores and omnivores that eat secondary consumers and are known as tertiary consumers.

Trophic level five consists of apex predators; these animals have no natural predators and are therefore at the top of the food chain.

Decomposers or detritivores are organisms that consume dead plant and animal material, converting it into energy and nutrients that plants can use for effective growth. Although they do not fill an independent trophic level, decomposers and detritivores, such as fungi, bacteria, earthworms, and flies, recycle waste material from all other trophic levels and are an important part of a functioning ecosystem.

Universe's existential threats

Species-extinction threats due to planetary, solar, galactic, or universal events, or some combination of these. The asteroid that took out the dinosaurs posed an existential threat and did, in fact, result in their extinction.

Zoonotic-based pandemic

A disease emergence driven by human-animal contact in a global viral ecosystem. The Covid-19 pandemic is an unrelenting demonstration of the devastating impact of zoonotic disease, whereby viruses jump from animals to infect humans.

Zoonotic diseases

An infectious disease that has jumped from a non-human animal to humans. Zoonotic pathogens may be bacterial, viral, or parasitic, or may involve unconventional agents and can spread to humans through direct contact or through food, water, or the environment. Zoonotic disease, also called zoonosis, is any of a group of diseases that can be transmitted to humans by nonhuman vertebrate animals, such as mammals, birds, reptiles, amphibians, and fish. Many domestic and wild animals are sources of zoonotic disease, and there are numerous means of transmission.

NOTES

CHAPTER 1
EARTH-LIFE ECONOMIES

5 **Earth-life economies, Earth-Life Species Economies**

Economies that result from foraging activities of Earth-life species.

6 **Sustainable-Capable Habitats** that would last for billions of years.

Habitats that can last for billions of years to ensure the evolution and sustainability of complex animal life and emergent intelligent species like *Homo sapiens*.

7 **Goldstar Traders**

A trader is an individual who engages in the buying and selling of assets in any financial market, either for themself or on behalf of another person or institution.

9 **Hunter-Gatherer economies, Mobile economies, Nomadic humans, Hunter-Gatherer Mobile economies**

Pre-agriculture hunter-gatherers were foragers and hence were mobile and consequently, their societies and economies were mobile.

12 **Trophic Level population limits**

Ecosystems manage and regulate energy usage and allowance through their trophic levels—the feeding positions in a food chain or web are called trophic levels. Food chains and their trophic levels create energy flow within a food web, so food is by far one of the most important environmental resources that affect population size.

All organisms need to take in nutrients in one way or another and will starve and die if they don't. Hence, the population of each trophic level must be in balance for the food web to remain intact. If one trophic level's population increases or decreases too much, it can decrease the number of producers, thus decreasing the amount of energy available in the food web, which can cause a reduction of the population due to lack of food.

13 **...within the limits of certain parameters,** A reference to planetary limits, or boundaries: Guiding human development on a changing planet.

The planetary boundary (PB) concept, introduced in 2009, aimed to define the environmental limits within which humanity can safely operate. This approach has proved influential in global sustainability policy development. Steffen et al. provide an updated and extended analysis of the PB framework. Of the original nine proposed boundaries, they identify three (including climate change) that might push the Earth system into a new state if crossed and that also have a pervasive influence on the remaining boundaries. They also develop the PB framework so that it can be applied usefully in a regional context.

18 **Adam Smith might have thought twice about excluding all nature from his theory of political economy.**

According to *Peter Ward and David Brownlee in their book "Rare Earth: Why Complex Life Is Uncommon in the Universe,"* the home star of a potentially life-evolving and sustaining planet will preferably be a single star.

CHAPTER 2
ECOSYSTEMS:
FOUNDATIONS OF EARTH-LIFE ECONOMIES

22 **Ecosystems,** as defined by Eugene P. Odum, in Science Direct, are "Living organisms and their nonliving (abiotic) environment are inseparably interrelated

and interact with each other. An ecological system, or ecosystem, is any unit (a biosystem) that includes all the organisms (the biotic community) in a given area interacting with the physical environment so that a flow of energy leads to clearly defined biotic structures and cycling of materials between living and nonliving parts. An ecosystem then is more than a geographical unit (or ecoregion); it is a functional system unit with inputs and outputs, and with boundaries that can be either natural or arbitrary," as defined by Eugene P. Odum, in ScienceDirect.

24 **What "Continuous Habitable Zones" are to stars, ecosystems are to planets**

These are zones and habitats. They are life-enabling environments evolved to meet the survival needs of all species sharing an ecosystem.

30 **Ecocide Hotspots**

Human progress is no excuse to destroy nature. A push to make "ecocide" a global crime must recognize this fundamental truth. Scientists recently confirmed the Amazon rain forest is now emitting more carbon dioxide than it absorbs, due to uncontrolled burning and deforestation. It brings the crucial ecosystem closer to a tipping point that would see it replaced by savannas and trigger accelerated global heating.

31 **A Fifth Crime: Ecocide**

The Pope describes ecocide as "the massive contamination of air, land and water," or "any action capable of producing an ecological disaster," and has proposed making it a sin for Catholics.

Ecocide is unlawful or wanton acts committed with knowledge that there is a substantial likelihood of severe and either widespread or long-term damage to the environment being caused by those acts.

31 **The Christian Bible claims** in Psalm 115—"The Heavens are the Lord's but the earth he has given to the sons of men"—or in Psalm 8—"Thou has given man dominion over the work of thy hands."

Clive Ponting notes that it should come as no surprise that early and medieval Christians accepted that their god had given humans the right to exploit plants, animals, and the whole world for their benefit. In this view, Ponting writes, "Nature is not seen as sacred, but open to exploitation by humans without any moral qualms—indeed humans have the right to use nature in whatever way they think best . . . Interventions and modifications to the natural world such as by extending cultivated areas, deforestation, and driving species to extinction and appropriating the planet's resources were readily interpreted as taking part in God's plan to improve upon creation."

34 **UN Secretary-General Kofi Annan commissioned a study of the state of the Earth's ecosystems.** *The Millennium Ecosystem Report of 2005*, the recent 2021 update, and other assessments lay out in stark detail these findings.

Scientists in these assessments refer to benefits humans and all species obtain from Earth-life ecosystems as *"ecosystem services"* and describe them in terms of *"Ecosystems And Human Well-Being,"* depicting them as free services intended primarily for human benefit with only casual references to the innumerable Earth-life species that once occupied, and to a large extent still do, those Earth-life ecosystems for millions of years.

34 ***The Millennium Ecosystem Assessment Report.*** This IPCC assessment notes that over the past 50 years, the human population has doubled. Between 1960 and 2000 the global economy increased more than sixfold, and the world population doubled to six billion people; with this growth the demand for ecosystem services grew significantly.

43 **How humans have changed the structure of Earth-life ecosystems.** The ecosystems and biomes most significantly altered globally by human activity include: marine and freshwater ecosystems, temperate broadleaf forests, temperate grasslands, mediterranean forests, and tropical dry forest.

54 **How humans changed the functions and cycles of Earth-life processes within ecosystems.**

Human-modified ecosystems are shaped by our activities and their side effects. They share a common set of traits including simplified food webs, landscape homogenization, and high nutrient and energy inputs. Ecosystem simplification is the ecological hallmark of humanity and the reason for our evolutionary success. However, the side effects of our profligacy and poor resource practices are now so pervasive as to threaten our future no less than that of biological diversity itself. The linked article looks at human impact on ecosystems and the consequences for evolution.

55 **The Gaia theory** posits that the Earth is a self-regulating complex system involving the biosphere, the atmosphere, the hydrosphere, and the pedosphere, tightly coupled as an evolving system. The theory sustains that this system, called Gaia, seeks a physical and chemical environment optimal for contemporary life. Scientists

now view the Earth as a system containing a fixed amount of each stable atom or element. Each element can exist in several different chemical reservoirs. Each element on Earth moves among reservoirs in the solid earth, oceans, atmosphere, and organisms as part of geochemical cycles. Movement of matter between reservoirs is driven by the Earth's internal and external sources of energy.

56 **Human modifications of Earth-life ecosystems** have changed not only the structure of ecosystems, such as what habitats or species are present in a particular location, but their processes and functioning as well. The capacity of ecosystems to provide services derives directly from the operation of natural biogeochemical cycles that in some cases have been significantly modified. Earth-life ecosystems, through their ecological and life-enabling processes (water, carbon, nitrogen, phosphorus, and oxygen cycles and energy and nutrient flows); sustains the quality of the air, fresh water, and soils on which all life, including humans, depend; distributes fresh water; regulates the climate; provides pollination and pest control; and reduces the impact of natural hazards.

58 **"Why Did Nobody See It Coming?"** Given the state of the world's ecosystems the question any normal person would ask is not unlike what Queen Elizabeth II asked when confronted with the worst economic downturn since the Great Depression (1929–c.1939) — *"Why Did Nobody See It Coming?"*

58 **The world's ecosystems and biodiversity allowed to get to the state where a fifth of countries are at risk of ecosystem collapse.**

59 **The world's wealth is built on our planet's natural ecosystems. Indeed.**

Nature is our most precious asset notes the Dasgupta Report on the Economics of Biodiversity. Yet most of the world's economists, those people who advise governments and companies regarding the best policies to pursue to ensure the economic well-being of companies, nations, international institutions, and peoples of the world, do not include in their advice and accounting the value of those countries nor the world's ecosystems and their services.

How do we fix this problem? The solution starts with understanding and accepting a simple truth: our economies are embedded within Nature, not external to it.

64 **Explosive human population growth** is a major component of the problem. This growth has driven and is driving the destruction of Earth-life ecosystems and biodiversity.

66 **"The Global Resources Outlook 2019 shows that we are ploughing through this planet's finite resources** as if there is no tomorrow, causing climate change and biodiversity loss along the way," said Joyce Msuya, Deputy Executive Director of UN Environment Programme.

67 **What does it mean to live and build human economies *inside versus outside* of Earth-life's ecosystems?** Hunter-gatherer humans who evolved and lived during most of the Pleistocene, a very cold and climatically unstable 1.8-million-year epoch, knew what it meant to live within Earth-life's ecosystems. They did so and experienced neither economic nor civilization collapse for nearly all of the 300,000 years of *Homo sapiens'* existence—all but the last 12,000 years when the Pleistocene began giving way to the Holocene, an increasingly warm and climatically more stable epoch; when rising CO_2-driven climate change began warming the Earth and bringing the last ice age to an end; a time when the Earth might have begun to be more conducive to growing crops.

68 ***It was during the relative climatic calm of the succeeding 10,000 years of the Holocene Epoch, human civilization as we have come to know it, evolved.***

72 **Living *within* as opposed to *without* Earth-life ecosystems** means following the survival-driven rules that enable life *within* ecosystems.

72 **Abandoning life in the ecosystem to farm and grow our own food** meant breaking out of Earth's biochemical-based, energy feedback network of animals, plants, water, air, soil, fungi, atmospheric and chemical cycles, and built-in waste recycling closed-loop networks—from the survival-driven network that has powered and sustained all Earth-life species and kept Earth alive for billions of years before Neolithic Revolution *Homo sapiens* showed up.

75 **Econocide.** The term "econocide" has also been used to describe decisions with catastrophic economic consequences. It is suicide seemingly catalyzed by an economic crisis.

"It is the most iconic image of the 1929 Wall Street Crash," Claire Prentice reported for the BBC, "financiers, having lost their fortunes, jumping to their deaths from the windows of skyscrapers." Now, 80 years later, American psychologists have coined the word "econocide" to describe a wave of suicides they say is linked to the current global economic crisis.

According to Price, the problem is not restricted to financiers. One doctor told her, "People think econocide is a problem on Wall Street, but it is also affecting people on Main Street, ordinary families who have lost their homes, their jobs, their savings."

In his 1977 book *Econocide: British Slavery in the Era of Abolition* Seymour Drescher argued that abolishing the slave trade in 1807 was tantamount to economic suicide.

77 Regardless of how humans may choose to build their economies using any of the many varieties: Free-Market Capitalism, Central Command and Control Communism, or anything else in between, if in order to build their economies, humans must raze Earth's forests, pave over its soil, pollute its atmosphere, boil its oceans killing phytoplankton that produce nearly 70 percent of Earth's oxygen, fish its oceans almost free of marine species, threaten most other species with extinction, eradicate most pollinators and insects, and chemically disrupt our human ability to reproduce, we inevitably end up breaking that *survival triad of life* we encountered earlier; that complementarity that must remain intact between Earth-life species, including humans, their economies, and Earth-life ecosystems—that must harmoniously inter-operate for life on Earth to survive.

78 In the words of **Marco Lambertini, Director General of WWF International in the 2020 Living Planet Report,** "Nature is declining globally at unprecedented rates not seen in millions of years. The way we produce and consume food and energy, and the blatant disregard for the environment entrenched in our current economic model, has pushed the natural world to its limits. A deep cultural and systemic shift is urgently needed, one that so far, our civilization has failed to embrace: a transition to a society and economic system that values nature. COVID-19 is a clear manifestation of our broken relationship with nature and highlights the deep interconnection between the health of both people and the planet."

We must rebalance our relationship with the planet to preserve the Earth's amazing diversity of life and enable a just, healthy, and prosperous society—and ultimately to ensure our own survival.

80 **It took humans quite a while, about 12,000 years of experimentation, to come up with various methods of growing food outside of Earth's ecosystems.**

86 **The key takeaway here, though, is that humans have not learned from the mistakes of their Neolithic Revolution ancestors** who abandoned foraging for farming, nor from those it has subsequently made during the last 400 generations—that human life and survival depends upon economies that must be built in harmony with its biodiversity and *within* Earth-life ecosystems as their pre-agriculture hunter-gatherer forebears did and survived for most of our species' existence.

CHAPTER 3
EARLY HUMAN ECONOMIES WERE WATERHOLE ECONOMIES

94 ***Hunter-Gatherer Economies in the Old World and New World***, Morgan et al., Agriculture and the Environment Online Publication, March 2017.

97 **James Suzman** in his book *Affluence Without Abundance: What We Can Learn from the World's Most Successful Civilisation.*

98 **There were an estimated ten million humans in the world on the eve of food production** (Price and Feinman, 2001: 194); now over eight billion people live on this planet, an increase of 700 percent in only ten millennia and growing 1.1 percent or 83 million per year. References: Price, T. D., & J. A. Brown, (1985). "Aspects of hunter-gatherer complexity". In T. D. Price and J. A. Brown, eds. YEAR. *Prehistoric hunter-gatherers: The emergence of cultural complexity* Orlando:Academic Press, 3-20.

98 **Animals that are commonplace today, including dogs, cats, sheep, geese, camels, cattle, pigs, and horses, started as wild animals** but over time were domesticated. (Zeder et al., 2006; Andersson, 2011)

99 **The Pleistocene - The Age of Ice** lasted 2.6 million years. Hunter-gatherers that lived during the Pleistocene (2.4 Mya - 11.8 Kya) confronted dramatically different climate and environments from hunter-gatherers and farmers during the Holocene (11.8 Kya to today).

101 Richerson, P. J., R. Boyd, & R. L. Bettinger (2001). **Was agriculture impossible during the Pleistocene but mandatory during the Holocene**? A climate change hypothesis.

101 **Hunting and gathering societies and their economies expanded into a broad range of habitats** during the Terminal Pleistocene and Early Holocene when approaches to foraging diversified (Steiner, 2001), in part due to the extinction of previously targeted, large-game species, but also because of the broad array of food resources that became available due to the warmer Holocene climate.

The Broad-Spectrum Revolution (BSR) is the term Kent Flannery (1969) used to describe change in hunter-gatherer subsistence practices from narrow (e.g., only large-bodied ungulates) to broad (e.g., including large and small mammals, birds, fish, amphibians, invertebrates, tree nuts, legumes, and grass seeds).

101 **Lee, R. B., & R. Daly (Eds.). 1999. *The Cambridge encyclopedia of hunters and gatherers*.** Cambridge, U.K.: Cambridge University Press.

101 **Diamond and Bellwood 2003.** Starting after about 13,000 BP (before the present) most foragers evolved into or were subsumed or replaced by groups practicing mixed foraging and cultivation and, ultimately, agriculture.

103 **This transition to agriculture** during the Holocene is thought by scientists to have been due, among other things, to changes in the environment brought on by climate change at the end of the Pleistocene Epoch and raises the question: Was agriculture impossible during the Pleistocene?

104 **How the Neolithic Revolution and the rise of agriculture hijacked civilization.** According to James C. Scott, it was this surplus grain, in particular, that enabled the rise of the state — James C. Scott in *Against the Grain*.

105 **Anthropogenic greenhouse gases began long before the Industrial Revolution but rather with the rise of agriculture** —according to William F. Ruddiman in his research entitled "*The Anthropogenic Greenhouse Era Began Thousands of Years Ago*."

106 **The change from hunting and gathering to farming and animal husbandry with the arrival of the Neolithic Revolution,** according to Jared Diamond, turned out to be the greatest mistake humans have made.

And according to Katherine J. Latham (DigitalCommons@University of Nebraska - Lincoln):

"The transition to agriculture in the Neolithic was arguably one of the most drastic lifestyle changes in human history. Changes in diet, living conditions, and subsistence activities had an enormous impact on human health, though effects varied from region to region. Skeletal analysis of these early agricultural communities suggests that the transition to agriculture had an overall negative impact on human oral health, increased the incidence of infectious disease and nutritional deficiencies, and contributed to an overall reduction in human stature."

CHAPTER 4
REDISCOVERING THE HUMAN ECONOMY — FOUNDATIONS

120 The **1987 Montreal Protocol**

An international treaty, adopted in Montreal on September 16, 1987, that aimed to regulate the production and use of chemicals that contribute to the depletion of Earth's ozone layer. Initially signed by 46 countries, the treaty now has nearly 200 signatories.

The initial agreement was designed to reduce the production and consumption of several types of CFCs and halons to 80 percent of 1986 levels by 1994 and 50 percent of 1986 levels by 1999. The protocol went into effect on January 1, 1989. Since then, the agreement has been amended to further reduce and completely phase out CFCs and halons, as well as the manufacture and use of carbon tetrachloride, trichloroethane, hydrofluorocarbons (HFCs), hydrochlorofluorocarbons (HCFCs), hydrobromofluorocarbons (HBFCs), methyl bromide, and other ozone depleting chemicals (ODCs). Several subsequent meetings of the signatory countries were convened to track overall progress toward this goal and to authorize new changes to the process of phasing out ODCs.

More ....

123 **What principles of economic production might one glean from those early human societies and their economies that enabled their longevity and survival?**

Hunter-Gatherer Economies in the Old World and New World.

Oxford Research Encyclopedia of Environmental Science

"Hunter-Gatherer Economies in the Old World and New World" by:

Morgan, Christopher, Shannon Tushingham, Raven Garvey, Loukas Barton, and Robert Bettinger, Subject: Agriculture and the Environment Online Publication Date: Mar 2017DOI: 10.1093/acrefore/9780199389414.013.164

Bicchieri, M. G. (Ed.). (1988). *Hunters and gatherers today: A socioeconomic study of twelve such cultures in the twentieth century*. Prospect Heights, IL: Waveland Press.

Ingold, T., D. Riches, & J. Woodburn (Eds.). (1988). *Hunters and gatherers vol. 1: History, evolution, and social change*. Oxford: Berg.

Ingold, T., D. Riches, & J. Woodburn (Eds.). (1991). *Hunters and gatherers vol. 2: Property, power, and ideology*. Oxford: Berg.

Keeley, L. H. (1988). Hunter-gatherer economic complexity and "population pressure": A cross-cultural approach. *Journal of Anthropological Archaeology*, 7(4), 373–411.

Kelly, R. L. (2013). *The lifeways of hunter-gatherers: The foraging spectrum*. 2d ed. Cambridge, U.K.: Cambridge University Press.

Ingold, T . 1980. The principle of individual autonomy and the collective appropnation of nature.

In *2nd international conference on hunting and gathering societies,* 19 to 24 September 1980. Quebec: Universite Laval, Departement d'Anthropologie. Lee, R. B . 1979. *The !Kung San: men, women, and work in a foraging society.* Cambridge: Univ. Press,

and I. DeVore (Ed.) 1976. *Kalahari hunter-gatherers: studies of the !Kung San and their neighbors.* Cambridge, Mass.: Harvard Univ. Press.

Woodburn. J. C. 1968a. An introduction to Hadza ecology. In *Man the hunter* (eds) R. B. Lee &. I. DeVore. Chicago: Aldlne.

____________1968b. Stability and flexibility in Hadza residential groupings. In *Man the hunter* (eds) R. B. Lee & I. DeVore. Chicago: Aldine.

1970. *Hunters and gatherers: the material culture of the nomadic Hadza.* London: The British Museum.

123 ***Egalitarian Culture: A societal prerequisite to human survival***

Pre-agriculture human economies emerged out of hunter-gatherer human societies organized in small, mostly mobile groups, that pursued a single goal and outcome — life and survival. They sought a living within Earth-life ecosystems and migrated when pickings grew sparse. They lived in harmony with other Earth-life species and, other than for food, sought neither to harm, farm nor domesticate animal or plant species, nor herd them. Culturally they were egalitarian and shared rather than hoarded food and other resources to ensure none would go hungry. In addition, when it came to Earth-life's ecosystems and biodiversity, they followed a kind of DOMC natural-resources-use principle — Don't Own, Modify or Control natural resources. They sought neither to own, significantly modify, nor control natural resources within the ecosystem they encamped and foraged. They were fiercely independent and obeyed neither king, queen, nor rulers of any kind, and believed neither in creator gods nor practiced religions.

"Egalitarian Societies" by James Woodburn. *London School of Economics and Political Science, University London* https://www.jstor.org/stable/2801707;

Cashdan, E. A. 1980. Egalitarianism among hunters and gatherers. *Am. Anthrop.* 82, 116-20. Dodd, R. 1980. Ritual and the maintenance of lnternal co-operation among the Baka hunters and gatherers. In *2nd international conference on hunting and gathering societies, 19 to 24 September.* 1980. Quebec: Universite Laval, Departement d'Anthropologie.

Lee, R. B. (1968). What hunters do for a living, or, how to make out on scarce resource. In R. B. Lee & I. DeVore (Eds.), *Man the hunter*. Chicago: Aldine.

Lee, R. B. (1984). *The Dobe !Kung*. New York: Holt, Rinehart, and Winston, Inc.
Lee, R. B., & I. DeVore (Eds.). (1968). *Man, the hunter*. Chicago: Aldine.

124 **Population Growth**

For most of human history, the global population was a tiny fraction of what it is today. Over the last few centuries, the human population has gone through an extraordinary change. In 1800, there were one billion people. Today there are more than eight billion of us.

126 **At a time when "Nobody Really Knows How the Economy Works,"** according to a recent FED Paper shared by Neil Irwin in an Oct. 1, 2021, *New York Times* article, if one were looking for takeaways on how best human societies might organize to survive, and how best to set up economies to achieve this original overarching goal, a summary comparison of the history of our species' economic past and present lists a few object lessons across eight categories.

What were the principles of economic production one might glean from those early human societies and their economies that enabled their longevity and survival?

126 **What can one glean from a review of these early human societies and economies? There are eight takeaways**

Takeaways on how best human societies might organize to survive.

126 —**Takeaway #1.** Life and Survival was paramount — ecosystems, biodiversity, and human life and survival were the overarching goal and desired outcome of these early human economies.

130 —**Takeaway # 2.** Population size matters: Small populations facilitate mobility and migration and enhance survivability; are more sustainable; reduce complexity; and enable humans' ability to live within the carrying capacity of ecosystems and the Earth.

131 —**Takeaway #3.** Mobility and Migration matter: Mobility and migration are indispensable to survival. Earth-life ecosystems and biodiversity productivity (plant and animal food sources, water, etc.) vary with location, seasons, weather, climate change and natural disasters, hence all Earth-life species must be mobile and prepared to migrate to find food and escape disasters to survive.

133 —**Takeaway #4.** Location matters: Species eke out a living inside Earth-life ecosystems (not outside), utilizing its natural processes and in harmony with its biodiversity.

133 —**Takeaway #5.** Ecosystem and biodiversity care can drive survival or extinction. Humans get to choose: Obey the DOMC rules: Do not seek to Own, Modify and/or Control Earth-life's natural resources: land, soil, water/seas, wind, atmosphere, forests, and most natural resources.

134 —**Takeaway #6.** Natural Resources Only: Use only the natural, recyclable, and biodegradable materials, and renewable energy sources available within Earth-life ecosystems.

134 —**Takeaway #7.** Share to survive; hoard to go extinct: Freely sharing food and other resources needed for life and survival prevents ecosystem resource exhaustion and biodiversity extinction, and thereby enables survival.

138 — **Takeaway #8.** Egalitarian Culture: A culture that prioritized life and survival above surplus and profits; with neither rulers, kings, queens, nor strongmen; nor entertained politicians, their politics nor elections; and acknowledged neither gods nor religions but regarded with fervor the sanctity of life—of human, ecosystems, and biodiversity life.

140 **Surviving hunter-gatherer peoples who are regarded as profoundly egalitarian** practice various leveling mechanisms that ensure social equality, usually by shaming or humbling members of a group that attempt to put themselves above other members. Such peoples include the Mbuti Pygmies of Zaire; the !Kung Bushmen (San) of Botswana and Namibia; the Pandaram and Paliyan of South India; the Batek Negritos of Malaysia and the Hadza of Tanzania. In all these six societies nomadism is fundamental.

Bicchieri, M. G. (Ed.). (1988). *Hunters and gatherers today: A socioeconomic study of twelve such cultures in the twentieth century*. Prospect Heights, IL: Waveland Press.

140 **Leveling mechanisms**

From cultural anthropology, a leveling mechanism is a practice that acts to ensure social equality, usually by shaming or humbling members of a group that attempt to put themselves above other members. They come into operation precisely at the point where the potential for the development of inequalities of wealth, power, and prestige is greatest.

Lee, R. B. (1968). What hunters do for a living, or, how to make out on scarce resources. In R. B. Lee & I. DeVore (Eds.), *Man the Hunter*. Chicago: Aldine.

Lee, R. B. (1984). *The Dobe !Kung*. New York: Holt, Rinehart, and Winston, Inc.
Lee, R. B., & DeVore, I. (Eds.). (1968). *Man the hunter*. Chicago: Aldine.

145 ***Sharing vs. hoarding; equality vs. inequality; and freedom to choose vs. control by others.***

In hunter-gatherer societies and economies then there could never have been the inequality that plagues twenty-first century societies and economies that Piketty so ably describes in *Capital in the Twenty-First Century.*

151 **Foundations of a *Survival Driven Pattern with mobility and migration at its very core.***

(1) *Life* is indispensable to all Earth-life species economies, including human economies, and emerges out of Earth-life ecosystems and biodiversity. No life, no economy.

(2) *Earth-life ecosystems and biodiversity*—the source of all life, yet depends upon Earth-life species to survive.

(3) *Small egalitarian human populations* are next. It won't be a human economy without humans. But these human populations must remain small, mobile, and egalitarian if they are going to rely on Earth-life ecosystems and biodiversity to survive, and vice versa.

(4) *Mobility and Migration.* All life must be mobile to exist and must migrate to survive.

156 **Work: A Deep History, from the Stone Age to the Age of Robots: Suzman ...**

CHAPTER 5
MODERN HUMAN ECONOMIES — TRANSITIONS

188 **Legal-person economies**

Economies dominated by corporations (legal persons) that has essentially replaced human economies. Whereas human economies evolved to enable human, ecosystem and biodiversity survival, legal-person economies evolved out of the human desire for economies dedicated to growing surplus, profits, wealth accumulation, and GDP growth.

188 **Legal person**

In law, a legal person is any person or "thing" that can do the things a human person is usually able to do in law—such as enter contracts, sue and be sued, own property, and so on. The reason for the term "legal person" is that some legal persons are not people: companies and corporations are "persons" legally speaking, but they are not people in a literal sense. Wikipedia.

188 **The Neolithic Revolution**

The Neolithic Revolution—also referred to as the Agricultural Revolution—is thought to have begun about 12,000 years ago. It coincided with the end of the last ice age and the beginning of the current geological epoch, the Holocene. And it forever changed how humans live, eat, and interact, paving the way for modern civilization.

During the Neolithic period, hunter-gatherers roamed the natural world, foraging for their food. But then a dramatic shift occurred. The foragers became farmers, transitioning from a hunter-gatherer lifestyle to a more settled one. A transformation, in the words of Jared Diamond, that turned out to be "The Worst Mistake in the History of the Human Race."

188 **Karl Paul Polanyi, an Austro-Hungarian economic anthropologist and politician, is best known for his book *The Great Transformation*,** which questions the conceptual validity of self-regulating markets.

To Polanyi, human economies were historically embedded in human societies. He was concerned that this society-economy relationship was being reversed with the emergence of the market economy; that human societies were being engulfed by human economies. This socioeconomic transformation would soon end up with legal persons replacing real humans, and legal-person economies replacing human economies; and humans reduced to human resources, a mere factor of production in these legal-person economies.

"In this classic work of economic history and social theory, Karl Polanyi analyzes the economic and social changes brought about by the 'great transformation' of the Industrial Revolution. His analysis explains not only the deficiencies of the self-regulating market, but the potentially dire social consequences of untempered market capitalism."

190 **The First Economic Revolution**

North and Thomas (1977, p. 230), in an article entitled "The First Economic Revolution" published in *The Economic History Review*.

191 **Civitas**

The Latin term "civitas", according to Cicero in the time of the late Roman Republic, was the social body of the cives, or citizens, united by law. It is the law that binds them together, giving them responsibilities on the one hand and rights of citizenship on the other. Wikipedia

191 **Hunter-gatherer egalitarian societies property ownership.**

191 ***Egalitarian Societies*** **by James Woodburn**

London School of' Economics and Political Science, University London

Greater equality of wealth, of power, and of prestige has been achieved in certain hunting and gathering societies than in any other human societes.

These societies. which have economies based on immediate rather than delayed return. are assertively egalitarian. Equality is achieved through direct, individual access to resources; through direct, individual access to means of coercion and means of mobility which limit the imposition of control; through procedures which prevent saving and accumulation and impose sharing through mechanisms which allow goods to circulate without making people dependent upon one another.

People are systematically disengaged from property and therefore from the potentiality in property for creating dependency.

A comparison is made between these societies and certain other egalitarian societies in which there is profound intergenerational inequality and in which the equality between people of senior generations is only a starting point for strenuous competition, resulting in inequality.

The value systems of non-competitive, egalitarian hunter-gatherers limit the development of agriculture because rules of sharing restrict the investment and savings necessary for agriculture: they may limit the care provided to the incapacitated because of the controls on dependency; they may in principle, extend equality to all mankind.

192 **On-Air dialogue** between Paul Krugman, Nobel Laureate, and Fareed Zakaria, host of GPS on CNN

203 ***The Pleistocene-Holocene transition***

The Pleistocene-Holocene transition, which occurred approximately 11,000 years ago, was a time of drastic climate fluctuations, which in turn had a great impact on the environment, atmosphere, ecology, and human populations. Not only were human settlement numbers affected, so too were settlement locations as well as subsistence patterns. According to archaeological indicators, the Pleistocene-Holocene climate was punctuated by repeated glacial cycles. The effects of mass glaciation and deglaciation were vast, intense, and felt globally. At its peak, approximately 30 percent of the Earth's surface was covered by glacial ice sheets. It is estimated that the average annual temperature near these glacial regions was about -6°C. During these glacial cycles sea-levels dropped 100 meters or more across the entire surface of the Earth, due to the large volumes of water contained in the glacial sheets. Major climatic events spanning the Pleistocene-Holocene transition included (1) The last Glacial Maximum, (2) Heinrich 1 Event, (3) the Bølling-Allerød, (4) the Younger Dryas, (5) the pre-Boreal, and (6) the 8.2k Event. Each of these events had extreme effects on the environment, as temperatures oscillated between warm, wet periods and dry, arid ones.

205 The Intergovernmental Panel on Climate Change (IPCC). Climate Change 2021: The Physical Science Basis. **The Sixth Assessment Report: AR6 Climate Change 2021: The Physical Science Basis**

Agricultural expansion and its impacts on tropical nature.

https://www.cell.com/trends/ecology-evolution/fulltext/S0169-5347(13)002929?_returnURL=https%3A%2F%2Flinkinghub.elsevier.com%2Fretrieve%2Fpii%2FS0169534713002929%3Fshowall%3Dtrue

Highlights:

- Agriculture will increase dramatically in tropical nations this century.
- This expansion will have major impacts on tropical forests and semiarid environments.
- The rapid proliferation of roads will strongly influence the footprint of agriculture.

Changes will be most dramatic in South America and Sub-Saharan Africa.

214 Archer, D. & V. Brovkin (2008). "The millennial atmospheric lifetime of anthropogenic CO2." *Climatic Change*, 90, 283–297.

Bala, G., K. Caldeira, A. Mirin, M. Wickett, & C. Delire (2005). "Multicentury changes in global climate and carbon cycle: Results from a coupled climate and carbon model." *Journal of Climate*, 18, 4531–4544.

Gabbatiss, J. (2017). Worst-case global warming predictions are the most accurate, say climate experts. December 6. The Independent

https://www.independent.co.uk/climate-change/news/global-warming-temperature-rise-climate-change-end-century-science-a8095591.html

Gowdy, J. & R. Juliá (2010). "Global warming economics in the long run." *Land Economics*, 86(1), 117–130.

Kasting, J. (1998). "The carbon cycle, climate, and the long-term effects of fossil fuel burning." *Consequences*, 4, 15–27.

Montenegro, A., V. Brovkin, M. Eby, D. Archer, & A. Weaver (2007). "Long-term fate of anthropogenic carbon." *Geophysical Research Letters*, 34, L19707.

215 **The Holocene droughts**

Ten Civilizations or Nations That Collapsed From Drought, Jeff Masters March 21, 2016

Drought is the great enemy of human civilization. Drought deprives us of the two things necessary to sustain life—food and water. When the rains stop and the soil dries up, cities die and civilizations collapse, as people abandon lands no longer able to supply them with the food and water they need to live.

While the fall of a great empire is usually due to a complex set of causes, drought has often been identified as the primary culprit or a significant contributing factor in a surprising number of such collapses. Drought experts Justin Sheffield and Eric Wood of Princeton, in their 2011 book, *Drought,* identify more than ten civilizations, cultures and nations that probably collapsed, in part, because of drought.

As we mark World Water Day on March 22, we should not grow overconfident that our current global civilization is immune from our old nemesis—particularly in light of the fact that a hotter climate due to global warming will make droughts more intense and impacts more severe.

215 **Cultural Responses to Climate Change** During the Late Holocene by Peter B. de Menocal. https://www.science.org/doi/10.1126/science.1059287. Historic and Prehistoric Drought in North America.

During the late Holocene, whole empires collapsed, and their people were diminished to much lower subsistence levels, whereas in other cases, populations migrated and adapted to new subsistence modes. In all cases, the observed societal response reflects an interaction between human cultural elements (socioeconomic, political, and secular stresses) and persistent multi-century shifts in climate.

These empires included: Akkadian (ca. 4200 calendar yr B.P.), Classic Maya (ca. 1200 calendar yr B.P.), Mochica (ca. 1500 calendar yr B.P.), and Tiwanaku (ca.

1000 calendar yr B.P.) empires. Cullen, H. M., P. B. Demenocal, S. Hemming, G. Hemming, F.H. Brown, T. Guilderson, & F. Sirocko (2000) "Evidence from the deep sea." *Geology,* 28, 379–382.

215 **The sixteenth-century drought** that ended the English settlers of northern Virginia.

A group of researchers who study tree ring records have found evidence of a "mega-drought" in the sixteenth century that wreaked havoc for decades in the lives of the early Spanish and English settlers and American Indians throughout Mexico and North America.

Early Settlers of Colonial Virginia.

216 **The Dust Bowl of the 1930s** lasted six years from 1933-1938 and was caused by a lack of precipitation across the northern Great Plains (climate change). It displaced millions of people and is believed to be a possible cause of the subsequent economic collapse.

The Dust Bowl was the name given to the drought-stricken southern plains region of the United States, which suffered severe dust storms during a drought in the 1930s. As high winds and choking dust swept the region from Texas to Nebraska, people and livestock were killed and crops failed across the entire region. The Dust Bowl intensified the crushing economic impacts of the Great Depression and drove many farming families on a desperate migration in search of work and better living conditions.

216 **The Little Ice Age** (1300 to 1870 CE) and the preceding medieval warm period (800 to 1300 CE). These represent the most recent millennial style Holocene climate cycle. While they did not terminate any human civilizations, they did manage to rearrange a few societies and economies. This warm period may have enabled the rise and expansion of the Norse under Erik the Red and enabled the Norse to colonize South Greenland. This expansion ended with the arrival of *the Little Ice Age* (during the late fourteenth century) that may have closed the trade routes with Europe.

About 1,300 years later, another warming of the Arctic caused by global climate change in the twenty-first century, is enabling sea routes that for centuries have been closed by sea ice, enabling a possible trade route to Asia. But this time around it is the Russians, not the Norwegians, that have begun to exploit this thawing of the Arctic, enabling ports and new shipping lanes, including the Northern Sea Route (NSR) and the Northwest Passage (NWP), with geopolitical implications that are just beginning to emerge.

220 **Economic Breakdown**

The economic impact of droughts is severe. Depending on the severity of the drought and the size of the area affected, the local, regional, or national economy might experience a massive setback.

A worldwide drought is in progress.

220 **Water Stress around the world.** Climate change is driving droughts.

222 **Climate Change will force a new climate normal.**

Over the coming 50 years, one to three billion people are projected to be left outside the climate conditions that have served humanity well over the past 6,000 years. Absent climate mitigation or migration, a substantial part of humanity will be exposed to mean annual temperatures warmer than nearly anywhere today.

222 (1) **It will be too hot to live for millions.**

Millions worldwide will face unbearable temperatures. A warming climate is likely to push entire regions out of their comfort zones—and make staying cool a matter of survival.

222 (2) **Climate change will alter where many crops are grown.**

223 (3) ***(Layne, Chapter 6, The Role of Climate Change in the making of an intelligent species, 2019).***

223 Peterson, L. C. & G. H. Haug (2005). "Climate and the collapse of Maya civilization: A series of multi-year droughts helped to doom an ancient culture." *American Scientist, 93*, 322–329.

224 (4) ***"Future of the human climate niche"*** All species have an environmental niche, and despite technological advances, humans are unlikely to be an exception. For thousands of years, humans have concentrated in a surprisingly narrow subset of Earth's available climates, characterized by mean annual temperatures around ~13°C.

224 (5) **THE GREAT CLIMATE MIGRATION**

Climate change will force a new American migration.

226 **Climate Change and Migration.** https://www.propublica.org/article/climate-change-will-force-a-new-american-migration

Migrating to escape global and/or local climate change to survive is *an "evolutionary survival pattern"* (Layne, Chapter 4)

237 **Impact of Covid-19 Pandemic.**

"How the COVID-19 Pandemic Will Permanently Change Society & the Economy" is the title of an article published Aug 17, 2021, in Finopulse.com.

CHAPTER 6
FROM MODERN HUMAN ECONOMIES TO LEGAL-PERSON ECONOMIES

250 **Life before civilization**

Was thought to be "solitary, poor, nasty, brutish, and short." This was the prevailing view of hunter-gatherer societies as propagated by Thomas Hobbes. Hobbes had a low view of human beings. Humans are all basically selfish, driven by fear of death and the hope of personal gain, he believed.

Until the 1960s, according to Serge Svizzero (2014), hunter-gatherer societies were mainly seen from Hobbes' perspective and this vision was also adopted by other authors, most famous among whom was E.R. Service (1966).

Subsequent scholarship demonstrated, to the contrary, that hunter-gatherers were comparably better than many modern humans and may even have been affluent—according to James Suzman, in his book about the San hunter-gatherers called *Affluence Without Abundance: What We Can Learn from the World's Most Successful Civilization.* The book demonstrated that this view was largely incorrect.

"Geneticists say that the oldest gene pattern amongst modern humans is that of the Khoe-San. It dates back to about 80,000 years ago. All other peoples on the planet, Europeans, Black Africans, Asians, North and South Americans, Australians are all descendants of this original gene type. The only possible exception is that of the Hadzabe hunter-gatherers of Tanzania who split off very early from the Khoe-San." Archaeologists now agree that the San are the descendants of the original *Homo sapiens* (anatomically modern humans) who occupied South Africa for at least 150,000 years. The hunting-gathering lifeway of making a living our forebears practiced for all but the last 12,000 years can be demonstrated in *A history of San Peoples of South Africa*."

257 **COP26 in Glasgow**. UN Climate Change Conference (COP26) at the SEC - Glasgow 2021

The UK hosted the 26th UN Climate Change Conference (COP26) in Glasgow from 31 October through 13 November 2021. The COP26 summit brought parties together to accelerate action toward the goals of the Paris Agreement and the UN Framework Convention on Climate Change.

257 **Net-zero does not equal zero CO2.**

Reaching net zero emissions means removing an equal amount of CO_2 from the atmosphere as we release into it.

Put simply, the term "net zero" applies to a situation where global greenhouse gas emissions from human activity are in balance with emissions reductions. At net zero, carbon dioxide emissions are still generated, but an equal amount of carbon dioxide is removed from the atmosphere as is released into it, resulting in zero increase in net emissions.

274 **The IUCN Red List of threatened species**

An indicator of the health of the world's biodiversity. More than 42,100 species are threatened with extinction.

This list of Categories and Criteria is intended to be an easily and widely understood system for classifying species at high risk of global extinction.

There is also an IUCN Red List of Ecosystems Categories and Criteria. It is a global standard for how the conservation status of ecosystems, applicable at local, national, regional, and global levels, is assessed.

280 **People have shaped most of terrestrial nature for at least 12,000 years.**

According to Erle C. Ellis, human populations, and land use over the past 12,000 years, with current biodiversity data, show that nearly three quarters of terrestrial nature has long been shaped by diverse histories of human habitation and use by indigenous and traditional peoples.

Archaeological and paleoecological evidence shows that by 10,000 BCE, all human societies employed varying degrees of ecologically transformative land use practices, including burning, hunting, species propagation, domestication, cultivation, and others that have left long-term legacies across the terrestrial biosphere.

Anthropogenic Transformation of the Terrestrial Biosphere.

Human populations and their use of land have transformed most of the terrestrial biosphere, according to Erle C. Ellis.

Twelve thousand years ago, nearly three quarters of Earth's land was inhabited and therefore shaped by human societies, including more than 95 percent of temperate and 90 percent of tropical woodlands. Lands now characterized as "natural," "intact," and "wild" generally exhibit long histories of use.

280 **Anthropogenic transformation of the terrestrial biosphere.** In the words of Erle C. Ellis, humans have significantly altered nearly all of Earth's systems, including its atmosphere, hydrosphere, lithosphere, and biosphere.

282 **Legal-person economies**

An economy comprised mostly *of legal persons, by legal-persons*, and *for legal-persons* with humans serving as mere employees and consumers. Today one no longer works for the "man," but rather for a legal person—a corporation in the legal-person's economy.

A human economy that has become dominated and displaced by legal person that seems to serve legal person more than humans.

An economy would come to exist for legal person that, according to David Korten in his book *When Corporations Rule the World*, "would emerge as the dominant governance institutions on Earth, with the largest among them reaching into virtually every country of the world and exceeding most governments in size and power."

283 **Legal-persons.** A legal person is any person or "thing" that can do the things a human person is usually able to do in law, such as enter into contracts, sue and be sued, own property, and so on. The reason for the term "legal person" is that some legal persons are not people: companies and corporations are "persons" legally speaking, but they are not people in a literal sense. Many legal persons have become corporations and are able to exercise all the powers of a human under the USA Constitution.

283 **Legal-person societies**

Human societies have now been mostly taken over and are run by legal-person societies. One shouldn't be surprised then, says Korten, "it is corporate interest rather than human interest that defines the policy agendas of states and international bodies."

287 **F.W. de Klerk & Apartheid**

F.W. de Klerk had to abandon what his ancestors had believed in. He was the last president of apartheid South Africa and died on November 11, 2021, aged 85.

De Klerk shared the Nobel Peace Prize in 1993 with Nelson Mandela "for their work for the peaceful termination of the apartheid regime, and for laying the foundations for a new democratic South Africa."

288 **Nelson Rolihlahla Mandela**

Was a South African anti-apartheid activist and politician who served as the first president of South Africa from 1994 to 1999. He was the country's first black head of state and the first elected in a fully representative democratic election.

288 **June 16, 1976 - The Day Apartheid Died**

On 16 June Youth Day is celebrated in South Africa in recognition of the role of the student uprising in June 1976 in the demise of apartheid. But 16 June is more than just a day of recognition; it serves as a stark reminder of the brutality of the apartheid regime and the futility of force in the face of social unrest.

294 **The health risks of leaded fuel**

295 **The oil industry was aware of the risks of climate change decades ago.** What Big Oil knew about climate change, in its own words.

296 **What Exxon Mobil Didn't Say About Climate Change**

297 **What Did Shell Know?**

"Internal Shell Climate Documents Revealed," Climate Investigations Center, April 5, 2018

297 **The Firms That Help Keep Oil Flowing**

298 **The coal industry knew about the danger of rising greenhouse gas emissions as early as 1966.**

And though Coal Powered the Industrial Revolution, it left behind an "Absolutely Massive" Environmental Catastrophe.

300 **The multinational corporation**

A multinational corporation (MNC) is a company that has business operations in at least one country other than its home country. By some definitions, it also generates at least 25 percent of its revenue outside of its home country.

Generally, a multinational company has offices, factories, or other facilities in different countries around the world as well as a centralized headquarters which coordinates global management.

Multinational companies can also be known as international, stateless, or transnational corporate organizations or enterprises. Some may have budgets that exceed those of small countries.

301 **How Corporations Rule the World**

According to David Korten in his book *When Corporations Rule the World,* the company has now replaced the household as the defining unit of economic analysis and organization.

"It is instructive to recall that the modern corporation is a direct descendant of the great merchant companies of the fifteenth, sixteenth-century England and Holland."

303 **How Corporations became people under the law**

Corporations first came into being as the instruments of colonial extraction, have emerged as instruments of natural resources extraction, as well as the dominant institutions on Earth.

304 It was President Abraham Lincoln who observed just before his death:

"Corporations have been enthroned . . . An era of corruption in high places will follow and the money power will endeavor to prolong its reign by working on the prejudices of the people . . . until wealth aggregated in a few hands and the Republic is destroyed. (See John Young, "Mining the Earth" in Lester R. Brown, *State of the World 1992*, New York W.W. Norton 1992.)"

305 **In 1886, in a stunning victory for the proponents of corporate power, the chief justice of the United States declared in Santa Clara County vs. Southern Pacific Railroad that *a private corporation is a natural person under the U.S. Constitution*** although the Constitution makes no mention of corporations.

Thus, corporations came to claim the full rights enjoyed by individuals while being exempted from many of the responsibilities and liabilities of citizenship.

305 **The takeover of human economies by legal-person economies**

Corporations came to claim the full rights enjoyed by individuals while being exempted from many of the responsibilities and liabilities of citizenship.

PART FOUR TECHNOLOGY AND HUMAN ECONOMIES

318 **The Green Revolution**

The Green Revolution refers to a transformative twentieth-century agricultural project that utilized plant genetics, modern irrigation systems, and chemical fertilizers and pesticides to increase food production and reduce poverty and hunger in developing countries. Over time, however, the techniques and policies of the Green Revolution were questioned as they led to inequality and environmental degradation.

318 **Agricultural runoff**

Happens when the water from rain, melted snow or irrigation doesn't sink into the soil for proper absorption. Instead, it moves over the ground, picking up natural and artificial pollutants along the way, contaminating groundwater, polluting lakes, rivers, and marine ecosystems.

CHAPTER 7
TECHNOLOGY
AND HUMAN ECONOMIES

329 **Leader in artificial intelligence will rule world.**

President Vladimir Putin warned that whoever reaches a breakthrough in developing artificial intelligence will come to dominate the world.

332 **Neil deGrasse Tyson & Avis Lang- *Accessory to War***

Modern humans pursue scientific research, new technologies, and innovations for numerous reasons, but seldom is the driving reason a desire to preserve Earth's ecosystems, biodiversity, and human survival.

332 **Technology Origins**

Technology predated early humans. *and* can be traced as far back as 3.3 million years ago (Mya). Stone tools, knives, hammers, and anvils were uncovered at Lake Turkana in Kenya and date back to the time of the *genus Australopithecus,* and *Lucy,* a famous member of this species who lived some 4.4 million to 1.4 (Mya) in Southern Africa.

333 **Oldest Stone tools** (3.3 million years) found at Lake Turkana in Kenya. Approximately 3.3 million years ago someone began chipping away at a rock by the side of a river. Eventually, this chipping formed the rock into a tool used, perhaps, to prepare meat or crack nuts. And this technological feat occurred before humans even evolved.

333 ***The genus Australopithecus and Lucy***

The best-known member of *Australopithecus* is *Au. afarensis*, a species represented by more than 400 fossil specimens from virtually every region of the hominin skeleton.

Dated to between about 3.8 and 2.9 Mya, 90 percent of the fossils assigned to *Au. afarensis* derive from Hadar, a site in Ethiopia's Afar Triangle. *Au. afarensis* fossils have also been found in Chad, Kenya, and Tanzania. The main fossil sample of this species also comes from Hadar, and the specimens found there include a 40-percent-complete skeleton of an adult female ("Lucy") and the remains of at least nine adults and four juveniles buried together at the same time (the "First Family").

333 **Southeast Asia was crowded with archaic human groups long before modern humans turned up.**

Around 55,000-50,000 years ago, a population of modern humans left Africa and started on the long trek that would lead them around the world. After rapidly crossing Eurasia and Southeast Asia, they travelled through the islands of Indonesia, and eventually as far as the continent of Sahul–modern-day Australia and New Guinea.

Their descendants are the modern human populations found right across this enormous region today.

Different genetic studies across this region tell us that the ancestors of modern humans appear to have met and mixed with four different archaic hominins, in at least six events. And this all happened in the very short window of time between leaving Africa 50,000-55,000 years ago and arriving in Australia and New Guinea no more than 5,000 years later.

334 **The Pleistocene - Holocene transition**

Occurred approximately 11,000 years ago and was a time of drastic climate fluctuations that had a great impact on the environment, atmosphere, ecology, and human populations. Not only were human settlements numbers affected, so too were their locations as well as subsistence patterns. It was a time when major shifts in climate and ecology were occurring, including the recolonization or colonization of previously uninhabited landmasses, the migration of human populations, the innovation of novel technologies, and the development of new subsistence strategies.

According to archaeological indicators, the Pleistocene-Holocene climate was punctuated by repeated glacial cycles. It is estimated that the average annual temperature near these glacial regions was about -6°C, and during these glacial cycles, sea levels dropped 100 meters or more across the entire surface of the Earth, due to the large volumes of water contained in the glacial sheets.

This resulted in unprecedented upheavals and disruptions for pre-agriculture hunter-gatherer humans with enormous consequences. Consequences included the expansion of deserts and grasslands and the fragmentation, or at least substantial modification, of the tropical rain forests. The transition from this situation to that characterizing the Holocene was far from straightforward. "Complex" and "oscillatory" better describe both the global and the African climate change at this time.

336 **Technology in the ancient world. A Primer on Paleolithic Technology.**

A Primer on Paleolithic Technology-The Holocene

337 **History of Earth's Climate. Temperatures of the Holocene.**

History of Earth's Climate—The Holocene

The interglacial Holocene has supported the development and growth of human civilisations and has been the cradle of civilizations.

See also: Holocene Epoch: The Age of Man

The Holocene Epoch began 12,000 to 11,500 years ago at the close of the Paleolithic Ice Age and continues through today.

339 **IPCC report**—the Intergovernmental Panel on Climate Change. Climate Change 2022: Impacts, Adaptation and Vulnerability

The IPCC Climate Change 2022 Impacts Report: Why it matters.

339 **Past Extinctions of *Homo* Species Coincided with Increased Vulnerability to Climatic Change**

Other *Homo* species that went extinct include *Homo habilis, Homo ergaster, Homo erectus, Homo floresiensis, The Denisovans, and Homo Neanderthals.*

339 **Ice Ages: What Causes the Earth to Freeze Over Every Few Million Years?**

At least five major ice ages have been documented in Earth's history. What causes ice ages? See also Milankovitch/orbital cycle.

340 **Economic impact of the Covid-19 pandemic.**

The Covid-19 pandemic-driven worldwide economic slowdown

345 **CRISPR - Wikipedia**

CRISPR (/ ˈkrɪspər /) (an acronym for clustered

Regularly interspaced short palindromic repeats is a family of DNA sequences found in the genomes of prokaryotic organisms such as bacteria and archaea.

These sequences are derived from DNA fragments of bacteriophages that had previously infected the prokaryote.

CRISPR is also the name given to a technology that can be used to edit genes and, as such, will likely change the world. The essence of CRISPR is simple: It's a way of finding a specific bit of DNA inside a cell.

347 **Crocodiles and Palm Trees in the Arctic?**

If we keep burning fossil fuels, Earth will be eight degrees warmer, returning to the climate of 52 million years ago, according to new research. It's the most dire prediction yet.

348 **Migration route of early humans out of Africa**

The environments of Eastern Africa, from whence Anatomical Modern Humans are thought to have migrated.

Carto, Shannon L., Andrew J Weaver, Renée Hetherington, Yin Lam, Edward C Wiebe, "Out of Africa and into an ice age: on the role of global climate change in the late Pleistocene migration of early modern humans out of Africa"

Human Migration. Humans left Africa and reached as far as Australia via a Southern Coastal Route.

CHAPTER 8
ENERGY AND HUMAN ECONOMIES: FROM RENEWABLES TO RENEWABLES

371 **Photosynthesis**

381 **The Biogeochemical Cycles**

A biogeochemical cycle or an inorganic-organic cycle is a circulating or repeatable pathway by which either a chemical element or a molecule moves through both biotic (biosphere) and abiotic (lithosphere, atmosphere, and hydrosphere) components of an ecosystem. Let us try to understand this definition. These cycles demonstrate the way in which the energy is used. These cycles move the essential elements needed to sustain life throughout ecosystems. They recycle, store, and regulate vital elements, through the physical facets of ecosystems, and they depict the association between living and non-living things in the ecosystems, thus enabling continuous ecosystems survival. There are two types of biogeochemical cycles:

Gaseous cycles – Includes the Carbon, Oxygen, Nitrogen, and the Water cycle.

Sedimentary cycles – Includes the Sulfur, Phosphorus, and Rock cycles.

381 **Chemotroph**

Photosynthesis

In the process of photosynthesis, plants convert radiant energy from the sun into chemical energy in the form of glucose—or sugar.

(water)		(carbon dioxide)		(sunlight)		(glucose)		(oxygen)
$6\,H_2O$	+	$6\,CO_2$	+	radiant energy	→	$C_6H_{12}O_6$	+	$6\,O_2$

(Source: Adapted from The National Energy Education Project (public domain))

Chemoautotrophs are cells that create their own energy and biological materials from inorganic chemicals.

A chemotroph is an organism that obtains energy by the oxidation of electron donors in its environments. These molecules can be organic or inorganic. The chemotroph designation contrasts with phototrophs, which use photons. Chemotrophs can be either autotrophic or heterotrophic. Chemotrophs can be found in areas where electron donors are present in high concentration, for instance around hydrothermal vents. More at Wikipedia

389 ***The Origin of Capitalism: A Longer View***

396 **Industrial Revolution**

In modern history, the process of change from an agrarian and handicraft economy to one dominated by industry and machine manufacturing. These technological changes introduced novel ways of working and living and fundamentally transformed society. This process began in Britain in the eighteenth century and from there spread to other parts of the world.

The energy revolution

One of the best ways of defining the essence of the Industrial Revolution is to describe it as the escape from the constraints of an organic economy.

CHAPTER 9
CLIMATE CHANGE, MIGRATION, AND HUMAN ECONOMIES

419 **C3 and C4 Grasses** –Wikipedia ; Science

Cool season grasses are C3 grasses, while warm season grasses are C4 grasses. The C refers to carbon and the number is the number of carbon atoms in the first compound produced by photosynthesis. So, cool season grasses produce a compound with 3-carbon atoms and warm season grasses produce a 4-carbon atom compound.

The two groups have different growth requirements, responding differently to temperature, moisture, and light. Warm season grasses require higher temperatures and light with lower requirements for moisture. For cool season grasses, it's the opposite.

In botany, C_4 carbon fixation is one of three known methods of photosynthesis used by plants. C4 plants increase their photosynthetic efficiency by reducing or suppressing photorespiration, which mainly occurs under low atmospheric CO_2 concentration, high light, high temperature, drought, and salinity.

C4 photosynthesis probably first evolved 30-35 million years ago in the Oligocene, and further origins occurred since, most of them in the last 15 million years. C4 plants are mainly found in tropical and warm-temperate regions, predominantly in open grasslands where they are often dominant. While most are graminoids, other growth forms such as forbs, vines, shrubs, and even some trees and aquatic plants are also known among C4 plants.

Grasses using the C4 photosynthetic pathway are ubiquitous across Earth's low to mid-latitudes, dominating modern tropical lowland, grassland, and savanna ecosystems. C4 grassy biomes play an important role in regulating global climate and have been linked to key adaptations and diversification in mammalian faunas. The C4 photosynthetic pathway is physiologically advantageous under conditions of aridity, higher temperatures and irradiance, seasonal climates, and low atmospheric partial pressure of carbon dioxide (pCO_2).

The assembly of Africa's iconic C4 grassland ecosystems is central to interpretations of many mammal lineages, including hominins. C4 grasses are thought to have become ecologically dominant in Africa only after ten million years ago (Ma). However, palaeobotanical records older than ten Ma are sparse, limiting assessment of the timing and nature of C4 biomass expansion.

420 **Richard Potts in "Hominin evolution in settings of strong environmental variability."**

Investigations into how climate change shaped human evolution have begun to focus on environmental dynamics, i.e., the nature and tempo of climate and landscape variability, an approach that de-emphasizes static reconstructions of early hominin habitats. The interaction among insolation cycles is especially apparent in the paleoenvironmental records of the East African Rift System, where the longest records of human evolution are preserved.

420 **A. Timmerman & T. Friedrich's Nature article entitled "Late Pleistocene climate drivers of early human migration."**

Based on fossil and archaeological data it has been hypothesized that the exodus of Homo sapiens out of Africa and into Eurasia between ~50-120 thousand years ago occurred in several orbitally paced migration episodes.

The findings document that orbital-scale global climate swings played a key role in shaping Late Pleistocene global population distributions, whereas millennial-scale abrupt climate changes, associated with Dansgaard-Oeschger events, had a more limited regional effect.

421 **Lawrence Barham** and **Peter Mitchell** in Chapter 8 entitled the "Transitions: From the Pleistocene into the Holocene" in their book *The First Africans*.

Africa has the longest record—some 2.5 million years—of human occupation of any continent. For nearly all of this time, its inhabitants have made tools from stone and have acquired their food from its rich wild plant and animal resources. Archaeological research in Africa is crucial for understanding the origins of humans and the diversity of hunter-gatherer ways of life.

422 **Last Glacial Maximum (LGM)**, (Britannica)

The most recent geologic interval, which spanned 29,000 to 19,000 years ago, in which the geographic extent of ice sheet and glacier coverage on Earth's surface peaked. Some 8 percent of the planet's total surface was covered in ice, and sea levels were approximately 125 meters (410 feet) lower than those of the present day. Often abbreviated to LGM, the Last Glacial Maximum was the most recent of the five glacial periods (ice ages) within the past 450,000 years, and it occurred during the final stage of the Pleistocene Epoch (2.58 million to 11,700 years ago).

422 **The Bølling–Allerød Interstadial** (also called the Late Glacial Interstadial), was an abrupt warm and moist interstadial period that occurred during the final stages of the Last Glacial Period. This warm period ran from 14,690 to 12,890 years before the present (BP). It began with the end of the cold period known as the Oldest Dryas and ended abruptly with the onset of the Younger Dryas, a cold period that reduced temperatures back to near-glacial levels within a decade.

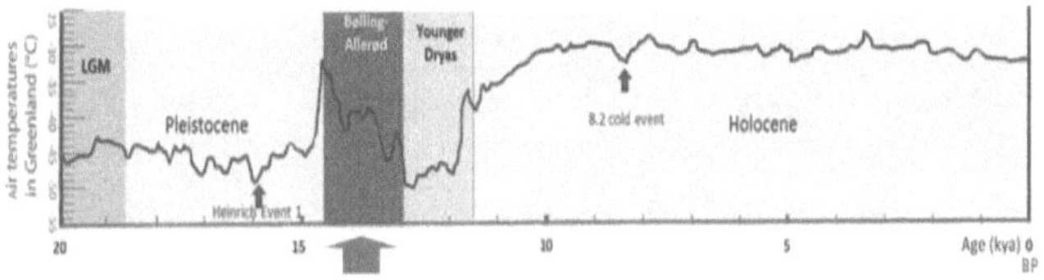

The Bølling–Allerød warming within the Post-Glacial period that followed the Last Glacial Maximum (LGM). Evolution of temperature in the Post-Glacial period according to Greenland ice cores. (Source: Wikipedia)

422 **The Younger Dryas,** which occurred circa 12,900 to 11,700 BP, was a stadial (cooling) event which marked a return to glacial conditions, temporarily reversing the climatic warming of the preceding Late Glacial Interstadial (also known as the Bølling–Allerød Interstadial, which spanned from 14,670 to 12,900 BP).

The Younger Dryas was the most severe and longest lasting of several interruptions to the warming of the Earth's climate.

The end of the Younger Dryas marks the beginning of the current Holocene Epoch.

422 **The Preboreal** is an informal stage of the Holocene epoch.

It lasted from 10,300 to 9,000 BP in radiocarbon years. It is the first stage of the Holocene Epoch. The Preboreal oscillation was a short (ca. 150 years) cooling episode within the Preboreal.

422 **The 8.2 ka cooling event** caused by Laurentide ice saddle collapse.

The 8.2 ka event was a period of abrupt cooling of 1–3°C across large parts of the Northern Hemisphere, which lasted for about 160 years. The original hypothesis for the cause of this event has been the outburst of the proglacial Lakes Agassiz and Ojibway. These drained into the Labrador Sea in ~0.5–5 years and slowed the Atlantic Meridional Overturning Circulation, thus cooling the North Atlantic region.

423 **Homo**

From Latin, homō ("human") is a genus of great ape that emerged from the genus Australopithecus and encompasses the extant species Homo sapiens (modern humans) and a number of extinct species classified as either ancestral to or closely related to modern humans, including Homo erectus and Homo neanderthalensis. The oldest member of the genus is Homo habilis, with records of just over two million years ago. Homo, together with the genus Paranthropus, is probably most closely related to the species Australopithecus africanus within Australopithecus. The closest living relatives of Homo are of the genus Pan (which includes chimpanzees and bonobos), with the ancestors of Pan and Homo estimated to have diverged around 5.7-11 million years ago during the Late Miocene.

https://en.wikipedia.org/wiki/Homo#List_of_lineages

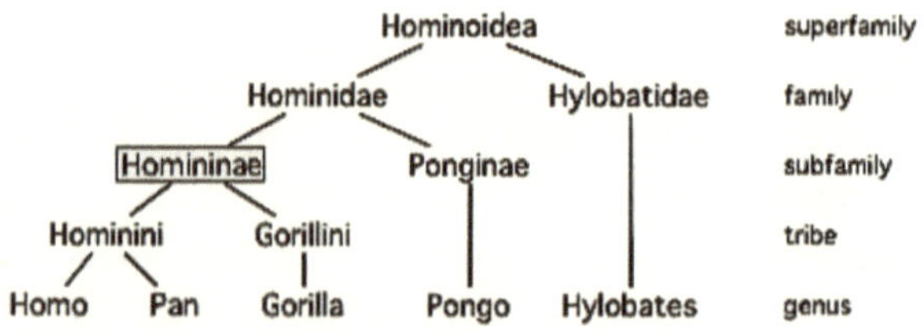

Evolutionary tree chart emphasizing the subfamily Homininae and the tribe Hominini. After diverging from the line to Ponginae, the early Homininae split into the tribes Hominini and Gorillini. The early Hominini split further, separating the line to Homo from the lineage of Pan. Currently, tribe Hominini designates the subtribes Hominina, containing genus Homo; Panina, genus Pan; and Australopithecina, with several extinct genera—the subtribes are not labelled on this chart.

433 **Mitochondrial Eve** – (Source - Wikipedia)

In human genetics, the Mitochondrial Eve (more technically known as the Mitochondrial-Most Recent Common Ancestor, shortened to mt-Eve or mt-MRCA) is the matrilineal most recent common ancestor (MRCA) of all living humans. In other words, she is defined as the most recent woman from whom all living humans descend in an unbroken line purely through their mothers and through the mothers of those mothers, back until all lines converge on one woman.

Haplogroup L

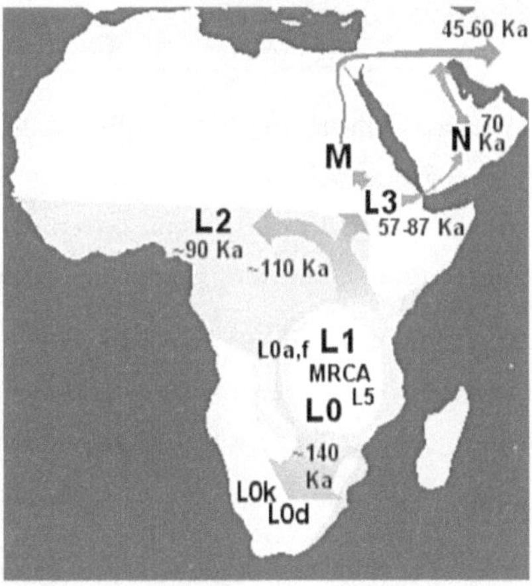

Possible time of origin	c. 100–230 kya
Possible place of origin	East Africa
Ancestor	n/a
Descendants	Mitochondrial macro-haplogroups L0, L1, and L5
Defining mutations	None

In terms of mitochondrial haplogroups, the mt-MRCA is situated at the divergence of macro-haplogroup L into L0 and L1-6. As of 2013, estimates on the age of this split ranged at around 155,000 years ago, consistent with a date later than the speciation of *Homo sapiens* but earlier than the recent out-of-Africa dispersal.

434 **Humans migrated out of Africa as the climate shifted from wet to very dry about 60,000 years ago**, according to research led by a University of Arizona geoscientist.

"Ancient Humans left Africa to avoid a drying climate" claims Jessica E. Tierney et al. of the University of Arizona.

"There's always been a question about whether climate change had any influence on when our species left Africa," said Tierney, UA associate professor of geosciences. "Our data suggest that when most of our species left Africa, it was dry and not wet in northeast Africa."

Genetic research indicates people migrated from Africa into Eurasia between 70,000 and 55,000 years ago. Previous researchers suggested the climate must have been wetter than it is now for people to migrate to Eurasia by crossing the Horn of Africa and the Middle East.

Tierney and her colleagues found that around 70,000 years ago, climate in the Horn of Africa shifted from a wet phase called "Green Sahara" to even drier than the region is now. The region also became colder.

The researchers traced the Horn of Africa's climate 200,000 years into the past by analyzing a core of ocean sediment taken in the western end of the Gulf of Aden. Tierney said before this research there was no record of the climate of northeast Africa back to the time of human migration out of Africa.

"Our data say the migration comes after a big environmental change. Perhaps people left because the environment was deteriorating," she said. "There was a big shift to dry and that could have been a motivating force for migration."

434 **Heinrich events**

Are any of a series of at least six large discharges of icebergs that carried coarse-grained rocky debris, apparently from North American ice sheets, into the North Atlantic Ocean at latitudes between 40° and 55° N, where the debris was later deposited on the ocean floor as the icebergs melted. Heinrich events are thought to be associated with sudden climate warming events that occurred between approximately 60,000 and 16,800 years ago during the most recent ice age of the Pleistocene Epoch (about 2.6 million to 11,700 years ago).

435 **The Great Rift Valley**

A geographical and geological feature running north to south for around 4,000 miles (6,400 kilometers), from northern Syria to central Mozambique in East Africa. Astronauts say it is the most significant physical detail on the planet that is visible from space.

The Rift Valley is the result of an ancient series of faults, rifts, and volcanoes deriving from the shifting of tectonic plates at the junction between the Somalian and the African plates. Scholars recognize two branches of the GRV: the eastern half—which is that piece north of Lake Victoria that runs NE/SW and meets the Red Sea; and the western half—running nearly N/S from Victoria to the Zambezi river in Mozambique. The eastern branch rifts first occurred 30 million years ago, the western 12.6 million years ago. In terms of rift evolution, many parts of the Great Rift Valley are in different stages, from pre-rift in the Limpopo valley, to initial-rift stage at the Malawi rift; to typical-rift stage in the northern Tanganyika rift region; to advanced-rift stage in the Ethiopian rift region; and finally to oceanic-rift stage in the Afar range.

438 **The human climate niche. (Source - Wikipedia)**

The temperature range that has sustained human life and activity, known as "the human climate niche," averages 11-15°C and we have been thriving in it for thousands of years. But the climate crisis has already put more than 600 million people outside of the climate niche.

The human climate niche is the ensemble of climate conditions that have sustained human life and human activities, like agriculture, on the globe for the last millennia. The human climate niche is estimated by calculating the human population density with respect to mean annual temperature.

The human population distribution as a function of mean annual temperature is bimodal and results in two modes; one at 15°C and another one at ~20 to 25°C. Crops and livestock required for sustaining the human population are also limited to the similar niche conditions.

Given the rise in mean global temperatures, the human population is projected to experience climate conditions beyond the human climate niche. Some projections show that considering temperature and demographic changes, 2.0 and 3.7 billion people will live in and out of the niche by 2030 and 2090, respectively.

440 **USDA Hardiness Zone Map**

The USDA Plant Hardiness Zone Map is the standard by which gardeners and growers can determine which plants are most likely to thrive at a location. The map is based on the average annual minimum winter temperature, divided into 10°F zones.

441 **Past Extinctions of Homo Species** Coincided with Increased Vulnerability to Climatic Change

At least six different Homo species populated the world during the Pleistocene. The extinction of all but one of them is currently shrouded in mystery, despite the enormous importance of the matter.

445 **Earth More Sensitive to Increasing Greenhouse Gas Than Thought**

Carbon dioxide is a so-called greenhouse gas: The more of it there is in the atmosphere, the more heat is trapped there and the higher the global average temperature climbs. Scientists have long debated how sensitive Earth's climate is to this planet-warming trace gas. Specifically, they ask, how much will worldwide temperatures rise if the level of CO_2 becomes double that seen in the era before human activity began spewing the gas into the atmosphere?

Current models and a range of observations suggest that Earth will warm somewhere between 1.5° and 4.5°C once carbon dioxide levels are twice the preindustrial concentration of about 280 parts per million and the climate system adjusts, says Steven Sherwood, an atmospheric scientist at the University of New South Wales in Sydney, Australia. That's a wide range, he notes—a range that hasn't narrowed since the first computer simulations of climate debuted in the 1970s. Broad analyses have hinted that a model's climate sensitivity depends, in large part, on how the model estimates cloud formation at low altitude, he adds. If a simulation produces generous amounts of low-level clouds, more sunlight is reflected back into space, and Earth, on the whole, is cooler than it would have been without the clouds.

447 **Arctic continental shelves.** (Source - Wikiversity)

Subsea permafrost carbon pools below the Arctic shelf seas are a major unknown in the global carbon cycle. Carbon from the Arctic ice escaping into the atmosphere makes knowing just how much CO_2 is heating the atmosphere at any given time an unknown. Thawing of Arctic permafrost could release significant amounts of carbon into the atmosphere, and with recent Arctic warming several degrees stronger than predicted, it is important to establish the vulnerability of permafrost to future warming. The study also suggests that a significant amount of old carbon is activated from ice–complex permafrost, with about two–thirds of this old carbon escaping to the atmosphere as carbon dioxide and the remainder being re–buried in shelf sediments.

The future trajectory of greenhouse gas concentrations depends on interactions between climate and the biogeosphere. Thawing of Arctic permafrost could release significant amounts of carbon into the atmosphere in this century. Ancient Ice Complex deposits outcropping along the ~7,000-kilometre-long coastline of the East Siberian Arctic Shelf (ESAS), and associated shallow subsea permafrost, are two large pools of permafrost carbon, yet their vulnerability to thawing and decomposition are largely unknown. Recent Arctic warming is stronger than has been predicted by several degrees, and is particularly pronounced over the coastal ESAS region. There is thus a pressing need to improve our understanding of the links between permafrost carbon and climate in this relatively inaccessible region.

Continental shelf is a portion of a continent that is submerged under an area of relatively shallow water, known as a shelf sea. Much of these shelves were exposed by drops in sea level during glacial periods. The shelf surrounding an island is known as an insular shelf.

The continental margin, between the continental shelf and the abyssal plain, comprises a steep continental slope, surrounded by the flatter continental rise, in which sediment from the continent above cascades down the slope and accumulates as a pile of sediment at the base of the slope. Extending as far as 500 km (310 mi) from the slope, it consists of thick sediments deposited by turbidity currents from the shelf and slope. The continental rise's gradient is intermediate between the gradients of the slope and the shelf.

Under the United Nations Convention on the Law of the Sea, the name continental shelf was given a legal definition as the stretch of the seabed adjacent to the shores of a particular country to which it belongs.

448 **Global warming**

Carbon dioxide in the atmosphere is increasing at a pace 100 times faster than it naturally should. Our planet is warming ten times faster than it has in 65 million years. Our oceans are acidifying 100 times faster than they have in at least 20 million years, and oxygen dead zones in our oceans have increased tenfold since 1950. "Right now, emissions are ten to 20 times higher than what happened at the end of the Permian mass extinction, which was the largest and biggest mass extinction," Professor Uwe Brand said. "Earth is amid what science says is an unprecedented rate of change, unlike anything seen in tens of millions of years."

"Earth may have already passed that crucial IPCC 1.5°C warming limit"

Global warming is the increase in the average temperature of the Earth's near-surface air and oceans since the mid-20th century and its projected continuation. Global surface temperature increased 0.74 ± 0.18°C (1.33 ± 0.32°F) during the last century. The Intergovernmental Panel on Climate Change (IPCC) concludes that increasing greenhouse gas concentrations resulting from human activity such as fossil fuel burning, and deforestation are responsible for most of the observed temperature increase since the middle of the 20th century. The IPCC also concludes that variations in natural phenomena such as solar radiation and volcanoes produced most of the warming from pre-industrial times to 1950 and had a small cooling effect afterward. These basic conclusions have been endorsed by more than 45 scientific societies and academies of science, including all of the national academies of science of the major industrialized countries.

449 **Oceans overheating beyond temperatures that drove The Great Dying.**

Climate change brings with it the increasing risk of extinction across species and systems. Marine species face particular risks related to water warming and oxygen depletion.

Carbon dioxide in the atmosphere is increasing at a pace 100 times faster than it naturally should. Our planet is warming ten times faster than it has in 65 million years. Our oceans are acidifying 100 times faster than they have in at least 20 million years, and oxygen dead zones in our oceans have increased tenfold since 1950." "Right now, emissions are ten to 20 times higher than what happened at the end of the Permian mass extinction, which was the largest and biggest mass extinction," Professor Uwe Brand said. "Earth is amid what science says is an unprecedented rate of change, unlike anything seen in tens of millions of years.

451 **Tipping Points**

Occur when change in large parts of the climate system—known as tipping elements—become self-perpetuating beyond a warming threshold and may lead to abrupt, irreversible, and dangerous impacts with serious implications for humanity.

457 **Economic Growth** Modern human economies. (Source - Investopedia)

Economic growth is an increase in the production of economic goods and services in one period compared with a previous period. It can be measured in nominal or real (adjusted to remove inflation) terms. Traditionally, aggregate economic growth is measured in terms of gross national product (GNP) or gross domestic product (GDP), although alternative metrics are sometimes used.

Economic Sectors (modern economies)

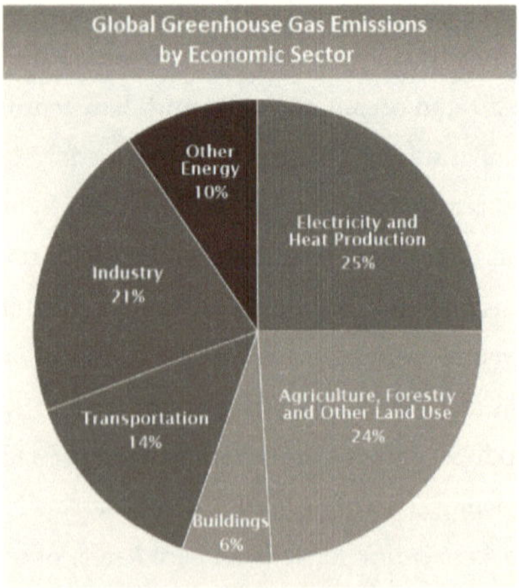

Source: IPCC (EPA's website. Based on global emissions from 2010.)

GDP: The most common measure of economic growth is the real GDP. This is the total value of everything, both goods and services, produced in an economy, with that value adjusted to remove the effects of inflation.

Economic variations on growth: Green Growth, Degrowth, No-growth, Postgrowth, and Decoupling growth and GHG generation.

Factors of Production: In economics, factors of production, resources, or inputs are used in the production process to produce output—that is, goods and services. Factors of production is an economic concept that refers to the inputs needed to produce goods and services. The factors are land, labor, capital, and entrepreneurship. The four factors consist of resources required to create a good or service, which is measured by a country's gross domestic product (GDP).

CHAPTER 10
SURVIVAL-DRIVEN ECONOMIES
WERE WATERHOLE ECONOMIES

483 **Planetary Boundaries**

Planetary boundaries are a framework to describe limits to the impacts of human activities on the Earth system. Beyond these limits, the environment may not be able to self-regulate anymore. This would mean the Earth system would leave the period of stability of the Holocene, in which human society developed. They are a set of nine planetary boundaries within which humanity can continue to develop and thrive for generations to come.

The concept of planetary boundaries has nine linear, delicately interconnected specific conditions: 1. Climate change 2. Rate of biodiversity loss (terrestrial and marine) 3. Interference with nitrogen/phosphorus cycles 4. Stratospheric ozone depletion 5. Ocean acidification 6. Global fresh water uses 7. Change in land use 8. Chemical pollution 9. Atmospheric aerosol loading.

488 **The Great Dying**

Permian–Triassic mass extinction pulses driven by major marine carbon cycle perturbations.

"The Permian/Triassic boundary approximately 251.9 million years ago marked the most severe environmental crisis identified in the geological record, which dictated the onwards course for the evolution of life. Magmatism from Siberian Traps is thought to have played an important role, but the causational trigger and its feedback are yet to be fully understood. Here we present a new boron-isotope-derived seawater pH record from fossil brachiopod shells deposited on the Tethys shelf that demonstrates a substantial decline in seawater pH coeval with the onset of the mass extinction in the latest Permian. Combined with carbon isotope data, our results are integrated in a geochemical model that resolves the carbon cycle dynamics as well as the ocean redox conditions and nitrogen isotope turnover. We find that the initial ocean acidification was intimately linked to a large pulse of carbon degassing from the Siberian sill intrusions. We unravel the consequences of the greenhouse effect on the marine environment, and show how elevated sea surface temperatures, export production and nutrient input driven by increased rates of chemical weathering gave rise to widespread deoxygenation and sporadic sulfide poisoning of the oceans in the earliest Triassic. Our findings enable us to assemble a consistent biogeochemical reconstruction of the mechanisms that resulted in the largest Phanerozoic mass extinction."

489 **Siberian traps** (see also The Great Dying)

These traps were the likely culprit for end-Permian extinction. New study finds massive eruptions likely triggered mass extinction.

492 **The 1987 Montreal Protocol to stop CFC-11** – Scientific Assessment

The global atmosphere has seen a decline in the burden of most ozone-depleting substances since the implementation of the Montreal Protocol on Substances that Deplete the Ozone Layer (Engel and Rigby, 2019). The Earth's ozone layer is on track to recover within four decades, a UN-backed panel of experts said. The overall phase-down has led to the notable recovery of the protective ozone layer in the upper stratosphere and decreased human exposure to harmful ultraviolet (UV) rays from the sun.

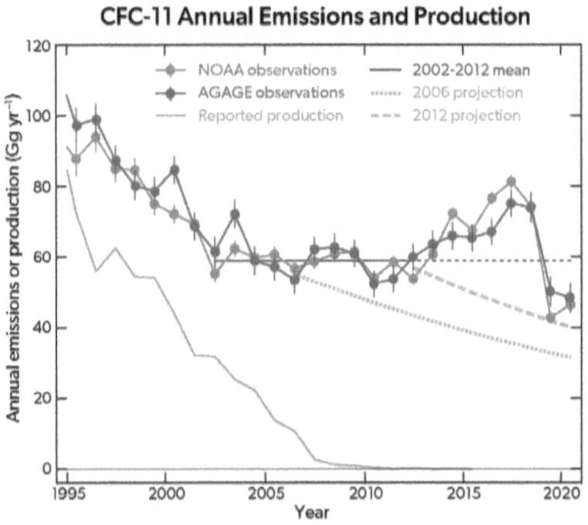

CFC-11 global emissions and reported production. Shown are emissions of CFC-11 derived from AGAGE (Advanced Global Atmospheric Gases Experiment; red)

and NOAA (National Oceanic and Atmospheric Administration; blue) global network measurements of CFC-11 abundances (see also Figure 1-3 of the Assessment) and a model using a CFC-11 lifetime of 52 years. Also shown is the production history reported to the UN Environment Program for all uses (green), the average of annual emissions over the 2002–2012 period (horizontal purple line) extended to 2020 (dashed purple line), and scenario projections based on observations through 2006 or through 2012 (grey dotted and dashed lines).

New technology warning: *stratospheric aerosol injection (SAI).*

However, *scientists also warned of the unintended impacts on the ozone layer of new technologies such as geoengineering.* For the first time, they examined the potential effects on the ozone arising from the intentional addition of aerosols into the stratosphere, known as a *stratospheric aerosol injection (SAI).* But they warned that an "unintended consequence" of SAI was that it "could also affect stratospheric temperatures, circulation, and ozone production and destruction rates and transport."

A renewed rise in global HCFC-141b emissions between 2017–2021

Despite a global ban on CFC production for dispersive uses, recent work found unexpected emissions of CFC- 11 (trichlorofluoromethane) between 2012 and 2017, likely stemming from CFC-11 produced in violation of the Montreal Protocol after 2010 (Montzka et al., 2018; Rigby et al., 2019; Montzka et al., 2021; Park et al., 2021).

492 **What Big Oil knew about climate change, in its own words**

493 **Investor-state dispute settlement (ISDS)**

How treaties protecting fossil fuel investors could jeopardize global efforts to save the climate—and cost countries billions.

496 **Wellbeing Economies**

Wellbeing Economics argues that a new way of developing our economies—around the well-being of people and planet—is not only possible, but our most urgent task. By letting go of GDP growth as the central gauge for economic policy and focusing on a new set of measures, Wellbeing Economists want to make the economy work for the many (not only the rich), and protect the planet at the same time. The Scottish First Minister recently gave a TED Talk about this. And you'll find more conceptual ideas around this on the WEAll website.

496 **Sustainable Development Goals**

The Sustainable Development Goals (SDGs), also known as the Global Goals, were adopted by the United Nations in 2015 as a universal call to action to end poverty, protect the planet, and ensure that by 2030 all people enjoy peace and prosperity.

The 17 SDGs are integrated—they recognize that action in one area will affect outcomes in others, and that development must balance social, economic, and environmental sustainability.

Countries have committed to prioritize progress for those who are furthest behind. The SDGs are designed to end poverty, hunger, AIDS, and discrimination against women and girls.

The creativity, know-how, technology, and financial resources from all of society is necessary to achieve the SDGs in every context.

499 **Humans must colonize another planet in 100 years or face extinction**, says Stephen Hawking. (https://www.cnbc.com/2017/05/05/stephen-hawking-human-extinction-colonize-planet.html)

499 **Kepler 186f 'Most Earth-like planet yet'** spotted by Kepler. https://www.bbc.com/news/science-environment-27054366.

The rocky planet, Kepler 186f, is close to the size of Earth and has the potential to hold liquid water, which is critical for life, the team says.

Nestled in the Milky Way, it is part of a five-planet system that orbits around a cool dwarf star. It was spotted by the Kepler telescope, which has found nearly 1,000 new worlds since its launch in 2009.

"This is the smallest planet we've found so far in the habitable zone," said Prof Stephen Kane, an astrophysicist from San Francisco State University, US.

Kepler 186f is about 500 light-years away from the Earth.

503 **Climate Tipping points**

Climate tipping points are conditions beyond which changes in a part of the climate system become self-perpetuating. These changes may lead to abrupt, irreversible, and dangerous impacts with serious implications for humanity. Armstrong McKay et al. present an updated assessment of the most important climate tipping elements and their potential tipping points, including their temperature thresholds, time scales, and impacts. Their analysis indicates that even global warming of 1°C, a threshold that we already have passed, puts us at risk by triggering some tipping points. This finding provides a compelling reason to limit additional warming as much as possible.

505 ***Fusion Energy***

Fusion energy is the source of energy at the center of stars, including the sun. Stars, like most of the universe, are made up of hydrogen, the simplest and most abundant element in the universe, created during the big bang. The center of a star is so hot and so dense that the immense pressure forces hydrogen atoms together. These atoms are forced together so strongly that they create new atoms entirely—helium atoms—and release a staggering amount of energy in the process. This energy is called fusion energy.

505 **How climate change is changing the planet**

Climate change has already destabilized the Earth's poles, putting the rest of the planet in peril.

The Thwaites ice shelf could collapse within the next three to five years, unleashing a river of ice that could dramatically raise sea levels.

The rapid transformation of the Arctic and Antarctic creates ripple effects all over the planet. Sea levels will rise, weather patterns will shift, and ecosystems will be altered. Unless humanity acts swiftly to curb emissions, scientists say, the same forces that have destabilized the poles will wreak havoc on the rest of the globe. For more see Arctic Report Card: Update for 2021.

510 **Humanity has used 50 percent of the world's habitable land and one-third of the world's forests for agriculture.** Today all but 3 percent of the Earth's ecosystems is left intact.

511 **World population reached eight billion in 2022.** It was less than five million 10,000 years ago.

514 **How Hunter-Gatherers Maintained Their Egalitarian Ways** by Dr. Peter Gray

Egalitarianism

The belief in human equality, especially political, social, and economic equality. Egalitarianism has been a driving principle of many modern social movements, including the Enlightenment, feminism, civil rights efforts, and the establishment of international human rights. Given that there are many ways in which people can relate as equals or be treated the same, egalitarianism as a concept is versatile and sometimes contentious.

Egalitarianism is often contrasted with hierarchy, the classification of people according to ability, economic power, social status, or other factors. While early human societies were often quite egalitarian, some scholars have proposed that the advent of agriculture and the consequent accumulation of wealth may have encouraged the development of hierarchical societies.

Egalitarianism

(1) The political doctrine that holds that all people in a society should have equal rights from birth.

(2) The doctrine of the equality of mankind and the desirability of political and economic and social equality.

REFERENCES

"1 d Milankovitch/Orbital Cycle." n.d. NOAA Climate.gov. Accessed December 27, 2024. https://www.climate.gov/teaching/literacy/1-d-milankovitchorbital-cycle.

"9.5: Anthropogenic Causes of Climate Change." 2020. Biology LibreTexts. Libretexts. June 5, 2020. https://bio.libretexts.org/Courses/Monterey_Peninsula_College/MPC_Environmental_Science/09%3A_Climate/9.05%3A_Anthropogenic_Causes_of_Climate_Change.

"10. Conclusions: Main Findings." n.d. Greenfacts.org. Accessed December 27, 2024. https://www.greenfacts.org/en/ecosystems/millennium-assessment-3/99-main-findings-0.htm.

"10 Pandemics That Changed the World." 2015. Cprcertified.com. October 27, 2015. Accessed December 27, 2024. https://www.cprcertified.com/blog/10-pandemics-that-changed-the-world.

"14 Ancient Civilizations That Collapsed." n.d. Ancientcivilizationsworld.com. Accessed December 27, 2024. https://ancientcivilizationsworld.com/collapsed/.

"A Primer on Paleolithic Technology." 2012. Nature.com. Accessed December 27, 2024. https://www.nature.com/scitable/knowledge/library/a-primer-on-paleolithic-technology-83034489/.

"About Homo Erectus and the First Fire." n.d. Actforlibraries.org. Accessed December 27, 2024. http://www.actforlibraries.org/about-homo-erectus-and-the-first-fire/.

Adam, David. 2021. "How Far Will Global Population Rise? Researchers Can't Agree." *Nature* 597 (7877): 462–65. https://doi.org/10.1038/d41586-021-02522-6.

Africa Center for Strategic Studies. 2021. "African Migration Trends to Watch in 2022." Africa Center. December 17, 2021. Accessed December 27, 2024. https://africacenter.org/spotlight/african-migration-trends-to-watch-in-2022/.

"Agricultural Runoff." 2019. Conservationlawcenter.org. August 2, 2019. Accessed December 27, 2024. https://conservationlawcenter.org/blog/wqm19-series-agricultural-runoff.

Ahmed, Nafeez. 2020. "Theoretical Physicists Say 90% Chance of Societal Collapse within Several Decades." VICE. July 28, 2020. https://www.vice.com/en/article/theoretical-physicists-say-90-chance-of-societal-collapse-within-several-decades/.

"Alaska Department of Revenue." n.d. Permanent Fund Dividend. Accessed December 27, 2024. https://pfd.alaska.gov/.

Aldern, Clayton, Christopher Collins, and Naveena Sadasivam. 2021. "How Texas's Zombie Oil Wells Are Creating an Environmental Disaster Zone." *The Guardian*, April 15, 2021. https://www.theguardian.com/environment/2021/apr/15/texas-zombie-oil-wells-environmental-disaster-zone.

Alves, Raquel Silva, Juliana do Canto Olegário, Matheus Nunes Weber, Mariana Soares da Silva, Raissa Canova, Jéssica Tatiane Sauthier, Letícia Ferreira Baumbach, et al. 2022. "Detection of Coronavirus in Vampire Bats (Desmodus Rotundus) in Southern Brazil." *Transboundary and Emerging Diseases* 69 (4): 2384–89. https://doi.org/10.1111/tbed.14150.

"Annual Report 2012." 2012. Worldbank.org. Accessed December 27, 2024. https://documents1.worldbank.org/curated/en/168831468332487486/pdf/730480AR0v10EP0nnual0Report020120En.pdf.

"Anthropocene." 2024. Wikipedia, The Free Encyclopedia. December 27, 2024. https://en.wikipedia.org/w/index.php?title=Anthropocene&oldid=1265563538.

Archer, D., and V. Brovkin. 2008. "The Millennial Atmospheric Lifetime of Anthropogenic CO2." *Climatic Change* 90: 283–97. https://doi.org/10.1007/S10584-008-9413-1.

Archer, David. 2005. "Fate of Fossil Fuel CO_2 in Geologic Time." *Journal of Geophysical Research* 110 (C9). https://doi.org/10.1029/2004jc002625.

Armstrong, Martin. 2022. "World Population Reaches 8 Billion." Statista. November 15, 2022. https://www.statista.com/chart/28744/world-population-growth-timeline-and-forecast/.

Armstrong McKay, David I., Arie Staal, Jesse F. Abrams, Ricarda Winkelmann, Boris Sakschewski, Sina Loriani, Ingo Fetzer, Sarah E. Cornell, Johan Rockström, and Timothy M. Lenton. 2022. "Exceeding 1.5°C Global Warming Could Trigger Multiple Climate Tipping Points." *Science (New York, N.Y.)* 377 (6611). https://doi.org/10.1126/science.abn7950.

Arsenault, Chris. 2014. "Only 60 Years of Farming Left If Soil Degradation Continues." *Scientific American*. December 5, 2014. Accessed December 27, 2024. https://www.scientificamerican.com/article/only-60-years-of-farming-left-if-soil-degradation-continues/.

"ATMO336 - Spring 2012." n.d. Arizona.edu. Accessed December 27, 2024. http://www.atmo.arizona.edu/students/courselinks/fall12/atmo336/lectures/sec5/pleistocene.html.

"Australopithecus." 2024. Wikipedia, The Free Encyclopedia. December 9, 2024. https://en.wikipedia.org/w/index.php?title=Australopithecus&oldid=1262018574.

Barham, Lawrence, and Peter Mitchell. 2008. "Transitions: From the Pleistocene into the Holocene." In *The First Africans*, 308–55. Cambridge, England: Cambridge University Press.

BBC. 2020. "How Covid-19 Put Our Food in Peril," October 14, 2020. https://www.bbc.com/reel/playlist/follow-the-food?vpid=p08vdj30.

———. 2021. "Pandora Papers: A Simple Guide to the Pandora Papers Leak," October 3, 2021. https://www.bbc.com/news/world-58780561.

BBC News. 2020. "FinCEN Files: All You Need to Know about the Documents Leak." *BBC*, September 20, 2020. https://www.bbc.com/news/uk-54226107.

———. 2021. "Canada Weather: Heat Hits Record 46.6C as US North-West Also Sizzles." *BBC*, June 28, 2021. https://www.bbc.com/news/world-us-canada-57634700.

Bearak, Max, and Manuela Andreoni. 2022. "Brazil, Indonesia and Congo Sign Rainforest Protection Pact." November 14, 2022. nytimes.com. Accessed December 27, 2024. https://www.nytimes.com/2022/11/14/climate/brazil-indonesia-democratic-congo-rainforest-protection-pact.html.

Behr, Felix. 2022. "Here's How Much the War Affected Ukraine's Grain Exports." Tasting Table. August 15, 2022. https://www.tastingtable.com/965662/heres-how-much-the-war-affected-ukraines-grain-exports/.

Berardelli, Jeff. 2021. "The Great Dying: Earth's Largest-Ever Mass Extinction Is a Warning for Humanity." CBS News. March 4, 2021. https://www.cbsnews.com/news/great-dying-permian-triassic-extinction-event-warning-humanity/.

Berwyn, Bob. 2023. "Relentless Rise of Ocean Heat Content Drives Deadly Extremes." Inside Climate News. January 11, 2023. https://insideclimatenews.org/news/11012023/relentless-rise-of-ocean-heat-content-drives-deadly-extremes/.

"Bezos Earth Fund." 2022. Bezos Earth Fund. #creator. August 29, 2022. https://www.bezosearthfund.org/.

Bhalla, Nita. 2019. "'No Tomorrow' Unless Natural Resource Consumption Falls: UN." Global Citizen. March 13, 2019. https://www.globalcitizen.org/en/content/natural-resource-consumption-danger-UN/.

Bhutto, Fatima. 2023. "Climate change is the catastrophe to end all catastrophes." October 16, 2023.Washingtonpost.com. Accessed December 27, 2024. https://www.washingtonpost.com/opinions/2023/10/16/climate-catastrophe-greece-wildfires-pakistan-super-floods/?_pml=1.

Bilmes, Linda J. 2021. "Putting a Dollar Value on Nature Will Give Governments and Businesses More Reasons to Protect It." *The Conversation*, May 11, 2021. http://theconversation.com/putting-a-dollar-value-on-nature-will-give-governments-and-businesses-more-reasons-to-protect-it-153968.

"Biogeochemical Cycle." 2024. Wikipedia, The Free Encyclopedia. December 17, 2024. https://en.wikipedia.org/w/index.php?title=Biogeochemical_cycle&oldid=1263558150.

"Biogeochemical Cycles." n.d. from *Introductory Biology: Evolutionary and Ecological Perspectives*. Umn.edu. Accessed December 27, 2024. https://pressbooks.umn.edu/introbio/chapter/ecosystemcycles/.

Blake, Tom. 2021. "14 Popular Side Gigs Reviewed - Best Ways to Make Extra Money" Money Crashers. May 24, 2023. https://www.moneycrashers.com/protections-gig-economy-workers/.

"Bølling–Allerød Interstadial" 2024. Wikipedia, The Free Encyclopedia. Accessed December 27, 2024. https://en.wikipedia.org/wiki/Bølling–Allerød_warming.

Borenstein, Seth and The Associated Press. 2022. "Landmark UN Climate Change Report: 'Parts of the Planet Will Become Uninhabitable.'" WHYY. February 28, 2022. https://whyy.org/articles/un-ipcc-climate-change-report-uninhabitable-planet-code-red/.

Borenstein, Seth, and The Associated Press. 2023. "Gen Z New Yorkers Are Furious with the UN: 'If You Do Not Want the Blood of My Generation to Be on Your Hands, End Fossil Fuels.'" Fortune. September 18, 2023. https://fortune.com/2023/09/18/gen-z-new-yorkers-un-climate-week-march-to-end-fossil-fuels/.

Bourne, Joel K., and John Stanmeyer. 2009. "The Global Food Crisis." *National Geographic*, June 1, 2009. https://www.nationalgeographic.com/magazine/article/cheap-food.

Braddock, Scott, Brenda L. Hall, Joanne S. Johnson, Greg Balco, Meghan Spoth, Pippa L. Whitehouse, Seth Campbell, Brent M. Goehring, Dylan H. Rood, and John Woodward. 2022. "Relative Sea-Level Data Preclude Major Late Holocene Ice-Mass Change in Pine Island Bay." *Nature Geoscience* 15 (7): 568–72. https://doi.org/10.1038/s41561-022-00961-y.

Brannen, P. 2017. *The Ends of the World: Volcanic Apocalypses, Lethal Oceans and Our Quest to Understand Earth's Past Mass Extinctions.* New York: Simon and Schuster.

Breitburg, Denise, et al. 2018. "Declining oxygen in the global ocean and coastal waters." Sciencemag.org. Accessed December 27, 2024. https://science.sciencemag.org/content/359/6371/eaam7240.

"Browse Films." n.d. Letterboxd.com. Accessed December 27, 2024. https://letterboxd.com/films/year/1974/.

Bruggers, James. 2021. "Coal Powered the Industrial Revolution. It Left Behind an 'Absolutely Massive' Environmental Catastrophe." Inside Climate News. December 12, 2021. https://insideclimatenews.org/news/12122021/coal-powered-the-industrial-revolution-it-left-behind-an-absolutely-massive-environmental-catastrophe/.

Burke, Anthony, and Danielle Celermajer. 2021. "Human Progress Is No Excuse to Destroy Nature. A Push to Make 'Ecocide' a Global Crime Must Recognise This Fundamental Truth." *The Conversation*, August 31, 2021. http://theconversation.com/human-progress-is-no-excuse-to-destroy-nature-a-push-to-make-ecocide-a-global-crime-must-recognise-this-fundamental-truth-164594.

Burke, K. D., J. W. Williams, M. A. Chandler, A. M. Haywood, D. J. Lunt, and B. L. Otto-Bliesner. 2018. "Pliocene and Eocene Provide Best Analogs for Near-Future Climates." *Proceedings of the National Academy of Sciences of the United States of America* 115 (52): 13288–93. https://doi.org/10.1073/pnas.1809600115.

"Burkina Faso." 2024. Wikipedia, The Free Encyclopedia. December 24, 2024. https://en.wikipedia.org/w/index.php?title=Burkina_Faso&oldid=1265062572.

"Can Europe Decarbonise Its Heavy Industry?" 2022. *Economist (London, England: 1843)*, September 19, 2022. https://www.economist.com/business/2022/09/19/can-europe-decarbonise-its-heavy-industry.

Cao, Qian. n.d. "What Are Atmospheric Rivers, and How Are They Changing?" *Scientific American*. Accessed December 27, 2024. https://www.activesustainability.com/water/atmospheric-rivers/.

Cardinale, Bradley J., J. Emmett Duffy, Andrew Gonzalez, David U. Hooper, Charles Perrings, Patrick Venail, Anita Narwani, et al. 2012. "Biodiversity Loss and Its Impact on Humanity." *Nature* 486 (7401): 59–67. https://doi.org/10.1038/nature11148.

Carey, Cayelan C., Bas W. Ibelings, Emily P. Hoffmann, David P. Hamilton, and Justin D. Brookes. 2012. "Eco-Physiological Adaptations That Favour Freshwater Cyanobacteria in a Changing Climate." *Water Research* 46 (5): 1394–1407. https://www.sciencedirect.com/science/article/abs/pii/S0043135411007883.

Carrington, Damian. 2014. "Earth Has Lost Half of Its Wildlife in the Past 40 Years, Says WWF." *The Guardian*, September 30, 2014. https://www.theguardian.com/environment/2014/sep/29/earth-lost-50-wildlife-in-40-years-wwf.

———. 2021. "Just 3% of World's Ecosystems Remain Intact, Study Suggests." *The Guardian*, April 15, 2021. https://www.theguardian.com/environment/2021/apr/15/just-3-of-worlds-ecosystems-remain-intact-study-suggests.

Cassella, Carly. 2020. "Chilling Report Suggests 1 out of 5 Countries Could Be Headed for Ecosystem Collapse." ScienceAlert. October 13, 2020. https://www.sciencealert.com/chilling-new-report-shows-1-out-of-5-countries-headed-for-ecosystem-collapse.

———. 2021. "Past 7 Years in a Row Were Hottest on Record, Harrowing WMO Report Confirms." ScienceAlert. November 1, 2021. https://www.sciencealert.com/provisional-un-report-confirms-past-7-years-have-been-the-warmest-on-record.

———. 2022. "Here's a Glimpse at a Future Hothouse Earth If Greenhouse Gasses Aren't Curbed." ScienceAlert. May 8, 2022. https://www.sciencealert.com/here-s-a-glimpse-at-a-future-hothouse-earth-if-greenhouse-gasses-aren-t-curbed.

———. 2023. "Domesticating Animals Changed Human Health Forever – and Not for the Better." ScienceAlert. October 28, 2023. https://www.sciencealert.com/domesticating-animals-changed-human-health-forever-and-not-for-the-better.

"Catastrophic Change Looms as Earth Nears Climate 'Tipping Points', Report Says." 2023. *Nature* 624 (7991): 233–34. https://www.nature.com/articles/d41586-023-03849-y.

"Chad." 2024. Wikipedia, The Free Encyclopedia. December 26, 2024. https://en.wikipedia.org/w/index.php?title=Chad&oldid=1265304736.

Chase-Lubitz, Jesse. 2024. "The Maldives Is Racing to Create New Land. Why Are so Many People Concerned?" Nature.com. April 23, 2024. https://www.nature.com/immersive/d41586-024-01157-7/index.html.

"Chemoautotroph." 2016. Biology Dictionary. December 10, 2016. https://biologydictionary.net/chemoautotroph/.

Cho, Adrian. 2022. "Mass of rare particle may conflict with 'standard model,' signaling new physics." Science.org. Accessed December 27, 2024. https://www.science.org/content/article/mass-rare-particle-may-conflict-standard-model-signaling-new-physics.

Cho, Renée. 2021. "Net Zero Pledges: Can They Get Us Where We Need to Go?" State of the Planet. December 16, 2021. https://news.climate.columbia.edu/2021/12/16/net-zero-pledges-can-they-get-us-where-we-need-to-go/.

Christian, Jordan I., Elinor R. Martin, Jeffrey B. Basara, Jason C. Furtado, Jason A. Otkin, Lauren E. L. Lowman, Eric D. Hunt, Vimal Mishra, and Xiangming Xiao. 2023. "Global Projections of Flash Drought Show Increased Risk in a Warming Climate." *Communications Earth & Environmen*t 4 (1): 1–10. https://doi.org/10.1038/s43247-023-00826-1.

Chu, Jennifer. 2015. "Siberian Traps Likely Culprit for End-Permian Extinction." MIT News | Massachusetts Institute of Technology. September 16, 2015. Accessed December 28, 2024. https://news.mit.edu/2015/siberian-traps-end-permian-extinction-0916.

Chu, Tooki. 2019. "Humans Interbred with Four Extinct Hominin Species." Gowing Life. October 13, 2019. https://www.gowinglife.com/humans-interbred-with-four-extinct-hominin-species/.

Clifford, Cat. 2022. "Democratic Lawmakers Accuse Big Oil Companies of 'Greenwashing.'" CNBC. December 9, 2022. https://www.cnbc.com/2022/12/09/democratic-lawmakers-accuse-big-oil-of-greenwashing.html?te=1&nl=david-wallace-wells&emc=edit_dww_20221215.

"Climate Change 2021: The Physical Science Basis." 2021. IPCC. August 6, 2021. Accessed December 27, 2024. https://www.ipcc.ch/report/sixth-assessment-report-working-group-i/.

"Climate Change 2022: Impacts, Adaptation and Vulnerability." 2022. IPCC. February 28, 2022. Accessed December 27, 2024. https://www.ipcc.ch/report/ar6/wg2/.

"Climate Change Will Alter Where Many Crops Are Grown." 2021. *Economist (London, England: 1843)*, August 28, 2021. https://www.economist.com/international/2021/08/28/climate-change-will-alter-where-many-crops-are-grown.

Climate Investigations Center. 2018. "Internal Shell Climate Documents Revealed." Climateinvestigations.org. April 15, 2018. Accessed December 27, 2024.

CNN. 2021. "On GPS: How Threatening Is Covid's Delta Variant?," August 1, 2021. https://www.cnn.com/videos/tv/2021/08/01/exp-gps-0801-krugman-covid-economy.cnn.

Collins, Chuck. 2024. "Updates: Billionaire Wealth, U.S. Job Losses and Pandemic Profiteers." Inequality.org. March 18, 2024. https://inequality.org/great-divide/updates-billionaire-pandemic/.

"COP15 Adopts Biodiversity Plan to Protect 30% of Land and Water by 2030." 2022. Bloomberg.com. December 19, 2022. Accessed December 27, 2024. https://www.bloomberg.com/news/articles/2022-12-19/cop15-adopts-biodiversity-plan-to-protect-30-of-land-and-water-by-2030?leadSource=uverify%20wall.

"Corporations." n.d. LII / Legal Information Institute. Accessed December 28, 2024. https://www.law.cornell.edu/wex/corporations.

"Cosmological Redshift." n.d. Western Washington University. Wwu.edu. Accessed December 28, 2024. https://www.wwu.edu/astro101/a101_hubble_redshift.shtml

"COVID-19 Cases." n.d. Datadot. Accessed December 27, 2024. https://covid19.who.int/.

Crane, Emily. 2022. "What Supreme Court's Leaked Decision on Roe v. Wade Means for Abortion Rights." *New York Post*, May 3, 2022. https://nypost.com/2022/05/03/what-supreme-courts-roe-v-wade-decision-means-for-abortion/.

Crenson, Matt. 2011. "In Ancient Southwest Droughts, a Warning of Dry Times to Come." *Science News Magazine*. August 1, 2011. https://www.sciencenews.org/article/ancient-southwest-droughts-warning-dry-times-come.

Crucifix, Michel, Marie-France Loutre, and André Berger. 2005. "Commentary on 'the Anthropogenic Greenhouse Era Began Thousands of Years Ago.'" *Climatic Change* 69 (2–3): 13–426. https://doi.org/10.1007/s10584-005-7278-0.

Dartnell, Lewis. 2019. *Origins: How Earth's History Shaped Human History*. La Vergne, TN: Basic Books.

Davis, Mark, dir. 2021. *Built for Mars: The Perseverance Rover*. United States.

"Deep-Sea Mining May Soon Ease the World's Battery-Metal Shortage." 2023. *Economist (London, England: 1843)*, July 2, 2023. https://www.economist.com/science-and-technology/2023/07/02/deep-sea-mining-may-soon-ease-the-worlds-battery-metal-shortage.

DeGrasse Tyson, Neil, and Avis Lang. *Accessory to War: The Unspoken Alliance Between Astrophysics and the Military*. Accessed December 27, 2024. https://www.amazon.com/Accessory-War-Unspoken-Alliance-Astrophysics/dp/0393357465.

deMenocal, Peter B. 2001. "Cultural Responses to Climate Change during the Late Holocene." *Science* (New York, NY) 292 (5517): 667–73. https://www.science.org/doi/10.1126/science.1059287.

Department of Economic and Social Affairs. n.d. "The 17 Goals." United Nations DESA. Sdgs.un.org. Accessed December 27, 2024. https://sdgs.un.org/goals.

Department of Economic and Social Affairs. 2016. *The Millennium Development Goals Report 2015*. United Nations.

Diamond, Jared. 1999. "The Worst Mistake in the History of the Human Race." *Discover Magazine*. May 1, 1999. https://www.discovermagazine.com/planet-earth/the-worst-mistake-in-the-history-of-the-human-race.

———. 2004. *Collapse: How Societies Choose to Fail or Succeed*. New York, NY: Viking Press, 2004.

"Doomsday Clock." 2024. Wikipedia, The Free Encyclopedia. December 10, 2024. https://en.wikipedia.org/w/index.php?title=Doomsday_Clock&oldid=1262236273.

"Drought Timescales: Short- vs. Long-Term Drought." n.d. Drought.gov. Accessed December 27, 2024. https://www.drought.gov/what-is-drought/drought-timescales-short-vs-long-term-drought.

Dubey, Anna. 2024. "Last Glacial Maximum." In *Encyclopedia Britannica*.

Dunham, Will. 2016. "Sea level rise projected to displace 13 million in U.S. by 2100." March 14, 2016. Reuters.com. Accessed December 27, 2024. https://www.reuters.com/article/idUSKCN0WG1YR/.

Easterbrook, Don. 2019. "Heinrich Event." In *Encyclopedia Britannica*.

"Economic Impact of the COVID-19 Pandemic." Wikipedia, The Free Encyclopedia. https://en.m.wikipedia.org/wiki/Economic_impact_of_the_COVID-19_pandemic.

"Ecosystem." 2024. Wikipedia, The Free Encyclopedia. December 26, 2024. https://en.wikipedia.org/w/index.php?title=Ecosystem&oldid=1265364416.

Editors of Encyclopedia Britannica. 2017. "East African Rift System." *Encyclopedia Britannica*. https://www.britannica.com/place/East-African-Rift-System.

"Edwin Hubble: 7 Facts About the Man Who Changed the Universe." 2015. *Biography*. December 29, 2015. https://www.biography.com/scientists/edwin-hubble-biography-facts.

Eldridge, Stephen. 2024. "Egalitarianism." In *Encyclopedia Britannica*.

El Gharib, Sarah. 2021. "5 Things to Know About COVAX, the Life-Saving Vaccine Initiative." Global Citizen. March 9, 2021. https://www.globalcitizen.org/en/content/what-is-covax/.

Ellis, Erle C. 2011. "Anthropogenic Transformation of the Terrestrial Biosphere." *Philosophical Transactions. Series A, Mathematical, Physical, and Engineering Sciences* 369 (1938): 1010–35. https://doi.org/10.1098/rsta.2010.0331.

"Emissions Gap Report 2023: Broken Record." 2023. UNEP. Accessed December 27, 2024. https://www.unep.org/interactives/emissions-gap-report/2023/.

"Eocene." n.d. Newworldencyclopedia.org. Accessed December 27, 2024. https://www.newworldencyclopedia.org/entry/Eocene.

"Ethyl Leaded Gasoline." 2012. *Environmental History*. September 23, 2012. https://environmentalhistory.org/about/ethyl-leaded-gasoline/.

ExamplesLab. 2021. "15 Examples of Hazardous Waste." Examples Lab. admin. December 12, 2021. https://www.exampleslab.com/15-examples-of-hazardous-waste/.

Farhoud, Nada. 2019. "Scientists Warn Raging Amazon Fires Could Tip Us beyond the Point of No Return." *The Mirror*. August 27, 2019. https://www.mirror.co.uk/news/uk-news/scientists-warn-raging-amazon-fires-19017448.

"File:Population Curve.Svg." Wikipedia, The Free Encyclopedia. https://en.wikipedia.org/wiki/File:Population_curve.svg.

Fishman, Andrew. 2021. "Brazil's Indigenous Groups Mount Unprecedented Protest against Destruction of the Amazon." *The Intercept*. August 28, 2021. https://theintercept.com/2021/08/28/brazil-amazon-indigenous-protest/.

Fletcher, Charles, et al. 2024. "Earth at risk: An urgent call to end the age of destruction and forge a just and sustainable future." PNAS April 2, 2024. Accessed December 27, 2024. https://academic.oup.com/pnasnexus/article/3/4/pgae106/7638480.

Floros, John D., Rosetta Newsome, William Fisher, Gustavo V. Barbosa-Cánovas, Hongda Chen, C. Patrick Dunne, J. Bruce German, et al. 2010. "Feeding the World Today and Tomorrow: The Importance of Food Science and Technology: an IFT Scientific Review." *Comprehensive Reviews in Food Science and Food Safety* 9 (5): 572–99. https://doi.org/10.1111/j.1541-4337.2010.00127.x.

Foden, Wendy B., Bruce E. Young, H. Resit Akçakaya, Raquel A. Garcia, Ary A. Hoffmann, Bruce A. Stein, Chris D. Thomas, et al. 2019. "Climate Change Vulnerability

Assessment of Species." *Wiley Interdisciplinary Reviews. Climate Change* 10 (1). https://doi.org/10.1002/wcc.551.

Franta, Benjamin. 2018. "On Its 100th Birthday in 1959, Edward Teller Warned the Oil Industry about Global Warming." *The Guardian*, January 1, 2018. https://www.theguardian.com/environment/climate-consensus-97-per-cent/2018/jan/01/on-its-hundredth-birthday-in-1959-edward-teller-warned-the-oil-industry-about-global-warming.

———. 2021. "What Big Oil Knew about Climate Change, in Its Own Words." *The Conversation*, October 28, 2021. http://theconversation.com/what-big-oil-knew-about-climate-change-in-its-own-words-170642.

Freedman, Andrew. 2013. "The Last Time CO2 Was This High, Humans Didn't Exist." Climatecentral.org. May 3, 2013. Accessed December 27, 2024. https://www.climatecentral.org/news/the-last-time-co2-was-this-high-humans-didnt-exist-15938.

"Freshwater Biodiversity." n.d. Panda.org. Accessed December 27, 2024. https://wwf.panda.org/discover/our_focus/freshwater_practice/freshwater_biodiversity_222/.

"F.W. de Klerk Had to Abandon What His Ancestors Had Believed In." 2021. *Economist (London, England: 1843)*, November 20, 2021. https://www.economist.com/obituary/2021/11/20/fw-de-klerk-had-to-abandon-what-his-ancestors-had-believed-in.

Gabbatiss, Josh. 2017. "Worst-Case Global Warming Predictions Are the Most Accurate, Say Climate Experts." *Independent*, December 7, 2017. https://www.independent.co.uk/climate-change/news/global-warming-temperature-rise-climate-change-end-century-science-a8095591.html.

"Gaia Hypothesis," n.d. Harvard.edu. Accessed December 28, 2024. https://www.sciencedirect.com/topics/earth-and-planetary-sciences/gaia-hypothesis.

Ganguly, Debjani. 2023. "'Now I Am Become Death, the Destroyer of Worlds' – the Bhagavad Gita Explained." *The Conversation*, October 24, 2023. http://theconversation.com/now-i-am-become-death-the-destroyer-of-worlds-the-bhagavad-gita-explained-214365.

Garland, Eric. 2012. "What Happens When There's No Growth to Manage," *Harvard Business Review*, September 28, 2012. https://hbr.org/2012/09/what-happens-whens-theres-no-g.

"Geologic Time Scale." 2024. Wikipedia, The Free Encyclopedia. December 24, 2024. https://en.wikipedia.org/w/index.php?title=Geologic_time_scale&oldid=1264884039.

Gibbens, Sarah. 2018. "Industrial Fishing Occupies a Third of the Planet." *National Geographic*, February 22, 2018. https://www.nationalgeographic.com/science/article/global-industrial-fishing-footprint-spd.

Gladstone, Rick. "Pandora Papers: A Money Bomb With Political Ripples." October 4, 2021. nytimes.com. Accessed December 27, 2024. https://www.nytimes.com/2021/10/04/world/pandora-papers.html?campaign_id=39&emc=edit_ty_20211011&instance_id=42550&nl=opinion-today&regi_id=76369677&segment_id=71322&te=1&user_id=cf3c5202536c3283927ea89694f95cce.

Glikson, Andrew. 2015. "Climate and the Rise and Fall of Civilizations: A Lesson from the Past." *The Conversation*, December 10, 2015. http://theconversation.com/climate-and-the-rise-and-fall-of-civilizations-a-lesson-from-the-past-51907.

Glikson, Andrew Y. 2014. "Climate and Holocene Civilizations." In *SpringerBriefs in Earth Sciences*, 91–102. Dordrecht: Springer Netherlands.

Global Challenges Foundation. n.d. "Ecological Collapse." globalchallenges.org. Accessed December 27, 2024. https://globalchallenges.org/global-risks/ecological-collapse/.

"Global greenhouse gas emissions and warming scenarios." n.d. Ourworldindata.org. Accessed December 27, 2024. https://ourworldindata.org/uploads/2018/04/Greenhouse-gas-emission-scenarios-01.png.

"Global Inequality." 2017. Inequality.org. May 25, 2017. https://inequality.org/facts/global-inequality/.

"Global warming." n.d. Phys.org. Accessed December 27, 2024. https://phys.org/tags/global+warming/.

"Global Wetland Outlook." 2021. Global Wetland Outlook. Accessed December 27, 2024. https://www.global-wetland-outlook.ramsar.org/.

Goddard, Taegan. 2024. "It's the Economy Stupid." *Political Dictionary* (blog). November 13, 2024. https://politicaldictionary.com/words/its-the-economy-stupid/.

Gowdy, John. n.d. "Our hunter-gatherer future: Climate change, agriculture, and uncivilization." Academia.edu. Accessed December 27, 2024. https://www.academia.edu/66550632/Our_hunter_gatherer_future_Climate_change_agriculture_and_uncivilization.

Gray, Peter. 2012. "Hunter-Gatherers and Play." Scholarpedia.org. Accessed December 27, 2024. http://scholarpedia.org/article/Hunter-Gatherers_and_Play.

"Green Growth." 2024. Wikipedia, The Free Encyclopedia. December 4, 2024. https://en.wikipedia.org/w/index.php?title=Green_growth&oldid=1261136932.

"Greenhouse Gas Emissions from Agriculture." Wikipedia, The Free Encyclopedia. https://en.m.wikipedia.org/wiki/Greenhouse_gas_emissions_from_agriculture.

"Green Revolution." Wikipedia, The Free Encyclopedia. December 16, 2024. https://en.wikipedia.org/w/index.php?title=Green_Revolution&oldid=1263427463.

Gricius, Gabriella. 2021. "Geopolitical Implications of New Arctic Shipping Lanes." *The Arctic Institute - Center for Circumpolar Security Studies* (blog). March 18, 2021. https://www.thearcticinstitute.org/geopolitical-implications-arctic-shipping-lanes/.

Gugliotta, Guy. 2008. "The Great Human Migration." *Smithsonian Magazine*. June 30, 2008. https://www.smithsonianmag.com/history/the-great-human-migration-13561/.

"Gulf of Mexico 'Dead Zone' Is the Largest Ever Measured." 2017. NOAA.gov. August 17, 2017. Accessed December 27, 2024. https://www.noaa.gov/media-release/gulf-of-mexico-dead-zone-is-largest-ever-measured.

Gustin, Georgina. 2021. "Trees Fell Faster in the Years Since Companies and Governments Promised to Stop Cutting Them Down." Inside Climate News. May 19, 2021. https://insideclimatenews.org/news/19052021/deforestation-climate-change-forest-trends-companies-governments/.

Hansen, Bent. n.d. "Holocene - History of Earth's Climate." Dandebat.Dk. Accessed December 27, 2024. https://dandebat.dk/eng-klima7.htm.

———. n.d. "Pleistocene - History of Earth's Climate." Dandebat.Dk. Accessed December 27, 2024. https://dandebat.dk/eng-klima5.htm.

Harrisson, Thomas. 2019. "Explainer: The High-Emissions 'RCP8.5' Global Warming Scenario." Carbon Brief. August 21, 2019. https://www.carbonbrief.org/explainer-the-high-emissions-rcp8-5-global-warming-scenario/.

Hauser, Christine. 2021. "Barbados Elects Its First Head of State, Replacing Queen Elizabeth." Nytimes.com. October 29, 2021. Accessed December 27, 2024. https://www.nytimes.com/2021/10/22/world/americas/sandra-mason-barbados.html.

Heffernan, Olive. 2019. "Seabed Mining Is Coming — Bringing Mineral Riches and Fears of Epic Extinctions." *Nature* 571 (7766): 465–68. https://doi.org/10.1038/d41586-019-02242-y.

Henry, Joseph. 2018. "Heinrich Events." Encyclopedia.com. Updated May 11, 2018. Accessed December 27, 2024. https://www.encyclopedia.com/earth-and-environment/geology-and-oceanography/geology-and-oceanography/heinrich-events.

Hessayon, Ariel, and Dan Taylor. 2022. "The Original Climate Crisis – How the Little Ice Age Devastated Early Modern Europe." *The Conversation*, March 7, 2022. http://theconversation.com/the-original-climate-crisis-how-the-little-ice-age-devastated-early-modern-europe-178187.

Hilton Johnson, W. 2024. "Pleistocene Epoch." November 23, 2024. *Encyclopedia Britannica*. https://www.britannica.com/science/Pleistocene-Epoch.

"Historic Hurricane Harvey's Recap." 2017. The Weather Channel. September 2, 2017. https://weather.com/storms/hurricane/news/tropical-storm-harvey-forecast-texas-louisiana-arkansas.

HM Treasury. 2021. "The Economics of Biodiversity: The Dasgupta Review: Headline Messages." Gov.uk. Accessed December 27, 2024. https://assets.publishing.service.gov.uk/government/uploads/system/uploads/attachment_data/file/957629/Dasgupta_Review_-_Headline_Messages.pdf.

"Holocene." 2024. Wikipedia, The Free Encyclopedia. December 26, 2024. https://en.wikipedia.org/w/index.php?title=Holocene&oldid=1265416564.

"Homo Habilis." 2024. Wikipedia, The Free Encyclopedia. November 25, 2024. https://en.wikipedia.org/w/index.php?title=Homo_habilis&oldid=1259436128.

Hood, Marlowe and Amélie Bottollier-Depois. 2021. Phys.org. April 30, 2021. Accessed December 27, 2024. https://phys.org/news/2021-04-climate-amazon-friend-foe.html.

Hooper, Ellie. 2020. "What Is Seabed Mining and Why Does It Threaten the Ocean?" Greenpeace Aotearoa. August 6, 2020. Accessed December 27, 2024. https://www.greenpeace.org/aotearoa/story/what-is-seabed-mining-and-why-does-it-threaten-the-oceans/.

Hopkin, Michael. 2005. "Ethiopia Is Top Choice for Cradle of Homo Sapiens." *Nature*. https://doi.org/10.1038/news050214-10.

"How Should Economists Think about Biodiversity?" 2021. *Economist (London, England: 1843)*, February 6, 2021. https://www.economist.com/finance-and-economics/2021/02/06/how-should-economists-think-about-biodiversity.

Howard, Brian Clark. 2015. "Photos: Indonesia's Rampant Fires Threaten Rare Orangutans." *National Geographic*, November 5, 2015. https://www.nationalgeographic.com/animals/article/151105-indonesia-fires-orangutans-photos.

Hulac Benjamin. 2016. "Tobacco and Oil Industries Used Same Researchers to Sway Public." *Scientific American*. July 26, 2016. Accessed December 27, 2024. https://www.scientificamerican.com/article/tobacco-and-oil-industries-used-same-researchers-to-sway-public1/.

"Human Climate Niche - 2020 and 2070." 2021. Science On a Sphere. July 21, 2020. Accessed December 27, 2024. https://sos.noaa.gov/catalog/datasets/human-climate-niche-2020-and-2070/.

Hurt, Avery. 2021. "Ice Ages: What Causes the Earth to Freeze Over Every Few Million Years?" Discover Magazine. February 3, 2021. https://www.discovermagazine.com/planet-earth/ice-ages-what-causes-the-earth-to-freeze-over-every-few-million-years.

"Impacts of a 4°C Global Warming." n.d. Greenfacts.org. Accessed December 27, 2024. https://www.greenfacts.org/en/impacts-global-warming/l-2/index.htm.

Imperial College London. 2024. "Global Warming Game-Changer: Plants Release Carbon Sooner Than Expected." Scitechdaily.com. June 25, 2024. Accessed December 27, 2024. https://scitechdaily.com/global-warming-game-changer-plants-release-carbon-sooner-than-expected/.

"Importance of Nutrition on Health in America." n.d. Feedingamerica.org. Accessed December 27, 2024. https://hungerandhealth.feedingamerica.org/understand-food-insecurity/hunger-health-101/.

Institute for Functional Medicine. n.d. "How Is Food Access Related to Chronic Disease?" Ifm.org. Accessed December 27, 2024. https://www.ifm.org/news-insights/food-insecurity-chronic-disease/.

International Energy Agency. 2021. "Net Zero by 2050." IEA. October 2021. Accessed December 27, 2024. https://www.iea.org/reports/net-zero-by-2050.

International Monetary Fund. 2024. "Moderating Inflation and Steady Growth Open Path to Soft Landing." Imf.org. January 2024. Accessed December 28, 2024. https://www.imf.org/en/Publications/WEO/Issues/2024/01/30/world-economic-outlook-update-january-2024.

International Rescue Committee. 2020. "The Human Stories of the World's Most Dangerous Migration Route." The IRC. August 5, 2020. https://www.rescue.org/article/human-stories-worlds-most-dangerous-migration-route.

International Rescue Committee. 2020. "These Illustrations Reveal the Human Stories of the World's Most Dangerous Migration Route." The IRC. July 17, 2020. https://www.rescue.org/uk/article/these-illustrations-reveal-human-stories-worlds-most-dangerous-migration-route.

IPBES, "IPBES Workshop on Biodiversity and Pandemics." 2020. Actu-environnement.com. Accessed December 27, 2024. https://www.actu-environnement.com/media/pdf/news-36397-resume-rapport-ipbes.pdf.

"It's the Economy, Stupid." 2024. Wikipedia, The Free Encyclopedia. November 10, 2024. https://en.wikipedia.org/w/index.php?title=It%27s_the_economy,_stupid&oldid=1256500723.

"IUCN Red List of Threatened Species." Accessed December 27, 2024. https://www.iucnredlist.org/.

"Jared Diamond on Our Species' Worst Mistake." 2010. A Fistful of Science (blog). October 23, 2010. https://fistfulofscience.wordpress.com/2010/10/23/jared-diamond-on-our-species-worst-mistake/.

Jennings, Ken. 2017. "The Making of the Siberian Traps Nearly Ended All of Life on Earth." *Condé Nast Traveler*. November 27, 2017. https://www.cntraveler.com/story/making-of-siberian-traps-may-have-killed-90-percent-life-on-earth.

Johanson, Donald C., and Henry McHenry. 2024. "Australopithecus." In *Encyclopedia Britannica*.

Jones, Nicola. n.d. "Redrawing the Map: How the World's Climate Zones Are Shifting." Yale E360. Accessed December 27, 2024. https://e360.yale.edu/features/redrawing-the-map-how-the-worlds-climate-zones-are-shifting.

Jurikova, Hana, et al. 2020. "Permian–Triassic Mass Extinction Pulses Driven by Major Marine Carbon Cycle Perturbations." *Nature Geoscience* 13 (11): 745–50. https://doi.org/10.1038/s41561-020-00646-4.

Kammeyer, Cora, et al. 2021. "The 2021 Western Drought: What to Expect as Conditions Worsen." Pacific Institute. June 4, 2021. https://pacinst.org/the-2021-western-drought-what-to-expect-as-conditions-worsen/.

Kaplan, Juliana, and Joseph Zebollas-Roig. 2021. "How Democrats Want to Give Money to Families: Childcare, Pre-K, College — Business Insider." August 15, 2021. Apple News. Accessed December 27, 2024. https://apple.news/A7ruw2tO-QUeQRaH1d1EVVw.

Kaplan, Sarah. 2021. "Climate change has destabilized the Earth's poles, putting the rest of the planet in peril." Washingtonpost.com. December 14, 2021. Accessed December 28, 2024. https://www.washingtonpost.com/climate-environment/2021/12/14/climate-change-arctic-antarctic-poles/.

Keaten, Jamey. 2024. "More than 8,500 migrants died worldwide last year, a record since the U.N. started counting in 2014." latimes.com. March 6, 2024.Accessed December 27, 2024. https://www.latimes.com/world-nation/story/2024-03-06/more-than-8-500-migrants-died-worldwide-last-year-a-record-since-the-u-n-started-counting-in-2014.

Kemp, L. et al. 2020. "Climate Endgame: Exploring catastrophic climate change scenarios." Europepmc.org. Accessed December 27, 2024. https://europepmc.org/article/PMC/PMC9407216.

Kennedy, Kelsey. 2016. "Orangutans Will Be Wiped Out by 2026, Thanks Largely to Fast Food and Face Wash." Quartz. August 24, 2016. https://qz.com/763732/borneo-orangutan-extinction-palm-oil.

Kintisch, Eli. 2016. "Why Did Greenland's Vikings Disappear?" November 10, 2016. Science.org. Accessed December 27, 2024. https://www.science.org/content/article/why-did-greenland-s-vikings-disappear.

Kiprop, Victor. 2018. "The Most Drought Prone Countries in the World." WorldAtlas. March 23, 2018. https://www.worldatlas.com/articles/the-most-drought-prone-countries-in-the-world.html.

Knight, Dacre. 2021. "COVID-19 Pandemic Origins: Bioweapons and the History of Laboratory Leaks." *Southern Medical Journal* 114 (8): 465–67. https://doi.org/10.14423/SMJ.0000000000001283.

Kohler, Timothy A., and Marcy Rockman. 2020. "The IPCC: A Primer for Archaeologists." *American Antiquity* 85 (4): 627–51. https://doi.org/10.1017/aaq.2020.68.

Kolus, Hannah, et al. "Pathways to Net-Zero: US Emissions Beyond 2030." Rhg.com. January 23, 2024. Accessed December 28, 2024. https://rhg.com/research/pathways-to-net-zero-us-emissions-beyond-2030/.

Kopittke, Peter M., Neal W. Menzies, Peng Wang, Brigid A. McKenna, Enzo Lombi. 2019. "Soil and the intensification of agriculture for global food security." 2019. *Environment International*. 132:105078. https://www.sciencedirect.com/science/article/pii/S0160412019315855.

Korten, David C. 2001. *When Corporations Rule the World*. San Francisco: Barrett-Kohler.

Kovarik, Bill. 2021. "A Century of Tragedy: How the Car and Gas Industry Knew about the Health Risks of Leaded Fuel but Sold It for 100 Years Anyway." *The Conversation*, December 8, 2021. http://theconversation.com/a-century-of-tragedy-how-the-car-and-gas-industry-knew-about-the-health-risks-of-leaded-fuel-but-sold-it-for-100-years-anyway-173395.

Kra, Gabriel. 2022. *5 Promising Factors Propelling Climate Action*. TED Talk, April 6, 2022. https://www.ted.com/talks/gabriel_kra_5_promising_factors_propelling_climate_action?subtitle=en

Krauss, Clifford. 2023. "Exxon Mobil Strikes $60 Billion Deal for Shale Giant." Nytimes.com. October 11, 2023. Accessed December 27, 2024. https://www.nytimes.com/2023/10/11/business/economy/exxon-mobil-pioneer-natural-resources.html.

Kusnetz, Nicholas. 2021a. "Big Oil's Top Executives Strike a Common Theme in Testimony on Capitol Hill: It Never Happened." Inside Climate News. October 29, 2021. https://insideclimatenews.org/news/29102021/big-oil-executive-testimony-capitol-hill/.

———. 2021b. "Canada's Tar Sands: Destruction So Vast and Deep It Challenges the Existence of Land and People." Inside Climate News. November 21, 2021. https://insideclimatenews.org/news/21112021/tar-sands-canada-oil/.

———. 2024. "Companies Are Poised to Inject Millions of Tons of Carbon Underground. Will It Stay Put?" Inside Climate News. March 20, 2024. https://insideclimatenews.org/news/20032024/louisiana-abandoned-oil-gas-wells-carbon-dioxide-storage/?utm_source=InsideClimate+News&utm_campaign=a609a0fcba-EMAIL_CAMPAIGN_2024_03_23_01_08&utm_medium=email&utm_term=0_29c928ffb5-a609a0fcba-328368532.

Lacey, Marc. 2021. "F.W. de Klerk, South Africa President Who Ended Apartheid, Dies at 85." Nytimes.com. November 11, 2021. Accessed December 27, 2024. https://www.nytimes.com/2021/11/11/world/africa/fw-de-klerk-dead.html.

LaFranco, Rob, Grace Chung, and Chase Peterson-Withorn. "Forbes 2024 Billionaires List - the Richest People in the World Ranked." n.d. Forbes. Accessed December 27, 2024. https://www.forbes.com/billionaires/.

Lanese, Nicoletta. 2020. "When Will 'Social Distancing' End?" Live Science. March 24, 2020. https://www.livescience.com/social-distancing-coronavirus-end.html.

Laurance, W. 2015. "The Scariest Part of Climate Change Isn't What We Know, but What We Don't." *The Conversation*. http://theconversation.com/the-scariest-part-of-climate-change-isnt-what-we-know-but-what-we-dont-45419.

Lauterwasser, David B. 2017. "The Collapse of Global Civilization Has Begun." Medium. November 14, 2017. https://medium.com/@FeunFooPermaKra/the-collapse-of-global-civilization-has-begun-b527c649754c.

Lavelle, Marianne. 2016. "Crocodiles and Palm Trees in the Arctic? New Report Suggests Yes." *National Geographic*, May 23, 2016. https://www.nationalgeographic.com/science/article/160523-climate-change-study-eight-degrees.

Lawless, Jill. 2024. "Online Misinformation Fueled Tensions over the Stabbing Attack in Britain That Killed 3 Children." AP News. July 31, 2024. https://apnews.com/article/uk-southport-stabbing-online-misinformation-1dcd23b803401416ac94ae458e5c9c06.

Layne, Samuel. 2020. *Survival: Evolutionary Rules for Intelligent Species Survival*. New York, NY: Maijai Press.

Leahy, Stephen. 2019. "How to Feed the World without Destroying the Planet." *National Geographic*, July 17, 2019. https://www.nationalgeographic.com/environment/article/how-to-feed-the-world-without-destroying-the-planet.

Leahy, Stephen, and Ian Willms. 2019. "This Is the World's Most Destructive Oil Operation—and It's Growing." *National Geographic*, April 11, 2019. https://www.nationalgeographic.com/environment/article/alberta-canadas-tar-sands-is-growing-but-indigenous-people-fight-back.

Lee, R. B. 1968. *What Hunters Do for a Living, or, How to Make Out on Scarce Resources*.

Lee, Richard B., and Irven DeVore, eds. 1976. *Kalahari Hunter-Gatherers: Studies of the !Kung San and Their Neighbors*. Cambridge, Mass. : Harvard University Press.

Lee-McGill, Cynthia. 2019. "Dams and Reservoirs Are Messing Up the World's Longest Rivers." Futurity. May 9, 2019. https://www.futurity.org/rivers-dams-reservoirs-2057882/.

Lenton, Timothy M., et al. 2023. "Quantifying the Human Cost of Global Warming." *Nature Sustainability* 6 (10): 1237–47. https://doi.org/10.1038/s41893-023-01132-6.

Leone, Anthony. 2022. "NASA Successfully Crashes DART Spacecraft into Asteroid." Spectrum News 13. September 22, 2022. https://www.mynews13.com/fl/orlando/space/2022/09/22/nasa-dart-mission.

"Life and Works of Anne Robert Jacques Turgot." 2001. Econlib. March 1, 2001. https://www.econlib.org/library/Essays/TurgotBio.html.

"Lifeway." 2023. Wikipedia, The Free Encyclopedia. April 13, 2023. https://en.wikipedia.org/w/index.php?title=Lifeway&oldid=1149582520.

Lindsey, Rebecca. 2024. "Climate Change: Atmospheric Carbon Dioxide." NOAA Climate.gov. April 9, 2024. https://www.climate.gov/news-features/understanding-climate/climate-change-atmospheric-carbon-dioxide.

"List of Countries by GDP (Nominal)." 2024. Wikipedia, The Free Encyclopedia. December 27, 2024. https://en.wikipedia.org/w/index.php?title=List_of_countries_by_GDP_(nominal)&oldid=1265547380.

Liu, Zekun, Zhanghao Chen, Jinyu Gao, Yaochun Yu, Yujie Men, Cheng Gu, and Jinyong Liu. 2022. "Accelerated Degradation of Perfluorosulfonates and Perfluorocarboxylates by UV/Sulfite + Iodide: Reaction Mechanisms and System Efficiencies." *Environmental Science & Technology* 56 (6): 3699–3709. https://doi.org/10.1021/acs.est.1c07608.

Livingston, Amy. 2020. "How to Get Emergency Financial Assistance & Help with Bills - Resources." Money Crashers. March 17, 2020. https://www.moneycrashers.com/coronavirus-emergency-financial-aid-stimulus/.

"Lucy's Story." n.d. Asu.edu. Accessed December 27, 2024. https://iho.asu.edu/about/lucys-story.

Lustgarten, Abrahm, and Meridith Kohut. 2020. "Climate Change Will Force a New American Migration." Propublica. September 15, 2020. https://www.propublica.org/article/climate-change-will-force-a-new-american-migration.

Lynch, David J. 2021. "Pandemic aftershocks overwhelm global supply lines." Washingtonpost.com. January 24, 2021. Accessed December 27, 2024. https://www.washingtonpost.com/business/2021/01/24/pandemic-shipping-economy/.

Madhani, Aamer, and Zeke Miller. 2022. "Biden Says Nuclear 'Armageddon' at Highest Risk since Cuban Missile Crisis." PBS NewsHour. October 6, 2022. https://www.pbs.org/newshour/politics/biden-says-nuclear-armageddon-at-highest-risk-since-cuban-missile-crisis.

"Mali." 2024. Wikipedia, The Free Encyclopedia. December 26, 2024. https://en.wikipedia.org/w/index.php?title=Mali&oldid=1265374328.

Margaritoff, Marco. 2020. "The True Story Of 'Houston, We Have A Problem' And What Went Wrong Aboard The Apollo 13 Craft." Allthatsinteresting.com. April 17, 2020. Accessed December 28, 2024. https://allthatsinteresting.com/houston-we-have-a-problem.

Marinelli, David. 2018. "Oceans without Fish by 2048, Extinction Happening Now." March 29, 2018. https://www.davidmarinelli.net/blog/oceans-without-fish-2048-extinction/.

Martucci, Brian. 2020. "Compassionate (Paid Family) Leave - What It Covers & How to Use It." Money Crashers. August 11, 2020. https://www.moneycrashers.com/compassionate-paid-family-leave/.

———. 2023. "Should You Pay Taxes with a Credit Card?" Money Crashers. April 1, 2023. https://www.moneycrashers.com/claiming-child-tax-credit/.

Maslin, Mark, and The Conversation. 2013. "How Climate Change and Plate Tectonics Shaped Human Evolution." *Scientific American*. November 24, 2013. Accessed December 27, 2024. https://www.scientificamerican.com/article/how-climate-change-and-plate-tectonics-shaped-human-evolution/.

Masters, Jeff. 2024. "A Record 63 Billion-Dollar Weather Disasters Hit Earth in 2023." Yale Climate Connections. January 18, 2024. https://yaleclimateconnections.org/2024/01/a-record-63-billion-dollar-weather-disasters-hit-earth-in-2023/.

Masterson, Victoria. "Degrowth – what's behind the economic theory and why does it matter right now?" Weforum.org. June 15, 2022. Accessed December 28, 2024. https://www.weforum.org/agenda/2022/06/what-is-degrowth-economics-climate-change/.

Matero, I. S. O., L. J. Gregoire, R. F. Ivanovic, J. C. Tindall, and A. M. Haywood. 2017. "The 8.2 Ka Cooling Event Caused by Laurentide Ice Saddle Collapse." *Earth and Planetary Science Letters* 473: 205–14. https://doi.org/10.1016/j.epsl.2017.06.011.

"Mauritania." 2024. Wikipedia, The Free Encyclopedia. December 26, 2024. https://en.wikipedia.org/w/index.php?title=Mauritania&oldid=1265312189.

Mazzai, Alessandra. 2022. "Decoupling (Emissions from Economic Growth)." Foresight. Foresight - the CMCC observatory on climate policies and future. May 17, 2022. https://www.climateforesight.eu/seeds/decoupling-emissions-from-economic-growth/.

McCulloch, Malcolm. 2024. "'A deeply troubling discovery': Earth may have already passed the crucial 1.5°C warming limit." Phys.org. Accessed December 27, 2024. https://phys.org/news/2024-02-deeply-discovery-earth-crucial-15c.html.

McGee, Michael. 2015a. "Daily CO2." CO2.Earth. August 29, 2015. https://www.co2.earth/daily-co2.

———. 2015b. "Earth's CO2 Home Page." Co2.Earth. September 12, 2015. https://www.co2.earth/earths-CO2-main-page.

McKenna, John. 2018. "Dead zones in our oceans have increased dramatically since 1950." Weforum.org. January 18, 2018. Accessed December 28, 2024. https://www.weforum.org/agenda/2018/01/dead-zones-in-our-oceans-have-increased-dramatically-since-1950-and-we-re-to-blame/.

Mecklin, John. (Ed.) 2024. "It is *still* 90 seconds to midnight." January 23, 2024. Thebulletin.org. Accessed December 27, 2024. https://thebulletin.org/doomsday-clock/.

"Media." n.d. Nationalgeographic.org. Accessed December 28, 2024. https://www.nationalgeographic.org/media/hominin-history/.

Melley, Brian, and Thomas Adamson. 2023. "6 Dead, More than 50 Rescued from Capsized Migrant Boat in the English Channel." AP News. August 12, 2023. https://apnews.com/article/migrants-small-boats-english-channel-crossing-drowned-4e3c6583d26e111fe1e1a62c8dffe7d3.

"Methane." n.d. Phys.org. Accessed December 27, 2024. https://phys.org/tags/methane/.

Micu, Alexandru. 2022. "Compound Droughts Risk Destabilizing the Global Food Supply If We Keep Burning Fossil Fuels." ZME Science. https://www.zmescience.com/science/compound-droughts-food-water-security-24636245/

"Middle Stone Age." 2024. Wikipedia, The Free Encyclopedia. July 8, 2024. https://en.wikipedia.org/w/index.php?title=Middle_Stone_Age&oldid=1233255353.

"Migrant Deaths and Disappearances." 2024. Migration Data Portal. Updated April 2, 2024. Accessed December 27, 2024. https://www.migrationdataportal.org/themes/migrant-deaths-and-disappearances.

Milka, Ruth. 2019. "'It Wasn't Just Big Oil That Knew about Climate Change Decades Ago': New Report Reveals Coal Knew Too." Nationofchange.org. November 23,

2019. https://www.nationofchange.org/2019/11/23/it-wasnt-just-big-oil-that-knew-about-climate-change-decades-ago-new-report-reveals-coal-knew-too/.

Millennium Ecosystem Assessment. 2005. Ecosystems and Human Well-being: Synthesis. Island Press, Washington, DC Millenniumassessment.org. Accessed December 27, 2024. https://www.millenniumassessment.org/documents/document.429.aspx.pdf.

Millennium Ecosystem Assessment. 2005. "Opportunities and Challenges for Business and Industry." Millenniumassessment.org. Accessed December 27, 2024. https://www.millenniumassessment.org/documents/document.353.aspx.pdf.

Miller, Anna. 2021. "Fossil Fuel Air Pollution Responsible for 1 in 5 Deaths Worldwide." Harvard T.H. Chan School of Public Health. February 9, 2021. https://www.hsph.harvard.edu/c-change/news/fossil-fuel-air-pollution-responsible-for-1-in-5-deaths-worldwide/?te=1&nl=david-wallace-wells&emc=edit_dww_20220708.

Miller, Scott, and Gregory N. Hicks. "Investor-State Dispute Settlement." Csis.org. Accessed December 28, 2024. https://www.csis.org/analysis/investor-state-dispute-settlement-0.

"Mitochondrial Eve." 2024. Wikipedia, The Free Encyclopedia. December 6, 2024. https://en.wikipedia.org/w/index.php?title=Mitochondrial_Eve&oldid=1261584981.

Monbiot, George. 2017. "Insectageddon: Farming Is More Catastrophic than Climate Breakdown." *The Guardian*, October 20, 2017. https://www.theguardian.com/commentisfree/2017/oct/20/insectageddon-farming-catastrophe-climate-breakdown-insect-populations.

Monteil, Abby. 2020. "50 Inventions You Might Not Know Were Funded by the US Government." Stacker. Stacker Media LLC. December 9, 2020. https://stacker.com/stories/5483/50-inventions-you-might-not-know-were-funded-us-government.

Montenegro, Alvaro, Victor Brovkin, Michael Eby, David Archer, and Andrew J. Weaver. 2007. "Long Term Fate of Anthropogenic Carbon." *Geophysical Research Letters* 34 (19). https://doi.org/10.1029/2007gl030905.

———. 2007. "Long Term Fate of Anthropogenic Carbon." October 10, 2007. American Geophysical Union. https://doi.org/10.1029/2007GL030905.

Moody, Kim. 2021. "Why It's High Time to Move On from 'Just-in-Time' Supply Chains." *The Guardian*, October 11, 2021. https://www.theguardian.com/commentisfree/2021/oct/11/just-in-time-supply-chains-logistical-capitalism.

Morgan, Chris, et al. 2017. "Hunter-Gatherer Economies in the Old World and New World." Researchgate.net. March 2017. Accessed December 28, 2024. https://www.researchgate.net/publication/316470697_Hunter-Gatherer_Economies_in_the_Old_World_and_New_World?enrichId=rgreq-7569630ccac85f-299fa7062c27b03346-XXX&enrichSource=Y292ZXJQYWdlOzMxNjQ3M-

DY5NztBUzo0ODc4MzA1NDQ3NTI2NDFAMTQ5MzMxOTI3MzE0O-A%3D%3D&el=1_x_3&_esc=publicationCover.Pdf.

Moseman, Andrew. 2024. "How Much Carbon Dioxide Does the Earth Naturally Absorb?" MIT Climate Portal. January 26, 2024. Accessed December 27, 2024. https://climate.mit.edu/ask-mit/how-much-carbon-dioxide-does-earth-naturally-absorb.

Mozée, Carla. 2021. "The S&P 500's Incredible Pace of Record Closing Highs Puts It on Course for the Best Run in 26 Years, an Investment Firm Says." *Business Insider*, July 13, 2021. https://markets.businessinsider.com/news/stocks/sp500-outlook-stock-market-record-highs-1995-stocks-bespoke-investment-2021-7.

Mulvaney, Kieran. 2022. "What Is a Carbon Footprint—and How to Measure Yours." *National Geographic*, June 24, 2022. https://www.nationalgeographic.com/environment/article/what-is-a-carbon-footprint-how-to-measure-yours.

Myers, Matthew. 2010."U.S. Supreme Court Upholds Verdict That Tobacco Companies Conspired to Deceive American Public and Addict Children." Press release. Campaign for Tobacco-Free Kids. June 29, 2010. https://www.tobaccofreekids.org/press-releases/id_1220.

Nag, Oishimaya Sen. 2018a. "What Causes a Wildfire?" WorldAtlas. September 21, 2018. https://www.worldatlas.com/articles/what-causes-a-wildfire.html.

———. 2018b. "What Are the Economic Impacts of a Drought?" WorldAtlas. October 10, 2018. https://www.worldatlas.com/articles/what-are-the-economic-impacts-of-a-drought.html.

Nakicenovic, Nebojsa, and Robert Swart. 2000. "IPCC Special Report on Emission Scenarios." ipcc.ch. 2000. Accessed December 27, 2024. https://www.ipcc.ch/site/assets/uploads/2018/03/emissions_scenarios-1.pdf.

NASA. 2009. "Habitable Zones of Different Stars." NASA. December 29, 2009. https://www.nasa.gov/ames/kepler/habitable-zones-of-different-stars.

National Academies. 2013. "Abrupt Impacts of Climate Change: Anticipating Surprises." Nationalacademies.org. Accessed December 27, 2024. https://nap.nationalacademies.org/catalog/18373/abrupt-impacts-of-climate-change-anticipating-surprises.

National Geographic Society, "Hunter-Gatherer Culture." 2024. Nationalgeographic.org. Updated November 20, 2024. Accessed December 27, 2024. https://education.nationalgeographic.org/resource/hunter-gatherer-culture/.

National Research Council. 1994. *Solar Influences on Global Change*. Washington, D.C.: National Academies Press.

National Research Council. 2011. "Understanding Earth's Deep Past." NAP.edu. Accessed December 27, 2024. https://www.nap.edu/read/13111/chapter/1.

Natter, Ari. 2021. "BP, Shell Leaders to Face Congress over Alleged Climate Cover-Up." October 12, 2021. Accessed December 27, 2024. https://www.stripes.com/theaters/us/2021-10-12/oil-companies-misled-public-fossil-fuels-allegation-3222114.html.

"Neanderthal." 2024. Wikipedia, The Free Encyclopedia. December 23, 2024. https://en.wikipedia.org/w/index.php?title=Neanderthal&oldid=1264692027.

Needleman, Herbert L. n.d. "History of Lead Poisoning in the World." Biologicaldiversity.org. Accessed December 27, 2024. https://www.biologicaldiversity.org/campaigns/get_the_lead_out/pdfs/health/Needleman_1999.pdf.

"News on permafrost soils." n.d. Phys.org. Accessed December 27, 2024. https://phys.org/tags/permafrost+soils/.

"News on warming World." n.d. Phys.org. Accessed December 27, 2024. https://phys.org/tags/warming+world/.

Nexus Media News. 2023. "'A Climate That No Human Has Lived Through.'" Nexus Media News. July 24, 2023. https://nexusmedianews.com/top_story/a-climate-that-no-human-has-lived-through/.

Nguyen, Amy. 2020. "S & S Decoded: Planetary Boundaries – A Safer Operating Space for Humanity." Sustainable & Social | Sustainable Business & Lifestyle. April 28, 2020. https://sustainableandsocial.com/planetary-boundaries/.

Nield, David. 2016. "Scientists Say It Could Already Be 'Game over' for Climate Change." ScienceAlert. November 10, 2016. https://www.sciencealert.com/scientists-say-it-could-already-be-game-over-for-climate-change.

Norman, Abby. 2017. "Stephen Hawking: 'I Am Convinced That Humans Need to Leave Earth.'" Futurism. June 20, 2017. https://futurism.com/stephen-hawking-i-am-convinced-that-humans-need-to-leave-earth.

North, Douglass C., and Robert Paul Thomas. 1977. "The First Economic Revolution." May 1977. *The Economic History Review*. Accessed December 27, 2024. https://www.jstor.org/stable/2595144?origin=crossref.

Odum, Eugene P. 2001. "Ecosystem, Concept of." Encyclopedia of Biodiversity, December 2001. https://www.researchgate.net/publication/288153910_Ecosystem_Concept_of.

"Oldowan and Acheulean Stone Tools." n.d. Missouri.edu. Accessed December 27, 2024. https://anthromuseum.missouri.edu/e-exhibits/oldowan-and-acheulean-stone-tools.

Onion, Amanda. 2015. "Ice Age." HISTORY. March 11, 2015. https://www.history.com/topics/pre-history/ice-age.

Osaki, Masakazu. "The Influence of Sedentism on Sharing Among the Central Kalahari Hunter-Gatherers." March 1990. *African Study Monographs*. Accessed December 27, 2024. https://repository.kulib.kyoto-u.ac.jp/dspace/bitstream/2433/68353/1/ASM_S_12_59.pdf.

Paddison, Laura. 2020. "Just 162 Billionaires Have the Same Wealth as Half of Humanity." HuffPost. January 20, 2020. https://www.huffpost.com/entry/billionaires-inequality-oxfam-report-davos_n_5e20db1bc5b674e44b94eca5.

Padilla-Iglesias, Cecilia. 2024. "The Hunter-Gatherers of the 21st Century Who Live on the Move." Aeon Magazine. March 5, 2024. https://aeon.co/essays/the-hunter-gatherers-of-the-21st-century-who-live-on-the-move?utm_source=Aeon+Newsletter&utm_campaign=a25e21c0de-EMAIL_CAMPAIGN_2024_03_08&utm_medium=email&utm_term=0_-b43a9ed933-%5BLIST_EMAIL_ID%5D.

Padmanaban, Deepa. 2020. "Climate Change May Have Been a Major Driver of Ancient Hominin Extinctions." Sapiens. November 6, 2020. https://www.sapiens.org/archaeology/hominin-extinctions/.

"Paranthropus." 2024. Wikipedia, The Free Encyclopedia. July 17, 2024. https://en.wikipedia.org/w/index.php?title=Paranthropus&oldid=1235136192.

Pariona, Amber. 2016. "Worldwide Population throughout Human History." WorldAtlas. July 13, 2016. https://www.worldatlas.com/articles/worldwide-population-through-out-human-history.html.

Parraga, Marianna, and Arathy Somasekhar. 2024. "Big Oil executives push back against calls for fast energy transition." Reuters.com. March 18, 2024. Accessed December 28, 2024. https://www.reuters.com/business/energy/ceraweek-big-oil-executives-push-back-against-calls-fast-energy-transition-2024-03-18/.

Parrish, Shane. n.d. "The Butterfly Effect: How Tiny Actions Unleash Global Consequences." Farnam Street Media. Accessed December 27, 2024. https://fs.blog/the-butterfly-effect/.

PBS NewsHour. 2021. "Severe Drought Reignites Decades-Old Conflict between Oregon Ranchers, Indigenous Peoples." YouTube. Accessed December 27, 2024. https://www.youtube.com/watch?v=YtYRKgpLz34.

Pells, Richard H., and Christina D. Romer. 2024. "Great Depression." In *Encyclopedia Britannica*. https://www.britannica.com/event/Great-Depression.

Penn, Justin L., and Curtis Deutsch. 2022. "Avoiding Ocean Mass Extinction from Climate Warming." *Science (New York, N.Y.)* 376 (6592): 524–26. https://doi.org/10.1126/science.abe9039.

Perkins, Sid. 2014. "Earth More Sensitive to Increasing Greenhouse Gas Than Thought." Science.org. January 2, 2014. Accessed December 27, 2024. https://www.science.org/content/article/earth-more-sensitive-increasing-greenhouse-gas-thought.

Perrone, Tommaso. 2017. "What Is Land Grabbing and Why Land Acquisitions Are Destroying the Planet." LifeGate. February 9, 2017. https://www.lifegate.com/land-grabbing.

Pethokoukis, James. 2020. "US Federal Research Spending Is at a 60-year Low. Should We Be Concerned?" Aei.org. May 11, 2020. Accessed December 27, 2024. https://www.aei.org/economics/us-federal-research-spending-is-at-a-60-year-low-should-we-be-concerned/.

Pettinger, Tejvan. 2017a. "Manufacturing - Secondary Sector." Economics Help. August 19, 2017. https://www.economicshelp.org/concepts/manufacturing-secondary-sector/.

———. 2017b. "Tertiary - Service Sector of the Economy." Economics Help. October 19, 2017. https://www.economicshelp.org/tertiary-service-sector/.

———. 2018. "Primary Sector of the Economy." Economics Help. December 18, 2018. https://www.economicshelp.org/concepts/primary-sector/.

Piketty, Thomas. 2017. *Capital in the Twenty-First Century*. Translated by Arthur Goldhammer. London, England: Belknap Press.

"Planetary Boundaries." 2012. Stockholmresilience.org. September 19, 2012. https://www.stockholmresilience.org/research/planetary-boundaries.html.

"Plio-Pleistocene." n.d. Amnh.org. Accessed December 27, 2024. https://research.amnh.org/paleontology/perissodactyl/concepts/deep-time/plio-pleistocene.

Plumptre, Andrew J., et al. 2021. "Where Might We Find Ecologically Intact Communities?" *Frontiers in Forests and Global Change* 4. https://doi.org/10.3389/ffgc.2021.626635.

Polanyi, Karl. 2002. *The Great Transformation*. 2nd ed. Boston, MA: Beacon Press.

Ponting, Clive. 2011. *A New Green History of the World: The Environment and the Collapse of Great Civilizations*. London, England: Vintage Digital.

Pope Francis. 2019. "Address of His Holiness Pope Francis to Participants at the World Congress of the International Association of Penal Law (15 Novembre 2019)." Vatican.Va. November 15, 2019. https://www.vatican.va/content/francesco/en/speeches/2019/november/documents/papa-francesco_20191115_diritto-penale.html.

"Portugal and the African Slave Trade." 2011. Nicole's Final Project. November 9, 2011. https://jicolerenaissance.wordpress.com/portugal-the-african-slave-trade/.

"Preboreal." 2023. Wikipedia, The Free Encyclopedia. November 22, 2023. https://en.wikipedia.org/w/index.php?title=Preboreal&oldid=1186316908.

Pross, Jörg, et al. 2012. "Persistent Near-Tropical Warmth on the Antarctic Continent during the Early Eocene Epoch." *Nature* 488 (7409): 73–77. https://doi.org/10.1038/nature11300.

"Putin: Leader in Artificial Intelligence Will Rule World." 2017. CNBC. September 4, 2017. https://www.cnbc.com/2017/09/04/putin-leader-in-artificial-intelligence-will-rule-world.html.

Rahn, Wesley. n.d. "Indonesia Forest Fires Spew Smoggy Haze over Malaysia, Singapore." Dw.Com. Accessed December 27, 2024. https://www.dw.com/en/indonesia-forest-fires-spew-smoggy-haze-over-malaysia-singapore/g-50489756.

Raia, Pasquale, et al. 2020. "Past Extinctions of *Homo* Species Coincided with Increased Vulnerability to Climatic Change." One Earth, October 23, 2020. Accessed December 27, 2024. https://www.cell.com/one-earth/pdf/S2590-3322(20)30476-0.pdf.

Ramsay, Adam. 2021. "COP26: How the UK Started the Climate Crisis." Resilience. Resilience.org. October 8, 2021. https://www.resilience.org/stories/2021-10-08/cop26-how-the-uk-started-the-climate-crisis/.

Randall, Patrick. 2015. "Take 5: Alarming droughts around the world." Worldcrunch.com. Accessed December 27, 2024. https://worldcrunch.com/world-affairs/take-5-alarming-droughts-around-the-world.

Rapier, Robert. 2019. "The Ten Countries That Dominate World Fossil Fuel Production." *Forbes*. July 14, 2019. https://www.forbes.com/sites/rrapier/2019/07/14/ten-countries-that-dominate-fossil-fuel-production/?sh=69a44375b133.

Ratu, Sintia. 2018. "Will Universal Income Ever Work?" May 3, 2018. Usnews.com. Accessed December 27, 2024. https://www.usnews.com/news/best-countries/articles/2018-05-03/will-universal-income-ever-work.

Raveena, K. 2021. "Global Wastage of Food and Rise of Food Insecurity." *Asiana Times* (blog). October 27, 2021. https://asianatimes.com/global-wastage-of-food-and-rise-of-food-insecurity/.

"RCP 8.5: Business-as-usual or a worst-case scenario?" n.d. Climatenexus.org. Accessed December 27, 2024. https://climatenexus.org/climate-change-news/rcp-8-5-business-as-usual-or-a-worst-case-scenario/.

Reiter, Bernd. 2022. "The African Origins of Democracy." Academia.edu. Accessed December 27, 2024. https://www.academia.edu/84263977/THE_AFRICAN_ORIGINS_OF_DEMOCRACY.

Renfrew, Colin. 2012. *Archaeology: Theory, Methods, and Practice*. Amazon.co.uk. Accessed December 27, 2024. https://www.amazon.co.uk/Archaeology-Theories-Practice-Colin-Renfrew/dp/0500290210.

"Report Card 2021." 2023. NOAA Arctic. April 27, 2023. https://arctic.noaa.gov/Report-Card/Report-Card-2021.

"Resources." n.d. Iucn.org. Accessed December 28, 2024. https://www.iucn.org/resources/issues-brief/ocean-deoxygenation.

Rettner, Rachael. 2020. "Should Schools Close for Coronavirus?" Live Science. March 5, 2020. https://www.livescience.com/should-schools-close-for-coronavirus.html.

Reuters. 2021. "De Klerk Apologizes for Apartheid in Posthumous Video," November 12, 2021. *New York Times*. https://www.nytimes.com/video/world/africa/100000008074093/de-klerk-south-africa-president-apartheid.html.

Reuters. 2021. "TC Energy seeks NAFTA damages over canceled Keystone XL project," Reuters.com. November 23, 2021. Accessed December 28, 2024. https://www.reuters.com/legal/litigation/tc-energy-seeks-nafta-damages-over-canceled-keystone-xl-project-2021-11-23/.

Richerson, Peter J., Robert Boyd, and Robert L. Bettinger. 2001. "Was Agriculture Impossible during the Pleistocene but Mandatory during the Holocene? A Climate Change Hypothesis." *American Antiquity* 66 (3): 387–411. https://doi.org/10.2307/2694241.

Rightmire, G. Philip, and Phillip Vallentine Tobias. 2024. "Homo Erectus." In *Encyclopedia Britannica*. https://www.britannica.com/topic/Homo-erectus.

Ritchie, Hannah and Max Roser, 2024. "Half of the world's habitable land is used for agriculture." February 16, 2024. Ourworldindata.org. Accessed December 27, 2024. https://ourworldindata.org/global-land-for-agriculture.

Ritchie, Hannah and Pablo Rosado. 2024. "Fossil fuels." Ourworldindata.org. Revised January 2024. Accessed December 27, 2024. https://ourworldindata.org/fossil-fuels/.

Rothman, Daniel H. 2019. "Characteristic disruptions of an excitable carbon cycle." PNAS. July 8 2019. Accessed December 27, 2024. https://pmc.ncbi.nlm.nih.gov/articles/PMC6660735/.

Russell, Stuart. 2020. *Human Compatible: Artificial Intelligence and the Problem of Control*. Amazon.com. Accessed December 27, 2024. https://www.amazon.com/s?k=Human+

Compatible&i=stripbooks-intl-ship&crid=1DGZ6D1RQV91L&sprefix=human+compatible%2Cstripbooks-intl-ship%2C227&ref=nb_sb_noss_1.

Robert Heilbroner, Peter J. Boettke. n.d. "Economic System." Encyclopedia Britannica. https://www.britannica.com/money/economic-system.

Roberts, Patrick, et al. 2023. "Assessing Pleistocene–Holocene Climatic and Environmental Change in Insular Near Oceania Using Stable Isotope Analysis of Archaeological Fauna." *Journal of Quaternary Science* 38 (8): 1267–78. https://doi.org/10.1002/jqs.3555.

Roncarolo, Federico, and Louise Potvin. 2016. "Food Insecurity as a Symptom of a Social Disease: Analyzing a Social Problem from a Medical Perspective." *Canadian Family Physician Medecin de Famille Canadien* 62 (4): 291–92, e161-3.

Roy, Diana. 2024. "Crossing the Darién Gap: Migrants Risk Death on the Journey to the U.S." Council on Foreign Relations. July 22, 2024. https://www.cfr.org/article/crossing-darien-gap-migrants-risk-death-journey-us.

Royte, Elizabeth. 2021. "Too Hot to Live: Millions Worldwide Will Face Unbearable Temperatures." *National Geographic*, June 17, 2021. https://www.nationalgeographic.com/magazine/article/too-hot-to-live-millions-worldwide-will-face-unbearable-temperatures-feature.

Ruddiman, W. F., F. He, S. J. Vavrus, and J. E. Kutzbach. 2020. "The Early Anthropogenic Hypothesis: A Review." *Quaternary Science Reviews* 240 (106386): 106386. https://doi.org/10.1016/j.quascirev.2020.106386.

Ruddiman, William F. 2003. "The Anthropogenic Greenhouse Era Began Thousand of Years Ago." Researchgate.net. Accessed December 27, 2024. https://www.researchgate.net/search.Search.html?type=publication&query=THE%20ANTHROPOGENIC%20GREENHOUSE%20ERA%20BEGAN%20THOUSANDS%20OF%20YEARS%20AGO.

"Russia-Ukraine Conflict: Vladimir Putin Threatens to Use Nuclear Weapons amid NATO Warning." 2022. Firstpost. February 25, 2022. https://www.firstpost.com/world/russia-ukraine-conflict-vladimir-putin-threatens-to-use-nuclear-weapons-amid-nato-warning-10408351.html.

Sanders, Nada R. 2021. "Why You Should Expect More Suez-like Supply Chain Disruptions and Shortages at Your Local Grocery Store." *The Conversation*, April 8, 2021. http://theconversation.com/why-you-should-expect-more-suez-like-supply-chain-disruptions-and-shortages-at-your-local-grocery-store-158266.

Sassaman, Kenneth E. "Complex Hunter–Gatherers in Evolution and History: A North American Perspective." *Journal of Archaeological Research*, September 2004. https://doi.org/10.1023/B:JARE.0000040231.67149.a8.

Schiermeier, Quirin. 2021. "Climate Change Made North America's Deadly Heatwave 150 Times More Likely." *Nature*. https://doi.org/10.1038/d41586-021-01869-0.

Schowalter, Timothy D. 2016. "Chapter 11: Ecosystem Structure and Function." *Insect Ecology (Fourth Edition)*. sciencedirect.com. Accessed December 27, 2024. https://www.sciencedirect.com/science/article/pii/B978012803033200011X.

Schwartz, John. 2017. "Exxon Misled the Public on Climate Change, Study Says." August 23, 2017. Nytimes.com. Accessed December 27, 2024. https://www.nytimes.com/2017/08/23/climate/exxon-global-warming-science-study.html

Scott, James C. 2017. *Against the Grain: A Deep History of the Earliest States*. New Haven: Yale University Press. https://yalebooks.yale.edu/book/9780300240214/against-the-grain/

Secretariat of the Convention on Biological Diversity. 2020. "Global Biodiversity Outlook 5." Convention on Biological Diversity. Accessed December 27, 2024. https://www.cbd.int/gbo5.

Sharma, Rakesh. 2021. "Non-Fungible Token (NFT): What It Means and How It Works." Investopedia. March 8, 2021. https://www.investopedia.com/non-fungible-tokens-nft-5115211.

Shaw, Al, and Abrahm Lustgarten. 2020. "New Climate Maps Show a Transformed United States." September 15, 2020. Oregon Institute for Creative Research: E4. Accessed December 27, 2024. https://oicr-e4.org/story-of-the-hour-1/2020/9/15/new-climate-maps-show-a-transformed-united-states.

Shaxson, Nicholas. 2021. "The City of London Is Hiding the World's Stolen Money." October 11, 2021. Nytimes.com. Accessed December 27, 2024. https://www.nytimes.com/2021/10/11/opinion/pandora-papers-britain-london.html.

Singh, Ishveena. 2017. "What Is Earth's Capacity and How Many People Can It Support?" Geoawesome. July 2, 2017. https://geoawesomeness.com/earths-capacity-many-people-can-support/.

"Slavery in the 21st Century." 2024. Wikipedia, The Free Encyclopedia. December 24, 2024. https://en.wikipedia.org/w/index.php?title=Slavery_in_the_21st_century&oldid=1264902011.

Smith, Adam. n.d. "Adam Smith on the Butcher, the Brewer, and the Baker." The Online Library of Liberty. Accessed December 27, 2024. https://oll.libertyfund.org/quotes/adam-smith-butcher-brewer-baker.

Smith, S. E. 2013. "Seven Companies Polluting the World without Consequences." Truthout. June 2, 2013. https://truthout.org/articles/seven-companies-polluting-the-world-without-consequences/.

Spacey, John. 2024. "91 Examples of Natural Materials." Simplicable.com. January 25, 2024. Accessed December 27, 2024. https://simplicable.com/en/natural-materials. https://simplicable.com/materials/natural-marterials#google_vignette.

Spanne, Autumn. 2021. "Green Revolution: History, Technologies, and Impact." Treehugger. June 23, 2021. https://www.treehugger.com/green-revolution-history-technologies-and-impact-5189596.

Specktor, Brandon. 2020a. "Coronavirus: What Is 'Flattening the Curve,' and Will It Work?" Live Science. March 16, 2020. https://www.livescience.com/coronavirus-flatten-the-curve.html.

———. 2020b. "Earth Barreling toward 'Hothouse' State Not Seen in 50 Million Years, Epic New Climate Record Shows." Live Science. September 10, 2020. https://www.livescience.com/oldest-climate-record-ever-cenozoic-era.html.

"Sperm Counts Are Falling Precipitously across the Rich World." 2021. *Economist (London, England: 1843)*, May 19, 2021. https://www.economist.com/graphic-detail/2021/05/19/sperm-counts-are-falling-precipitously-across-the-rich-world.

"Standardized Precipitation Evapotranspiration Index (SPEI)." n.d. Ucar.edu. Accessed December 27, 2024. https://climatedataguide.ucar.edu/climate-data/standardized-precipitation-evapotranspiration-index-spei.

Stanford University. 2013. "Climate change occurring 10 times faster than at any time in past 65 million years." Phys.org. Accessed December 28, 2024. https://phys.org/news/2013-08-climate-faster-million-years.html.

"State of Nature: How Modern Humans Lived as Nomads for 99 Per Cent of Our History." 2009. *Independent*, February 11, 2009. https://www.independent.co.uk/news/world/world-history/state-of-nature-how-modern-humans-lived-as-nomads-for-99-per-cent-of-our-history-1604967.html.

Stechemesser, Annika, et al. 2024. "Climate Policies That Achieved Major Emission Reductions: Global Evidence from Two Decades." *Science (New York, N.Y.)* 385 (6711): 884–92. https://doi.org/10.1126/science.adl6547.

Steffen, Will, et al. 2015. "Planetary boundaries: Guiding human development on a changing planet." Sciencemag.org. January 15, 2015. Accessed December 28, 2024. https://science.sciencemag.org/content/347/6223/1259855.full.

Steiner, Philippe. 2001. "The Sociology of Economic Knowledge." *European Journal of Social Theory* 4 (4): 443–58. https://doi.org/10.1177/13684310122225253.

Stromberg, Joseph. 2012. "Why Did the Mayan Civilization Collapse? A New Study Points to Deforestation and Climate Change." *Smithsonian Magazine*. August 23, 2012. https://

www.smithsonianmag.com/science-nature/why-did-the-mayan-civilization-collapse-a-new-study-points-to-deforestation-and-climate-change-30863026/.

"Subsidies Hurt Environment, Critics Say before Talks." 1997. Nytimes.com. June 23, 1997. Accessed December 27, 2024. https://www.nytimes.com/1997/06/23/world/subsidies-hurt-environment-critics-say-before-talks.html.

Supran, Geoffrey, and Naomi Oreskes. 2017. "What Exxon Mobil Didn't Say About Climate Change." Nytimes.com. August 22, 2017. Accessed December 27, 2024. https://www.nytimes.com/2017/08/22/opinion/exxon-climate-change-.html?_r=0.

Surma, Katie. 2021. "Lands Grabs and Other Destructive Environmental Practices in Cambodia Test the International Criminal Court." Inside Climate News. March 23, 2021. https://insideclimatenews.org/news/23032021/land-grab-deforestation-international-criminal-court-cambodia-ecocide/.

"Sustainable Development Goals." n.d. UNDP. Accessed December 28, 2024. https://www.undp.org/sustainable-development-goals.

Sutherland, A. 2015."The 'Anasazi' Mystery: Sophisticated Civilization That Disappeared." *Ancient Pages* (blog). September 20, 2015. https://www.ancientpages.com/2015/09/20/the-anasazi-mystery-sophisticated-civilization-that-disappeared/.

Suzman, James. 2017a. *Affluence Without Abundance: The Disappearing World of the Bushmen*. New York, NY: Bloomsbury.

———. 2017b. *Affluence Without Abundance: What We Can Learn from the World's Most Successful Civilisation*. New York: Bloomsbury.

Suzman, James. 2021. *Work: A Deep History from the Stone Age to the Age of Robots*. Amazon.com. Accessed December 28, 2024. https://www.amazon.com/Work-Deep-History-Stone-Robots/dp/0525561757.

Svizzero, Serge, and Clement A. Tisdell. 2016. "Economic Evolution, Diversity of Societies and Stages of Economic Development: A Critique of Theories Applied to Hunters and Gatherers and Their Successors." *Cogent Economics & Finance* 4 (1): 1161322. https://doi.org/10.1080/23322039.2016.1161322.

Svizzero, Serge, and Clement Allan Tisdell. 2014. "Hunter-Gatherer Societies: Their Diversity and Evolutionary Processes." August 2014. Researchgate.net. Accessed December 27, 2024. https://www.researchgate.net/publication/265215014_Hunter-Gatherer_Societies_Their_Diversity_and_Evolutionary_Processes.

Tan, Ming. 2023. "Tech for good: What it means and how we can deliver on it." Weforum.org. May 21, 2023. Accessed December 27, 2024. https://www.weforum.org/agenda/2023/03/tech-for-good-what-does-it-mean-and-how-can-we-deliver-on-it/.

Taylor, Caroline, Tom R. Robinson, Stuart Dunning, J. Rachel Carr, and Matthew Westoby. 2023. "Glacial Lake Outburst Floods Threaten Millions Globally." *Nature Communications* 14 (1): 1–10. https://doi.org/10.1038/s41467-023-36033-x.

Tebor, Celina. 2021. "The current drought is worldwide. Here's how different places are fighting it." July 19, 2021. Phys.org. Accessed December 27, 2024. https://phys.org/news/2021-07-current-drought-worldwide.html.

"Temperatures - Climate Action Tracker." n.d. Climateactiontracker.org. Accessed December 27, 2024. https://climateactiontracker.org/global/temperatures/.

"Ten Civilizations or Nations That Collapsed from Drought." n.d. Weather Underground. Accessed December 27, 2024. https://www.wunderground.com/blog/JeffMasters/ten-civilizations-or-nations-that-collapsed-from-drought.html.

"The 5 Ways Tobacco Companies Lied about the Dangers of Smoking Cigarettes." 2017. Truth Initiative. December 21, 2017. https://truthinitiative.org/research-resources/tobacco-prevention-efforts/5-ways-tobacco-companies-lied-about-dangers-smoking

"The Economics of Climate Change: The Stern Review." 2006. Grantham Research Institute on Climate Change and the Environment. October 30, 2006. https://www.lse.ac.uk/GranthamInstitute/publication/the-economics-of-climate-change-the-stern-review/.

"The Growing Demand for More Vigorous Antitrust Action." 2022. *Economist (London, England: 1843)*, January 10, 2022. https://www.economist.com/special-report/2022/01/10/the-growing-demand-for-more-vigorous-antitrust-action.

"The State of Food Security and Nutrition in the World 2021." 2021. FAO, IFAD, UNICEF, WFP and WHO. https://doi.org/10.4060/cb4474en.

"The Story behind the Discovery of the Ozone Hole." n.d. UKRI.org. Accessed December 27, 2024. https://www.ukri.org/our-work/responding-to-climate-change/topical-stories/the-story-behind-the-discovery-of-the-ozone-hole/.

"The Value of Pollinators to the Ecosystem and Our Economy." 2019. Forbes. October 14, 2019. https://www.forbes.com/sites/bayer/2019/10/14/the-value-of-pollinators-to-the-ecosystem-and-our-economy/?sh=34493c727a1d.

"They Fired on Us Like Rain." 2023. Hrw.org. August 21, 2023. Accessed December 27, 2024. https://www.hrw.org/report/2023/08/21/they-fired-us-rain/saudi-arabian-mass-killings-ethiopian-migrants-yemen-saudi.

Thomas, Leah. 2018. "Earth Will Start Becoming a Desert by 2050 If Global Warming Isn't Stopped, Study Says." *Newsweek*. January 2, 2018. https://www.newsweek.com/earth-desert-2050-global-warming-768545.

Thompson, Helen. 2015. "The Oldest Stone Tools yet Discovered Are Unearthed in Kenya." Smithsonian Magazine. May 20, 2015. https://www.smithsonianmag.com/science-nature/oldest-known-stone-tools-unearthed-kenya-180955341/.

Tirado, Reyes. 2008. "Dead Zones: how agriculture fertilizers kill our rivers, lakes and oceans." Researchgate.net. Accessed December 27, 2024. https://www.researchgate.net/publication/267639399_Dead_Zones_how_agriculture_fertilizers_kill_our_rivers_lakes_and_oceans.

Tollefson, Jeff. 2021. "IPCC Climate Report: Earth Is Warmer than It's Been in 125,000 Years." *Nature* 596 (7871): 171–72. https://doi.org/10.1038/d41586-021-02179-1.

Tondo, Lorenzo. 2021. "Revealed: 2,000 Refugee Deaths Linked to Illegal EU Pushbacks." *The Guardian*, May 5, 2021. https://www.theguardian.com/global-development/2021/may/05/revealed-2000-refugee-deaths-linked-to-eu-pushbacks.

Turnbull, Colin. 1968. *The Forest People*. London, England: Simon and Schuster.

"U.S. Market Data." n.d. Marketwatch.com. Accessed December 27, 2024. https://www.marketwatch.com/market-data/us.

UCL. 2021. "Limiting Fossil Fuel Extraction to Meet 1.5°C." UCL News. September 8, 2021. https://www.ucl.ac.uk/news/2021/sep/limiting-fossil-fuel-extraction-meet-15degc.

Umar, Baba. 2021. "Brazil's Bolsonaro Sued at ICC for 'Genocide', 'Ecocide.'" TRT WORLD. August 9, 2021. https://www.trtworld.com/americas/brazil-s-bolsonaro-sued-at-icc-for-genocide-ecocide-49052.

UN Environment Programme. 2022. "COP15 Ends with Landmark Biodiversity Agreement." United Nations Environment Programme. December 20, 2022. https://www.unep.org/news-and-stories/story/cop15-ends-landmark-biodiversity-agreement.

UN News. 2021. "António Guterres Secures Second Term as UN Secretary-General, Calls for New Era of 'Solidarity and Equality.'" UN News. June 18, 2021. https://news.un.org/en/story/2021/06/1094282.

"UN Report: Nature's Dangerous Decline 'Unprecedented'; Species Extinction Rates 'Accelerating.'" United Nations Sustainable Development Goals. May 6, 2019. https://www.un.org/sustainabledevelopment/blog/2019/05/nature-decline-unprecedented-report/.

UNESCO. n.d. "The Ocean We Need for the Future We Want." Unesco.org. Accessed December 28, 2024. https://www.unesco.org/en/ocean.

USEPA. 2015. "Current State of the Ozone Layer." https://www.epa.gov/ozone-layer-protection/current-state-ozone-layer.

USEPA. 2024. "Greenhouse Gas Equivalencies Calculator." Environmental Protection Agency. Updated November 2024. https://www.epa.gov/energy/greenhouse-gas-equivalencies-calculator.

UNFCCC. 2006. "Technologies for Adaptation to Climate Change." Unfccc.int. Accessed December 27, 2024. https://unfccc.int/resource/docs/publications/tech_for_adaptation_06.pdf.

"United Nations Launches Extensive Study of Earth's Ecosystems." 2001. Sdearthtimes.com. Accessed December 27, 2024. https://www.sdearthtimes.com/et0701/et0701s11.html

University of Arizona. 2017. "Ancient Humans Left Africa to Escape Drying Climate." *Science Daily*, October 4, 2017. https://www.sciencedaily.com/releases/2017/10/171004151231.htm.

University of Copenhagen. 2023. "Six of nine planetary boundaries now exceeded." Phys.org. September 13, 2023. Accessed December 28, 2024. https://phys.org/news/2023-09-planetary-boundaries-exceeded.html.

UNODC. 2022. "Smuggling of Migrants in the Sahel." Unodc.org. Accessed December 27, 2024. https://www.unodc.org/documents/data-and-analysis/tocta_sahel/TOCTA_Sahel_som_2023.pdf.

Valla, François R., Hamoudi Khalaily, Nicolas Samuelian, and Fanny Bocquentin. 2002. "From Foraging to Farming." *Bulletin Du Centre de Recherche Français de Jérusalem*, no. 10: 71–90. https://journals.openedition.org/bcrfj/1272.

van Ewijk, Stijn. 2018. "Sustainable use of materials in the global paper life cycle." July 2018. Researchgate.net. Accessed December 27, 2024. https://www.researchgate.net/publication/327032452_Sustainable_use_of_materials_in_the_global_paper_life_cycle.

Von Rueden, Christopher,, Michael Gurven, Hillard Kaplan, and Jonathan Stieglitz. 2014. "Leadership in an Egalitarian Society." *Human Nature (Hawthorne, N.Y.)* 25 (4): 538–66. https://doi.org/10.1007/s12110-014-9213-4.

Wallace-Wells, David. 2017. "When Will Climate Change Make the Earth Too Hot for Humans?" Intelligencer. July 14, 2017. https://nymag.com/intelligencer/2017/07/climate-change-earth-too-hot-for-humans-annotated.html.

———. 2021. "Ten Million a Year." London Review of Books. December 2, 2021. https://www.lrb.co.uk/the-paper/v43/n23/david-wallace-wells/ten-million-a-year?utm_source=firefox_pocket_save_button.

Walters, Sam. 2021. "How Humans Survived the Ice Age." Discover Magazine. December 9, 2021. https://www.discovermagazine.com/planet-earth/how-humans-survived-the-ice-age.

Wamsley, Laurel. 2021. "Mackenzie Scott Is Giving Away Another $2.7 Billion to 286 Organizations." Npr.org. Accessed December 27, 2024. https://www.kpbs.org/news/2021/06/15/mackenzie-scott-is-giving-away-another-27-billion.

Ward, Peter, and David Brownlee. n.d. *Rare Earth: Why Complex Life Is Uncommon in the Universe*. Copernicus Books. Springer Verlag, 2000.

Wardle, David, et al. 2004. "Ecological Linkages Between Aboveground and Belowground Biota," Researchgate.net. Accessed December 27, 2024. https://www.researchgate.net/publication/8515633_Ecological_Linkages_Between_Aboveground_and_Belowground_Biota.

Watson, Traci. 2017. "Oldest Homo Sapiens Fossils Ever Found Push Humanity's Birth Back to 300,000 Years." *USA Today*, June 7, 2017. https://www.usatoday.com/story/news/2017/06/07/oldest-homo-sapiens-fossils-ever-found-300000-years/102585284/.

Weinzettel A, Jan, Edgar G. Hertwich A, Glen P. Peters B, Kjartan Steen-Olsen A, and Alessandro Galli. 2013. "Affluence Drives the Global Displacement of Land Use." *Global Environmental Change*. https://www.sciencedirect.com/science/article/pii/S0959378012001501.

Weisberger, Mindy. 2019. "This One Number Shows Why Measles Spreads like Wildfire." Live Science. February 8, 2019. https://www.livescience.com/64727-measles-contagious.html.

"Wellbeing Economies." 2021. David Suzuki Foundation. February 24, 2021. https://davidsuzuki.org/project/well-being-economies/.

"Wellbeing Economy Governments (WEGO): Wellbeing Economy Alliance." n.d. Wellbeingeconomy.org. Accessed December 27, 2024. https://wellbeingeconomy.org/wego.

Western, David. 2001. "Human-Modified Ecosystems and Future Evolution." *Proceedings of the National Academy of Sciences of the United States of America* 98 (10): 5458–65. https://doi.org/10.1073/pnas.101093598.

Western, Luke, et al. 2022. "A renewed rise in global HCFC-141b emissions between 2017–2021." Copernicus.org. Accessed December 28, 2024. https://acp.copernicus.org/articles/22/9601/2022/acp-22-9601-2022-discussion.html.

"Western North America extreme heat virtually impossible without human-caused climate change." 2021. Worldweatherattribution.org. July 7, 2021. Accessed December 27, 2024. https://www.worldweatherattribution.org/western-north-american-extreme-heat-virtually-impossible-without-human-caused-climate-change/.

Weyler, Rex. 2019. "Nine Ways Humans Have Altered Earth's Holocene Climate." Greenpeace International. June 30, 2019. Accessed December 27, 2024. https://www.greenpeace.org/international/story/22792/nine-ways-humans-have-altered-earths-holocene-climate/.

"What Do Volcanoes Have to Do with Climate Change?" 2015. Nasa.gov. April 29, 2015. https://climate.nasa.gov/faq/42/what-do-volcanoes-have-to-do-with-climate-change/.

"What Is Biomimicry?" 2024. The Biomimicry Institute. July 29, 2024. https://biomimicry.org/what-is-biomimicry/.

"What Is Sustainable Agriculture?" n.d. Union of Concerned Scientists. Accessed December 27, 2024. https://ucsusa.org/resources/what-sustainable-agriculture.

"Why Is the Stock Market Surging during a Pandemic?" 2020. AARP. June 9, 2020. https://www.aarp.org/money/investing/info-2020/what-stock-market-surge-means.html.

"What Was the Great Dying That Almost Wiped Out Life on Earth 252 Million Years Ago?" 2021. ScienceAlert. December 10, 2021. https://www.sciencealert.com/what-is-the-great-dying.

"William Ruddiman." 2024. Wikipedia, The Free Encyclopedia. July 30, 2024. https://en.wikipedia.org/w/index.php?title=William_Ruddiman&oldid=1237531889.

Winck, Ben, and Juliana Kaplan. 2021. "The Richest 1% of Americans Dodge $163 Billion in Taxes Yearly: Treasury — Business Insider." September 8, 2021. Apple.News. Accessed December 27, 2024. https://apple.news/ARL1Oy0rrSnuLWB6A7IUNfg.

Winkler, Adam. 2018. "'Corporations Are People' Is Built on an Incredible 19th-Century Lie." *Atlantic Monthly (Boston, Mass.: 1993)*, March 5, 2018. https://www.theatlantic.com/business/archive/2018/03/corporations-people-adam-winkler/554852/.

Winn, Zach. 2023. "Cleaning Up One of the World's Most Commonly Used Substances." MIT News | Massachusetts Institute of Technology. October 13, 2023. Accessed December 27, 2024. https://news.mit.edu/2023/cleaning-common-substance-cement-alternative-1013.

Winterhalder, Bruce, and Douglas J. Kennett. 2019. "1. Behavioral Ecology and the Transition from Hunting and Gathering to Agriculture." In *Behavioral Ecology and the Transition to Agriculture*, 1–21. University of California Press.

Wilson, Tom. 2022. "Fusion Energy Breakthrough by US Scientists Boosts Clean Power Hopes." *Financial Times*. December 12, 2022. https://arstechnica.com/science/2022/12/fusion-energy-breakthrough-by-us-scientists-boosts-clean-power-hopes/.

Wood, Johnny. 2021. "What does net-zero emissions mean and how can we get there?" Weforum.org. Accessed December 28, 2024. https://www.weforum.org/agenda/2021/11/net-zero-emissions-cop26-climate-change/.

Woodburn, James. 1982. "Egalitarian Societies." *Man*. September 1982. Royal Anthropological Institute of Great Britain and Ireland. Jstor.org. Accessed December 27, 2024. https://www.jstor.org/stable/2801707.

"World on fire: Scorching heatwaves spark wildfires around the globe." 2021. Reuters.com. August 13, 2021. Acessed December 27, 2024. https://www.reuters.com/news/picture/world-on-fire-scorching-heatwaves-spark-idJPRTXFJPKU

Worrall, Simon. 2017. "Without Bugs, We Might All Be Dead." *National Geographic*, August 6, 2017. https://www.nationalgeographic.com/animals/article/insect-bug-medicine-food-macneal.

Wrigley, E. A. 2013. "Energy and the English Industrial Revolution." *Philosophical Transactions. Series A, Mathematical, Physical, and Engineering Sciences* 371 (1986): 20110568. https://doi.org/10.1098/rsta.2011.0568.

Wu, Shuang-Ye. 2023. "2023's Extreme Storms, Heat and Wildfires Broke Records – A Scientist Explains How Global Warming Fuels Climate Disasters." *The Conversation*, December 19, 2023. http://theconversation.com/2023s-extreme-storms-heat-and-wildfires-broke-records-a-scientist-explains-how-global-warming-fuels-climate-disasters-217500.

Wuebbles, Donald. 2024. "Ozone Layer." *Encyclopedia Britannica*. https://www.britannica.com/science/ozone-layer

Xerces Society. n.d. "The Risks of Pesticides to Pollinators." xerces.org. Accessed December 27, 2024. https://xerces.org/pesticides/risks-pesticides-pollinators.

Xu, Chi, et al. 2020. "Future of the Human Climate Niche." *Proceedings of the National Academy of Sciences of the United States of America* 117 (21): 11350–55. https://doi.org/10.1073/pnas.1910114117.

"Y Combinator." Wikipedia, The Free Encyclopedia. https://en.m.wikipedia.org/wiki/Y_Combinator.

"Younger Dryas." 2024. Wikipedia, The Free Encyclopedia. December 12, 2024. https://en.wikipedia.org/w/index.php?title=Younger_Dryas&oldid=1262713328

Zandt, Florian. 2022. "The Most Dangerous Migration Routes." Statista. May 18, 2022. https://www.statista.com/chart/27466/minimum-estimate-of-recorded-migrant-deaths-on-major-migrant-routes-since-2014/.

Zapata, Christian. 2009. "Dust Bowl." HISTORY. October 27, 2009. https://www.history.com/topics/great-depression/dust-bowl.

———. 2017. "Manhattan Project." HISTORY. July 26, 2017. https://www.history.com/topics/world-war-ii/the-manhattan-project.

Zeballos-Roig, Joseph. 2021. "House Democrats Propose Extending Biden Child Tax Credit until 2025—Business Insider." September 11, 2021. Apple.News. Accessed December 27, 2024. https://apple.news/Aa_2uEHk_SCasXXcrWPROZQ

Zerbe, James G. 2021. "Hunter-Gatherer Societies." In *Encyclopedia of Evolutionary Psychological Science*, 3962–64. Cham: Springer International Publishing.

Zimmer, Carl, and Benjamin Mueller. 2022. "New Research Points to Wuhan Market as Pandemic Origin." *The New York Times*, February 26, 2022. https://www.nytimes.com/interactive/2022/02/26/science/covid-virus-wuhan-origins.html.

LIST OF PHOTOS & CHARTS

Figure I-1. Animals converging around a waterhole at Amboseli national park Kenya. xiv

Figure 2-1. Aerial view of the Suncor oil sands extraction facility on the banks of the Athabasca River near Fort McMurray in Alberta, Canada. 28

Figure 2-2. Aerial view of a chemically deforested area of the Amazon jungle caused by illegal mining activities in the river basin of the Madre de Dios region of southeast Peru. 29

Figure 2-3. Ecocide Hotspots. 30

Figure 2-4. Ecosystems and selected services. 41

Figure 2-5. Examples of Earth's biomes. 43

Figure 2-6. The world's eight major biomes are distinguished by characteristic temperatures and precipitation. Polar ice caps and mountains are also shown. 44

Figure. 2-7.	Land grabbing: the race for hectares.	46
Figure 2-8.	The Sahel is the semi-arid transition region.	49
Figure 2-9.	Deforestation in the Brazilian Amazon, one of the few fragments of wilderness undamaged by human activities.	50
Figure 2-10.	Soil biodiversity.	53
Figure 2-11.	Miscellaneous insects.	54
Figure. 2-12.	Too much nitrogen and phosphorus in the water can have diverse and far-reaching impacts on public health, the environment, and the economy.	57
Figure 2-13.	Excess nitrogen in the air can impair our ability to breathe, limit visibility, and alter plant growth.	58
Figure 2-14.	A climate map showing the last 66 million years of Earth's history. The next 300 could be unlike anything we've ever seen.	65
Figure 2-15.	Holocene temperature variations.	67
Figure 2-16.	The Holocene cold and warm periods represent only small temperature changes compared to both the glaciation periods and the other interglacial periods.	68
Figure 2-17.	Science instruments on NASA's Mars 2020 Perseverance rover.	69
Figure 2-18.	NASA's new Mars rover landing successfully.	70
Figure 2-19.	Modern Hadza hunter-gatherers collecting tubers, a staple food of the community, in the Yaeda Valley, Tanzania. The Hadza are a modern hunter-gatherer tribe.	71
Figure 2-20.	Sunken treasure.	84
Figure 2-21.	Indigenous Brazilians sing while protesting outside the Supreme Court in Brasília, Brazil, on August 26, 2021, as they await an important ruling from the court.	86
Figure 3-1.	Human species during Pleistocene.	99
Figure 3-2.	Milestones in human evolution correlated with climate variability.	100
Figure 3-3.	Animals around a waterhole in the Etosia salt pan.	110
Figure 4-1.	Foundations of human economies.	128

Figure 4-2. The sudden, exponential growth of sedentary human populations. 132

Figure 4-3. Planetary boundaries. The Earth System has passed six of nine planetary boundaries. 162

Figure 4-4. Moderate or severe food insecurity has been climbing slowly for six years and now affects more than 30 percent of the world population. 169

Figure 4-5. Global wastage of food and rise of food insecurity. 170

Figure 5-1. CO_2 levels from 800,000 years ago. 208

Figure 5-2. Resources that must remain off-limits. 210

Figure 5-3. Global greenhouse gas emissions and warming scenarios. 211

Figure 5-4. Global average surface temperature. 212

Figure 5-5. Map of states and counties affected by the Dust Bowl between 1935 and 1938. 217

Figure 5-6. GISP2 ice core temperature and accumulation data. 218

Figure 5-7. U.S. Drought Monitor. 219

Figure 5-8. Water stress around the world. 221

Figure 5-9. New climate maps show a transformed United States. 225

Figure 5-10. More deaths due to undervaccination in red states. 237

Figure 5-11. Wildlife Trade. Stop Wildlife Trade, Stop Wildlife Consumption, and Stop Destroying Nature, and We Will Stop Pandemics. 239

Figure 5-12. Global GDP growth, 1995-2020. 240

Figure 5-13. WHO Coronavirus (Covid-19) Dashboard. 241

Figure 5-14. The five risks that will have the biggest impact in the next ten years. 244

Figure 6-1. Foundations of human economies. 264

Figure 6-2. Global land use for food production. 274

Figure 6-3. De Klerk shared the Nobel Peace Prize with Nelson Mandela. 290

Figure 6-4. Lead in gasoline and human exposures in the U.S. 295

Figure 6-5. Coal is king for carbon dioxide emissions. 298

Figure 7-1.	A stone tool revolution occurred some 300,000 years ago.	333
Figure 7-2.	Human migration out of Africa via the Southern coastal route.	349
Figure 8-1.	Human energy transitions: From renewables back to renewables.	374
Figure 8-2.	World human population (est.) 10,000 BCE–2000 CE.	376
Figure 8-3.	Global fossil fuel consumption through 2021.	377
Figure 8-4.	The relentless rise of carbon dioxide.	378
Figure 8-5.	The relentless extraction of fossil fuels.	387
Figure 8-6.	Shares of total U.S. energy consumption by major sources, selected years (1776-2023).	388
Figure 8-7.	U.S. primary energy consumption by energy source, 2023.	389
Figure 8-8.	Minerals required for green energy technologies.	402
Figure 8-9.	Global reserves of minerals required for green energy technologies, overlaid with fragility and corruption measures.	403
Figure 9-1.	Fleeing Hurricane Harvey.	426
Figure 9-2.	Missing Migrants Project.	428
Figure 9-3.	Migrants flock to the Darién Gap, a remote jungle region bridging Central and South America.	429
Figure 9-4.	Map of the migration route from Ethiopia to Saudi Arabia through Yemen.	429
Figure 9-5.	Saudi Arabia: Mass killings of migrants at Yemen border.	431
Figure 9-6.	The most dangerous migration routes: Eastern, western, and central.	432
Figure 9-7.	Possible migration routes taken by ancient humans starting from Africa.	433
Figure 9-8.	The countryside in Samangan Province in north-central Afghanistan, where water for agriculture and even drinking is scarce.	437
Figure 9-9.	The tropics are expanding by half a degree per decade.	440
Figure 9-10.	Hardiness zones in the U.S., which track average low temperatures in winter, have all shifted northward by half a zone warmer since 1990.	440

Figure 9-11. Past and future trends in global mean temperature spanning the last 67 million years. 443

Figure 9-12. IPCC CO2 and temperature projections. 445

Figure 9-13. Texas's zombie oil wells are creating an environmental disaster zone. 446

Figure 9-14. Migrants from Venezuela making their way through the Darién Gap between Colombia and Panama last year. 452

Figure 9-15. GHG output by sector of modern human economies compared with pre-agriculture hunter-gatherer mobile economies. 455

Figure 9-16. The relentless rise of carbon dioxide. 456

Figure 9-17. Mauna Loa CO_2 annual averages versus humanity's efforts to restrain or remove GHGs. 461

Figure 9-18. Global GHG output by economic sectors: Modern sedentary human economies versus pre-agriculture hunter-gatherer mobile economies. 463

Figure 10-1. DART spacecraft near the two asteroids, Didymos and Dimorphos. 488

Figure 10-2. Fossilized crinoids, marine invertebrates that lived during the Permian Period. 489

Figure 10-3. U.S. 2020 billion-dollar weather and climate disasters. 501

Figure 10-4. More dangerous heat waves are on the way. See the impact by state. 502

Figure 10-5. Exceeding 1.5°C global warming could trigger multiple climate tipping points. 503

Figure G-1. Planetary boundaries that have been breached (in orange), 2009-2025. 539

LIST OF TABLES

Table 2-1.	Earth-life ecosystems	36
Table 2-2.	Ecosystem services	37
Table 2-3.	Key trends in ecosystems and their services	42
Table 2-4.	Estimated human population worldwide	65
Table 4-1.	Takeaways on how human societies might organize to survive	127
Table 4-2.	Early versus modern human economies	153
Table 5-1.	Sectors of the modern economy	189
Table 5-2.	Human Economies - Transitions	199
Table 5-3.	List of epidemics and pandemics with at least one million deaths	234
Table 6-1.	Comparison of the socioeconomic lifeways of foraging versus farming and their respective impact on Earth-life ecosystems and biodiversity	271

INDEX

Page numbers followed by f indicate figures; t, tables.

A

Abiotic parts of ecosystem, 23–24

Aboriginal humans
- Amazon protection advocated by, 85
- ecosystem repurposing impact on, 45–46
- ecosystems inhabited by, 35–36

Aborigines, 220

Abortion, 270

Accessory to War (DeGrasse Tyson and Lang), 332

Aché, 507

Acid rain, 279, 383

Acquisition and consumption, socioeconomic goal of, 480–481

Add-ons, 73, 76, 81

Aesthetic values, 39

Affluence, 45

Affluence Without Abundance (Suzman), 97, 141, 250, 499

Afforestation, 358

Afghanistan, migration from, 226

Africa
- climate conditions in, 434
- continent, reshaping of, 435
- desertification in, 437–438
- migration out of, 113, 181, 223, 287, 336, 342, 348, 349, 349f, 350, 359, 409, 411, 415, 420, 422, 425, 432, 434–435, 436
- parts uninhabitable, 502
- pillaging of, 292
- population of, 267–268
- slave trade, 291
- southern tip of, 501

Africans, enslavement of, 160

Afrikaners, 292

Against the Grain (Manning), 499

Against the Grain (Scott), 156

Agrarian societies
- binding commitments and dependencies of, 142
- rise of, 442

Agrarian socioeconomic lifeways, 272–280

Agricultural-based socioeconomic lifeways, 512
Agricultural civilization, 182
Agricultural communities, xv, 106, 180, 182, 232, 242, 243, 264, 307, 373, 414, 512
Agricultural economies
 abandonment of, 452, 453–454
 adopting of, 414
 characteristics of, 124
 collapse of, xxi, 97
 ecosystem destruction and, 126, 285
 growth of, 125
 hunter-gatherer economies compared to, xx, 267–268
 limitations of, 20
 population growth in, 10–11
Agricultural Revolution, 268
Agricultural societies
 collapse of, 97
 economic disasters impact on, 108
 and economies, 376
 and hunter-gatherer societies compared, 124–125
Agriculture
 adoption of, 24, 78, 79, 95, 105, 110, 121, 127, 159, 172, 174, 203, 229, 232, 239, 258, 272, 385, 393, 403, 437
 advent of, 201, 226–227, 228, 334, 336, 345, 444, 502, 515
 from animal-assisted to machine-assisted, 404
 and beyond, 133
 cancel culture beginning with, 60
 carbon dioxide release, contribution to, 490
 civilization collapse since dawn of, 164
 civilization without, 205
 climate favorable to, 181, 337, 377
 conditions enabling, 100, 101, 204, 205, 208, 214
 development of, 343, 344, 437
 driven northward, 215
 drought impact on, 220
 ecological cheating in, 74
 as economic development stage, 251
 economies before, 190
 economies giving rise to, 88
 economies outside of ecosystems with, 68
 elevation of, 157
 end to, 205, 209, 337
 energy needs of, 378, 386, 404, 455
 environmental impact of, 275, 356, 510
 expansion of, 44–45, 103, 233, 238, 274, 501
 failure of, 263–264
 fire use in, 376
 food production capacity in, 188
 foraging *versus,* 262–263
 forests cleared for, 232
 freedom, loss of, 281–282
 goal and outcome of, 116–117
 greenhouse gases contribution by, 456
 hunting and gathering giving rise to, 94
 impact of, 264–265, 275
 industrialization of, 330
 intensification of, 275
 population growth relationship to, 104
 processes, 71
 rejection, hypothetical of, 506–507
 rise of, 180, 208–209, 467
 runoff, 55, 318
 socioeconomic lifeway, 271t
 start of, 181
 subsistence changes starting with, 200
 surface water shortages for, 221
 survival odds reduced by, 223
 survival threatened by, 329–330
 technologies, 80, 105, 276t–277t, 279
 triad of life, breaking away for, 77
 water use for, 48
Agriculture transition
 choice made, 306–307, 390, 393
 climate change preceding, 227, 425
 consequences of, 483–484, 497
 downside of, 79
 economic development approach change with, 95
 economic rights and freedoms, loss due to, 200
 economies emerging from, 124
 ecosystem and biodiversity destruction in wake of, 96, 259
 ecosystem boundaries, collision with, 162–163
 energy consumption increase during, 371
 energy demand increase during, 373, 404, 406
 energy transition compared to, 391–392
 environmental impact of, 16–17, 75,

278–279
experimentation following, 80
facilitation of, 330
global warming as factor in, 206, 334
goal and outcome swapped through, 155
during Holocene, 203–204
impact of, 101–102, 116, 183, 190–191, 207, 242, 261, 262, 276–277, 343–344
mistakes during and since, 86
motivation for, 284
oral health, impact on, 106
overview of, xxiii, 181–182, 188, 258, 300
plant and animal domestication, 103–104
societal consequences of, 278, 306–308
transitions, other compared to, 288
Agro-chemicals, 134
Agro-pastorlists, 251
Agta, 507
Air pollution, 57, 74, 382
Air quality, 38, 310
Aka, 507
Alaska, palm trees in, 425
Alaska Native people, 236–237
Alaska Permanent Fund, 143–144
Algae, growth of, 57, 81, 318
Alliance, 60
Alternative energy sources, 296
Amazon (company), 283
Amazon rain forest
burning of, 29, 29f, 30
climate change impact on, 50
deforestation in, 50f
drying, potential of, 46
loss of, 412
protecting, 85
American Constitution, 149, 161, 303, 305
American Indians, 220, 236–237
American Petroleum Institute, 296
American Southwest, 215, 216
American West, 220
Ammonia, 57–58
Anasazi, 453–454, 466
Ancestral Pueblo, 215, 223
Ancient Pueblo, 453–454
Andes range, 334
Animal diseases. *See* Zoonotic diseases
Animal domestication
biodiversity species, 175
and crops, timelines for, 103–104
for food production, 285
hunter-gatherer economy abandonment including, 105–106
inability to practice, 252
lack of, 107
no requirement for, 256
populations of, 125
process of, 98
societies and economies characterized by, 124
start of, 204, 239, 242
zoonotic diseases arising from, 172, 229, 343
See also Farm animals
Animal husbandry, 229, 239, 242, 243, 258
adoption of, 181, 200, 203
carbon dioxide release, contribution to, 490
food production through, 392
technologies needed for, 101
transition to, 188, 397
zoonoses and, 278
Animal life
complex, 486–487
evolution and survival of, 70
planetary conditions enabling, 7, 19
Animal products, 278
Animal reservoirs, 238
Animals
around waterhole, 110f
classification as pests, 72
disappearance of, 206
foraging wild, 231
herding of, 201
humans as, 253, 314
hunter-gatherer relations with, 202
migration of, 424
oxygen used and carbon dioxide given off by, 73
PFAS in bodies of, 159
small species, emergence of, 181
status *versus* humans, 32
Annan, Kofi, 34
Antarctica, ice caps over, 296
Anthropocene epoch
climate change during, 209, 422
dawn of, 181, 425
emergence from Holocene to, 81–82, 117, 167, 182, 280

hot temperatures of, 337–338
human extinction risk during, 384
second chance, potential offered by, 227
start of, 43
transitions prior to, 198
Anthropocentric perspective
belief systems incorporating, 31–32
in research, 27
Anti-abortion laws, 270
Anti-immigrant pushback, 454
Apartheid
versus coexistence, 111
dismantling, 288, 289
as slavery legacy, 292
Apollo 13 disaster, 457–458, 459, 461
Application services, 235–236
Aquatic ecosystems, 23, 311, 318
Aquatic life, death of, 81
Aquatic plants, 57
Aquifers, depletion of, 48
Archer, D., 214, 358
Arctic meltdown, 357
Arctic ports, 219
Arctic Report Card, 506
Arctic shipping lanes, 219
Armies, rise of, 485
Artificial intelligence (AI)
corporate behavior resembling, 310
Earth-life species economies and, 300
extinction, potential due to, 175, 324
global dominance through, 329
maturity test applied to, 328
power to rule, 308
unknown impact of, 318
See also Superhuman artificial machine intelligence (Superhuman AI)
Asia, 437–438, 502
Asphalt roads, 55
Assets, owners of, 302
Association, choice of, 142
Asteroids
collision, 488
deflecting, 500
mining, 500
spacecraft near, 488f
Asylum seekers, 430
Atmosphere
changes to, 502–503
excess nitrogen in, 57–58, 58f
gas composition of, 19
harm to, 383
polluting, 30, 77
threat targeting, 230
Atmospheric aerosol loading, 74
Atmospheric chemistry, anthropogenic changes in, 102–103
Atomic bomb, 330
Australia
desertification in southern, 437–438
droughts in, 220
migration to, 349
Australopithecus, 333, 422
Auto emissions tests, 73–74
Auto exhausts, 74
Automobile-dependent infrastructure, 302
Automobiles, invention of, 387
Autonomy, individual, 145, 201

B
Bab-el-Mandeb Strait, 433
Bacteria, 66
Bala, G., 213
Bank failures, 194
Banking, economies before, 190
Barbados, 289–291
Barham, Lawrence, 421
"Basic reproduction number" (term), 235
Batek Negritos, 140, 507
Bees, 54
Behavior, cultural services bound to, 40
Belize, 453
Best-countries-to-live-in lists, 152
Bethel, Alaska, 441
Bezos, Jeff, 107
Bezos Earth Fund, 353
Biden, Joe, 107, 146, 195–196, 197, 245, 504
Billionaires
absence of, 197
aspirations for becoming, 353
existence, conditions enabling, 146
life and survival *versus* becoming, 286, 287
wealth, increasing among, 195
wealth owned by, 480
Billion-dolar disasters, 501f, 502
Bill of Rights, 305
Biochemical-based, energy feedback network, breaking out of, 72
Biochemicals, 37

Biodiversity
abandonment of, 366
advance of, enabling, 106
agrarian socioeconomic lifeways impact on, 272–273
agricultural societies and economies control over, 97
agriculture impact on, 275
agriculture transition impact on, 242
biomass comprising, 363
changes in, 335, 337, 502–503
climate change impact on, 409, 425
coexistence with, 264, 265, 351, 359–360, 472
as complementary biological species-set, 73
components of, 15
concern for, 286
conditions enabling, 19
control over, 98
damage to, 264–265
dependence on, 253
depletion of, 125
destruction of, 17, 22, 64, 83, 86, 96, 122, 174, 176, 183, 184, 200, 230, 239, 243, 246, 247, 265, 294, 299, 300, 301, 312, 313, 343, 345, 366, 385, 393, 466–467, 468, 474
displacing of, 232
early humans interaction with, 344
Earth-life economies benefit to, 16
Earth-life economies dependent on, 475
Earth-life support for, 503
economies, modern and, 457
economies at odds with, 95
economies in harmony with, 86, 94, 108, 174, 176, 197, 395
economies out of harmony with, 103
economist views concerning, 58–59
ecosystem processes and services dependent on, xxi
ecosystem products and services dependent on, 256
ecosystem repurposing impact on, 45–46
elimination of, 67, 273
enabling, 483
end of, 132
energy needs, 372
evolution of, 418
exhaustion of, 311
exploitation of, 260, 480
extinctions not driven by, 355
foundations of, 300
goals, 63, 405
harm to, 318
health of, 274
human dependence on, 64, 252
humanity acting within, 371–372
humans as part of, 79
hunter-gatherer economies relationship with, 9
hunter-gatherer impact on, 97
interchangeability of, 157
life dependent on, 477
life evolving out of, 129
as life source dependent on earth-life species, 152
living in harmony with, 77, 86, 95, 96, 129, 167, 174, 177, 190, 229, 231, 243, 254, 256, 257, 258, 259, 262, 263, 272, 273, 285, 300, 308, 309, 313, 315, 320, 323, 348, 377, 384, 393, 413, 473, 512, 513–514, 516
living out of harmony with, 102, 247, 372, 380, 385, 390, 478
loss of, 51–54, 74, 233, 238
loss of, ending, 168
maintaining, 183–184
making a living within, 128, 164, 252
market growth harm to, 310
modern economies impact on, 10, 275
outputs, 165
perceptions of, 6
preservation of, 116, 137, 138–139, 168, 231–232, 240, 245, 253, 259–260, 263, 279, 321, 322, 331, 332, 491
pressures on, 274
prioritizing, 403
products and services, 131, 144
public education on, 64
reducing impact on, 284–285
re-engineering, 56
restoration of, 380, 498
role of, understanding, 314
sacrifice of, 284
sanctity of, 166
sanctity of life and, 138
species, no domesticating, ownership,

modification, or control of, 266
survival, role in, xvii, 133
survival of, 110, 126, 167, 171, 173, 234, 247–248, 258, 259, 261, 262, 264, 287, 309, 316, 317, 396, 478, 497, 510, 516
survival without destroying, xviii, 13
transformation of species, 183
Biodiversity extinction
accelerating, 134
agriculture as cause of, 278
approaching, 188
avoiding, 136
conditions leading to, 126
continuing, 117
corporation role in, 310
economic goal and outcome change resulting in, 156
economies driving, 78
eliminating possibility of, 124
failure to prevent, 279
forces driving, 20, 102, 121, 137–138, 163, 188, 207, 243, 255, 257, 268, 375, 396, 474, 479, 486, 495
halting, 506
hoarding role in, 137
population growth role in, 164
potential risk of, 120, 125
preventing, 232, 293
sedentary societies and economies pushing, 132
societies and economies built off of, 110
socioeconomic approach built on, 491
start of, 104
stopping, 123, 238, 240
technologies and innovations role in, 317, 323
Biodiversity products and services
as commodities, 310
demand on, reducing, 266
Biogeochemical cycles, 56
Biogeochemical flows, 64
Biological altruism, 328
Biological control, 38
Biological life forms, 75–76
Biological wiring, 329
Biomass
carbon as component of, 401–402
changes in, 418
as energy source, 361, 363, 364, 370, 379, 380–381, 391
fire consumption of, 376
fishing impact on, 47
reduction in, 54
resource conversion into, 52
wood as form of, 388
Biomes
adapting to, 348–349, 420
change in, 337
climate change impact on, 181, 424, 425
definition and overview of, 23
destruction of, 301
energy obtainable throughout all, 364
examples of, 43f
global remodeling of, 335
habitats equipped with, 256
human activity impact on, 43–44
hunter-gatherer adaptation affected by, 99
overview of, 44f
products and services, 439
shift in temperature, 100
Biomimicry, 319
Biosphere
changes to, 502–503
Earth-life species adapted to, 439
economic value of, 16
ecosystems as base of, 23
harm to, 383
integrity, loss of, 74
Biotechnology, 309
Biotic conditions, changes in, 418
Biotic parts of ecosystem, 23
Bioweapons research, 331
Birth control, natural, 267
Birth rate, increase in, 278
Birth rate, low, 510
Bison, driving to near-extinction, 137
Bitcoins, 156
Black holes, 2
Blackouts, 25
Blacks, 236–237
Bølling-Allerød, 422
Bolsonaro, Jair, 85, 269
Border walls, 26, 270, 428–429
Boreal forests, 44
Botha, P. W., 288
Botswana, 154
Brand, Uwe, 450
Brazil

droughts in, 220
as Rainforest Protection Pact co-signer, 85
slavery in, 291–292
British Columbia, 222–223
British Crown corporations, 304
Bronze Age, 344
Brovkin, V., 214, 358
Brownlee, Donald, 18, 486–487
The Btritish East Company, 304
"Bubble of life" (term), 24
Bushmeat, 61
"Bushmen" peoples, 250
"Bushmen" peoples, descendants of, 107
Business address, 508
Businesses, 235
Businesspeople, 145
Bycatch, 47

C
California, 220
Cambodia, 45
Cambrian Explosion, 66, 299
Cambrian Revolution, 439
Camels, 98, 104
Canada
British colonization of, 304
habitability niche driven toward, 225
permafrost line shift in, 441
tar sands, 269, 446
territorial claims against, 151
Cancel culture, 60
Cancer-causing agents, 158–159
Capital in the Twenty-First Century (Piketty), 146
Capitalism, 207, 468
Capitalist economies
alternative to, 123
commodities bought and sold in, 310
economic-sharing system *versus,* 135
global system, 260
goal of, 115
greenhouse gases and, 345
human economies differing from, 200
hunter-gatherer economies compared to, 11
origin of, 79
property ownership in, 191
Capitalist societies and economies, 146, 153–154
Carbon
capture and storage (CSS), 279, 358
in ecosystems, 401–402
release of, 214, 448
removing from atmosphere, 358, 448–449
reservoir for, 382
Carbon 14, 489
Carbon cycle, 76, 402
Carbon dioxide (CO_2)
annual averages, 461f
anthropogenic, 490
arresting, 394
automobiles spewing, 319
average lifetime number for, 358
capture, 357, 447
climate change driven by, 405
coal role in, 298f
concentrations, increase in, 204–205, 213–214
concentrations, variations in, 420
cyclic increases in, 208
death and extinction driven by, 367
economic growth connection to, 341
economic production activity driven by, 230
excessive, impact of, 50–51
fossile fuel connection to, 228
global warming driven by, 175, 182, 206, 212, 227, 281, 295–296, 340–341, 385, 392, 393, 445, 445f, 486
oceans, impact on, 449
past and present, 422
persistence and impact of, 75, 214
plant processing of, 482
plant productivity enabled by change in, 203
during Pleistocene, 101, 103, 181
point of no return on, 64
polar cap melting caused by, 347
quantity, estimating, 449
reducing, need for, 257
release by humans, 71, 74, 75, 105, 219, 221, 490
removing from atmosphere, 311, 358
respirated, 76
rising levels of, 338, 357, 378, 378f, 379, 383, 456f, 457, 461
solar radiation trapped by, 459
sources of, 297

total volume of, 358, 457
weaning humanity off of, 173
Carbon dioxide (CO_2) buildup
activities contributing to, 209, 376
efforts to end, 172, 176, 212
impact of, 319
market growth role in, 310
stopping, 340, 342
Carbon emissions, 56, 275, 358
Carbon energy sources, 302
Carbon footprint, 281, 505
Carbon-free economy, 494
Carbon monoxide, 318
Carbon-neutral economy, transition back to, 389
Carbon system, 28f
Cardinale, B., 52
Carnivores, food source for, 26
Carson, Rachel, 59, 62
Carto, Shannon L., 434
Carville, James, 505, 515
Catastrophe, climatic change combined with, 443
Catastrophe assessment, 441–442
Cattle, domestication of, 98, 104
Cattle-supporting arable land, 49
Central Africa, tropical forests in, 348
Central African Republic, 412
Central American countries, migration from, 226
Central American migrants, 16
Central Kalahari San, 154
Central Mediterranean Route, 431
Cereal crops, yields of, 443
CFC-11, 120, 121, 157, 257, 492
CFC emissions, 120
CFCs, ban on, 120, 157
Charles, King of England, 289–290, 293
Chemical-dependent factory-farming techniques, 80
Chemical fertilizers, 318
Chemical pollution, 74, 134
Childbirth, forced spacing of, 131, 270
Childcare, 196, 301–302
Child mortality, 218
Children
behavioral problems in, 170
malnutrition and death of, 509
raising, 514
as soldiers, 160
Child tax credit, 236
China
climate change and mobility in, 224
coal in, 299, 376
economic and humanitarian issues, 245
greetings in, 136
population of, 512
rare-earth metals controlled by, 83, 85, 398
Christianity, 141
Christians, nature as viewed by, 31–32
Chronic diseases, 170
Church, rise of, 126
Cigarette manufacturers, 158
Cities and towns
abandonment of, 223
animal migration into, 424
climate change impact, potential on, 225–226
ecosystem and biodiversity impact of, 242
features of, 124
growth of, 188
lack of, 115
rise of, 307
in sedentary societies, 9, 182, 343, 413, 484, 497, 513
surplus, profits, and wealth accumulation-driven, 2
Citizenship, responsibilities and liabilities of, 305
City-states, 125, 204, 258
Civilization
climate conditions enabling, 337, 377, 411
dropping out of, 282
end, potential of, 337
evolution of, 68, 418
human intelligence responsible for, 327–328
life before, 250
potential future, 227, 231, 343, 344
rise of, 171, 180, 182, 228, 258, 259, 283, 307, 336, 344, 345, 386, 393–394, 397, 444, 467, 490, 491, 502, 503
subjects, slaves, and peasants of, 343
undoing, 462
Civilization collapse
agriculture paving way for, 264–265
avoiding, 410–411
climate change as factor in, 215, 219, 223

diseases plaguing, 80
Earth-life support system modifying followed by, 273, 274
economic production prone to, 229
economies driving, 177
economy collapse followed by, 454
energy transitions and, 393–394
failure to foresee, 62
growth obsession as cause of, 468
during Holocene, 200
human economies driving, 120–121
life elsewhere following, 453
local ecosystem decimation role in, 27
mistakes leading to, 86
numerous, 117
reasons for, xv, xviii, 95–96, 125, 163, 167, 384, 475
rise and, 98, 208–209, 243, 286, 453–454
risk factors for, 246, 469
socioeconomic transitions leading to, 180, 481
technologies and innovations role in, 323
Civilizations
agriculture hijacking of, 104
city-states with, 204
climate change impact, past on, 214–215
conditions enabling, 205
Earth's carrying capacity exceeded by, 231
economies giving rise to, 88
evolution of modern, 99–100
formation of, xvii
future, 204
outside of ecosystems, 81–82
problems accompanying, 171, 244–245
rise of, 98, 125, 200, 214, 226–227
surplus-driven, 244–245
transforming, 173
Clarion-Clipperton zone (CCZ), 84f
Class-action lawsuits, 159
Class structures, 126, 468
Clean air, 310
Clean energy, 85
Climate
behaviors and innovations impacted by, 101
humanity no ability to manipulate or control, 327
maps, 65f
movement based on changes in, xix
regulating, 38
stability of, 15, 19, 336
Climate architecture, survival-enabling, 490
Climate catastrophe, sleepwalking to, 341
Climate change
escaping, 129, 130
evoltutionary priority in face of, 234
migration in response to (*see* Climate migration)
survival knowledge needed in light of, 108–109
world economy *versus,* 464
See also Global warming
Climate change, anthropogenic
agriculture role in, 105
carbon buildup role in, 76
carbon dioxide-driven, 89, 163, 205, 376
catastrophes driven by, 389–390
causes of, 244, 246, 255, 261, 412
climate niche shift due to, 439–442
combating, 449
conditions leading to, 126
corporation role in, 310
crop production impacted by, 426
economic expansion and, 71–72
economic goal and outcome change resulting in, 156
economic impact of, 100
economic opportunities made possible through, 218–219
economic systems and lifeways, seeking improved, 468
economies and societies ended by, 230
ecosystem collapse brought on by, 49–51
ecosystem repurposing combined with, 46
ecosystems affected by, 44
environmental changes driving, 233
examining, 233
as existential threat, 405
extinction risk due to, 117, 317, 328, 384
fossil fuels role in, 55, 324, 396, 501–502
funding, 245
funding for reducing, 146
future impact, potential of, 213, 338–339, 344, 474
future scenarios, 441–443, 444–446
greenhouse gases role in, 359, 512
halting, 297, 394
Holocene-Anthropogenic transition

accompanied by, 345
human economies threatened by, 246
human impact on Earth including, 43
human survival impacted by, 246
human vulnerability to, 438, 441, 443
impacts of, 182, 204, 222–223, 297, 309, 419, 441, 443
increasing, 340
industries fueling, 494
insect diversity loss due to, 54
knowledge of, 61, 295–296, 297, 298
mass extinction due to, 504–505
mitigation of, 246, 448–449
mitigation policies, 213–214
modern humans confronting, 117
pandemics and, 230, 238
planetary boundaries, crossing with, 74
planet carrying capacity and, 385
public misled on, 158
rates of, 280
risks posed by, 243
shortages due to, 112
societal and economic disruptions unleashed by, 205
technologies role in causing (*see* Technologies: climate change caused by)
technology use, potential in fighting, 339, 344, 357, 359, 450
threat of, 319
trajectories and potential future impact, 208, 209–210, 221–222, 227–228
triggering of, 397
unknowns, 445–446, 450, 451
viral spillovers accelerated by, 175
Climate change, past
adapting to, 181
carbon dioxide-driven, 205
civilization collapse preceded by, 95–96, 125
at end of Pleistocene Epoch, 103
during Holocene Epoch, 68, 214–215
human evolution correlated with, 100f
human survival impacted by, 223
hunter-gatherer experience of, 411, 436–437
impacts of, xvii, 214–215, 343
inter-epoch transitions, role in, 337
migration, human economies and, xxiii
during Pleistocene, 100, 101, 180–181, 423
Pleistocene-Holocene transition, 203, 205–206, 247, 421
steady states, changing, 198
Climate change, past and present compared, 214–223, 346–350, 411, 417–422, 424–425, 433–436
economies, 100
Eocene, 425
extinction risk due to, 410
human transition accompanied by, 81
intensifying, 82
intersection of two regimes of, 346
localized *versus* global, 454
natural *versus* anthropogenic, 340, 345, 436, 444–445
Pliocene, 437
technology use, potential in fighting, 344
transformation of Earth, 183
Climate disasters, 2023, 426
Climate issues, operational scrutiny and investor pressure on, 297–298
Climate migrants
migrants, past compared to modern, 113
no room for, 340
reception of, 342
Climate migration
current conditions, 16, 128, 427–428
extraterrestrial (*see* Migration: extraterrestrial)
past, 8, 10, 215, 223, 242, 247, 287, 340, 409, 411, 418, 423–424, 425, 432
past and present compared, 113, 342, 411, 425, 432–436, 452–454
potential future, 226, 338, 418, 424, 426–427, 436, 439, 440, 451–452
Climate niche, 224–225, 225f, 438, 439–441, 442
Climate policies, potential future scenarios, 210–211
Climate refugees, 506
Climate system, unknowns, 445–446
Climate tipping points, 503f, 504
Climate transition to steady-state phase, 496
Climate zones, shift in, 440
Climatic conditions, variability of, 107
Clothing, 114, 115
Coal
abandonment of, 375, 391

carbon dioxide emissions due to, 298f
climate change and, 298
discovery of, 376
as energy source, 361, 372, 387–388
geopolitics impacted by, 397
global phaseout of, 299
machinery powered by, 387
mining and combusting, 357
phasing out, 494
pros and cons of, 81
reserves, 209–210
use of, 362
Coastal cities, 298, 348
Coastal communities, 48
Coastal regions, 338, 340
Coastlines, submerging of, 225
Cobalt, 404
Coexistence
with ecosystems and biodiversity, 264, 265, 472
importance of, 111
knowledge of, 516
mutual preservation and, 497
survival, role in, 141, 260
Cold climate in art and literature, 218
Command, economies based on, xviii
Commerce
as economic development stage, 251
versus essential needs, 119, 121, 187
lack of, 114
Commodities, production of, 98
"Common prosperity," 245
Communications, economies before, 190
Communism, economies based on, 77
Communist leaders, 303
Communities
activities and services, 302
health and well-being of living, 301
Community college, tuition-free, 196
Community of species, 24
Companies
climate policies *versus* oil and gas production, 212–213
earnings of, 147
Companionship, animal role in, 98
Competitive advantage, 316
Complex hunter-gatherers, 254
Compulsion to reproduce, 224
Computing technologies, 342, 345
Conflicts
climate change-triggered, 441
food access affected by, 168
Congo, 85
Congo tropical forest, 46
Constitution, 143, 149, 161
Construction, economies before, 190
Consumer goods, shortages of, 61
"Continuous Habitable Zones," 24–25
Contract, societies based on, 191
Contract workers, protections for, 236
Convention on Biodiversity, 2002, 63
Convention on Biological Diversity (CBD), 60
Cooler climes, migration to, 227
Coolhouse Earth, 422, 444
Cooperation, 141, 302
Copenhagen Agreement COP15 (2009), 63, 172, 314
Copenhagen Agreement COP26, 172, 252, 257, 258
Copenhagen Agreement COP27, 172, 209
Coral bleaching, 47
Coral reefs, 47, 311, 338
Corporate charter, 304
Corporate-infrastructure-driven economic activity, 122
Corporate ownership, 111
Corporations
artificial intelligence, behavior resembling, 310
choices made by, 282
control of choices, wresting from, 312
as dominant governance institutions, 250
economic behavior of, 310
economy working only for, 196
ecosystem products and services commandeered by, 147
employees of, 308
environmental ignorance of, 311
government relations with, 304, 309
human-economy functions turned over to, 184
as legal-persons, 303
making a killing, 301, 317
making a living, role in, 310
as "persons," 198, 305
power to rule, 308, 312
products and services, 157

proliferation of, 308
rise of, 303–305
size and power of, 250, 283, 304–305, 306
surplus generation in hands of, 306
survival, attitudes concerning, 309
taxes charged to, 245
tax exemptions for, 197
working for, 283
Corridor of survivability, 438
Costanza, Robert, 15–16
Counties, 124
Countries
caring, socioeconomic image as goal of, 152
economic system comprising, 207
financial health and well-being of, 198
in sedentary societies, 124
Covid-19 pandemic
causes of, 244
climate change and, 230
corporation role in, 310
deaths, 234f, 236–237, 237f, 241–242, 241f
economic and societal changes resulting from, 232
economic impact of, xvi, 61, 195, 225, 229, 240–241, 246, 340–341
failure to foresee, 62, 278
home schooling during, 508
impact of, 204, 234–237
inequality laid bare by, 192–193
lessons from, 233–234, 256
as manifestation of broken relationship with nature, 78
pandemics, other compared to, 237–238
recovery from, 443
supply chain shortages stemming from, 135
vaccines, 146, 172, 192, 194, 235, 237, 331
variants, 294
as wake-up call, 82
work from home during, 10, 508
zoonotic diseases resembling, 80, 106
Creator god(s)
belief in, 160, 173, 485
nonbelief in, 107, 109, 112, 123, 161, 292, 468
Crime, increasing, 225
Crimes against humanity, 430–431
Criminals, 156
Crinoids, 489f
CRISPR, 345
Cropland, land converted to, 44–45
Crops
before animal domestication, 103
emerging new, 336
failure of, 218
growing, 68
harvesting, 484
location, change in, 222
pollination, 56
production, 46, 426
raising, 104
types, 56
yields, poor, 225
Cuban Missile Crisis, 491, 504
Cultivated areas, extending, 31
Cultivation, 44, 101
Cultural diversity, 39
Cultural heritage values, 39
Cultural services, 36, 37t, 39–40
Cultural wars, 235
Cultures, xv, xvii
Cyanobacteria, 367

D
Dams, 48
Darién Gap, 429f, 430, 452f, 453
DART spacecraft, 488, 488f
Dasgupta Report on the Economics of Biodiversity, 60
Dead zones, 30, 55, 81, 246, 279, 311, 449
Death
of children, 509
Covid-19 epidemic, 234f, 236–237, 237f, 241–242, 241f
instruments of, 322
technologies and innovations role in, 323
Decarbonization, 399, 400, 402–403, 404, 405, 462
Deceased, treatment of, 241
Declaration of independence, 161
Deforestation
in Amazon, 50f
civilization collapse as consequence of, 21–22, 163
economic growth driving, 269–270
justification for, 31
land grab and ecosystem repurposing

leading to, 46
mining activities, illegal as cause of, 29f, 30
stopping, 275
DeGrasse Tyson, Neal, 332
Degrowth, 465
De Klerk, F. W., 287, 288–289, 290f, 291, 292, 293
"Delayed return economy," 202
De Menocal, Peter, 215, 218
Democracies, 149, 150, 282, 346
Democratic leaders, 303
Denisovans, 99, 339
Desertification, 435, 437–438
Diamond, Jared, 191
DiCaprio, Leonardo, 21, 22, 67, 163
Dickens, Charles, 218
Dictators, 173, 303, 485
Didymos (asteroid), 488f
Diesel power, 386–387
Dimorphos (asteroid), 488f
Dinosaurs
Earth system shift not seen since time of, 65
epoch of, 43
extinction of, 22, 488
human survival skills *versus,* 500
Disaster
catastrophe combined with, 442
population density compounding, 166
Diseases
chemicals causing, 71, 159
civilization collapse preceded by, 62
emergence of, 46, 233
during Little Ice Age, 218
spread of, 442
Disinformation, 158
Diverse communities, 52
Dogs, domestication of, 98, 103
DOMC (Domesticate, Own, Manage, or Control)
customs concerning, 111–112, 123, 131, 133–134, 164
early human approach to, 321, 413, 508
hunter-gatherer approach to, 266, 407, 466, 468
hunter-gatherers and modern humans compared, 151, 153t, 166
lifeways, 372, 468
technologies and innovations aimed at, 322
Dominica, 290–291
Doughnut economics, 163
Drinking water
clean, 310
nitrates in, 57
source of, 47–48
Droughts
adaptation to, 48
carbon dioxide role in, 50
future, 426, 438, 506
impact of, 215–216, 219–221
mitigating, 15
natural changes in, 420
shrinking supplies due to, 62
DuPont, 159
Dust Bowl, 1930s, 216, 217f
Dutch trade, 304

E
Early Africans, 336
Earnings, maximizing, 286
Earth
atmosphere, human changing of, 490
carrying capacity of, 12, 231, 314, 360, 385, 484, 501
climate history, 444
dominant species, 330
early conditions, 66
functioning independent of human control, 355–356, 500
habitability of parts of, change to, 436
as habitat for life, 6–7, 18, 19
history, 65f
learning to survive away from, 452
migration from, 350–351, 436
new steady-state, shift to, 65
transformation of, 183
Earth 2.0, 499, 500
Earth at risk, 86
Earth-life economy
life and survival in, 77, 475
purpose of, 16–17
Earth-life energy system architecture, 372–373
Earth-life processes
functions and cycles of, human changes to, 54–58
interaction with, 300

Earth-life species
chemicals harmful to, 134
codependence of, 24, 472–473, 485
coexistence with other, 12, 497
collaboration between, 53
complementarity and interoperability of, 77
death of, 74
degradation of, 42
destruction of, 67, 111
displacement of, 27, 45, 85, 111, 112, 484
distribution of, 51
domestication of, 104, 108, 322
economies destructive to, xxii
economies ensuring survival of, xxiv, 88
ecosystems, interaction with, 482
ecosystems occupied by, 35
energy needed by, 364–365, 372, 373, 406
energy source known to, 400
energy stored and distributed within and by, 363
evolution and survival of, 3, 7, 72–73, 420, 439, 483
extinction of, 208, 256, 257, 259, 335, 371, 419, 484, 485, 496, 510
extinction threat, 274, 299, 366, 383, 449
foraging activities of, 87, 483–484
freshwater harboring, 48
goals enabling, 479
greenhouse gas threat to, 458
harnessing, 386
human relationship to, 55
hunter-gatherer societies compared to, 88
interactions of all, 355
life and survival of, 166, 240, 370, 475
lifeways of, 243, 284, 312, 335, 409
living in harmony with other, 79, 109, 123, 343
location of, 17
mobility of, 424
modern economies not prioritizing, 195
ownership of other, 104, 111–112, 133
preservation of, 136, 137, 360
removal of, 52
socioeconomic lifeways for, 89, 263
stranding diversity of, 412
survival in harmony with, 314
survival of, 13, 165, 174, 180, 234, 252, 256, 262, 265, 279–280, 294, 311, 391, 406–407, 478, 481–482, 500
vanishing of, 338
wisdom of the waterhole, 109
Earth-life species economies
components of, 254
early human economies integrated with, 12
ecosystems as foundation of, 23, 24
emergence of, 25, 322, 478
evolutionary function of, 472
goal and outcome of, 244, 299–300, 473, 492
goal and purpose of, 90
human economies in contrast to, 8, 20
life indispensable to, 152
overview of, 5–6
requirements for, 87, 255
studying, 481
success of, 244
survival, design for, 18
technologies and innovations emergence from, 315
Earth-life support system(s)
abandonment of, 80
collapse of, 274
components of, 73
destroying elements of, 78
functioning of, 15
harm to, 503
modifying, 273–274, 279
species lifeways, encoding in, 272
Earth-life systems
altering of, 280
carbon dioxide emissions not recycled by, 76
need to learn about, 280
Earth Summit and follow-up, 63
Earth system
cyclical rotation of, 424
damage done to, 505
Earth system states, emergence of, 444
East Africa
environments in, 349
landscape, changing, 336–337, 435
East Africa Rift Valley, 335–336, 348
East Asian financial crisis, 193
Easter Island, 35
Ecocide
causes of, 301

as crime, 31, 269
government and corporate committing of, 309
Ecocide hotspots, 30f
Ecolization, 227
Ecological systems and services
economies dependent on, 16
habitats and ecosystems providing, 15
Econocide
avoiding, 77
risk of, 75, 309
Economic activity
hunting and gathering as only, 190
legal-persons driven *versus* survival-driven, 122
Economic collapse
drought as factor in, 216
exploring reasons for, 95
foundation for, xviii
growth obsession as cause of, 468
local ecosystem collapse as factor in, 27
production prone to, 229
risk of future, 62, 67
socioeconomic transitions leading to, 180
Economic crisis, 464–465
Economic development
differing approaches to, 106
gains in, 40
push for, 341
technologies and innovations to achieve, 332
Economic expansion, 392
Economic gain, 132, 160
Economic goals, 332
Economic growth
climate change impact on, 426
consequences of unchecked, 379, 387
economies not emphasizing, 467
elevation of, 160
energy hunt driven by, 457
focus on, 404
global warming, relationship with, 340–341, 459
greenhouse gas emissions, decoupling from, 464–465
versus human survival, 341, 405
life and survival *versus,* 357, 475, 480, 495
no growth, 465–466
outside of ecosystems, 371, 372
policies promoting, 196
pursuit of, 200, 255, 284, 316, 378, 468
survival chances inversely proportional to, 125
survival *versus,* 154–155, 294
technologies and innovations for, 322
Economic (GDP) growth. *See* GDP growth
Economic hierarchy, 200
Economic migrants, past and modern compared, 113
Economic opportunity, 360
Economic order, new, potential, 227
Economic organization, 40, 301
Economic output, 404
Economic production
activity, reduction of, 230
change in, 191, 207–208, 243
climate change impact on, 206–207
lack of, 114
lesson in, 229
living within *versus* living without as method of, 229
principles of, 123, 125
Economic recovery, 196
Economic refugees, 506
Economic rights and freedoms, robbing people of, 200
Economics
as dismal science, 176
of evolution, 229
falsehoods propagated in, 2
modern, focus of, 198
Economic sectors
as carbon dioxide and methane generators, 209
carbon dioxide increase driven by, 212
decarbonization transformation of offending, 462
greenhouse gas emissions by, 462–464
modern economy comprised of, 175–176
overview of, 189t
Economic slowdowns and downturns, 168–169
Economic systems, seeking improved, 468
Economic transformation, agriculture transition as, 105
Economic transition, next, goal and outcome of, 184
Economies

collapse, pathway to, 176
collapse of, 239
definition and overview of, xviii, 471–475
ecosystem destruction wrought by human, 2
emergence of, xvi–xviii, 5–6, 243, 322–323, 482
managing, 176
nature of, 262, 477–478
pandemic impact on trajectory of, 234
pre-humanity, 87, 472
purpose of, 87, 250
Economists
ecosystems and biodiversity, views on, 58–59
lack of, 197
survival, attitudes concerning, 309
wisdom of the waterhole rejected by modern, 116
Economy
building, 273–274
concept, 14, 471
foundational components underpinning, 15
hallmarks of, 254
purpose of, 301
requirements for, 472, 477
term, xvi
Economy and human well-being, disconnect between, 192–195
Ecosystem footprint, 107, 108
Ecosystem processes and services
damage done to, xxi
Earth-life processes, 54–58
economy operation within *versus* outside, 244
human-modified, 58
human participation marginal in, 33–34
space station processes compared to, 32–33
Ecosystem products and services
biodiversity species maintaining, 256
climate change impact on, 419
continued access to, 424
corporation inability to account for, 310
demand on, increasing, 268–269
demand on, reducing, 168, 266
dependence on, 253
driven to poles, 165
Earth-life species thriving on, 439
energy, 25–26, 108, 319
extracting, 175
hunter-gatherer and modern societies and economies compared, 147
no domesticating, ownership, modification, or control of, 266
seasonal shift in, 467
Ecosystems
abandonment for farming, 50–51, 202, 366
abusing, 175
add-ons (*see* Add-ons)
advance of, enabling, 106
agrarian socioeconomic lifeways impact on, 272–273
agricultural societies and economies control over, 97
agriculture as war on, 72
agriculture impact on, 275
agriculture transition impact on, 242
balance within, 12
biomass comprising, 363, 364
carrying capacity of, 11, 163, 360
categories, 36t
change in, 337, 418, 502–503
climate change impact on, 49–51, 181, 409, 424, 425
coexistence with, 265, 472
collapse of, 27, 56, 61, 62, 67, 125, 131–132, 164, 188, 268, 278, 279, 293
concern for, 286
as condition for life, 8
control over, 98
cycles within, 76
damage to, reversing, 498
danger to, 102
defined, 22
degradation of, 42
departure from, 75
depletion of, reducing, 131, 268
description of, 23–24
destruction of, 17, 20, 22, 27–28, 29–31, 51, 64, 67, 71–72, 78, 96, 110, 117, 121, 122, 123, 126, 132, 174, 176, 183, 184, 188, 200, 207, 229, 238, 239, 240, 243, 246, 247, 255, 257, 265, 285, 294, 299, 300, 301, 312, 313, 317, 323, 343, 345, 366, 385, 393, 396, 404, 468, 474, 479, 485, 491, 495, 496, 506, 510
disruptions within, 350

diversity of, 420
early human economy coexistence with, 94, 197, 316
early humans interaction with, 344
Earth-life economies dependent on, 475
Earth-life support for, 503
economic systems inhibiting, 264
economic value of, 59, 60
economies, modern and, 457
economies dependent on, xvii, 21
economies destructive to, 12
economies embedded in, 14–15
economies enabling, 88
economies ensuring survival of, xxiv
economies in harmony with, 13, 254
economies outside of, 401, 474, 478, 483, 503
economies within, 3, 25, 86
economist views concerning, 58–59
as economy component, 6
enabling, 138–139, 483
energy needs, 372
energy obtainable throughout all, 364, 370
energy sources outside of, 370, 373, 377, 378, 386, 390, 392, 397, 400, 407, 412, 486
energy sources within, 372, 373, 374, 376, 378, 380, 386, 390, 397, 399–400, 406, 412, 455
evolution of, 36, 69–70
exhaustion, avoiding, 136
exhaustion of, 124, 125, 132, 137–138, 163, 164, 175, 311
exploitation of, 104, 260, 480
food production outside of, 392
food search within, 272
foraging activities within, 179
foundations of, 300
function(s), 23, 24, 51–52
global remodeling of, 335
goal of, 35, 405
goods and services provided by, 2, 15, 33
growing food outside of, 80
harm to, 120, 310, 318
human activity impact on, 43–44, 360
human dependence on, 64, 252
human economies outside of, 25, 34, 35, 68, 71–72, 77, 78, 81–82, 96, 103, 110, 114
human economies within, 12, 67–68, 71, 77, 79, 82, 86, 95, 151, 187, 190
humanity acting within, 371–372
human life outside of, 24, 33, 34, 67, 68–69, 76, 82, 102, 105–106, 108, 151
human modification of, 56
human needs met by, 28–29
human split with, 102
human use of, 27
hunter-gatherer economies relationship with, 9
hunter-gatherer impact on, 97
ignorance concerning, 28, 29
impact on, limiting, 360
importance of, 32
interchangeability of, 157
inventions functioning outside of, 76
life and survival of, 166, 167, 258, 259, 316, 497
life dependent on, 477
life evolving out of, 129
as life source dependent on earth-life species, 152
as life support systems, 33
life support systems embedded in, 81
lifeways lived within, 407
life within, 72, 79, 105, 106, 109, 129–130, 151, 163, 174, 256, 258, 273, 308, 313, 351, 359, 467
maintaining, 183–184
making a living outside of, 95, 96, 116, 133, 134, 159–160, 162–163, 174, 247, 369, 370–371, 380, 383, 385, 390, 392, 397, 400, 403, 404, 405, 479, 485, 490, 491, 496, 497
making a living within, 88, 90, 95, 96, 105, 106–107, 116, 128, 133, 151, 159–160, 164, 165, 167, 174, 176, 177, 180, 229, 231, 243, 252, 257, 259, 262, 263, 264, 265, 285, 300, 309, 313, 315, 317, 320, 321, 322–323, 343, 364–365, 370, 377, 383, 384, 393, 395, 400, 404, 405, 472, 473, 478, 482, 485, 486, 496, 497, 513
modern economies impact on, 10, 195, 275
modification of, 466–467
paving, 124
pillaging of, 24, 43
preservation of, 86, 116, 133–134, 137, 139, 177, 231–232, 240, 253, 259–260, 263,

321, 322, 331, 332, 360, 491
prioritizing, 403
public education on, 64
rearranging, 34
reducing impact on, 284–285
re-engineering, 56
repurposing of, 45–46, 486
resources extracted from, 60, 134
resources provided by, 482, 508
restoration of, 358, 380
role of, understanding, 314
roles, playing in, 79
sanctity of, 166
sanctity of life and, 138
sharing of, 232
societies and economies outside of, 371, 372, 374–375, 376
socioeconomic lifeways outside, 366, 384
species foraging activities within, 87
species needs met through, 25–27
species threatened within, 449
state of, 34, 35
survival, design for, 391
survival of, xviii, 110, 126, 171, 173, 174, 180, 234, 247–248, 261, 262, 265, 284, 287, 309, 396, 478, 481–482, 500, 510, 516
sustenance extracting from, 202
threat targeting, 230
transformation of, 183, 348
universal income available through, 144
value offered by, 16
waterholes used within, 110
worry over state of, 32
Ecosystem services
agriculture impacts on, 276t–277t
biogeochemical cycles role in, 56
changes in, 51
combinations of, 40, 41f
degradation of, 42
demand for, 40
freshwater support for, 48
GDP impacted by, 59
growth limited in use of, 20
human survival impacted by, 28
overview and types of, 36–40, 37t
population strain on, 113
sharing, 133–134
trends in, 42t
Ecotourism, 39
Education, 189, 190
Educational values, 39
Efé, 507
Egalitarianism
departure from, 306–307
hierarchical communities, transition to, 258
hierarchy *versus,* 514–515
of hunter-gatherer societies, 107, 112, 123, 126, 138–140, 142, 143, 150, 160–161, 191, 269, 285, 292, 303, 306, 313, 343, 468, 513–515
and kinship, 191
return to, 308
society and economy transformation, potential toward, 154, 171
as survival prerequisite, 150
term, 140
8.2 ka event, 422
Einstein, Albert, 1, 2, 108
Eldredge, Niles, 72
Electrical grid system, 16
Electronic waste, 9
Elements, movement of, 55–56
Elites, 156, 192, 204
Elizabeth II, Queen, 58, 61
Ellis, Erle C., 102–103, 280
Elosia salt pan, 110f
El Salvador, 453
Emissions Gap Report, 445, 448
Empires, 156
Empire State Building, 508
Employee protections, 236
Employees of corporations, 308
Employers, 149, 190, 201
Employment, lack in hunter-gatherer societies, 190
Energy
access to, 373
demand for, 378, 379
fire relationship to, 375–376
forms, exploring, 351
heat and mechanical, 371
and human economies, xxiii
producing and consuming, 78
rising costs, 225
triad of life, breaking away for, 77
See also Renewable energy

Energy architecture, 363, 364, 366, 370
Energy consumption, 373, 379, 389, 389f
Energy grid system, 26, 400
Energy industry, 120, 212
Energy production, freshwater role in, 48
Energy sector, 297
Energy shortage, 365
Energy sources
abandonment of, 385
changes in, 344
climate impact of, 281
consumption by, 388f
Earth's, 56, 232
ecosystems equipped with, 25–26, 108, 319
fossil fuels *versus* sun, 78
low-carbon, 362
man-made, 382
no need to increase, 469
overview of, 361–364
search for new, 102, 372, 376, 377, 380, 384, 386–387, 397, 403, 404, 406, 407, 411, 455–456, 457, 464
sun, 26, 78, 114, 361–362, 363 (*see also* Solar energy)
See also Nonrenewable energy sources; Renewable energy sources
Energy storage and distribution, 364–365
Energy storage and distribution grid, 26, 370
Energy superpowers, 397
Energy technologies, 334, 338
Energy transition, second
agriculture leading to, 392
fossil fuels role in, 394
Energy transition, third
embarking on, 394, 406
goal of, 404
human survival in face of, 367, 399
outcome unknown, 397
overview of, 392
solutions to, 405
Energy transitions, first (during agriculture transition), 373, 391–392, 396–397
Energy transition(s)
green energy transition, 493
from nonrenewables to renewables, 397, 398–399, 405, 406
opposition to, 459
renewables to nonrenewables, 396–397, 406, 412
from renewables to renewables, 374, 374f, 391–393
survival and, 404, 406
English settlers, Virginia, 215–216
The Entrepreneurial State (Mazzacuto), 309
Entrepreneurs, 145, 352, 353
Environment
agriculture impact on, 274
changing, 238, 335
climate change impact on, 419
conditions, 15
crimes against, 269
damage, 63
degradation, 318
destruction of, 343
harm to, 383
market growth harm to, 310
modern farming techniques impact on, 80
ravaging of, xxi
threat targeting, 230
Environmental destruction
civilization collapse preceded by, 62, 95–96, 233
growth obsession as cause of, 468
Environmental disasters, 107, 242
Environmental disaster zones, 446, 446f
Environmental pollution, 134
Eocene epoch
carbon dioxide increase during, 347
climate conditions, repeated, 445
climate of early, potential repeat of, 425
Early, 442
extinctions at end of, 347
Hothouse conditions, 338, 412
ice caps absent during, 440
temperatures, rising during, 345–346, 444, 450
Epidemics, 234f
See also Covid-19 pandemic; Pandemics
Equality
allegiance to, 172
emphasis on, 140
shift away from, 191
upholding and rewarding, 171
Eric the Red, 216
Erosion, 15, 38
Ethiopia
environments in, 349
human fossils in, 432

land grabs in, 45
migration from, 429f, 430
rifting process grabs in, 335
EU citizenship, 291–292
EU policy toward migrants, 428–429
Europe
climate change and mobility in, 224
desertification in, 437–438
ice, 342
European Union (EU), 398
Evolution
Earth-life species location favored by, 17
economics of, 17, 229, 256
economies, role in, 7–8
ecosystems designed for survival by, 391
food, following and, 130
human limitations within, 355
life and survival enabled by, 486
life on Earth developing from, 6–7, 20
life support mechanisms put in place by, 279, 280
modern human economies *versus,* 20
push-back, 399
survival, investment in, 17–18
survival traits, 224
zone and habitat conditions favorable to, 24–25
Evolutionary biology, 230
Evolutionary goal, 287
Evolutionary goal and outcome, 77, 90, 155, 273, 299, 312, 314, 316, 332, 372, 406, 463, 473, 474, 491, 492
Evolutionary goal and purpose, 319–320
Evolutionary life-sustaining mechanisms, re-engineering, 312
Evolutionary lifeways, 264, 467
Evolutionary mature human lifeways, 314
Evolutionary maturity, 314, 328, 329, 356
Evolutionary socioeconomic goal, 265
Evolutionary survival-driven economic principles, 195
Evolutionary survival-driven economy, 495
Evolutionary survival-driven energy architecture, 363, 370
Evolutionary survival-driven lifeways
benefits of, 508–509
continuing, 507
goal, 394
readopting, 313
Evolutionary survival-driven pattern
abandoning, 284
egalitarianism as component of, 292
existence of, 256
following, 280, 300
return to, 287
surplus-driven economic focus, replacing with, 294
Extinction
avoiding, 311
biosphere integrity loss as, 74
conditions leading to, 7, 22
danger of, 62–63, 74
economies carrying risk of, 20
ecosystems at risk of, 13
fossil fuels as potential source of, 365
global warming as cause of, 317, 374, 387, 399, 474, 492
near-total, 355, 488
risk of, 77, 94, 117, 120, 121, 328
species driven to, 27, 31, 43, 45, 73, 98
survival *versus,* 18, 133–134
technologies and innovations role in potential, 323, 324
See also Biodiversity extinction; Human extinction; Self-extinction
Extracting, impact of, 55
Extractive industries, 30, 35–36
Extraterrestrial attacks, 230
Extraterrestrial species, extinction of, 312–313
Extreme weather events
future, 426
ongoing, 435
past, 427–428, 427t
Pleistocene, 247
reducing risk of, 15
risks posed by, 243, 246
Exxon, 158, 405
Exxon Mobil, 296

F
Facebook, 115, 147, 283, 303, 321
Facial masks, 235
Fake news, 235, 513
Families, separation between, 412
Family leave policies, 236
Famine
civilization collapse preceded by, 62

during Little Ice Age, 218
reducing, 80
risk of, 80
Farm animals, 206, 227, 231, 331, 373, 381, 386, 404, 414, 484, 497, 513
Farming. *See* Agriculture
Farming socioeconomic lifeways, 286
Farmland
land converted to, 44, 72, 112
as private property, 191
Farms
abandonment of, 223
carbon dioxide destruction of, 50–51
maintaining, 124
Fascist leaders, 303
Fauna and flora changes, 181
Federal Reserve Bank of the United States, 236
Fertilizers, 71, 80, 81, 279, 318
Feudal economy, 201
Fiber, 37, 44
Financial beings, humans as, 301
Financial risk, systemic, climate change-triggered, 441
Financial services, 190
Financial services industry collapse, 148
Fire, use of, 333, 344, 375–376
The First Africans (Barham and Mitchell), 421
Fish
depleting, 137
destroying, 30
drought impact on, 221
pesticide killing of, 81
threats to, 57
Fisheries, degradation of, 47
Fishing
economic sectors emergence after, 189
to exhaustion, 269
foraging replaced by, 204
"Flatten the curve" (term), 235
Flies, 54
Floods
coastal regions, 338
at end of ice age, 247
future, 426
mitigating, 15
Food
access to, 168–169, 275
alternative, knowledge of, 215
availability, shrinking, 506
as common resource, 114
consuming, 78
delivery of, 301
demand for, 44
as ecosystem benefit, 37
energy in form of, 26, 370
following, 113, 130, 179, 423
gathering, 145
growing own, 71, 72, 80, 114, 483–484 (*see also* Agriculture)
hoarding, 171, 256
hunting for, 124, 145
lack of, 10
owning, controlling, and managing, 115
procuring, 307
search for, 121, 188
sharing of, 123, 168, 170–171, 206, 284
species following, 25
surplus, 104, 145, 156, 285
Texas blizzard, 2021 cutoff of, 16
triad of life, breaking away for, 77
varieties of, reduced, 206
worldwide food crisis, 112
Food and life support systems and technologies, 80
Food crisis, 112, 356
Food insecurity
absence in hunter-gatherer societies, 11, 270
climate change exacerbation of, 443
food sharing *versus,* 168
health impact of, 169–170
increase in, 169f, 170f
species free of, 25
Food production
absence of, 508
agricultural, socioeconomic consequences of, 278
animal domestication for, 285
built-in, 272
and consumption, 78
economies giving rise to, 180, 507
energy-intensive, 392, 404
food procurement *versus,* 285
foraging *versus,* 284
human population and, 98
increase in, 40, 318, 321, 404
land use for, 274, 274f, 275

modern capacity, 188
nature role in, 256
people required for, 267
pollination role in, 54, 55
population growth and requirements, 275
Food sources, 253, 335, 364, 381
agriculture impact on, 102
climate change impact on, 181
energy transition impact on, 404
freshwater and marine systems as, 48
for hunter-gatherers, 97
loss of, 412, 413
making a living, 483
plants as, 203
pursuit of changing, 128
Food supply
drought impact on, 48
energy transition impact on, 399
increasing, 80, 277
threats to global, 394
Food waste, 170f, 171
Food Waste Index, 169
Foraging
abandonment of, 181, 183, 207, 226, 232, 239, 242, 243, 261, 281, 306–307, 371, 378, 385, 386, 390, 392, 403, 414, 480, 483–484
advantages of, 359, 419, 509
in Africa, 182
agriculture *versus,* 103, 172, 175, 259, 262–263, 272, 300
bands, 340
changes in, 336
communities based on, 174
continuation, hypothetical of, 292–293, 506
critique of, 479
crops, protecting from, 191
cultivation combined with, 101
diversified approaches to, 101
economy emergence from, 322
within ecosystems, 179
ecosystems as setting for, 90
enabling, 510
farming combined with, 206
fishing *versus,* 204
versus food production, 284
knowledge acquired during, 215
lifeways, 395
for a living, 472
mobility needed for, 129
overview of, 266
purpose of, 507
return of, 281–282
socioeconomic constraints coming from, 273
socioeconomic lifeway, 271t
tools for, 316
transition from, 227, 229, 258, 268, 277, 278, 284, 334, 343, 373, 393, 404, 406, 425
Foraging area, farmland carved out of, 191
Foraging lifeways, 88–89, 425
Foreign investment, 45
Foreign investors, treaties protecting, 493
Foreign trade, 251
Forest fires, 9
Forests
clearing of, 30, 77, 232, 239
destruction, ceasing, 246
destruction of, 63
farmland, conversion to, 44
nitrogen, excess impact on, 58
potential loss of, 412
services provided by, 36
transformation of, 336, 412, 420
For-profit firms, 148
Fossil energy-driven products, 257
Fossil fuel companies and corporations, 492–493, 494
Fossil fuels
abandoning, 331, 369, 375, 391, 399, 457
addiction to, 351
adoption of, 159, 232, 281, 319, 352, 369, 372, 388
availability of, 398
burning, 28f, 214, 257, 328, 358, 375, 382, 450, 456
capabilities of, 75
as carbon dioxide increase factor, 209, 228, 490
climate impact of, 281, 324, 385, 387
combustion of, 51, 55
consumption of, 377f, 378
cutting emissions, 449
dependence on, 459
discovery of, 330, 455
doubling down on, 296, 297

ecosystem goods and services prior to, 15
energy mix dominated by, 362
as energy source, 176, 277
energy technologies, 334
existence of, 390
extinction driven by, 489–490
extraction of, 28f, 105, 387f, 460
financing of, 395
global warming, role in, 158, 278, 394, 405, 459, 489, 505
infrastructure projects, 494
leaving in ground, 246
mass extinction, potential driven by, 489
production of, 461
profiting from, 492
reserves, 209–210
solar energy compared to, 364
stopping use of, 281, 282
versus sun, 78
supply chains, 309
survival at risk from, 121, 223, 329–330, 356, 365, 366, 374
triad of life, breaking away for, 77
use of, 460–461
France, 81
Francis, Pope, 31
Franta, Benjamin, 297
Freedom
forebears' dedication to, 172
in hunter-gatherer societies, 269, 285, 292
loss of, 281–282, 306–307
politicians, Western governments, and, 282
return to, 311
upholding and rewarding, 171
Free-market capitalism
economies based on, 16–17, 77, 115, 260
rise of, 278
Free-market imperatives, 17
Free speech, corporation right to, 305
Freshwater consumption, 74
Freshwater depletion, preventing, 275
Freshwater diversity, decline of, 52–53
Freshwater ecosystems, 47–48, 81, 220
Friedrich, Thomas, 420
Froitzheim, Nikolaus, 447
Fuel
demand for, 44
as ecosystem benefit, 37
use of, 296
See also Fossil fuels
Fungicides, 71
Fur trade, 304
Fusion, 391, 505

G
Gaia theory, 55–56
Gain, capitalist economies focus on, 11
Galaxies, movement of, 1
Gambling, 148
Game species, extinction of, 101, 103
Garvey, James R., 298
Gas
abandonment of, 375, 391
as energy source, 361
as nonrenewable energy source, 397
pros and cons of, 81
restricted access to, 112
use of, 362
Gas companies, 212–213, 269
Gases, 73, 75–76
Gas industry, 446
Gasoline, leaded, 74
Gasoline, shortage of, 112
Gas reserves, 209–210
GDP
country breakdown, 373
county benefits as share of, 225–226
as economic success measure, 60
ecosystem services relationship to, 59
generation of, 188, 319
humanity *versus,* 193–194
poverty, unalleviated in spite of, 171
See also Global GDP
GDP growth
abandoning, 500
accelerating, 184
capitalist economies focus on, 11
desire for, 396
economies based on, xviii, 82, 473, 491, 496
generation of, 209, 317
during global pandemic, 11
as goal, 115, 346
lack of, 190, 231
maximizing, 261
nonrenewables exploited for, 391
obsession with, abandoning, 360
pursuit of, 82, 85, 90, 127, 176, 238, 240,

247, 284, 301, 392, 394, 415, 468, 481, 503
survival *versus,* 20, 77, 88, 154–155, 299–300, 320, 474, 498
technologies and innovations to achieve, 332
Generational wealth, 508
Genetic diversity, decline in, 51
Genetic engineering, 72, 77
Genetic resources, 37
Geo-engineering, 450
Geographic areas and regions, 483
Geographic location, fixed, 508
Geographies, energy obtainable throughout all, 364
Geological epoch, 99, 103
Geology
changes, 412
climate change impact on, 419
shaping, 418
transition of, 335
Geothermal energy, 391
GHGs. *See* Greenhouse gases
Gies, Erica, 45
Gig economy, 283
Gig workers, protections for, 236
Glacial-age permafrost bodies, 447
Glacial cycles, 421
Glacial ice sheets, 421
Glacial-to-interglacial transitions, 203
Glaciation periods, 68f, 165
Glaciation temperatures, cooling to, 100
Glaciers
disappearance of, 347
melting of, 412
meltwater from receding, 336
in most recent ice age, 334
thawing, 357
Gleick, Peter, 436
The Global Assessment Report on Biodiversity and Ecosystem Services 2021, 9
Global banks, 156
Global Biodiversity Outlook 5, 62–63
Global Biodiversity Outlook Report (GBO), 60
Global capitalism (term), 284
Global climate, anthropogenic changes in, 102–103
Global climate agreements, 460
Global ecological systems and services, 16
Global economy
emergence of, 444
growth of, 11, 40
undoing modern, 462
Global financial crisis, 2007-2008, 443
Global free-market capitalist system, 278
Global GDP
drop in, 241
growth, 240f
pandemic cost as share of, 193–194
Global gross national product, 16
Global hydrological cycle, 74
Global migration, 224
Global North, 289, 291
Global pandemic, 11, 394
The Global Ramsar Wetlands Outlook 2018, 52
Global Resources Outlook 2019, 66
Global trade, 11
Global vaccine distribution strategy, 234
Global warming
accelerating, 311, 449
agriculture facilitated by, 209
anthropogenic, 412, 421
Apollo 13 disaster, comparison to, 458
carbon buildup role in, 76
carbon dioxide-driven, 89, 163, 212, 310, 379, 385, 392, 486
civilization emerging in wake of, 204
civilization threatened by, 265, 278
climate tipping points, 503–504, 503f
confronting, 275
containing, 312
corporation role in, 310
dilemma of, 385
duration of, 450–451
economies and economic forces driving, 78, 175–176
ecosystems triggered with, 74
energy source role in, 362
events leading to, 79, 268
extinction driven by, 317, 374, 387, 399, 474, 492
failure to halt, 384
forces driving, 240, 261, 375
fossil fuels role in, 158, 405, 489, 505
greenhouse gases role in, 334, 345, 414, 455, 459, 505
heat waves resulting from, 223

human extinction threat due to, 319
human impact of, 340–341
hunter-gatherer experience of, 211–212, 411
intensifying, 82
knowledge of, 295–296
limiting, 74, 299, 357–358, 448
marine ecosystems destruction contribution to, 86
migration in face of, 165
modern humans confronting, 117
ozone depletion and, 120
pause in, 341–342
potential future scenarios, 210–211, 211f, 213, 438–439
response to, 344
reversing, 341, 348
risks accompanying, 328
scientific literature on, 225
slowing, 357
socioeconomic collapse due to, 497
socioeconomic disruptions due to, 182
solution pros and cons, 279
survival threatened by, 329
technologies role in fighting, 341, 358
technology, past no impact on, 337
threat posed by, 394
unprecedented, 357
as warning sign, 294
Global warming climate change, past and current compared, 198, 334, 336, 337–338, 345–346
Glyphosate-based weed killers, 158
Gods
absence of, 115, 201, 306
belief in, 124
nonbelief in, 138
See also Creator god(s)
Goods and services, shortages of, 135–136
Google, 283, 303, 321
Government actions, foreign investors protected from, 493
Government ownership *versus* coexistence, 111
Governments
absence of, 115, 149, 258
carbon dioxide buildup, decisions concerning, 212
control of choices, wresting from, 312
corporation relations with, 304, 309
corporation size and power compared to, 250, 283, 304–305, 306
ecosystem products and services commandeered by, 147
power remaining in hands of, 311–312
reclaiming power yielded to, 313
returning control to, pitfalls of, 306
rise of, 283
struggling under thumb of, 173
survival, attitudes concerning, 309
technological breakthroughs, role in, 309
Gowdy, John, 213
Grain
growing, 484
loss of ability to farm, 224
scarcity of, 206
shortages, 112
surplus, 104, 156
Graphite, 404
Grasslands
expansion of, 420, 422
farmland, conversion to, 44
forests transformed into, 336
services provided by, 36
Graven, Heather, 448
Gray, Peter, 514
Great Drought, 1280s, 215
Great Oxygenation Event, 367
Great Plains, northern, 216
Great Rift Valley, 412, 435
The Great Transformation (Polanyi), 14, 188
Greece, 222
Green corridors, 420
Green economy, 401
Green energy
conversion to, 402
minerals needed to produce, 83, 402f, 403f, 404
return to, 400
search for, 456
transition to, 405, 493
Green energy technologies, 402f, 403f
Green growth, 464
Greenhouse gases
burning, 450
as climate change factor, 419, 444, 512
as commercial product, 341
continuing, 336

duration of, 281
Earth sensitivity to, 445
economies powered by, 359
effect of, 297
as energy sources, 328
escape of, 447
extinctions driven by, 488–489
fossil fuels role in, 331, 455
global warming, role in, 459, 505
human extinction threat due to, 319
impact of, 334, 450–451, 469
inability to stop, 345
increases in, 208, 279, 446, 449, 455, 456–457
origin of, 105, 382
output by economic sector, 209, 454–455, 455f, 457, 463f
plastics role in, 311
producers of, 414
production of, 460, 505
release of, 450, 458
removing, 450, 461, 461f
science and innovations role in, 457
solar radiation trapped by, 459
stopping, 461, 461f, 506
trajectories and potential future scenarios, 209, 210–211, 211f
undercounting, 460
Greenland, 151, 216–218, 296
Greenland Ice Sheet Project 2 (GISP2) ice core, 217, 218f
Greenpeace, 494
Green Revolution, 80, 318
Green Sahara, 434
Green technologies, 86
Greetings, sharing reflected in, 136
Groundwater
depletion of, 48, 221
filtering, 55
nutrient pollution in, 57
Group action, 114
Guaranteed basic income, 143–144
Guatemala, 453
Gulf County, Florida, 226
Gun violence, 11, 194, 270
Guterres, António, 292, 299, 341
Guyana, 290–291

H
Habitability niche, northward movement of, 225
Habitable land, reclaiming, 348
Habitats
agriculture impact on, 275, 285
biomass comprising, 364
biomes within, 256
change in, 337
climate change impact on, 181, 409, 424
components of, 15
as condition for life, 8
conversion into agricultural systems, 51
destruction of, 17, 20, 22, 45, 46, 232, 301, 312
development of, 6
early human economies coexistence with, 94
economies dependence on, xvii
economies embedded in, 14–15
as economy component, 6
evolution of, 69–70
failure of, xxi
global remodeling of, 335
human economies outside of, 25
human-made problems affecting, 26
life dependent on, 477
life evolving out of, 129
life support systems embedded in, 81
living within, 273
loss of, 47, 54, 62, 275
making a living within, xviii, 243, 263, 265
market growth harm to, 310
preservation of, 263, 360
provisioning of, 40
resources provided by, 482
seizing, 331
services as commodities, 310
survival without destroying, xviii
value offered by, 16
Hadza (Hadzabe) hunter-gatherers, 507
creator-god, nonbelief in, 160–161
decision-making among, 150
food and sexual boundary, 145
hunting weapons, 143
Khoe-San, split from, 251
living within ecosystems, 70–71, 71f
modesty expected of, 146–147
possessions, accumulation discouraged

among, 148
as sources of knowledge, 142
Hardiness zones, 440, 440f
Hate speech, 513
Hauer, Matthew, 438
Haves and have-nots, 168, 192
Hawken, Paul, 305
Hawking, Stephen, 451, 499
Hayes, Rutherford B., 305
Hazardous waste, 102
Health, climate change impact on, 426
Health systems, 310–311
Heat, deaths due to, 338
Heat waves
carbon dioxide role in, 50
future, 426, 502, 502f
threat in form of, 230
unprecedented, 222–223
Heffernan, Olive, 83
Heinrich 1 event, 422
Heinrich events, 434
Herbicides, 55, 318
Herbivores, energy obtained by, 26
Herding, 39, 175, 201, 331
Hess, Hannah, 226
Hickel, Jason, 465
Hierarchical communities, transition to, 258
Hierarchy, egalitarianism *versus,* 514–515
Hitler, Adolf, 303
Hoarding
absence of, 190, 268–269
as economic transformation factor, 284
energy sources driving, 376
as farming goal and outcome, 116–117, 171
inequality resulting from, 468
in modern economies, 195, 275
of natural resources, 124
problems stemming from, 174
rejection of, 172
versus sharing, 111, 113, 137, 141, 145–147, 171, 172, 174, 231, 238–239, 258, 268, 270, 278, 285, 312, 343, 352, 359, 373, 480, 483, 497
See also Surplus: hoarding
Hobbes, Thomas, 141, 250, 251, 252, 253, 255, 257, 258, 259, 260–261, 270, 272, 314, 491, 492, 499
Holocene epoch
agriculture transition during, 203–204, 391–392
alternative path, hypothetical during, 394
carbon dioxide increase during, 105
civilization collapse during, 468
civilization rise during, 214, 411, 454
climate and temperature variations during, 67f, 68
climate architecture during, 490
climate change during, 219, 226, 227, 452
climate conditions during, 101, 181, 203, 208, 214–215, 223, 228, 421, 422, 423, 425, 444
dawn of, 330, 337
Early, 101
emergence from, 81–82, 198
end of, 117, 167, 424
energy sources search during, 387
energy transitions during, 393–394
greenhouse gases during, 456
human species during, 334
modern economies and civilizations evolving during, 99–100
socioeconomic lifeways and methods developed during, 505
subsistence changes during, 200
temperatures of, 183, 337, 345
transition to, 103
warming temperatures of, 212, 343, 353–354
Holocene-to-Anthropocene transition
climate change, 337, 345, 347, 421
Pleistocene-Holocene Transition compared to, 424–425, 436
Home, modern, 301–302
Homeless
resource sharing with, 124
super-rich *versus,* 192
Homelessness
avoiding, 113, 468, 509
causes of, 244
end to, 194
mobile and sedentary societies compared, 142
mobile economies, absence in, 10, 11
sharing *versus,* 270
species free of, 25
in surplus economy, 244
Homes *versus* schools and offices, 507–508

Hominin species
  diversity of, 336
  energy available to, 370
  evolution of, 423
  extinction of, 117, 181, 183, 223, 335, 343, 344, 346, 410, 418
  habitation of, 349
  humans, modern compared to, 299
  lineage, 444
  migration of, 420
  sole surviving intelligent, 329
  tools developed by, 316
  transformations, 105–106
  See also Homo genus/genera
Homo erectus
  descendants of, 253
  extinction of, 339
  fire use associated with, 333
  food search by, 200
  migration of, 420
  physical abilities, 99
  technologies and innovations of, 339
Homo ergaster, 339
Homo floresiensis, 99, 339
Homo genus/genera
  appearance of, 422, 444
  climate change impact on, 425
  dispersal of, 422
  evolution of, 99, 409, 410, 417–418
  extinction of, 413, 418, 423, 424, 436
  migration threats greater than encounters with, 428
  technologies and innovations of, 339
Homo habilis, 99, 339
Homo heidelbergensis, 99, 420
Homo neanderthals, 99, 339
Homo sapiens
  climate change impact on, 425
  destructive bent of, 200
  economies older than, 99
  environmental conditions and ecosystems, exposure to new, 420
  evolution and survival of, 422
  fossils of, 432
  health of, 410
  as last surviving intelligent species, 313, 335, 336
  lineage, 444
  mass extinction, potential driven by, 299
  migration, 451
  technology predating, 332–333
Honduras, 453
Horn of Africa, 434
Horses, 98, 104
Hospitality and leisure, economies before, 190
Hothouse Earth
  of the Anthropocene, 422
  of the Eocene, 338, 412
  from Icehouse Earth to, 496
  lurch toward, 341
  of the Paleocene, 444
Household as economic unit, 301
Housing, permanent, 285
Houston, 225–226
Hu, Akielly, 464–465
Hubble, Edwin, 1
Huber, Matthew, 437
Hudson's Bay Company, 304
Human choices, manipulating, 321
Human civilization. *See* Civilization
Human diseases, regulating, 38
Human economies
  abandonment of, 452
  activity impact on, 244
  animal and plant domestication role in, 104
  building, impact of, 34, 81
  capitalist economies differing from, 200
  climate change impact, potential on, 105
  climate change impact on, 409, 410
  collapse of, 102, 106, 122, 200, 244, 475
  control of, 282, 309
  definition and overview of, 198
  destruction caused by, 77
  Earth-life economies in contrast to, 8, 24
  Earth-life support for, 503
  ecological value contributed to, 16
  economies predating, 2–3, 5–6
  ecosystem resources, dependence on, 60
  ecosystems and biodiversity advance enabled within, 106
  ecosystems as foundation of, 23
  ecosystems impacted by, 33
  ecosystems pillaged to build, 24
  emergence of, 18, 22, 25, 121, 129, 138, 187, 322–323
  end of, 132

evolution of, 121, 507–508
factors shaping, 418
foundations of, 127–129, 128f, 263–264, 264f
functions turned over to legal-person economies, 184
goal and outcome, replacing, 82, 90
goal and outcome of, 85, 116, 154–155, 245, 405, 414, 475, 495
greenhouse gases output by, 456
greenhouse gases output by sector, 454–455, 455f
human survival risks posed by, 246–247, 359
legal-person economy, transformation into (*see* Legal-person economies: human economies transformed into)
longevity of, 140
nature of, 471
nature's role in, 485
purpose of, 139, 474
rediscovering, xxii
requirements for, 129–130, 245–246, 248, 263, 478, 482
rise of, 200
role of, 309
technologies and innovations focus no longer within, 317
threats to, 246
transformation of, 461–462
in triad of life, 243
Human economies, early
economic activities comprising, 122
evolutionary function of, 472
evolving and enduring, 121
foundation supporting, 114, 123, 174, 180
goal and outcome of, 126–130, 155, 187–188
immediate-use economies, 111
and modern compared, 153t, 197
persistence of, 94
studying, 481
survival of, 88, 122, 499
tools developed within, 316
See also Hunter-gatherer economies
Human economies, modern
building, 482
changed needed for, 499
collapse, risk of, 481
everything for sale in, 115
expectations of, 194
role and purpose of, 193
socioeconomic goals and outcomes of, 473
survival, requirements for, 197
Human evolution
as adaptive response, 423
animal domestication and, 104
climate change as factor in, 223, 418, 419–420
conditions enabling, 129, 439
economies before, 472
factors influencing, 336–337
during ice age, 346–347
milestones in, 100f
Human existence, dawn of, 242
Human extinction
add-ons role in, 73
agriculture adoption and, 159
architects of own, 151
avoiding, 516
chemicals potentially driving, 81, 134
climate change-driven, 79, 238, 374, 439, 441–442
economic and societal transitions leading to, 242
economic production change contributing to, 207–208
economies leading to, 82, 177, 244, 257
ecosystem collapse leading to, 22, 27–28
global warming-driven, 319
greenhouse gases role in potential, 359, 459, 469
human desires *versus,* 120
life support system tampering leading to, 279
marine ecosystems destruction increasing, 86
path leading to, 160, 163, 294, 299, 415
preventing, 329
socioeconomic transformation needed to counter, 259
technologies and innovations role in potential, 323, 357
threats contributing to, 175–176, 384
See also Self-extinction
Human food chain
insect role in, 54
integrity of, 310

ecosystems, relationship to, 110
lifeways, 466–469
living, 79
natural resources, use of, 420–421
resource demands, 379–380
spenind time, 201
technologies and innovations, 336, 351–353, 360, 379, 410–411
in transition, 81–82, 351
Human social relations, 14
Human societies
activity impact on, 244
collapse of, 246, 442, 443
enabling, 140
evolution and economic development of, 251
factors shaping, 418
human economies embedded in, 14, 128, 128f, 263–264, 264f
injustice in, 272
longevity of, 138
manipulating, 321
requirements for, 263
survival of, 262
transformation of, 442
Human societies and economies
building of, 183
characteristics of, 125–140, 128f
climate change impact, past on, 214–218, 343
climate change impact, potential future on, 228, 345
collapse of, 127, 174, 177, 230, 256–257, 351, 481, 492, 497
core components of, 191
ecosystems, biodiversity, and life preserved through, 321
ecosystems and biodiversity, bringing into harmony with, 313
egalitarian, 166
energy sources, 371
goal and outcome of, 264, 312, 314, 316, 357, 406, 473, 491, 492, 500
harmful effects of, 312
hoarding impact on, 171
hunter-gatherer and modern compared, 115–117, 123–125, 135, 138, 149–150, 156–157, 164, 166–167, 168, 170–171, 172–173, 174–175, 176–177, 180, 231, 238–239, 254–255, 256, 265, 466–469, 473–474
inequality in, 145–146
life and survival as goal of, 114, 171, 173, 322, 346, 357
life and survival enabled by, 90
local nature of, 112
longevity of, 122, 135, 231, 322
loss of control over, 283
potential future, 171–172
purpose of, 309
rearrangement of, 344
requirements for successful, 243, 255
survival of, 126, 127, 224, 252, 256, 378, 395, 502–503, 506
technologies and innovations disassociated from, 317
transformation of, 183
transitions, 197–202, 199t, 227–228, 242
waterhole perspective, 109, 110–114
Human societies and economies, early and modern compared, 127, 127t, 154, 473
overview of, 253
transformation of, 180–181
Human socioeconomic lifeways
changes in, 343, 344, 345, 353–354, 394, 461–462, 473, 479, 483
choreographing, 337
destruction of, 300, 301
factors shaping, 418
life and survival enabled by, 372–373
nonrenewables exploited by, 391
transformations, 302, 393
Human species, 99f, 336
See also Hominins
Human stature, reduction in, 106
Human survival
abilities, 500
economic growth *versus,* 341
economic incentive to maintain, 357
economies, modern and, 457
economies role in, 245–246
enabling, 407, 413, 478, 483, 497, 516
endangering, 184, 485
energy sources and, 362, 363, 366, 406
energy transition, third and, 367
energy transitions and, 40, 399, 404
ensuring, 173, 180, 265
evolution and, 223

focus on, 346
future of, 183
goal and outcome, 309, 316, 405
greenhouse gas as threat to, 458
versus hominin extinctions, 343
individual choices and actions determining, 342
location, mobility, and migration role in, 165–166, 223–224, 347
modern human approach to, 332
natural environment, dependence on, 252
organization for, 512
path to, 486
planning for, 293
population size and, 161–164
preserving, 480
prioritizing, 403
profits and wealth *versus,* 212–213
prospects for, 380
requirements for, 140, 150, 152, 234, 247–248, 252, 256, 259–260, 287, 355–356, 406–407, 478, 496, 500, 510
rules enabling, 500
societies and economies embodying, 230
socioeconomic mechanism for, 138
socioeconomic system enabling, 261
versus surplus, 195
surplus-driven agendas *versus,* 312
technologies and innovations not required for, 330–331, 342, 344
technology corporations not prioritizing, 212
temperature increase *versus,* 402–403
threats to, 240, 243, 244–245, 246–247, 301, 317, 329–330, 332, 334, 345, 347, 396, 491, 493
threats to (nonrenewable energy sources), 366, 388–389
urge for, 359, 392
weakened ability to ensure, 356–357
and well-being, 171, 193, 239
Human trafficking, 160, 244, 270
Human values, 40
Human welfare, 15, 27
Human well-being
ecosystem services described in terms of, 35
increase in, 40
programs to improve, 42–43
survival and, 171, 193
Humility, 313
Hunan wet market, 229
Hunger
alternative foods, knowledge in times of, 215
avoiding, 112–113
causes of, 244
end to, 194
prevalence of, 168
reducing, 318
Hungry, resource sharing with, 124
Hunter-gatherer communities, 160, 263
Hunter-gatherer economies
abandonment of, 68, 414, 474
archaeological evidence of, 93
benefits of, 86
characteristics of, xviii–xxi, 20, 126–140, 419
endurable nature of, 121
global warming impact on, 334
goal and outcome of, 245, 497
greenhouse gas output low in, 454–455, 455f
levelling mechanisms in, 68
longevity of, 473–474
mobility of, 424
modern alternatives to, 122
modern economies, comparison to, 8–13
production factors not crucial in, 465–466
sectors, 462–464
social life, xix
socioeconomic transitions in, 180
subsistence model, 253
survival-driven, 32, 155
survival of, xv–xvi, 88, 190, 462–464
transformation of, 415
Hunter-gatherer lifeways
abandonment of, 79, 207, 280, 284, 286, 287–288, 343–344, 356–357, 373, 437, 491, 512–513
characteristics of, 266–270, 407, 466–469, 516
critique of, 479
development of, 473
egalitarianism in, 140, 141, 292, 514
emanation from communities, 263
evolutionary, 303
feasibility of, 259

foraging giving rise to, 179–180
forces shaping, 349
legacy of, 352
rediscovering, 313
return to, 173, 183, 258–259, 287, 288, 294, 306, 311, 312, 353, 359, 379, 398, 481, 498
survival enabled by, 360
survival of, 515

Hunter-gatherers
adaptation, factors affecting, 99
all humans as, 190
belief system of, 160–161
businesspeople compared to, 145
climate change impact on, 203, 205–206, 209, 211–212, 226, 228, 247, 334, 339, 342–343, 412–413, 415
complex, 254
deviation from pattern of, 260
Earth-life economies benefit to, 16
economic goals as seen by, 195
energy source used by, 365, 371, 400, 412
evolution of, 329
food and diet, 96, 97
freedom of, 282
humans from Neolithic Revolution compared to, 34
in Pleistocene epoch, 67–68
legacy of, 60
making a living, 486
migration by, 8, 113, 223, 226, 287, 340, 425, 428, 432–434, 453
modern, 70–71, 71f, 79, 107, 175, 250, 307, 424, 507
natural resources, use of, 420–421
perceptions of, 250, 251, 252
planetary boundaries, ignorance of, 164
population size, 161, 251
renewable energy, access to, 401
sharing among, nullification of, 192
survival of, 177, 197, 253, 279–280, 294, 316, 330, 334, 339–340, 342, 351, 360, 379–380, 398, 406, 407, 410–411, 420–421, 468, 481, 483, 501, 513
technologies and innovations of, 320, 323, 349, 351–352, 379–380, 410–411
way of life, 201–202

Hunter-gatherer societies, 148, 167–168, 269
nature, relationship with, 98
views concerning, 251

Hunter-gatherer societies and economies
best organization for survival, 125–140, 127t, 261
characteristics of, 118, 123, 306
critique of, 255, 491
egalitarianism in, 141–142
emergence of, 94–95
energy source supporting, 371, 374, 377
equality emphasized in, 140
forces shaping, 349–350
foundations for survival of, 88–89, 151–152, 174, 176, 180
goal and outcome of, 258
goals, aspirations, and priorities of, 343
habitats, expansion into range of, 101
leadership and decision-making in, 149
levelling mechanisms in, 145–147
lifeways and customs of, 172
Neolithic Revolution societies and economies, comparison to, 106–107, 254
practices, 360
rebuilding, 231
success factors, 96–97
survival of, 108–109, 243, 252, 254, 320, 351, 394, 474–475, 491, 509
transition from, 190–191
universal income in, 144
variations in, 98–99
wealth accumulation discouraged in, 148
See also Human societies and economies: hunter-gatherer and modern compared

Hunting and gathering
as economic development stage, 251
energy needs met through, 364–365
methods and tools needed for, 181
shift from, 42, 201, 206–207
skills and equipment, access to, 144
as subsistence method, 197

Hunting weapons, 143
Hurricane Harvey, 426f, 427
Hurricane Ian, 490
Hydrocarbon liquid gas, 376
Hydroelectricity, 220
Hydrology, 420
Hydropower, 361, 362, 391
Hypertension, 159, 170

I

Ice age
in Europe, 349
Pleistocene, 425, 444, 467
survival during, 360
Ice age, last, end of (Last Glacial Maximum), 68, 167, 172, 180–181, 212, 247, 334, 343, 344, 346–347, 377, 411, 421, 422, 436, 462
Ice ages, lifeways and economies shaped by, 410
Ice caps
absence during Eocene Epoch, 440
melting of, 296, 298, 347
Icehouse Earth, 444, 496
Icehouse state, 411
Ice sheets, 421
"Immediate return economy," 202
Immediate-reward economic system, 268
Immediate-use economies, 111
Immunity, weakened, 159
Independence, lack of, 201
India, 299, 304, 512
Indigenous Brazilians, 85, 86f
Individualism, 269, 281
Individuals
corporations *versus*, 305
freedom of choice limited for, 282
Indonesia, 45, 85, 193
Industrial economies, 20
Industrial expansion, 501
Industrial goods, shortages of, 61
Industrialization, 184
Industrial Revolution
carbon dioxide and, 319, 422
carbon system in place since, 28f
climate stability enabling, 68f
coal powering of, 299
commercial society development with, 251
ecological cheating since, 74
economies predating, 467
ecosystem goods and services prior to, 15
energy sources prior to, 371
forces bringing about, 284
fossil fuel adoption during, 281, 352, 372, 396
greenhouse gas emissions after start of, 455
greenhouse gas emissions prior to, 105
hydrocarbon burning during, 204
legal-person economies rise accompanying, 456–457
technologies and innovations of, 344, 345, 360
temperature increase after start of, 459
temperatures predating, 342
Industries
collapse of, 230
drought impact on, 220
economies before, 190
goals and practices of, 245
lack of, 114
Inequality
alternative to, 509
civilization collapse preceded by, 62
conditions leading to, 111, 172
Covid-19 pandemic exposing, 192–193
emergence of, 192, 258, 285
ills resulting from, 270
in modern societies and economies, 145–146, 156–157, 195, 272, 286
Neolithic Revolution bringing, 204
persistence of, 169, 171
prevention of, 468
Infant mortality, 270
Infectious diseases, 106
Infectious disease spread, 442
Inflation, 164, 194, 195, 506
Influenza viruses, 237
Information technology, 190
Inheritance, 148, 167–168
Inhumanity, ills resulting from, 270
Initial Eocene Thermal Maximum (IETM), 345–346
Innovations
ability, overestimating, 348
climate change caused by, 337, 411
continued focus on, 341
creating, reasons for, 319
destructive use of, 329
emergence of, 323, 475
evolutionary goal and purpose, 319–320
goal and outcome of, 321–322, 324
goals enabled by, 284, 332
greenhouse gases, role in, 457
historic overview, 315–317
lack of direction for, 320
life and survival *versus* pursuit of, 357

limitations of, 336
making a living, enabling through, 331
making a living, task delegated to, 300
maturity test applied to, 328
motivations for pursuing, 332, 352
pros and cons, 345
threat posed by, 177
unproven, 469
In-person customer presence, businesses requiring, 235
An Inquiry into the Nature and Causes of the Wealth of Nations (Smith), 141, 479
Insect biodiversity, 53–54, 54f
Insecticides, 55, 71, 318
Insects
beneficial, 81
eradication of, 77
population decline, 63–64
Inspiration, ecosystems as source of, 39
Intelligent species
advancing, 329
conditions leading up to, 19, 66
evolution and survival of, 70
making a living, 483
maturity of, 328
planets capable of supporting, 25
Inter-city flying, 81
Inter-continental migration, 224
Inter-country migration, 224
Inter-ecosystem wanderings, 26
Interglacial periods, 68f, 100
Intergovernmental Panel on Climate Change (IPCC), 426, 442, 444–445
founding of, 297
mitigations identified by, 341
projections put out by, 338–339
warming scenario, 449
Internal combustion engines, 73, 318–319
International bodies, 250
International conflict, 442
International Criminal Court, 31
International Energy Agency report, 2021, 74, 383
International Land Coalition, 45
International Monetary Fund, 459
International Rescue Committee, 431
International Seabed Authority (ISA), 83
International Space Station, 32, 33, 36, 332
International Union for the Conservation of Nature, 274
Internet, 283, 309, 345, 513
Internet technologies, 235–236
Interpersonal relationships
in hunter-gatherer socieites, 142
property relations as basis of, 191, 206
Intra-country migration, 224
Invasion, civilization collapse preceded by, 62
Invasive species, 61
Inventions, 331, 348
Investment industry, 298
Investment mega-corporations, 212
Investors, 195
Investor-state dispute settlements (ISDS), 493
Invisible hand, xvii, 2, 18, 163
IPhones, 222, 345
I Robot (movie), 64
Iron Age, 344
Irrigation, 71, 114, 239, 343, 344
IRS enforcement, 196
Irwin, Neil, 126
Island nations, 338, 348
Israeli-Palestinian conflict, 345
IUCN Red List, 274

J

Jamestown, Virginia, 216
Java, agricultural economy in, 98
Jefferson, Thomas, 161
Jet Propulsion Lab, 69, 70
Jobs
absence of, 201
access to, 302
hunting for, 124
Jobs report, 195
Jones, Nicola, 440, 441
Ju/'hoansi, 107, 507

K

Kalahari, 250, 348
Kammeyer, Cora, 221
Kasting, J., 213
Kemp, Luke, 441
Kenya, 333
Kepler 186f, 499
Kepler-452b, 499
Khoekhoe peoples, 250
Khoe-San, 160–161, 250, 251
Kinship-based societies, 191

Knowledge areas, traditional and formal, 39
Knowledge economy, 189
Kopp, Bob, 437
Korea, 193
Korten, David C., 250, 283, 301, 303–304, 306
Krugman, Paul, 192, 193–194, 195
K Street, 305
Kumming-Montreal Global Biodiversity Framework (GBF), 168
!Kung Bushmen
  boasting discouraged among, 146, 148, 150
  egalitarianism among, 140
  hunting weapons, 143
  meat distribution among, 147
  possessions, accumulation discouraged among, 148
  traditional ways maintained by, 507
Kusnetz, Nicholas, 447
Kyoto Protocol (1997), 63

L

Labor, division of, 144, 145
Labor force, size of, 130
Labor productivity, lower, 225
Lahaina, Maui fires, 2023, 427
Lakes, creation of, 336, 412, 435
Lake Turkana, 333
Lambertini, Marco, 78
Land
  acquisition of, 105–106
  attachment to, 107
  clearing, 484, 510
  converting to farmland, 44, 72, 112
  global displacement of, 45
  as life requirement, 114
  management, sustainable, 358
  ownership, lack of, 483
  as personal property, 192
  pollution of, 81, 383
Land-air temperatures, increase in, 448
Land bridges, disappearance of, 412
Landfills, 121
Land grabs
  versus coexistence, 111
  impact of, 45–46
  maps, 46f
  marine ecosystem seizing compared to, 85
  wildlife habitats destroyed by, 232
  by world leaders, 354
  zoonotic diseases, role in, 331
Land Matrix, 45
Landowners, humans as, 104
Landownership, societies based on, 191
Landscape, diversity in, 420
Land subsidence, 221
Land system change, 74
Land use
  in agriculture, 275, 285
  as carbon dioxide increase factor, 209
  change, impact of, 46, 51
  change in, 232, 238
  for food production, 274, 274f, 275
  modern practices, 420
  terrestrial biosphere transformed through, 280
Lang, Avis, 332
Language, 99, 105
Laos, 45
Large animals (non-game), extinction of, 335, 343, 344, 346, 410
Large-game species
  extinction of, 101, 181, 412–413
  hunter status, kill impact on, 145
Last Glacial Maximum. *See* Ice age, last, end of (Last Glacial Maximum)
Latham, Katherine J., 106
Latinos, 236–237
Laurence, Bill, 450
Lauterwasser, David B., 62, 63
Law enforcement, 143
Law(s), lack of, 115, 143, 258
Layne, Samuel, 201–202, 261, 310, 328, 369
Leadership, 125–126, 149–150
Least Cost Pathway, 448
Lee, Richard B., 146, 147
Legal-person corporations, 387
Legal-person economies
  abandonment of, 452
  change needed fir, 499
  characteristics of, 260–261
  corporations as, 303
  economies built to serve, 197
  economies identified as, 194–195
  emergence of, 397
  fossil fuels dredged up by, 395
  goal and outcome of, 85, 495, 498
  greenhouse gases and, 345, 414, 454, 457
  human economies transformed into, xxiii,

184, 188, 190, 260, 262, 302, 306, 479, 480, 497
human survival risks posed by, 246
legal-persons and, 190
powers and capacities of, 319
rise of, 282–283, 405, 456–457
socioeconomic goals and outcomes of, 473
socioeconomic lifeways enabled by, 391, 457
technologies and innovations hijacked by, 317
Legal-person economies and societies
aspects of our lives managed by, 294
human societies and economies replaced by (*see* Modern human societies and economies: legal-person economies and societies replacing)
residents in, 283
Legal persons
choices made by, 282
climate change fueled by, 494
control of choices, wresting from, 312
economic growth as priority of, 459
economic pursuits of, 301
economic system comprising, 207
economies built of, by, and for, 200
financial health and well-being of, 198
human socioeconomic lifeways dominated by, 302
human survival not a priority for, 212
humans *versus,* 241
making a living, task delegated to, 300
powers and capacities, 319
power to rule, 308
Legal-persons-driven economic activity, 122, 193, 198
Legal systems, absence of, 149, 270
Leisure, time for, 201
Leveling mechanisms, 140, 142, 145–147, 155
Life
activity impact on, 244
attitude, changing toward, 313
carbon dioxide role in, 50–51
catastrophe for life on Earth, 213
conditions necessary for, 7, 439
destroying, 329, 330, 383
Earth ability to support, 439
economies, role in, 7–8, 127–128, 152
end of, 132
energizing/energy indispensable to all, 364, 370, 371, 373, 377
evolution of, 129, 263
foundation of, 256
foundation of, destroying, 78, 384
human activities posing risk to, 55
interchangeability of, 157
money and profit *versus,* 77, 157–159, 239
possible future scenarios, 210
preservation of, 321
versus profit, 139
requirements for, 243, 248, 472, 477, 486–487
resources required for, 114
sanctity of, 138
Life, triad of
economies as component of, 323
evolutionary, xxii, 3, 87, 179, 248, 481, 510
survival-driven, xvii, 3, 77, 243–244, 482
Life and survival
abandoning goal of, 156
achieving, 415
countries and nations prioritizing, 171
cultures prioritizing, 138
economies enabling, 177, 188
economies prioritizing, 82, 88, 116, 123, 126–130, 154–155, 171, 174, 197, 264, 301, 357, 414, 463, 474, 495, 497
energy needed for, 372
evolutionary foundations for, 314, 486
evolutionary prerequisite for, 96
foundations enabling, 183, 474
as goal and outcome, 166–167, 173, 299–300, 331–332, 475, 480–481, 496, 498, 500
inventions and innovations for the purpose of, 320
lifeways prioritizing, 321, 360
materials enabling, 121
norms of, xxii
prioritizing, 392, 406
versus profits, 240, 301
pursuit of, 161, 359
reigniting purpose, 312
relationships essential to, 482
return to, 499
technologies and innovations role in, 323, 324, 331
versus wealth accumulation and economic

growth, 294
Life on other planets, 32
Life-sustaining mechanisms, destruction of, 312
Lincoln, Abraham, 304–305
Liquefied gas, 397
Lithium, 404
Lithium-ion batteries, 85
Little Ice Age, 216, 217–218, 221
Livable space, reduction in, 438
Livestock
contact with humans, 233
husbandry, 246, 455
production, 44, 46
raising, 104
Living beings, humans as, 301
Living organisms, 381
Living Planet Report 2024, 51, 78
Local economies and societies, 112, 115
Local ecosystems, 124
Location, 133, 165–166
Logging, impact of, 64
London Company, 304
Love, human economies energized by, 302
Lovell, Jim, 457–458
Low-carbon future, 494
Low-energy system, 372–373, 406, 407
Low-income households, 220
Lustgarten, Abraham, 224
Lytton, British Columbia, 223

M
Machines, power to rule, 308
Madagascar, 220
Madre de Dios region, Peru, 29f
Magna carta, 161
Main street, 283
Making a living
across ecosystems, 129–130
across millennia, 200
alternative ways of, 123
ancient knowledge of, 94
climate change impact on, 337
corporation role in, 310
delegation to innovations, 300
destruction resulting from ways of, 122
economics insights on, 176
economy emergence and, 243
flaw in manner of, 121
fossil fuels, burning for energy, 176
within habitats and ecosystems, 243
in harmony with nature, 128, 258, 265
households, supporting in, 250
hunter-gatherers and modern humans compared, 108, 114, 133, 134, 151, 167, 175, 253, 264–265, 272
pre-agriculture, 88, 250
requirements for, 256
shift in ways of, 183, 201, 206–207, 257, 307
species way of, 262
stable, long-lasting way for, 202
success, requirements for, 255, 256
supporting and enabling, 301, 317
transitions, impact on ways of, 201
unintended consequences of, 280, 299
wild food collecting, 94
without committing econocide, 77
See also Ecosystems: making a living within/outside
Malnutrition, 278, 338
Maloney, Carolyn, 296
Malthus, Thomas, 14
Mammals, 488
Manchin, Senator, 146
Mandela, Nelson, 288–289, 290f, 293
Mangroves, 36
Manhattan Project, 340
Manning, Richard, 499
Manufacturing, 190, 251
Manufacturing sector, 189
Mao Zedong, 303
Margaritoff, Marco, 458
Marine biodiversity, extinction of, 82
Marine ecosystems
carbon emissions impact on, 56
destruction of, 86
nutrient system in, 81
protection lacking for, 85
seabed mining impact, potential on, 82–83, 85
threats to, 47
Marine invertebrates, 489f
Marine species
depleting, 137
destroying, 30, 55, 77, 246, 318
exploitation of, 85
extinction of, 83

population declines, 47
risks to, 449
Marine systems, 48
Market economies
alternative to, 123
economic-sharing system *versus,* 135
emergence of, 188
goal of, 115
human lifeways transformed by, 302
human survival and, 117
hunter-gatherer economies compared to, xx, 114
overview of, xviii
Market growth, 308, 310
Market movements, 310
Markets, 10, 14
Mars
atmosphere, absence of, 76
exploration of, 66, 69, 70
migration to, 79–80, 350–351
mining, 500
Marshall, John, 147
Mars rover, 70f, 75
Maslin, Mark, 335
Massachusetts Bay Company, 304
Mass extinctions
danger of future, 280, 299, 407, 441, 450, 497, 504–505, 507
evolution following, 18
fossil fuel-driven, 503
human survival of, 500
ocean-driven, 449
past, 343
past and potential future compared, 367, 442, 488–489
Mass migration, 418
Materials, new, invention of, 102
Maternal behavior, 17
Matter, movement of, 56
Mauna Loa, 461f
Maya, 98, 215, 223, 453–454, 466
Mazzacuto, Mariana, 309
Mbuti, 143, 145, 507
Mbuti Pygmies, 140
Meat distribution, 147
The Meat Fight (film), 147
Medieval warm period, 216–217, 221
Mega-cities
concentration in, 224
overpopulated, 166
population mainly in, 340
Megafauna-sized predators, 247
Meiksins Wood, Ellen, 389
Mental health risks, 170
Merchant companies, 303–304
Metals, search for, 84f
Methane gas (CH_4)
cyclic increases in, 208
escape from permafrost, 447
release by humans, 105, 209, 221
solar radiation trapped by, 459
temperatures, impact on, 281
Miami, 225–226
Microbes, 70, 238
Micronutrient deficiencies, 170
Middle class, 195, 196
Mid-Pliocene Epoch, 445
Migrants
border walls lacking for, 26
climate change, flight from, 16
conditions faced by, 353, 428–433, 432f
deaths, 428f, 430–431, 431f, 432f
deterrents, 270
opposition to, 342
past and present compared, 413, 454
from Venezuela, 452f
Migration
adaptation through, xix
built-in compulsion for, 423–424
climate change, human economies and, 181, 215, 226, 242, 247 (*see also* Climate migrants; Climate migration)
corridors, 422
cultural and ecological adaptations in course of, 348
and dispersal, 418
energy used during, 370
extraterrestrial, 350–351, 436, 451–452, 499–500
global warming driving, 334
green corridors supporting, 420
human economy, role in, 129
hunter-gatherers and modern humans compared, 113, 226, 253, 413, 414, 428, 432–433
modern attitudes toward, 130
potential future, 227
routes, 429f, 430, 431–433, 432f, 433f

sea-level rise forcing, 103
seasonal, 467
for survival, 12, 125, 130, 131–132, 151, 152, 161, 165–166, 223–224, 340, 348
See also Africa: migration out of
Milankovitch cycles, 421, 451
Military, lack of, 115
Military goals, technologies and innovations to achieve, 332
Millennium Ecosystem Assessment Report of 2005, 9, 23, 27, 34
Millennium Ecosystem Assessment Report of 2015, 40–41
Millet, 103
Minerals
for green energy technologies, 83, 402f, 403f, 404
mining and extracting, 246, 404, 500
search for, 86
shortages of, 83
Minimum wage, 245
Mining activities, 29f, 55
Mining companies, 83
Miocene epoch, 444
Missing Migrants Project, 428f, 430
Mississippi River Valley, 225
Mitchell, Peter, 421
"Mitochondrial Eve" (female migrant), 433
Mobile economies
advantages of, 128
characteristics of, 8–10, 20
of Earth-life species, 424
as evolutionary lifeway, 264
functioning of, 13
migration along with, 453
modern, 507
for survival, 419
transition from, 425
Mobile lifeways, 424
Mobile to sedentary economies, transitíon from, 10, 174–175, 277–278, 343
Mobility
abandonment of, 484, 513
advantages of, 125, 266–268, 284–285, 411, 465–466, 467, 509–510
ecosystem and biodiversity, preserving through, 138–139
human economy, role in, 129–130
as leveling mechanism, 142
population size impacted by, 130, 131, 139
resources, finding through, 113
retaining, 360
sedentism replacing, 172, 206
shift from, 201, 242
species population and economy shaped by, 20
survival value of, 107–108, 131–132, 151, 152, 161, 165–166, 253, 419
Modern economies
alternative approaches to, 122–123, 135
boundary delineating, 14
envisioning, 13–15
evolution of, 99–100
evolution *versus,* 20
foundations of, 96–97
goals and outcomes, 498
hunter-gatherer economies compared to, 8–13
as legal-person economies, 405
surplus-driven socioeconomic lifeways of, 268
survival-driven economies, return to, 498
Modern human societies and economies
characteristics of, 152, 255
collapse, potential of, 89
evolution of, 507–508
forces driving, 346
goals and outcomes of, 316, 481, 495, 496–497
goals of, 90
humans viewed as lesser beings by, 160
hunter-gatherer societies and economies compared to, 107, 270
ills plaguing, 11, 244–245
legacy to pass on, 167
legal-person economies and societies replacing, 283, 284, 294, 301, 317, 480, 497
lifeways, 330
longevity of, 122, 135
problems plaguing, 509
remaking, 154–155
socioeconomic goals and purpose of, changing, 258–259
survival-driven lifeways abandoned by, 89
survival of, 407
Modern mobile economies, 9–10
Modern socioeconomic lifeways, critique of,

89–90
Money
creation and allocation of, 302
humans following, 25
versus life, 77, 157–159
and market economy, human lifeways transformed by, 302
mobile economies lacking in, 10
no need for, 114
Monocrop industrial agriculture, 207
Monocultures, 420
Monsanto, 158
Montenegro, A., 214, 358
Montreal Protocol, 1987, 120, 157, 492
Moon, landing man on, 340
Morgan, Christopher, 94
Morocco, migration from, 226
Mount Kilimanjaro, 334
Mozambique, 45
MRNA vaccines, 331, 345
Msuya, Joyce, 66
Multinational corporate economies, 473
Multinational corporations
choices made by, 282
economic activities of, 193
economic pursuits of, 301
economic reach and power, 303
fossil fuels dredged up by, 395
legal-person societies and economies operated by, 283, 405
making a living, task delegated to, 300
reclaiming power yielded to, 313
rise of, 397
Murphy, Christopher, 197
Musk, Elon, 451
Mutuality, relationships stressing, 142
Mutual survival. *See* Survival: mutual, enabling

N
Nasser, Amin, 459
National leaders, planning for human survival, 293
National paid family leave policy, 236
Nations
collapse of, 454
growth of, 188
rise of, 182, 258, 307, 484
surplus-driven socioeconomic lifeway, hypothetical abandonment of, 294
warring nation-states, 411
Native plant species, 72
Natural assets, destruction of, 286
Natural capital, 60
Natural disasters
civilization collapse preceded by, 125
at end of ice age, 247
escaping, 128, 129, 130
risks posed by, 243, 246
shrinking supplies due to, 62
Natural environment, human survival dependent on, 252
Natural gas
cut-off of, 356
discovery of, 376
mining and combusting, 357
as nonrenewable, 388
as nonrenewable energy source, 397
processing plants, 447
restricted access to, 112
terminals, 494
Natural medicine, 37
Natural resource industries, 30
Natural resources
carrying capacity of, 132
depletion and exhaustion of, 268–269, 311
diversity of, 420–421
domestication, ownership, modifciation, and control, rejection of, 123, 133
extraction and exploitation of, 260, 304
hoarding of, 124
mining of, 246
plundering, 27
use of, 109, 134, 420–421
Nature
as asset, 60
bio-inspired-eco-friendly solutions, 319
climate change, role in mitigating, 448–449
collision with, 280
contract with, 202
decline of, 78
destruction of, 239f
energy transition forced by, 399, 400
exploitation of, 31–32
food produced by, 256
human economies view excluding, 2, 22
humans seen as separate from, 6

making a living in harmony with, 160
modern economics removed from laws of, 116
pillaging of, 302
preserving assets of, 231
products and services obtained free from, 144, 466
regard for, 98
secrets of, 321
state of, 62–63
survival of, 312
tug-of-war with, 375
war, declaring on, 229, 484
well-being of, 173
Nayaka, 507
Neanderthals, extinction of, 165, 339, 340
Neighbor, loving, 139
Neighbors, not knowing, 302
Neoclassical economics, 141
Neolithic Revolution
agriculture adopted during, 95, 96, 157, 174, 204, 239, 259, 344, 345, 385
alternative path, hypothetical during, 292–293
civilization following, 68
dawning of, 336
Earth's survival-driven networks prior to, 72
economic choices since, 121
economic collapse after, 197
economic failures during, 229
economic goal and purpose replaced during, 90
economic sectors emerging after, 189–190
economics falsehoods propagated since, 2
economies emerging since, xviii, xxiv, 3, 68, 88, 127, 172, 175, 246, 247, 252, 267, 313
energy sources during and after, 378
energy transition during, 373, 374–375
farming villages in, 224
food production since, 272
forces bringing about, 284
habitats and ecosystems deemphasized since, xix
humans from, 34
hunter-gatherer lifeways abandoned during, 79, 474, 479
hypothetical non-occurrence of, 506–507
impact of, 75, 106
lifeways changes coming with, 188
mistakes made during, 86
modern problems, origin during, 331
modern societies and economies emerging from, 124, 176
overview of, xv
perceptions of, 251
population growth after beginning of, 130, 131
progress, perceived with, 251
property rights and, 190–191
societies and economies outside of ecosystems during, 110
societies and economies prior to, 117
societies and economies purpose and goal, 156
socioeconomic changes beginning with, xxii
socioeconomic goal and outcome swap since, 155, 156, 159
socioeconomic lifeways adopted during, 479
socioeconomic traits dating to, 254
survival-driven lifeways abandoned during, 89
survival knowledge forgotten with, 94
technologies and innovations as applied after, 323
technologies and innovations during, 334
technologies and innovations since, 329
Neolithic surplus, 301
New England, 304
A New Green History of the World (Ponting), 31
NFTs (Non-Fungible Tokens), 156
NIMBY (concept), 509
Nitrogen, 49, 56–58, 57f, 58f, 74
Nitrous oxide (N_2O), 459
Nitrous oxide (N_2O) emissions, 279
Nix, Elizabeth, 453
Nobel Peace Prize, 289, 290f
No growth, 465–466
Nonnatural processes and materials, 102
Nonprofits, 148
Nonrenewable energy sources
abandonment of, 375, 391, 395
adoption of, 396, 474
agriculture use of, 392

attraction to, 365–366, 393
availability of, 376
carbon dioxide increase due to, 490
cost of, 387
current uses, 362–363
death and destruction driven by, 391
as ecosystem renewables, 34
excavating, 75
existence of, 390
extinction driven by, 365, 374, 383
impact of, 344, 382–383
invention of, 102, 376
lack of, 379
leaving in Earth, 402
machines using, 386–387
modern economy use of, 412
reluctance to give up, 395
renewable energy sources compared to, 364–365, 381
resorting to, 486
solar energy compared to, 370–371
survival independent of, 379, 380
threat posed by, 405
transition to, 388–389, 390, 396–397
See also Energy transition(s): from nonrenewables to renewables
Non-target organisms, pesticide killing of, 81
Norse colonies, 216–218
North, Douglass C., 190–191
North America
British colonization of, 304
climate change and mobility in, 224
droughts impact on, 219, 220
ice, 342
ice sheets covering, 334
wildfires in, 222
Northern Africa, migration to, 353
Northern Europe, 218, 334
Northern regions, temperatures rising in, 441
Northern Sea Route, 219
Northwest Passage, 219
Not-for-profit corporations, 308
NRNA vaccines, 234
Nuclear Armageddon, 503
Nuclear bomb, 175, 330
Nuclear energy, 361, 362, 376
Nuclear power, 391, 397
Nuclear war, 359, 443, 504
Nuclear weapons, 329, 354, 355, 356, 491, 504
Nutrient cycling, 40
Nutrient deficiencies, 170
Nutrient pollution, 56–57
Nutritional deficiencies, 106

O

Obama, Barack, 494
Ocean acidification
advance of, 47
carbon dioxide role in, 449
climate change driving, 71
coral reefs affected by, 63
gradual, 435
planetary boundaries, crossing with, 74
practices contributing to, 450
shelled animals impacted by, 489
Ocean energy, 391
Ocean floor, ores and minerals on, 83, 84f
Oceans
as carbon reservoir, 382
changes to, 502–503
damage to, 311
decimation of, 393
extinctions in, 458
heating of, 337
icebergs released into, 434
as life requirement, 114
pollution of, 51
rising of, 166, 296, 337, 412
Ocean temperature
boiling, 77
increase in, 156, 338, 435, 449
Odum, Eugene P., 22
Offices, homes *versus,* 507–508
Oil
abandonment of, 375, 391
as energy source, 361
geopolitics impacted by, 397
mining and combusting, 357
pros and cons of, 81
use of, 362
Oil companies
actions taken against, 74–75
climate policies *versus* profits, 212–213, 295, 296–297
industrial development, 269
no liability for, 30
public misled by, 158
Oil industry, 245

climate change, knowledge of, 295, 296
energy transition opposed by leaders in, 459
in post-carbon world, 492–493
Oil refineries, 447
Oil reserves, 209–210
Oil spills, 383
Oil wells, 446, 446f
Oligarchs, 156
Oligocene epoch, 444
OPEC, 398
Open carry, 143, 270
Oral health, 106
Orangutans, 35, 36
Orbital-scale changes, 417–418
Orbital-scale forcings, 419
Ores, harvest of, 83
Organic molecules, elements associated with, 381–382
Organization for Economic Co-operation (OECD), 144
The Origin of Capitalism (Meiksins Wood), 389
Ornamental resources, 37
Overconsumption, 450
Overpopulation
civilization collapse preceded by, 62
climate migration prior to, 434–435
migration challenges combined with, 411
problems stemming from, 468
Ownership
caring *versus*, 359
versus coexistence, 111
economic ways characterized by, 278
lack of, 114, 256, 482–483
privileges of, denying, 145
shift to, 206
wealth accumulation and, 258
Oxfam International, 45
Oxygen
algae role in reducing, 57
depletion in water, 81, 449, 450, 458
life dependent on, 114
photosynthesis role in producing, 487
production of, 40, 77
sources of, 311
Ozone
depletion of stratospheric, 64, 74
production of, 57–58, 279
Ozone layer
hole in, 120, 157, 176, 232, 257, 341, 494
protecting, 492
Ozone pollutants, phasing out of, 120

P

Pacific Northwest, temperatures in, 223
Paleocene-Eocene Thermal Maximum (PETM), 345–346
Paleocene epoch, 444
Paleolithic period (Old Stone Age), 334
Palm oil, 81, 246
Palm oil plantations, 30
Palm trees, 347, 425, 440
Pandaram, 140
Pandemics
causes of, 240, 244, 246
climate change and, 230, 238
economic and societal changes resulting from, 228
economic impact of, 11
economies and societies ended by, 230
emergence from, 394
evictions during, 194
frequency, increasing, 237–238
historical overview of, 234f
horrors of living through, 236–238
impact of prior, 234
invasive species role in, 61
land use change as driver of, 46
lockdowns, 130
preventing, 232–233, 238, 239f
recovering from, 443
risk of, 233
as sedentary economy phenomenon, 10
spread of, 233
. *See* Covid-19 pandemic; Zoonotic diseases: pandemics
Parakaná, 507
Paranthropus, 422
Paris Agreement (2016)
climate commitments, 213, 465
goal of, 209, 210–211, 299, 438
impact of, 63
Least Cost Pathway, 448
Parraga, Marianna, 459
Particle physics research, 350
Partitions *versus* coexistence, 111
Pastoralism, 251

Pathogens, 46
Paull, Charles, 447
Peace and prosperity, 496
Pearce, Fred, 460
Peasants, 126, 200, 201
Penicillin, 331
People
corporations *versus*, 305–306
harm to groups of, 42
power to rule, 307, 308
People of color, 220, 289
Perfluoroalkyl and polyfluoroalkyl compounds (PFAS), 158–159
Permafrost, thawing, 447
Permafrost line, 441
Permian Basin, 446
Permian mass extinction, 450, 489f
Perseverance Rover, 69, 69f, 70, 70f, 75, 77
Personal possessions, 148, 270
Personal property, 191, 192
Personal use items, 114
Pesticides
agricultural runoff created through, 55
harmful effects of, 71, 81, 279, 318
increase in, 80
insect diversity loss due to, 54
Peters, Glen, 460
Petroleum, 376, 388
Petroleum industry, 446
PFOA, 159
Phanerozoic Earth history, 442
Pharmaceuticals, 37, 309
Phosphorus, 49, 56–57, 57f, 58, 74
Physical capabilities, hunter-gatherer adaptation affected by, 99
Phytoplankton, killing, 77, 311
Pigs, domestication of, 98, 103
Piketty, Thomas, 138, 146
Piotrowski, Jan, 308–309
Place, sense of, 39
Planet
colonizing other, 499
crippled, 458
life evolving and sustaining, 486–487
life-support systems of, 13, 328
rebalancing relationship with, 78
Planetary boundaries
crossing, 74, 275
living within, 360, 397, 399, 501
nonrenewable energy sources, crossing with, 406
overview of, 162f
pushing, 161
pushing past, 511–512, 511t
term, 64–65, 399
Planetary infrastructure, 483
Planets, migration to other, 350–351, 436, 451–452, 499–500
Plant hardiness zones, 440, 440f
Plants
carbon stored by, 448
changes in, 181
domestication of, 98, 104, 105–106, 107, 124, 252, 256
emergence of new, 206
as energy producers, 26
energy sources not used by, 102
exploitation of, 335
extinction of, 343
foraging for, 202, 231
photosynthesis, 371, 372, 487
during Pleistocene, 101, 203
productivity, improved of, 103, 206, 208
Plastics
islands of, 311
as modern economies by-product, 9
as pollutants, 61
pros and cons of, 81
as waste, 246
Plate tectonics, 337, 412, 435
Plato, 140–141
Pleistocene epoch
atmosphere and vegetation during, 101
climate change during, 103, 410, 421, 423, 425
climate conditions during, 100, 209, 247, 421, 444, 467
disruptions of, 205
economies during, 100
environmental changes during, 335–336
human species during, 99f, 333–334, 420
hunter-gatherers living during, 67–68
ice ages of, 198, 203, 339, 347, 411, 425
migration during, 165
Terminal, 101, 107, 212, 345
transitions during, 197–198
Pleistocene-Holocene Transition
aftermath, 167

climate change during, 180–181, 182, 227, 228, 232, 247, 334–335, 338, 340, 345, 377, 422, 423, 425, 436–437, 462
end of, 346
Holocene-to Anthropocene transition compared to, 424–425, 436
hunter-gatherer response to, 205
hunter-gatherer survival of, 117
ice age transition, 501
technology during, 347
Terminal, 336
Pliocene Epoch
climate conditions during, 421, 445
hominins during, 333
temperatures during, 82, 437
Plio-Pleistocene transition, 422
PNAS NEXUS, 86
Polanyi, Karl, 8, 14, 15, 188
Polar caps. *See* Ice caps
Poles
climate change impact on, 440, 505–506
ecosystem products and services driven to, 165
migration toward, 452
Police, lack of, 115, 143
Political contributions, 304
Political instability, 441
Political organization, 40
Political-oriented economies, 126
Political parties, 149
Political problems, 513
Political structures, 125–126
Political systems, 173, 269, 272
Political willpower, 341
Politicians
on freedom and democracy, 282
hunter-gatherer socieities lacking, 138
societies and economies without, imagining, 171
Politics, absence of, 112, 171, 410, 468
Pollination, 54, 56
Pollinators
destroying, 30, 55, 71, 77
disappearance of, 311
ecosystem changes impact on, 38
killing, 318
in soil habitats, 53
Pollution
absence of non-biodegradable, 26
cutting, 275
deaths due to, 338
Ponting, Clive, 31, 35
Poor, 171, 195
Population
rearranging and redistributing, 227
small egalitarian, 152
Population, sedentary, 373
Population control, 277–278
Population density
climate connection to, 442
disaster compounded by, 166
of hunter-gatherers, 97, 253
hunter-gatherers and agricultural economy compared, 98
hunter-gatherers and modern economies and societies compared, 468
survival at trophic level, 12
Population growth
addressing, 276
Agricultural Revolution, 269
agriculture and, 104, 124–125, 277–278
alternatives to rapid, 231
balance disregarded by, 12
conditions favoring, 378
as ecosystem and biodiversity destruction driver, 64, 102, 164
ecosystem demands increased due to, 44
ecosystem services pushed to limits by, 113
energy consumption increase coinciding with, 373
energy sources and, 344, 376
fear of, 379
food production and, 275
historic and projected, 65t
impact of, 10–11, 40, 278, 511–512
mobility as check on, 131, 139, 267–268, 360, 466, 510, 513
Neolithic Revolution and beyond, 130, 131
pattern, 376f
reducing and restraining, 314
resource exhaustion due to, 125
of sedentary societies, 131–132, 132f, 340, 484
slowing, 340
unchecked, 42–43, 279
Population size
human survival, role in, 161–164
small, 130, 339

Portland, Oregon, 222
Portugal, 291–292
Possessions, transmission of, 148
Post-agriculture societies and economies, 89, 103
Post-industrial economies, population growth in, 10–11
Post-Neolithic human economies, xvii
Potts, Richard, 420, 422
Poverty
- avoiding, 113, 468, 509
- causes of, 169
- decline in, 40–41
- ending, 496
- during global pandemic, 11
- reducing, 275, 318
- sharing *versus,* 270

Power cutoff, 16
Power failures, lack of, 25
Power plants, 447
Power struggle, 149
Power to rule, 307, 308
Pre-agriculture societies and economies, survival of, 95
Preboreal, 422
Precambrian geologic eon, 66
Precipitation, lack of, 216
Precipitation patterns, future changes in, 426
Predators, 114
Pregnancy-induced hypertension, 159
Pregnancy-related complications, 170
Pre-industrial societies and economies, energy supply of, 372
Presidents, 303
Pre-Stone Age technologies, 321
Primary forest ecosystems, repurposing, 45–46
Primary production, 40
Primary sector of economy, 189, 189t
Private equity firms, 297
Private property
- absence of, 192
- farmland as, 191
- land as, 285

Private sector, absence of, 190
Proceedings of the National Academy of Sciences (PNAS)
- NEXUS, 86
- research papers, 224, 447

Product, humans as, 115
Production, factors of, 465, 480
Production disruptions, 62
Professional service providers, working class dependence on, 302
Professions, maintaining, 124
Profits
- abandoning, 500
- common prosperity *versus* corporate, 245
- corporation communication in, 310
- desire for, 396
- economies based on, xviii
- ecosystem products and services resold for, 147
- elevation of, 160
- enabling, 322
- energy hunt driven by, 457
- generation of, 209, 299–300, 301, 317, 319, 473
- goal of, 491
- *versus* life, 77, 82, 213, 320
- life and survival prioritized over, 138, 155, 240, 405, 474, 475, 498
- life and survival *versus,* 480
- making, 90, 111, 112, 115, 116–117, 247, 346, 495
- maximizing, 261, 308, 310
- nonrenewables exploited for, 391
- obsession with, abandoning, 360
- oil industry prioritizing, 296
- *versus* people, 240
- pursuit of, 84, 85, 127, 156, 167, 176, 238, 255, 284, 301, 316, 392, 394, 403, 415, 481
- *versus* self-subsistence, 17
- technologies and innovations to achieve, 332

Property
- concept of, 508
- interpersonal relations impacted by, 191, 206
- ownership, 191, 206
- personal, 191, 192

Property damage, 221
Property rights, 190–191, 192
Prosperity, 496
Provisioning services, 36, 37–38, 37t
Public, misleading of, 158
Public education on ecosystem and biodiver-

sity importance, 64
Public sector, absence of, 190
Public thought and discourse, corporate domination of, 305
Putin, Vladimir
on artificial intelligence, 329
conditions giving rise to, 107
corporate power, hypothetical in hands of, 303
resources cut off by, 356
territorial claims by, 151, 293, 354–355
weapons in hands of, 357, 491, 504–505

Q
Quantum computing, 342
Quaternary sector of economy, 189, 189t

R
Racism, 288
Racketeers, 158
Radiation, impediment for, 296
Radu, Sintia, 143
Rain, ecosystems irrigation with, 114
Rainfall
climate change impact on, 225
natural changes in, 420
torrential, 204
Rainforest Protection Pact, 85
Rand, Ayn, 375
Rare Earth (Ward and Brownlee), 18, 486–487
Rare-earth metals, 83, 85, 398
Raw materials, 189, 190
Real estate, 190, 508
Recession, 2008/9, 148
Recreation, 39
Recyclable materials, 134
Red Cross, 502
Regions in sedentary societies, 124
Regulating services, 36, 37t, 38
Religion(s)
in agrarian societies, 126, 278
ecosystems before, 32
hunter-gatherer societies lacking, 112, 115, 118, 123, 138, 139, 201, 292, 306, 410, 468
misguiding by, 397
rise of, 307–308, 343
Religious leaders, 282
Religious-oriented economies, 126
Remote communications, 236
Remote work, 235, 236
Renewable energy
abandonment of, 278, 319, 344, 392
advantages of, 364–365, 383
current practices, 362
discovering new, 505
energy disconnect problem, 401
foraging for, 75
historic, 361–362
investment in, 297
life grid powered by, 400
return to, xxiii, 366, 369, 375, 383–384, 387, 389, 391, 392, 394, 396, 398, 399–400, 402–403
technologies, 365
transition from, 390
Renewable energy sources
of ecosystem, 376, 381, 390, 482
reliance on, 386
search for, 365
sun, 78, 363, 370
use of, 134
Rent collection, 112
Rent-free living quarters, 80
Representative Concentration Pathway 8.5 (RCP 8.5), 225, 225f, 444–445, 449
Research and development
continued focus on, 341
curiosity, 322
economies before, 190
goals and purposes of, 332
life and survival *versus,* 357
overview of, 189
Reservoirs, elements moving among, 55–56
Resources
allocation of, 478
appropriating, 31
exhaustible nature of, 113, 125
extraction of, 29
finding, 113
free access to, 112–113
grabbing, 111
as life requirement, 114
off-limits, 210f
ownership *versus* equal access, 111–112
owning, controlling, and managing, 115
seasonal nature of, 113

sharing, 124, 136, 145
use, rampant, 163
Respirated gases, 75–76
Respiratory diseases, 55
Retail, economies before, 190
Retirement, saving for, 148
Reverse dominance, 514
Rhodium Group, 225, 226
Ricardo, David, 14
Rice, 103, 104
Rich
power to rule, 307
proposals to tax, 194
tax evasion by, 195–196
Rift Valley. *See* East Africa Rift Valley; Great Rift Valley
Rivers, flow of, 48
Roads, ownership of, 115
Roanoke, Virginia, 216
Robots, 300
Royal Dutch Shell, 75, 158
Royal power, 304
Royalty, factors of production owned by, 480
Royte, Elizabeth, 222
Ruddiman, William F., 105
Rule of law, 143
Rulers
in agrarian economies, 126
emergence of, 278, 285, 307–308, 397, 485
freedom lost to, 282
hunter-gatherers lacking, 107, 112, 114, 123, 138, 143, 172, 201, 258, 269, 292, 306, 311, 468
impact on nations, 303
power, source of, 307
societies and economies without, imagining, 171
subjugation to, 343
surplus, profits, and wealth siphoned off by, 156
Ruling class, rise of, 278
Rural areas, climate change impact on, 226
Rural communities, drought impact on, 221
Russell, Stuart, 327
Russia
buildings condemned in, 441
climate change and mobility in, 224
fossil fuels witholding, threats of, 398
natural gas denied by, 112
sea routes, potential open to, 218
strongmen in, 149

S
Safety net cuts, 196
Sagan, Carl, 76
Sahara, 434
Sahel Desert, 420
Sahel region, 49–50, 49f, 226, 353
Sahlins, Marshall, 499
Samangan Province, Afghanistan, 437f
San, 250
SARS, 237
SARS-CoV-2, 228–229, 260
Saudi Arabia, 353, 429f, 430, 431f
Saudis, migrants killed by, 430
Savannas, 412, 422
Savings, absence of, 190
Schiermeier, Quirin, 222
School closures, 235
Schools, homes *versus,* 507–508
Schopenhauer, Arthur, 140–141
Science
denial of, 235
growing knowledge of, 182
and real threats compared, 230–231
Science fiction, 356
Scientific advances, 345
Scientific discoveries, 331
Scientific explorations, 341
Scientific research
infections resulting from, 331
motivations for pursuing, 332, 352
Scientific solutions, 280
Scott, James C., 156
Seabed mining, 82–83, 84f
Seafood, livelihoods dependent on, 246
Sea levels
decreases in, 100, 421
during Pliocene Epoch, 82
rise in, 103, 225, 226, 247, 338, 426, 435, 438
Seas, rising, 357
Season, movement based on changes in, xix
Sea sponge skeletons, 448
Sea surface temperatures, increase in, 346
Seattle, Washington, 222
Secondary sector of economy, 189, 189t
Sedentary activity, 155

Sedentary agrarian socioeconomic lifeways, 272–280, 452
Sedentary communities
- characteristics of, 373
- ecosystems and biodiversity impact of, 242, 285
- mobility shift to, 201, 480
- overcrowded, 413
- polarization within, 410
- societies and economies built around, 264
- towns and cities, 497, 513

Sedentary economies
- collapse of, 454
- limitations of, 20, 126, 343, 425
- past and present, 424, 452, 454
- *See also* Mobile to sedentary economies

Sedentary lifestyle, 166, 484
Sedentary lifeways, 424
Sedentary societies
- economic disasters impact on, 108
- economy evolution, impact on, 507–508
- emergence of, 182
- food production in, 182
- housing, permanent on, 285
- mobile societies replaced by, 172, 174–175, 268
- Neolithic to modern, 130
- population growth in, 131–132, 132f, 163, 174, 340
- units comprising, 124

Sedentary societies and economies
- advent of, 376
- choice of, 165
- ecosystems, impact on, 131–132
- food hoarding in, 171
- hunter-gatherer economies compared to, 468
- jump-starting, 467
- migration challenges, 411–412

Sedentation
- adoption of, 258, 336
- economies giving rise to, 88, 180
- forced adaptation to, 154
- mobility replaced by, 206, 437
- mobility *versus,* 360
- as new economic brief, 188
- as norm, 512
- shift to, 201
- socioeconomic lifeways of, 515

Segregation, human, 126
Self, focus on, 285
Self-employment, hunting and gathering as, 201
Self-extinction
- climate change-driven, 351
- global warming role in potential, 319
- greenhouse gas-driven, 359
- maturity past level of, 328
- path to, 357
- preventing, 353
- retaining right to, 355
- risk to, 481
- survival *versus,* 151
- technology misuse resulting in, 316–317

Self-subsistence, 17
Self-sustaining economies, 10
Semi-arid transition region, 49f
Semi-tropical climates, 97
Sense of place, 39
Service, E. R., 141, 250, 251, 252, 260–261
Service for a fee, 115
Service sector, 189t
Sexes, division of labor between, 144, 145
Sex trafficking, 160
Sexual slavery, 160
Shareholder and stakeholder value, survival *versus,* 20
Sharing
- abandonment of, 239, 242, 278
- critique of, 479
- dedication to, 172
- economies based on, xxiv, 134–137, 138, 141, 174, 245, 253, 266, 411, 465, 467, 468, 483, 508–509
- economies prioritizing, xx, xxi, 292
- ecosystem and biodiversity, preserving through, 138–139
- of food, 123, 168, 170–171, 206, 284
- hoarding *versus* (*see* Hoarding: *versus* sharing)
- hunger and thirst avoided due to, 113
- market-based economies compared to, 114
- norms of, xxii
- relationships based on, 302
- relationships stressing, 142
- of resources, 516
- return to, 353
- shift away from, 191, 192, 206, 258, 343

as survival requirement, 111, 167–168, 231
of water, 515–516
Sheep, domestication of, 98, 104
Shell (firm), 297
Shelled animals, bleaching of, 489
Shelley, Mary, 218
Shelter
availability of, 25
as common resource, 114
owning, controlling, and managing, 115
Shoemaker-Levy (comet), 487
Shorelines, 48
Shortages
avoiding, 112
failure to foresee, 61, 62
hunter-gatherer economies and modern economies compared, 136–137
Short-term problems, response to, 328
Siberia
traps, 489, 490, 504
wildfires in, 222
Silent Spring (Carson), 59
Sinema, Senator, 146
Slavery
abolition of, 291
absence among hunter-gatherers, 111–112, 161, 292
birth of, 104, 200, 278, 308
causes of, 244
condemnation of, 289, 290
corporate profits from, 311
emergence of, 258
introduction of, 126
legacy of, 292
modern-day, 485
Neolithic Revolution bringing, 204
slave trade, 291, 292
western world practice of, 160
Small egalitarian human populations, 152
Smith, Adam
economic development described by, 251
economies not invented by, 88
economy as understood by, 471
economy purpose as understood by, 474
human self-interests cited by, 141
hunter-gatherer societies as perceived by, 252
legal-persons, hypothetical views on, 260–261, 480
lifeways not understood by, 108, 479
nature importance discounted by, 2, 18, 22
wisdom of the waterhole rejected by, 116
Smog, 279
Social and political unrest, 62
Social classes, 143, 278, 285
Social diseases, 169
"Social distance" (term), 235
Social equality, 140
Social groupings, 142
Social ills, 11
Social issues, 9, 170
Social justice, 60
Social life, xix
Social media, 345, 395, 513
Social organization, 40
Social relations, 39
Social safety nets, 236
Social structures, 262
Societal goals, 332
Societal lifeways, relationship with global warming, 340–341
Societal structures, xvii
Societies
ability to shape, 262
activities of, 22
climate change impact, potential on, 105
collapse of, xv, 2, 102, 106
pandemic impact on trajectory of, 234
Society
just, healthy, and prosperous, 78
organization, change in, 190–191
Socioeconomic evolutionary survival mechanism, 127
Socioeconomic issues, Neolithic Revolution and modern humans compared, 275, 513
Socioeconomic lifeways
adoption of new, 334–335
changes in, 188, 307–308, 322, 336, 369, 396, 480–481
foraging and farming compared, 271t
goals, 394
hunter-gatherer and modern compared, 266–272, 271t
market-based, surplus-driven economies and, 117
modern, 89–90
outside ecosystems, 366

overview of, 265
return to, 398
return to early, 293, 395
successful, experience with, 176
surplus, need for, 389
survival-driven economy and society, 405
unwillingness to give up, 82
waterhole-inspired, 117
See also Hunter-gatherer lifeways; Survival-driven lifeways
Socioeconomic models, 77
Socioeconomic philosophy, 321
Socioeconomic practices, 123
Socioeconomic solutions, pros and cons, 280
Socioeconomic system
everything for sale in, 115
of individuals, 302
new, building, 503
new, transition to, 192
Socioeconomic transition, potential future, 182, 258
Socioeconomic woes, avoiding, 113
Soil
bacteria, 55, 81
formation and retention, 40
nitrogen, excess impact on, 58
paving over, 77
plowing, 55
polluting, 30
tilling, 71
Soil biodiversity, 53, 53f
Solar energy
generation, storage, and distribution of, 363–365, 370
interest in, 361
investment in, 297
too late, 505
use of, 362, 370–371, 391
Solar irradiance variations, 216, 221
Solar radiation management, 279
Solar renewable survival-driven energy architecture, 366
South Africa, 250, 288–289, 292, 340
South America, 136, 342
South China Sea, 151, 355
Southern Coastal Route, 349, 349f
South Koreans, 193
South Pole, 82, 347
"Spaceship Earth," 13, 36, 56, 458–459
Space station Earth, 33
Space stations, 182, 345
SpaceX supply delivery, 33
Speciation, 418
SPEI Global Drought Monitor Index, 220
Spending time, 201
Spillover risk, 442
Spiritual and religious values, 39
Starvation, 224
State
institutions of, 192
political power of, 303
rise of, 104, 126, 283
States
corporations as virtual, 304
economic system comprising, 207
financial health and well-being of, 198
growth of, 188
policy agendas of, 250
in sedentary societies, 124
surplus-driven socioeconomic lifeway, hypothetical abandonment of, 294
Stechemesser, Annika, 461
Stock market crash, 194
Stock market during global pandemic, 11
Stone Age
early human preparation for, 329
human survival of, 344
mitigations and adaptations, 339
stages of, 422
technologies and innovations, 321, 336, 337, 344, 345
tools, 316
Stone tools
advances in, 334–335
evidence of, 332–333
hunter-gatherer use of, 334
industries, 422
revolution, 333f
Storage, 137, 270
Storm protection, 38
Street address (concept), 508
Stress, 170
Strongmen, 138, 149, 171, 173
Sub-Saharan Africa, 226
Subsistence economy, 202
Subsistence lifestyle, 94
Subsistence method, 24
Sumatra, Indonesia, 30

Sun
as energy source, 26, 78, 114, 376, 391
selection of, 18
Suncor oil sands extraction facility, 28f
Superhuman artificial machine intelligence (Superhuman AI)
aspirations for, 355
as biggest event in history, 327–328
Earth's thermostat, lowering with aid of, 342
extinction, potential due to, 324
inventing, 329, 350
potential use as weapon, 356
rogue, 357, 359
Supermarkets
clearing of shelves in, 136
goods and services, abudance in, 135
hunter-gatherer economies in contrast to, 136
Super-predator, humans as, 12
Super-rich *versus* homeless and unemployed, 192
Supply chains
building, 130
dependence on, 309
dependence on global, 302
disruptions, shrinking supplies due to, 62
disruptions to, 112
energy architecture and, 364
energy transition and, 399
failing, 506
hunter-gatherer economies in contrast to, 136
redundancy lacking in, 61
reliance on, 113
shortages, 135
Supporting services, 36, 37t, 40
Surplus
abandoning, 287, 500
absence of, 190, 231, 253, 268–269
accumulation of, 124, 126, 155, 188, 238, 258–259, 285, 301, 352
desire for, 120–121, 389, 394, 396
economies based on, xviii
elevation of, 157, 160
as farming goal and outcome, 116–117, 307
free-market capitalist system stemming from, 278
gathering, 90
generation of, 209, 275, 299–300, 306, 317, 473
goal of, 115, 127, 156, 167, 176, 491
hoarding, 137–138, 192, 197, 202, 231, 268, 278, 286, 292, 312, 467, 468
life and survival prioritized over, 138, 475
life and survival *versus,* 480
maximization of, 284, 285, 300
Neolithic Revolution bringing, 204
nonrenewables exploited for, 391
obsession with, abandoning, 360
preferential treatment for those with, 234
pursuit of, 244–245, 247, 284, 301, 403, 415, 481
reduction of, 194
versus sharing, 111
versus survival, 195, 239, 498
technologies and innovations to achieve, 332
Surplus-driven agendas, 312
Surplus-driven companies, alternatives to, 308
Surplus-driven economies
departure from, 293
divorced from ecosystems and biodiversity, 260
human survival and, 117, 244–245, 246, 247
reclaiming power yielded to, 313
socioeconomic lifeways of, 268
Surplus-driven entities, 301
Surplus-driven socioeconomic lifeway
abandoning, 294, 308
adopting, 300, 479
human socioeconomic lifeways replaced by, 302
survival-driven lifeways replaced by, 301, 313
taking down, 288
Surplus owners, 193, 194
Survivability niche, 225, 439–440, 441
Survival
catalyst of, xxii
choices based on need for, 107
economic activity apart from, 121
economic growth *versus,* 125
economies prioritizing, 17, 18, 20, 136
ecosystem and other species survival

linked to human, 110
endangering, 111
energy role in, 370, 372
ensuring, 78
as evolutionary priority, 234
versus extinction, 133–134
hoarding not conducive to, 138
mutual, enabling, 265, 407, 472–473, 481–482, 485, 491, 497, 514–515
prospects, enhancing, 106
requirements for, 263, 272
sharing role in, 136, 137
surplus at expense of, 124, 126
surplus *versus,* 139
urge for, 359
wealth accumulation and GDP growth *versus,* 77, 115
See also Life and survival
Survival-driven architecture, 163, 481, 482, 483, 485, 486, 488, 490, 499, 502–503
Survival-driven Earth-life-system architecture, 500
Survival-driven economies, 477–516
abandonment of, 157, 257, 260
changes to, 413
characteristics of, 261
goal and outcome of, 284–285, 480
versus market-driven economies, xvii–xviii
overview of, xxiv
policies, adopting, 245
rediscovering, 90, 197
return to, 293
sedentary farming communities *versus,* 264
versus surplus-driven economies, 244
Survival-driven energy architecture, 363, 364, 366, 370
Survival-driven lifeways
abandonment of, 2, 89, 255, 286, 300, 313, 343–344, 483, 491, 495
benefits of, 321, 395
continuation, hypothetical of, 506–507
foundations supporting, 486
goal and outcome, 294
rejection of, 354
return to, 288, 294, 308, 313, 353, 359, 498–499
surplus-driven lifeways replacing, 301
Survival-driven pattern, evolutionary. *See* Evolutionary survival-driven pattern
Survival-driven principle, 360, 385
Survival-driven societies and economies
pre-Neolithic Revolution, 254
return to, 359
socioeconomic lifeways fitting within, 405
Survival-driven socioeconomic goal and outcome, 496
Survival-driven socioeconomic systems
agriculture transition impact on, 268
ecosystem, biodiversity, and human coexistence in, 265
hunter-gatherer and agrarian compared, 268
Survival-driven startup companies, hypothetical, 308
Survival-driven technologies and innovations, 323
Survival: Evolutionary Rules for Intelligent Species Survival (Layne), 201–202
Survival-threatening mistakes, avoiding, 457
Sustainable agriculture, 246, 273
Sustainable Development Goals, 43, 169, 496, 498
Sustainable society and economy, 312, 319
Suzman, James
on commerce *versus* essential needs, 187
on early human economies, 499
on hunter-gatherer food sources, 97
hunter-gatherer lives analyzed by, 141, 250
on modern hunter-gatherers, 107
on original affluent society, 463
on wheels of commerce, 119, 121
Svizzero, Serge, 251
Swigert, John L, Jr., 457–458
Synchronous failures, 443
Systemic climatic risk, 443
System of Environmental Economic Accounting, 60

T
Taiwan
Chinese claims on, 355
droughts in, 220
greetings in, 136
invasion of, 293
territorial claims against, 151
Tanzania, hunter-gatherers in, 70, 71, 71f
Tar sands, 269, 446

Tax code reform, 196
Tax cuts to wealthy, 196
Tax evaders, 156
Tax evasion, 137, 195–196
Tax havens, 156
Tax inequality, 197
Taylor, D., 217
Technologies
  adapting and innovating, 329
  advances, foundations of, 345
  agriculture combined with other, 330
  breakthroughs, 309, 475
  climate change caused by, 337, 343, 411
  creating, reasons for, 319
  destructive use of, 329
  emergence of, 323
  evolutionary goal and purpose, 319–320
  expansion, foundation for, 337
  forces driving modern, 346
  goal and outcome of, 321–322, 324
  goals enabled by, 284, 332
  growing knowledge of, 182
  historic overview, 315–317
  hunter-gatherers lacking, 117
  lack of direction for, 320
  life and survival *versus* pursuit of, 357
  limitations of, 336, 450
  making a living, enabling through, 331
  motivations for pursuing, 332, 352, 354–355
  pre-human, 344
  pros and cons, 345
  rise of, 235–236, 343
  threat posed by, 177, 354–355
  unintended consequences of, 80, 81, 279, 280
  unproven, 469
Technology
  for good, 319
  and human economies, xxiii
  hunting and fishing aided by, 12–13
  origin of, 332–333
  pinning hope on, 342
  wish lists and fantasies, 356
Technology corporations, 212
Telemedicine, 235–236
Teller, Edward, 295–296
Temperate climates, northward drift of, 215
Temperature, lowering, 341–342
Temperature niche, migration in response to, 440
Temperature records in sea sponge skeletons, 448
Temperatures, global, rise in
  alternative scenarios, 280
  anthropogenic, 490
  average survace temperature, 212f
  carbon dioxide role in, 257, 445
  CFCs ban role in slowing, 120
  economic system, modern role in, 207
  efforts to cap, 172, 460
  future impact, potential of, 213, 225, 296, 345, 426, 437, 438–439
  future projections, 445f
  greenhouse gases role in, 281, 458
  human survival *versus,* 402–403
  mean temperatures, 443f, 444
  northern region temperatures compared to, 441
  past impact of, 347
  poles impacted by, 505–506
  species extinction driven by, 335
  as unintended consequence of human activity, 183
  unscheduled, 495–496
  See also Global warming
Temperatures past and present, 421–422
Temperature variations
  Holocene, 67f, 68f
  natural, 420
  oscillations, 422
Terraforming, 80
Terrestrial biosphere, transformation of, 280
Terrestrial ecosystems
  carbon emissions impact on, 56
  as category, 23
  destruction of, 83
  marine ecosystems compared to, 82
  nitrogen and phosphorus in, 49
  protective measures, 85
  repurposing of, 45–46
Terrorists, 156
Tertiary sector of economy, 189, 189t
Texas blizzard, 2021, 16
Texas oil wells, 446f
Third World countries, 220
Thirst, avoiding, 112–113
Thomas, Robert Paul, 190–191

Thwaites ice shelf, 506
Thyroid disease, 159
Tibet, peaks of, 335
Tibetan plateau, 412
Tierney, Jessica E., 433–434
Timber, demand for, 44
Timmermann, Axel, 420
Tiwanaku civilization, 98, 215
Tobacco companies, 158
Tobacco industry, 120, 245
Toolmaking, advances in, 334
Topography, transition of, 335
Town council meetings, 162
Toxins, dependence on harmful, 302
Trade, lack of, 114
Tradition, economies based on, xviii
Transactions, neutralization and depersonalization of, 148
Trans-Arctic routes, opening of new, 219
Transformation, current, predictions concerning, 183
Transitions
  geologic and climate, 338
  human societies and economies, 197–202, 199t, 227–228, 242
  overview of, xxii–xxiii
Transport, freshwater role in, 48
Transportation
  of early humans, 11
  economies before, 190
  limited choices concerning, 282
  ownership of, 115
Trees, 73, 449
Trickle-down economics, 163
Trinidad and Tobago, 290–291
Tropical climates, food sources in, 97
Tropical forests, 336, 348
Tropics, expansion of, 440, 440f
Trump, Donald, 107, 151, 293, 508
Tubers, 71, 71f
Tundra, 44
Turkey, 222
Turnbull, Colin, 146
Tutu, Desmond, 288, 293

U
UK, migrant policy, 429
Ukraine
  grain exports, 356
  invasion of, 293, 329, 346
  territorial claims against, 151, 354
  war in, 61, 62, 135, 341, 345, 491
Ukrainians, migration of, 338
UN Convention on Biodiversity, 63
Undervaccination, 237, 237f
Unemployed, 192
Unemployment
  during global pandemic, 11
  hunter-gatherers unaware of, 164
  insurance, 236
  lack in hunter-gatherer societies, 190
UN Environment Program Food Waste Index, 169
UNFCCC (United Nations Framework Convention on Climate Change), 460
Uninhabitable parts of Earth, 338, 502
U.N. Intergovernmental Panel on Climate Change (IPCC). *See* Intergovernmental Panel on Climate Change (IPCC)
United East India Company, 304
United Nations, 502
United Nations Environment Program (*later* U.N. Environment), 45, 66
United Nations Sustainable Development Goals, 43, 169, 496, 498
United States
  border wall, 428–429
  climate change impact on, 224–226, 225f
  droughts in, 220
Universal basic income, 80, 113, 143–144, 236
Universe, 2
  expansion of, 1
  exploring, 321
  research on, 350
Upper Paleolithic period, 334
Urban areas
  drought impact on, 221
  overpopulated, 166
  services provided by, 36
Urbanization, 46
Urbanized agrarian societies, 442
U.S. Constitution, 149, 161, 303, 305
U.S. Drought Monitor, 219, 219f
U.S. Environmental Protection Agency, 158
U.S. House of Representatives reports, 212–213
U.S. Supreme Court, 158, 270
Utilities

economies before, 190
ownership of, 115

V

Vaccines
sharing, 172
uneven distribution of, 234
See also Covid-19 pandemic: vaccines
Vancouver, British Columbia, 222
Vassals, 201
Vegetables, loss of ability to farm, 224
Vegetation
trends or oscillations in, 420
unpredictable conditions affecting, 419
Venus, atmosphere, absence of, 76
Vestager, Margrethe, 309
Villages
lack of, 115
population concentration in farming, 224, 242
in sedentary societies, 124, 182, 484
Virginia
colony of, 304
drought in, 215–216
Viruses, undiscovered, 233
Vital resources, depletion of, 62
Vogel, Jefim, 465
Volcanoes, active, effects of, 216, 221

W

Wallace-Wells, David, 74
Wall Street, 283
War, weapons of, 332
Ward, Peter, 18, 486–487
Warfare
animal role in, 98
avoiding, 468
civilization collapse preceded by, 62
emergence of, 258
rare in hunter-gatherer societies, 514
Warmhouse state, 411
Warriors, 278
Wars
current conditions, 394
political systems accompanied by, 173
products and services for, 341
supply chains disrupted by, 112
waging, 167, 321
Waste disposal
freshwater role in, 48
volume of, 188
Waste generation, 383
Waste recycling, ecosystems equipped for, 25–26, 72
Waste treatment, 38
Water
access to, xix–xx, 25, 112
agricultural consumption of, 124, 275
conservation of, 215
cycling of, 40
demand for, 44
as ecosystem benefit, 38
movement of, 382
overview of, 48
oxygen in, 81
planet providing, 19
pollution of, 81
purification of, 38
regulating, 38
on surface, 487
as survival requirement, 110
Texas blizzard, 2021 cutoff of, 16
use of, 40, 48
Water crises
at end of ice age, 247
risks posed by, 243, 246
Waterhole economy
characteristics of, xxiv
overview of, xix–xxi
Waterhole-inspired socioeconomic lifeways, 322
Water pollution
impact of, 383
nitrogen and phosphorus as source of, 57, 57f
Water quality, 220
Water stress, 220, 221f
Water supply
climate change-driven shrinking, 61
climate change impact on, 426
Water temperatures, 220
Waterways, nitrogen, excess impact on, 58
Wealth
capitalist economies focus on, 11
distribution, hypothetical of, 147
generation of, 188, 317, 319, 322, 341
goal of, 115
hoarding of, 124

human survival *versus,* 210, 213
inequalities of, 145
maximizing, 286
rejection of, 172
society tiered by, 111
surplus of, 200
technologies and innovations to achieve, 332
trading humans for, 292 (*see also* Slavery)
Wealth accumulation
abandoning, 500
absence in hunter-gatherer societies, 148, 150, 190, 292
adoption of, 258
animal domestication for, 285
desire for, 286, 396
as economic goal and outcome, 156, 167, 258–259, 491
economies based on, xviii, 82, 88, 90, 127, 473
elevation of, 160
enabling of, 468
energy consumption increase coinciding with, 373
energy hunt driven by, 457
energy sources and, 376
as farming goal and outcome, 116–117
focus on, 346
foundation of, 111
generation of, 209
goal of, abandoning, 287
hierarchical society development stemming from, 515
versus human well-being, 240
inequality resulting from, 172
life and survival *versus,* 240, 294, 312, 474, 475, 480
maximizing, 261, 284
nonrenewables exploited for, 391
obsession with, abandoning, 360
opportunity for, 112
pursuit of, 85, 176, 247, 255, 301, 392, 394, 403, 415, 481
versus survival, 77, 154–155, 239, 299–300, 498
Wealth gap, 245
Wealth management industries, 148
Wealth of Nations (Smith), 141, 479
Weaponry, advances in, 334
Weapons of mass destruction (WMDs), 151, 244, 246, 247, 345, 352, 355
Weather and climate disasters, 501f, 502
Weaver, Andrew J., 434
Weeds, 72
Wellbeing economies, 319, 496, 498
Wellbeing Economy Alliance, 152, 155
Wells, drying of domestic, 221
Welsby, Dan, 209–210
Western Africa, tropical forests in, 348
Western governments on freedom and democracy, 282
Wetlands, loss of, 51
Weyler, Rex, 205
Wheat, 104, 112
Wheat belt, 440
When Corporations Rule the World (Korten), 283, 301
White House, 508
WHO Coronavirus (Covid-19) dashboard, 241–242, 241f
Wilderness, 274
Wildfires, 204
drought-related increase in, 220, 221
unprecedented, 222–223
Wildlife
drought impact on, 221
loss of, 63, 85
plunder of, 229
trade and consumption of, 233, 238, 239f, 240, 331
Wildlife habitats
destruction of, 484
human settlement in, 46
restructuring and/or destroying, 124
Wilson, Jim, 297
Wind energy
interest in, 361
investment in, 297
too late, 505
use of, 362, 391
Winkler, Adam, 198, 200
Winner-take-all capitalist societies and economies
best-countries-to-live-in-lists among, 153–154
hunter-gatherer societies and economies compared to, 146
Winner-take-all socioeconomic system, 135

Winters, Joseph, 464–465
Wisdom of the waterhole, 108–114, 115–116, 117, 163, 164, 174, 321, 359, 407
Wood, replacement as energy source, 387–388
Wood harvests, 40
Work from home, 10, 236
Working class, 302
Working people, 196
World domination, innovations and technologies used for, 329, 330
World Economic Forum, 243, 244, 246
World economic system, discriminatory, 234
World economy, climate change *versus,* 464
World GDP, 373
World Health Organization, 158
World leaders
  economic goals of, 195–196
  fossil energy financed by, 395
  human survival, need to plan for, 293
  surplus-driven socioeconomic lifeway, hypothetical abandonment of, 294
World War I, 78–79
Worldwide food crisis, 112
Woudenberg, Carina, 453

X
Xi Jinping, 107, 151, 245, 293, 355
Xu, Chi, 441

Y
Yaeda Valley, Tanzania, 70, 71, 71f
Yang, Andrew, 80
YC companies, 308
Y Combinator (firm), 308
Yemen, 429f, 430
Yiwara, 507
Younger Dryas, 422
Yucatán Peninsula, 453

Z
Zakaria, Fareed, 192
Zombie oil wells, 446, 446f
Zoonotic diseases
  absence in hunter-gatherer economies, 10, 232
  animal domestication and, 10, 172, 229, 331, 343
  animal husbandry and, 278
  causes of, 238, 309
  corporation role in, 310
  incidence of, 106, 206, 233
  prevention of, 232
  risk of, 80, 312
Zoonotic pandemics, 172, 175, 228–229, 230
  absence of, 232
  origins of, 126, 156, 163, 233, 278

www.ingramcontent.com/pod-product-compliance
Lightning Source LLC
Chambersburg PA
CBHW030536080526
44585CB00012B/180
* 9 7 8 1 7 3 3 7 5 5 5 4 2 *